NATURAL RESOURCE MANAGEMENT AND PUBLIC ADMINISTRATION

NATURAL RESOURCE MANAGEMENT AND PUBLIC ADMINISTRATION

Edited by

RAKESH HOOJA
SUNIL DUTT

Indian Institute of Public Administration
in association with

KANISHKA PUBLISHERS, DISTRIBUTORS
NEW DELHI-110 002

KANISHKA PUBLISHERS, DISTRIBUTORS
4697/5-21 A, Ansari Road, Daryaganj
New Delhi-110 002
Phones : 2327 0497, 2328 8285
Fax : 011-2328 8285
e-mail: kanishka_publishing@yahoo.co.in

First Published 2009

ISBN 978-81-8457-152-3

PRINTED IN INDIA

Published by Madan Sachdeva for Kanishka Publishers, Distributors, 4697/5-21A, Ansari Road, Daryaganj, New Delhi-110 002, Typeset by Sunshine Graphics, Delhi, and Printed at Rajdhani Printers, Delhi.

Foreword

In a country like India where the majority of people subsists on the locally available natural resources and depends on them for their survival, livelihood, health, and future development with dignity, many development projects reduce the access and rights of communities to livelihood resources and impinge on community lands and possessions. There are instances of the diversion of forest lands to non-forest purposes, and a major increase in the number of such 'development' projects being given environmental clearance. The unplanned spread of mining operations is another such example.

The Green Revolution made India self-reliant in foodgrains, but the long-term impacts of this phenomenon are a matter of concern. In a concerted bid to fill the country's granaries, several water-thirsty and hybrid crops were inducted into our agricultural system. Their intense irrigation requirement and the adverse impact on the traditional crop mixes of coarse grains, cereals and pulses that optimize water use, have taken their toll on the irrigation system and groundwater availability. Ironically, groundwater irrigation has been instrumental in enhancing food security and mitigating hunger and poverty but it has also contributed most to the depletion of groundwater reserves.

Falling water tables, premature silting of dams, increasing desertification, droughts and other ecological deprivations continue to haunt modern-day India. Our irrigation infrastructure has rested primarily on large dams, canals and ground water mining. The ecological degradations can, in a large measure, be attributed to this dominance of supply-side hydrology. The unfair and inequitable consumption of water for more than a century has meant that a large portion of population continue to depend on rainfall and fall prey to the frequent hazards of floods and droughts compounded by the effects of global warming.

The depleting agricultural output and earnings result in a large scale destabilizing of economy with a cascading effect on the other rural economic activities and livelihoods. For this compelling reason the natural resource management must be linked to human welfare as the major motivating force. This brings out significance of natural resources and their sustenance into sharp focus, because the crisis facing land, water, forests, and air needs to be tackled for strengthening livelihoods options, checking migration and long-term food and livestock security. The sustainable management of natural resources can be recontextualised as sustainable governance of natural resources. This in turn makes it possible to place the politically neutralising discourse of 'management' in a space for a wider societal debate, in which the different stakeholders deliberate and negotiate the norms, rules and power relations related to natural resource use and sustainable development. At best it can evolve as a social learning process involving scientists, experts, politicians and communities and their corresponding scientific and traditional knowledge.

There have already been significant moves of assertion by communities themselves. Whether it is the resistance of villagers in Plachimada (Kerala) against a multinational bottling plant that sought to draw the groundwater and polluting the land, the intensification of legal dispute against the unpalatable 'development' by citizens, the regeneration of forests and wetlands by thousands of villages across India, and the increasing number of farmers switching to organic cultivation are several noteworthy initiatives that demonstrate the will of rural and urban communities to take matters into their hands. Some governments too have acted in response, by granting greater powers to local bodies, promoting organic farming, or bringing in other eco-friendly policies and schemes. Several self-motivated officials have also shown the way by promoting unconventional water harvesting, clean energy sources, and participatory forms of resource management.

There is an imperative need for regeneration of land and water, which are degraded to abysmally low levels of productivity over more than 60 per cent of India's area. This cannot be done by centralised bureaucracies, but by empowering and providing resources to rural and urban communities. The amazing regeneration of forests under joint forest management over millions of hectares, or of wetlands through decentralised water harvesting, despite inadequate power-sharing in such programmes are encouraging signs. These systems had a crucial mix of creativity to match the varied agro-ecological conditions and of management to sustainably maintain them without external assistance. Where it has worked, water harvesting in rural areas has remained a symbol of community ingenuity, ownership and control.

Besides local resources, trans-regional issues can be resolved by arriving at an agreement that each basin state is entitled to a reasonable and equitable share, and once considerations in determining equity, i.e. population dependent on water, contribution of water by each basin state, availability of alternate water sources and maximum satisfaction of the need of a state without causing substantial injury to other states—are all agreed upon, specific disputes could be decided within the framework of these parameters.

The chapters in this volume throw further light on the nuances of natural resource management through research, study and field experiences of the learned authors who are known authorities in the respective fields. It is hoped that the issues, alternatives and strategies underlined in these contributions will impact resource management regimen in the country.

Bhartendra Singh Baswan
Director
Indian Institute of Public Administration
New Delhi

Preface

Natural Resource Management (NRM) involves considerations of sustainability; participation and involvement of multiple stakeholders including users, the community and government; appropriate technology (both traditional as well as modern, scientific and innovation-based); appropriate use of each resource (and sub-categories within each resource) according to the natural or physical context as well as the socio-cultural and politico-economic context; appropriate mix of community or user-based NRM and government sponsored or government managed NRM; use of social capital as well as government institutions and capabilities based upon experience; as well as balancing between environmental sustainability, equity and social justice, and developmental efficacy. In today's world appropriate Natural resource Management, and the likely impacts of its management or mismanagement, has become extremely vital. It cannot be left only to individual users or to the community (or to NGOs), and government and public administration have to continue to play a significant and pro-active role. It certainly cannot be left to the market as some thinkers were inclined to favour in the last couple of decades before the recent global economic meltdown.

The natural environmental resources of the earth are getting ever more depleted by diminution through gross mismanagement and increased consumption by the burgeoning population with its ever expanding living standards. As such the preservation of these resources necessitates that new strategies for their conservation, optimum utilization, and management are urgently developed. An upgradation of these resources can also be achieved by an adequate mix of technology, capital, scientific planning and institutional arrangements. The increase in the population of developing countries is one of the major causes of shortage and shrinking due to overuse or suboptimal use of key resources like land and water since the sizeable chunk of this populace supports their livelihood by the existing resources. The need to produce increasing quantities of food has put a greater strain on agriculture and natural inputs.

Natural Resource Management can be looked at through efforts in individual sectors like agriculture, forestry, groundwater, irrigation, or through multisectoral programmes such as watershed development or Command Area Development or Desert Development.

Agriculture represents a pristine bounty of nature which sustains millions of families globally. For generations they have been making indiscriminate use of environmental resources as if they were inexhaustible or infinite. We are just past the green revolution era and experts have started warning us of food insecurity of a different kind which is driven by the over use of land, water, fertilizers and hybrid crop varieties. Pushing agriculture to marginal lands has often resulted into large scale soil erosions and floods. The perils of decades of extensive farming without appropriate crop rotation or other techniques to prevent erosion are sending warning signals through abrupt climatic changes. In the last century itself deep plowing of the virgin topsoil of the Great of USA had killed the natural grasses that normally kept the soil in place and trapped moisture even during periods of drought and high winds. The Kansas Dust Bowl is the most dramatic example of this phenomenon.Similarly the Aral Sea has become a disaster area due to improper planning and management of the waters that flowed into the area. While such examples are well known, at the local levels many such instances covering smaller areas exist.

Droughts have been affecting lives, livelihoods and the economic condition of the people who are dependent on agriculture in the arid zones of country. Policies and action plans have been formulated both at the Central and state level to tide over the difficult situations arising out of drought conditions. However, a successful drought policy framework needs to look not only at drought relief and rehabilitation in affected areas, but also measures at drought proofing of the economy of the region and drought prevention in the non-drought periods and years.

In such a milieu the foremost challenge facing the task of natural resource management is to arrive at a pragmatically structured agenda of an accurate assessment of problems related to such management and evolve a definite matrix of policy design and implementation of interventions embedded more in the considerations of food, livelihood and environmental security than the political calculus. Apart from the felt need for greater investments in natural resource management, the governance of these resources should be done through institutional mechanisms of Central and state governments, users and community groups, and other stakeholders. One may observe that hitherto most of the state interventions have been top down in character and ignore the value of involving all stakeholders in the process of implementation.

Then there can be a India-specific strategy for propagating Participatory Irrigation Management (PIM). There is a need for discussion on the type of approach to PIM that needs to be followed and the efforts that are required to be undertaken to ensure the acceptance, adoption and spread of PIM in India, including a scheme of what should form part of state-level legislations on PIM in India. The strategy and approach could make water users develop a sense of ownership in water users associations and to develop deep involvement in their working, rather than merely being silent members who become members of Water Users Associations due to legislative fiat or governmental orders.

The plans to conserve and augment the energy and environmental resources like forests, farmlands, rivers, watersheds, and flora and fauna, that have suffered extensive damage and degradation need to concentrate on the factors that affect critical resources and their management. These are all part of a vital chain supporting each other yet susceptible to a cascading effect in the event of injudicious tampering with the intricate and vulnerable balancing mechanism. Joint Forest Management has emerged as a possible strategy for popular participation in forest management through micro-institutional solutions. The experiment has been introduced in various states with varying degree of success. Efforts are afoot to create a space for the local populace, mostly through their local representatives, to participate in this innovative scheme. There are limited institutional options for strengthening protection and management activities. Confidence building measures between local institutions, NGOs and administration and the reduced dependence on the forest bureaucracy are key to the success of this venture. It calls for a greater financial stability and commitment from all concerned to impact sustenance to the mechanism.

India has almost 20 per cent of the world's irrigated land and one of the biggest irrigation infrastructures. Nearly two-thirds of the available water is consumed by the agriculture sector. In order to effect greater efficiency in the use of water for agriculture better management of irrigation networks, revamping of cropping patterns, preservation of water tables and maintenance of green cover of land are needed on priority. The fact remains that the water resources are intricately linked to rural livelihood support systems besides the livestock and consumption needs. The central concern behind all policies, interventions and strategies is the livelihood perspective of a very large segment of the population. There is much more to livestock-environment-watershed relationship than meets the eye. A whole lot of micro and macro issues need to be addressed in the context of this relationship for achieving greater synthesis between livestock and watershed development. One of the most important issues hampering livestock and watershed development happens to be a total lack of coordination among various government agencies that work in the related fields. Several inadequacies and drawbacks have been witnessed in the policies that have been perused hitherto pointing towards the need to frame a holistic development policy keeping in mind the crucial dimension of livelihood dependence of poor on the livestock and the significance of livestock assets in poverty reductions

The planning and development for water resources projects necessarily entails coordination among different users of water as well as many state agencies/ undertakings for optimal utilisation of available water and to formulate and operate water resources projects within the framework of overall basin/sub-basin plan of various uses of water and meeting conflicting demands of water users. That brings into focus governance and institutional mechanisms to ensure integrated water resources management. Agriculture being the largest consumer of water, it will be wise to adopt water-conserving cropping patterns, water harvesting and water pricing policies to discourage waste. The core strategy of watershed management lies in a combination of protection, regeneration and production along with appropriate land and water management.

Planned development and modernising outlook brought the gigantic and ambitious irrigation or multipurpose projects in to focus after India's independance. These ventures have come to be known as temples of the modern India. Many a time these schemes have ignored equity and entitlements of the people in the project and led to large scale displacement and acute human misery. Any development to be sustainable and inclusive has to steer clear of creating disparities and imbalances. There are instances where downstream areas do not receive any or very little water violating riparian rights of the people along the river besides endangering the aquatic life which is again a means of livelihood for many. While planning large and mega multipurpose irrigation projects a deliberate and conscious deliberation is needed to cater to livelihood water and energy needs of the entire community base on a realistic assessment of their rightful claims. Water management within such projects has to be meticulously planned out and appropriate water management systems put into place. On-field water application and appropriate drainage measures also have to be catered for.

The flawed perception that all rivers have surplus water is often born out of the stark ignorance their complex ecosystems. The proposed river inter-linking projects are the part of such a belief. But from the floodplains to delta and estuarine zones, rivers have cradled communities who have had an intrinsic link with resources in a subsistence economy. With a structural intervention of engineering a lake from a gulf, the subsistence economy is certain to receive more blows. The change of land relations and its effect on claims on estuarine and marine resources must be studied Undertaken on political or emotional considerations rather than scientific investigation, such projects may meet the fate of Kalpsar project which was recommended by four expert committees after detailed studies. Gujarat's governments have continually failed to commit themselves to the cause of Salinity Ingress Prevention. The project as of now is in a state of abandonment after huge investments in terms of time and money.

Traditionally people had evolved sound methods to conserve water resources. But the ever increasing pressure to grow more has condemned this traditional wisdom as backwardness. Of late, watershed development, ground water conservation and recharge techniques have tried to revive these resources but over bureaucratization and misplaced technological interventions, oblivious of scale, have undermined their potential. The issue of natural resource management is much beyond demand-supply dichotomy. It involves greater critical facets including environmental concerns, ecological disorders and alarming onset of pollution, aridity and land infertility amongst growing consumption and developmental demands. Technological breakthroughs as well as institutional innovations are both essential for improved NRM.

The limited availability of fresh water calls for appropriate exploitation of all potential storage sites and replenishable groundwater resources, which is indeed a tall order. Low water charges or irrigation rates in most states do not convey the scarcity value of water and on the contrary encourage overuse and misuse. The collection of water charges as a percentage of demand is also very low in most states. The Tenth Plan strategy was aimed to link reforms in water sector to Central funding. One of the problems being faced in the rural drinking water sector is slippage of habitations from fully covered to partially covered and partially covered to not covered habitations due to increase in population, fall in groundwater, and water quality problems, etc. The sustainability issues in this regard focus on revival of traditional rain water harvesting techniques. A National Water Code could clearly define the parameters within which watershed development should take place. The issue of sustainability of assets created merit attention along with embarking on a massive programme to conserve water.

The essays by the authorities in the respective fields contained in the volume have been drawn from the treasure trove of successive volumes of *Indian Journal of Public Administration over the last more than fifty years.* Practically all the authors are well known and have contributed comprehensively on the related areas. The pieces were authored over a period of time, which would enable readers to appreciate changes in thinking and implementation over the years. These writings address the problems and challenges of natural resource management and have suggested strategies for approaching the task both at the national and local levels.

The editors spent long hours going through all the back issues of Indian Journal of Public Administration. While 32 articles were finally selected, the 10 odd articles originally part of our short list had to be finally excluded which involved a lot of agonizing reflection. The selected articles cover a wide gamut from environment protection machinery, to forestry management, land-water management, watershed plus, integrated water resource management, irrigation and PIM, groundwater, hydroelectricity, agriculture and food production, and droughts. We found the task of reading through the articles to be extremely stimulating and thought provoking as well as informative, containing numerous meaningful ideas. We hope that the comity of researchers, scholars, policy-makers and experts will find the collection of essays equally relevant and useful.

RAKESH HOOJA
SUNIL DUTT

Contents

SECTION IV
LAND-WATER MANAGEMENT AND WATERSHED MANAGEMENT

SECTION V
OVERVIEW OF INTEGRATED WATER MANAGEMENT

SECTION VI
IRRIGATION AND PARTICIPATORY IRRIGATION MANAGEMENT

SECTION VII
GROUND WATER AND HYDRO-ELECTRICITY MANAGEMENT

SECTION VIII
AGRICULTURAL, FOOD PRODUCTION AND DROUGHT MANAGEMENT

SECTION I: ENVIRONMENT PROTECTION MACHINERY

1

Environment Protection in India

R.B. Jain and Kanchan Sharma

Environment has become a paradigm, a hold-all term in recent years. Environment is an all-embracing concept. It means different things to different people. The variations in individual's notion of environment ranges from one's immediate physical surroundings to political set-up or socio-economic conditions. In fact, environment is everything that affects not only man but other organisms also. In this sense, environment is a multi-dimensional system. It has spatial, temporal and functional dimensions.

In the recent past, environmental issues have resulted in environmental conflicts. These conflicts have resulted in certain political movements based on ecological issues concerning the quality of man's habitat. In order to reconcile the interests of various groups which are involved in environmental conflict, society has to evolve certain rules and regulations and a legal framework.

I. NATURE OF ENVIRONMENTAL PROBLEMS

Protection of environment is a major problem of the present society. Man's desire for more joy and comfort has led him to exploit nature's free goods to the extent of reducing its natural capacities for self-stabilisation. Up to now, man has been indiscriminately manipulating the environment and nature to fulfil his narrow selfish interests. In the process, he has sometimes left the environment so badly mauled and mutilated that it is proving harmful to the humanity itself. As a consequence of this outright disregard of the impact of these activities on the environment, numerous environmental problems have arisen.

Most of our environmental difficulties originate from man's ecological misbehaviour. The most alarming of man's assaults on the environment is pollution of air, earth, river and sea with dangerous and even lethal substances. This pollution is generally irreversible; the chain of evil it initiates in the life support systems of the world as well as in living tissues is for most part irreversible. In this, often unnoticed calamity, radiation caused by these substances is changing the very nature of the life. Chemical released through nuclear explosion come to earth in rain or drift down as fall out, get deposited in soil, enter into the grass or ears of grain and ultimately the bones of a human being to remain there until their death. Similarly, chemicals sprayed on croplands or forests or gardens lie along the soil, entering into living organisms, and keep passing on from one to another. These chemicals dissolve into stream water and get converted into clouds and come down with rain and wreck unknown havoc. Today, horrors of terms like 'acid rain' and 'nuclear winter' have become well-known.

The nature of environmental problems is different in developed and underdeveloped societies. In developed countries, these problems have emerged due to the advancement of scientific and technological development, whereas the environmental problems of developing countries are in large measure those that have arisen from the lack of development. They are problems; in other words, of both, rural and urban poverty. In both the towns and the countryside not merely the quality of life but the life itself is endangered by poor water, housing, sanitation and nutrition and by sickness, disease and by natural disasters. They are problems which affect the great mass of mankind. It is also true that problems arising out of the process of development are also evident in these countries. Indeed as the process of development gets underway the latter type of problem is likely to assume increasing importance (as India is facing now-a-days). The process of agricultural growth and transformation, for example, involves construction of reservoirs and irrigation systems; clearing of forests; use of fertilisers and pesticides, etc. These processes certainly have environmental implications. Similarly, industrialisation results in the release of pollutants and react on the environment in a number of ways.[1]

It is clearly evident that environmental deterioration is not a new phenomenon. But both the rate of deterioration and its critical impact have risen sharply in the years since the Second World War. In the post-Second World War period, environmental pollution has emerged as one of the main health hazards in the West. Rapid population growth, fast industrialisation and urbanisation, the technological explosion and the patterns of economic growth have all directly contributed to growth of this irritant. While growth has brought extraordinary benefits, it has not been accompanied by sufficiently farsighted efforts to guide its development.

In India, people have been conscious about environmental problems ever since the Vedic times. It is clearly mentioned in the scriptures that nature and humankind (i.e. Prakriti and Purush) form an inseparable part of the life support system. This system has five elements—air, water, land, flora and fauna—which are interconnected, interrelated and interdependent and have co-evolved and co-adapted.[2]

As long as humankind, as a part of this system, worked in harmony with nature and used the resources for its normal sustenance, damage to the system was minimal. With the process of development, human activities assumed such enormous dimensions that the life support system could no longer sustain these. As a result, the waste generated through human activities was much more than the system could absorb or assimilate. This has caused the problem of pollution. While everyone agree that development is necessary for raising the living standards and affording a quality of life to the people, it is but certain that all major development is associated with some negative environmental impact. The need of the hour is to ensure that the biogenetic shocks from such development should not cross the threshold limit of resource sustenance.

India is also facing a serious problem of environmental pollution Methyr-Iso-Cynate (MIC) gas tragedy of Bhopal is a pointer in that direction. That the problem of this type of catastrophe exists in all industrial cities of India was again highlighted by the acid gas leak in the Shriram Foods and Fertilisers Industries Ltd., Delhi which created near panic conditions in the capital city though the leak was much less in magnitude and effects.

In India, the environmental pollution is a multi-causal phenomenon. The principal reason of this pollution is rapidly increasing industrialisation. The indiscriminate and mushrooming growth of industries in and around residential colonies has complicated the scenario. The smoke from the chimneys, the untreated effluents discharged in river and canals, and mixing of chemical gases in the atmosphere are the three main sources of industrial pollution.

Since Independence, India has made tremendous progress on all fronts. We are, today, among the first ten industrialised nations. We have also achieved near self-reliance in core sectors such as, iron and steel, crude refining and petrochemicals, drugs and pharmaceuticals, fertilisers and engineering goods and many essential commodities. With the rising population the demand for these commodities is also increasing. Evidently, such a major industrial transformation has some costs associated with it. These are in the form of generation of solid, liquid and gaseous pollutants.

Of the various kinds of pollution (air, water, land, noise, radiation and odour) that affect the quality of life in India, water pollution is by far the most serious in its implications for the health and well-being of the citizens. The major sources of pollution of natural waters, including coastal waters, is the discharge of industrial and residential wastes from cities, towns and industries. Most of the cities and towns in India do not have sewerage treatment facilities and where they do exit, such facilities are in the form of primary treatment. According to the Central Board for Water Pollution, only eight cities in India are provided with complete sewerage and sewage treatment facilities. Thus, most of the community and industrial waste finds its way into water courses without treatment, rendering the water downstream unsafe. The problem is further compounded by agriculture run-offs, which contain chemical nutrients, pesticides, and other hazardous chemicals, the use of which is continuously increasing. Another survey carried out by National Environmental Engineering Research Institute (NEERI) on pollution of rivers and streams in different parts of the country indicate that between 50 per cent to 70 per cent of the pollution load in a stream is contributed by domestic sewage and the rest by industrial wastes. In a predominantly industrialised area, this ratio may be reversed in respect of industrial wastes.[3] It is generally accepted that 80 per cent of all diseases are due to water-borne infection. Thus, the problem of water pollution is a gigantic one.

The problem of air pollution is also associated with industrial growth and urbanisation. It is contributed mainly by industrial, domestic and vehicular sectors. The problem of air pollution, although it is not as major as those faced by highly industrialised countries, nevertheless presents itself in large cities of the country. Apart from industrial units, automobile is another source which add to air pollution to a considerable extent in urban areas. Delhi's case is a pointer to the future. According to J.N. Dave, it is the most polluted city in the country as far as vehicle exhausts are concerned. Dave and his team of researchers conducted a survey and found that 400 tonnes of pollutants are emitted every day by nearly 5,00,000 vehicles. This amounts to 34 per cent of the smoke and dust emitted in the city, a higher proportion than anywhere else. What is worse is that over the past decade the pollution in Delhi has increased to 75 per cent.[4]

The indiscriminate felling of trees for timber and firewood and a fastly shrinking forest area is the country is another major factor for disturbing the ecological balance. The percentage of forest areas is shrinking drastically. The latest satellite data confirm that India is losing 1.3 million hectares of forests a year, nearly eight times the annual rate put out by forest departments.[5] Commercial exploitation of the forests and faulty land-use are the two factors responsible for deforestation.

The blind land reclamations programme have further contributed in disturbing the ecological balance. A sharp decreasing population of wildlife also has a telling impact on environmental hazards.

The accumulated results of the above mentioned factors has been that a poor and underdeveloped country like India is confronted with a very serious problem of environmental pollution. Earlier, it was thought that environmental pollution is a problem of affluent West, but it is becoming more of a problem of the poor orient.

II. LEGAL AND CONSTITUTIONAL PROVISIONS FOR PROTECTION OF ENVIRONMENT

Environment protection is a major problem of the present society. Global environments and the entire biosphere is changing fast as a result of the impact of science and technology. Pollution of air, space, outer space, land areas and oceans is taking place rapidly. Because of the application of global technology, ecological changes are occurring in the structures of the earth with an adverse impact on global environment. According to the United Nations Declaration of 1972, maintenance of wholesome human environments is, therefore, the concern of all mankind.[6] A clean and healthy environment is essential in both industrialised and developing societies.

India is one of the very few countries of the World which has enshrined in its Constitution a commitment to environment protection and improvement.[7] The environmental law is a new division of law. The environmental law appears to be a recent origin but it is not a sudden creation. Many provisions dealing with the environment are scattered in pieces and found in the different enactments of this country. Although some provisions in the Constitution relating to improvement in the quality of life had been made since its proclamation in 1950, but a direct reference to environmental protection and improvement was introduced with the Constitution (42nd Amendment) Act of 1976. It was perhaps, the UN Conference on Human Environment held in Stockholm in 1972, which significantly influenced the government's awareness regarding the necessity of legal and organisational framework for protection of environment. It has interjected a new dimension to public responsibility by making it obligatory for the Central Government, state government and every citizen to protect and improve the environment.[8]

The 42nd Amendment Act has made certain changes in the Seventh Schedule of the Constitution. In the Concurrent List after entry 17, entry 17A was inserted which provided for 'forests'. Originally, forests were a subject of State List. As there was no uniform policy followed by the State in respect of protection of forests, this subject was transferred to List III. Now on this subject the Parliament and the State Legislature both may pass legislation. The subject of protection of wild animals and birds was also transferred from List II, entry 20, and inserted in List III, entry 17B.[9] Further the Amendment Act for the first time introduced a new entry, 20A in List III after entry 20. Entry 20A deals with population control and family planning. Today, the greatest pollutant is the number of people—the enormous increase in population is mainly responsible for the modern environmental problems.[10]

The legal sanction to protect different segments of environment in India, has been provided by successive enactments of certain laws. During the period immediately after independence, decision makers were more interested in the problem of economic development in general; therefore, environmental issues were largely ignored. It is a well-known fact that Pandit Nehru had tremendous interest in wildlife, but the honour goes to Indira Gandhi for enacting the Wildlife (Protection) Act, 1972. It is clearly evident from the title of the Act that its main objective is to protect the wild animals and birds, particularly the rare species, such as the lion and the great horned rhinoceros, which are fast disappearing. The Wildlife Protection Act was followed by the Water (Prevention and Control of Pollution) Act 1974. This is another major and significant Act in environmental protection in India. The Act came into force in 12 states. The intention of the Government of India was to extend the Act to the whole country and hence a provision was made in the Act (Section (3) of the Act)—that any state can adopt the Act and the Act would come into force in that state from the date of adoption.[11] The objective of the Act is to prevent and control water pollution and also to maintain and restore the wholesomeness of water. For achieving the objectives of the Act, provisions were also made for setting up of Central and State Boards for prevention and control of water pollution in their respective areas.

Of all the environmental problems facing the country, the problem of deforestation has received maximum public attention. Despite the law on the subject (Indian Forest Act, 1927) deforestation has reached such a state that it has created havoc in the economic system. Thousands of trees are killed daily for commercial and non-commercial purposes. But one must appreciate the fact that when the enactment was made in 1927, the socio-economic and political conditions were vastly different. In order to accommodate diverse interest associated with forest resources, under the changed socio-economic and political environment after independence, the Forest (Conservation) Act 1980 was passed by the Government. Under the Act, the Central Government may constitute an Advisory Committee to advise the Government regarding grant of approval under Section 2 and any other matter connected with the conservation of forests which may be referred to it by the Central Government.[12] The Central Government makes rules for carrying out the provisions of the Act.

The Air (Prevention and Control of Pollution) Act, 1981, is another important Act which has been passed by the Government of India. The Act makes provisions for prevention, control and abatement of air pollution, for establishment of Boards for conferring powers and functions relating thereto for matters connected therewith. These Boards have been empowered to establish air laboratories, to enable them to perform their functions efficiently.

Recently, the Government of India has enacted another important Act, in order to protect the environment, known as the Environment (Protection) Act, 1986, which has been brought into force with effect from November 19, 1986. The Act was passed for the following objectives: protection, regulation of discharge of environmental pollutants; handling of hazardous substances; speedy response in the event of accidents threatening environment; and giving deterrent punishment to those who endanger human environment safety and health.[13] The Act is said to be a more effective and bold measures to fight the problem of pollution as compared to all the previous laws in this regard. Under the Act, the Central Government has been empowered to take all appropriate measures to prevent and control pollution and to establish an effective machinery to achieve this objective. The Act has adopted a new stand with regard to the question of *locus standi* so that now even a citizen has the right to approach a court provided he has given a notice of not less than 60 days of the alleged offence and his intention to make a complaint to the Central Government or the concerned authority. The Central Government has been vested with powers of entering and inspecting any place through any person or agency authorised by it. The Act also authorises the Central Government to issue direction for the closure, prohibition or regulation of any industry's operation or process. It also authorises Central Government to stop or regulate the supply of electricity or water or any other service directly without obtaining a court order.[14]

III. IMPLEMENTATION MACHINERY FOR ENVIRONMENTAL PROTECTION IN INDIA

In order to implement the rules and regulations mentioned in the preceding section of the article, the government has evolved overtime different ministries, boards and departments as a machinery to translate these Acts into reality.

Since 1971, the Government of India has taken commendable initiative to inject environmental considerations into the processes of planning for national development. These included comprehensive preparatory activities for India's participation in Stockholm Conference and Indira Gandhi's landmark keynote address at the conference, the setting up of National Committee on Environmental Planning and Coordination (NCEPC), constitution of state environment committees, undertaking of environmental research programmes, incorporation of environment related subjects in school and college curricula, enactment of laws for environmental protection, formation, in November 1980, of a full-fledged Department of Environment (DOE) at the Centre, programme for spread of environmental awareness through a spate of seminars, World Environment Day celebrations and eco-development laws. All of these are indicators of Government's recognition of the need to check environmental degradation, and to plan for environmentally sound development.

The present integrated Department of Environment, Forests and Wildlife, in the Ministry of Environment and Forests, was created in September 1985. The Ministry serves as a focal point in the administrative structure of the Central Government for planning, promotion and coordination of environmental and forestry programmes. The Ministry's main activities include survey and conservation of natural resources, protection of environment and its regeneration, and development of the degraded parts of the environment. The main tools utilised for this include surveys, impact assessment, control of pollution, regeneration programmes, support to organisations implementing such programmes, research to evolve solutions, extension, education and training to augment the requisite manpower collection, collation and dissemination of environmental information and creation of environmental awareness.

We will provide below the details of various action plans as envisaged by the different departments associated with the Ministry of Environment and Forests.

Control of Water and Air Pollution

The Water (Prevention and Control of Pollution) Act 1974 and the Air (Prevention and Control of Pollution) Act 1981 continued to be implemented through the Central Pollution Control Board and the State Pollution Control Boards. During the year 1988-89, Goa and Tripura have constituted State Boards[15] with this all states excepting the States of Manipur, Nagaland, Sikkim, Arunachal Pradesh and Mizoram have constituted their State Boards. Followings the enactment of the Environment (Protection) Act 1986, mere responsibilities have been placed on the Central and State Boards. The Central Board, in collaboration with the Department of Ocean Development, established 173 monitoring stations all along the 6,000 km. of the Indian coast for purposes of water quality measurement. The programme also involves the State Pollution Control Boards.

Thirty-four, national ambient air quality monitoring stations were sanctioned during the year 1988-89 out of which nine are operational. The National and Zonal Task Forces set up to pursue the implementation of effluent standards in industries, have been reconstituted. So far, 3,270 prosecution have been launched by the Central and State Pollution Control Boards since the enactment of the Water and Air Acts in 1974 and 1981 respectively. Under the Environment Protection Act 1986, the Central Government has taken action against 47 units, which resulted in close down of 28 units and 19 units have been directed to set up their effluent treatment plants.[16]

Two multi-parameter continuous ambient air monitoring stations were installed in Delhi with financial assistance from European Economic Community (EEC).

Ganga Action Plan

An action plan was drawn up for cleaning the polluted stretches of the Ganga. To oversee its implementation, a Central Ganga Authority was set up by Government of

India's Resolution dated February 15, 1985.[17] The authority is under the chairmanship of the Prime Minister and its membership includes Chief Ministers of U.P., Bihar and West Bengal. The steering committee has identified schemes to be taken up under the Ganga Action Plan for the states of U.P., Bihar and West Bengal. So far 262 schemes have been sanctioned under the Ganga Action Plan at a cost of Rs. 250.44 crore covering the states mentioned above. Of thee, 50 schemes have been completed and the rest are in good progress.[18]

Wasteland Development

The National Wasteland Development Board was established in May 1985, primarily to formulate, coordinate and catalyse programmes for management and development of wastelands in the country. Computer based monitoring cells were set up in 15 states to monitor and evaluate various projects in afforestation, social forestry, etc. An interdisciplinary committee of the representatives of the Land Development Banks (LDB) has been constituted to make policy recommendations for promoting greater involvement by LDBs in afforestation projects.

The scheme of Rural Fuel-wood Plantations is being implemented in 159 fuel-wood deficient districts in 25 states and the Union Territory of Delhi.[19]

Besides its regular programmes for afforestation and wasteland development, the National Wasteland Development Board has initiated new schemes of aerial seeding for development of remote and inaccessible wastelands in various hills, mountains, etc.

Survey of Natural Resources

Flora: The Botanical Survey of India (BSI) continued its activities on the survey, identification and exploration of the plant wealth of our country. Under the plant conservation programme, a Red Data Book on Indian Plants covering 235 species has been published and plant survey in certain priority areas of Andaman and Nicobar, Sikkim, U.P., Jammu and Kashmir, South Western Ghats and Pondicherry, were initiated by BSI and 25 per cent of the work was completed during the last year. The BSI garden planted 560 plants of 50 species of rare and potentially useful plants for conservation and multiplication.[20]

Fauna: The Zoological Survey of India (ZSI) has been engaged in the survey of faunal resources and collection of baseline scientific data with regard to their taxonomy, ecology, behavioural patterns, impact of pollution, etc. One hundred twenty-six Faunostic Surveys, covering various ecosystems of 40 districts of several states of the country were conducted by the ZSI.

Conservation of Natural Resources

1. *Forest Conservation*: In the implementation of the provisions of the Forest (Conservation) Act, 1980, greater emphasis is being laid on compensatory afforestation while allowing diversions in unavoidable cases, of forest lands for non-forestry purposes.

The new National Forest Policy lays emphasis on maintenance of environmental stability, restoration of ecological balance and preservation of the remaining natural forests. In view of the symbiotic relationship of the tribals with the forests, the policy emphasises meeting the basic needs of the tribals living within forests. Afforestation and tree planting to meet the needs of the poor in one of the aims of the policy.

The Forest Conservation Act, 1980 has been amended to facilitate its stricter implementation and to provide for penalties for violators. During the year 1988-89, diversion of 18,765 hectares of forest land was permitted for development projects under strict conditions of compensatory afforestation.[21] The six Regional Offices have been set up to monitor and evaluate ongoing forestry development projects.

2. *Wildlife Protection*: Amendments to the Wildlife (Protection) Act 1972 have been initiated to make the laws more effective. Sixty-seven National Parks and 394 Sanctuaries have been set up so far all over the country representing four per cent of the total geographic area. Captive Breeding and Rehabilitation Programmes were continued to cover nine species, including the endangered ones. Under the "Snow Leopard Conservation Project", it has been decided to create a network of 12 Snow Leopard Reserves throughout the Himalayas. The 17th Tiger Reserve has been established in Tamil Nadu. These 17 Tiger Reserves cover 26,643 sq. kms. in 13 states.[22]

3. *Biosphere Reserve*: Out of the 13 identified potential sites for setting up Biosphere Reserves, four have been set up so far. These are located in: Nilgiris in Tamil Nadu, Kerala and Karnataka, and Nanda Devi in U.P., Nokrek in Meghalaya and the Great Nicobar in Andaman and Nicobar Islands.

Environmental Impact Assessment

The divisions in the Ministry dealing with impact assessment have been strengthened to cope with the expanded work. Two hundred fifty-two development projects were appraised during the year, out of which 96 were cleared. Thirty-two projects were rejected out of which six were on grounds of environmental incompatibility. Narmada Control Cell has been created in the Ministry for follow up action on the environmental aspects of Narmada Sagar and Sardar Sarovar Projects. The Doon Valley has been designated as an ecologically fragile area under the Environment Protection Act, 1986. An expert group for recommending norms for determining ecologically fragile areas in the country has been set up.[23]

Environmental Research

Under the environmental research promotion programmes, research projects have been executed by universities, R&D institutions and NGOs concerning studies on impact of developmental activities on natural ecosystems, survey and monitoring of environmental indications, alternative approaches to environmental parameters, pollution control, energy use, instrumentation, etc. The entire area of forestry research was reorganised during 1987-88. The Indian Council of Forestry Research and Education (ICFRE) has been set up to coordinate research activities in this field. In addition to the Forest Research Institute, Dehradun, five more research institutes are being set up.

Environmental Education, Awareness and Information

Under the scheme of Centres of Excellence, two centres, viz., the Ecological Research and Training Centre at the Indian Institute of Science, Bangalore, and the Centre for Environmental Education at Ahmedabad have been established for strengthening country's environmental education, research and training base. During the year 1987-88, the Indian Forest College was upgraded to the status of a National Forest Academy and named after the late Indira Gandhi.[24]

Thirty one-week training courses were organised to train about 800 officers of the Indian Forest Service. November 19 to December 18, 1988 was observed as National Environment Month (NEM). During the NEM, National Museum of Natural History, New Delhi, organised a large number of programmes for various target groups.

A detailed analysis of the budget allocations of the Ministry of Environment and Forests since 1985 clearly reveals that a significant proportion of the budget allocations goes to Ganga Action Plan and Wasteland Development Project. It is also evident that relatively their share is increasing overtime. This shows the manifest bias of the statistic policy on environment whereas Wasteland Development project is basically meant for augmenting the agricultural output. The Ganga Action Plan has more or less urban bias in favour of cities located along the river coast and to appeal to the Hindu sentiments.

IV. PROBLEMS OF IMPLEMENTATION OF ENVIRONMENTAL PROTECTION

The preceding sections (Sections II and III) make it explicit that Government of India has taken a large number of steps in constitutional, legal and administrative fields, in order to protect the environment from further degradation and pollution. In spite of such efforts made on part of both the Central and State Governments, the problem of environmental degradation and pollution has not been controlled to the extent to which it can be. The fault must lie with the institutional set-up or with the people, or with both.

To understand the causes of our failure to tackle environmental problems, one must have some idea of the kind of perceptions that different sections of our society, including our planners and decision makers, have of such problems. Around the time of Stockholm Conference, people in India were not very much aware about the development related to environmental hazards. Even the most educated classes in our society considered all references to the environment in India to be merely fashionable-conservation subjects at best, borrowed from among the issues considered important by the advanced nations. The academics and professionals were, of course, fully aware of the environmental hazards but only in narrow sectoral contexts, such as public health, forestry, etc. What was not perceived was the totality of the linkages between these problems. Towards the mid-seventies, high level committees were set up to look into environmental safeguards but little was really accomplished in practical terms. This was partly due to the usual bureaucratic perversity and inertia towards any innovative thinking. It was also due to one basic misperception. This was the tendency even in the minds of well-intentioned planners and government technocrats, to think of environmental protection as a new and additional sector of government for which fresh allocations of men, money and material would have to be found amidst other competing demands of traditional sectors, like industry, agriculture, transport, health, energy, education. Environment, thus, was not seen as a dimension having to do with the wise management of physical and human resources in each of the above mentioned sectors. Because of these misperceptions and a lack of sincere commitment in following up 'paper initiatives', it is not surprising that governments, both at the Centre and states, have achieved very little in building a firm institutional base in order to tackle the staggering environmental challenges that face us. One crucial function that the government will have to undertake itself at various levels and to varying extent is in environmental appraisal. It has to become an integral part of all planning programmes. To achieve this goal, methodologies appropriate to Indian conditions must be worked out[25] and analysts, trained for the job.

Over the last decade or so, though new legislative enactments related to the environmental have paved the way for protection of environmental resources, yet several problems still persist. Anyone, who closely reads the provisions in these Acts, may wonder why no perceptible steps have been taken by the authorities for their enforcement. One of the serious problems in implementing these laws is that the importance attached to environmental protection is of much recent origin, as such it has not got penetrated deep into the government working, and public servants continue to work with the same glaring neglect of environmental factors as before. Despite the presence of these provisions, we find squalor and unhygienic conditions in villages, towns and cities. This shows there is a laxity in the enforcement of the legal provisions.

From legislation point of view, some loopholes in the Acts hinder the progress of implementation. For instance, Acts have been passed to control the air and water pollution, but they have lost their significance in the absence of similar steps taken for the control of noise pollution. So the requirement is to have a coordinated and broader policy. In particular, one of the main defects of the Water (Prevention and Control of Pollution) Act 1974 itself is that it is not uniformly applicable to the whole of India. In India, water of rivers is subject to the jurisdiction of different states. This is the main obstacle that comes in the way of framing a uniform law and adopting a national policy.

With the coming into force of the Environment (Protection) Act 1986 in November, the Government succeeded in pushing through a cleverly tailored piece of legislation. While at one level, it gave legislative form to the environmental concerns of the people, the Act continues to give ample protection to the interests of industry. Clearly, the Act was not a legislative necessity. For after all there already exist over 300 Central and State Government Acts which generally or specifically deal with such matters. The problem has always been in implementing them. In fact, ironically enough, the new act does not make earlier legislations invalid. There are inadequate linkages in handling matters of industrial and environmental safety.

If the authority contemplated by the Central Government to be charged with its implementation is similar to those of pollution control boards, then it is feared that the entire exercise if foredoomed to failure. This is so because the Boards seem to have adopted a soft line *vis-à-vis* the industry and prefer to be persuasive rather than punitive.[26]

The Act is criticised on the ground that its radical approach regarding the sale of *locus standi* is rendered ineffective by the requirement of 60 days notice which gives a long enough time to the offender to make amends and escape liability under the Act. This is a loophole which needs to be plugged.

Yet another criticism is that there is undue centralisation under the Act and power is vested in the Central Government and even the authorities constituted to implement it are subject to the supervision and control of the Central Government.[27]

In the context of events after Bhopal—and the growing awareness among all sections of the people—the act was a political necessity. For one thing, the increasing pressure being put on the government to take cognisance of the appalling status of industrial safety was not merely a lay instinctive response in the wake of the Bhopal disaster. During the last few years, several State Governments have set up expert groups to study the situation and everyone has come down heavily not only on industry but also on the regulatory machinery as well. In Punjab, for instance, the committee found that the government did not even know the total number of registered factories—while Industries Department listed 80,000 units—the factory inspectorate recognised only 10,000. Of the 258 factories inspected, only one had any kind of pollution control equipment.[28]

However, although the new Act was given the President's assent in May, there are no signs of the new 'nodal agency' which was to be constituted for implementing the legislation. Thus, the rules, formulated under the Act, are in effect nothing more than guidelines. In short, industry is quite safe and protected by a piece of legislation which is quite important even while seeming to be progressive.

The Act is also surprisingly silent with regard to conservation of forests which is a subject of supreme importance in a country like India. One would naturally expect an appropriate amendment to rectify this lacuna in this revolutionary piece of legislation. The government, particularly the Ministry of Environment and Forests, has its work cut out in strengthening the existing environmental legislation and studying areas where it may be worthwhile to enact new ones.

Another point of criticism is that several crore have so far been spent by the Government of India on environmental research without any development. Under the Man and Biosphere Research Committee, research projects have been founded all over the country. Neither the selection of the projects for research funding, nor the practical application of the fruits of research have been anywhere near adequate. In the early stages of the programme, a majority of the projects submitted for approval were little more than classical problems of botany, zoology, medicine, public health, town planning, etc. which had been camouflaged by adding a reference or two to environment and ecology. The concept of multi-disciplinary studies, aimed at solving the real life environmental issues, was practically absent.[29]

Lack of proper coordination and cooperation among the administrative institutions is an important loophole in the whole institutional set-up. Greater degrees of coordination and cooperation is needed for the implementation of environmental programmes, between Central, State and local governments, between different administrative institutions and ministries, and between institutions themselves. If environmental crisis is to be overcome, the Ministry of Environment and Forests and the eco-development agencies will have to make efforts to ensure that environmental awareness spreads to bureaucracies within the government. Environment should not be regarded as just another sector of development. It should form a crucial guiding dimension in each department and ministry.

In 1987, a conference on the "New Environment Protection Act" sponsored by the Indian Law Institute, New Delhi and the Consumer Education and Research Centre, Ahmedabad—a proposal to establish a National Environment Protection Authority (NEPA) with various sub-groups, like an environment impact assessment group, environment courts, an interim relief cell, and a standards and enforcement divisions were mooted. The NEPA should consist of about 20 eminent public citizens, scientists, several activists, representatives from labour, industry, consumers and women's groups and governmental officials.[30] The functions of this agency would be to monitor implementation of various environmental protection laws in the country, and to serve as a coordinating body on environment protection measures taken or proposed to be taken by various State Governments. However, so far, such an agency has not been established in India.

A further weakness of the present official programme for environmental protection is its lack of recognition of the crucial role that NGOs can play in complementing the government's own efforts. A large number of environmental NGOs are working in India on various aspects of environmental protection. By the very nature of their functioning, such NGOs get a much more practical, people-based view of environmental issues that the government—with its unimaginative, inflexible structure—could ever get on its own. Thus, the involvement of NGOs as the eyes and ears of the government in terms of the grassroot monitoring of environmental quality, needs to be properly recognised. In turn, steps should be taken to strengthen the NGOs, to enable them to perform the above mentioned functions.

Highlighting weakness in Government of India's present approach to environmental protection does not in any way change one basic fact. This is that in the present Indian socio-political set-up no environmental programme or improvement on any significant scale can take place without the direct or indirect involvement of the Central and State Governments. Very creditable work by private groups in fields, like social forestry, rural sanitation, environmental education, etc. notwithstanding, it is governmental intervention at all levels—whether by providing finances or other incentives or expertise or equipment and other infrastructure support—that will determine the success or otherwise of environmental management programmes. This is not necessarily a very desirable state of affairs, but it is a hard reality that must be faced and "internalised" by all those concerned about the environment.[31]

CONCLUDING OBSERVATIONS

The Responsibility for Environment Protection

The problem of conserving the environment while proceeding with necessary development is a colossal one. It is so huge that in a country like India, it presents a great challenge to those who have to implement the policies and programmes. The problems encompass many fields, and therefore, vast areas of the subject are handled at the national level by various ministries and departments of the Government of India. However, India being a federal system, much of the action in this field has to be decentralised and entrusted to the states. It is mainly the State Governments, who have to carry out the necessary measures. The implementation of environmental policies and evaluation of their impact would necessarily have to be devolved on the local administration and the local self-governing institutions in the cities, towns and villages.

At the behest of the NCEPC, established in February 1972 to provide a focal point in the structure of the government where environmental considerations could receive close attention in an integrated manner, almost all the states and the Union Territories of India have established environmental boards/committees with the terms of reference almost similar to the national committees. These boards/committees are chaired by the respective Chief Ministers because it was thought that chairmanship by head of government would give stature and executive authority to the boards. An official of the Union Department of Environment, which is responsible for evolving national policy on environment commensurate with the needs of development, is invariably a member of the State Board Committees. This arrangement has been thought necessary to enable good liaison between the national committees and the State Boards.

However, at present the state environmental committees or the state departments of environment lack necessary technical expertise. These administrative bodies suffer in their work and effectiveness due to utter paucity of staff. A further handicap is the non-availability of funds or financial support for setting up necessary expert committees, visits to project sites, and preparation of environmental appraisal of projects handled by state governments. The situation is really serious, in the sense that in most states, these environmental committees are not at all active. Financial stringency, coupled with inadequate attention being paid by State Governments to whatever meagre environmental departments/committees that exist there, is affecting the dedication and motivation of the Centre's leadership and its officials.

The net result of this state of affairs is that at the decentralised levels of administration, i.e., the districts and the cities, the official institutions, which are charged with the responsibility of action for protection of environmental concerns are unable to act effectively. The main obligation of the state to meet its constitutional requirements—such as enact appropriate laws, rules and regulations; set up enforcement and review mechanism; and invite the public to participate in the environmental policy process—remains largely unfulfilled. Despite the indifference shown by the administration in the cities and towns in India in either enforcing the laws to protect the quality of environment or to take constructive or punitive action in preservation or improvement of environment, the voluntary NGOs and the judiciary, in some cases, have been quite active in bringing to the notice of the administrative authorities in the cities the damages caused to the environment as a result of government's development policies or commercial exploitation of the forests or wildlife by private organisations. The NGO's crusade against the Silent Valley Project, the Mathura Refinery, the West Coast Fertiliser Plant, the Dal Lake Project, the Berisal Project, and the famous Chipko Andolan provide some hope for creating awareness in public and authorities about the kind of catastrophes the people in India are heading for through environmental degradation.

We may now conclude by saying that in India all the life support systems are now under serious stress and strains. Both the human and animal population pressures have reached a level where the flora, fauna, soil and water and also the atmospheric conditions are becoming more and more depleted, polluted and adversely affected. Consequently, in a predominantly agricultural country, the renewable base of land resources has been eroded and environmental degradation has taken place in the name of development. The situation calls for a bold approach to development which should be based on techno-environmental and socio-economic evolution of each development project, if the human beings are to be spared of the recurrent of tragedies like the Bhopal Gas or Shri Ram Fertilisers leaks or the hazards of river, water, or air pollution.

REFERENCES

1. United Nations, *Development and Environment*, 1972, pp. 7-8.
2. Ramakrishna Mission, *Cultural Heritage of India*, Vols. I, II and III, 1972.
3. Arun C. Vakil, *Economic Aspects of Environmental Pollution in India*, Bombay, Arun C. Vakil, 1984, p. 98.
4. CSE, *The State of India's Environment: 1984-85, The Second Citizen's Report*, Centre for Science and Environment, New Delhi, 1985, p. 13.
5. *Ibid.*
6. S. Bhatt, *Environmental Protection and International Law*, New Delhi, Radiant Publishers; 1985, p. 1.
7. Suresh Jain and Vimla Jain. (eds.), *Environmental Law in India*, Indore, The Lawyers Home, 1984, p. 3.
8. *Forty Second Constitutional Amendment Act*, 1976.
9. S.M. Jain (ed.), *Legal Control of Environmental Pollution*, New Delhi, Indian Law Institute, 1980, p. 3.
10. *Ibid.*
11. Suresh Jain and Vimla Jain (eds.), *op. cit.*, p. 38.
12. *Forest Conservation Act*, 1980.
13. The Statement of Objects and Reasons of the Environment Protection Act, 1986.
14. Ibid.
15. Government of India, Ministry of Environment and Forests, *Annual Report*, 1988-89, p. 6.
16. Ibid.
17. Government of India, Ministry of Environment and Forests, *Annual Report*, 1985-86 p. 4
18. Annual Report, 1988-89, *op. cit.*, p. 7.
19. *Ibid.*, p. 8.
20. *Ibid.*, p. 3.
21. *Ibid.*, p. 4.
22. *Ibid.*, p. 4.
23. *Ibid.*, p. 5
24. Government of India, Ministry of Environment and Forests, Annual Report, 1987-88, p. 8.

25. Thomas Mathew, "Governmental Response to Environmental Needs in India, *India International Centre, Quarterly*, Vol. 9, Nos. 3 and 4, December, 1982, pp. 240-42.
26. Refer *Ecology* Vol. 1, No. 3, August, 1986, p. 89.
27. *Ibid*, p. 91.
28. Refer *Economic and Political Weekly*, Vol. XXII, No. 4, January 24, 1987, p. 106.
29. Thomas Mathew, *op. cit.*, pp. 243-44.
30. See Times of India, April 10, 1989, p. 7, col. 5 & 6.
31. Thomas Mathew, *op. cit.*, p. 247.

Section II: AREA DEVELOPMENT APPROACH

2

Area Development Approach to National Resource Administration

Rakesh Hooja

The Command Area Development Approach was first thought of 25 years ago in 1972. It would be appropriate to look back and see how the concept/approach has evolved since then, starting with the reasons for the need of such an approach.

MULTIDISCIPLINARITY OF CAD COMBINING THE TECHNICAL AND INSTITUTIONAL ASPECTS

Perception of the Concept

Today, there are many in Irrigation Departments throughout India for whom an irrigation scheme or project one concerned basically with construction of dams and canals and their maintenance. In fact, for many of them even proper running of water in the canals and the functions of (to use terms used by Uphoff, Meinzen-Dick and St. Julien; and Coward)[1] water acquisition, allocation, distribution (if necessary drainage) and conflict management and recourse mobilization are unnecessary botherations which they have to cope up with when they would much rather be dealing with the design, construction, and maintenance of structures of with maintenance of the physical system. Perhaps this is because Irrigation Departments in India are manned almost exclusively by engineers, who have not been brought up to study writers like Coward who states that "irrigation development requires successful joining of irrigation technology and appropriate institutions and organizations to govern that technology."[2] Since most present-day project commands already have settled populations, it is also now forgotten by many in India (and abroad) that irrigation projects also may need to concern themselves with settlement/colonization in the early stages of their development.

However, even outside India, writers have had to caution against the tendency of many irrigation bureaucrats to consider irrigation schemes [according to Kellar this term includes watershed, and irrigation system(s) which deal(s) with the capture, delivery, application and removal of water from agriculture land, the people, information systems, and the necessary production, financial and institutional inputs all put together] as being limited in scope to aspects related to developing and managing irrigation systems.[3] As Lowdermilk had written, irrigation management is "the process by which water is manipulated (controlled) and used in the production of food and firbre... (It) is not water resources, dams or reservoirs to capture water; nor codes, laws or institutions to allocate water; nor farmers organizations, nor soils or cropping systems. It is, however, the way these skills and physical, biological, chemical and social resources are utilized for improved food and fibre production."[4]

Similarly Uphoff, Meinzen-Dick and St. Julien point out that "there are many ways in which an irrigation enterprise can fail. Engineering designs and technical operations need to be correct and efficient... if soils are not suitable for irrigation, productivity may be poor and decline. Factor and market prices have to be 'right'... Physical and economic factors will not be productive unless the many activities associated with irrigation are integrated into an operational system. The human efforts that transform material relationships to make irrigation feasible establish a socio-technical process that is much more complex than the observable acquisition and distribution of water to the fields. Getting this larger process 'right' is essential."[5]

Wade and Seckler talk about the need to integrate physical and managerial design.[6] Wade also shows how any sharp distinction between technical and institutional aspects is bound to breakdown.[7]

In similar vein, Kellar has paraphrased Peterson (1984) to state that what is required is "multidisciplinary diagnosis, study, thought and action."[8]

Keller went to suggest, in Sampath and Young, a more disciplinary framework leading to multi-disciplinary action, backed up by an interdisciplinary framework, leading to inter-disciplinary action.

Dimension of Coordinated, Integrated and Multidisciplinary Development

Western countries do not have to worry about whether as sufficiently developed physical and economic infrastructure along with provision for amenities and services exists as a given part of the environment within which an irrigation scheme can function, with the irrigation scheme itself forming the external environment for an irrigation system. Hence, for irrigation schemes, such as those in India, we have to think beyond the watershed, water supply and agricultural domains of Kellar[9] in an irrigation scheme and also consider the dependency of the irrigation scheme on the larger human and natural eco-systems. Thus, irrigation schemes cannot be considered separately from area development schemes but, in fact, need to be considered instead as multi-disciplinary, integrated and interdependent area development schemes based on irrigation and involving occupational changes, fresh settlement of resettlement of populations, infrastructure development, agriculture, irrigation, individual beneficiary schemes and coordinated and integrated functioning of various sectoral programmes in the area.

It is to ensure coordinated, integrated and multidisciplinary planning and implementation of irrigation schemes that India's National Water Policy of 1987 had advocated that all irrigation projects should adopt the Command Area Development (CAD) Approach, A CAD approach can be said to be one based on multidisciplinary, interdependent and integrated area development based on irrigation and water management. The Ninth Five Year Plan Working Group defines the broad-based objective of CAD to improve water-use efficiency by way of increasing agriculture production and/or by reducing water expense through efficient management of various production factors, such as land, water, other inputs, crops, credit, etc. Such measures include increasing cropping intensities, adopting high-yielding varieties, ensuring adequate irrigation in space and time, adequate fertilizer use, plant protection measures, minimizing application losses of water through On Farm Development (OFD), and cultivation of climatically efficient crops of varying water requirement in a combination which is affordable in terms of availability of water supply and attainment of optimal crop production.

CAD Conception in India: Historical Perspective

Evolution of the Concept

The Irrigation Commission (1972) suggested constitution of special administrative units for coordinated and expeditious development of command areas of major and medium irrigation projects. A Ministers Committee of Government of India (1972-73) had similar views. This led to a new programme of CAD for which Government of India issued circular letters in August and September 1973 for setting up of CAD Authorities under Area Development Commissioners to take measures for optimum utilization of irrigation potential and for stepping up agriculture production through coordinated, multidisciplinary efforts. Sivamohan and Scott have rightly pointed out that India's CAD concept is unique: aiming to integrate a very wide range of developmental, sectoral and functional components and sub-components through articulation of a comprehensive strategy of development which includes disparate fields previously (and even now by many) thought to be unrelated to irrigated agriculture.[10] Their analysis of the reasons why CAD was initiated based on concern for the gap in utilization of already created irrigated potential, a change in the concept of irrigated agriculture, recognition of the need of infrastructure development below the outlet level, and concerns for distributive justice, is unexceptionable and the very brief summary of the subsequent shifts in CAD policy quite perceptive.

Incomplete View of CAD Experience and Need for a Unified Set-up

However, by only listing the components recommended by the National Commission on Agriculture and the 14 activities originally envisaged in 1973[11]—not including Government of India's amended list of September 1976, or the objectives of CAD recommended by Administrative Staff College of India (ASCI)[12] in a study conducted for the Government, or the functions for CAD Authorities suggested by the Task Force (1990), or the discussions by the 1983 Task Force, the 1987 Indian Institute of Management Study, the 1988 National Workshop, and the Working Group on preparing

Eighth Plan proposals for CAD (1990)—and only mentioning the 1981 High Level Committee in a different context in a footnote, they have not managed to explain the rationale of all the changes, or the interplay of different forces and different experiences of the CAD approach being tried out in Indian irrigation. Thus, at least to the mind of this commentator (who has been at the helm of affairs in large CAD Projects and has tied to keep himself abreast of governmental thinking and mid-course corrections in the CAD programme, both due to his academic interest and compulsions of his responsibilities as he has been Secretary to Government of Rajasthan for Command Area Development and Water Utilization since January 1994), they ended up conveying an incomplete impression to the reader of the mosaic of different CAD experiences in the country.

It is not true (as suggested by Sivamohan and Scott)[13] that CAD merely became a part of either the Agriculture or the Irrigation Department in every Indian state, thus neglecting one or the other aspects. Some states did set up integrated and separate organizations with officers from concerned departments being seconded to the CAD set-up. Though now only one or two states retain such integrated organization and the Ninth Five Year Plan Working Group on CAD has again had to emphasize the need for a unified administrative set-up for CAD Projects. Nevertheless, it is correct that tensions between people from different departments exist and attempts at integration face major difficulty and that no workable solution has so far been found for unsatisfactory man system operations or for lack of success of farmers organizations. Also, the change in emphasis from "full package". The OFD (for discussion on full package of OFD see Hooja)[14] to concentrate on construction of field channels and *warabandi* (rotational water supply) did occur. But, the comprehensive area development approach, with focus on increased agricultural production and investment aimed at rural prosperity, was never abandoned by the government, and the conclusions of Sivamohan and Scott that the policy thrust developed in the earlier years has been more or less lost in all the states in perhaps partially true only for some states.

EVOLVING AN IDEAL CAD ORGANISATION

In this article, I have undertaken to supplement the analysis already available in *ODI Irrigation Management Network Paper 20,* with my views about the objectives of CAD and the activities which should be implemented directly by a CAD project. I will also make some comments about the ideal CAD organization. As a first step, I will attempt a summary of the approach set forth in the Government of India, Eighth Five Year Plan Working Group on CAD[15] in the Task Force 1990, and in the Ninth Plan Working Group for CAD.[16] These embody the latest government pronouncements about the CAD Programme in India.

In Eight Plan Working Group indicates that (building on the Seventh Plan's thrusts on Integrated Water Management, OFD works and Agriculture Inputs Supply) the core CAD items should be to ensure reliability of irrigation water supply through unified control and adoption of management approach and intensification of software components, such as adaptive trials and demonstrations, farmers' participation and training, staff training, conduct of crop cutting and farm management studies, and communication. The future thrust of the programme is to be towards better water management. There is need to consider the entire distribution system from headworks to farm gate as one management unit to ensure that irrigation water releases follow a pre-determined plan and any deviation from planned and publicized releases should be identified and corrective action taken. Wireless communication system would be a major requirement for effective operation of the distribution system.

Involvement of farmers in irrigation management, though it has begun, should be converted into a mass movement of farmers for their effective participation below the minor outlet level and, to this end, voluntary agencies may be involved in action research projects.

Surface and ground water resources have been considered so far more in isolation than in conjunction. This has often resulted in inadequacy and unreliability of water during the period of peak demand, on the one hand, and waterlogging and related problems of salinity, on the other. CAD projects should, therefore, plan conjunctive use to ensure that water distribution is so regulated that farmers are induced to switch over to cropping patterns more consistent with the soil characteristics of the land on which the crops are grown and a balance is struck between the draft from ground water and the recharge of ground water from surface sources.

Changes Suggested by Planning Commission

The Eighth Five Year Plan Working Group had also suggested changes in the existing pattern of central financing as described by Sivamohan and Scot[17] in such a manner that field channels are constructed on grant basis from the Central and state governments without any liability on the farmers; 100 per cent Central assistance is provided for *warabandi* in case the same is implemented through an organized farmers' association; assistance is extended for field drains on the same pattern as for field channels; and the establishment of a monitoring cell at project level through 100 per cent Central assistance has been proposed.

In April 1996, the Government of India slightly modified its financing pattern for matching grants and loans to the states. For field drains, Central assistance was brought at par with that of field channels (50% of cost from canal outlet to channel). Arrangement subsidy for Farmers Associations, which get registered and take over distribution of water in a canal, get a one-time functional grant of Rs. 500 per hectare to be shared between Government of India, State Government and Farmers Association in the ratio of 9:9:2 has been provided for Cost of reclamation of irrigated waterlogged areas up to a maximum of Rs. 12,000 per hectare would be shared on a 50:50 bass between Central and State Governments.

Even though the Ninth Plan Working Group (1996) recommendations succeeded the 1990 Task Force recommendations, we are summarizing there here in continuation to those of the Eighth Plan. There should be a unified administrative set-up for CAD Authorities (CADAs) which should have complete technical and administrative control over officers from various departments deputed to it. The CADA should also have unified command from headworks down to last level in field and up to the last outfall of drainage network. Participatory Irrigation Management should necessarily be promoted as part of CAD. Enhanced subsidy should be given for development of ground water and conjunctive water use be encouraged. In addition to major and medium projects, minor irrigation projects (500 ha. to 2000 ha.) should also included udder Centrally sponsored CAD. Emphasis on sprinkler and drip should be given to economise on use of water. Adaptive trials and demonstrations on farmers fields and training of functionaries, farmers and NGOs, as well as monitoring and evaluation by a multidisciplinary team, should receive 100 per cent Central Grant. A 100 per cent Grant to be shared on 80:20 basis by Center and States should be provided for: (*i*) Survey, Planning and Construction of OFD, (*ii*) Construction of field channels, (*iii*) construction of field, and collector, drains (collector drains were not covered earlier under Central assistance for CAD), (*iv*) reclamation and survey of waterlogged areas, (*v*) rehabilitation of minor/distributories linked to Participatory Irrigation Management, (*vi*) enforcement of *warabandi,* (*vii*) Partial subsidy to small and marginal farmers and SC/ST against loan's being taken by them, (*viii*) crop compensation, (*ix*) establishment costs of work items, and (*x*) one-time functional grant to water-users associations.

The Working Group has also suggested setting up of State Level Advisory Council for CAD activities.

The shortcoming and constraints which the Ninth Five Year Plan Working Group hopes CAD would enable the country to overcome are: (*i*) lack of reliability of water supply at the canal outlet due to inadequate maintenance of irrigation system, (*ii*) difficulty in obtaining land for field channels due to lack of consolidation of holdings, and lack of proper alignment of field channels in the absence of consolidation, (*iii*) existence of unlined field channels which can easily be ploughed over leading to conflicts, (*iv*) lack of coordination between CAD and Irrigation Departments, (*v*) lack of *warabandi,* (*vi*) lack of maintenance of field channels and field drains and drainage system below field channels, (*vii*) absence of collector and intermediate drains, (*viii*) problem of waterlogging, soil salinity and alkalinity, (*ix*) lack of Extension Service support, (*x*) lack of attention to development of wireless communication and farm roads, (*xi*) lack of coordination among different departments at State level concerned with CAD, (*xii*) lack of farmers participation, (*xiii*) lack of marketing infrastructure, (*xiv*) lack of On Farm Water Management, and (*xv*) lack of proper Crop Management.

Performance Indicators of CAD and Recommendations of National Workshop

Accordingly, the Ninth Plan Working Group has suggested the following performance indicators for the CAD Programme: (*a*) equitable distribution of water, (*b*) Production and productivity enhancement, (*c*) water supply augmentation to command additional areas, (*d*) demand based average water availability, (*e*) sustainability of resource base, (*f*) adequate and balanced level of input use, (*g*) adoption of appropriate technology, and (*h*) optimizing water use efficiency per of unit of land and per unit of water.

The Ninth Plan Working Group report is still to be processed and implemented. The 1990 Task Force,[18] however, has already had an impact on Government of India's policies regarding CAD.

Since the Task Force 1990 was set up as a result of a National Workshop on CAD held in February 1988, the recommendations of that workshop are being reproduced in part below:

It is recognized that removal of uncertainty in irrigation water supply is the key element is meeting the basic objective, of the Programme. Reliability of supply is most cases is impeded by:

- Lack of unified control of water management from headworks to farm gate;
- System inadequacies, such as lack of control structure, measuring devices and absence of distribution system within an outlet command;
- Inadequate preventive and operation maintenance of water distribution system; and
- Lack of farmers' participation in irrigation management.

1. The Workshop recommends that removal of uncertainty in the supply of irrigation water be treated as the core be element in the CAD programme.
2. The Workshop feels that there should be unified control of irrigation water management and recommends that management of irrigation system right from headwork to farm gate should rest with CADA.
3. Keeping in view the crucial importance of modernization and maintenance, the Workshop recommends that adequate funds be mobilized for modernization to correct system inadequacies and for meeting maintenance requirements.
4. Participation of farmers in irrigation management is more widely recognized than practiced. With active participation of beneficiaries, effectiveness of the programme would improve and maintenance of the irrigation at micro level be better achieved. The Workshop recommends intensification of efforts to secure participation of irrigators in the CAD programme.
5. The Workshop recommends closer interaction of agriculture research and extension service with CADA to ensure adoption of suitable cropping pattern and better crop water management practices.
6. Promotion of conjunctive use of surface and ground water not only enhances water availability but also leads to avoidance of deleterious effects, such as waterlogging and salinity, or excessive fall in the water table noticed when development of surface water or ground water projects are taken up in isolation. The Workshop recommends that in keeping with the National Water Policy, conjunctive use of water be made an integral part of all projects.
7. To alleviate, if not eliminate, problems of waterlogging and salinity, the Workshop recommends that drainage works be given high priority in the existing projects and should form an integral part of all new projects.
8. The workshop recommends that lining of channels be taken up only to the extent needed, based on soil characteristics and cost effectiveness.

9. Land leveling is capital intensive and expensive to implement if benefits are marginal. When technical considerations require land shaping the Workshop recommends that project authorities should involve specialists of high caliber in drawing up plans and ensure that such works are taken up only where benefits substantially exceed the costs.
10. Constraints on achievements of Programme objective are project specific. The Workshop recommends that project-wise identification of bottlenecks and formulation and implementation of action plans should be given due recognition.
11. Since CAD Programme and CAD Authorities are widely known and states have evolved arrangements for administration of the Programme best suited to their local conditions, the Workshop does not consider it necessary to rename the Programme or suggest allocation of the Programme to any particular administrative department at the state level.
12. The Workshop recognizes the need for management oriented multidisciplinary teams working at the CAD project level to ensure efficient discharge of the core function of providing reliable water supply at the farm gate, and such other functions that may be assigned to CADA's to fulfill the basic objective of improving utilization of irrigation potential and increasing productivity in irrigated agriculture.
13. The Workshop recommends setting up of a Task Force to suggest a suitable indicative organizational model for CADA having due regard to economy.
14. There is need for improvement in the quality of personnel and their training, particularly at the level of CAD workers; farmers' training is also equally important. The Workshop recommends that training programmes be reviewed; facilities in Water and Land Management Institutes (WALMIs) be strengthened and intensively utilized for this purpose.
15. Irrigation water rates, in most cases, do not cover even maintenance charges and do not convey the scarcity value of water. Water charges are often substantially higher in the case of ground water, thereby rendering conjunctive use less attractive to the farmer. Water rates for surface water and ground water need to be rationalized and should be adequate to cover the annual maintenance and operation charges as also a part of the fixed cost. It should be the endeavour to reach this ideal over a period of time while ensuring, assured and timely supplied of irrigation water.

Task Force View on Functions of CADA

The Task Force 1990 reminds us that "when the CAD programme was initiated in 1973-74, the main objective was to increase agriculture production in irrigated areas. Agricultural productivity was sought to be maximsed by bridging the gap between creation of irrigation potential and its utilization together with efficient management of irrigation water, soil and various inputs, provision of extension and credit facilities, scientific crop planning etc... However, this has not happened primarily due to organizational deficiencies." The report goes on to state, "this task force feels that the concept of CAD Programme is a very well conceived one and it is as relevant today as it was at the time of its introduction. The primary objective of the Programme can, therefore, be said to be the optimization of production in irrigated agriculture through a multi-disciplinary, integrated and well coordinated approach to development of the Command Area."

The functions of CADA recommended by the Task Force 1990 also include construction and maintenance of main and link drains, modernization of the main and distribution irrigation system, developing solutions for the ill effects of irrigation on the environment, and the marketing and processing of agricultural produce and establishment of agro-based industries.

Demand based water supply, based on dynamic regulation for diversified cropping to provide water at critical stages of each crop (as mentioned in *ODI Irrigation Management Network Paper 20*) is being talked of in the Irrigation Departments in recent years. But this approach has not yet found a mention in official CAD policy documents; though one suspects, it would soon become a major concern of CAD.

The September 1992 Irrigation Ministers' Conference also mooted the idea of Command Area Management to supplement CAD, thus reemphassing that CAD should not focus merely on engineering construction activities but also on management recourses.

The *Planning Commission Approach Paper for the Ninth Five Year Plan,* recently approved, has also stressed the need to continue the Centrally sponsored CAD Progamme.

Objectives of CAD

As regards the objectives of CAD, enlarging on Kathpalia Hooja, Hooja, Hooja, ORG and Jayaraman[19] we can list the following as appropriate:

1. Full utilization of created irrigation potential (potential can be deemed to have been created when delivery system up to 5-8 hectare level is in place).
2. Increased productivity per unit of water and per unit of land.
3. Provision of predictable water supply to all farmers.
4. Efficient use of water with equitable distribution at minimum administrative cost.
5. Evolving appropriate cropping pattern and persuading farmers to follow them.
6. Conservation of soil and water resources.
7. Planned and regulated development of the command area and its inhabitants in harmony with the land and its agro-climate conditions.
8. Settler motivation in case of virgin area being brought under irrigated cultivation for the first time, and resettlement assistance, in case population is being displaced.

9. Attainment of cost effectiveness and productive returns on investments of the farmers.
10. Protection of the developed command area to avoid environmental damage and loss of valuable command area due to waterlogging, salinity, erosion, gully formation, pest infestation, canal siltation, etc.
11. Providing the organizational means and incentives for effective and constructive farmers participation in system operation and maintenance.
12. Balancing industrial, domestic, livestock, drinking water and irrigation demands for water.
13. Smoothen transformation of labourers, rainfed farmers or pastoralists into irrigated cultivators with improved living standards.
14. Providing basic infrastructure improved amenities and services, and increased employment opportunities.
15. Creating coordinated and well integrated government delivery system for the command area.
16. Adopting a holistic project approach for each irrigation project.

Activities to be Performed in a CAD Project

As regards the activities which should be performed by CADA, a list originally prepared for Hooja[20] based on Pande[21] and Sarupria[22] which was subsequently modified for Hooja[23] and Hooja[24] is being further refined as follows:

A. Watershed Management above the headworks and management of the headworks.

B. Improvement of existing Irrigation System (including minor and sub-minors).

1. Lining, desilting and deweeding of canals (and redesigning canal systems, if necessary), including deferred maintenance or rehabilitation of canals where necessary.
2. Construction and operation of control structures.
3. Rationalization of outlets.
4. Proper maintenance.
5. Canal capacity works and canal modernization as well as constructing intermediate storage for better water regulation.
6. Enforcing water discipline and *warabandi* (rostered rotational water supply).
7. Stabilization of canal banks through: (*a*) planning, and (*b*) engineering works.
8. Rotational running of canals and *warabandi* within the outlet chack.
9. Maintaining full supply levels of canals for reliable, timely an adequate supply of water.
10. Conjunctive use of ground, surface and drainage water for irrigation.
11. Wireless communication for better canal management.
12. Weed-control and prevention of canal management.
13. Control of unauthorized use of water.

C. Drainage Works

1. Construction of main drains, carrier (or linkage or intermediate) drains and seepage (or interceptor) drains, skimming wells etc.
2. Maintenance of the above.

D. Flood Control Measures

E. On Farm Development (OFD)

1. Farm drainage works.
2. Watercourse construction works, including re-alignment of water courses, where necessary.
3. Farm road works.
4. Realignment of field boundaries and updating of land records and land revenue maps.
5. Lining of water courses.
6. Land leveling and land shaping.
7. Individual wells for supplemental irrigation.
8. Protection of marginal lands and already developed OFD lands through soil conservation and afforestation techniques for gully and ravine control.
9. Reclamation of saline and alkaline lands.
10. Suitable treatment of unirrigated or non-command patches that fall within the larger command area.
11. Monitoring of water table.

F. Agricultural Activities

1. Intensive Agriculture Extension system which also undertakes irrigation extension.
2. Adaptive and adoptive research to feed the extension system.
3. Provision of and/or monitoring of supplies of inputs, including water and services and tie-up of the extension system with co-operatives and canal water distribution.
4. Propagation of better on-farm water application and cultivation techniques and diffusion of innovations.
5. Popularising water users associations and Participatory Irrigation Management.
6. Conduct of soil and hydrogeological surveys.
7. Conduct of Farm Management surveys, crop cutting experiments, etc.
8. Farmers training.
9. Evolving and promoting optimal cropping patterns.
10. Recording agro-meteorological date to determine crop water requirements.

G. Macro Development of Command Areas

1. Land allotment and motivation of new settlers or resettlement of displaced persons.

2. Roads for opening up the command area for irrigated agriculture.
3. Market yards and storage facilities.
4. Processing Industries.
5. Forestry, pastures and horticulture.
6. Development of human settlements in virgin areas being brought under irrigation, including town and country planning, provision of schools/ dispensaries, etc.
7. Development of both milch and drought animals.
8. Containment of water-borne human and animal diseases.
9. Aquaculture.
10. Development of rural artisans and rural industries.
11. Special programmes for the rural poor, like IRD of Government of India.
12. Land reforms and consolidation of holding, if necessary.
13. Afforestation to keep soil from blowing into canals.
14. Provision of drinking water in newly settled areas.
15. Settling pastoralists for pasture development and livestock breeding on lands not fit for crop husbandry.
16. Planning studies to decide future priorities.

H. Institutions

1. Integrated managerial control of the system, the area, and of irrigation engineers, agriculture engineers, (land) revenue staff, agriculture extension and research set-up, cooperative structure, Public Works Departments (PWD) and Ground Water Department (GWD) staff, afforestation staff, Agriculture Producer Marketing Committees, dairy and animal husbandry staff, and district level functionaries of various government departments, who are placed under the supervision, control and/or coordination of the Project Administrator or Area Development Commissioner.
2. Coordinating with special credit institutions for providing: (*a*) short-term credit for agriculture inputs, (*b*) Term credit for OFD and related works, and (*c*) IRD credit for small and marginal farmers, agricultural labourers, rural artisans and other rural poor.
3. Coordination with peoples representatives, panchayats and farmers outlet committees.
4. Systematic implementation.
5. Concurrent evaluation and monitoring for self-assessment and mid-course corrections.

Physical Achievements of CAD

From its inception to 1994, 14.8 million hactare was included under CAD Project of which 11.4 million hectare irrigation potential has been utilized (*i.e.*, 77% utilization). Field channels have been constructed in 13.5 million hactare, field drains in 0.7 million hactare, land leveling done in 2.1 million hactare and *warabandi* enforced in 8.2 million hactare up to March 1995. However, as already indicated above, these achievements are not very relevant performance indicators from the point of view of assessing the impact of CAD Programme.

NEEDS OF CAD

An Integrated Organizational Structure

Now to turn to the question of appropriate organizational structure. The ASCI study,[25] Sing[26] and the Task Froce[27] 1990 have all commented favourably on the CADA set-up in the Indira Gandhi Canal Project (IGCP; formerly Rajasthan Canal) as incorporating all the objectives of CAD laid down by the Central Government with all relevant functions under the direct control of the CAD authority and linkages established with CADA through the budgetary process. Here (Hooja, Hooja and Kaudia),[28] the Area Development Commissioner (ADC) has been delegated powers of Chief Engineer (Irrigation); Chief Engineer. (Ground Water), Chief Engineer, IGCP; Director of Agriculture; Registrar of Cooperative Societies; Chief Town Planner; Director of Animal Husbandry; Director, Sheep and Wool; and Divisional Commissioner, has been authorized to coordinate the work of the Colonization Commissioner as well as of the District Collector.

The Area Development Commissioner directly administers operation, maintenance and regulation of Canals, Left-over Canal Construction works, construction of water courses, agriculture extension, farmers training, adaptive research and trials in CAD run farms, and on farmers fields, water application trials, settler motivation, monitoring of roads, drinking water arrangements, conduct of planning studies, including hydrogeological barrier studies, afforestation, anti-waterlogging and drainage, and certain aspects of animal husbandry, sheep and wool, and cooperatives development works and two World Food programme Projects—one for settlers and the other for labourers, and for infrastructure development. Thus, the state government is funding some activities in addition to those funded by the Central Government as part of CAD.

The Area Development Commissioner also coordinates works relating to land allotment and colonization, *mandi* towns developments, agricultural marketing and some aspects of canal construction. Each state government department seconds, or deputes, its staff to the CAD set-up where they work directly under the ADC as part of one organization. Thus, the CAD set-up corresponds to what Jayaraman[29] had called a new concept in rural development strategy where instead of separate departments, each having its own autonomy, the new strategy is to create an administrative unit, based on natural resource activity, that cuts across the usual administrative boundaries.

Rajasthan, like a few other states, also has a separate state level CAD department headed by a full-time Secretary.

However, while such an integrated CAD set-up has helped in smoother implementation, it has certainly not been plan sailing. The Irrigation Department and the Indira Gandhi Canal Board (responsible for canal construction) have often wanted to take away functions assigned to the CADA. The Forest Department has resisted its officers and staff being placed under the ADC and afforestation works being done by the CADA. The Colonization Department would prefer to go its own way rather than having to coordinate its land allotment and land possession, giving work with that of canal construction or with CAD; and the placing of the Colonization Commissioner fully under ADC has been resisted.

A similar integrated set-up of CAD-IGNP also exists in CAD-Chambal Rajasthan project, though one CAD project in Rajasthan-Mahi does not have a unified set-up. Recently, for Sidhmuck-Nauhar also, the government has opted for a unified and integrated CAD set-up.

Even within CAD, staff of various wings tend to look at the work of their own wing as a separate water-tight compartment, if not viewing other wings like separate department, with whom they tend to have traditional departmental rivalries, or on whom they can try to pass on blame for non-achievement of the impact of the CAD project as a whole. Trying to get the staff to take a holistic or comprehensive overview of issues proved difficult and the comments of Jayaraman[30] for non-integrated CADAs that "much of the CADA commissioner's time is wasted because of the... time consuming procedures needed to attain coordination...often the personal appeals of the Commissioner to all units and his very senior status are the only means for achieving coordination" is partially applicable even for Rajasthan's interacted CADA set-up. The Ids study[31] has also indirectly referred to this problem when they mentioned the frequent recourse to meeting by the ADC, the Additional Area Development Commissioner and the heads of various wings of CAD.

Sarupria had noted not he context of one Indian State which does not have an integrated CAD organization that irrigation and agriculture staff attach little significance to the CAD approach "the atmosphere being one of total indifference if not outright hostility. In particular, irrigation officials, especially at the project level, were emphatic in their view that irrigation management was a techno-legal problem and only the Irrigation Department officials, mostly engineers were competent to handle it". Wade's[32] observation that "the Irrigation Department is powerful, wealthy and accustomed to going its own way; and on the whole has been slow to sympathies with CAD ideas" is still relevant. Dandeker[33] has bemoaned the defective planning and execution of irrigation projects in India and attributed it to the fact that planning of irrigation projects in India and attributed it to the fact that planning of irrigation projects is mostly done by State Irrigation Departments which still continue to be the monopoly of civil engineers and, therefore, the inputs from other disciplines, such as agronomy, agro-economy, social sciences, etc., is not up to the desired level.

However, the longer an integrated CAD set-up remains in existence, the lesser the likelihood of such intra-discipline tensions and of excessive display of loyalty towards the parent department continuing, as instead, the CAD approach gets entrenched in tradition. (At least Kathpalia's recommendation that the CAD department be dispensed with the irrigation and the agriculture departments strengthened and that a coordinating committee be set up, does not appear to be valid to this commentator.) As noted above, the Ninth Plan Working Group has emphasized the need for integrated organizational set-up.

Farmers Participation

More disturbing is the failure of even the best CAD organizations to evoke much farmers participation except in some rare instances. Partly this may be because as Champers said "to a remarkable degree, many writers on irrigation ignore and even appear to be unaware of the relationship between people and irrigation water. Attention is usually fixed on hydrological, engineering, agricultural and economic aspects. Especially in official documents, it is rare to find described, let alone analyzed, the human side of the organization and operation of irrigation systems, the management of those who manage water, the procedures of allocation of water to groups of individuals, and the distribution of water within groups. There may be almost as may instances of these omissions as there are reports on irrigation."[34] (To Chambers list, we may add that analysis of farmers likely behaviour in varying circumstances also fails to find place in reports regarding CAD and irrigation). Hence, efforts to involve farmers in water management are like grouping in the dark due to insufficient knowledge and understanding.

Siva Mohan and Scott[35] are correct in their assertion that water shortages (and also in this writer's view, uncertainty about supply of water) due to main system operation lead to conflict, "erosion of communal ethics" and breakdown of farmers associations. Here, the argument repeatedly being set forth by Freeman[36] and Freeman and Lodermilk (in Cernea 1991 – the earlier version is the 1985 edition)[37] that main irrigation system requirements, knowledge, attitudes and environment differ drastically from those existing at the farm of outlet level and accordingly that a middle-level agency is required to function as an interface between the central irrigation system and the farmer/water user appears sound. In fact, even if participation of farmers' organization was not an immediate objective, a middle level organization whose short-term goals, working, and administrative style, would differ both from those of the central main line agency and from those of the farmers within the outlet command (what we call the Chak committee) is likely to prove effective. Perhaps initially, this middle level wing could be a governmental organization with CAD, which would also continue to perform the main line central agency tasks through a separate wing of CAD, and gradually the middle level organization could become a farmers' organization which would then interact better with a grassroots farmers association. Such organizational reform has not yet been fully integrated into India's CAD approach even though Participatory Irrigation Management (PIM) is now vigorously being advocated for CAD projects both by Government of India and by State Governments.

In fact, since 1995 the Government of India has organized two national PIM Conferences and has sponsored through the CAD Progamme 14 Regional PIM Workshops, over 60 Project level PIM Workshops, and countless PIM training programmes. It has also, as already mentioned, provided for one-time grants to water-users associations for PIM and has sponsored PIM action research projects through NGOs and is acting as a clearing house for information on PIM.[38]

Nonetheless, we should not forget that farmers' organization is not a panacea for all problems and that the costs involved may not always be worth it (Parlin and Luke)[39] as participation may be a very good solution or remedy for only some problems, and that there is a need to achieve a fit between irrigation organizations and the technology in both type and scale for achieving improved water management.

CONCLUSION

However, despite the differences from state to state in the extent to which the CAD approach is applied, and to which the CAD organization is integrated into a unified and comprehensive set-up, the fact that the CAD approach exists (one that envisages interdisciplinary effort and unified career structure for integrated and comprehensive area development based on water management using the skills, orientation and methodologies of all relevant disciplines), along with its emphasis on the need for PIM itself provides hope for the future of water management in India.

REFERENCES

* The ideas expressed in this article are personal and put forth for only academic purpose and can not be construed to be those of the organization where the author work. This article is the by-product of a larger study on *Settler Motivation in Indira Gandhi Canal Project: A Study in Policy and Administration being conducted by the author.*

1. N.R. Upoff, Meinzen-Dick and N. St. Julien, *Improving Policies and Programmes for Farmers Organization and Participation,* Water Management Systems Project Paper 1, USA, Cornell University, 1985, and Jr. EW. Coward, "Planning Technical and Social Change in Irrigated Areas", in M.M. Cernea (ed.), *Putting People First,* Oxford, Oxford University Press, 1991.
2. Jr. E.W. Coward (ed.), *Irrigation and Agricultural Development in Asia,* Cornell, Cornell University Press, 1980.
3. J. Keller, *Irrigation Scheme Water Management, Water Management Synthesis,* Professional Papers, Utah State University, 1988.
4. M.K. Lowdermilk, "Social Organizational Factors of Irrigation Systems" Diagnostic Analysis of Farm Irrigation Systems, Training Curse in Water management. *Annual,* 1981.
5. Uphoff, Meinzen-Dick and St. Julien, *op. cit.*
6. R.E. Wade and Seekler in R.K. Sampath and R.A. Young (eds.), *Social Economic and International Issues in Third World Irrigation Management,* Westview Press, 1990.
7. *Ibid.*
8. Keller, *op. cit.*
9. *Ibid.*
10. Sivamohan and Scott, *op. cit.*
11. *Ibid.,* p. 15.
12. Administrative Staff College of India (ASCI), *Comprehensive Study of Organization* and *Monitoring and Multi-Level Coordination, Problems of CAD Authorities,* Hyderabad, 1979.
13. Sivamohan and Scott, *op.cit.*
14. R. Hooja, "Development of Catchments in Chambal Rajasthan Projects" in M. Mukerjee (ed.), *Administrative Innovations in Rajasthan,* Associated, 1982; reprinted in R. Hooja, *Administrative Interventions in Rural Development,* Jaipur, Rawat, 1987.
15. Ministry of Water Resources, India, *Report on Working Group in Command Area Development for Formulation of Plan Proposals for Eight Five Year Plan 1990-95, 1996.*
16. India, *Report of Working Group on Command Area Development Programme,* New Delhi, Ministry of Water Resources, 1996.
17. Sivamohan and Scott, *op. cit.,* p. 17.

18. India, *Report of Task Force on Organizational Models for CAD Programme,* New Delhi, Ministry of Water Resources, 1970.
19. G.N. Kathpalia, "Command Area Development Programme in India—Progress and Future," *Wamana,* Vol. 4, No. 3, 1989; R. Hooja, Command Area Development—Development of Governmental Thinking About its Objectives and Components", in P.C. Mathur and R.K. Gurjar (ed.), *Land and Water Management in Arid Ecology,* Jaipur, Rawat, 1991; and R. Hooja, "CAD" Approach to Water Management Driven Development—Reflections on DDA Irrigation Management Network Paper No. 20", *ODI Irrigation Management Newsletter,* 1993; and *Multidisciplinary Management of Irrigation Schemes and the Command Area Development Approach in India,* HCM-RIPA Occasional Paper No. 2, 1995; operations Research Group (ORG), *Evaluation of CAD Programme in IGNP*—Approach Paper (mimeo), 1991; and. T.K. Jayaraman, M.K. Lowedermilk and W. Clyma, *Command Area Development Authorities for Improved Water Management,* Synthesis Report No. 8, Colorado State University and Utah State University, 1982.
20. R. Hooja, "Rural Credit in CAD Area: OFD and SFDA Loaning", *The Administrator,* Vol. 27, No. 1, 1982, reprinted in *Symposium on Water School on Integrated Agriculture Development in the Command Areas of Irrigation Projects* INSA, 1983, also reprinted in R. Hooja, Administrative Interventions in Rural Development, Jaipur, Rawat, 1987.
21. V. Pande, "Planning and Implementation of Command Area Development", paper presented in Command Area Development Training Seminar for Chambal Project Personnel, Jaipur, HCM-RIPA, 1976.
22. S. Sarupuria, "Irrigation Agriculture—A Regional Planning Approach to Command Area Development", *Asia Economic Review,* Vol. 19, No. 4, 1977.
23. R. Hooja, "Command Area Development— Development of Governmental Thinking about its objectives and Components" in P.C. Mathur and T.K. Gujarat (eds.) , *op. cit.*
24. Hooja, 1997, *op. cit.*
25. ASCI *op. cit.,* Vol. 1, p. 18.
26. K.K. Singh, "Alternative Organizational Strategies for Command Area Development" in A.O. Elman, 1978.
27. India, Tasks Force, 1990, *op. cit.,* p. 18.
28. R. Hooja, "Intermediate Level Planning—The Case of a CAD Project", *The Administrator,* Vol. 36, No. 3, 1991; and R. Hooja and R.S. Kavdia (eds.), *Planning for Sustainability is Irrigation – Command Area Development and the Indira Gandhi Canal Project,* 1994.
29. T.K. Jayaraman *et. al., op. cit.*
30. *Ibid.*
31. Institute of Development Studies, *Report of the Mentoring and Evaluation System of Rajasthan CAD Settlement Project,* Jaipur, 1996.
32. R.E. Wade, "Water to the Fields: India's Changing Strategy" *South Asian Review,* Vol. 8, No. 4, 1975.
33. M.M. Dandeker, "Some Aspects of Irrigation Water Management in Development Counties" in J. Singh, M.S. Acharya and A. Sharma (eds.). *Water Management – Problems and Prospects in Command Areas,* Himanshu, 1990.
34. R. Chambers, "Men and Water: The Organization and Operation of Irrigation" in B.H. Farmer (ed.), *Technology of Change in Rice Growing Areas of Tamil Nadu and Sri Lanka,* West view Press. 1977.
35. Sivamohan and Scott, *op. cit.*

36. D.M. Freeman, "Designing the Organizational Interface Between Users and Agencies" in B.W. Parlin and M.W. Lusk (eds.), *Farmer Participation and Irrigation Organization*, Westviewz Press, 1991.
37. D.M. Freeman and M.K. Lowdermilk, "Middle Level Farmer Organisations As Links Between Farms and Central Irrigation Systems" in M.M. Cernea (ed.), *Putting People First*, Oxford, Oxford University Press. 1991.
38. L.K. Joshi, *Management of Irrigation: A New Paradigm – Participatory Irrigation Management*, New Delhi, Ministry of Water Resources, Government of India 1979.
39. B.W. Parlin and M.W. Lusk "International Irrigation Development—Factors Affecting Project Success", in *Society and Natural Resources*, Vol. 1, No. 2, 1980.

3

Reforming Desert Development Administration and Strategies in Rajasthan*

An Extension Approach for Desert Development and Environmental Preservation

Bhupendra Hooja

Any progamme of desert development or controlling the process of desertification must ultimately mean the judicious, scientific and balanced management or use of the natural resources – water, soils flora and fauna and all the mineral wealth which lies under the ground. This also means scientific use or management of both the traditional or commercial and non-conventional sources of energy-solar or wind energy, electricity or petroleum products, coal or fire-wood, farm manure or farm-waste. And in the final analysis, management means acquisition of adequate knowledge, appropriate technologies, suitable skills and careful or judicious investment of financial, technical or manpower resources, not only by the government agencies but also by the people at large, the communities which live in the desert lands. That in brief is the challenge of our times. For which, keeping in view the schemes and programmes required a suitable administrative apparatus may also have to be evolved.

Deserts are primarily the "gifts of nature to man (and how man has used them) because all the deserts around the earth have grown out of the interplay of natural forces or natural circumstances, though man has also made his contributions to accelerate or accentuate the conditions of desertification. But on the whole, and in the desert lands, various human communities, once driven into the harsh and unhospitable

---

* This paper on completely modifying present desert development administration has resulted from the authors work as Chairmen of the Sub Groups on (1) Desert Development and (2) Modernisation of Agriculture set up for Formulation of the Seventh Five-Year Plan by the Government of Rajasthan 1984.

environments for some political or substantial physical reasons, have learnt to adapt and adjust themselves to their environment. Their survival or prosperity has depended upon the ecological balance they have been able to maintain over a long span of time.

In fact, there are very few deserts which may be called 'living crowded deserts, so to say, or where there are large concentration of human population. Wherever conditions are hostile and harsh, people have avoided venturing into the desert heart land unless compelled by some whelming pressures from outside.

The desert in Rajasthan, which is a part of the Thar Desert of the Indian sub-continent is no exception. But as far as human settlements go, the Rajasthan desert is comparatively more settled or inhabited than many deserts in other parts of the world. But the population pressure or its density has been in close correspondence with the life-sustaining factors or natural assets, particularly on rainfall or moisture regime and the soil conditions. Thus, as we proceed north, north-west or westwards from the Arawali range, the great divide between the arid and sandy parts of the country and the fertile Yamuna-Ganga plains, we come across less and less human population with isolated and scattered settlements at a great distance from each other and vast stetches of barren, sandy tracts infested with sand dunes, both of the shifting type and those which are comparatively more stabilized. The economy or even the pattern of social life naturally has been well-suited and oriented to the environmental conditions. It has been basically pastoral, even nomadic, with the local people raising a variety of hardy breeds of cattle, sheep or goats and camels, so that animal husbandry has been the mainstay or goats and camels, so that animal husbandry has been the mainstay or the main way of their life and culture. Rainfed and dry-land agriculture through cultivation of coarse and hardy crops like bajra has also been their supplementary occupation as well as a supplementary source of nutrition.

Over the centuries, the people of the desert have evolved their own ways of life, their animistic or pastoral gods and goddesses, their ceremonial rites and rituals, their festivals and cattle-fairs, their cropping patterns and practices such as crop rotation or leaving the hard-pressed lands fallow; and even social customs to maintain a kind of ecological balance or a viable equation between the natural resources and the growing human needs. Thus hospitality to the stranger, whether a casual visitor or fugitive, has been one of their local cultural traits. Just as self-reliance and autonomy have been the features of their socio-economic and political organization; and infanticide, particularly of the girls, has been a sort of cruel necessity with which they have had to adjust themselves in the past. As far as the protection of environment is concerned, their religious beliefs, social customs and traditions have seen to it that there is no willful waste or wanton destruction so that all over the land there have been local forests or tree groves, oran lands and gochars dedicated to or associated with the protection of local village dieties, and the catchments or water reservoirs have been left undisturbed. Unlike the tribals and the present-day hoards of contractors who have roamed around the forests and jungles with their axes and tree felling machines, in the desert areas the ordinary people have tried to protect their very scarce tree cover and vegetation. In fact, we have had the well known historical incident when the Bishonois sacrificed themselves to protect their khejri trees.

By and large, people living in the Rajasthan desert have neither been callous for indifferent towards their environment. They have learnt to make do with their natural resources, content with their meals of coarse grains, milk or butter-milk and with their simple rural with its pastoral socio-economic patterns and cultural traditions.

This has been possible because each child, each person, each family, each caste and community and each village society has been able to understand or appreciate the natural local surroundings in which a person or a community or a society has been born or placed Apart from this, understanding knowledge has flowed down through the ages by oral tradition or exchange of personal and mutual experiences and observations. There has been no need or urge for innovations or concerted efforts to search for new sources of hidden wealth in the midst of sand dunes, except perhaps the continuous an endless search for drinking water (though mostly, the search for drinking water from underground sources has resulted in disappointment). The residents of a dhani or a hamlet in the desert areas may not have a global view of the desert, but they know enough to help and guide them in their day-to-day existence, about their little patch of the desert or about their immediate neighbourhood.

On the other hand, today when there is a great rush going on for discovering the hidden wealth under the earth (or discovering the potentials of various natural regions of the world) so as to exploit them with the latest scientific knowledge and technologies, our scientists and experts, explorers and adventurers, travellers and the surveyors have managed to gather a lot of knowledge and scientific data so as to have a global and comprehensive view of the desert and its characteristics. But, unfortunately many such experts and research scientists have very little or limited knowledge of the micro level or local settings of the desert, its potentials and problems. If we look at the pile of research studies and experiments or surveys which have been conducted even in India during the last few decades, particularly since after Independence, we cannot but appreciate the fact that quite a large number of unknown and baffling secrets pertaining to the desert have come to light. A series of research institutes, experiment centers for applied research, and technology and demonstration stations have been established. Data relating to meteorology or landscape and geological features and about the hidden wealth of the desert lands have also been spoiled and programmes outlined for their exploitation.

But the gap between these research scientists and the average desert-dwellers still remains there, or perhaps it has widened because the research scientists have added to their knowledge and expertise by leaps and bounds thus increasing the distance between their laboratories and desert lands. This is a challenge which needs to be faced and met boldly and immediately. The knowledge available in our research stations and with our scientists and experts must be pooled and coordinated and then channelised or amplified as a flexible and variable package management practices and brought within the reach of the ordinary people those who have live in desert. This knowledge should be as much about the limitations of the desert environment or its problems as much as about the potentials and the appropriate or available technologies to harness the same. This effort must be the starting point of any programme for the development of desert lands or for protective and preventive measures.

In fact, what required is a systematic approach for data collection and analysis, and then bringing this knowledge or awareness come not only to the user agencies or the government sponsored authorities, but also within easy reach of the widely spread-out and scattered desert communities through proper channels of the information or communication networks supplemented by suitable educational or training efforts and the so-called extension machinery. In fact, since the desert environment is rather fragile and subject to agroliimatic or geophysical variations and pressures, self-discipline born out of a proper monitoring understanding and appreciation of the nature and problems of the environment is perhaps more necessary in the desert areas than elsewhere. If proper care and caution are not exercised, the damage to the natural resources will be far quicker and greater or more serious in the desert areas than elsewhere. That is why, all over the world, same and concerted voices are being raised against the free and uncontrolled play of forces and factors which have led to and are continuously leading to the process of desertification or the continuation of man-made conditions which accentuate and extend the frontiers of the desert. The balance or the relationship between man-animal-land-water and natural resources has got to be properly understood and strictly applied or enforced. And this is possible only on the basis of the proper acquisition and transmission of scientific knowledge and technology and with the creation of suitable socio-economic political motivation or an emotional and intellectual, cultural well as religious climate and the creation of a new desert-base 'modern' culture supplemented and enriched with the latest gifts modern science and technology.

Needless to suggest that the immediate threat to the desert land as to any other land or ecological system arises from what is emmistically called "the process of modernisation" or the expand horizon of new science and technology aimed at maximum output free land or returns from these investments.

These were some of the problems or challenges which came up surface when the problems of the desert were brought under discussion in Seventh Five-Year Plan Working Group on Rural Development and more so in the Sub-Group on Desert and DPAP. The Sub-Group set up by Rajasthan Government to help formulate proposals far development of the desert and drought-prone areas.

Ours was a small 'working' group with which experts and administrators and those connected with the formulation and implementation of projects in the desert areas were associated. The group had general overall review of the desert scene as well as the efforts initiated and implemented by the state government and other authorities by way of development efforts over the past few decades, more so during the Fifth and Sixth Five-Year Plan periods. However, came to the sad and unfortunate conclusion that although see serious attempts have been made in the recent past to improve the social and economic conditions of the desert communities through various schemes, including schemes for individual beneficiaries, particularly for the landless, artisans, cattle-breeders and sheep breeders or by way of improving the infrastructural facilities like the networks of roads, transportation and communication services and other social or civic facilities, including particularly driving water facilities in many parts of the desert, as far as measure for environmental control or improvement were concerned, not enough has been achieved or attempted. This view has also been expressed recently by the Planning Commission's Committee on Backward Areas.

On the other hand, it was also our sad observation that through the sustained and coordinated scientific efforts put in by institutions like the CAZRI (Central Arid Zone Research Institute) and other agencies and organizations of the Government of India and the state government though these have enlarged the horizons of our knowledge and the scope of what was and is technically feasible and viable, all this fund of new knowledge, expertise and field experience has failed to reach the homesteads or dhanis of the scattered agro pastoral communities.

It was, therefore, but natural that our sub-group should come to the unanimous conclusion and present its consensus view before the meeting of the full Working Group (and through it before the State Government) that, whatever may be programmes by way of environmental control or management of natural resources or for the benefit of individual or group beneficiaries are initiated during the Seventh Plan and subsequently, simultaneously a basic or integral component of the planning effort must be directed towards the collection and analysis of relevant data with regard to the natural resources and their regular monitoring, followed next by the identification and adaptation of suitable or proper management techniques or practices both for productive as well as long-term protective measures.

The second stage should be of communicating both these types of knowledge or experience to the rural communities through the various local institutions like panchayats or cooperatives, schools and colleges as well as through all the modern methods or media of mass communication, the spoken and printed word as well as the electronic devices like the radio, TV and films, etc. so that, on the basis of growing popular understanding and appreciation, mass mobilization in the desired direction may be made possible.

Naturally, the next step would be of making his knowledge or information an integral part of the process of education and training for developing proper skills in the handling of tools and equipments as well as in the application of these skills or tools in the proper management or environmental control measures such as forestation or development of grasslands and pastures, and dry-land or rain fed farming of coarse grains of fodder crops and the whole gamut of activities connected with the social life and economy of the area.

Last but not the least our sub-group was prompted to recommend that a massive effort for extension is also called for in the desert areas so that there can be a continuous practical or work-and-activity oriented extension of the knowledge of research to the farmer's fields and pasturelands. Naturally it was recommended that extension in the desert areas need not be based on or directed only towards 'crop husbandry', though the management of dry-land Kharif crops of coarse grains or fodder crops and pulses and oil seeds is quite necessary and relevant; but the core or the message of the extension work in the desert areas ought to be based on or related to 'land management' or 'land husbandry' so that the particular features, problems, potentials and limitations of each piece of land or each land unit or natural water-shed are properly grasped and appreciated; and related to such knowledge, suitable, proper and viable and technically feasible practices for the use of the natural resources can be evolved, adopted or recommended.

It has been the view of our sub-group that not only such a "land husbandry based extension work" is necessary or imperative in the desert areas, but it will also prove to be a continuous, regular and an all-time absorbing activity, in season and out of season, until it becomes an integrated part of the day-to-day life of the life, until the new practices and techniques, the do's and don'ts become acceptable parts of their way of the people and the administrators or of the desert culture. Extension work in the desert lands has both a short-term target, that of protection or prevention of further damage, as well as a long-term objective, that of creating a sort of new and modern but scientific culture.

During the rainy season, when suddenly there are heavy rains washing away the lands or when there are rain failures (such as during the lean or dry seasons) when the high temperatures and high velocity winds begin to play havoc with the top soils of the desert lands, it becomes a really challenging task to ensure that the cultivable lands where fairly reasonable or adequate rainfall has occurred should be brought under the plough in the shortest possible time; or where (and in case) rains have failed or have been insufficient or the summer season has been prolonged with its long spell of hot winds and dust storms, something tangible should be done to reduce the hazards of wind erosion. These two possibilities are being mentioned as indicative of the types of activities or the strategies which the farming communities may have to adopt with suitable guidance and support from the experts of the agriculture, soil and water conservation, animal husbandry, sheep and wool development organizations or departments of the State Government in keeping with the research support provided by institutes like the CAZRI or the Central Sheep Research Center, Avika Nagar and so on.

Some suitable practices or preventive and protective measures are also necessary in the desert conditions to see that the productive lands are properly looked after when there are no standing crops on them or when the hoards of sheep, goats, cattle and camels began to roam across them in search of grass, fodder; suitable measures are also called for to prepare these soils for the next crops. Unfortunately, this happens to be an almost neglected activity in the western districts of Rajasthan particularly in the sand-dunes affected desert areas. Over the centuries, a tradition or a psychology or a general belief seems to have developed according to which, if the lands are left fallow or uncultivated, open to the sky and to the interplay of natural forces, automatically these would acquire or regain their productive capacity. This seems to be the basic assumption amongst the local people who still cling to largely pastoral or nomadic traditions, not appreciating that cultivation means (or should mean) first of all, adequate and repeated care of the land sources all the year round to maintain its productivity. unfortunately, our scientists and technical experts and extension workers or administrators have done nothing to end this 'fatalistic' dependence of the local people on the 'natural' recovery of their local environment in spite of human encroachment followed by neglect.

It is felt that if the whole problem is looked at from a different perspective and basically the environmental angle, it will be appreciated that as far as looking after the productivity of the national assets, particularly the local soils, is concerned, much more needs to be done than is being attempted at present. Today, modern research in soil chemistry has developed a new filed of knowledge about its natural characteristics. Bio-genetic or chemical and civil engineering measures have been identified in various parts of the world which can be suitably adopted to the environmental conditions of western Rajasthan, even in the sand-dune infested desert areas; though, of course, the cost of some of these measures may be prohibitive. There are also long-term soil and environment monitoring and management activities which can help in the reclamation or rehabilitation of the degraded forests, denuded hills or the depleted soils, such as aforestation measures, development of grasslands or shelter belts and sand dune stabilization in addition to various programmes and activities of a localized nature for soil and moist conservation. The point is that the sources of knowledge and suitable or proper technologies are there. These have to be demonstrated, adopted and applied at all the field levels or, so to say, these have to be ultimately accepted and adopted by the local communities themselves, provided the relevant parts of this vast fund of information and knowledge are made available to them transmitted and explained to them, and provided that the local communities are further assisted in planning out their local programmes or projects for the adoption of technical practices and undertaking short-term, medium-term or long-term programmes for managing their soil and water resources in particular and the environment in general. It is not an easy task. After all the desert is a vast stretch of land.

To make a beginning, the sub-group on the Seventh Five-Year Plan for desert development and DPAP areas has proposed an investment of about Rs. 500-600 crores on various activities in the desert or the core and fragile areas of the desert, largely for the management of the local land and water resources and for environmental control. In other words, investments by way of help, subsidy or assistance to individual beneficiaries or target groups have not been included in the core plan for desert development; and it has been suggested that these activities should be taken up separately and additionally under the normal plan programmes of the state government or its various departments. The programme recommended under that has been called the 'core sector' which includes *inter alia* stabilization of sand-dunes, development of range lands and pastures, shelter belts to protect natural and man-made assets or key installations as well as agricultural lands, aforestation for fuel and timer and for improving the climate, soil and water management on water shed basis, and development of drinking water and alternative energy sources.

The sub-group has also identified various broad sub-regions in which these core activities or their suitable permutations and combinations can be initiated, depending upon the specific characteristics or special features and problems of each such region. *For example* if we take up the Gang-Bhakra-RCP (Indira Cannal) belt of command areas along the western border land, the introduction of irrigated crops with flow irrigation facilities available throughout the year on a fairly liberal scale have created its own peculiar challenge for the experts, administrators, extension workers and the people who have been brought from here and there to colonies the areas. How much water to give? When, or for what crops! Without treating water-logging or salinity or without washing away the top soils? At the same time, there are certain other location specific problems such as of sand dunes, or of salinity, or of varying soil depths and the nature of the sub-strata which are likely to raise yet another set of problems, if these have not appeared already. There are fairly high sand dunes in between the command areas which cannot possibly be levelled for cultivation or for any other related use. In fact, these need to be stabilized. Similarly, water discipline and careful or cautions management in its application is necessary, particularly in areas where the sub-soils are impervious and where due to poor drainage there may soon be a hazard of perched water-table rising at a fast rate, as indeed it has occurred in some villages of Gananagar and Bikaner districts adjoining the RCP canal system. Naturally, these problems need to be identified and trakeled as a part of the command area or desert development programmes; and once some suitable treatments or techniques have been identified or established as practical, serious steps have to be taken to demonstrate and explain the same amongst the people particularly amongst the leaders of public and officers, and to educate and motivate the people to adopt them with necessary technical guidance or material support from the government agencies.

Elsewhere in the desert the problem ma be somewhat different. *For example*, flow irrigation facilities may not be available and lift irrigation may be expensive, or the ground water may also be found at fairly deep levels and may turn out to be saline or of very poor quality. Proper agriculture or animal husbandry practices and activities need to be identified for such area; and these may largely be related to the development of grass-lands, pastures, tree-belts or fuel or fodder reserves or the development and rehabilitation of natural vegetation growth. *For example*, in the extreme west and south-west in the sand dune infested belt along the Indo-Pak border where the Indian territory makes a bulge into Pak territory, such a situation does exist. Here a different set of activities or land management techniques will be necessary, and especially in areas where the density of population is very little and there is also little intrusion by herds of stray or wandering cattle, sheep or goats, perhaps it may be necessary to undertake departmental activities or to reserve these areas as some sort of natural 'sanctuaries' or natural desert park.

Then again, there may be lands with rocky outcrops or rocky upper strata, though denuded and barren, *i.e.*, there are two such identified tracts south-west of Jaiselmer and Barmer commonly named as Malani tract, where perhaps in the absence of topsoil or because of stony or granular surface, it is very difficult to grow even a blade of grass; but here and there, on the barren rocky surface, it may be possible to control and store the run-off of the erratic and infrequent rains by suitable civil engineering works such as anicuts, bunds, or by gully-plugging, etc. so that ultimately, over the years, some vegetation may be restored to these areas. In these or similar parts, some reclamation may be possible through classing or fencing off the areas. Years ago, some such experiments and demonstrations were launched by the CAZRI and the State Soil Conservation Board with mixed results. However, the local people have to be told about such activities and duly compensated if they are deprived of some rights of facilities of land use.

Similarly, in the Luni Basin area, the problems are of a somewhat different nature, and these have been identified by the CZARI as well as other agencies and experts.

Naturally, the remedial measures including flood protection measures or channellising the water streams and soil conservation measures on a fairly large scale in the Godwar sub-mountainous area along the western slopes of the Arawali will require a different package of programmes and activities than in other parts of the sandy desert.

Same may be said about the Arawali range itself which, for the first time, is proposed to be included in the programme of desert development, because it has been rightly stressed that, unless this major dividing line between the desert and the fertile plains of north India is properly managed or rehabilitated or made to bloom, it may not be possible to bring about an effective control on the agro-climatic or environmental conditions of the desert lands. The Arawali range also does not have the same type of problems or environmental hazards along its entire length. In the north-east, the problems are different than near about the Sambhar Gap, where the western desert or the desertic winds have plenty of scope or opportunity to penetrate castwards and where already the sub-soil and ground water conditions are more saline. Problems would naturally be for a different complexion in each district segment of the Arawali range, as also on the eastern or western slopes. Ajmer Beawar area is yet another sub-zone; and further south towards the east in the Udaipur-Jhadole-Gogunda Khunbhalagarh area, the problems are of a different nature, while westwards in the Sirohi and Mount Abu area or along the Godwar ware, the problems are of somewhat different type.

We have not said much about other parts of the desert for example the non-command areas of Ganganagar, Bikaner and Jaiselmer districts or the area comprising of Churu, Sikar, Jhunjhunu in the north or Nagpur and Jodhpur in the center of Pali, Barmer and Jalore areas towards south-west. Suffice it to say that the sub-group has broadly identified or recommended about a dozen distinct regions or sub-regions in western Rajasthan where location-specific environmental control or use and management progammes of a long-term nature, alongwith land and water management for day-to-day economic activities like dry farming or animal husbandry, etc. need to be taken up in a systematic or integrated manner.

The sub-group has also strongly recommended that the starting point of all these programmes or activities should be a careful and detailed survey or inventory or stock-taking of the natural resources of the desert for which modern techniques of survey such as satellite imagery or areal photography may also be pressed into service, in addition to ground survey of a semi-detailed or detailed type, as well as surveys of ground water potential and other problems of the sub-soil or through the soil survey units of Agriculture Department or the sub-strata with the help of the Geological Survey Organization. There should also be a central agency or nodal organizations where all the data from different sources or organizations can be brought together, suitably cross-checked, co-related and analyzed, and made more intelligible (even fore the non-experts) and then made available in more easily understood (even in non-technical) terms.

On the basis of such data, suitable progammes or projects, both of a medium-term nature and for detailed long-term exercise, can be devised. In other words, project formulation should be the next stage of action after data compilation. These projects will have to be of a specific nature for each specific area or watershed. For that, perhaps nodal institution like the CAZRI can do a lot of ground-work, at least as far as the technically feasible or viable large 'area projects', or the location suited programmes or activities need to be identified. It may also be necessary to suitably strengthen the staff and organization of the concerned state department dealing with desert management and the desert development commissioner by inducting technical experts or desert area experts in these organizations. The University set-up may also need to be toned up or suitably restructured particularly for applied research, education and training and extension through the 'Lab to Land' strategy. As mentioned earlier, further detailed and local exercises with regard to data compilation, analysis and assimilation as well as monitoring of the local environment in addition to 'local' Project formulation and implementation will have to be carried out on a regular and sustained basis at the various regional or sub-regional levels, whether we opt for independent regional authorities or agencies of the Desert Development Department.

Then will come the stage of implementation by local communities wherever the people are available in sizable numbers, and by departmental agencies where due to low density of population, the shortage of manpower is likely to be a deciding factor. Once we have sketched out such a broad strategy and attempt to work out its details for application and implementation, it will be appreciated that in addition to data compilation , project formulation and research activities in institutes like the CAZRI there is a whole gamut of activities which need to be set into motion so that, over the years, the local communities (including the present generation and the new or younger generation) may become not only acquainted with but fully conversant with the problems of the desert, the environment or technical nature of these problems and how these can be controlled or solved and the various strategies or measures necessary for a proper, balanced and scientific long-term use of the natural assets.

This brings one back to the point already mentioned above, *i.e.*, the process of education, training and extension of applied knowledge,. Knowledge about he environment needs to be communicated to all and sundry, both though the formal educational system as well as through informal or adult education activities; and a conscious and sustained effort has to be done in this regard by all concerned and at all levels.

Perhaps the time has come when the contents of the formal educational system and of the text-books used in the primary or secondary schools or in the colleges in the desert areas need to be somewhat different from the contents of such books in other parts of the state. Similarly, suitable curricular or extra-curricular activities of a practical natural on the lines of the Gandhian concept of work oriented basic education need to be initiated on a large and extensive scale. In the desert areas, it may be necessary for the schools or colleges and such other institutions, to have their own plots of desert or marginal lands for necessary experimentation or application of new techniques for local desert control or land and water management measures.

Similarly at the level of village panchayats or cooperative institutions or in respect of oran lands or pastures and grazing lands, programmes and activities on a community or cooperative basis need to be initiated. Even when the more recent target group programmes like IRDP or NREP or 'Trysem' or 'Set-up', etc. are taken up which are meant to give individual help and guidance to the young and old for their economic upliftment, it is urged that these activities should also be co-related to and integrated with the overall local programmes of desert control or management of land and water recourses.

While all this is being done at the ground level, it may be necessary for other institutes and agencies like the CAZRI or the Agricultural University or the Desert Development Commissioner's organization and their subordinate filed-level organizations to established suitable experimentation or research stations, demonstration plots and so on, so that each such farm or demonstration plot or research center may also become a center for training and extension activities in the local area which it serves. In these centers, all locally necessary or desirable and feasible activities for management of the local, natural or environmental resources need to be applied both for research purposes as well as for demonstration and training purposes.

In addition to these arrangements, it may be necessary to have extension staff located at the village level or in each watershed or such other natural land unit, an extension worker for land management who should become ultimately the 'friend, philosopher and guide' in the true sense of the word, as was the original concept or intention with regard to such functionaries. It must be appreciated that the knowledge or understanding of each such functionary must be reasonably adequate and at the same time, he also must be a natural, lead man capable of good public relations work and of leadership for sustained day-to-day activity in the area of this his operations.

Naturally, we cannot possibly except to have such qualified and experienced individuals and educated workers to start with. Such workers will have to be discovered and trained so that each one of them is able to function on his own. Perhaps to some extent the process of training or continuous training can be speeded up and kept in good gear by the adoption of the concept or technique of T & Y extension system which has been adopted in the extension network elsewhere in the state or in the country, so that the village extension workers get their fortnightly training or message of programmes of work at the fortnightly get-together or meetings, which also provide them opportunities for updating their knowledge and they return to their fields with their batteries duly charged. But in the desert areas where the problems and challenges are much more complex and difficult fortnightly training exercises and visits will need to be supported by formal, although capsule, programmes of institutionalized education and training; and for that the research stations, demonstration plots and other institutional farms or controlled pasture-lands in the neighbouring area can be selected. In fact, it may be worthwhile to have the fortnightly or monthly training programmes at these institutional centers where, in addition to lifted and trained experts, all kinds of facilities will be available and many experiments and demonstrations will be going on.

In the extension set-up, it will also be necessary to have qualified and experienced Subject Matter Specialists (SMS) or experts connected with soil chemistry, land and water management, land engineering, aforestation, pest or rodent control, animal husbandry and the like. These SMS teams may be ultimately located at the panchayat samiti/tehsil level, but in any case, such teams should be available and work in a coordinated manner at least at the district level, as well as at the level of each distinct sub-regional or regional unit of project or work organization.

A word about the ICAR/Government of India backed programme of extension under the broad title 'From Lab to Land'. If we under-stand it correctly, this is a kind of extension programme to be initiated and conducted by the research laboratories or institutes like the CAZRI or the ICAR as well as by the universities on their own. But I may be permitted to say that this parallel or somewhat competitive arrangement, though it has its own utility or necessity, not be made universal and it cannot cover the entire ground. At least, at the lower and actual filed operational level, this project needs to be joined up or connected with the extension channels of the various government departments or project agencies at the state, regional, sub-regional, district or panchayat samiti level. My suggestion would be that the Lab to Land programme should be extended up to the level of a field research station or a demonstration centre or a demonstration campaign center. Beyond that and up the grassroot level, the major concern or the responsibility devolve upon and must be borne by the extension set-up of the state government or its various departments and project agencies.

Perhaps it will not be out of place to attempt a brief thought tentative exercise sketching out the organization or technical so up for the extension machinery in the desert area. As we have see the major challenge or task before the extension staff in the desert area will be the communication of scientific practices and techniques alongwith the development of local technical or manager skills for a more balanced and judicious use or upkeep of the desert environment and its natural physical resources. This means that the extension staff even at the grass root level should be proper qualified, trained and motivated, and kept in constant harms. This also means that as far as possible, the staff should have local origin or it must feel at home in the desert environment or in the midst of the desert ways of life The staff should conservation minded with firm belief in the policies of preservation and protection of the natural resources, more than in the mode cult of increased production or marketing operation, etc.

Perhaps this can be (or will be) a major difference between work and role of the extension staff in the so-called agricultural potential areas of the state in the country and those placed in less potential or comparatively more backward or dry and arid regions. In the case of farmers, the main responsibility of the extension staff has been to guide and motivate the farmers for higher production through the application of new and improved technologies or new and improved inputs such as high yielding varieties (HYV) seeds fertilisers, pesticides, more and liberal use of water and farm implements. Because, over the years, separate agencies government departments, concerned with various types of inputs has been created, the role of the extension staff has remained some limited to the supply of knowledge of guidance, at least in the recent or the on-going tax phase of extension, though in the earlier phase, the extension workers were also closely and directly involve in the handling or management of the supply of inputs as well. In very rare circumstances the agriculture extension workers or the supervisors and guides were (have been) called upon to display practical terms their own knowledge or to do something concrete and tangible by way of field action or performance. When some new techniques and practices or inputs etc. had to introduced, displayed or demonstrated, the extension workers would refer the keen or enthusiastic cultivators to the nearest reason center and demonstration farm or some demonstration or trial plots nearby, or in the alternative, the sales and marketing networks of various inputs or farm equipments would arrange such visits or demonstrations for the farming communities. By and large, the extension staff remained advisory in character and at the most, interested spectators or demonstrators of the changes or improvements being introduced.

However, in the case of desert development work, the extension staff will have to themselves become performers or doers of actual field work and if they have to act as demonstrators, they will have to demonstrate something practical or concrete in actual practice not only at the research stations or demonstration farms but by putting their own head, and shoulders to some specific or clearly set out technical practice or field task.

For example, an essential component of the programme for desert development or protection of the desert environment against further degeneration should be to bring about a very efficient and closely monitored use of the conventional sources of energy, specially where the domestic fuels or kitchen fires are concerned (whether in the form of firewood, dry bush or cattle-dug, etc. or whether it is in the form of kerosene or diesel or electricity) . In fact, on the farm energy or the fuel scene, the conservation of the natural vegetation cover on the desert or marginal lands is not possible, unless the supply lines of conventional as well as modern commercial sources of energy, petroleum products or cooking gas or coke, etc. are made more easily accessible and manageable. In fact, wherever possible the system of electricity generation, transmission and consumption will also need to be improved. If this can be done, and if these efforts are further supplemented by necessary research support and adoption of techniques in respect of alternative and non-conventional sources of energy, it may be possible to protect the rather scarce and poor quality cover of trees and bushes on the desert landscape.

It has been suggested, and in the case of desert scene, this is being stressed with all the necessary emphasis, that the abundant sources of solar and wind energy can and should be utilized both at the farms (*for example*, for pumping water or for post harvest technology) as well as in the kitchens through solar cookers or boilers or even gober gas plants and for street-lighting.

For this type of programme, our sub-group has recommended that the Government of India and its various allied or subordinate agencies should undertake the full responsibilities of basic and applied research, and the adoption of suitable tools and techniques, followed by education training motivation and popularization. Without some positive beginning having been made in this varied directions of use of alternative energy sources the programme for afforestation, social forestry, shelter-belt plantations or farm plantation, etc. cannot be taken up on a large scale with a fair measure of promise of success.

We need not detail out the programme responsibilities of the research organizations or of the units of administrations or of educational institutions, etc. but if we look at the responsibility of the extension staff we can soon appreciate the point that to be a good motivator or a demonstrator, the successful extension workers must be able to handle and install and demonstrate or actually run some of the new gadgets or appliances for harvesting solar energy, wind energy, gas plants or electric installations, etc. unless the filed demonstration and training agencies are already there in the field. Similarly, they should be able to not only advise but actually help and guide the local community, the school children, youth or women and skilled or unskilled labourers in afforestation or tree plantation or social forestry programmes. Subsequently, the extension staff must lend support to the local bodes or the administration in enforcing necessary rules or byelaws or guidelines for proper management, maintenance and protection of such community assets.

This has been sketched out by way of an illustration. It is felt that in respect of other activities connected with land management or improvement, soil and water conservation, range land or pasture management, horticulture, sand dune stabilization and dealing with problems of saline lands or saline or breackish pockets of water, the extension workers at the field level with proper support or guidance from their superiors or the subject matter experts should be able to demonstrate or explain these activities and even perform some local achievements or success story on their own and in association with different sections of local society, so as to established their credibility and usefulness.

This means that the extension workers need to be picked up or selected very carefully and put through a fairly long and elaborate process of training, including institutional training as well as in field works. It has to be ensured that the extension worker continues to implement or display a fairly high standard of practical knowledge or experience of current scientific technologies. If young persons or even old experienced hands with some academic background and keen minds to learn new things are selected for such field level jobs perhaps they will have to be put through at least a year or two years course of training or working experience with facilities available at CAZRI or other such institutions, so that after training or reorientation, they are able to stand on their own in the filed and achieve something new or concerted in at least a few selected areas of work They must be able to work with the local people and not avoid dirtying their hands in the process. They must feel at one or at home with the local communities, speak their dialects and dream their dreaming. Even local retired personnel, civil pensioners or service-men can be involved in these tasks of land improvement and energy conservation.

Our aim should be that there should be at least one full time extension worker in every village whose efforts can be supplemented, supported and helped by small groups of part-time workers or local agents, village experts, artisans and craftsmen or such other types of professional workers even teachers or workers besides forest guards who can and should be drawn into the extension net-work.

For every group of 10-village extension workers, there should be a coordinator, not just a supervisor or an inspector but a coordinator and a practical guide. At this level it may also be desirable to have in each Panchayat Samiti a widely diverse and disbursed team of skilled professioned workers with necessary academic or scientific background in various disciplines so that they can help the field level extension staff in their day-to-day problems, particularly in two or three specific areas or spheres of work, *viz.*, (1) Energy, fuel economy and use or installation of non-conventional items such as solar cooking gas plants, or windmills, etc. (2) Soil and water management techniques including soil survey, soil testing and simple engineering works. (3) Problems relating to grass lands, pasture development dry land agronomy and afforestation. Some of these professional staff may be available or posted at the local research or demonstration centers or projects of work. If not, they may have to be recruited and incorporated in the extension set-up.

If the academic and actual field training level of the village extension staff may be equated to that of a qualified and trained ITI passed or matriculate person, we can think in terms of the coordinators or the next supervisor or guide level persons having the same or coequal qualifications or experience as a diploma holder or higher secondary passed young man in various relevant streams of scientific knowledge in respect of the aforementioned process of coordination. Generally speaking this level of coordinators may be the same as that of a revenue inspector or a cooperative inspector, etc.

At the Panchayat Samiti (PS) level or at the various demonstration farms and applied research stations located at the PS head-quarters (or elsewhere in the PS) Subject Matter Specialists (SMS) with more through and up-to-date practical training and experience and with academic professional qualifications at least up to the graduate level will need to be posted. Once again, two or three major specialties or disciplines mentioned above will need to be adequately covered at this level. Other subject matter specialized or experts like animal husbandry or veterinary experts or soil scientists and agronomists can and should also be made available at the PS level to supplement the efforts of these experts. However, it is strongly urged that each one of these PS level experts should either be based or closely linked with some research institution of a practical nature or with some educational and training institution or a demonstration farm or a soil and water testing laboratory or a project engineering and mechanical unit, etc. The present-day basis of the so-called SMS experts located at the PS/Sub Districts or District level without any place, without any mooring in any institution or practical field of work, has not proved much conductive or useful. This needs to be avoided.

At the district level attention needs to be given (at the district level or the local project area level) that adequate or satisfactory arrangements exist for the compilation or collection of all types of scientific survey and monitoring data and the necessary technical support of staff laboratories and equipments to guide and coordinate field level extension or project activities. A general and universal staffing pattern cannot be suggested at this level because it is felt that the staff should be posted according to the nature of the development work and its quantum and as far as possible, all the activities to be taken up in a particular area (a satiable or manageable land unit for a viable project) should be brought together under the fold of a comprehensive or multi-purpose, but an integrated, 'area development project'. The project organization will thus provide for the necessary type of staff component, according to the nature of complexion and duration of the project. But since the fight to control, manage and improve the desert will be long-drawn it may soon become necessary to make such area project organizations or the field agencies of extension or technical agencies, integral parts of the District or Sub-District development set-up. The same will hold good for the next higher coordinating or controlling authority or authorities at the level of the Desert Development Commissioner/ Additional Commissioner.

This entire field-level exercise will need a considerably strengthened net-work of field stations, data collection centers, monitoring out-posts, soil and water testing laboratories, experimentation farms, training or orientation centers, desert based Vigyan Kendras for additional and continuous academic and scientific support to the formal and informal education system at the primary, secondary or university levels, as well as through new institutions like rural ITIs and polytechnics and the local university and ultimately the national or state level institutions or training centres like CAZRI or control sheep and wool Research Institute, etc.

It is also recommended that the propagation of dry land farming techniques through the extension method based on continuous training of the field staff followed by their visits to the beneficiaries fields should be continued and improved upon in respect of cultivable lands. But the fortnightly or monthly training meets of evaluation and briefing sessions of the field staff should be organised at the nearest research and demonstration or experimentation station or a project farm where the field staff can be given first hand experience of the various processes and techniques for conservation measures or development activities. However, the dry land agriculture extension workers must be thoroughly exposed to and trained in soil and water conservation techniques or in the management of fuel and alternative energy sources or in the use of new gadgets and appliances. Such personnel will be useful only in areas where the production of annual crops, mostly cereals and oil seeds, may be possible without detriment to the local soils or depletion of water source.

A Tentative Organizational Chart for Extension Staff in Desert or Dry land areas is produced on next page.

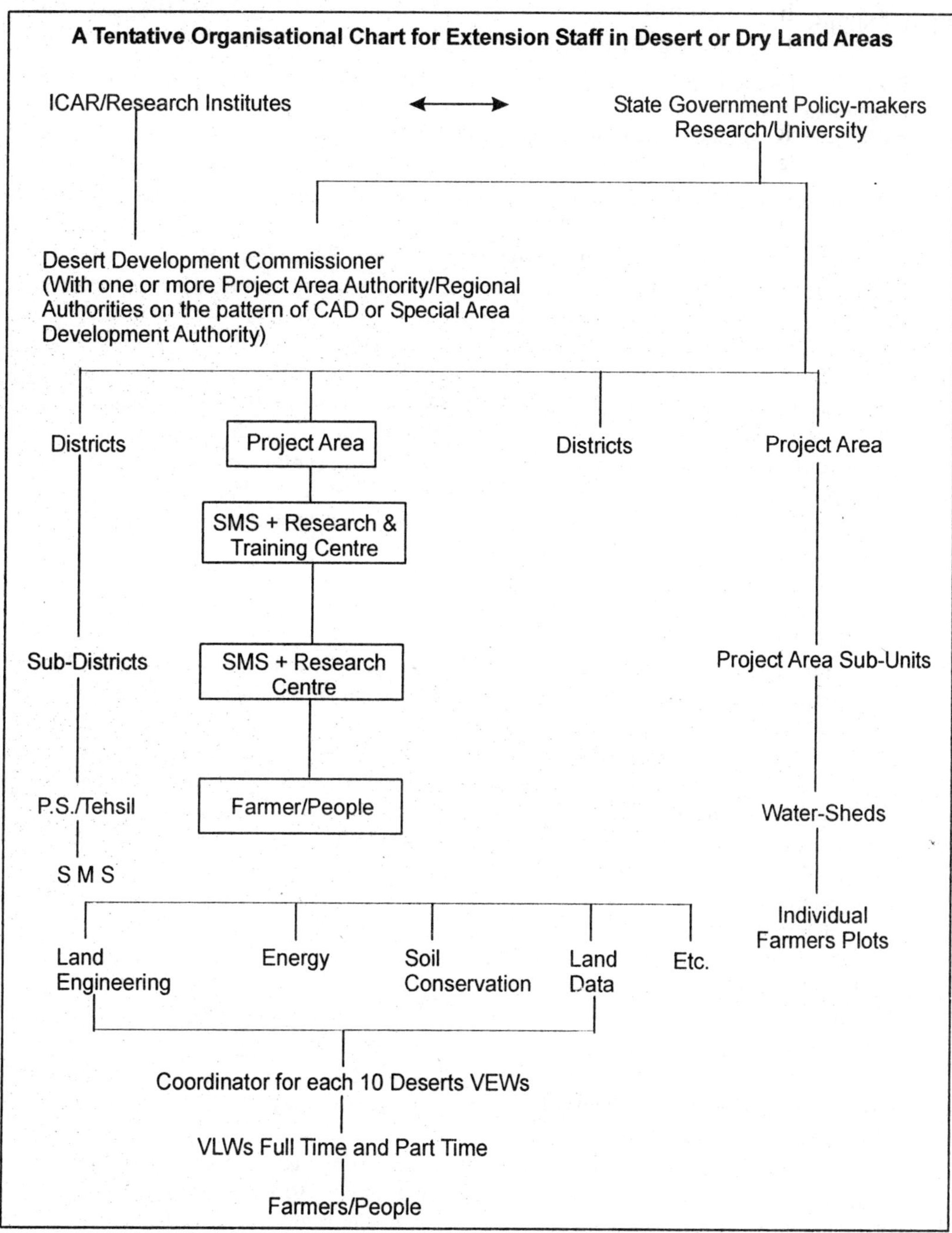
A Tentative Organisational Chart for Extension Staff in Desert or Dry Land Areas
ICAR/Research Institutes
State Government Policy-makers
Research/University
Desert Development Commissioner
(With one or more Project Area Authority/Regional
Authorities on the pattern of CAD or Special Area
Development Authority)
Districts
Project Area
Districts
Project Area
SMS + Research &
Training Centre
Sub-Districts
SMS + Research
Centre
Project Area Sub-Units
P.S./Tehsil
Farmer/People
Water-Sheds
S M S
Individual
Farmers Plots
Land
Engineering
Energy
Soil
Conservation
Land
Data
Etc.
Coordinator for each 10 Deserts VEWs
VLWs Full Time and Part Time
Farmers/People

REFERENCES

1. Rural Development in India – Some, Factors, National Institute of Rural Development, Hyderabad, 1979.
2. Ramesh K. Arora (ed.), Peoples Participation in Development Process, HCM SIPA, Jaipur, 1979.
3. N.K. Jaiswal and N.V. Kolte, Development of Drought Prone Areas, NIRD, Hyderabad, 1981.
4. Report of the Seminar on Drought Prone Areas, HCM SIPA, Jaipur, 1981.
5. Development and Transfrer of Technology for Rainfed Agricu!ture and SAT Farmer, ICRISAIT, Hyderabad, 1980.
6. Horst G. Mensching and R.C. Sharma (ed.), Resource Management in Drylands, Rajesh Publications, Delhi, 1984.
7. Bhupendra Hooja and Rakesh Hooja, "Government Development Schemes and the Modernization of Agriculture in India", The Administrator, Vol. 25, No. 4, 1980.
8. Bhupendra Hooja, "Land and Water Management—Some Points for an Agenda of Action", Paper presented at Seminar on Desert and Drought Prone Areas, Jaipur, March 6, 1982.
9. (a) Bhupendra Hooja, "Some Challenges and Strategies of Agriculture and Land Water Management in the 1980s", Prashasnika, Jan.-March, 1983.
   (b) Bhupendra Hooja, "Planning Priorities and Development Policies in Agriculture", in Development Policy and Administration Review, Vol. IX, Nos. 1-2, Jan.-December 1983, Printed (1985).
10. Bhupendra Hooja, "Natural Resources and Livestock Development in Rajasthan-Need for Integration". Paper presented at National Seminar on Problems and Prospects of Livestock Management, IDS, Jaipur, November 26-30, 1982.
11. Bhupendra Hooja, "Some Notes on Working Animals and Milch Cattle in Rajasthan". Paper Presented at National Seminar on Problems and Prospects of Livestock Management, IDS, Jaipur, November 26-30, 1982.
12. Rakesh Hooja and Bhupendra Hooja, "Land Water Management Productivity", Indian Journal of Public Administration, Vol. 28, No. 3, 1982.
13. Rakesh Hooja, "Government Developmental Delivery System for Desert Districts, The Administrator, Vol. 28, No. 2, 1982."
14. Rakesh Hooja, "Machinery for Delivering Benefits to the Rural Poor", Indian Journal of Public Administration, Vol. 28 No. 1, 1982.
15. Rakesh Hooja, "Development Role of the District Collector-The Case of Rajasthan", Development Policy and Administration Review, Vol. IX, No. 1-2, Jan.- Dec. 1983 (Printed 1985).
16. Rakesh Hooja, "India's Credit Based Anti-Poverty Programmes", The Administrator, Vol. XXX. No. 1 Jan.-March 1985.
17. Rakesh Hooja, "Peoples Participation in Comprehensive Watershed Development Programmes", in Hoshiar Singh (ed.), Rural Development Administration in India, 1984.
18. Government of India, National Commission on Agriculture, Interim Report on Desert Development, New Delhi, 1974.
19. Government of India, Ministry of Rural Development, Report of Task Force on the Drought Prone Area Programme and Desert Development Progarmme, New Delhi, 1982.
20. Government of India, Planning Commission, "National Committee on the Development

of Backward Areas", Report on Development of Drought Prone Areas and Desert Areas, September 1981.

21. "Interim Report of the Sub-Group on Desert and Drought Prone Areas of the Working Group for Preparation of Seventh Plan for Rural Development", Jaipur (mimeographed), August 1984.
22. Rakesh Hooja and Yogeshwar Sharma (eds.) Energy Alternatives for Rural Development, HCM SIPA, Jaipur, 1985.

4

Organization for Command Area Administration in India[1]

V.S. Gopalakrishnan

Crores of rupees have been spent by Indian Government in constructing major and medium irrigation projects, and yet the returns have been partial due to under-utilization of irrigation potential. Of late, stress is being laid *on* the application of the principles of scientific soil and water management with a view to obtaining optimum benefits from each unit of available irrigation water. However, what is rather striking is that innovations in the organizational set-up have not kept pace with the development of techniques in water utilization. It is high time that a complete change is brought about with a view to constituting a highly efficient organizational structure responsible for command area administration. Any amount of improvement in scientific techniques of water management would be of little avail without there being a suitable self-contained and efficient administrative machinery to bring about the development of the command envisaged.

Extent of Under-Utilization

Land and water are basic to agriculture. Where there is no adequate support of water to the land, agriculture becomes hazardous. The bulk of Indian agriculture is carried under the vagaries of rainfed conditions. Therefore, it is only in respect of the areas where both protective and productive irrigation has been made available with the construction of major, medium and minor irrigation projects, that there is a scope to combine the soil and the water in the best manner possible with a view to obtaining maximum agricultural production. Compared to the total sown area, the irrigated area being fractional, there is need for total concentration in maximizing production in the command of major and medium irrigation projects. Any amount of efforts made in the dry land areas in the manner of various scheme, like soil

1. The views expressed here are meant to be personal and not official.

conservation, dry farming practices, etc. can make no significant impact on production statistics. If a 'big leap' in agricultural production is to be brought about, we have to operate mainly on those areas where water is available as a result of the existence of irrigation projects. Some statistics in this regard would amplify the position. The net area cultivated in the country in 1967-68 was 139.7 million hectares, whereas the net area irrigated was 27.5 million hectares. The percentage of irrigation out of cultivated area comes to 19.7 per cent only. In the year 1970-71, the total irrigated area was estimated to have been 39.0 million hectares, out of which the area irrigated by major and medium projects was 19.0 million hectares and the area irrigated by minor irrigation projects was 20.0 million hectares. According to the information available, the percentage? of utilization of the irrigation potential which has been created is 83 per cent. If we roughly assume the non-utilization percentage as 20, the underutilized potential for major and medium projects comes to roughly 4 million hectares. Assuming an investment of Rs. 2,500 per hectare, the underutilized potential would represent an investment of nearly 1,000 crores that is now almost a dead loss. Even the figure of 83 per cent of utilization would give us an exaggerated picture since the efficiency of utilization is very much below the optimum level. In fact, some studies made in irrigation projects have indicated that only about 40 per cent of the water delivered at the canal head reaches the field. All this would point out to the greatest need of the hour to concentrate on maximizing foodgrains production out of the irrigation potential created in India rather than scattering away our energies in various types of schemes applicable to dry lands and other areas.

Factors Responsible for Under-Utilization of Irrigation Potential

The utilization of irrigation potential of major and medium projects is 50 per cent in Bihar, 40 per cent in Madhya Pradesh, and 56 per cent in Maharashtra. The picture in other States is better, but that is still a far cry from the ideal. The reasons for under-utilization can be enumerated briefly as follows:

(*i*) Lack of coordination between the Departments, especially the Department of Irrigation and the Department of Agriculture;
(*ii*) Lack of land development in the command area, i.e., land levelling and land shaping, etc;
(*iii*) Absence of well designed field distribution system consisting of water courses, field channels, etc.
(*iv*) Lack of adoption of proper cropping patterns based on water availability and soil characteristics;
(*v*) Lack of adequate soil surveys;
(*vi*) Lack of proper extension services;
(*vii*) Seepage losses in the distribution system;
(*viii*) Untimely supply of input facilities;
(*ix*) Poor infrastructure facilities in the manner of roads, markets, etc.; and
(*x*) Incomplete work in the consolidation of land holdings.

Remedies have already been evolved in respect of items (*ii*) onwards in the list of reasons indicated for poor utilization of water. It has been suggested that the development of Ayacut should go hand-in-hand with the construction of the dam. The World Bank/International Development Agency (IDA) now-a-days insist that irrigation engineering works and agricultural development programmes should go on simultaneously. The new planning methodology would consist in ensuring that when a dam is completed along with its canals, distributories, etc., the command area is also simultaneously ready for irrigation after the completion of all the required developmental work, like land levelling, shaping, construction of water courses, etc. This would also obviate delays between the Commissioning of the projects and commencement of use of water. As regards the field distribution system, there is an attempt to take over the work of construction of water courses, field channels, etc. by the Government Departments rather than leave it to the will and mercy of the cultivators. In respect of cropping patterns, emphasis is being laid on zoning of the crops to suit the nature of soil, climate, natural protection available, etc., with a view to optimising the yields from every unit volume of water. In order to reduce seepage losses, lining of water courses is being widely recommended. The importance of soil surveys is being stressed more and more since soil information is most essential to ensure efficient water management. There is a growing awareness to the question of strengthening the extension services as well as in ensuring timely supply of inputs and other facilities to the farmers in the command area. The State Governments have been giving serious attention to the consolidation of holdings, especially in areas of high-agricultural potential on a priority basis. Though provision of infrastructure facilities call for tight financial outlays, its importance is being increasingly realized.

Integrated Area Development Approach

Realising that a wide range of activities have to go together simultaneously, like land levelling and shaping, drainage, prescription of proper cropping patterns, construction of water courses and field channels, provision of necessary inputs, building of adequate infrastructures, etc. the Government have adopted an integrated area development approach in respect of the command area with a view to bringing about maximum utilization of water and maximization of agricultural production. Accordingly, during the Fourth Plan, a Central Sector Scheme for the Integrated Area Development of Commands has been launched. A second programme of Soil and Water Management—Pilot Projects in Selected Irrigation Commands—has been taken up during the Fourth Plan, the main purpose of which is to demonstrate to the cultivators the introduction of improved irrigation techniques. These two schemes are said to be working successfully.

Innovations in Command Area Administration

Any amount of physical support for best water management, like land development, proper water courses and field channels, etc., coupled with timely supply of inputs and facilities will make no sense unless a suitable organizational set-up is evolved for their administration of the same. The impression of the author is that sufficient attention has not been paid to the aspect of evolving a suitable administrative machinery for the management of command areas, although many improvements in scientific techniques of water management have been brought about. A beginning has however, been made, as in evident from the fact that most States have accepted the need for providing a single planning and coordinating authority for the command area projects. It appears that Project Coordinators/Administrators are now in position in Pocharapad, Mahi, Kadana, Tawa, Tungabhadra, Jayakwadi, Chambal, Kosi, Gandak, and Sone Projects. It also appears that action to set up such organizations has also been initiated in some other commands. It has been recognized that 'there should be a single planning and Coordinating authority to look after the working of all the Departments and agencies concerned. Such an agency has not only to be under an officer of proper status and seniority, but he has also to be provided necessary support in technical disciplines.'

Departmental Chauvinism and Inadequacies in Present Management Set-up

What strikes one's eyes most is lack of coordination between the Department of Irrigation and the Department of Agriculture. This position obtains not only at planning and construction stage of a project, but also during the maintenance stage. During the project formulation and constructs on stage, the Irrigation Department does not have sufficient liaison with the Department of Agriculture. The construction of dam and canals is not coordinated with development of command area. The Agriculture Department remains in the dark as to the nature and extent of benefits the project would offer to the cultivators. The Irrigation Department is likewise bereft of any conception as to how well the farmers would benefit from the irrigation project. The Departments of Irrigation and Agriculture often function in isolation with the result that it is the poor cultivator, who should be the primary concern, is left high and dry. Very often the end is forgotten arid only the means are remembered. The Irrigation Engineers often forget that their activity only constitutes a means and is not an end in itself. The Agricultural Officers also generally consider the dam and the impounded water as alien. They do not have any sense of belonging to the dam, canals and distributories, but have a sense of belonging only to the fields.

The cultivators, when questioned or even without it, have many complaints against the working of the Department of Irrigation or the Department of Agriculture. One of the usual complaints is that the water is not being released by the irrigation people in a timely manner. Another complaint that crops up quite often is that supply of inputs to the farmers has not been effected on time. The combined result of these two types of complaints is that the proper recommended varieties of crops are not raised and even if raised, they suffer from inadequate irrigation. The Irrigation Engineer would deny the charge on him but would readily point out that the Agriculture Department has failed to make timely supply of inputs and therefore, the expected crop production is not there. The Agricultural Officers would claim that they are not at fault, but the Irrigation Department did not release the water on time and, therefore, the expected crop production is not there. There is hardly any coordination between these two Departments. In many states, the Collector is the coordinating authority and there are even Coordination Committees constituted. The Collector is, however, a busy man and his main attention is taken away by matters pertaining to law and order, revenue administration, civil supplies, etc. The Coordination Committee meets once in three months or so and except for conducting some reviews by way *of post-mortem* accomplishes nothing. This points out to a sad lack of coordination between the various departments operating in the command area. The cultivator is the eventual victim, who does not even know as to who is the single top authority he can approach to obtain redress for his grievances.

Irrigation Officers, who maintain the dam, feel responsible to their bosses only (like Superintending Engineers), and the Collector, who is the Coordinator, has no control over these officers. Similarly, the agricultural extension machinery operating in the command area has no allegiance to the Collector and its loyalties rest only with the district level agricultural officer who is generally a member of the District Development Office. The work of Ayacut development, namely, construction of water courses, levelling, etc., is undertaken by specialized State Governmental Agencies, like Soil Conservation Department in full independence of the Collector or the district developmental authorities, like Zila Parishad. Quite often, the drainage schemes in the command areas are undertaken by the Irrigation Departments, whose officers are naturally independent of the Collector. The District Deputy Registrar of the Cooperative Societies controls cooperative credit in respect of inputs, like seeds, fertilizers, etc., but this officer is normally independent of the District Developmental Officer as well as the Collector. We thus have a multiplicity of functionaries and departments operating in the command area, whose work the Collector or the Committee is supposed to coordinate but over whom he has no real control. There is no machinery to ensure day-to-day coordination in the working of these departments. The departmental functionaries in the Command Area also lack being supervised since their superiors are normally located at District or Divisional Headquarters, way away from them.

PROPOSAL FOR AN ORGANIZATION FOR COMMAND AREA ADMINISTRATION

The integrated area development approach has come to stay. Mere integration is not enough, but day-to-day coordination with control is also a must. I would, therefore, make a plea for both integrated and coordinated area development approach. The coordination without control, as in the case of the Collector today, can offer little benefits. It is, therefore, necessary to set up a command area authority which will be able to bring about, on a day-to-day basis, coordination with control and supervision. Therefore, what is envisaged is a Project Administrator who will have full control and supervision over the following agencies working in the command area : (*i*) officers of the Irrigation Department, (*ii*) officers of the Extension Wing of the Agriculture Department, (*iii*) officers in-charge of Ayacut development wing of Agriculture Department, etc. If this set-up is possible, there is no reason why the Project

Administrator should not be delegated with the powers of Registrar of Cooperative Societies so that he can control cooperative credit to the primary societies and to the farmers and bring about a link-up between supply of inputs and supply of credit, in a timely manner. (Quite often we now find that the credit operations controlled by the Deputy Registrar and the supply of inputs controlled generally by the district developmental body do not go hand-in-hand). The unit in-charge of soil survey, working in the Command area can also be made directly responsible to the Project Administrator who can supervise its work administratively at close quarters on a day-to-day basis. A Soil Testing Centre can also be located in the Command area which would function under the administrative supervision of the Project Administrator though technically it would be guided by the State Departmental Officers. The Project Administrator should also be put in-charge of planning and development of infra-structure Facilities required for the Command area. The continuous presence of the powerful and influential Project Administrator at the site of the Command area itself would be a helpful factor to ensure that the cultivators follow the cropping patterns as prescribed. He can also establish personal contacts and bring about a larger activization of the Land Consolidation Officers. In effect, the Project Administrator will be a leader, friend, philosopher and guide to the farmers in the Command area as well as a leader, supervising and guiding force for the multi-departmental set-up operating in the Command area itself. In such a set-up, there will be a close day-to-day watch and supervision exercised on the work of the multi-departmental officials in the Command area by the Project Administrator who will be ultimately responsible to the project as a whole. The present situation, in which the district level irrigation officer, the district level agricultural officer, the district level cooperative officer, etc., or their supervisors maintain only occasional supervision over the work of the subordinate officials in the Command area due to the factor of long intervening distances, can thus be remedied with the appointment of a Project Administrator located at the dam site itself.

It may be possible to make a further extension to this proposed picture, by putting the Project Administrator as in-charge of fisheries development in the tank area and also for soil conservation measures in the catchment area. We would thus have a single unified, apex authority, *viz.*, the Project Administrator with lines of control running down from him. Consisting of irrigation officials, agricultural extension officials, etc. This entire administrative set-up should be located right near the dam with suitable office and housing facilities.

A Few Details of the Proposed Organization

About 600 major and medium irrigation projects have been taken up on hand in the Plan era—1951-72. Of these, 42 major projects with potential of 3.5 million hectares, and 326 medium projects with a potential of 2.1 million hectares have been completed. It is felt that the Project Administration required for major projects may have to be slightly different from that required for medium projects.

Medium Projects

Apart from 326 medium projects with a potential of 2.1 million hectares that have been completed already as Plan works, 153 medium projects are under execution with the targeted irrigation of about 1.0 million hectares. The importance of efficient project administration for medium projects cannot, therefore, be over-emphasized. Normally, a medium project costs anything between Rs. 25 lakhs to Rs. 5.0 crores and would be in a position to irrigate anything between 1,000 hectares and 20,000 hectares. It would be reasonable to assume that the Project Administrator for command area of 15,000 acres (about 6,000 hectares) and above should be an officer of the rank and status of a District Collector. For projects with command of less than 15,000 acres, the Project Administrator should be of the rank at least of a Sub-Divisional Officer.

For projects above 15,000 acres, the Project Administrator of the rank of a Collector will be located near the dam and would be fully in-charge of the development, administration and management of the command area. He should be assisted by a Class I Agricultural Officer, who should be at least M.Sc. in Agriculture and trained in Extension work. For every 5,000 acres, there may be a Graduate Agricultural Officer, who would be responsible for extension and who would be located in one of the major villages in his jurisdiction. For areas of 1,000 acres, we may have Agricultural Assistants who should be generally Matricultates and products of Agricultural Schools. This agricultural extension machinery, though directly responsible to the Project Administrator, should maintain close technical liaison with the District Agricultural Office. Similarly, the Executive Engineer or/Distant Engineer of Irrigation Department, who is in-charge of maintenance and management of the dam, canals and distributaries, should also function directly under the Project Administrator though he should derive technical assistance and guidance from higher level departmental officers, like the Superintending Engineer. The Project Administrator can also be entrusted with the supervision and the governance of the functioning of trial-cum-demonstration farms in the command area. The officers of the Agriculture Department concerned with land development in the command area would also be directly responsible to the Project Administrator though they would derive technical guidance and help, apart from supplies of machinery, etc., from their superior officers working in the State Agriculture Departments. The Soil Survey Unit and the Soil Testing Laboratory should be put under the administrative control of the Project Administrator. The Project Administrator would also be Deputy Registrar, Cooperative Societies for the Command area villages in respect of primary societies. The planning and development of infrastructure facilities would also be the charge of Project Administrator. Likewise, the Fisheries Officers entrusted with the development of fisheries in the tank as well as the officers in-charge of soil conservation projects in the catchment area can also be put under the charge of the Project Administrator.

We would, therefore, have a self-contained administrative machinery fully controlled and coordinated in a day-to-day basis and fully alive to the developmental needs of the command area. In such a set-up, the goals become clear and common to all the functionaries. In this set-up, the Agricultural Officer would regard the dam and the canals as belonging to the common organization and, therefore, unto himself. The Irrigation Engineers would regard the command fields and the farmers as very close to themselves.

Projects of Less than 15,000 Acres

Here the Project Administrator should be at least an officer of the rank of a Sub-Divisional Officer. The set-up that may consist of officers of the concerned departments would be identical except in respect of their levels. Here also, there will be a unified command and a clear line of control. There will be coordination with control and responsibility with authority.

Set-up for Major Irrigation Projects

With the in-flow of aid from World Bank/L.D.A. and the interest shown by the A.R.C. in financing of command development programmes, perhaps, the most ideal set-up would be to have a corporation or an authority which can be in a position to draw upon funds from the financial bodies for carrying out the developmental programmes. Command Area Boards or Authorities have already been set up in respect *of* some major irrigation projects, and Projects Administrators on a whole-time basis *of* a sufficiently high rank and status have been appointed. However, the Project Administrator often functions in isolation, with the power to coordinate but without any control over the officers of various departments, as in the case of Jayakwadi project. Even though such Project Administrator may be a full-time officer, the lack of control over the officers renders attempts of coordination often infructuous. He is vested with responsibility to coordinate, but he has little authority over the officers. Therefore, what is suggested here is that in respect of such major command areas where a Project Administrator has been functioning independently or as a member of the Project Developmental Board/Authority, the officers of various departments responsible for development or administration of the command area should be brought directly under his control and supervision so as to facilitate coordination. The constitution of a Corporation or an Authority may not be always possible in respect of all the major projects. Even in such cases, a Project Administrator should be appointed along with a complete set-up of various departmental officers concerned with command area development and administration under him. A major irrigation project normally commands an area of 50,000 acres and above and, therefore, very often the catchment and the command over-run more than one District. The Project Administrator for major projects should, therefore, be at least of the status of a Commissioner.

Likely Difficulties in Constituting Proposed Organization

Finance may be argued as the main constraint in bringing about the proposed organizational set-up for command area administration. However, strictly speaking, there is no reason why Finance should come in the way. Let us assume that a project with a command of 50,000 acres has been constructed with a cost of Rs. 5.0 crores. The Project Administrator in this case of the rank of a Collector and his own personal office set-up may cost the Exchequer something like only Rs. 30,000 per year. All the rest of the staff working under the Project Administrator will not be new since the existing departmental officers would be simply transferred under his control. It has been estimated that the cost of development of land and provision of various facilities, like soil survey, extension and demonstration, communications, markets, etc., would work out to, on a very rough and average basis, Rs. 400 per acre. On this basis, the developmental cost of the command of 50,000 acres would work out to Rs. 2.0 crores. Considering the expenditure of Rs. 5.0 crores for the Project (dam, canals, etc.) and Rs. 2.0 crores on the command area development, the cost of running the proposed organizational set-up would be negligible.

Another argument against the proposed set-up may be that it would cut across the concept of democratic de-centralization. Here also, this argument cannot hold much water. Since the irrigation department in-charge of dam and canals, and the agriculture department in-charge of Ayacut development are already independent of the district local development body, the proposed set-up cannot make inroads into the authority of the district local body. The district level local body may be affected only to the extent that the agricultural extension machinery would be transferred over to the Project Administrator.

CONCLUSION

About 600 major and medium irrigation projects have taken birth since 1951, out of which 42 major projects and 326 medium projects are already completed. The major and medium projects alone offer irrigation facilities to 20 million hectares of land. Since minor irrigation is mostly under the control of private individuals, and is also largely managed in an efficient manner, the Government can do very little for it. However, since major and medium projects are those over which the Government have invested crores of rupees and are under the control of the Government, it should be Government's endeavour to derive fullest benefits from optimum utilization of water from such projects. It is in this context that it is urged that the proposed type of machinery for project administration should be set up for each, and every major and medium project.

SECTION III: FOREST MANAGEMENT

5

Conserving India's Forests, Protecting India's People

Vandana Shiva

When the British colonized India, they first colonized her forests. Ignorant of their wealth and of the wealth of knowledge of local people to sustainable manage the forests, they displaced local rights, local needs and local knowledge and reduced this primary source of life into a timber mine. Women's subsistence economy based on the forest was replaced by the commercial economy of British colonialism. Teak from Malabar was extracted for the King's Navy, and the sal of Central India and the conifers of the Himalayas were exploited for the railway system. Although, it is always local people who are held responsible for deforestation, it is commercial demands that have more frequently resulted in large-scale forest destruction. In the Himalayan region, there is evidence that it were the needs of the Empire and not of the local people that led to rapid forest denudation. According to Atkinson Gazetteer:

> The forests were denuded of good trees in all places. The destruction of trees of all species appears to have continued steadily and reached its climax between 1855 and 1861, when the demands of the Railway authorities induced numerous speculators to enter into contracts for sleepers, and these men were allowed, unchecked, to cut down old trees very far in excess of what they could possibly export, so that for some years after the regular forest operations commenced, the department was chiefly busy cutting up and bringing to the depot the timber left behind by the contractors.

When the British started exploiting Indian timber for military purposes, they did it rapaciously and in ignorance, because the "great continent appeared to hold inexhaustible tracts covered with dense jungles; there was no apparent necessity for their detailed exploration, there had been a possibility thereof. In the early years of occupations, the botany of the forest, species of trees, these and their respective values was an unopened book."

THE COLONIAL POLICY OF DEFORESTATION

To the colonial government and its officials, the critical role that forests play in nature and the great influence they exercise on the physical well-being of a country went unrecognized. In view of the large forest wealth that existed, the government for some years obtained its full requirement without difficulty, while local needs were also met. The early administrators appear to have convinced that this state of affairs could go on for an unlimited period. In many localities, forests were viewed as an obstruction to agriculture, which was taxed, and were seen, therefore, as a limiting factor to the prosperity of the coloniser. The policy was to extend agriculture and the watchword was to clear the forests with this end in view. Virgin forests of the Doon Valley were, thus, clear felled for land grants made exclusively to British settlers.

The military requirement for Indian teak led to an immediate proclamation declaring that the royalty right in teak trees claimed by the former government in the south of the continent, was vested in the East India Company. In the year 1799 alone, 10,000 teak trees were brough down by the Beypur River in Malabar. Under further pressure from the Home Government to ensure the maintenance of the future strength of the King's Navy, a decision was taken to appoint a special officer to superintend forest work—his duties were to preserve and improve the production of teak and other timber suitable for ship building. Captain Watson of the Police was appointed the first Conservator of Forests in India on November 10, 1806. Under the proclamation of April 1807, he weilded great powers. He soon established a timber monopoly throughout Malabar and Travancore and furnished the government, as did his immediate successors, with a plentiful supply of cheap timber. But the methods by which this was done were intolerable and gradually gave rise to seething discontent amongst both local peasants as well as proprietors. The feeling rose to such a pitch that the Conservator ship was abolished in 1823.

The introduction of colonial forestry was, thus, established not because of superior forestry knowledge or scientific management, but through dominant military need and power. It was only after more than half a century of uncontrolled forest destruction by British commercial interests that an attempt was made to control exploitation. In 1865, the first Indian Forest Act (VII of 1865) was passed by the Supreme Legislative Council, which authorized the government to declare forests and wastelands (*benap* or unmeasured lands) as reserved forests.

The introduction of this legislation marks the beginning of what is called the "scientific management" of forests; it amounted basically to the formalisation of the erosion both of forests and of the rights of local people to forest produce. Commercial forestry, which is equated with 'scientific forestry' by those narrow interests, exemplified by western patriarchy, is reductionist in intellectual content and ecological impact, and generates poverty at the socio-economic level for those whose livelihoods and productivity depend on the forest. Reductionism has been characteristic of this forestry because it sunders forestry from water management, agriculture and animal husbandry. Within the forest ecosystem, it has reduced the diversity of life to the dead product, wood, and wood in turn to commercially valuable wood only. A commercial interest has the primary objective of maximizing exchange value on the market through the extraction of commercially valuable species—forest ecosystems are, therefore, reduced to the timber of such species. By ignoring the complex relationship within the forest community and between plant life and other resources, like soil and water, this pattern of resource use generates instabilities in the ecosystem and leads to counter-productive use of nature as a living and self-reproducing resource. The destruction of the forest ecosystem and the multiple functions of forest resources in turn hurts the economic interest of those groups of society, mainly women and tribals, who depend on the diverse resource functions of the forests for their survival. These include soil and water stabilisation and the provision of food, fodder, fuel, fertilizer, etc.

FOREST STRUGGLES

The dispossession of the local people of their rights, their resources and their knowledge has not gone unchallenged. Forest struggles have been taking place throughout the country for over two centuries to resist the colonisation of the people's forests in India. The access and rights of the people to forests were first severely encroached upon with the introduction of the forest Acts of 1878 and 1927. The following years witnessed the spread of forests *Satyagrahas* throughout India as a protest against the reservation of forests for exclusive exploitation by British commercial interest, and their concomitant transformation from a common resource into a commodity. Villagers ceremonially removed forest products form the reserved forests to assert their right to satisfy their basic needs. The forest satyagrahas were especially successful in regions where survival of the local population was intimately linked with access to the forests, as in the Himalaya, the Western Ghats, and the Central Indian hills. These non-violent protests were systematically crushed by the British; in Central India, Gond tribals were gunned down for participating in the protests; in 1930, dozens of unarmed villagers were killed and hundreds injured in Tilari village in Tehri Garhwal, when they gathered to protest against the Forest Laws of the local rulers. After enormous loss of life, the Satyagrahis were successful in reviving some of the traditional rights of the village communities to various forest products. The Forest Policy of post-colonial India continued on the colonial path of commercialisation and reductionism, and with it continued people's resistance to a denial of their basic needs, both through alienation of rights and through ecological degradation. In the mountain regions of the Himalaya, the women of Garhwal started to protect their forests from commercial exploitation even at the cost of their lives, by starting the famous *Chipko,* Movement, embracing the living trees as their protectors. Beginning in the early 1970s, in the Garhwal region of Utter Pradesh, the methodology and philosophy of *Chipko* has now spread to Himachal Pradesh in the north, to Karnataka in the South, to Rajasthan in the west, to Orissa in the east, and to the Central Indian highlands.

There are in India, today, two paradigms of foresty—one life-enhancing, the other life-destroying. The life-enhancing paradigm emerges from the forest and the feminine principle; the life-destroying one from the factory and the market. The former creates a sustainable, renewable forest system, supporting and renewing food and water sources. The maintenance of conditions for renewability is its primary management objective, while the maximising of profits through commercial extraction is the primary management objective of the latter. Since the maximizing of profits is consequent upon the destruction of conditions of renewability, the two paradigms are cognitively and ecologically incommensurate. The first paradigm has emerged from India's ancient forest culture, in all its diversity, and has been renewed in cotemporary times by the women of Garhwal though *Chipko*.

It is these two distinct knowledge and economic systems which clashed in 1977 in Adwani when the *Chipko* Movement became explicitly an ecological and feminist movement. The women, of course, had always been the living, natural forest. But in the early days, when it was directed against removing the non-local forest contractors, local commercial interest had also been part of the resistance. Once non-local private contractors were removed and a government agency (the Forest Development Corporation) started working through local labour contractors and forest cooperatives, the women continued to struggle against the exploitation of the forests. It did not matter to them whether the forest was destroyed by outsiders or their own men. The most dramatic turn in this new confrontation took place when Bachni Devi of Adwani led a resistance against her own husband, who had obtained a local contract to fell the forest. The forest officials arrived to browbeat and intimidate the women and *Chipko* activities, but found the women holding up lighted lanterns in broad daylight. Puzzled, the forester asked them their intention. The women replied, "we have come to teach you forestry". He retorted, "You foolish women, how can you who prevent felling, know the value of the forest? Do you know what forests bear? They produce profit and resin and timber". And that women immediately sang back in chorus:

> What do the forests bear?
> Soil, water and pure air
> Soil, water and pure air
> Sustain the earth and all she bears.

The Adwani *Satyagraha* created new directions for *Chipko*. The movement's philosophy and politics now evolve to relect the needs and knowledge of the women. Peasant women came out, openly challenging the reductionist commercial forestry system, on the one hand, and the local men, who had been colonized by that system, cognitively, economically and politically, on the other.

ANTI-SOCIAL "SOCIAL FORESTRY"

Social forestry projects are a good example of single species, single commodity production plantations, based on reductionist models which divorce forestry from agriculture and water management, and needs from markets.

A case study of World Bank sponsored social forestry in Kolar district of Karnataka is an illustration of reductionism and maldevelopment in forestry being extended to farmland. Decentred agro-forestry, based on multiple species and private and common tree-stands, has been India's age-old strategy for maintaining farm productivity in arid and semi-arid zones. The bonage, tamarind, jackfruit and mango, the jola, goblin, kagli and bamboo traditionally provided food and fodder, fertilizer and pesticide, fuel and small timber. The backyard of each rural home was a nursery, and each peasant women the silviclututurist. The invisible, decanted agro-forestry model was significant because the humblest of species and the smallest of people could participate in it, and with space for the small, everyone was involved in protecting and planting.

The reductionist mind took over tree-planting with social forestry plans were made in national and international capitals by people who could not know the purpose of the bonge and the neem, and saw them as weeds. The experts decided that indigenous knowledge was worthless and 'unscientific' and proceed to destroy the diversity of indigenous species by replacing them with row after row of eucalyptus seedlings in polythene bags, in government nurseries. Nature's locally available seeds were laid waste; people's locally available knowledge and energies were laid waste. With imported seeds and expertise came the import of loans and debt and the export of wood, soils—and people. Trees, as a living resource, maintaining the life of the soil and water and of local people, were replaced by trees whose dead wood went straight to a pulp factory hundreds of miles away. The smallest farm became a supplier of raw material to industry and ceased to be a supplier of food to local people. Women's work, linking the trees to the crops, disappeared and was replaced by the work of brokers and middlemen who brought the eucalyptus trees on behalf of industry. Industrialists, foresters and bureaucrats loved the eucalyptus because it grows straight and is excellent pulp-wood, unlike the long which shelters the soil with its profuse branches and dense canopy and whose real worth is as a living tree on a farm. The longe could be nature's idea of the perfect tree for arid Karnataka. It has rapid growth of precisely those parts of the tree, the leaves and small branches, which go back to the earth, enriching and protecting it, conserving its moisture and fertility. The eucalyptus, on the other hand, when perceived ecologically, is unproductive, even negative, because this perception assesses the 'growth' and 'productivity' of trees in relation to the water cycle and its conservation, in relation to soil fertility and in relation to human needs for food and food production. The eucalyptus has destroyer the water cycle in arid regions due to its high water demand and its failure to produce humus, which is nature's mechanism for conserving water. Most indigenous species have much higher biological productivity than the eucalyptus, when one considers water yields and water conservation. The non-woody biomass of trees has never been assessed by forest measurements and quantification within the reductionist paradigm, yet it is this very biomass that functions in conversing water and building soils. It is little wonder that Garhwal women call a tree dali or branch, because they see the productivity of the tree in terms of its non-woody biomass which functions critically in hydrological and nutrient cycles with the forest, and through green fertilizer and fooder in cropland.

'Greening' with eucalyptus is a violence against nature and its cycles, and it is a violence against women who depend on the stability of nature's cycles to provide sustenance in the form of food and water. Eucalyptus guzzles nutrients and water and, in the specific conditions of low rainfall zones, gives nothing back but terpenes to the soil. These inhabit growth of other plants and are toxic to soil organisms which are responsible for building soil fertility and improving soil structure. The eucalyptus certainly increased cash and commodity flows, but it resulted in a disastrous interruption of organic matter and water flows within the local ecosystem. Its proponents failed to calculate the costs in terms of the destruction of life in the soil, the depletion of water resources and the scarcity of food and fodder that eucalyptus cultivation creates. Nor did they, while trying to shorten rotations for harvesting, see that tamarind, jackfruit and bonge have very short rotations of one year in which the biomass harvested is far higher than that of eucalyptus, which they nevertheless declared 'miracle' tree. The crux of the matter is that fruit production was never the concern of forestry in the reductionist paradigm—it focused on wood, and wood for the market, alone. Eucalyptus, as an exotic, introduced in total disregard of its ecological appropriateness, has, thus, become an exemplar of anti-life afforestations.

Women throughout India have resisted the expansion of eucalyptus because of its destruction of water, soil and food systems. On August 10, 1983, the women and small peasants of Barha and Holahalli village in Tumkur district (Karnataka) marched en masse to the forest nursery and pulled out millions of eucalyptus seedings, planting tamarind and mango seeds in their place. This gesture of protest, for which they were arrested, spoke out against the virtual planned destruction of soil and water systems by eucalyptus cultivation. It also silently challenged the domination of forestry science that had reduced all species to one (the eucalyptus), all needs to one (that of the pulp industry), and all knowledge to one (that of the World Bank and forest officials). If challenged the myth of the miracle tree; tamarind and mango are symbols of the energies of nature and of local people, of the links between these seeds and the soil, and of the needs that these trees—and others like them—satisfy, in keeping the earth and people alive. Forestry for food—food for the soil, for farm animals, for people—all women's and peasants' struggles revolve around this theme, whether in Garhwal or Karnataka, in the Santhal Parganas or Chhattisgrah, in reserved forests, farmlands of the commons. Destruction of diversity and life, and colonization of the commons is built into reductionist forestry and its new avatar, 'wasteland development'

WASTELAND DEVELOPMENT AND THE TRAGEDY OF THE COMMONS

Recovering five million hectares of the commons in India each year could signal the end of rural poverty and a reversal of the ecological collapse of critical life-support systems like soil, water and vegetation. Yet the wasteland development programme, far from being a recovery of the commons project, will, in fact, privatise the commons, accentuate rural poverty and increase ecological instability. In one stroke, it will rob the poor of their remaining common resources, the only survival base to which they have access. The usurpation of the commons, which began with the British, will reach its final limit with the wasteland development programme as is evident from what Chattrapati Singh of the Indian Law Institute argues;

> It is evidence that till end of the last century and in all historical periods before that, at least 80 per cent of India's natural resources were common property,

> with only 20 per cent being privately utilized ... This extensive common property has provided the resource base for a non-cash, non-market economy. A whole range of necessary resources has been freely available to the people. Thus, commonly available wood, shrubs and cowdung have been utilized for cooking and heating mud, bamboo and palm leaves for housing, wild grass shrubs as animal fodder, and variety of fruits and vegetables as food.

These free commons have historically been the survival base for rural India and the domain of productivity of women. With the reservation of forest a century, ago, the first step towards the privatisation of commons took place. Today, 'wasteland development' constitutes the last step in their disappearance. *N.S. Jodha*, who has worked extensively on common property resources, has shown how women's work and the livelihoods of poorer sections of rural society are intimately linked to trees and grasslands in the commons, which support the farm animals and, thus, take pressure off cropland, while increasing organic inputs to crop through animal waste. Small peasants and landless laborers can own livestock largely because of the existence of the commons. Further, in arid zones, traditional farming systems partly derive their stability and viability form the commons which allow for an integrated and diversified production strategy using crops, livestock and trees, which cushion the dry-land economy by supplying food, fodder and fuel in years of crop failure. Nearly 10 per cent of the nutrition of poorer families have been found to come directly from the commons. Women's work in the sustenance economy of the poorest groups is, this, closely tied to the existence of the commons.

'Wastelands' as a land-use categories, like much else, a part of our colonial heritage, loaded with the biases of colonial rule, where meaning was defined by the interest of the rulers. The colonial concept of waste lands was not an assessment of the biological productivity of land, but of its revenue generating capacity; 'wateland' was land that did not pay any revenue because it was uncultivated. Under such wasteland came the forested districts of Chittagong, Darjeeling, Jalpairguri, Chota Nagpur and Assam—and the vast trail of forest land towards the mouth and delta of the Hooghly and other rivers, known as the Sundarbans.

It was not until later n the nineteenth century that the value of forests was realized. Ecological considerations were not, however, the central objective of the reservation of forests through the notification of the Forest Act of 1878. It was the revenue generating capacity of forests which led to their reservation, and protection was defined as the exclusion of villagers, access to forests as a common resource. Forests in themselves now constituted a property of great value and might be made to yield an annual revenue equal to cultivation. The shift in the colonial perspective of seeing forests as wealth and not waste also led to their conversion from a common resource for local use, under local community control, to a commodity for commercial use under bureaucratic control. This robbery of the commons was seriously resisted through 'forest *satyagrahas*' throughout the country.

A second robbery of the commons is now under way through 'waste-lands development' , which is a euphemism for the privatization of the commons.

An example of how such a scheme goes away can be taken from the Karnataka experience. Village commons in *Shimoga* and *Chikmagalur* are being taken away from people for wasteland development. These village commons are 'C' and 'D' class lands in revenue records. Categorised as wasteland, they are meant for fulfilling the basic needs of villages, for whom 'wasteland' are their common wealth, supporting their agricultural ecology. Attempts to change the vegetational and land-use characteristics of these village commons are, in their perception, attempts at robbing their land of its biological wealth. There is a proposal for transferring all these village commons, within a radius of 100 kms of Harihar Polyfibres, and utilizing about 45,000 acre of commons for growing eucalyptus and selling it to Harihar Polyfibres. The commons are to be leased individually to a few landless beneficiaries.

The people of the affected villages have protested by uprooting newly planted eucalyptus seedlings from these 'wastelands' in large numbers. (Some of the wastelands are, in fact, under natural evergreen of semi-green forests, and the average tree population has been found to be 50-200 per acre of diverse tree species). The cultivation of eucalyptus in the village commons consisting of these 'C' and 'D' class lands is seen by the people as a progamme for the creation of wastelands, not a progammes for their development. The conversion of ecologically productive village commons to feedstock for the wood and fibre industry is in direct conflict with the basic biomass needs of the local villages, and their diversion to industrial plantations through a project for wasteland development has generated a major popular resistance movement for the protection of the commons, called "Mannu Rakshana Koota" or "Movement for Saving the Soil". The government seems determined to take over the commons and manage them commercially throughout the country. Poor people's needs and the need for ecological stability are to be sacrificed in this ultimate privatization of the commons.

There is, of course, the popular triage thesis that the poor have no right to survival and should be dispensed with. Hardin's tragedy of the commons scenario emerges from male reductionist assumptions about nature and the logic off triage that such reductionism and its principles of exclusion and dispensability that they entail. Hardin is just a symbol of the new trend in reductionist science which uses the language of ecology and conservation to unleash another attack of violence against nature. More centralization, more uniformity, and more manipulation become new and false prescriptions for overcoming the ecological crisis. Yet neither nature nor people can be saved when the destruction of the former and the dispensability of the latter are the presuppositions for creating the new reductionist science of nature.

6

Social Forestry: Roots of Failure

Kamla Chowdhry

India's population by the year 2000 will have increased from its present 800 million to 1000 million. Cultivable land per capita which declined from 0.48 ha to 0.26 ha between 1951 and 1981, will decline further to 0.14 ha per capita, half of what it is today. With the present rate of deforestation, there will be hardly any forest cover left by the year 2000. Already there are acute shortages of fuel wood and fodder. Even to sustain present demand, fuel wood production must increase from its present 100 million tonnes (mt) a year to about 300 mt and green fodder from about 230 mt to about 780 mt. Survival for the poor is becoming precarious. Women are forced to walk miles in search of fuelwood and fodder. Acute shortages of other forest products, such as bamboo, reed, raisin and other such forest-based raw materials have destroyed the livelihood of millions of tribals and others dependent on forests, as also their culture and way of life. India's future depends on its ability to regenerate its degraded forests and other cultivable and non-cultivable land resources.

In 1976, the National Commission on Agriculture, in its review of the forestry sector, suggested two new directions. Firstly, a greater emphasis on production forestry through establishing Forest Development Corporations. Secondly, a programme of Social Forestry to deal primarily with fuelwood and fodder production for the rural poor. This is not the place to discuss the role of the Forest Development Corporations, but suffice to say, that many agree with the opinion of the late Salim Ali that these should more aptly be called the Forest Destruction Corporations.

Social Forestry was supported by government and considerable funds allocated for its development, especially from the Sixth Plan onwards. Centrally sponsored schemes were promoted for increasing fuelwood in the fuelwood deficient districts. Bilateral and international agencies gave generous support for Social Forestry not only to increase the supply of fuel-wood and fodder, but also to ensure the participation of the rural poor so that the control of these resources would be in the hands of the poor. Social Forestry was to be a programme of the people, for the people, and by the people. Because Social Forestry is labour intensive, it was also hoped that it would contribute significantly to rural employment. Social Forestry, with its village woodlots, farm forestry and other afforestation activities seemed to promise the greening of the country. And, in the long run, this would have meant halting deforestation and significant contribution to the ecological regeneration of the country. Social Forestry had the promise of a many splendoured thing.

By now, we have had over two decades of experience in Social Forestry. An analysis of the programme indicates that the Forestry Department has not really understood the mission of Social Forestry. Various studies have shown that Social Forestry has not achieved its objectives of increasing fuel-wood and fodder and that the major beneficiaries have not been the rural poor. We discuss in the following pages why Social Forestry failed. What assumptions went wrong, and more importantly, what can we learn from experiences gained so far?

TRADITION AND CULTURE OF FORESTRY DEPARTMENT

Social Forestry is much more 'social' than 'forestry' in its essence. By assigning Social Forestry to the Forestry Department, whose early traditions and culture were anti-people, the likelihood of promoting fuelwood and fodder with people's participation seemed somewhat doomed. The first Inspector-General of Forests, appointed in 1864, Dietrich Brandies, brought in a Germanic culture of discipline and of managing forests. Forests were considered resources owned by the Raj, meant for exploitation for the benefit of the colonial rulers, with severe restrictions and limitations on people's rights. The system was based on Germany's version of the enclosure movement. The pattern of reserving forests and restricting forest rights built up resentments amongst the people against the Forest Department. Violations and encroachments intensified the Germanic para-military aspects of protecting the forests. Social Forestry, which required a people-centred approach and special sensitivities in dealing with the rural poor, was located in such a para-military culture and tradition. The forest officials, entrusted with Social Forestry, were expected to work collaboratively with village communities when their whole tradition and approach was to keep people away from 'their' forests. It was, therefore, not surprising that afforestation schemes of roadside plantations, village woodlots, nurseries for saplings, etc. became essentially departmental programmes with the 'enclosure mentality'. The question may well be asked if Social Forestry was conceived as a people's programme, was the Forestry Department with its tradition and culture of 'enclosures' the best place to nurture it? New objectives require new strategies, new structures and new working cultures. Social Forestry, to be successful, must have enabling structures and appropriate administrative policies for its mission of enabling the rural poor to grow fuelwood and fodder for their needs.

CENTRALISED SCHEMES

One of the most successful aspects of Social Forestry has been farm forestry, that is, saplings distributed to farmers essentially for afforestation on their field bunds. Further, in order to encourage farmers, especially poor farmers, to take to afforestation, saplings, were distributed free. The Department established large centralised nurseries, primarily of eucalyptus, for distribution to farmers. Eucalyptus was selected not because the poor farmers wanted it for fuelwood or fodder but because it was easier and cheaper to raise eucalyptus saplings, and because they were non-brow-sable and had a ready market. In reality, farm forestry became a subsidised programme for the bigger fanners. They came in their trucks and tractors and collected thousands of free saplings, planting them in their fields. Many converted their agriculture lands to eucalyptus plantations because of the promise of higher profits. And, when the trees were ready, sold the produce in the market as poles or as wood for paper and pulp industry. The mission of fuelwood and fodder for the rural poor seemed sidetracked by the strategies followed.

Another reason for large centralised nurseries and free distribution was the pressure to achieve targets. A formula of conversion of 2,000 saplings distributed was interpreted as a hectare of land planted. What land, what survival rates, who benefited, these became inconvenient questions to be set aside.

The National Wasteland Development Board encouraged decentralised nurseries, a nursery for every two or three villages, that is, within walking distance. A poor farmer was given the necessary facilities and training to raise the nursery. The species selected were in response to what people wanted, and the enterprise meant employment for a poor person. The cost of such decentralised nurseries was also cheaper.

Who Benefited?

Various independent studies of Social Forestry, including an evaluation by the Programme Evaluation Organisation of the Planning Commission, have indicated that the major beneficiaries have been the larger farmers, on the one hand, and paper and pulp and building industry, on the other. Acute shortages of fuelwood and fodder continue to persist. The road-side plantations are auctioned, where the bidding is by the contractors from the city and not the local poor. Administrative procedures developed during the colonial period continue and the poor farmer, who is the reason behind Social Forestry, gets ignored, bypassed and shoved aside.

Importance of a Local Organisation

In West Bengal, Social Forestry has been more successful because the village panchayats were actively involved in identifying land and beneficiaries. The revitalisation of village panchayats in West Bengal was based on implementation of land reforms and distribution of surplus lands. A group scheme of Social Forestry emerged in these villages by landless people who were distributed surplus land. Fuelwood, fodder and also cash incomes increased. The Forest Department also negotiated with several village communities to protect forests on the basis of an agreed sharing scheme. The protection of forests by village communities has been so successful that the West Bengal Government has extended the scheme to other parts in the state as well. Without a local organisation, active participation and involvement of people is difficult to achieve.

Equity

In many successful projects of afforestation and the sustainable use of forests, the principle of equity in distribution of local resources has contributed significantly to the success of the project. In the *Chipko* villages in the Himalayas, the women in the villages have organised themselves for safeguarding their ecosystems and in developing fuelwood and fodder resources in their common lands. They identified fragile slopes and planted them to prevent landslides. They planted species that the women wanted. The *Chipko* women have developed an equity approach to sharing biomass. Every woman is entitled to a head-load from the commons on a given day of the week, and this is strictly adhered to. When the Sarpanch's wife in one village tried to get an extra head-load on a different day, her head-load was confiscated. Although the Sarpanch tried to create trouble for the women—his dignity and pride were deeply hurt—the women were able to resist his threats. With subsistence needs of fuelwood and fodder ensured, with confidence gained in dealing with local issues (including village tyrants), they have extended their efforts to larger issues of ecology and hill development.

Another successful example of a local organisation based on equitable sharing of resources is the *Sukhomajri* project in the Shivalik hills. The *Sukhomajri* village has been able to protect its watershed, save the village from falling into a widening gorge because of massive erosion, and has been able to increase the social and economic well-being of the village community in a span of three to four years. *Sukhomajri* has established a Water Users' Association, which provides an equal share of the rain-water collected by building a small dam. Even the landless are entitled to an equal share, which they can barter for share-cropping, money, etc. Everyone in the village has a vested interest in safeguarding the watershed, so that the dam does not get silted. Earlier the trees were planted in the watershed by the Forestry Department to stop soil erosion, but the villagers did not cooperate. The forest officials threatened the villagers and imposed heavy fines when caught with their cattle grazing in the watershed. But these mechanisms, as we know from experience elsewhere, will not work and did not work. Only when the community established its own organisation and assured equitable distribution of benefits that every member of the community endeavoured to safeguard the afforestation in the watershed.

With the building of the check-dam, with the availability of harvested rain-water, with the consensus on equitable sharing of water, the economy of the village boomed. In 1977, there were 250 quintals of wheat, 500 quintals of wheat-straw and 196 quintals of maize. In 1981, the production had increased to 1,015 quintals of wheat, 2,031 quintals of wheat-straw and 356 quintals of maize. The milk yield increased from 2,196 litres to 4,405 litres. The grass in the catchment area increased from 200 kgs in 1977 to 2,500 kgs in 1981.

The use of common property resources, such as harvested water, common grazing lands, and traditional uses of forests over a period of time, confers a form of right in the eyes of the users. If changes in use rights are to be formulated for the common good, these change must be agreed to by consensus by *Gram Sabhas* and village communities, as happened in Sukhomajri and in many other successful projects.

LAND-USE POLICY

Land can be classified as agriculture, forests, revenue and community land. A large-scale programme of afforestation, especially for fuelwood and fodder, cannot be undertaken on private agriculture lands. With a population of 800 million, even marginal lands are being used for subsistence farming adding to rapidly increasing wastelands. Food production must increase from about 170 mt to about 240 mt to take care of the increased population by year 2000.

As far as revenue and community lands are concerned, a great deal of these have disappeared as common lands. Illegal occupation, largely by the more powerful rural elites, is one reason, and distribution by government to the rural poor as part of their anti-poverty programme is another reason—although Jodha has shown that even here the larger farmers were able to corner this land. The remaining revenue and community lands, the left overs, are so degraded, so poor in quality, that unless heavy investments are made, there is very little hope of bringing them to productive use. The only realistic possibility of increasing fuelwood and fodder and other timber needs for the rural poor is the use of 'degraded' forest land with little or no tree cover.

The Forest Department has 75 m. ha of land under its control and management. Out of this, about half has tree cover and the other half is treeless for a variety of reasons-illegal cutting by contractors (with the involvement of politicians and forest officials), submergence due to building dams, diverting forest land for agriculture and other so-called public purposes, etc. Even the poor have assaulted the forests. As long as people have no fuel, fodder, timber, they will invade the remaining forests, however stringent the laws of enforcement may be. The solution is not in keeping people out by more stringent laws or arming the forest guards, as is being suggested, but evolving schemes for people's involvement and participation as has been achieved by the West Bengal Social Forestry programme and many other agencies

Tree Patta Scheme

As part of Social Forestry and rural development a 'tree patta' scheme was jointly evolved by the National Wastelands Development Board (NWDB) and the Ministry of Rural Development. The scheme involved access to common land for afforestation purposes. The patta holder was given access to land with usufruct rights of trees and grasses grown on the land. The scheme did not take off primarily because land was not available for the purpose—only very rocky and degraded land was offered and even that meant various political and bureaucratic hurdles. The policy in terms of treeless forest land-about 35 to 40 m ha—has been that this is to be safeguarded and not allowed to be used even for afforestation purposes under the guidance of the Forestry Department. Without access to land, Social Forestry and other afforestation schemes can only be on paper and rhetoric for the birds.

Land-Use Policies for Afforestation

The land-use policy for afforestation purposes must be clearly stated. Unutilised land, whether with forest, revenue, or panchayats, should be made available for afforestation on a 'contract basis' to the people. In China 20.67 m ha of barren hills were contracted for tree planting to 50 million households since 1979; coal mines were allotted 260,000 ha to grow their own wooden rops to be used in the mines; light industry was allotted 66,000 ha of wastelands to produce their own pulpwood requirements rather than the Forest Department providing it. Unfortunately in India, there is no holistic approach to land- use. Administrative jurisdictions and territorial concerns dictate fragmented and conflicting land-use policies. For a holistic approach to land-use, contributing to the welfare of the people, present and future, it is appropriate to consider the spirit of the saying *Sabhi Bhoomi Gopal ki*—all land belongs to the Lord.

SUMMARY AND CONCLUSIONS

Social Forestry was conceived as a people-centred programme, a programme to empower the rural poor for their fuelwood, fodder and other timber needs. In fact, Social Forestry became a government programme, a programme of the Forest Department. Major funds of Social Forestry were used in protected and reserved forests, and the only benefit to the poor was in terms of employment; it is sad to observe that even here, in some instances, it was found that minimum wages were not paid.

People's participation, which was to be the central thrust of Social Forestry, was the first casualty. It was said that people were difficult to work with, they were not interested in assuming responsibility, etc. People's participation cannot be achieved through bureaucratic structures. Experience of the last 40 years has amply made this clear. The very bureaucracy hired to service the poor, including the Social Forestry programme, drained development funds from those who were too weak to protest.

There has been a neglect of land-use policies, especially for the uncultivated half of India, that is, forest lands, revenue and community lands. The poor have paid a heavy price for this neglect. Further, different administrative jurisdictions of land have lent property and custodial approaches to land-use policies irrespective of their best use and contribution to social welfare.

Lack of appropriate policies regarding access of land to the poor for afforestation purposes, defunct Acts and laws, which hinder rather than motivate people, resulted in vested interests controlling the Social Forestry programme. Instead of fuelwood and fodder, Social Forestry has largely provided raw materials to paper, pulp and building industry, bypassing the rural poor.

New programmes, new strategies require new structure. Social Forestry too needs to be housed in an appropriate organisation structure which encourages and promotes people's participation. One such structure promoted was the Rashtriya Vrikshamitra Sahyog Mandal (RVSM), an agency jointly sponsored by the National Wastelands Development Board, and the National Dairy Development Board (NDDB). The RVSM has promoted tree growers cooperatives for fuelwood and fodder in several states.

Social Forestry and massive afforestation by the people cannot be a programme of a single government department. Social Forestry must be a people's movement.

Schools, colleges, mandis, municipalities, government departments, and other identified institutions should share the responsibility to plant trees and maintain them either directly or through a contract system with local people.

The current political discussion on *panchayati raj* and the devolution of powers to village panchayats can be a significant step in achieving the objectives of Social Forestry. West Bengal's considerable success in Social Forestry is due to the active involvement of village panchayats and an active programme of distribution of surplus ceiling lands to the poor.

Gandhiji's talisman seems appropriate for those in charge of Social Forestry:

> I will give you a talisman. Whenever you are in doubt, or when the self becomes too much with you, apply the following test:
>
> Recall the face of the poorest and the weakest man whom you may have seen, and ask yourself, if the step you contemplate is going to be of any use to him. Will he gain anything by it? Will it restore him to a control over his own life and destiny?

7

Development of People's Institution in Joint Forest Management: Assumptions, Realities and Opportunities

P.K. Das

It has been progressively realised that managing forests "with the people" rather than 'from the people' is rewarding for both the state and the village communities. The concept of forest management 'with the people' recognises that local authority over forest management is a crucial determinant towards success. Historically, such authority has been exercised by she state, forest departments (FDs). However, by and large, the FDs have failed to manage the forests properly basically due to non-cooperation from the local village communities. The National Commission on Agriculture (1976) recommended to seek people's involvement in forest management in order to reverse the trend of deforestation. This had prompted the states to initiate local level forestry with the involvement of village communities. To begin with, attempts were made to assign the responsibilities of forest management to the local self-government (panchayat) during 80's under the community woodlot programme. Over a period of time, it was found that in most pan of the country, these woodlot enterprises were not very successful. Panchayat was identified to be still a higher order of threshold in managing the forest resources. Its perspective in managing the woodlots could hardly match with the needs of the poor strata of the village community who were most in need of what the woodlots could produce. In many cases, panchayats saw woodlots as income generators more than as resources to meet public needs.

Since, 1990s, the focus for participatory forest management has shifted to Joint Forest Management (JFM) and the user groups in the village society are contemplated to be the co-managers of local forest resources. The user groups include those who want to participate and who have a common material interest, linking them together in protecting the local forest resources. The user groups have been brought under an institutional structure, variously known as Forest Protection Committee, Vana Samrakshana Samithi, Village Forest Committee, etc., in different states (hereafter mentioned as PI, *i.e.*, People's Institution). These institutions are expected to provide a forum for developing participatory approach and to manage the sharing of responsibilities and benefits. Conceptually, they are envisaged as local level forest management units as well as an interface between FD and village community. In pursuance of their mutual obligation with FD, they are required to perform tasks mostly related to protection of forests, including regeneration and fire and theft prevention. In return, they are assured to have a share in the forest produce. To translate the concept of JFM into action, so far 25 states have passed their respective resolutions based on the guidelines of the Central government issued in June 1990. They have formulated institutional frameworks for the PIs, sphere of which ranges from hamlet to cluster of villages. With the introduction of JFM, popular participation in forest management through micro-institutional solution like PI of user groups is being seen as an innovation. Many of the states have experience of almost one decade or more with the functioning of PIs. Ever since the introduction of JFM, a considerable body of literature has been generated on the concept and functioning of these PIs. Its implementation has led to a host of issues related to the applicability of the institutional frameworks of PIs crafted by the forest bureaucracy. These issues are being discussed and analysed nationwide in order to arrive at a common understanding. The present paper is an addendum to this initiative. Its genesis owes to author's field exposure and supporting literature on conceptual inputs (references appended).

INSTITUTIONAL OPTIONS

For building up local capacity for participatory forest management, few options are available. The first and foremost among them is a decision on the existing and new institutions. In the case of participatory forest management, the dispute still continues on whether FD and NGO should work through the existing traditional institutions or through newly created ones. Much before the introduction of JFM, many forest villages across the country initiated informal (and sometimes formal) local institutions for the purpose of village level decision-making towards protection of forest resources. Such initiatives have been traced in the states of Orissa, Jharkhand, Chhattisgarh, Karnataka, Gujarat, Madhya Pradesh, Rajasthan and Andhra Pradesh. These efforts in some cases received support in the form of leadership and encouragement from political movement like Jharkhand Mukti Morcha in the Jharkhand state. In Orissa the traditional village governance system provides the supportive socio-political environment. In Karnataka, such initiatives were legally recognised during the British period itself. In Chhattisgarh and Madhya Pradesh, the Adivasi Mukti Morcha, led by an elite group, provides back-up support to the tribals to stake their claims over the local forests. However, most of these initiatives can be traced to the tribal areas where the bondage between forests and local socio-cultural habits are strong. These village groups have a strong economic dependence on forests and their internal stability is often dependent on the equitable sharing of costs and benefits among members, and a system of accountable decision-making. As the local contexts differ from place to place, there remains diversity among the institutions of these groups. Some are small and informal, others are large with more formal rules and regulations. Leadership structure also vary from a single natural leader to a collective leadership selected from sub-groups, hamlets or neighbourhoods. With the introduction of state-sponsored JFM, an attempt has been made to impose a uniform institutional framework on the PIs across the state irrespective of their local contexts. The concern for such a decision revolves around few arguments. The existing organisations are viewed to be too 'traditional' to be able or willing to take on 'modern' forest management tasks. In fact, FD's primary management objective is of timber production, be it JFM or otherwise, which is non-negotiable. The JFM rules and regulations implicitly indicate this. The state owns the timber and sets rules for its protection, production and harvest. This is because of the fact that the traditional management system is less likely to accept such priority in forest management. *Secondly,* it is viewed that the traditional management system is controlled by rural elites and. hence, may not be able to serve the marginalised majority. *Thirdly,* while the world view is in favour of making forestry projects more gender sensitive, women are virtually excluded in the traditional community management system. Apart from such problems of intra-group equity, the issue of inter-village equity (generally in terms of access to forest resources) warrants external intervention (may be from NGO or FD). For smooth external intervention, it is desired that the PIs are obliged to the external agency for their creation and thus act according to its instruction. These views have reinforced the bureaucratic disposition to avoid the old institutions and create new ones, which are more amenable to FD.

Such views favouring creation of PIs uniformly ignoring the local context, however, require reconsideration. In fact, in the field situation. PIs undertaking the responsibilities of forest resources management may exist either in functioning or weak condition. In other situations, they may not exist at all. These three situations are quite different from each other and, thus, need different treatment. Where the existing PIs are functioning (informal or formal) and they [ire able to identify their problems; formulate rules for access, extraction and benefit sharing; and execute them; they may require assistance in terms of encouragement for gaining full control of community management, training on micro planning and small amount of capital to execute works beyond their capacity to fund, etc.

Then there are PIs which are relatively weak in performing protection and management activities. Youth clubs, mahila mandals and other such institutions had undertaken social forestry activities and in some places they have been protecting forests under JFM. They may be wet behind the ears in discharging their new roles of forest protection and management, but they already have pattern of cooperation, procedures, sanction etc. within the group. In such cases, a larger role for FD and NGO through facilitation may be appropriate to help create greater local capacity.

In both the above mentioned situations, the requirement is flexibility in the state prescription of rules and regulations to accommodate these attributes of the PIs. Imposition of rigid and uniform institutional norms may weaken their internal strength as these may not be compatible to their existing management procedure and they may find it difficult to accommodate these new rules and regulations. More so, the experience in JFM implementation has already established how much involvement of time, energy and money is required to create new institutions.

However, in the third situation, where the tradition of community management has been lost and the traditional community institutions have collapsed, attempt for re-establishment of traditional community management system may prove to be futile. There may be no option but to promote new institutions to meet the challenge. The requirements of these three types of situation, thus, indicate that FD needs to redirect its focus in handling issues related to institutional framework. This will not only enhance the chances of success but also save considerable time, energy and money.

TRUST BUILDING

It has been conceptually accepted and practically experienced that forest resources can be managed successfully in collectivity. But then all PIs are not equally efficient. There are situations where both efficient and inefficient PIs exist side by side. Obviously, the question arises on the conditions that promote or strengthen collective action. The primacy of two basic conditions is under debate. While one school of thoughts emphasises on institutional norms, the other focuses on trust among members of the group as the central to the problems of collective action. This is, however, apparent that institutional norms minus trust is less effective in eliciting cooperation among the members of PIs. Institutional rules defining appropriation, enforcement and monitoring would be effective only when individual members abide by them and trust others to abide by them. In other words, rules work in a group effort when members perceive assurance of cooperation from each other. Truly speaking, eliciting assurance of cooperation among stakeholders remains a serious concern in collective forest resource management. More than two decades have passed with the attempt of creating a participatory environment in forest management at local level, but building trust among members of PIs, and also between FD and PIs still remains a myth.

In the absence of trust among members, formation of social capital has not taken place in the PIs. As a result, good forest has come up in many places especially due to 'front-end loading' of capital investment in the donor propelled JFM projects. But, the present stock may not sustain in the absence of trust and cooperation among the stakeholders. The suspicion gains ground when it is found that emphasis is being laid on institutional strengthening in the states where the JFM project enters the second phase. It is prudent at this stage to, think over few modalities of eliciting cooperation and trust among the members of the PI.

Creation of core group: One of the ways may be to form a core group within the PI wherein the members get assurance from each other to abide by the rules and help alleviate the problems of collective action. The members of the core group should comprise an optimal number to infuse encouragement among other members for extending cooperation subsequently. The key issue here is delineation of circumstances to identify the core groups m the village setting. Generally, the forest dependent villagers fall into two main categories based on their extent of dependence on forests. One category includes those who primarily depend on forests for their livelihood like bamboo basket makers, leaf plate makers, graziers, fuel wood collectors, etc. Due to their near total dependence on forest produces for subsistence and livelihood, these groups usually live closer to forest areas and have maximum stake in improving the productivity of forest lands. Since they live closer to the forest area, these groups are in advantageous position so far the protection and monitoring are concerned. The other category includes people who have some other sources of livelihood like agriculture, small business, daily wage work, salaried employment, etc. They are relatively better off and fall in the category of local elite. They generally reside away from the forest and depend on it to support their subsistence requirements. Since the distance between forest and their settlement is more, and their dependence on forest is not so acute, they may be constrained to effectively participate in day-to-day protection activities. It is this group that breeds more number of passive members. Share in revenue from final harvest is the primary incentive for their participation in JFM programme. They are better placed in the local decision-making process. The poor are dependent on them basically for land, labour and credit and. thus, it will become difficult for them to voice their opinion at the time of benefit distribution against the will of elite group.

Multi-tier memberships: In view of such differential stake of the members on the local forests, a system of differential membership can be introduced to protect and manage them. Those who primarily depend on forests for their livelihood, seem to be better placed to form the core group of cooperators. If they can share a common understanding of their situations, trust each other and have autonomy to make their own rules, they are more likely to organise themselves and lay the foundation of the PI. The other peripheral members may be of two categories: (*a*) one who cannot participate in the day-to-day management activities but are willing to perform reduced duties; and (*b*) the other who can not extend active participation of any kind. While those falling in category (*a*) may pay an extra fee in exchange of reduced duties. others in category (*b*) may pay special membership fee for availing forest products at a special but below the market rate. The experience of pani panchayat introduced in several states indicates that such a multi-tier system of user groups has the potential to sustain in forestry management as well. In fact, many community initiated forest protection groups in Orissa have crafted rules for special membership which are working satisfactorily. The core groups have the feeling that they are duly rewarded for their initiative as they need not pay anything in lieu of the benefits they obtain from the forest.

Pro-participatory rules and regulations: More pro-people JFM rules and regulations, awarding PIs greater autonomy, may be another way to evoke cooperative behaviour among the members of PI. Forests are associated with multiple products (wood, leaves, fodder, fruits, seeds, shade, wildlife, etc.) and multiple user groups (in terms of income, caste, location, access, etc.). The success of forest management depends on the complex interaction between the user groups and the forest products at local level, which varies significantly across the regions. This warrants that the institutional rules ought to be framed depending on the nature of such interaction in a specific location. Any kind of template rules imposed on a vast geographical area (state) ignoring the diversity of such interaction is unlikely to work, in JFM the rules that govern the PIs are common to all. The members do not have power to change them even though they do not find them 'fair' to evoke their willingness to protect the forest. Conversely, in case the members perceive particular rules workable, they cannot adopt it for their own benefit. Under the circumstances, how the members of PI or even of core group can be expected to cooperate each other to protect the forest?

The state resolutions on JFM seem to owe to the parable of Prisoners' Dilemma. For example, the resolutions generally prescribe to hand over the forest offenders to FD for taking action under the provisions of forest Acts and laws. This is indicative of FD's perception that the PIs are not competent enough to sustain the restrained access to the forest resources. Thus, delegating them the power to control access may prove to be disastrous. Hence, FD should control them through imposing penalties as laid by the stale. Though such prescription sounds well, it ends with little fruition on the ground. Cases are booked against offenders apprehended by the PIs but months and years roll without any concrete action by the concerned authority. The legal mechanisms and the authority of the government in the country are not so powerful to create a threat to the rule breakers across the micro situations. Thus, alternatively the power has to be delegated to the local management systems.

PIs have demonstrated their effectiveness in curbing forest offences wherever they themselves handled them directly. Depending on their respective socio-cultural values and the forest condition, they adopted various penalty systems for violation of rules. For example, many self-initiated PIs in Orissa decide higher penalty for illicit cutting of more valued species, consider the capacity of the offender for payment of penalty and also the circumstances under which the offence is committed, obtain undertaking from the offender as well as the local influentials for not repeating the offence in future, work out innovative graduated sanctions at times culminating into *nak khat* (rubbing the nose on the ground for a distance in the presence of all villagers) and seeking intervention of the federation of PIs in case of failure of execution of local penalty system. Such arrangements may not undermine the role of FD in handling offences. Since the legal property rights to the forest lay in the hands of the state, FD can intervene where externalities (like over extraction by non-participating villages) threaten the cooperation strategy among members of PIs. There are cases where the members of PIs could succeed in achieving cooperation among themselves but when they failed to stop outsiders from extracting from the protected areas, their interest in protecting the forests gradually eroded. However, the aspect of how the inter-village conflict affects the cooperation among members of PIs has been dealt separately.

REDUCING DEPENDENCE OF PI ON FOREST BUREAUCRACY

The notion of building trust between FD (particularly the front line forest bureaucracy) and PIs, perhaps, has not worked well on the ground. Even after more than two decades of implementation of participatory forest management, the relation between people and FD has not been smoothened. At the best, the front line staff of FD interact with the members of PI as patron or implementor. In many situations, they are apathetic to work with the villagers. Of course, at this stage also one can hope that productive relationship between them is achievable. But time is running out and a hard decision on this issue has to be taken so that whatever resources have been created under JFM may sustain. Since trust building between these two sets of stakeholders still remains a debatable issue, why can't the government policy and actions be diverted to reducing the need for PIs to trust the from line forest bureaucracy? In other words, the dependence of PIs on forest bureaucracy needs to be reduced on matters related to management decisions, particularly in protection, extraction and management priorities. The front line staff may be engaged for assessment and monitoring of PI's activities and facilitating their access to information, credit, etc. As experienced elsewhere, such a situation will evoke a sense of realisation among the members that the forest is theirs and they have legitimate rights to manage it in view of their specific contexts. This requires a clear hand-over point where FD's jurisdiction ends and PI's jurisdiction begins.

SIZE OF PIs

In the implementation of JFM the FDs are generally influenced by the dominant school of thoughts that advocates 'small is beautiful'. According to it, smaller size of the group has greater chance of ensuring homogeneity within the group. Homogeneity in turn facilitates cooperation among members. Hence, hamlet has been the centre of focus for constituting PIs in some states. Though it is believed that this approach would facilitate alleviation of cooperation-related problems within the group, in reality, it suffers from some deficiencies which act as major disincentive in the process of creation of sustained cooperative environment. Success of forming a group may come easier to smaller groups, but success in protecting the forest resources under JFM arrangements may be difficult for such small group, particularly where protection from outsiders is of vital concern. However small the PI is, it is really difficult to ensure equal participation of all the members in the protection activities, basically due to higher opportunity cost of patrolling and poverty of the members. In many cases, watchers have been employed as an alternative measure. But due to their poverty and limited number, the members of such PIs are highly constrained to raise adequate surplus fund that would enable them to engage paid watchers on long-term basis. It is common observation that the system of employing paid watch and ward personnel is dispensed with shortly due to fund scarcity. In situations where external threat to the forest is more acute, the small PIs may find it difficult not only to protect the forest, but also to maintain the cooperation among members.

By now, in quite a good number of cases, inter-village conflict has surfaced over the use of forest allocated to the PIs. There are other villages around the same forest patch with entitlement to benefits under the old forest settlement. But they have been excluded under the new management system, *i.e.*, JFM. However, these villages continue to stake their claim over the forests allocated to PIs. Their action sometimes results into over-extraction of the forest resources. The small PIs are constrained to counter such external threats due to the reasons mentioned above. As a result, when the members find it difficult to protect forest from the rule breakers, they may realise that it does not make sense to contribute to an unsuccessful endeavour. Sensing such danger in providing continued protection to the forest, FD, perhaps, encourages the members of the PI to work in the forest against wage employment. Apart from providing additional income to the members, such an arrangement ensures protection to the resources also. Here again, when such provision of employment is withdrawn with the termination of the project, the frequency of visit of the members to the forest has been observed to recede considerably. Such experience is contrary to the prevailing belief that collective action in forest management can be better ensured when the group size is small. In a small group it may be easier to form PI and make sure that meetings take place regularly. But it may be equally difficult to ensure adequate protection to the forest, particularly where the external threat is pronounced. In other words, in small group approach, it may be relatively easy to organise collective action, but achieving the objective of protecting the forests, particularly where the external threat is more, may be difficult in the long run. In contrast, the larger groups may have some comparative advantages in achieving the objective of providing protection to the forests. They may be better placed to create adequate funds from internal sources for executing protection measures. Their heterogeneity itself in some situations may appear as a privilege to self-organisation if the collective action is initiated by those who have command over the community and have genuine interest in forest protection. The Vana Panchayat in the hills of Uttaranchal is generally dominated by a single caste As the dominating caste also has genuine stake in the health of the forests, the core group for managing the forests emerged from it and there was proper enforcement of protection measures. Whereas in the Shivalik areas of Haryana, Some HRMS (Hill Resource Management Society), which have widely distributed economic and caste groups with varying degree of forest dependence, face severe difficulty for self-organisation. It is apprehended that under the circumstances, if the management responsibility is left to the dominant leaders, the most dominant sub-group within the community easily appropriate control of the PI to serve its own interest.

Thus, the basic issue perhaps is not the size of the PI. but the ground reality of who forms the core group to initiate collective action. The implicit message of the above arguments is that uniform decision on small or large group is not the solution. The problem needs to be viewed from different angle. Few things need to be taken care of while deciding the size *of* the PI. *First,* the potential threat for offence or any conflict to the PI. In the event of perceived threat lo smaller PIs, possibility of getting assurance for protection support from neighbouring settlement (main or adjoining village) on some agreement (for example, share in the benefits) may be thought of. For instance, it was observed in Orissa that one Vana Samrakshana Samithi included the main village as well as the hamlet, despite the fact that the main village was located quite far from the allocated forest patch. The forest patch had potential threat from the neighbouring villages. To counter such threat, the core group was formed in the hamlet, inhabited by poor tribals and the supporting group from the main village, inhabited by influential well-off people. In lieu of their support to the core group, the residents of main village were getting small timber/poles as and when required. The system worked well. On several occasions, the residents of main village extended full cooperation to foil the offensive bid by other villages. *Secondly,* funding from external sources to encourage protection behaviour of locals may not help sustenance of the mechanism. The local mechanisms will grow stronger if funded through local sources of revenue. Depending on the local dynamics, communities have to decide on the group size so as to tackle the problems of funds for protection as well as threat from outsiders. FD or NGO may act as facilitator to establish and strengthen the local network of PIs which, in turn, will have bearing on reduction in internal as well as external threat of tree-riding on the protected forests.

FUNDING PATTERN

The funding pattern of the project has a link with the institutional development at local level. The mode of investment and expenditure followed by the government as well as donor agencies creates hindrance for the programme to build effective PIs. The tendency of 'front-end loading' of capital investment and expenditure in the projects puts pressure on the authority to exhibit measurable results within a short span of time. This hardly leaves any opportunity to the project implementing agency for assigning adequate priority to institutional development. The mid-term evaluation reports of first phase of JFM projects are the examples of how the achievements in physical aspects override the social sector in terms of importance. No doubt such pressure on physical achievement has resulted into good forests in many places, but after the expiry of the first phase, it has been realised that PIs are not confident of maintaining them in future without FD's support. As a result, in the second phase of donor propelled projects, the programme thrust is on strengthening PIs.

There is thus, need for a shift in priority in the investment pattern. Instead of 'front-end loading' of capital investment and expenditure, particularly for providing employment in forestry activities, the strategy of slow and gradual release of funds based on performance of PIs, in institutional development after a substantial period of interaction with them, may improve upon the situation. This would mean that initial investment in the project would be low in terms of intensification of employment in forestry activities, but significant in terms of institutional strengthening for establishment of community control. This has become essential in view of the existing situation that the PI members, particularly the poorer groups, perceive the arrangement for employment in forestry activities as payment against the protection work they perform simultaneously. Thus, their protection activities are linked with employment they get in the forest. In other words, they are virtually paid for providing protection to the forest. The social capital for conservation and protection of forests has not been formed. As a result, after the expiry of the project period, in many cases the visit of the members to 'their' forest is reduced considerably. It may be argued here that shifting the focus from employment generation to institutional development is likely to have deleterious effect on the JFM programme as a whole. Staggering the employment generation activities may lead to higher opportunity cost for members who are wage earners, headloaders, graziers and NTFP collectors. On one hand, their family earning is severely affected due to sudden regulation of access to the forest as a result of introduction of JFM, and on the other hand, alternative employment opportunities in forestry activities is also squeezed. Obviously, they may lose interest in protection of forests. The argument is genuine due to obvious reasons. The problem can be overcome by creating alternate productive sources of income in the village society itself by way of intensifying the village development activities. If resources outside forests become more productive, villagers' dependence on forest may be reduced with simultaneous reduction in protection problems. Attempts are being made, for example in Andhra Pradesh, to make village development an integral component of JFM. In Dewas district of Madhya Pradesh, a concerted effort is on to augment village development funds and its appropriate utilisation. However, such endeavour will have to go a long way for its meaningful conceptualisation and implementation as well.

COMMITMENT OF FRONT-LINE STAFF

The diffusion of JFM depends largely on the nature of role played by the front-line forest functionaries. It is commonly held opinion that the front-line staff are not so responsive to JFM activities. As a result, the aspect of institution building, a slow and strategic process in itself, has been neglected so far. It is generally prescribed that they require more and more training to get motivated for their intense involvement in JFM, particularly for institution building. It is not very clear what motivates the front-line staff to support and promote 'power reducing' policies like JFM and establish working relation with the client-communities to execute policy actions. Why the forest officials, particularly those at grassroots level, will respond favourably lo such reform which aims at reducing their authority in forest management? While the answer to such question is yet to be obtained on a firm basis, the dynamics of reality have demonstrated that a demand-driven situation can lead to improved performance of public agencies. However, in forestry sector, such situation is uncommon as PIs are yet to be established on a stronger footing. Then what is the alternative to mobilise large scale support for JFM among the front-line staff? There is perhaps no template solution for this problem. Little is known till today about what actually motivates public officials. In forestry sector, the problem of front-line staff seems to be little different. They are generally held responsible by the senior officials for forest degradation. Such pressure affects their mindset to have a preference for policing the forest. More so, due to obvious reason, they are reluctant to support and promote 'power-reducing' policy like JFM. The biggest challenge, thus, relates to identifying the factors that facilitate the motivation of field staff to have strong PIs. If the case of West Bengal is any indication, perhaps, the work situation is one of the dominant factors for behavioural motivation of the front-line functionaries. In West Bengal, the front-line staff of FD and their union played progressive role in supporting JFM. They facilitated the dialogue between FD and villagers for a more collaborative style of forest management by organising workshops, seminars, forestry week, etc. Their union lobbied the forest minister and proposed a participatory approach to forest management. The basic reason for such support for participatory approach by the front-line staff was that their work became more dangerous due to violence from villagers and simultaneous accusation by senior officials for rapid degradation of forests. During 70's there were many confrontations between villagers and foresters throughout the state over illegal telling of timber resulting into physical assault and even murder of several foresters. Since these staff were expected to live in forested areas with their families, the issues of their safety became a central concern for their union which realised that cooperation with people might be the only option to ensure the safety of the field staff. They were motivated to support any policy that would improve their work situation. They acted through their union to press the administration for changing the overall approach towards forest management. The analysis gives an impression that the nature of the work situation was one of the dominant compelling factors for the front-line staff to promote favourable attitude towards participatory forest management. The situation provides cue for two things:

- The actual work situation plays an important role in shaping the behavioural motivation of the field staff.
- The other thing relates to the need for creation of space within the organisation for inner democratisation. The situation of the field staff was highlighted by their union which was considered sympathetically by the decision-makers in the department.

Both these aspects are vital to the field staff who are responsible for building or strengthening local institutional capacity. Regardless of varying local contexts, the forest bureaucracy tends to formulate uniform role-prescription for the field staff. Where as the ground reality is that the PIs are to respond adequately to the local context which may differ from place to place. But, in view of their prescribed roles, front-line staff are constrained to accommodate these variations. *Secondly,* the physical target in terms of area to be regenerated/planted and number of PIs to be formed are prescribed for them. Due to obvious reasons, they devote much of their time to fulfil these two targets. The activities related to strengthening of PIs are relegated to the background. Due to rigid hierarchy in the organisation, there remains a wide gap between the realisation of field problems by the field staff and their reporting in the process of monitoring. Under the given circumstances, inner democratisation is necessary for free flow of feedback about ground reality to the project leadership. It is a kind of situation where the frontline staff will have the opportunity to speak up and criticise policy decisions and the leadership will actively search out ways to change and improve the management system. There is a need for introspection by the leadership in forest bureaucracy on how far it can afford to reverse its trend of ordering the front-line staff to implement decisions taken at the top and solicit criticism and redirection from lower levels.

PARTICIPATORY DEMOCRACY WITHIN PI

PIs are deemed to be participatory democratic institutions where the members can have intense interaction among themselves in decision-making on the strength of being aware and informed about their lights and responsibilities. But, in effect, their style of functioning has been more akin to representative democracy. As crafted in most of the state resolutions, the elected members of the management committee should meet once monthly. So far the frequency of meeting of general body is concerned, while some states specified once in six months, others are silent on it. The impact of this is pronounced on the ground. The long gap between the opportunities (general body meetings) for interaction among the members makes them lose track of the situation. Progressively the PI turns to become leader centred institution with members as passive observers. The decisions and their enforcement strategy generally remain confined to leaders or at the most, few members of the management committee. The members of PI are not aware and informed of its objectives even after several years of its implementation. In many cases, they even do not have the knowledge of the members of the management committee. On the contrary, in the smaller PIs where there prevails confusion over the concept of general body and management committee and, as a result, all the members meet frequently to discuss issues related to access control, employment distribution in forestry activities, dispute resolution, benefits distribution, etc., members are not only better informed but also more vibrant and enthused about the JFM.

It is thus apparent that despite the stated objective of bringing about participatory democracy within the PIs, the strategy prescribed to achieve it is felt to be not very supportive. For a genuinely participatory mechanism within the PI there is need to create a space for the members at large to play important role in crafting the decisions on for management and also for the members of the management committee to consult the general membership on critical decisions. In the PRI system, when the representative democracy by and large failed to evoke people's participation in developmental activities, as a corrective measure, focus has been shifted to Gram Sabha so as to facilitate the general membership to actively participate in decision making on strength of being aware and informed about their rights and responsibilities in village development activities. The minimum number of Gram Sabha meetings have also been increased to make the participation of members more effective.

CONCLUSION

The National Forest Policy (1988) made an emphatic departure from the conventional approach of forest management wherein forest was regarded mainly as a source of revenue to the government and village communities residing in and around forests as its enemy. The JFM resolution (1990), crafted in the light of the National Forest Policy (1988), highlighted the approach towards mobilising people's participation in development and protection of forests. For building up meaningful and sustained people's participation the need for development of local level institution cannot but be over emphasised. But the spirit of involving village communities through the local institutional arrangements has hardly reflected on the ground. Centralised management practice in the name of decentralisation continues. Though the local institutions have been created at grassroots level, attempt for making them responsive to the local context has not been made on serious footing. The overall approach under JFM has still remained target-oriented.

The short-term perspective of forest departments to protect the forests during project period might have made them disinterested in taking the risk of experimenting with varied institutional arrangements for doing the job. Thus, it strives for centralised decision by way of structured management system executed through PIs. Decentralisation of institutional framework (site specific) ensuring autonomy to the PIs is still a far cry. The consequence is not very palatable. Forests have come up well in many areas, but PIs are too weak to manage them in future. It is thus high time that the forest bureaucracy develops its own capabilities to initiate introspection on how far it can afford to modify its present approach for institution development so that the PIs would have relevance and be responsive to the local context.

A SELECT READING

Blair, H.W., 1996. Democracy, equity and common property resource management in the Indian sub-continent. *Development and Change,* 27: 475-99.

Blair, H., 2000. Participation and accountability at the periphery: Democratic local governance in six countries, *World Development,* 28 (1), 21-40.

Blair, H.W. and P.D., Olpadwala, 1988. *Forestry in Rural Development Planning-Lessons from the Rural Experience,* London Westview Press.

Colchester, M., 1994. Sustaining the forests: The community-based approach in South and South-East Asia. *Development and Change,* 25, pp. 69-100.

Clooster, D., 2000. Institutional choice, community and struggle: A case study of forest co-management in Mexico, *World Development,* 28 (1), 1-20.

Hill, I. and D. Shields, 1998. *Incentive for Joint Forest Management in India-Analytical Methods and Case Studies.* Washington D.C., World Bank.

Joshi, A., 1998-99. Progressive bureaucracy: An oxymoron? The case of Joint Forest Management in India, Rural Development Forestry Network, Network paper 24a, Winter.

Kumar, N.N. Saxena; Y. Alagh and K. Mitra, 2000. India—Alleviating poverty through forest development—Evaluation country case study series, Washington D.C., World Bank.

Sarin, M., 1996. *Joint Forest Management—The Haryana Experience.* Ahmedabad: Centre for Environment Education.

Uphoff, N., 1986. *Local Institutional Development: An Analytical Source Book with Cases,* Kumarian Press.

Uphoff, N., 1989. Approaches to community participation in agriculture and rural development, Economic and Development Institute of the World Bank.

Varughese, G. and E., Ostrom, 2001. The contested role of heterogeneity in collective action. Some evidence from community forestry in Nepal, *World Development,* 29 (5), pp. 747-76.

8

Changes in Governance to Achieve Forest Development

M. Kamal Naidu

Historically forests have always been a people-centred 'Common Property Resource' (CPR). In due course the ancient *Rishis* in the *Ashram* areas imposed certain restraints in using the forest. It is to the credit of Kautilya to have codified and place certain forests areas into five different categories according to their use in his *Arthashastra* in 320 BC. He classed them with specific purposes and uses as for recreation and hunting, for economic useful forest produce, for elephant's maintenance, for aesthetics and Brahmins schools, and the un-classed forests remained as the CPR. To administer the classified forests two officers were designated as Superintendent of Forest Produce and Chief Elephant Officer. Accordingly, rules were prescribed for management, and controls with penalties for violations, keeping in view social and religious norms, customs and courtesy as the traditional control mechanisms.

Kautilya's codification remained without any attempt of elaboration or modification, or with any serious implementation. Forests continue to be used by the people mostly as a CPR till the beginning of the 19th Century, when the valuable forests came to be destroyed heavily with the coming in of the East India Company and other European traders. They exploited the forests rampantly for ship-building, furniture making, and construction of mansions in Europe throwing all rules against exploitation to the wind.

ESTABLISHMENT OF FOREST ADMINISTRATION FOR DEVELOPMENT

The period 1799-1856 was one of informal control under the British East India Company when there were no organised efforts at administration or management. The forests gradually came under progressive stern measures after the first systematic investigation on the availability of teak in 1800 AD revealed the depressing situation. This resulted in the appointment of the first Conservator of Forest in 1806 for stabilising the exploitation of forest areas, and their development for higher productivity, to meet the increasing global demand for shipping, railways and construction.

With the advent of British rule, Lord Dalhousie finalised the outline for forest administration in 1 855 with a view to consolidate the forests for development. The period 1856-96 was the transitional period towards more active state control of forest areas. The first Inspector General of Forest (IGF) was appointed in 1864 for regulating forests, their development and sustained supplies. Dalhousie was responsible for the effective steps in the formation of the Forest Organisation and enacted the first forest legislation of 1865. This empowered the state's claim to forests by demarcation and reservation of forest areas, with regulations in its use by settlement of rights. With more forest areas being brought under government control, the Forest Act of 1878 was amended to make a distinction between Reserved and Protected Forests. extinguishing all customary rights of people in the former and gave them only restrided concessions in treating forests as CPR.

In 1894, the first Indian Forest Policy was enunciated laying down sound principles for the preservation of forests. Besides this, all the previous legislations were consolidated. The forests came to be recognised as the 'Hand-made of Agriculture'. From 1900 to 1947 a strong foundation was laid for research, education and training to help in the administration for improvement and higher productivity. During this phase an approach was made towards regulated production of timber for commercial and social needs, with revenue to government as the prime consideration. The several Forest and Wildlife Acts and Regulations were consolidated in 1927. These were done with a view to incorporate the new developments and their regulation, including wildlife protection as the important constituents in conservation. This period also witnessed the entire planning and development of forests in jeopardy and heavy destruction due to the inexhaustible demands of the two World Wars.

The Government of India Act of 1935 entrusted the forest administration to the states, whereby IGF became responsible only for forest research, education, and policy. The forest administration of the states was entrusted to the Chief Conservator of Forests as solely in-charge, assisted by Conservators, and DFO with ranges, sections and beats.

CHANGES IN FOREST ADMINISTRATION AFTER INDEPENDENCE

The administrative set-up and the measures that existed at the time of Independence largely continued. Large extents of ex-princely and proprietary forests were transferred and consolidation done, when forests came to occupy 22.7 per cent of the geographical land area.

In 1952 a new Forest Policy was enunciated with the aims and objectives of development based on a demand-supply frame, to provide the greatest good to the largest number. This policy emphasised 'production and protection' with a significant feature of putting one third of the land area under forest cover, and more balanced land-use to prevent denudation and soil erosion, while meeting the needs of grazing, small-wood and firewood needs of the poor. The policy of 'maximum revenue and production of timber' continued with the growing needs of industry and commerce. Therefore, a programme of raising quick growing species like eucalyptus and bamboo, and extensive teak was embarked in the 60s in degraded areas for meeting industrial needs and generating rural employment. To check inaccurate inventories being done by field sample plots, Pre-Investment Survey of Forest Resources (PISFR) was established in 1965 in collaboration with UNDP/FAO at the national level to improve the accuracy of the inventory. This organisation became the present Forest Survey of India (FSI) in 1981. These enabled to investigate and report on the raw material status, and made proposals to set up many wood-based industries in select areas based on the type and potentialities of the forest. With Independence, there had been a decline of respect for law, accentuated by increased human and livestock population, and biotic interferences. This had an adverse impact on the forests decline qualitatively. The changing needs of the country added new dimensions to the management of forests in the field of production and harvesting. Therefore the Estimates Committee of Parliament in 1969 initiated rethinking for a more purposeful, realistic and effective forest policy.

In 1972, an International Understanding for Sustainable Development at the UN Conference on Human Development and Environment recognised the value of forests in the global context as:

1. Regulators of climate,
2. Repository of species and potentially valuable new products, and
3. Conservation of soil and water resources.

Since the 70s social goals like poverty alleviation and income distribution became prominent features in forestry objectives. Even funding agencies expressed the need to help societies and communities to evolve ways, compatible with their traditions, culture and aspirations. Therefore Forest Development changed from their production and industrial orientation in the 60s towards Rural Development approach in 70s. The real impetus to social forestry came from the Interim Report on Social Forestry submitted by National Commission on Agriculture (NCA) in 1973 after the National Workshop at Gandhinagar, which recommended farm forestry as a component of Economic Development Programme for creating adequate resources to supply fuel, food, fodder, small timber and Miscellaneous Forest Produce (MFP) for the many uses of the rural people. This emphasis reflected the unique potential of forest to produce goods, income, services and homes for low income people, many of whom had been pushed to the margins of society or left out of the development process. In 1976 NCA made three important policy recommendations, namely:

1. Institutional financing through Forest Development Corporations to raise industrial plantations,
2. Removal of middlemen in forest produce trade, and
3. Emphasis on Social Forestry to meet local needs.

This set a new trend in forest management for development of the degraded forests with the objective of creating high productivity and greater employment generation as against the traditional conservation forestry with very low economic returns practiced hitherto. This was achieved by recourse to higher investment through institutional financing in mechanisation of planting and logging operations to improve the efficiency in working and productivity, with a view to meet the growing industrial needs for pulp, paper and plywood, etc. There was also a focus on elimination of middlemen and contractors by resorting to state trading in timber and other forest produce to enhance revenue and ensure fair wages to forest labour, like departmentally working of logging and marketing, *beedi* leaves, etc.

With drastic changes that had taken place in the role of FD after Independence, the forest organisation responded to the 1952 policy of meeting rural and industrial demands, and NCA 1976 recommendations of production and social forestry by rapid expansion of the forest department, enlarging its size two to three-folds, in terms of manpower and structure, by increasing the number of functional and territorial division under different schemes. This resulted in lop-sided expansion in functional areas overlapping the traditional territorial jurisdictions of the main structure. This brought unplanned fragmentation of existing middle level districts structure, resulting in intrigues and displeasures within the organisation, with too many hierarchy levels. This created considerable gap between the FD and its working environment.

Since the NCA report on forestry was given greater importance, the forests were transferred from state to concurrent list through the 42nd Amendment to the Constitution in 1976. However the forests continued to be policed rigidly, excluding any form of people's interferences.

Inspite of all efforts in conservation and development of potentiality, tremendous destruction continued. As the FD failed to stop the forest degradation owing to many external factors—social, political and developmental-the Forest Conservation Act was passed in 1980 banning conversion of forests to non-forestry purposes. This had a very salutary effect on forest by preventing further decline at least in extent.

Afforestation gained impetus with its incorporation in the new Socio-Economic Development Programme announced by Indira Gandhi in 1980, and subsequently incorporated as "Afforestation and Tree Planting" in its 20-point programme. This focused the state governments attention for according higher priority to afforestation in the Fifth Plan (1980-85) with emphasis on 'Ecological Security' and linking forest development with tribal economy. With this emphasis, social forestry was extended to outside the forest areas along roads, canals, railway lines, agricultural field bunds, barren lands, and wastelands to meet local needs of fuel, food, fodder, small timber and MFP. Realising the vital role of forestry in far-reaching socio-economic changes, particularly in rural development, Rajiv Gandhi created a new Department of Forest and Wildlife under the Ministry of Environment and Forests in 1985. His concern for forestry was evidenced in his address to the nation in January 1985: "Continuing deforestation has brought us face to face with a major ecological and socio-economic crisis. The trend must be halted. I propose immediately to bring five million hectares of land every year under fuelwood and fodder plantations". Thus in 1986 a new strategy for Forest Development was incorporated in the new 20point programme with the following objectives:

- Grow more trees and raise more forest with full people's participation;
- Protect the traditional rights of tribal people and local communities regarding access to fuel wood and forest produce;
- Reclaim wastelands for productive uses; and
- Plant appropriate species to verdure with the hills, deserts and coastal belts.

About this time XI World Forestry Congress at Mexico in 1985 stated: "The changing world situation requires a new definition of the relationships between forest resources and society, harmonising the human being with the natural environment through a clear awareness of the technical, social, economic and political changes needed within a new forest strategy". It elaborated by stating "The Forestry Sector must be a part of the integral development of society contributing to the welfare of both the rural and urban communities by making full use of its productive, protective and social potential".

FOREST MANAGEMENT IN 21ST CENTURY

The 21st Century poses difficult choices to the forest department. On the one hand it has to deal with the problems of declining areas of natural forest, timber supplies and availability of financial resources (a huge gap between supply and demand for wood, which is 25-30 per cent of the demand). On the other hand it will have to cope with pressures to do more with less human resources provided.

Since last three decades there had been increased concern about wildlife protection, bio-diversity conservation and people's participation in protection and management of forests. These concerns were reflected in the revised National Forest Policy of 1988, which has taken into consideration the symbiotic relationship between forests and the local indigenous people, and their role in protection, regeneration and development of forests. As a consequence of this policy, Government of India issued a landmark notification in 1990 making "Participatory Forestry Management" an important feature of forest management. As a result, there has been a paradigm shift in the forest management objectives from working the forests for timber and maximisation of revenue with rigid policing, to managing for providing various goods and services for local societal needs by participation, keeping in mind the environmental conservation.

The World Bank was primarily involved in projects on 'Extraction and Processing of Timber' initially. In 1994 the World Bank and other lending agencies revised their priorities for funding forest development projects. They are insisting on people's participation to achieve social goals like poverty alleviation and income distribution. The problems and changes in thinking made the department to reassess its approaches in management and make drastic changes in its outlook. Presently the overall structure of the forest administration remained unchanged over 150 years, except in terms of regulations, manpower and norms. The structure and administration were evolved primarily to protect and manage forests.

The change in the mindset of the foresters requires accepting an attitude of 'sharing and caring along with the people' with the realisation of the fact that despite stringent laws and their rigidity in patrolling, they did not succeed in preventing destruction of forests. Hence change in outlook of the department is desired through developing a new vision, and appropriates goals to be achieved through pursuing appropriate strategies. Accordingly the structure and systems in the department need to be revamped and implemented to achieve the new development objectives.

Therefore a five-pronged approach is recommended to bridge the gap in production:

1. Need to reduce total demand by rationalising the utilisation of available wood resources through appropriate technological intervention.
2. Need to develop wood alternates from other natural/renewable sources.
3. Need to exposed forest area and adopt an aggressive afforestation programme.
4. Need to protect the existing forests and improve its productivity; and
5. Need to strengthen policy and institutional framework keeping in view people's participation.

Section IV: LAND-WATER MANAGEMENT AND WATERSHED MANAGEMENT

9

Land Water Management and Watershed Development

Rakesh Hooja and Bhupendra Hooja

Perhaps the biggest challenge of the campaign for productivity lies in the agricultural sector, or to be more precise, in respect of land use and water management. Yet unless this challenge is met successfully, the other more threatening and persistent challenge is met successfully, the other more threatening and persistent challenge, that of poverty which besets half the world and mostly the third world or developing countries like India cannot be resolved or mitigated.

Unlike the industrial sector where productivity is linked with the scale of the venture or the level of technological or administrative efficiency, the human skills or the relationship of man to machine, land and water management has also a concern itself with the immediate and the long range objective so that the productivity (or fertility) of land does not decrease through constant or unplanned use, over-exploitation and threats of wind or water vision etc. Further, it has to be adjusted to the fact that different categories of land, because of their potentialities and limitations related to soil and agro-climatic conditions, are suitable only for specific though different uses like afforestation, agriculture, pasture development, animal husbandry or non-agricultural use like residential houses or industries. (Even within the sphere of crop husbandry different lands are suitable for different crops).[1] Therefore, lånd productivity cannot be measured merely in quantitative terms, but in terms of whether a particular type or class of land is being prepared and used to produce the type (or a mix) of products it is best suited for in view of its features, the local weather conditions, rainfall patterns, etc.

Of course, the conventional productivity issues like management, research and extension, inputs including credit, seeds, fertilizer, pesticides and tools, skills and processes of manufacture, etc., also become relevant for particular holdings of land. Whether the best seeds are being used or the best implements and the best input-mix and agronomic practices? Whether the ownership and management (*e.g.*, absentee landlord *versus* peasant proprietor) patterns are suitable? And whether or not the size of operational holdings is viable or optimal, and so on, there are some illustrative considerations for land uses.

The first two issues of land water management are best examined through the comparatively more recently developed concept of the watershed, which we describe in detail later.

Another difference between the agriculture sector (which includes animal husbandry, farm forestry, etc., also or production on or from the land) and industry is that agriculture is indeed a way of life at least in countries like India, in spite of all the changes which have taken place during recent times. So many of our social customs, cultural traditions and religious rituals, the way our rural masses live and function are in fact the results or off-shoots of the manner in which the land resources have been managed in the past.

Agriculture is also the largest private sector enterprise in which the decision-making ultimately vests with millions of big and large as well as small and marginal farmers and not on government rules, controls, licensing or restrictions and policies or policy guidelines (like the Industrial Policy Resolutions). Even government incentives or subsidies or the market pulls and price factors occasionally tail to make a dent in the decision-making process of the millions in the set-up of a subsistence economy. The farmer's goals of greater profits and risk reduction may, in fact, conflict with the government goals[2] of: (*i*) uplift of the poor farmers and agricultural labourers, (*ii*) increased aggregate agriculture production, and (*iii*) more production per unit of input be it land, water, credit, seeds and fertilizers, manpower of managerial stall (with some attention now being paid to optimum land utilization) which themselves may prove contradictory in practice. In agriculture, the human factor and the institutional support, the environmental limitations of land-type and water availability, as well as the tools and technologies and village social customs and land ownership and cultivatorship break-ups, etc. interact upon each other and play a major role thus complicating matter more than in the organized industrial and service sectors.

Response of the farmers brings to the problem of what is euphemistically called 'people's participation' in the development process.[3] This situation also creates and administrative-cum-managerial problem which is that for industries or mining or for the services sector there is normally only one concerned nodal government department or ministry. And even where more departments or agencies exist, over the years systems of dovetailing them have evolved, *e.g.*, the industries department concerns itself with sales tax concessions or the provision of power to industries, etc. In the agriculture (or rural development) sector on the other hand, there are many departments of the government like agriculture, cooperatives, animal husbandry, sheep and wool forests, soil conservation, ground water, irrigation, public works department, power, community development and panchayats and even departments which are normally considered to be regulatory (as opposed to developmental) like (land) revenue, (land) survey and settlement, civil supplies, police, etc., which provide the pre-requisites for development.

Though the initiative chiefly lies with the beneficiaries, each one of these departmental or their service agencies have to contact or cater to hundreds and thousands of individual farmers and beneficiaries without any effective inter-linking, institutions having been built up to bride the gaps between each department or its agencies. This creates immense problems of coordination due to the inbuilt departmentalism and inter-departmental and even intra-departmental if more than one wing exists in a department) rivalries that pervade the Indian administrative delivery system.[4] Then various departments have difficulty in working together, the chances of their managing to evoke people's participation on a large scale in government projects (like those of soil conservator, etc.) are scanty. Similarly they seldom manage to influence the decision-making of the farmers, livestock breeders, agricultural labourers, etc. Thus in a way the government has developed a split or splintered personality in respect of the agriculture sector causing in beneficiary-supplicants to run from pillar to post. In fact as no single window on behalf of the government exists for the agriculturists; the district rural development agency (DRDA) dealing only with some aspects of agriculture and rural development, unlike the district industries center (DIC) which deals with all aspects of industrial developmental) the government's efforts at land-water management or optimal land water utilization can seldom affect the farmers n a coordinated manner.

Another difference between industries and agriculture which flows from the above-mentioned differences is that while more industrial projects are formulated by private individuals who intend to implement the projects themselves (even in the case of the public sector projects, the implementing organization is provided for in the project itself), in the case of agriculture projects the government formulates projects which it hopes individual farmers shall (separately or jointly as a community group, or co-operative society) implement, or make use of, under government sponsorship.

Small wonder that increasing productivity in the agriculture (or land water management) sector is more complex a task than in other sectors. The complexity increases when we try to decide whether productivity per unit land or water is more important than productivity per unit credit, or inputs, or manpower.

DISCIPLINE IN WATER USE

The question of agrarian productivity is becoming vital for India not only because India is a primarily agrarian country, but also because there is a limit to which increased water or fertilizer application or increase in cultivated area, or irrigated area, or decrease in absentee landlordism and decrease in mismanagement, can increase productivity. All lands or soils are not suitable for cultivation, or even for aforestation, or pasture development and livestock rearing. Similarly, while the network of irrigation has expanded at great cost, even if the entire surface and ground water irrigation potential is tapped (and conjunctive use of surface and ground water stepped up) large tracts in many states are likely to remain uncovered. Even in the irrigated areas we remain dependent upon, and constrained by, the monsoon factor.

Thus the cost in real terms of each unit of water available for irrigation emphasizes the need for a controlled and regulated use of water (and in drier areas even moisture) so that maximum production per unit of water can be achieved. This shall also naturally lead to the development of various crops, trees and grass varieties to suit different soil and agro-climatic conditions.

Many experts have commented that in India (especially in the natural), well endowed areas there is a tendency to waste our land, water and other inputs in an extravagant manner, while other countries with less quantities of water available, and less variety of soil and agro-climatic conditions have achieved miracles through emphasis indiscipline in irrigation and application of other inputs only at critical stages of plant growth and only in the required quantities, no more and no less.

Even for brought prone of arid and semi-arid areas, and areas of adverse soil or whether conditions, techniques of dry land farming for rainfed drought resistant, and saline water tolerant, crops have been developed by institutions like central arid zone research institute (CAZRI) Jodhpur and international crop research institute for the semi-arid tropics (ICRISAT). However, their impact on the mass of farmers has so for been marginal.

It is of course true that the country has progressed in respect of the production, distribution and application of modern and sophisticated inputs like high yielding and hybrid seeds, chemicals, fertilizers and pesticides for different crops, soils and agro-climatic conditions, new tools and machines, and credit (both short term and long term). An agriculture extension network has also been evolved based on a training and visits (T&V) system.[6]

However, while new peaks of production have been achieved, it appears that perhaps the existing methodologies and tools have brought us to a plateau where all productive efforts seem to indicate almost a stagnant level of growth and there are still many institutional, technological and even physical constraints which need to be surmounted.

OPTIMAL STRATEGY

It is our contention that one of the basic reasons for the stagnation like situation is that different efforts have been going on in different directions by different agencies,[7] and sufficient and continued attention is not being and towards the very base of agriculture production which is the identification and harnessing of the potentials of our national resources such is land, forests, water, the sun and the wind.

Future efforts a greater agricultural productivity will have to follow the dictum that each unit, or tract or region of land should be looked upon in an integrated or holistic manner and provided with a comprehensive multi-disciplinary, multi-sectoral mix of governmental activities and inputs that the region or tract requires, and from each such unit, tract, or region, we should only hope and endeavour to obtain what it can offer according to its capacity or potential and no more (despite the pressure of human and livestock population on the land). Each tract may require that a different strategy be adopted. We shall also have to ensure that the inhabitants of the tract can be persuade to accept the optimal strategy including its strong points and its limitations whatever they be.

Only this can be the key to productivity.

PROTECTION OF LAND RESOURCE

We are concerned with the challenges and strategies of land and water management for increasing or even maintaining productivity levels in the agricultural or pastural spheres because of the following important considerations, among others.

Since agriculture has been a continuous activity in many so called fertile parts of India for thousands of years, the soil has been continuously under cultivation. It is doubtful whether, in the past, our ancestors, even though they were good at their job, really managed to put back into the soil all that was taken out or used from season to season or year to year. Besides, the pressure of human population (and successive waves of invasions) and of cattle have been constantly on the increase. More and more aborigines or original settlers have been pushed down into the harsh and inhospitable interior in the hills or on the desert under the pressures of fresh inroads and invasions. For centuries, the fertile plains have remained the battlefield of constant internecine warfare. Then these lands have passed through long phases of feudal regimes and land structure as also of colonial rule with the inevitable impoverishment of the people and their basic land resources.

Before amends could be made and remedial measures initiated on scientific lines with available technical skills and tools, the demands of 'social justice' and immediate welfare or social security of the rural masses resulted in allotment of millions of hectares of government surplus land or land vested n the government as a result of land ceilings. Thus even marginal and sub-marginal lands have been allotted or taken possession of and brought under the plough causing much widespread irrespirable damage. Trees and woodlands and even shrubs have been cleared in a haphazard manner, baring and exposing the dry soils to the hazards of wind, sun and rain.

It is indeed alarming that as per the trends of the last two census operations, the density of human and cattle population has been increasing in the hilly tribal areas or in the desert lands where poor soil conditions cannot sustain such pressures.

To some extent, even the programme of land reforms and land ceiling, has proved counter-productive. First, because the new tenants, though secure in their direct relations with the state, and more so the fresh allottees of small parcels of land, did not have the wherewithal to look after and tend their holdings or to repair the past damage and to rebuild their fertility, Secondly, even after ceilings the 'social institution' of absentee landlords and the existence of large 'benami' holdings have combined to prevent proper investments in the protection or preservation of the land resource.

According to the Ministry of Agriculture estimates, which have been repeatedly quoted by crusaders for land and water management like B.B. Vohra, Dr. Swaminathan and many others, out of neatly 143 million hectares of agricultural land in use in the country nearly 87 mill. ha. or 61 per cent are 'sick lands'. Leaving aside urban and non-agriculture lands or those which are barren and uncultivable, we have nearby 226 mill. ha. including agricultural lands, forests and permanent pastures, culturable wastes and fallows. Of these 175 mill. ha. are degraded land affected by soil erosion, water-logging and salinity. With such a poor base how can any one expect better yields? We wish to emphasize the point that our poor or degraded soils can only breed poverty.

Or, to put it differently, if we wish to remove poverty, we have no choice but to improve out soil and water resources.

It has been estimated that if a fairly long-term or medium-term programme is drawn up for reclamation, an investment of at least Rs. 50,000 crores with corresponding human efforts will be needed during the next 15 years or so. Such is the dimension of this challenging task.

While the programme of land reclamation and soil or water conservation ought to and must be taken up a sustained and systematic manner, we wish to suggest that such efforts should not be separated from the programmes or on-going activities of land and water use. Reclamation, conservation, protection and preservation and such other works programmes on a macro or mini-scale should be taken up and dovetailed or integrated with cultivation of crops, raising of cattle, sheep, goats, management of fallows, waste lands or grazing-lands, the up-keep and management of water (irrigation) sources, the preservation of vegetation cover, the bushes and trees and so on. Agencies or techniques may be different for different purposes or soils, but the approach should be common, integrated, mutually supporting and complementary.

Fortunately, such a concept has emerged at least at the thinking and planning levels in different parts of the country over the recent years under the special area development programmes. But corresponding administrative changes have not yet taken place.

Another reason why we wish to advocate and emphasize the adoption of an integrated approach for development and use of land resources according to their respective area or region wise potentials emanates from a comparative view of agricultural developments or achievements of different regions and states. Per hectare yields of different crops in different states can be taken as good indicators of these differences, which have become all the more prominent in respect of crops mainly covered under the green revolution strategies. For example average yields of rice are higher in Punjab, Haryana, Tamil Nadu and Karnataka, according to 1978-79 data than other states. Similarly in wheat, also Punjab and Haryana lead the way with Gujarat, West Bengal, Orissa and UP or Bihar trying to catch up. In jowar Karnataka, Tamil Nadu, Maharashtra and UP are quite high. Gujarat leads in bajra with Punjab and Tamil Nadu just trailing behind (The dry lands of Rajasthan are far behind).

An analysis of such available data viewed against the neutral physical features, the soil an whether conditions of the area and the technologies evolved or put in use can help in working out a reasonably scientific pattern of land use with proper guidelines for present and long-term management. But a more correct picture will emerge if the various regions or their smaller manageable segments are identified and taken up on the basis of soil classification or soil zones (as is presently done in the land settlement operations in a slightly less scientific though pragmatic manner).

It is the intention of this paper to examine in the light of the above comments the watershed concept of land-water management, and the administrative or organizational arrangements required for better land-water management and productivity.

WATERSHED PLANNING

As one of the authors has written elsewhere:[8] ··· Watershed management requires an integration of all scientific knowledge from many disciplines and a combination of technologies, strategies and techniques with the development and use of available but appropriate tools. In other words, it should be conceived as a multi-disciplinary, or inter-disciplinary development effort, within the natural boundaries of an established but identified drainage area so that the land or water and plant resources can be identified, conserved and developed in such a manner that both the immediate and long term needs of the people continue to be met in a somewhat regulated but sustained manner." We may add that the human and livestock resources of the area and even the industries and service sector ventures should be taken into account while planning the land and water utilization in a watershed and persuading the local people to follow the land-water use break-ups and land-water management practices being recommended. Watershed development is not a single department activity, not is it only soil conservation or duty farming as many seem to believe.

It must once again be stressed that land must be looked upon as a multi-purpose but basic factor of production rather than as incidental to various schemes of various governmental departments or to the diverse plans of various private individuals. In the words of B.B. Vohra:[9] "The habit of considering land as incidental to narrowly conceived departmental schemes, instead of a single indivisible resource which needs attention in its own right, needs to be rooted out. Today the irrigation engineer looks at the land as something to terrace and bund, the forester as something to grow trees, and planner as something which can create large scale employment opportunities."

A watershed[10] has been loosely defined as a catchments or drainage basis. We may say that it refers to an area which has a ridge-line on three sides and whose surplus run-off (of water) is drained from a drainage point. Thus even the catchments area of a small seasonal stream may be considered a watershed. Big watersheds separate drainage basins. Each watershed or catchments is a pat of some bigger and larger watershed—and cannot be developed in isolation. The smaller unit ultimately has to fit into the misgsaw of the larger area.

A watershed[11] may be 50 hectares in a hilly area (and consist of even a single holding) and may even go upto 10,000 hectares or more (covering more than one district) elsewhere. It is rarely that a watershed's boundaries coincide with the boundaries of existing administrative units or of existing landholdings, both of which have evolved historically.

The size of the watershed to be selected for land-water management or development will depend upon the main use or mix of uses that the area is to be put to, which in turn depends upon agro-climatic and soil conditions, the density of population, the proximity to and links with commercially developed areas, the presence of minerals, or of water and of energy sources, and the life-styles and skills of the population inhabiting the area.

The above would influence the main objective or objectives of watershed planning in a region. The objectives of such planning can be one or more of the following : (*a*) conservation of moisture in rainfed areas for optimal production, (*b*) to check soil erosion, (*c*) to control problems of drainage, salinity, alkalinity, etc., (*d*) flood prevention and flood control, (*e*) to check siltation in reservoirs, (*f*) collection of surplus run-off in farm ponds and is recycling for crop use, (*g*) to recharge ground water or increase the water table in wells, (*h*) collection of surplus run-off for meeting the drinking water requirement of the cattle and human population in desert areas, (*i*) to improve the main and on-farm irrigation systems for increased area under irrigation, increased irrigation efficiency and thus increased productivity in the crop-husbandry, afforestation, horticulture sylvipasture fields, etc; (*j*) better industrial and other commercial uses of land and water, and (*k*) the setting up of a new human settlement or the expansion or improvement of an old settlement leading to changes in the land-water utilization pattern, etc. The dominant objectives in a region would affect the watershed management practices adopted for watersheds in the region.

The size of the watersheds is also affected by the factor of how big the beneficiary group (or the population) living off the watershed can be and still permit meaningful interaction. Linked to this is the question of how many different groups and factions are likely to be covered by a watershed, for the lesser number of groups, factions and villages, the easier it would become to ensure meaningful participation on the part of all beneficiaries.

Similarly sometimes the optimal land water use patterns, cannot be achieved because the objectives of the local populace clash too drastically with the optimally recommended solutions. 'Second best' options may have to be accepted in such cases. However there is a limit to which technical considerations can be sacrificed for administrative or socio-political convenience for otherwise the entire objective of watershed development and management may be lost. For example at many places the boundaries of existing holdings may have to be changed on technical grounds.

Detailed and uniformly acceptable guidelines and norms for watershed selection are yet to be evolved.[12] However the selection of each individual watershed would entail detailed soil, topographical, hydrological, land holdings and land use pattern, population occupational break-up and live-stock, etc., surveys and a study of the potential for agriculture, industries animal husbandry, horticulture afforestation, etc., in the area. We may call such a study an "Integrated Basic Resource Survey".

After the identification of watersheds comes the issue: which watersheds should be picked up for early development? Priority watersheds can be selected on the basis of the following: (*i*) maximum returns per upper investment on unit area. (*ii*) availability of technical manpower for survey planning and implementation of watershed management programmes, (*iii*) availability of inputs, (*iv*) availability of good water, (*v*) availability of suitable soils, (*vi*) socio-economic return, (*vii*) intensity of problems, (*viii*) willingness or keenness of the local farmers for the work, and (*ix*) awareness of the local farmers (or livestock breeders, etc.) so that they shall be able to benefit from the watershed development through use of appropriate cropping pattern/animal husbandry techniques, etc.

Then for each watershed a suitable mix of developmental works as well as land and water use practices shall have to be worked out and got implemented both by the government and by the private landowners and other dwellers in the area.

WATERSHED MANAGING AGENCIES

This brings up the question of who will undertake the watershed development and land water management work especially since departmentalism as it exists today in India) is the very anti-thesis of good land water management.

One response can be the people themselves through either beneficiary associations,[13] or through existing panchayati raj institutions,[14] of which more later.

A second response can be that special integrated watershed development agencies be set up like some of the more comprehensive command area development (CAD) projects[15] where staff from various disciplines and field of expertise is placed directly under the agency which is asked to both man and implement in an integrated and coordinated manner for the area assigned to it. A list of the activities that can be assigned to such an agency in the irrigated area is being provided below[16] (a similar list could be worked out for such an agency in dry rainfed, areas).

A. Watershed Management above the headworks

B. Improvement of Existing Irrigation System (including minor and subminors)

1. Lining, desilting and deweeding of canals (and redesigning canal system, if necessary).
2. Construction and operation of control structures.
3. Rationalization of outlets.
4. Proper maintenance.
5. Canal capacity works and canal modernizing.
6. Enforcing water discipline and warabandi (rostered rotational irrigation).
7. Stabilization of canal banks through: (*a*) plantation, and (*b*) engineering works.
8. Rotational running of canals.
9. Maintaining full supply levels of canals.
10. Conjunctive use of ground and drainage water for irrigation.

C. Drainage Works

1. Construction of main drains, carrier (or linkage) drains and seepage (or interceptor) drains.
2. Maintenance of the above.

D. Flood Control Measures

E. On Farm Development (OFD)

1. Farm drainage works.
2. Watercourse works including re-alignment of water-courses where necessary.
3. Farm road works.
4. Realignment of field boundaries and updating of land records and revenue maps.
5. Lining of watercourses.

6. Individual wells for supplemental irrigation.
7. Protection of marginal lands and already developed OFD lands through soil conservation and afforestation techniques for gully and rain control.
8. Reclamation of saline and alkaline lands.
9. Suitable treatment of unirrigated or non-command patches that fall within the larger command area.

F. Agricultural

1. Intensive agriculture extension system.
2. Adaptive and adoptive research to feed the extension system.
3. Monitoring of supplies of inputs and water and tie up of the extension system with co-operatives and canal water distribution.
4. Popularizing better on farm irrigation and cultivation techniques.
5. Popularizing water users associations.

G. Macro Development of Command Areas

1. Roads.
2. Market yards and storage facilities.
3. Processing Industries.
4. Forestry and pastures and horticulture.
5. Development of Human settlements in virgin areas being brought under irrigation.
6. Development of both milch and drought animals.
7. Containment of water borne human and animal diseases.
8. Aquaculture.
9. Development of rural artisans and rural industries.
10. Special programmes for the rural poor like the Government of India programme of integrated rural development (IRD).
11. Land reforms and consolidation of holdings, if necessary.

H. Institutions

1. Integrated management of irrigation engineer, agriculture engineers, (land) revenue staff, agriculture extension and research set-up, cooperative structure, PWD, afforest ton staff, agriculture produce marketing committees, dairy and animal husbandry staff, and district level functionaries of various government departments who are placed under the supervision control and/or coordination of the project administer.
2. Coordinating with special credit institutions[17] for providing: (*a*) short term credit for agriculture inputs, (*b*) Term credit for OFD works, and (*c*) IRD credit for small and marginal farmers, agricultural labourers, rural artisans and other rural poor.

For the coordination of such agencies, reorganization at the state government level[18] would also be necessary so that proper coordination of the work of such integrated multi-disciplinary project agencies can be achieved. Instead of the existing functional departments two different wings of the land water management department should be set up, one for irrigated areas and the other for rain fed areas. While government managed implementation can be more emphasis may get paid to achievement of physical and financial targets than to the actual impact of the government work.

SELF-MANAGING AGENCIES

As regards implementation through the beneficiaries,[19] one possibility is that the land, water and natural resources of each village may be placed at the disposal or under care of the various gram panchayats, or panchayat samities for them to manage themselves with some technical advisory being given by the government functionaries or other agencies of experts and consultants. The local populace knows best its area and its problems as they crop up from day to day and season to season and it has learnt to live wit these problems or challenges according to the indigenous pool of knowledge, technology, skills and resources available at that level. But if the local community can be provided with the latest knowledge about the limitations and potentials of its natural resources or the environment and about the techniques for optimal utilization of these resources and provided with necessary wherewithal beyond what it can mobilize through its own initiative and organization, then it can easily set up its own multi-discipline teams and feel much more responsible or involved in the planning an implementation of various programmes, than even functionaries of the above recommended special multi-disciplinary government agencies or who as often reluctant or shy of exploring the rural areas. Self-management, not merely participation, should be the key-word for mobilizing the local communities into the campaign for rehabilitating or rebuilding, conserving an developing the basic land and water resources of any single or group watersheds linked together in easily manageable units of development administration.

This process requires almost at the start a fresh orientation or reorientation of the outlook and approach of the rural communities or masses. For example, after the basic survey is over they have to be made aware of both the limitations and possibilities of development or exploitation of the available resources, motivated about the need for discipline use, imparted with and the acquisition of skills and then induced to proceed with the programme through their own efforts in the first instance and with outside support or help from other neighbouring communities where necessary and to the extent possible.

Broadly speaking the development effort of the local communities will have 3 or 4 segments of activities: (*a*) entirely local or more or less self-sustained schemes or programmes based on their own resources and efforts and leading towards self-sufficiency, (*b*) schemes of programmes requiring help or guidance or technical and financial support from outside, (*i*) either from the nearby or neighbouring communities, or (*ii*) some specialized vacancies of the government or the cooperative and private sector; or (*c*) economic programmes and efforts dependent on outside trade or aid in procurement of raw material, energy, machinery or credit and channels, for made and marketing, through private or co-operative or state trade channels.

But in the case of managing land and water resources, it may be appreciated that much work can be accomplished at the local level at least in respect of micro-watersheds. It is only when a number of watersheds, complementing each other, are linked or strung together, and large tracts of lands with different types of physical features, soil profiles, etc., are taken up for a large watershed, or sub-regional and regional or area development approach that a more sophisticated type of managerial and coordinating agency with suitable field level set-up, is required.

A number of organizations of the latter type have been established (with more or less integration within the organization's structure) all over the country in the command areas, desert or drought prone areas, the tribal or valley areas and so on. But their one weakness which is now becoming more and more noticeable has been that such organizations have not had their or solid (grass) roots in the collective mind of the local people. Their field level agent has been a paid or hired functionary, not the local community organized on a representative or functional basis. If the base of any local areas development organization can be built or rooted in the local community or its representative body, and then the organizational hierarchy sought to be built up, we can have not only the participation but actual development of the beneficiaries in the process of development—prospecting, running, implementation and monitoring—in a more responsive and responsible manner.

Of course where the local communities fail to undertake their responsibilities seriously (or to give up factional interests[20] for the sake of general communitarian interests) safeguards can be built into the system so that the government can then assume powers to undertake watershed development and ensure proper land water management through its special integrated multi-disciplinary agencies. Such an approach, should also be available to (and within reach of) the local community, which should also have the opportunities to develop and utilize the local skills or to import skills from outside. Education, training, and employment facilities should be land oriented; at least that must be their common main thrust. The local community should then proceed to create and build up suitable technical representative managerial and operational as well as economic institutions, to subserve its needs and the takes of land and water management. Perhaps the existing departmental set-up, controlled and regulated from the remote state headquarter, will have to go. That seems to be the broad approach or possibility. The local community, the local farmer, forester, cattle breeder on the spot will have to enter the state and become its center, if ultimately productivity per unit of manpower has also to be ensured with the productivity of per unit of land or per unit of water or pr unit of any other input.[21]

SUMMARY

To recapitulate, the watershed concept of land-water management envisages the following steps:

1. Identification and demarcation of watersheds.
2. Survey or natural resources physical features, soil conditions and characteristics, land use and ownership-management patterns, pressure of human and cattle population and identification of problem areas of over-exploited, degraded, eroded-lands as also untapped resources.
3. Technical understanding and appreciation of existing problems and hazards and identification of appropriate remedial preventive, protective, productive and appropriate technologies suitable for the area.
4. Identification of available local tools and technologies, skills and experts so as to list out the spheres of activity in which outside help or guidance would be necessary.
5. Assessment of requirement of funds for immediate medium term and long term operations for works required to protect or develop the land, water and forest resources, etc. (through rural works like contour bunding, terracing, training of streams and gullys, sand dume stabilization, aforestation, range management, and soil conservative works, small anicuts and, development or rehabilitation of waste lands and saline lands and the like.
6. To inform, educate and motivate the local people affected by the problems or the hazards and who are likely to benefit from the protective and development measures so as to prepare them for necessary community effort at the local or mini- or micro-watershed level. This process of dissemination of information or extension both by the official and technical departmental agencies and through voluntary action must necessarily become a continuous ongoing activity.
7. On the basis of the existing cropping patter and land use data particularly in the rain fed and dry land areas to evolve and propogate a suitable but more scientific and planned land use system so as to maintain the natural balance between the land capability and the actual production. This process may involve (in certain watersheds) actual reduction in the cultivated area and earmarking of more and more lands for permanent pastures grazing lands, grove lands or tree crops for fuel, fodder and other purposes. Or it may involve decrease in the area under cereal crops with more and more lands earmarked for, say, fodder development.
8. The preparation (after compilation of the above indicated data about the natural resources, the problems and hazards, the remedial measures, the possible directions of change, the requirement of necessary inputs) of local watershed development plans including both measures of immediate urgency and programmes of long term gestation. This plan should also contain marketing and raw material input the ups and linkages with allied activities like sheep, goat and cattle rearing, rural industries, etc.
9. To create and establish suitable organizations, institutions, agencies, and services for carrying out in a comprehensive, integrated and multi-disciplined manner the above mentioned watershed development plans, either singly or in manageable groups of two or three or more watersheds, depending upon the nature of the area, its problems means of communication resources, etc.

10. Implementation of the various programmes in a dovetailed manner with proper coordination, control, supervision and monitoring so as to ensure that all necessary segments activities are taken up side by side. It may be mentioned that the programme requires constant attention and concurrent evaluation so that the shortfalls and distortions can be checked at the earliest. The constant evaluation should not only be of the programme's implementation but also of the still available resources of the area and their possible new use.
11. The planning or coordinating agency should not only be able to win popular support and confidence, but also should be armed with the necessary authority to enforce discipline, for example against uncontrolled and overgrazing, or against indiscriminate lopping off trees, or damaging of soil conservation and protective works, cultivation of marginal lands, and uncontrolled or extensive irrigation, as also to ensure realignment of field boundaries where technical desirable.
12. The community must also be taught and trained to maintain and look after the works and to exercise self-restraint from over exploitation or use of uneconomic and inefficient land-water use practices.

END NOTES

1. For example for Rajasthan Bhupendra Hooja has made certain suggestion on Land Use Pattern in Rajasthan—A Plea to Change the Priorities" in *Prashasnika,* Vol. IX, Nos. 1 and 2, January, June 1980, a point indirectly borne out by B. Hooja and Pathak, "Production and Availability of Foodgrains in Rajasthan During Seventies", *Rajasthan Economical Journal,* Vol. 4, Nos. 1 and 2, Jan., July 1980, where it is stressed that greater emphasis needs to be placed on production of coarse grains in Rajasthan.
2. Also see Bhupendra Hooja and Rakesh Hooja, "Government Development Schemes and the Modernization of Agriculture in India", *The Administrator,* Vol. XXV, No. 4, Winter 1980.
3. See Ramesh K. Arora (ed.), *People's Participation in Development Process.* HIMSIPA, Jaipur, 1979.
4. For example N.K. Jaiswal and N.V. Kolte, *Development of Drought Prone Areas,* MRD, Hyderabad, 1981 have quoted the *Report on Integrated Rural Development of* The Task Force on Integrated Agriculture Development in Drought Prone Areas of the Planning Commission, Government of India, 1973 which states: "In this administrative backward and there is a real danger that any integrated plan of development of a drought-prone area may flounder on the rock of departmentalism."
5. See for example *Report of the Seminar on Development of Drought Prone Area* HIMSIPA and IIPA, Rajasthan Regional Branch, Jaipur, 1981 as well as: (1) *Development and Transfer of Technology for Rainfed Agriculture and the SAT Farmer* ICRISAT Hyderabad, 1980, (2) *Socio-Economic Constraints to Development of Semi-Arid topics Agriculture,* ICRISAT, Hyderabd, 1980, (3) *Desertification and Its Control,* ICAR, New Delhi, 1977; (4) Special Issues on Arid Zone Research and Development (in two parts) of *Annal of Arid Zone,* Vol. 19, Nos. 3 and No. 4, September 1980, and December 1980. And other back issues of the Annals; (5) *Improved Dryland Agriculture for Western Rajasthan, Technical Bulletin,* No. 1, CAZRI, Jodhpur, September 1976; and (6) *Outlines of the Techniques for Reconstruction of the Arid*

Zone, Technical Bulletin, No. 7, CAZR, Jodhpur, December 1980.

6. On the T&V system see: (1) Daniel Benor, *Report on Chambal Command Area Development Project Extension Service,* World Bank, Washington, January, 1974; (2) Bhupendra Hooja, "Agriculture Extension—A New Programme for Continuous Training at All Levels". Kurukshetra Vol. XXVII, No. 7, January 1, 1979; and (3) Rakesh Hooja, "T&V" in Rajasthan—An attempt at Better Downward Communication Through Agriculture Extension in CAD and non-CAD Area". The *Administrator,* Vol. XXIII, Nos. 3 and 4, July, Dec. 1978.
7. For an overview of governmental developmental programmes being implemented is rural India, see: (1) *Rural Development in India – Some Facts,* NIRD, Hyderabad 1979; *Rural Development Administration in India – Some Emerging Policy Issues,* ESCAP, Bongkok DP/AARD/18, 1979; (3) *Public Service Delivery Systems for the Rural Poor,* SCAP, Bangkok, ST/ESCAP; 105. 1980 and Rakesh Hooja, "Machinery for Delivering Benefits to the Rural Poor", *Indian Journal of Public Administration,* Vol. XXVIII, No. 1 January-March 1982.
8. Bhupendra Hooja, "Land Utilization and Watershed Management", (micro) inaugural address delivered at a workshop on Watershed Management at CAZRI, Jodhpur, 5 February 1981.
9. B.B. Vohra while inaugurating a seminar o Land-use Planning at Trivandrum, October 21, 1980.
10. On watershed development also, see: (1) *Guidelines for Watershed Management,* FAO, Rome, 1977: (2) B.B. Vohra, *Land and Watershed Management Problems in India,* Training Division Cabinet Secretariat, Government of India, New Delhi, 1979; (3) N.K. Jaiswal and N.V. Kolte, *op. cit.*
11. The ensuing paragraphs are based on certain portions of Rakesh Hooja, "People's Participation in Comprehensive Watershed Development Programmes" forthcoming in Hashiar Singh (ed.), *Rural Development Administration in India,* 1982.
12. *Though Operation Watershed Management* proceedings of the National Seminar on Watershed Management, Jan. 28-February 2, 1980, Ministry of Agriculture, Government of India, New Delhi, 1980 (mimeo) is a useful guide.
13. See Bhupendra Hooja, "Beneficiary Participation Through Irrigation Sichai Groups", *The Administrator,* Oct.-December, 1979.
14. See Bhupendra Hooja: (*a*) "Managing Rural Development Through Panchayats—A Functional Approach", *The Administrator,* Vol. XXV, No. 4, 1980; (*b*) "Functional Approach to Panchayats—A Post Asoka Mehta Committee Perspective", *Administrative Change,* Vol. 6, Nos. 1 and 2, July 1978 and June 1979.
15. See K.K. Singh, "Alternative Organisational Strategies for Command Area Development" and Anthony Bottial, "Evaluating the Organizational and Management of Irrigation Agriculture" both in *Proceedings of the Commonwealth Workshop on Irrigation Management* Hyderabad, India, 17-27 October, 1978 (mimeo), Commonwealth Secretariat, London. Also see Rakesh Hooja, B.N. Maheshwary and S.R. Mittal, "On Farm Development in Chambal Rajasthan Project", forthcoming in S. Betra (ed.), *Administration in an Indian State* (Associated, Delhi). For the description of a particular CAD Project's organization.
    For the desert areas the need for an integrated or coordinated agency has been suggested by Rakesh Hooja in "The Development Delivery System in a Desert District", paper presented at a seminar on Desert and Drought Prone Areas, 6 to 8 March, 1982.
16. An earlier version of this list had been prepared for Rakesh Hooja, "Area Development for Land and Water Management—A Preliminary Prospective Report on A Winter School on CAD projects" *Rural Development Digest,* Vol. 2. No. 3, 1979. The related problems of a particular CAD Project have been set forth in Rakesh Hooja "Effective Land and Water

Management—A Statement of Issues from the Rajasthan Viewpoint", *The Administrator,* Vol. XXV, No. 4, Winter 1980.

17. See Rakesh Hooja, "Rural Credit in CAD Areas—OFD and SFDA Loaning", incoming in *The Administrator,* No. 1, 1982. Also see Bhupendra Hooja, "Rural Credit Development in India—An Overview", Occasional Paper, Series No. 2, Paper No. 1, *Journal of Development Studies,* Jaipur, 1982.
18. The idea of a Land Use Commission at the all India level with a Ministry of Natural Resources (dealing with land water management) and a separate Division of the Planning Commission with similar reorganization at the inter-state and state as well as lower levels has been suggested in Bhupendra Hooja, "Land and Water management. Some Points on Agenda for Action", (mimeo) paper presented at seminar on Desert and Drought Prone Areas at Jaipur, 6 to 8 March 1981.
19. See n. 14. Also see T.K. Jayaraman, "Strategy for Mass Mobilization and people participation in the Implementation of Watershed Management Programme" in seminar on *Strategy of Mass Mobilization and People's Participation in Implementation of Watershed Management Programme,* (mimeo), Central Board of Irrigation and Power, New Delhi, October, 1980.
20. A description of how the various vested interests of, and conflicts between, intra-village groups may affect development programmes has been given in Rakesh Hooja, "Agrarian Structure and Rural Development", *New Quest,* No. 27, May-June, 1981.
21. An earlier attempt at applying the authors thinking which is being set forth in this paper, in the Rajasthan context, is Bhupendra Hooja, "Rajasthan in the Eightees—Some Challenges and Strategies of Agriculture Development" paper presented at the seminar on Administrative Reforms organized by IIPA, Rajasthan Regional Branch, Jaipur, 2-4 July, 1981. That paper is now being re-developed as an occasional paper in the Rajasthan context for the recently established Institute of Development Studies, Jaipur.

10

Experiences of Participation in Integrated Watershed Development Project in Himachal Pradesh

S.S. Negi

THE PROJECT

The Shiwalik Hills are amongst the youngest mountain ranges in the World having being formed 2.02 to 2.5 million years ago. These hills are extremely fragile and highly degraded mainly due to the unstable geology, fragile rocks, steep slopes and heavy biotic pressure. The Shiwalik hills form the transition between the main Himalayan mountain ranges to the north and the Indo-Gangetic plains in the south.[1]

Even though the average rainfall in these hills is between 1,000 and 1,500 mm, there are acute shortages of water, fuelwood, fodder and other goods and services based on natural resources. The area is subject to severe soil erosion and land degradation. Rainfed agriculture is the main source of income for the rural population, 35 per cent of whom live below poverty line.

A World Bank supported Integrated Watershed Development Project (Hills) was launched in July 1990 in selected subwatersheds of the Shiwalik hills of Himachal Pradesh and also in the adjoining states of Punjab, Haryana and Jammu & Kashmir. This is now commonly referred to as the first phase of the project.

The integrated Watershed Development Project (Hills II) started from 1999-2000 in 32 new subwatersheds of the Shiwalik hills of Himachal Pradesh with the main object of restoring the productive potential of the project area by using evolving watershed and participatory approaches. Participation of local communities in project interventions is now the main thrust of this multi-disciplinary project.

EXPERIENCE OF PARTICIPATORY APPROACHES IN IWDP (HILLS) (PHASE I)

The participatory approaches, as we know them today, evolved through experience, learning by doing and recognition of the fact that people's involvement in natural resource management is the cornerstone of success and it brings about sustainability.

In the first phase of this project which extended from 1990-91 to 1998-99, people's participation in watershed management was evoked only towards the fag end. Participation of people in watershed development picked up with the constitution of Village Development Committees (VDCs) formed to facilitate project implementation and managing/maintaining the assets created. By the time the project ended, 114 VDCs had been constituted in different parts of the project area.

However, the new project (Phase 1) is primarily a participatory one designed in such a way that local communities will play a vital role in planning, implementation, monitoring and evaluation of the project.

Pre-MTR Period

The project started at a slow pace in 1990-91 with the practice of top down planning and implementation. The participatory approaches as we know them today were largely absent and planning and implementation was primarily done by the staff. The procedures adopted for the project in watershed planning and development had a limited scope for involving the local communities. The population in the project area were treated only as beneficiaries and not as stake-holders. Areas to be covered were identified on the basis of technical needs and activities carried out without appropriate consultation with local communities.

Post-MTR Period

The Mid Term Review (MTR) was carried out in August 1994 and recommendations were made for strengthening project implementation In involving local communities, which continued to be looked upon as beneficiaries and not stake-holders.

Participation of people in watershed development picked up with the constitution of VDCs formed for facilitating project implementation and managing/maintaining the created assets. Out of the total 114 VDCs constituted in different parts of the project area, only about one-fourth could become sustainable on a long-term basis.

PARTICIPATORY APPROACHES OF IWDP (HILLS II)/ (PHASE II)

In the new project (IWDP—Hills II) a Participatory Watershed Development approach is being followed which revolves around integrating participation of local communities with all project interventions. The local population is now actively involved in assessment of natural resources, identification and ranking of problems, planning, implementation, monitoring and evaluation. Thus, there is now a major shift in the new project towards social development and sustainability of social institution.

The following participatory process is being adopted for this project:

Participatory Assessment and Planning (PAP)

PAP is the basic tool being used for development of a Village Development Plan (VDP).

Village Development Plan (VDP)

A VDP is a community generated, condensed, site-specific, need-based and people-oriented plan covering the specific micro-watershed for a village or group of villages. The usual Participatory Rural Appraisal (PRA)[2] tools are used for developing the VDP which is a flexible document and may be changed during its implementation if necessary.

Stake-holder Capacity Building

Lack of stake-holder capacity building was one of the major lacunae in social development during the previous project. Adequate provisions have now being made for capacity building of stake-holders.

Roles and Responsibilities of Local Communities and the Project.

The roles and responsibilities of the local communities and project have been made clear from the onset.

Village Development Committee (VDC)

The VDC is the basic functional unit of the project responsible for development and implementation of the VDP with the project being a partner. All house-holds falling in the micro-watershed constitute the general house of the VDC through one male and one female member. An executive body consisting of a President, Vice-President, General Secretary, Treasurer and eight other members is elected by the general house. The executive committee has at least 50 per cent women members. A project staff is nominated as an *ex-officio* member of the VDC to facilitate its functioning.

Women have been identified as the priority stake-holders in this project in the Shiwalik hills of Himachal Pradesh, where they are actively involved in on-farm as well as off-farm activities. A significant percentage of stakeholders in the sub-watersheds are women as many males go out of the village in search of work leaving the women folk behind to look after the fields, animals, raising the family and taking care of all other house-hold activities.

Special attention is being given to the problems and needs of women. The project supports a number of initiatives that give direct benefit to women through greater access to resources, technical know-how and opportunities for additional income.

Several self-help groups are now operating in the project area with the active support of the project. Each group has a savings account in a registered bank with the savings generated by them being used for self-loaning. The project supports these groups and has taken initiatives for their capacity building. Now these self-help groups are taking up income generating activities for women at the grassroots level.

CASE STUDIES

The Gol Jamala Experience

Gol Jamala and Amlidol are two villages of subwatershed No. 4 of Sirsa catchment in

Solan district. The major problems of this micro-watershed before intervention of the project were high-level erosion, acute scarcity of water and shortages of fuelwood and fodder. There are 49 families in Gol Jamala and 19 families in Amlidol. Most of these families joined the VDC set-up to support watershed development.

The turning point came with the construction of a 10 m high earthen dam at Gol Jamala between February 1996 and May 1996. The stored water of this dam has the capacity of irrigating more than 20 hect. of land (two life saving irrigations each). The local community put in all the manual labour for laying of pipelines and constructed proper channels for distribution of the water. After the water became available for irrigation they began to collect money for operation and maintenance of this dam. The villagers have evolved an interesting system of sharing the available water for irrigation.

Up-stream of the large earthen dam at Gol Jamala a perennial How exists and the VDC came up with a proposal to construct a head wall there so that the water could be used for irrigation. The project agreed to this provided the VDC contributed all manual labour for laying the two km long pipeline from the headwall to their fields. This was constructed during 1998-99 and the VDC shared the cost by collecting more than Rs. 45,000, for laying the two km pipeline. The committee is now also managing this water which is available in plenty with the surplus water being allowed to replenish the reservoir of the Gol Jamala dam.

The VDC is also managing and protecting three plantation areas in the upper catchment. They auction the grass from two of these areas while the third one remains available for grass cutting by the poor families. The sources of income of this VDC are:

(*a*) Sale of grass.
(*b*) Cess on irrigation: This money is kept in separate bank accounts. While they have set aside the money from water cess for maintenance of water harvesting structures, the money from the sale of grass has been used to buy utensils and other articles for use in community events. They also rent these articles to adjoining villages on payment of a nominal fees.
(*c*) Contribution from members.

Katola Experience

Katola is a village situated on the Sainwala-Barampapri road in sub-watershed No. 8 of Moginand-wali-khad in Sirmour district. This area was subject to severe erosion caused by the *nallah* that was eroding the agricultural land. The Katola micro-watershed was taken up for treatment during 1997-98 under the first phase.

There are 45 families in Katola and surrounding hamlets. Most of these families joined the VDC for supporting watershed development.

The main problems of this micro-watershed before intervention of the project were severe soil erosion; scarcity of water for irrigation and cattle; low agriculture productivity and shortage of fodder; and fuelwood.

The construction of a small dam across the main *nallah* near Katola has provided irrigation to about 19 hect of land besides reducing the intensity of floods and soil erosion. The villagers parted with the land submerged under the reservoir. They also put in all manual labour for laying of the pipeline. The VDC is responsible for maintenance of this asset and distribution of the irrigation water amongst its members.

The VDC has also introduced fishing in the reservoir of this dam on an experimental basis.

The VDC at Katola is also responsible for managing other assets created under the previous project. They hold regular meetings and keep detailed records. The VDC also has a bank account.

ACTIVITIES OF VDCS OF IWDP HILLS II

Nurput Unit VDC's

Bari Khad

- The local leadership is dynamic, effective and far-sighted. The VDC is functioning as a cohesive team.
- The villagers feel that the most important benefit of the project is that it has brought people of the three hamlets together. They are able to sit together and plan for the future.
- The VDC has executed many works like afforestation, construction of village ponds, grass plantation, cement masonry structure, etc.
- In this VDC, the women have formed eight self-help groups (SHGs). The motivator is very active and guides all these groups. The SHGs have saved Rs. 20,248.
- One SHG has constructed a footpath in the village.
- The VDC has auctioned surplus grass from the plantation area to supplement its income.
- The VDC has a bank saving of Rs. 54,000.
- One natural breeding centre was opened and VDC contributed Rs. 950 as community share.
- VDC imposed a fine to the tune of Rs. 4,205 from the persons who damaged/ destroyed the plantation.

Bhadroya

- In initial stages there were conflicts among the members.
- Subsequently, the executive members have emerged as good team leaders.
- The women have organised themselves into seven SHGs. The SHGs have a saving of Rs. 9,400.
- The women are also receiving training in tailoring.
- The VDC has a bank balance of Rs. 25,060.
- The VDC has executed many works like plantation, fish ponds, strengthening of footpath, terrace repair and vegetative field boundaries.
- One natural breeding centre was opened and VDC collected Rs. 950 as community share.

Thora-Baloon

- The women have organised themselves into four SHGs and have saved Rs. 13,200.
- Women are also receiving training in tailoring.
- The VDC has a bank balance of Rs. 33,420.
- De-worming of sheep/goats of tribals was done with the participation of VDC.
- Two natural breeding centres were opened and Rs. 950 was collected as public share for each centre.
- VDC has executed works like afforestation construction of farm ponds, terrace repair, vegetative field boundaries and strengthening of footpath.
- The VDC is also looking after the protection of the plantation and imposes fines on the defaulters.

Chakki

- This is the remotest located community of the project. All the residents of this village are tribals. They are migrant shepherds. Most of menfolk move around with their herd of sheep for a major part of the year while women and children remain in the village.
- VDC has taken up many works like forest plantation, construction of farm pond, strengthening of footpath, etc.
- One natural breeding centre was opened.

Patka

- The VDC has a woman Pradhan who is successfully leading the VDC.
- The VDC has taken up execution of plantation, shrub hedge, village pond, cement masonry structure and vegetative field boundaries.
- The women have organised themselves into two self-help groups and saved Rs. 2,200.
- The VDC has Rs. 15,295 in its bank account.
- One natural breeding centre was opened. VDC contributed Rs. 950 by way of public share.

Lahru

- The VDC has been active in execution of works like construction of footpath, farm ponds, improvement of drinking water source, vegetative field boundaries and strengthening of footpath.
- The women have formed two SHGs and have saved Rs. 3,550.
- The VDC has a bank balance of Rs. 6,000 only.

NAHAN UNIT VDCS

Shambhuwala

- VDC Shambhuwala is one of our forward looking VDCs. The leadership of the pradhan and the executive has been exemplary. The record keeping is also very meticulous. The pradhan made an appeal through 'Kandi Sandesh' to all his counterparts to make the project a success.

- The VDC has taken the responsibility of protection of the area planted by them and have appointed a caretaker for Rs. 500 per month, they have also decided to impose fines on the violators.
- The VDC had taken up the work of construction of a footpath. The people have provided free labour and a passage longer than actually estimated has been constructed.
- The women have organised themselves into a SHG. They have received training in bee keeping and tailoring.
- The VDC has Rs. 50,000 in its account.

Suketi

- Suketi has a Tribal Development Committee (TDC) as most of its residents are migrant Gujjars (cattle-rearers). The village is known for its cattle shows.
- The TDC has undertaken execution of works like footpaths, farm ponds, etc.
- The women have been provided training in bee-keeping and tailoring as per the tribal development plan.
- The TDC has Rs. 11,300 in its savings account.

Surla

- VDC Surla has elected a lady as its Pradhan, therefore, women's participation is enthusiastic.
- The VDC has decided to tackle the problem of drinking water as its first priority. The repair and rejuvenation of old wells and *bowries* (water bodies) has been taken up.
- The people have greatly appreciated the field visits to successfully managed areas. Its impact is visible.
- The VDC has Rs. 30,000 in its savings account.

Nihog

- The VDC Nihog has a good leadership in its Pradhan. He has been able to convince the villagers to work in close coordination with each other.
- The VDC has constructed water tanks and irrigation channels. The VDC has provided free labour for laying of this irrigation channel.
- The VDC has also taken up the responsibility of protecting the plantations. The VDC charges Rs. 10 per cattle head as a fine for grazing in plantation.
- Women have received training in income generating activities.
- The VDC has Rs. 17,000 in its savings account.

Chabahan

- The first priority of this VDC was the construction of a footbridge over the stream so that the school children could safely cross the torrential stream in the rainy season and agricultural produce can be transported to the market. The footbridge has now been constructed.

- The VDC has undertaken execution of works like farm, ponds, cattle stalls, etc.
- The VDC has about Rs. 22,000 in its saving account.

Koti Kalyanpur

- This is one of the model VDCs, which has had maximum number of visitors and yet people are eager to share more and more.
- The VDC has executed several works like construction of a footpath, irrigation tanks, afforestation, etc.
- The motivator of this VDC is a dedicated lady. The SHG has a contribution of Rs. 50 per month from each member per month.
- The ladies are getting trained in tailoring. They pay Rs. 20 per month to the SHG as a token fee.
- The VDC is also raising a nursery for income generation.
- The VDC has Rs. 42,000 in its savings account.

Batol Dagshsi

- The lady Vice-President of this VDC is an able leader. She has seen able to facilitate participation by women in project interventions.
- The VDC has taken up execution of works like construction of footbridge, village ponds, etc.
- The VDC has Rs. 18,500 m its saving account.

Bhojnagar

- The VDC is working in close coordination with the panchayat. It has appointed panchayat pradhan as its auditor.
- The VDC has also appointed advisors for forestry, agriculture, horticulture and animal husbandry who are responsible for works in their respective fields.
- Bhojnagar had the first SHG in the state under the project. This oldest SHG is now giving loans to its members.
- The SHG has executed the construction of a farm pond to supplement its income.
- The VDC has also taken up execution of works like construction of a footpath, plantation, etc.
- The VDC has Rs. 20,900 in its savings account.

Khadin

- Accessibility to this village is difficult in absence of a proper road. The school children had to take a steep and dangerous track and accessibility to market was hazardous. A footpath was constructed by the VDC on priority.
- The VDC has also constructed irrigation tanks as irrigation was a major problem.

- The SHG is receiving training in tailoring and cutting for income generation.
- The VDC has Rs. 47,000 in its savings account.

NALAGARH UNIT VDCs

Mandiarpur

- This VDC is one of the model VDCs. The VDC has a good leadership in its lady vice pradhan who is able to convince the villagers to work in close coordination and the project.
- Women are active stakeholders. They have formed a SHG and collect Rs. 20 per month from each member.
- To supplement the household income the SHG set up a forest nursery and is also preparing nutrified bricks for animals. They are also receiving training in tailoring.
- The VDC has undertaken useful activities like afforestation strengthening of footpaths, potable water supply and lying of RCC pipe, village ponds, cratewire structures, etc.
- The VDC is also protecting the plantation area.
- The VDC has a cash balance of Rs. 47,000.
- One natural breeding centre was opened and VDC contributed Rs. 950 as community share. Community is also contributing for maintaining the bulls.

Teliwal

- VDC has executed many works like afforestation, construction of village ponds and a potable water supply scheme to argument the drinking water.
- The women have organised themselves into a SHG.
- The VDC has a cash balance of Rs. 65,000.
- One natural breeding centre was opened and VDC had borne five per cent cost of the bull purchased by the project.

Aduwal

- The VDC has executed works like construction of farm ponds, dry stone structure, afforestation, etc.
- A SHG has also been formed by women in Aduwal.
- One natural breeding centre was opened by VDC.
- The VDC has a cash balance of Rs. 65,000.

Mittian

- The VDC has executed works like strengthening of footpath, construction of village ponds and also contributed labour for execution of WHS, cement structure, etc.
- One natural breeding centre was opened by VDC.
- The VDC has a cash balance of Rs. 47,000.

Raitwari

- The VDC has executed works like afforestation, pasture development, construction of village ponds, vegetative shrub barriers, etc.
- The VDC has a bank account of Rs. 42,000.
- One natural breeding centre was opened.

Dhang-Plasi

- This is the richest VDC in terms of its bank account. It has collected Rs. 1,15,000.
- Women are active stakeholder. They have formed a SHG and collect Rs. 20 from each member per month.
- The VDC has executed works like construction of village ponds, contributed labour for WHS, potable water supply and cratewire structures.
- One natural breeding centre was opened.

Sitalpur

- The VDC has executed works like construction of cratewire structure, village ponds, afforestation and raising of forest nursery.
- The women have organised themselves into a SHG which has raised a forest nursery of 20,000 seedlings.
- The VDC has a cash balance of Rs. 37,000.

Alyon

- The VDC is actively involved in the execution of works like construction of village ponds, afforestation and raising of nursery, etc.
- VDC also takes keen interest in all the project interventions.
- One natural breeding centre was opened by VDC.
- The VDC has raised a cash balance of Rs. 49,835.

Salehra

- The VDC has constructed very good farm ponds besides raising a forest plantation.
- The VDC has a cash balance of Rs. 27,675.
- One natural breeding centre was opened by VDC.

UNA UNIT VDC'S

Thana Kalan

- The is a progressive VDC. It has executed a number of works like construction of a footpath, farm pond, keeping of wells for potable water, etc.
- The women have organised themselves into a SHG. The group has collected Rs. 3,600.
- An income generating group has also been formed which undertook 'namkeen (snack) making' for income generation. At the cost of Rs. 950 in the first trial

they have made a profit of Rs. 500.
- They VDC has a surplus of Rs. 39,000.

Lamlehri

- This is also one of the model VDCs of the project. The villagers have very small land holdings and depend on 'labour' as an alternate livelihood. The villagers keenly undertook the execution of works like construction of a cement masonry structure, farm pond, live hedge spurs, brushwood check dams, landslide treatment, etc.
- The record keeping by this VDC is meticulous.
- The SHG is quite active and has collected Rs. 5,320.
- The VDC has made a saving of Rs. 39,666.

Balliwal

- The VDC has executed works like farm pond, terrace repair, etc.
- The women have formed a SHG. It has a saving of Rs. 8,000.
- The VDC has Rs. 13,127 in its saving bank account.

Bhadsali

- It has taken execution of works like footpath, cratewire structures, farm pond, etc.
- The women have formed a SHG and taken up knitting for income generation. The group has loaned Rs. 1,700 to help a member tide over rough circumstances.
- The VDC has Rs. 42,000 in its savings account.

Jadla

- The VDC has executed works like construction of a farm pond, footpath, water tank, etc.
- The women have formed a SHG and have started knitting for income generation. They have saved Rs. 7,245.
- The VDC has Rs. 13,800 in its saving account.

Ghanari

- The VDC has executed works like construction of a farm pond, terrace repair, etc.
- The women have formed a SHG. They have saved Rs. 12,250.
- The VDC has Rs. 8,551 in its savings account.

Polian Purohitan

- The VDC has executed a number of works like strengthening of a footpath, terrace repair, etc.
- The VDC has Rs. 6,765 in its savings account.

Paloh

- Village Paloh, Khawarian and Suri remained cut off from the main road in the rainy season. Crossing the torrential stream in rains was dangerous for adults what to say of the school children and the old. The first priority of the VDC was to construct a footbridge over the stream. This footbridge has now been constructed.
- The VDC has executed a number of works like construction of a water tank, footpath, etc.
- The women have formed a SHG. They have saved Rs. 1,200.
- The VDC has Rs. 37,000 in its savings bank account.

REFERENCES

1. S.S. Negi, *New Delhi, Handbook of the Himalaya IPC; and Discovering the Himalaya,* Vol. I & II, IPC.
2. B. Singh and V. Varalakshmi, New Delhi, *Micro-planning Manual for JFM Areas,* TERI, 1998.

11

Policy Interventions and Administrative Instruments for Sustainable Livestock Development in Watersheds: Some Suggestions Based on the Lead Study of Five Watersheds

Rakshat Hooja and Ranjitha Puskur

INTRODUCTION

The Livestock-Environment-Watershed Interactions in India (LEAD) study[1] undertaken by the International Water Management Institute (IWMI) along with its partners *Samuha* (Karnataka), *Sampark* (Madhya Pradesh), WOTR (Maharashtra), WASSAN (Andhra Pradesh) and *Sevamandir* (Rajasthan) aimed to identify, document and analyse livestock-environment-watershed interactions in five selected watersheds, one in each of the above mentioned states, located in the semi-arid areas of India. The study focused on the inter-linkages between livestock production, natural resource endowment and management, market access, watershed development interventions and the policy environment as it examined the importance of livestock in rain-fed areas.

One of the most clear cut findings of the LEAD study, which reinforced an already existing notion, was that livestock is an important means of livelihood (in terms of income and security) for the resource poor households in drought-prone watersheds who depend on rain-fed mixed farming for their livelihoods. Keeping this fact in mind and looking at the knowledge base created as a result of the LEAD study, IWMI is also trying to develop actionable policy threads for further improving and incorporating livestock production in watershed development programmes. The aim is to take these suggested changes in policy, procedures, administrative instruments etc. to the stakeholders and the policy makers for feedback[2].

As part of the effort to develop policy recommendations based on the LEAD study, an earlier document in this series[3], based on state level policy reports prepared by the five partners, had identified the macro issues that need to be addressed in the context of livestock-environment-watershed interactions and recommended a need for greater synthesis between livestock and watershed development along with a few general policy recommendations.

This article adopts a rather different approach; it tries to look at the problem from a micro perspective. Using the specific study findings of the LEAD study for each of the five watersheds that were extensively surveyed as a foundation, it tries to arrive at specific interventions and improvements that would be useful for optimising the positive benefits and minimising the negative impact of watershed development on livestock and environment and *vice versa*. These interventions or improvements can be made at various levels—at the level of policy or operational and implementation procedures (administrative instruments) or in terms of awareness, training and capacity—building. But before moving on to the watershed-specific analysis let us once again briefly look at some of the main concerns in the livestock and watershed sectors that need to be addressed.

LIVESTOCK AND WATERSHED DEVELOPMENT: SOME ISSUES AND CONCERNS

One of the most important issues that seriously hampers livestock and watershed development is that the coordination among various government departments that work in related fields and between government and NGOs is not strong enough for a holistic development policy for an area to be adopted. The list of government departments itself is long enough (water resources, agriculture, animal husbandry, forests, panchayati raj, rural development, etc.,) and achieving effective coordination between them at the field level, middle level and the top level is not an easy task. Some efforts are being made in these regards and these efforts need to be strengthened. Only through such coordination will it be possible to include the crucial dimensions of livelihood dependence of poor on the livestock sector and the value of livestock assets in poverty reduction (especially small ruminants) in the watershed development strategy of the Government.

The importance of common property resources and pasturelands, for sustainable livestock activity in watersheds is also something that needs to be looked at. In many areas the common lands and pasturelands have been encroached and land for free grazing of livestock is not easily available. From the watershed point of view the degradation of land due to overgrazing and other such reasons also needs to be seriously addressed and there is a need for greater policy and ground-level interventions for controlled grazing and community management of common and revenue lands with clear usufruct rights regarding investments in biomass. The problem of encroachment is more complex, but various options for addressing this problem need to be explored as in low input-low-out-put livestock production systems community resources play a very important role. On a related note the problem of shortage of fodder and feed because of an inadequate fodder policy is another aspect that needs attention. Emphasis needs to be on developing common property resources;

productivity enhancement activities including diversification of crop patterns and fodder production in such a way that these pave the way for high value crop-livestock integrated mixed farming as an income generation activity in the rainfed areas. There is also a need for assessment and inclusion of livestock fodder rquirements in social forestry projects.

Treatment in resource scarce watersheds may introduce tradeoff between livestock and crop development, between upstream and downstream users, or between free grazing and stall-fed livestock. Long—term sustainability of natural resources and livelihood assets like livestock must be given a priority while planning watershed development programmes.

The importance of draught animals for marginal farming is something that has been neglected in India. Despite increasing mechanisation of traction, electrification of pumps and post harvest operations, draught animals still provide most of the power for marginal and small farmers in many semi—arid areas. A clear policy needs to be worked out for draught animals in areas where their use is still in vogue.

Though veterinary services are available and subsidised/free, accessibility and effectiveness (of these services) is still a problem area. In terms of infrastructure the number of veterinary hospitals, dispensaries, primary veterinary centres, mobile dispensaries, artificial insemination centres seem to be adequate, yet the returns on these investments have been very low and it seems to be a case of quantity over quality. There is a need to make efforts to increase the awareness of the benefits of health care among the livestock owners as well as to make timely and appropriate service available.

The government it seems has also not made too much effort to organise the livestock owners into user, self-help or beneficiary groups. Some organisations at district level do exist but there is a need to take them down to the watershed/ panchayat level for the livestock owners in semi-arid areas to give them a strong voice in the local decision-making process. Formation as a user group will allow the livestock owners to take advantage of institutional support, like credit, etc.

Market access for livestock producers also needs to be looked at. Except for areas where dairy cooperatives are very active and for large—scale poultry farming, the marketing of livestock and livestock products is not well organised. Effective use of Watershed Development Programmes and institutions created thereby needs to be made to build necessary linkages to develop and exploit markets for livestock and their products. The government does not seem to be playing a major role in livestock marketing and the livestock owners are mainly dependent on middlemen. The dependence on middlemen is especially acute in meat markets and serious policy interventions are required in this regard as the benefit to the actual producer is extremely low compared to the market price of meat.

Before turning to a micro-level watershed by watershed analysis based on the study of the selected watersheds under the LEAD project, it would be useful to look at the recommendations of Government of India guidelines regarding implementation structures and processes which were in force at the time of the field study (*i.e.*, in 2002, 2003).

INSTITUTIONAL AND ADMINISTRATIVE ARRANGEMENTS AS PER GOVERNMENT OF INDIA WATERSHED GUIDELINES[4]

The guidelines for watershed development had been revised in 2001 by the Department of Land Resources of the Ministry of Rural Development and circulated as the Guidelines for Watershed Development (Revised 2001)[5] (Also referred to as the common guidelines)

The common guidelines, as they had been revised and reformulated in 2001 in order to redress a number of emerging issueds, infused a greater degree of flexibility which made them easier to implement. The approach followed in the common guidelines aimed to bring people to the centre stage and push the administration towards a facilitating and assisting role.

The main institutional and administrative arrangements as prescribed in the common guidelines of 2001 can be summarised as follows:

1. A State Watershed Development Committee (SWDC) was constituted to ensure coordination among various government departments/institutions and voluntary agencies. This committee was to meet twice a year to monitor, review and evaluate the progress of implementation of watershed development programmes.
2. The Watershed Development Programmes were to be implemented through the Zila Parishads/District Rural Development Agencies (DRDAs).
3. To ensure coordination at the district level, a District Watershed Development Committee (DWDC) was constituted under the Chairman Zila Parishad or DRDA with a multi–source membership of officials and non-officials. The role of DWDC was to advise and assist the ZP/DRDA on matters regarding selection of Project Implementation Agencies (PIAs), and of members of Watershed Development Teams, as well as training, community organisation, etc. The committee was also supposed to approve the detailed action plan for watershed development projects in the district.
4. The Panchayati Raj Institutions (PRIs) had an important role to play in Watershed Development Programmes. The PRIs had the right to monitor and review the implementation of the programmes and provide guidance for improvements in the administrative arrangements and procedures with a view to ensuring convergence with other programmes of the Ministry of Rural Development. At the village level, the gram panchayat was to be involved in the implementation of the programme, especially in community organisation activities and in training programmes. The zila parishads, panchayat samitis and the gram panchayats were also entitled to take on the responsibility of implementing a cluster of watershed projects in the capacity of PIA, however in all such cases they had to follow norms prescribed for PIAs, under the guidelines and had to compete with other NGOs, GOs, or community based organisations or other support organisations to get selected as a PIA.

5. The projects at the field level were implemented by the Watershed Committees (WC) under the over all supervision and guidance of PIAs. PIAs were to normally be assigned 10-12 watershed projects covering an area ranging between 5,000-6,000 hectare and were to be responsible for appointment of the four-member Watershed Development Teams (WDT) for planning, implementing and reviewing of watershed programmes through village level organisations, and for maintenance of accounts. The PIAs were to be preferably selected from amongst PRIs, government departments or a reputed NGO, which had been active in the field of watershed development or any similar area of development.
6. The WDT had a minimum of four members, one each from the disciplines of forestry/plant science, animal sciences, civil/agricultural engineer and social sciences. The appointment of the WDT was to be completed within a period of two months from the date of nomination of PIA.
7. The common guidelines envisaged the following institutions at the village level in order to enable the communities to take up participatory watershed management:

   (*a*) Self-Help Groups (SHGs)—Constituted in the watershed area with the help of the WDT, these groups were to be homogenous groups having common identity who are dependent on the watershed but not owning land in the watershed areas such as agricultural labourers, shepherds, etc.

   (*b*) User Groups (UGs)—These groups were to consist of persons most likely to derive direct benefits from particular watershed work and holding land within the watershed areas. The UGs were to eventually take over the operation and maintenance of completed community works.

   (*c*) Watershed Associations (WAs)—Members of the community who are directly or indirectly dependent on a watershed area were organised into a WA, which should be a registered society as per Registration of Societies Act 1860. The WA was to meet at least twice a year to improve, monitor and review the watershed development plan, nominate members of the watershed committee, etc. Wherever a watershed was coterminous with a village panchayat, the gram sabha of the panchayat concerned could be designated as the Watershed Association.

   (*d*) Watershed Committee (WC)—The WC was to consist of members nominated by WA from amongst the user groups, self help groups, gram panchayat and a member of the WDT for carrying out the day-to-day activities of the watershed development project. Each WC was to have a secretary who was to be paid on an honorarium basis by the WA.

It may be added that many states had developed their own detailed guidelines based on the 2001 Common Guidelines. An example of this lies in the process guidelines for watershed development issued in 2002 by Government of Andhra Pradesh (*see* Diagram 1).

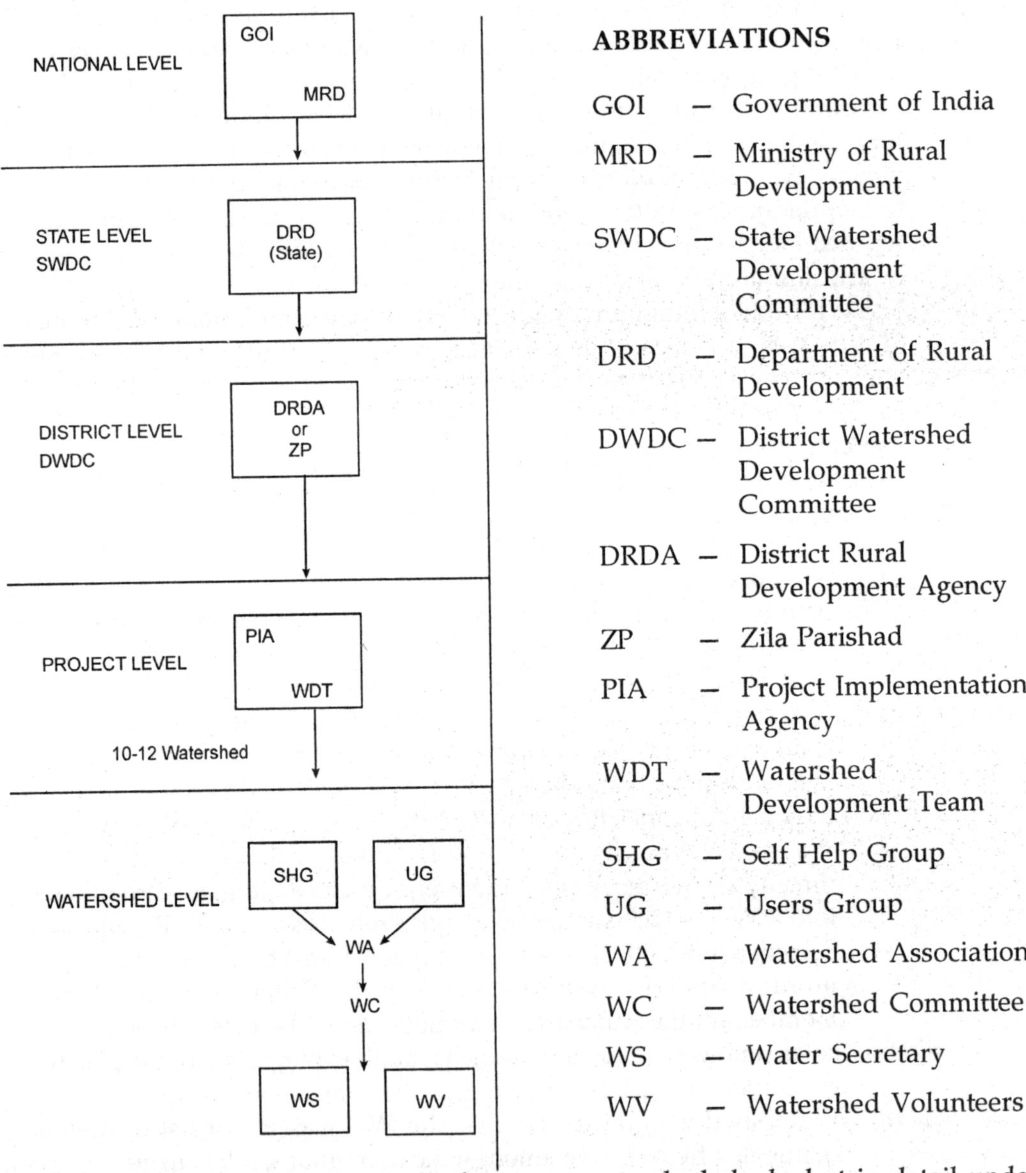

Let us turn our attention to the five meso-watersheds looked at in detail under the LEAD study.

THE LEAD STUDY WATERSHEDS

The five watersheds, which were part of the LEAD study, are Kalyanpur in Rajasthan, Kosgi in Andhra Pradesh, Ladki Nadi in Madhya Pradesh, Kanaknala in Karnataka and Vaiju Babulgaon in Maharashtra. The studies were undertaken at the meso-watershed scale and not at the 500 hectare advised for watershed development programmes in the government guidelines. Thus a number of project watersheds fell within the research area boundaries, which ranged in size between 3460 hectare and 13064 hectare. The Table 1 provides more details of the LEAD study watersheds.

Table 1: Summary Statistics of the Study Watersheds

Name of watershed	*V. Babulgaon*	*Kanakanala*	*Kalyanpur*	*Kosgi*	*Ladki Nadi*
State	Maharashtra	Karnataka	Rajasthan	A.P	M.P.
District (s)	Ahmednagar	Koppal	Udaipur	Mehbubnagar	Jhabua
LEAD partner	WOTR	Samuha	Sevamandir	WASSAN	Sampark
Implementing arrangement	NGO	GO-NGO to	NGO and GO NGO-CBO	GO	GO-NGO
Scale of watershed	4876 ha	13064 ha	7488 ha	3460 ha	5838 ha
Major focus	NRM	NRM	NRM	SWC	NRM
Average annual rainfall	430 mm	499 mm	584 mm	739 mm	1024 mm
Livestock intensity (ACU/ha)	0.99	1.39	1.54	0.71	1.56
Proportion of area treated	24%	43%	44%	56%	90%
Average HH income (Rs)	58,146 (52,285)	15,704 (11,135)	11,727 (11,227)	17,824 (25,687)	21,955 (21,522)
Average income from LS (Rs)	18,879 (29,852)	1,652 (2,835)	457 (2,021)	855 (2,684)	1,238 (3,495)
Livestock income as % of total	32.5%	10.5%	3.9%	4.8%	5.6%
LR/hh	3.21 (3.70)	3.04 (3.08)	4.39 (2.86)	2.45 (4.93)	3.59 (2.71)
SR/hh	4.24 (7.54)	6.48 (17.42)	6.29 (7.72)	1.04 (4.80)	2.53 (3.11)
Average no. of HH members	5.6 (2.34)	6.7 (2.5)	6.6 (2.18)	6.6 (2.58)	5.9 (1.95)
Caste	1% ST` 8.8%SC 8.8% BC 81.4% OC	10.6% ST 5.6%SC 70.6% BC 13.1% OC	94% ST 1.5% SC 4.5% OC	15% SC 67.5% BC 12.3% OC	87% ST 13% OC
Average education per HH (years)	5.14 (2.41)	1.61 (1.71)	2.69 (2.29)	3.12 (2.38)	2.27 (2.34)
Average landholding (acres)	5.40 (7.84)	8.89 (7.75)	2.64 (4.31)	3.10 (5.12)	3.72 (4.13)
Average irrigated area (acres)	0.38 (1.01)	0.92 (2.75)	0.78 (1.29)	1.25 (3.23)	2.19 (2.61)
% Irrigated area	7%	10.4%	29.5%	40.3%	58.9%
Local wage agricultural labour men (Rs/day)	57 (14.13)	38 (23.15)	44 (6.63)	48 (4.86)	23 (7.64)
City wage agricultural labor men (Rs/day)	96 (17.45)	55 (16.21)	65 (25.01)	74 (16.5)	36 (16.06)

Source: Lead Household survey, 2004. Figures in parentheses are standard deviations.

It would be best to look at the main characteristics and the livestock-environment-watershed interaction within each of the study watersheds separately and also suggest some possible intervention for each case, as the watersheds vary not only in terms of their biophysical conditions but also in terms of their socio-economic setting.

Kalyanpur

Kalyanpur has very poor biophysical conditions with a terrain that is hilly and steep, and prone to erosion. Cultivation is only possible in valleys and downstream areas. Only a small part of the total area has been treated and the open wells make main source of irrigation. Given the conditions, the overall biomass is not very low, but still in terms of robustness of the watershed as defined in the LEAD Study, Kalyanpur was ranked fifth and last among the five watersheds studied.

Despite the poor biophysical conditions, the livestock density in Kalyanpur is high with 1.27 large ruminants and 1.30 small ruminants per hectare. In terms of livestock population per household the figure for Kalyanpur is 4.16 large ruminants and 4.76 small ruminants. Eightysix per cent of the households own small ruminants while 93 per cent of the households own large ruminants. Among the 200 households surveyed the specific livestock holdings were as follows—bullock (166), indigenous cattle (134), buffalo (97), goat (158) and sheep (46). None of the households owned any crossbred cattle and breed improvement among indigenous breeds is not common either. During 2002-2003, Kalyanpur witnessed a significant decline in goat population and this can be attributed to disease, drought and fodder shortages in the watershed.

Looking at the determinants of livestock holding, total irrigated area, number of household members and downstream location seem to be important factors in determining large ruminant holdings in Kalyanpur. For small ruminants holding, availability of fallow lands seem to be an important factor, while lower castes seem to have a greater tendency to keep goats and sheep. There is also a link between availability of common lands and small ruminant holding. In Kalyanpur forestlands outside the village are sometimes used for grazing and villages that have large forest and non-arable areas have greater livestock density.

The household survey conducted in Kalyanpur reviled no landless families. The holding of large ruminants seems to be concentrated among the semi-medium and medium farmers. The marginal and small landholders keep greater number of small ruminants than large ruminants, but again the greatest concentration is between the medium and large landowners.

Kalyanpur is a watershed where the livestock plays a very important role as during summer the main occupation of 55 per cent of the household members is looking after the livestock.

In the form of subsistence farming that exists in Kalyanpur no fodder (except for drought relief) can be imported from outside. All the feed needs to come from within the watershed itself. There is little fodder production in the watershed. Farmers mainly depend on grass grown during the kharif season, crop residues and grazing on own land and common properties (contours and bunds). During summer, grazing on neighbours' fallow pasture also takes place.

In terms of cash income the contribution of livestock in Kalyanpur is very low (4% of the total income) and most of it comes from sale of animals. But livestock does provide security and liquid assets during the regular droughts and production for self-consumption. Also as the large number of bullocks suggests livestock is an important source of draught power in Kalyanpur. Manure is another product of livestock and in Kalyanpur an astonishing 91 per cent of the manure is collected and mostly used as fertilizer in the fields.

The people of Kalyanpur have almost zero access to organised livestock markets. Villagers still prefer to purchase livestock from *Banjaras* or within the village. Due to non-availability of formal credit, villagers seem to depend on moneylenders or family/ friends for credit with interest rates around five per cent per month. In normal circumstances loans are not taken for livestock production.

Of the five watersheds studied, Kalyanpur has the lowest costs associated with the production of various livestock species, but this also has a direct bearing with the low level of health care for animals in the area.

On the question of gender roles in livestock production, Kalyanpur is a very clear example of women shouldering the bulk of the load, i.e. milking, cleaning, feeding and collecting manure, associated with keeping livestock, with the men having a monopoly over the transportation of animals.

Let us now explore some policy and administrative instruments that may be used to enhance the livestock productivity in Kalyanpur.

SUGGESTED INTERVENTIONS IN KALYANPUR

As we have seen the livestock in Kalyanpur are mainly dependent on feed produced within the watershed, as such common property resources and pasturelands become very important, as they are the main grazing source for the animals and a direct relationship between and the availability of common land and number of ruminants per household can be observed. But over time most of the arable common property has been encroached leading to greater pressure on pasturelands and the still remaining common properties like contours and bunds as well as the forests being used for grazing (leading to degradation associated with overgrazing). For the sustainable development of livestock and other natural resources in the area the issue of common property needs to be addressed as a priority. Some methods to tackle this rather problematic issue are given here:

- *Option A*—Officially lease out the encroached area to the person illegally occupying it for a basic sum of money and for a fixed tenure after which he/ she will have the option of either buying the land or once again re-leasing it as common land. The money collected in this fashion could be used to develop the remaining pastureland, grow subsidised fodder and other biomass development activities.
- *Option B*—Regularise the encroachment on condition that though the ownership rights will be transferred to the current occupier, a certain portion

of the land would be used for growing fodder and a certain portion be allowed to remain fallow for grazing activities. The PRI or the watershed institutions could be used to govern this process.

- *Option C*—Try to get the encroachment removed and get the land *de-facto* back into the common property resource pool.

Given the political problems involved in dealing with common resources, it may be the best, in an area like Kalyanpur where cash incomes are not very high, to give option A and B to all the people who are encroaching land that the official records show as common property. This method will help to clearly define the land titles, improve feed availability and also contribute to the development of cultivable wastelands within the watershed.

The coordination among the various government functionaries working for development within the watershed is also not as good as it should be. Though in name there exists a WDT consisting of animal husbandry and agriculture experts along with a hydrological/civil engineer and a social scientist, they are in no way responsible to the project coordinator of the project implementing agency, nor is the project coordinator in a position to judge the usefulness and applicability of suggestions made by the various functionaries. Fig. 1 demonstrates the existing set-up in Kalyanpur.

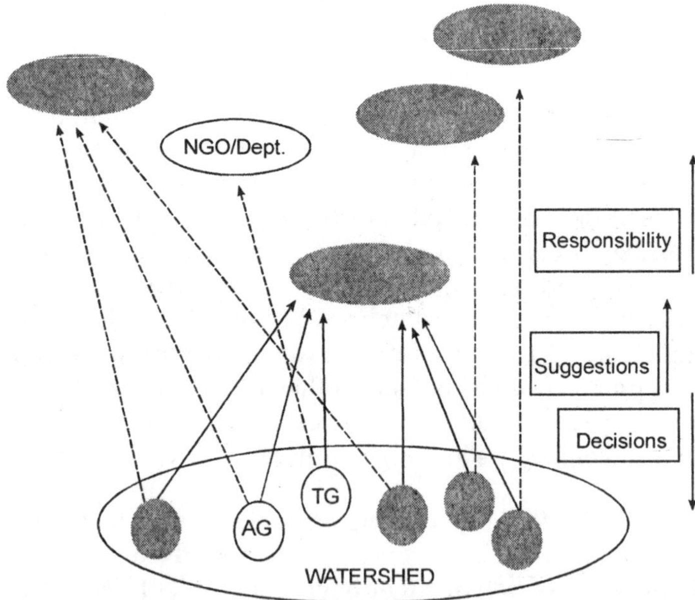

Note: AH—Animal Husbandry, AG-Agriculture, TG-Training, EN-Engineering, WE-Watershed Committee, PRI-Pancyayati Raj Institution, ZP-Zila Parishad.

Fig. 1

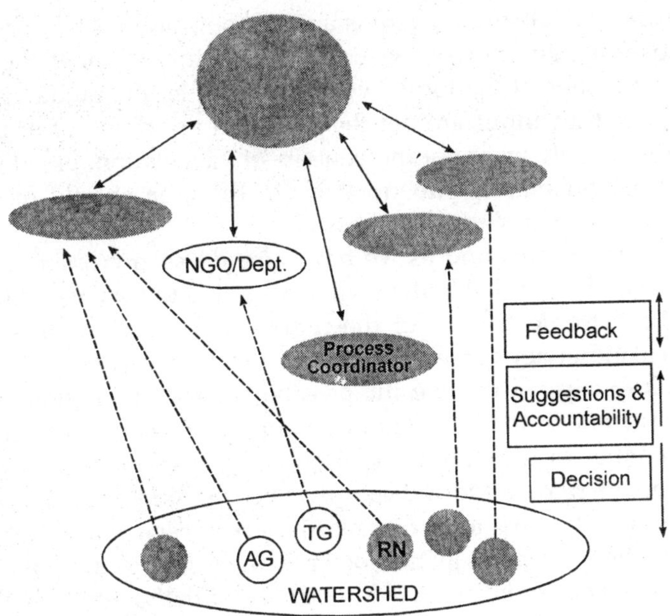

Note: AH—Animal Husbandry, AG-Agriculture, TG-Training, EN-Engineering, WE-Watershed Committee, PRI-Pancyayati Raj Institution, ZP-Zila Parishad.

Fig. 2

As the Fig. 2 demonstrates the responsibility and accountability of the field level functionaries are not interlinked with their duties in watershed development, the existing model post project sustainability suffers as the activities undertaken as part of the watershed development may have little linkage with the activities planned by the government departments like animal husbandry, agriculture or forests. In order to improve coordination and post project sustainability, a slightly modified setup is being suggested.

The suggested structure would allow for greater continuity between project and post project activities in the watershed area, allow for inputs from all concerned government departments and other involved parties as well as make the field level functionaries indirectly accountable to the project coordinator.

Along with the implementation set-up another factor that hampers livestock development in the Kalyanpur watershed is that there is no core budget for livestock available as part of the watershed development programme. Also it is difficult to undertake a plethora of activities on the limited watershed budget of Rs. 6,000 per hectare. Greater coordination with the animal husbandry department would allow for their budget to be used as a supplement to the livestock budget in an integrated manner. This would also make it possible to organise a greater number of health camps, as has been the demand and need in Kalyanpur.

On the topic of healthcare, the lowest field level functionary is the point of contact with the people and in Kalyanpur there is a need to improve his capacity as well as empower his position. The person needs to be capable to meet the needs of the people and take decisions at the local level. For example, the medicines available to the vet looking after Kalyanpur are not the ones that are required at the local level. Also villagers are not fully aware of the benefits of vaccination, breed improvement, etc., and the animal husbandry functionaries in the area should make use of the watershed institutions to spread awareness.

Kalyanpur is a tribal area and as we have already seen crossbreds are not very common in the area. Most probably they will not be able to survive within the limited resources and the extreme climate of the region. But there exists a possibility of improving the local indigenous breeds to improve productivity. The animal husbandry department needs to explore the specific possibilities for this region.

The low cash income from livestock in Kalyanpur can be attributed to some extent on the non-availability of a market. The high number of goat population and the equally high turnover rate would indicate that buying and selling does take place, though mostly locally. If access to an organised market, especially meat market could be provided, with the watershed institutions playing a role in maintaining price and quality, the income levels in the area could rise substantially. Similarly the watershed development programme-based institutions should also play an important role in making credit available at low interest rates.

KOSGI

Kosgi has a flat terrain and not much erosion. There are several tanks in the watershed, though most of them are not perennial. Irrigation levels are high (40% of cultivated area) with tanks being used in the rabi season and bore-well irrigation in summer and early kharif. In terms of the robustness of the watershed, Kosgi has by far the greatest biophysical potential among the studied watersheds, but despite livestock favourable conditions, the villagers seem to prefer agriculture and migration labour as their main sources of income and employment.

Interestingly in contrast to Kalyanpur, despite good biophysical conditions, the livestock density in Kosgi is much lower (.58 large ruminants per hectare and .65 small ruminants per hectare). Also only 14 per cent of the households own small ruminants while the corresponding figure for large ruminants is 35 per cent. The livestock holdings as per the household survey are as follows—bullock (70), indigenous cattle (30), crossbred cattle (2), buffalo (41), sheep (1) and goat (26). As seen some crossbred cattle are there in the watershed but farmers are not too interested in breed improvement due to lack of awareness. Kosgi witnessed a moderate increase in livestock populations during 2002-2003.

The determinants of livestock holding in Kosgi can also be contrasted with Kalyanpur as the availability of total irrigated area is a strong negative factor for keeping livestock, especially large ruminants. The number of household members is a positive factor for keeping livestock, both small and large. This may be linked to the fact that a number of the smaller families migrate during off-season for work.

The large landholders are also the main owners of large ruminants with a staggering 29 large ruminants per household among large farmers. A significant number of the landless also own small ruminants and the small ruminant population seems to be more concentrated among the landless, marginal, small and the semi-medium farmers with the large land holders owning no small ruminants.

Livestock again is not one of the main sources of cash income in the area (only 5%) with the bulk of the income coming from agriculture and wage labour. Milk is the main livestock product that is sold with buffaloes playing an important role here. The bullock is also a minor source of income in contributing in terms of rental income and manure (though only 37% of the manure is collected) along with the self-consumption of its draught power.

Grazing and crop residues are the main sources of animal feed in Kosgi. In fact crop residues are very critical in Kosgi and in their non-availability farmers tend to sell their livestock. The availability of crop residue has also been going down over time, as farmers have tended to shift towards cash crops like red gram. Fodder cultivation is undertaken by only a few select buffalo owners in Sampally village in Kosgi. Grazing takes place mostly in own lands/pastures and contour bunds, as there is an acute shortage of common land in Kosgi. Most of the common land is encroached, with neither the villagers nor the panchayat having any control.

Out of the five watersheds, Kosgi is one of the two (V. Babugaon being the other) having good access to the market (as well as access to chilling plants and being on the milk route). But compared to V. Babugaon (as we shall see later) the development in Kosgi has been minimal. Some farmers have reported that the markets have deteriorated in the recent past and are exploited by middlemen in the absence of formal control of state/other organisations. In Kosgi SHG seem to have helped in dairy production. Access to some form of credit also exists in Kosgi with over eight per cent of the surveyed households having taken loans specifically for livestock production. Moneylenders are the main source of credit though bank/SHG/farmers association credit also seems to be available.

The cost associated with livestock production in Kosgi, though higher than the subsistence based on livestock production in Kalyanpur, is still low. Regarding health care, in a couple of villages a Gopal Mitra and a livestock activist team are present but mainly the livestock rearers seem to follow their own control and preventive measures.

SUGGESTED INTERVENTIONS FOR KOSGI

Kosgi is a watershed where conditions are perfect for large-scale livestock production; high biophysical potential in terms of rainfall and vegetation, access to market and credit, availability of some kind of animal healthcare; but for some reason animal husbandry has failed to take off in this watershed. The focus of any intervention in Kosgi has to be to kick start the livestock sector in Kosgi and make it a major economic activity. Along with the need to look at the problem of common property resources and greater coordination among the various government and NGO functionaries working in the watershed, as already outlined for Kalyanpur and also applicable for Kosgi, the suggested interventions should be around the following four areas—creation of awareness about the potential of livestock rearing, market integration, breed improvement, and fodder cultivation. The Fig. 3 lists some of the possible intervention.

DEVELOPING LIVESTOCK IN KOSGI

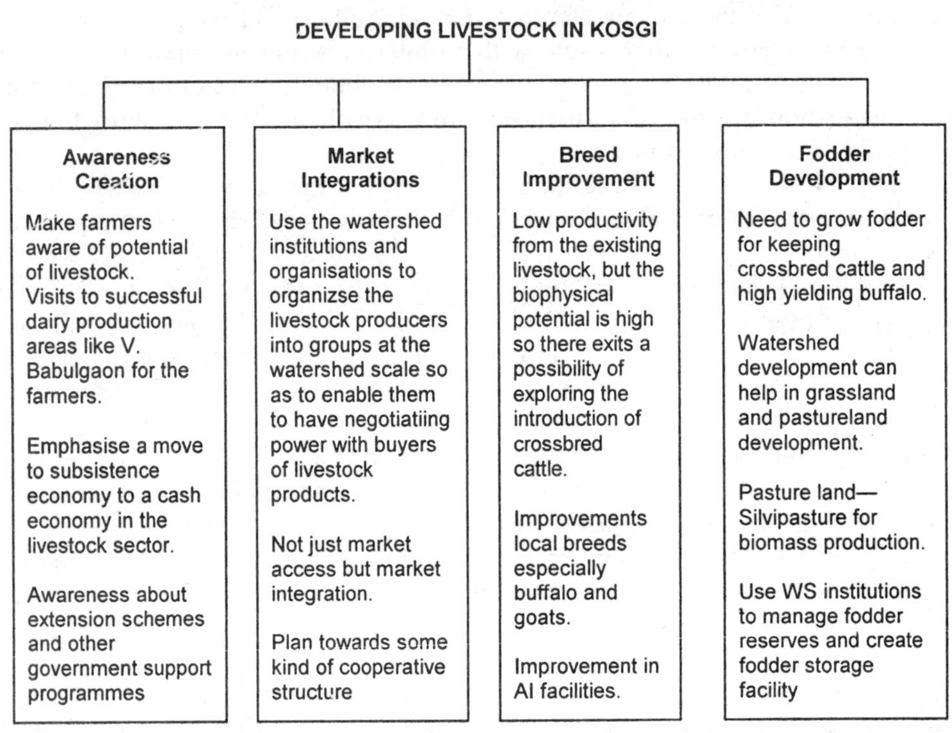

Fig. 3

Ladki Nadi

Inspite of good climatic conditions the overall biomass in Ladki Nadi is low with little horticulture or shrub lands. Deforestation has had an impact on the area and the terrain is also poor. Midstream areas are rainfed while there is irrigation in the in the downstream areas where soils are also good. Tanks are the most important source of irrigation but in some cases bore wells are also used. The entire area has been treated and the difference in soil fertility and water access between the upstream and downstream is noticeable; upper caste farmers inhabit the downstream areas and are much better off than the tribals in the upstream areas. In the robustness of the watershed indicator, developed during the LEAD study, Ladki Nadi was rated second overall but when greater weightage is given to terrain and vegetation than climate its position falls to third.

Ladki Nadi has the highest livestock density out of five watersheds studied. The density of large ruminants is 1.29 per hectare while that of small ruminants, mainly consisting of goats, is 1.35 per hectare. Looking at livestock per household one notices that the number for small ruminant at 3.91 per household is impressive. Among the household surveyed 58 per cent owned small ruminants and 86 per cent large ruminants. Specific livestock-wise holdings were as follows—bullock (153), indigenous cattle (96), cross breed cattle (11), buffalo (84), sheep (2), goat (124). Ladki Nadi is the only watershed where efforts at breed improvement of small ruminants have been made. Ladki Nadi has shown across the board increase in livestock holding during 2002-2003.

The determinants of livestock holding in Ladki Nadi are very interesting. The location in a watershed is a negative determinant for keeping both large and small ruminants, with the tribals in the upstream hilly areas preferring to keep livestock and the farmers in the irrigated plains less inclined to do so. Social position also is an important factor in determining small ruminant holdings, which are concentrated among the tribals.

The highest number for the average large ruminant holding per household among the landless category is in Ladki Nadi (exactly 1.0), though the number is much greater for medium and large landholders (7.71 and 6.0 respectively). Interestingly the landless own no small ruminants, which seem to be evenly distributed among the marginal, small and semi-medium farmers with a much greater holding per household among the large farmers.

In Ladki Nadi again crop residues and grazing on own pasturelands are the main sources of food for the animals as there is relatively little grazing land and the forestland is degraded.

Crops provide 81 per cent of the cash income in Ladki Nadi, and livestock only six per cent with milk contributing highest livestock income in 62.2 per cent of the houses and manure in 30.03 per cent (this is the highest contribution to livestock income from manure among all the five watersheds—82 per cent of the manure is collected and out of this almost one-sixth is used as fuel. The figure for fuel use of manure is very high compared to the other watersheds). In view of the above it is no surprise that the main determinants of livestock income in Ladki Nadi are the buffalo and the bullock.

Easy access to markets is restricted to a couple of villages, which are nearer to the towns and as such are more active in dairy production. Again there exist no formal markets for meat. Bank loans are available but the householders need to approach moneylenders for large amounts.

The costs associated with production of various livestock in Ladki Nadi are higher than Kalyanpur and Kosgi but lower than Kanaknala and considerably lower than V.Babulgaon. Regarding healthcare, a vet has been trained as part of the watershed project and is providing services at low costs.

SUGGESTED INTERVENTIONS IN LADKI NADI

Ladki Nadi is a watershed where the differences between the upstream and downstream are visibly acute. Traditionally the poorer tribals have lived in the upper areas and the richer farmers in the fertile land downstream and the watershed treatment had made this difference even greater with the soil fertility and water availability improving considerably in the lower areas. Any intervention in the area should ideally address the problems faced by the tribals. Some suggestions for Ladki Nadi are as follows:

1. Greater focus on rainfed plantations and vegetative cover as well focus on reforestation efforts to increase biomass in the area. Deforestation has had a severe impact in Ladki Nadi and the primary focus of the Watershed Development Programme now should be to counter this impact. Rainfed plantations and vegetative cover will also help in providing greater grazing area for the livestock. Simultaneous efforts to develop the remaining common lands and the pasturelands should also be taken up and these should be placed under the control of the PRI or the institutions created as part of the watershed programmes.
2. There is a great potential in developing the meat market in Ladki Nadi and this is an activity that will benefit the tribals the most. Currently, the tribals sell their livestock to middlemen at very low rates. A formally organised market with the support of the government and the watershed institutions would be very beneficial for the tribals. Credit at low interest rate should also be made available to the inhabitants to assist them in the market integration activities. At the same time possibilities of the expansion of the milk market should also be considered.
3. Along with the development of grazing areas, stricter norms related to free grazing of livestock and use of forest produce need to be enforced in the watershed.
4. The introduction of a vet as part of the project is a good step. This needs to be carried forward and options for greater coordination with the Animal Husbandry Department need to be looked at along with the organisation of health camps and a focus on animal vaccination. Breed improvement should also be considered. Some crossbred cattle are there in the area and based on how they have fared strategies for increasing their population in the area should be formed. But large-scale breed improvement in the tribal areas may not be possible.

Vaiju Babulgaon

Vaiju Babulgaon has a steep hill range as the upstream border of the watershed and plains in the downstream area. Treatment has taken place in the upstream areas but rainfed agriculture dominates with the irrigated area being low. In the downstream areas a decent amount of vegetation growth can be found and the biomass is fair with protected shrub lands on the slope. The wastelands are affected by erosion and grazing pressure. On the watershed robustness indicator index used for the study Viju Babulgaon was ranked third behind Kosgi and Ladki Nadi.

The livestock population density in V. Babulgaon is not very high but productivity per unit livestock is very high because of the presence of a large number of high yielding crossbred cattle and the resulting dairy activities. The density of large ruminants per hectare is .81 and that of small ruminants .90. The large ruminant holding per household is 2.63 and small ruminant holding 2.98. 67 per cent of the households own small ruminants and 78 per cent of the households own large ruminants. While looking at the number of specific livestock in the households surveyed one can clearly see the higher number of crossbred cattle in V. Babulgaon as compared to the other watersheds. The specific livestock numbers are as follows—bullocks (98), indigenous cattle (39), crossbred cattle (99), buffalo (17), sheep (4) and goat (142). Almost 50 per cent of the households in V. Babulgaon own crossbred cattle, though the number has gone down during 2002-2003 due to drought.

Total irrigated area is an important positive determinant for keeping large ruminants, as is the number of household members. Livestock density in a village is also an important determinant for large ruminants and chances of keeping a large ruminant in a village that already has a large number of livestock are higher. The determinants for small ruminant holding are very similar to the determinants of large ruminant holding in V. Babulgaon.

Some landless in V. Babulgaon do keep large ruminants as cattle is mainly stall-fed and therefore land is not a prerequisite for keeping them. As expected the medium and large farmers are the ones keeping the maximum number of large ruminants per household. The landless, marginal, small, semi-medium and the medium farmers, all keep a significant number of small ruminants per household.

In terms of occupation livestock is very important as between 17-28 per cent of the time (depending on the season of the year) the main occupation of household members is looking after the livestock.

With the livestock incomes in V. Babulgaon being high, it no longer represents the general feed source structure of the subsistence livestock production systems and fodder and crop residues are also imported into the watershed. Cut and carry and stall-feeding are widely practiced and strict rules are enforced. Supplements are also used for the dairy animals. But overall own pastures/contour bunds and own crop residues remain the main food sources for the animals with the goats being heavily dependent on grazing on the contour bunds.

During the study year 2003-2004, livestock was the most important cash income source in V. Babulgaon contributing 33 per cent of the total income. Milk and sale of animal were the two main sources of income for most of the households and the contribution of crossbred cattle is very significant here. Overall livestock income and income per unit livestock is also very high in V. Babulgaon.

V. Babulgaon benefits immensely from integration with the market and access to the chilling plant. The management of the market by co-operative institutions have also allowed the inhabitants of the watershed to be able to bypass the middlemen and all the disadvantages that come along with them. The adoption of crossbreeds in V. Babulgaon is a direct impact of the dairy development in the area.

With livestock being a major source of income, loans for livestock are not uncommon in V. Babulgaon. Over 26 per cent of the households surveyed had taken loans for livestock production; most of them from co-operative bodies or banks.

As can be accepted with the presence of crossbred cattle, the costs associated with cattle production in V. Babulgaon are almost ten times the cost in Kalyanpur. For other animals also the costs are considerably higher.

Healthcare-wise, mostly traditional medicines are used for the livestock and only a few farmers seek veterinary treatment for the animals because of the costs involved.

SUGGESTED INTERVENTIONS FOR VAIJU BABULGAON

The livestock production system in V. Babulgaon is very robust even though the biophysical conditions are not ideal. There really is no need to tamper with a successful model that V. Babulgaon has for livestock so the focus of any intervention should be on developing the biophysical potential of the region. But as a cautionary note one needs to make sure that in the future dairy production remains linked with the sustainable development process of the area and does not run away on its own steam. For this cooperation and coordination between the dairy co-operatives, animal husbandry department and the other functionaries and institutions that are part of the watershed development process needs to remain strong.

Another danger that V. Babulgaon needs to protect itself against is degradation of land due to overgrazing. For this the watershed institutions, with heavy fines, should strictly enforce the existing rules regarding grazing and cut and carry.

The focal point of the watershed activities should be wasteland development as this may provide extra land for fodder/grass cultivation in the long run and will anyway lower the erosion potential of the area.

V. Babulgaon has comparatively low rainfall and a steep incline therefore it is essential that the water harvesting processes are efficient and more importantly the stored water (surface or ground) is available to all the villagers during times of water stress. As V. Babulgaon suffers frequent droughts, the idea of increasing tank storage capacity should also be given a thought.

Kanaknala

The Kanaknala watershed in Karnataka is characterised by low rainfall and high evaporation. Both the fertile black and the red soil can be found in this watershed but the surface stoniness and gravel amount are also very high. Upstream treatment has led to some groundwater level increase in the downstream areas. Though irrigation is still limited, bore well use for irrigation is increasing. The wastelands are highly degraded and the overall biomass/vegetative cover in this watershed is very low. Kanaknala was ranked fourth on the roboustness of watershed indicator used in the LEAD study.

Like Kalyanpur, Kanaknala too has low biophysical potential but a high livestock density, especially in terms of small ruminants. The figure for large ruminants per hectare is .71 and for small ruminants 3.40. On an average a household owns 3.20 large ruminants and 10.85 small ruminants. It is interesting to note that despite the high density of small ruminants only 34 per cent of the households surveyed owned small ruminants. The corresponding figure for large ruminants was 67 per cent. The numbers for specific livestock among the surveyed households were as follows—bullocks (130), indigenous cattle (93), crossbred cattle (1), buffalo (33), sheep (41) and goat (48). It should be noted here that all the goats and sheep reported here are from one village within the watershed itself. Kanaknala recorded substantial growth in all livestock populations except crossbred cattle in spite of drought year in 2002-03.

The number of people in a household seems to a positive determinant for keeping large ruminants, but it is a negative determinant for small livestock holding. Exactly opposite is the case of household income being below lower than the average watershed income where it is a negative factor for keeping large ruminants; it is a very strong positive determinant for keeping small ruminants. This suggests that the poorer people generally tend to keep the smaller ruminants and this is corroborated by the fact that high caste is a negative determinant for small ruminant holding.

As per the information collected in the household survey, even the landless households in Kanaknala keep 3.36 small ruminants on average. The concentration of large ruminants per households is much greater among the medium and the large farmers.

Community grazing and crop residues are the important sources of feed for the animals in Kanaknala with little or no grazing taking place in own pastures of contour bunds. Unlike the other watersheds, the large ruminants in Kanaknala are also allowed and left for free grazing.

The cash income contribution of livestock is slightly higher in Kanaknala (11%) compared to the previous three watersheds. Manure is the main source of livestock income in over 30 per cent of the houses, but sale of animals and milk also make important contributions.

Some parts of Kanaknala do have access to markets, but in other villages the situation is not very good. As per the survey, 6.21 per cent of the households had taken loans for livestock production. The main source of the credit were the SHGs, which seem to be active in the area.

The costs associated with livestock production in Kanaknala appear to be on the higher side and this could be probably accounted for by the higher use of veterinary and animal health services.

SUGGESTED INTERVENTIONS IN KANAKNALA

The Kanaknala watershed has low biomass cover but a large livestock population with the lower income group holding a large number of goats. The amount of non-irrigated land is also very high. The interventions in Kanaknala should follow a two-path approach in order to achieve holistic development in the area (*a*) intensive water harvesting to increase the water storage in the area, bring more land under irrigation, and develop the vegetative cover in the area; and (*b*) develop clear and organised linkages in terms of producer→processor→consumer channels and a strong livestock market.

(*a*) *Intensive water harvesting*—Kanaknala receives very little rainfall and most of the area is rainfed only. But the soil is fertile. So it would be advisable to build water-harvesting structures not just as per requirements of the watershed drainage system but also as per need at the village level. The village level structures will not only help to increase the water storage in the area, but also provide direct and visible benefits and are thus likely to be better maintained. These structures will also provide contours for grazing the livestock and take the pressure away from the remaining commons/ forest/pasture land (Kanaknala is the only watershed where grazing on contour bunds and own fields is not the key source of feed for the livestock).

(*b*) The small ruminant owners within the watershed need to be organised for them to take full advantage of the market and derive a substantial income from livestock. Clear controls governing pricing of animals and quality controls need to be put in place so that the livestock rearers do not remain at the mercy of the middle men. It would be best for Kanaknala if milk and meat marketing were treated as key livelihood activities of the villagers within the watershed development programme itself.

REFERENCES

1. For more detailed information about the LEAD study and its findings see (insert correct ref later) IWMI, Patencheru, *Livestock – Environment Interactions in Watersheds: Some Preliminary Results from the Study*, 2004.
2. In this regard a Policy Round Table was organised with the Rajasthan Government on 10th August 2004. More Round Tables with other state governments and a National Workshop are also planned.
3. Rakshat Hooja "Towards a Policy for Livestock in Watershed Development Programmes Livestock-Environment-Watershed Interactions in India: A Draft Document based on Five State Level Studies", IWMI 2004 unpublished paper LEAD Project IWMI, Patancheru, July 2004. Also see Rakshat Hooja "The Need for Synergies Between Watershed and Livestock Policies" forthcoming in *Social Change*.
4. This section is based upon Rakesh Hooja and Rakshat Hooja "The Changing Role of Panchayat Bodies in Watershed Development" paper presented at National Seminar on Panchayats at Madhya Pradesh Institute of Social Science Research" Ujjain in December 2003, and being published in the seminar volume D.C. Shah and Y.K. Sisodia (ed.) *A Decade of Panchayati Raj in India*, forthcoming, Rawat Publications; this paper was also invited for Tata-IWMI Partnership Annual Researchers Meet on Water at Anand from 17 to 19 February 2004 and discussed in a session on watershed development.
5. The Haryali Guidelines of 2003, which made the Panchayati Raj Institutions responsible for Watershed Development Programmes, had not yet come into force while the detailed study of the selected watersheds was being carried out under the LEAD study of IWMI.

12

Wasteland Development, Environmental Protection and the Poor*

N.C. Saxena

The Term wasteland in India refers to such degraded land which has deteriorated for lack of appropriate water and soil management, but which can be brought under vegetative cover with reasonable effort.[1] Out of a total geographical area of 329 m ha, the area of culturable wasteland is considered to be 84 m ha.[2] This includes 36 m ha of forest degraded land, a similar area which is privately owned or encroached upon, and the rest is under the control of Revenue Departments, which is used as open access lands and for grazing by the village communities. This article discusses only forest and revenue wastelands, as regeneration of private degraded lands through agro-forestry raises entirely different kind of policy issues.

Indian forests are capable of producing at least 2 cubic metres of wood per ha per year[3], as against the present productivity of 0.47 cubic metres. For the other category of degraded land, the Agriculture Finance Corporation (a Government of India Undertaking) estimated[4] that an investment of Rs. 9 to 15,000 per ha (including overheads) in irrigation, soil improvement and protection would increase the productivity of vast blocks of village wastelands from almost nil at present to four to eight cum per ha per year.

Deforestation and low productivity of public lands has caused immense harm to the poor who depend on these sources. Unfortunately, changes in gathering by the poor are not reflected in the Gross National Product, and, hence, do not attract the attention of the policy-makers.

---

* Views expressed are personal, and do not bind the organisation for which the author works, or has worked in the past. The ideas presented in this article have been analysed in greater depth in the books. *To the Hands of the Poor: Water and Trees*, by Robert Ghambers, N.C. Saxena, and Tushaar Shah, being published by Oxford and IBH, New Delhi, and Intermediate Technology Group, London.

ANALYSIS OF PRESENT POLICIES

Reasons for low productivity of forest and revenue lands, and consequent harm to the poor, are several and complex, we describe some of them.

As compared to agriculture, uncultivated lands got a very low priority in development plans. Before 1980, the share of forestry was less than one per cent of the development budget, whereas agriculture got between 20 to 24 per cent. A *laissez faire* policy was followed with respect to revenue lands. There was neither any fund allocation for them, nor was any specific government department made responsible for grasses and pasture development.

OLD FOREST POLICY

The 1952 National Forest Policy declared that village community should in no event be permitted to use forests at the cost of 'national interest', which was identified with defence, communications and vital industries. It stated that national forests should be used to produce valuable timber for industry and other national purpose.

In Kerala, for instance, 1.5 lakh ha of area between 1970-80 was brought under man-made plantations replacing mixed forests.[5] This policy deprived the poor of the livelihood goods that they used to get from mixed forests. Till 1981, Karnataka supplied eucalyptus to the paper industries at Rs. 24 per tonne,[6] when the cheapest wood in the market sold for Rs. 300 a tonne.

Neglect of people's demands during 1960-80 exacerbated biotic pressure which made regeneration of natural forests further difficult. The ratio of firewood to foodgrain price doubled in 1975-85 which made headloading an attractive economic activity leading to further deforestation.

Social Forestry Policy

Social Forestry programmes, although extremely successful in terms of wood production, could not achieve its social objectives. Between 1980-87, the Government claims to have raised 18,865 million trees. If survival rate is assumed to be 60 per cent, the average number of new trees per village (the number of villages in the country is around six lakh) since 1980 comes to 18,865! This is by all means an impressive achievement. The impact of economic activity of such a magnitude is already being felt in the pole and pulp market. However, a recent note prepared by the NWDB admits that there has been a big gap between the stated objectives and the actual outcome as shown in Table 1.

Rights and Distribution Policy

People are far from fully informed about what they can legally collect from forests, and what is prohibited. A government evaluation of tribal districts[7] revealed that out of 767 trebles interviewed, only 145 said that they had the right to the collection of timber from forests for making agriculture implements, 222 could send their cattle for grazing, 143 said that they had no rights in forests and the rest did not know the precise position for sure in this regard.

Table 1: Stated objectives and actual outcome in social forestry projects

S. No.	*Stated Objective*	*Actual Outcome*
1.	Produce fuelwood and fodder	Market oriented trees were planted which did not improve consumption within the village. Fodder trees were generally ignored. As spacing was kept low to accommodate more trees to meet the targets, grass production suffered.
2.	Reduce pressure on reserved forest land	As demand of the poor for fuelwood and fodder was not met from projects, pressure on forest land continues unabated.
3.	Regenerate wastelands, hills, barren slopes and eroded terrains	Trees have come up on farm land, specially irrigated land, and strips belonging to government. Block plantation on degraded wasteland had low priority and survival rate remained poor. 'Wasteland Development' was the slogan, tree farming the reality.
4.	Involve community in management	Communities were generally not given government funds. Instead, Forest Department raised trees on common lands which were seen as government trees. Problem of handing over these plantations to Panchayats remains unsolved.
5.	Help the poor through improved access to forestry products, and higher incomes through asset creation	Participation of small farmers in farm forestry has remained poor. Diversion of land from agriculture to forestry reduced employment opportunities, specially for women. Tribal areas, where dependence on forest is acute, were generally ignored in social forestry projects. Raising of MFP trees and strengthening the position of 'gatherers' were not the objectives of the projects.

In social forestry projects, rights to trees and procedures for marketing and allocating benefits have not been defined or established, or these have not been publicised.

Several villagers, when asked as late as in 1988 in Karnataka about distribution[8] said, "We know nothing about this". Even forestry officials disagreed with each other about the rules. The share which would go to the individuals, village, mandal panchayat and the Forest Department (FD) were not clearly laid down in Karnataka till 1988.

A government evaluation of Orissa Social Forestry Project[9] indicated that 82 per cent of the villages did not know how the produce from village woodlots would be distributed. Most of the people did not expect any share from the final output. They looked upon such woodlots as another category of reserved forests. Wide variation in the pattern of grass, an early output of social forestry projects was seen in Madhya Pradesh villages.[10] In some villages, grass is rationed to, every household, in others to those only with cattle, in had been beaten and politically powerful villagers had grazed their cattle on the community plantations.

During field visits by the author, it was found that even where a government order existed on distribution, filed staff had little knowledge about it. Their interpretation of Government orders varied from place to place. The villagers considered social forestry trees as Government property, and were generally reluctant to get involved in their maintenance. Uncertainty about the distribution of benefits and who will gain and how is the most important factor in explaining the poor response of the people in community forestry, and to people's indifference to regeneration of public lands.

Neglect of Minor Forest Products

Minor Forest Produce (MFP) in India provide to the trebles and forest dwellers the major portion of their food, fodder, fruits, herbal medicine and several other items for sale. Although Government revenue form MFP has increased substantially in the past few decades, employment and income of the poor have declined. The production of *lendu* leaves in MP fell from 5.09 million bags in 1981-82 to 3.9 million bags in 1985-86.[11] *Tendu* workers in Orissa were being paid only 40 per cent of the minimum wages.[12] Despite nationalisation, the collection of sal seeds fell from two lakh tonnes in 1979 to only 60,000 tonnes in 1987,[13] causing a loss of income of Rs. 140 million to the poor, besides increasing import bill.

Nationalisation has hardly helped forest dwellers as, in almost all cases, the FD has appointed agents formally and informally.[14] This means that the tribals are now at the mercy of two different sets of people, the contractor as well as government department, and any payment that the tribals get has to be routed through both of them. Nationalisation has also meant that forest dwellers are no longer owners of trees on their private land. For instance, in block Karjat (Maharashtra), tribals cannot dispose of forest product in the open market. The net result is that contractors buy mixed wood from them at Rs. 30-50 a ton and sell it to the FD in the name of the tribals at Rs. 500-800 a ton.

Regeneration of MFP has attracted only a token effort so far. It is unfortunate that there is no place for MFP in social forestry schemes. Large scale propagation techniques in important MFP like *tendu* and *mahua*, are still to be developed. The Seventh Five Year Plan target for MFP species is only 85,000 ha as against a likely achievement of 9 million ha for total afforestation. During 1983-88, only four per cent of all trees planted in Orissa were of MFP variety.[15]

New Forest Policy

The new Forest Policy announced in December, 1988 and which replaced the 1952 document, expresses several sentiments in favour of tribals and the people, but an amendment to the Forest Conservation Act introduced in 1988 has restricted plantation of horticulture crops, palms, oil bearing and medicinal plants on forest lands, a provision which seems to show total insensitivity to the lifestyle and the needs of the tribals and the poor. On several occasions, it had been stated that a people's movement would be launched in forestry, but the 1988 amendment to the Act did not permit any assignment of forest lands to the people.

The new forest Policy wishes to curtail the rights and concessions of forest dwellers by relating them to the carrying capacity of forests. It also looks down upon entry of forest dwellers into forests and bans free gathering of forest produce by them, as it declares that the domestic requirements of tribals should be made available through conveniently located depots at reasonable prices.

Reading the new policy together with the amended Forest Conservation Act gives an impression that government wishes to have exclusive rights to management and ownership over forest lands, both reserve and non-reserve. This monopoly, it may be noted, was diluted to some extent during the social forestry phase when some states tried to secure people's involvement on forest lands through usufruct sharing social security schemes, and others included degraded forest lands in social forestry projects, intending to transfer their management to village committees. On these lines, the social forestry projects of Tamil Nadu, Bihar and Orissa have an important component on forest lands for meeting people's requirements. The mid-term evaluation of the Andhra Pradesh social forestry project also recommended[16] strengthening the social security plantation scheme on forest lands through sharing of usufruct with the poor. Haryana FD transferred the responsibility of protection of some government forests to 50 village societies *a la* Sukhomajri. In return, the villages harvested the enhanced production of *bhabbar* and other grasses.

The future of these schemes is now in jeopardy, as the Forest Conservation Act frowns upon management sharing schemes. It is doubtful if the West Bengal Government will be permitted to go ahead with the largescale replication of Arabari model for rehabilitation of degraded forests. Even where the programme is intended on road strips (as in Uttar Pradesh where road strips have been declared as protected forests) or unclassed forests (Himachal Pradesh), the programme has been held back due to lack of permission from the Central Government.[17] Environmental benefits cannot be realised by ignoring people's demands, nor is it possible to enforce exclusive property rights,[18] given the open and unguarded nature of forests in India. Working with the people and for them, howsoever desirable, is still a far cry, slogans notwithstanding.

POSSIBLE SOLUTIONS

Part of the difficulty in seeing what best to do arises from the conflict model in policy-makers' minds. They perceive the poor, and not market forces, as responsible for deforestation, and hence seek to restrict only their consumption. That the poor have played a part in deforestation is not in dispute. But to blame them is a convenient diversion. Moreover, the prescription which follows is counterproductive. The prescription is not, as we argue it should be, policies to meet people's needs for forest products, such as fodder, MFPs, and fuelwood. It is to demand and impose more stringent laws, with military style controls, compulsory contraction of bulls, banning people from entering forests, and curtailing the rights and concessions of forest dwellers. These measures have their roots in the bureaucratic psyche which believes firmly in the power of the stick and in rewards to those who wield it.

The poor and the environment are seen, all too often, as antagonistic. The extreme bureaucratic view is then that people should be excluded from forests. The extreme humanist view is that the FD should be excluded from forests. In our view, the conditions in which either is feasible and right are quite rare. Nor is the conflict model necessary or useful. To the contrary, ways can be sought in which the interests of people and of long-term sustainability are harmonised in a mutually supporting manner.

As a practical policy, it is suggested that social forestry should be extended to reserved and protected forest lands by changing the nature of species from teak, eucalyptus and pine to usufruct based trees, such as neem, mahua, tendu, sal, arjun, and palmyrah. These should be supplemented with shrubs and bushes to yield fuelwood and fodder in the shortest possible time.

This would strengthen access of the poor to forests as species suitable for individual gathering by households are planted, and therefore benefits would be directly appropriated by the poor. Unlike commercial timber species, relatively low value non-rotational trees for recurrent products would not so much attract the attention of rich farmers and contractors.

The implementation of social forestry programmes in India has been heavily influenced by the perspectives of foresters and of foreign experts who advise Central Government and the donor agencies. Both of them, because of their training and experience, have looked upon trees as timber, to be obtained after clear felling.

The traditional Indian way of looking at trees has, however, been different. As opposed to trees for timber, Indian villagers for centuries have depended on trees for livelihood. There has been little clear felling. In-stead, trees have been valued for the intermediate products they provide. Trees were valued for the diversity of their products and the many ways in which they helped to sustain and secure the livelihoods of the people.

Thus, there would be a world of difference between plantation of eucalyptus and of *prosopis juliflora* on roadsides. Eucalyptus benefits urban markets and industry, whereas prosopis cannot only solve the fuelwood problem of poor families, but would also generate self employment for the poor. What is significant bout *prosopis, ber, neem, mahua, agave* or other low market value but high bio-mass trees is that they do not require decisions about market shares between rich and poor. Their usufruct is not of much interest to the rich, or is available to them only through gathering by the poor, so that by default the benefits are available for the poor. Given the inefficiency of administration and 'soft' character of the political system, one could generalise that out of a tree the stem goes to the rich and the towns, whereas branches, leaves and twigs belong to the poor. Therefore, the strategy should be to opt for species which have high proportions of branches and twigs relative to stem wood.

A further advantage of planting "trees of the poor" (which are essentially employment augmenting trees, as they require labour for gathering and collection, as opposed to trees which are felled) on forest and revenue lands is the likelihood of improved cooperation. People are reluctant to protect trees which will be auctioned or clear felled to the benefit of Government, contractors and forest staff. They are much more likely to collaborate in protection of trees from which they, much more than others, are in a position to benefit.

TREES, LIVELIHOODS AND THE ENVIRONMENT

We shall now discuss the environmental impact of our recommended in preceding paras.

For forest and revenue lands, we have recommended livelihood forestry with usufruct based people-oriented trees (which may sometimes be slow growing, like *mahua,* but may be fast growing like *prosopis juliflora* or *arjun*) but supplemented by an understory of quick growing bushes, grasses and shrubs. This would mean that benefits in the form of fodder and fuelwood would be quickly available to the poor and would continue for 8-15 years or so (depending upon silvicultural maturity period of the tree), till the canopy of the main trees closed, preventing sunlight reaching the understory. At this time, benefits from the main trees in forms, such as leaves, branches and fruit, would start flowing to the poor.

This would provide soils with a good cover of litter. The maintenance of life-support systems is a function performed mainly by the crown biomass of trees. It is this component of trees that can contribute positively towards the maintenance of the hydrological and nutrient cycles.[19] Treeswhich provide a lot of leaves, twigs, and branches enrich the soil much better than those which provide poles and timber alone.

The objective of soil and moisture conservation would be better achieved through grasses and shrubs, rather than with plantations.[20] In the latter case, there is progressive suppression of the grass growth by the closure of the tree crowns after the first few years of plantation. Leaf litter from plantations is collected by the villagers, and thus does not help in soil/moisture conservation. An understory of shrubs, grasses and bushes is more suitable for site stabilisation and reduction of run-off, given the practical conditions of acute shortage of fodder in India.

Conventional forestry based on clear felling disrupts the annual circulation of nutrients, and increases soil erosion.[21] Monoculture plantation forestry is also prone to pest attack. Thus, eucalyptus plantations in Kerala raised after clear felling dense green and deciduous forests, have been devastated by fungal diseases, and the consequent low productivity defeated the very purpose for which they had been raised.[22] Similar was the experience of teak plantations in North Bastar, Madhya Pradesh.[23] On the other hand, mixed forests draw and give nutrients to the soil at different stages of their growth, and hence are ecologically far more beneficial than plantations. As opposed to timber, which is product of the dead tree, we have emphasised products of the living tree-fruits, nuts, flowers and twigs.

Sometimes land is too degraded and has little soil to support trees, specially in arid and semi-arid areas. Tree growth is so slow that barely one tonne of wood gets added per hectare per year. This is then not sufficient to cover the cost of seedings, planting and protection. But such lands can often support improved varieties of grasses.[24] Even with scanty and irregular rains four to five tons of dry matter from *stylosanthes* and *Cenchenn (anjan)* grasses can be produced from one hectare of such waste land. Besides grass cover can reduce run-off of rain and soil loss. It also starts yielding income within two years. Despite suitability of grass plantation on degraded lands on technical grounds, an official paper from Maharashtra, presented in the seminar organised by BAIF at Pune in June 1988, admitted that trees were being planted indiscriminately even where soil was less than 30 cm in depth. Only 45 per cent of land taken up under social forestry in Maharashtra qualifies for tree plantation as a technical solution. The remaining 55 per cent required revegetation through grasses, legumes and soil bunding, yet only three per cent of sites were actually given this treatment. Rather, trees were being planted on such soils leading to further soil erosion. Such is the fascination of the FD for timber and non-browsable species that they ignore their own technical prescriptions.

In sum, non-rotational trees, which provide permanent cover, and give recurrent annual yields in forms, such as mulch leaves and wild fruits combined with grasses, bushes and shrubs are environmentally superior to raising timber trees which have their value only in the stem.

The poor have suffered in social forestry programmes because they are not organised, and bureaucracy has failed to deliver the share from timber and pulpwood trees to them. Usufruct-based trees overcome both these problems. Under the new policy suggested by us, technology produces an output which eliminates the need for political and bureaucratic fine tuning.

GAINERS AND LOSERS

What are the possibilities of our suggestions being accepted by the Government? With the measures suggested by us, the rural poor gain, but the rural rich do not lose. This promises a solid rural interest group of rich and poor with considerable potential political clout.

Major losers are lower-level officials. Losing contacts with middlemen means less power and less income for the petty officials. The change in the nature of species from timber to usufruct based trees would surely hurt petty officials.

Higher up the scale, assessment of gains and losers is more difficult but more hopeful. It is widely believed that forest officers, contractors and politicians profit from commissions and illicit felling of trees. To the extent this prevails, it will be an obstacle. But on the positive side, there are gains as well as possible losses to each group.

Forest officers, especially the younger lot, are more honest a compared to other class I services, and do not take a share from the ill-gotten wealth of their subordinates. But, being attacked from the press and environmentalists for having failed to protect forests, they have developed a defensive mentality and have thus become emotionally dependent on their subordinates. They are initially likely to support the lower level officials against reforms proposed here. But their long-term interest lies in 'earning' a good name for their profession, by joining the mainstream of rural development, and in identifying with the rural poor. Having no vested interest in corruption, they could be made to support our proposals through suitably designed training programmes.

Of all the groups in India, who have made money since independence industrialists, rich farmers, politicians, bureaucrats, and urban professionals—it is the contractors who as a group enjoy least degree of political support. They have made good despite being condemned by all and sundry. Bureaucrats avoid being seen with them, politicians give speeches against them, and policies are made with a view to curb their hold over the economy. This is not to deny the clout that they as individuals enjoy with the political system because of money power. Contractors in the Indian system are an enigma—individually powerful but powerless as a group. Thus, we are hopeful that they would not be able to scuttle the progressive measures that we have suggested.

For their part, politicians stand to gain widespread support from their electorates if they espouse these reforms as their own (rather than stemming from bureaucracy), and promote their implementation. The gains to the poor rural majority are so large and so consistent that they should ensure popularity and votes to any leader who advocates and supports these measures, especially when the rural rich are also gaining.

The problem remains of the lower-level staff who stand to lose. If anti-people policies still continue, the question arises, "who rules the country"?

REFERENCES

1. NWDB, *Description and Classification of Wasteland*, New Delhi, National Wastelands Development Board, 1987.
2. Robert Chambers, N.C. Saxena and Tushaar Shah, *To the Hands of the Poor: Water and Trees*, New Delhi, Oxford and IBH (forthcoming).
3. Forest Survey of India, *State of India's forests*, Dehradun, Forest Survey of India (mimeo), 1988.
4. NWDB, *Note for the Meeting of the Consultative Committee of Parliament: Afforestation*, February 19, 1988 (mimeo).
5. FAO, *Intensive Multiple-use Forest management in Kerala*, FAO Forestry Paper 53, 1984, p. 37.
6. S. Shyam Sunder and S. Parmeswarappa, "Social Forestry in Karnataka", *Economic and* Political Weekly, November 21, 1987.
7. Government of India *Evaluation Report on Integrated Tribal Development Projects*, Programme Evaluation Organisation, Planning Commission, Government of India (mimeo), 1987.
8. David Brokensha, *Village-level Management of Common Property Resources, Especially Fuelwood and Fodder Resources, Karnataka, India.* A Report Prepared for the World Bank, (mimeo), 1988.
9. Government of Orissa, *Evalution of Orissa Social Forestry Project*, Phase I, Government of Orissa, Bhubaneswar (mimeo), 1987.
10. USAID, *Second Mid-term Evaluation Report, Madhya Pradesh*, USAID, New Delhi (mimeo), 1985.

11. Government of Madhya Pradesh, *Forestry Project of Rehabilitation of Degraded Forests and Afforestation in M.P.*, Madhya Pradesh Forest Department, July 1987 (mimeo), p. 32.
12. Tirath Gupta, and Amar Guleria, *Some Economic and Management Aspects of a Non-Wood Forest Product in India: Tendu Leaves,* New Delhi, Oxford and IBH, 1982, pp. 85-86.
13. Government of India, *Commodity Studies* (in six volumes) (conducted by Progressive Agro-Industrial Consultants), New Delhi, Ministry of Welfare, 1988.
14. Government of India, *Background Note Prepared for the Seminar on Welfare and Development of Tribals,* New Delhi, Ministry of Tribals (typescript), 1987.
15. SIDA, *Forestry for the Poor: An Evaluation of the SIDA Supported Social Forestry Project in Tamil Nadu, India,* SIDA, Stockholm, (Sweden), 1988.
16. CIDA, *Andhra Pradesh Social Forestry Project: Mid-term Review,* New Delhi, Canadian International Development Agency, 1988.
17. USAID, *National Social Forestry Project:* Mid-*term Review,* USAID, New Delhi, 1988.
18. Simon Commander, "Managing Indian Forests: A Case for the Reform of Property Rights", *Development Policy Review,* Vol. 4, 1980.
19. V. Shiva and J. Bandyopadhyay, *Ecological Audit of Eucalyptus Cultivation,* Dehradun, English Book Depot, 1985, p. 36.
20. G.P. Maithani, *et al.*, "Survey of Shrubs for Hastening the Process of Reclamation of Ecologically Vulnerable Areas of Central Himalayas", *Indian Forester,* May 1988, Dehradun.
21. Stephen Spurr and Burton Barnes, *Forest Ecology,* New York, John Wiley, 1980, p. 240.
22. M. Achuthan Nair and C. Sreedharan, "Farming Systems in the Homestead of Kerala," *Agro-Forestry Systems,* Vol. 4, No. 4, 1986.
23. Robert Anderson and Walter Huber, *The Hour of the Fox: Tropical Forests, the World Bank and Indigenous People in Central India,* New Delhi, Vistaar Publications, 1988, p. 83.
24. B.V. Nimbkar, "The Greening of Maharashtra", *Economic and Political Weekly,* February 20, 1988.

Section V: OVERVIEW OF INTEGRATED WATER MANAGEMENT

13

Issues in Water Resources Administration in India*

K.L. Rao

Water resources in India very from region to region. There are tracts where rainfall in heavy. The highest rainfall in the world (the maximum ever recorded 1,042† inches) occurs in Assam. In some areas, there is scarcity of rainfall—less than 5 inches. The average rainfall is about 45 inches. Also, there are two distinct monsoons—one is the southwestern starting from the southernmost point in Kerala in May and sweeping across the entire country during June to September, and the other, the northeastern occurring in October to March. The rainfall is much smaller and is confined to Kerala. Tamil Nadu and to a few showers in the Northern States of Punjab, U.P. and Bihar. Also due to deep deposit of alluvium in Gangetic Basin and some coastal regions, and fault zones in river basins like that of Narmada, there are large areas where water is stored underground and can be exploited. Thick clouds floating over India during monsoon months have possibilities of extraction of water from clouds at required locations at a future date when rain making technology is fully developed. Desalination may yield some small quantities of fresh water for domestic use. Thus, water resources in India are principally from surface runoff and the ground water.

Quantitative estimates of different sources of water are based mostly on reasonable assumptions. Measurements are being done now and it will take some time before these can be used for an accurate assessment of water. Assuming 45 inches rainfall per year spread over the entire area of the country (850 million acres), the total runoff comes to 3,000 million acre ft.‡ Allowing for a third of this quantity for losses due to evaporation, water falling on the ground will be 2,000 million acre ft., out of this, the surface runoff is 1,350 million acre ft. and the rest soaks into the ground. Of the water that goes into the ground, two-thirds is partly retained as moisture in the soil and partly lost due to evapotranspiration and sub-surface flow. The water that seeps down to porous strata and represents the annual reserve works out to 217 million acre ft. or say 220 million acre ft.

---

* It was contributed to the United Nations' Inter-regional Seminar on "Current Issues of Water Resources Administration" held in New Delhi on December 7-16, 1971.

† 1 inch = 2.54 centimetres.

‡ 1 million acre feet = 1,233.5 million cubic metres.

The surface runoff in India is estimated at 1,350 million ft. International comparisons indicate that India's surface flows are more than favourable. Similarly, ground water resources may be considered quite good. Some of the wells in the Gangetic Basin, apart from accidental ones in Rajasthan deserts, yield 150,000 gallons an hour (*i.e.* seven cusecs). One can, therefore, conclude, in a Broadway, that India has adequate water for exploitation, but this requires skilful management to achieve maximum benefits and to conserve for the needs of growing population.

EXPLOITATION

The waters in India are used mainly for irrigation. This is by consequence of its tropical climate and food and fibre requirements of its millions of people. India's population stands today at 550 million and this may go up to 900 million by the end of this century. Agriculture is practised on 400 million acres and about a fourth of it is irrigated. Of this irrigated area 27 per cent is served by ground water and the rest by surface flows. We may assume that the portion of India below the Tropic of Cancer, *i.e.* 23½° to 20° is Central India (the States of Gujarat and Madhya Pradesh) and below it is southern or Peninsular India. Areas cultivated and irrigated from ground and surface water resources in these regions are shown in the following Table 1.

Table 1: Areas Cultivated and Irrigated in the Three Regions of India

(in Million Acres)

Regions	*Area Cultivated*	*Area Irrigated*		
		Surface	*Underground*	*Total*
North	181	41	17	58
Central	74	5	3	8
South	145	27	7	34
Total	400	73	27	100

Surface irrigation is obtained through: (i) construction of small tanks; (ii) diversion barrages; and (iii) storages. It is roughly estimated that the extent of land irrigated by small tanks is about 15 million acres and the rest is from barrages and storages. Besides these, in areas where there is inadequate rainfall, contour bunding is also adopted to retain whatever rainfall occurs in the local areas.

Ground water is exploited through: (i) shallow wells generally up to 50 ft. depth; (ii) medium wells up to 300 ft.; and (iii) deep wells up to 1,000 ft. In Tamil Nadu, at the southern tip of India, appreciable irrigation is done through wells, mostly shallow. Thus, 2.3 million acres are irrigated by this source. In Uttar Pradesh, in Gangetic Basin, 9 million acres are provided with deep tubewell waters.

WATER RESOURCES ADMINISTRATION: IRRIGATION

Water resources are managed in different ways in India. India is divided into 18 States and Development of irrigation in India is reserved for its 18 States, that is, States are responsible for the development of irrigation in their respective States. The central Government deals with inter-State rivers and in general assists, examines and finances irrigation projects sent by the States. The Ministry of Irrigation and Power, of which Central Water and Power Commission forms the technical part, coordinates and handles development of irrigation and power of the entire country. In many States, there are separate departments under Ministers for Irrigation.

Ground water exploitation by shallow wells is generally in the hands of individual farmers. State Governments provide finances in the shape of loans for digging of wells. There are at present seven million wells in the country. There is a great demand for electrification of the wells as the farmers have found that it is more economical to pump the water by using electric motors than use of animal power as has been the practice. Electrification is done through the State Government agencies known as State Electricity Boards. Deep and medium tubewells, which number 30,000, are generally constructed and managed by State Governments. At the Centre, there is an Exploratory Tubewells Organization. It digs deep tubewells and if the yields are more than about 18,000 gallons an hour, the wells are handed over to the State governments for exploitation. Recently, in order to expedite ground water exploitation, a Central Ground Water Board has been set up. This works under the Ministry of Agriculture. The Agriculture Ministry, as the name indicates, deals essentially with the growth of agriculture and the food problems of the country. These subjects are again State subjects and in the States are dealt with by the Departments of Food & Agriculture. They deal directly with farmers. Thus, in India, which is a federal country, there is a harmonious blending of functions of both State and Central Governments in the field of agricultural production and in the most important and basic input, that is, water management.

At the Centre, irrigation activity is divided into two categories: (i) major and medium; and (ii) minor. Major and medium projects are those which cost more than Rs. 25 lakh each. Minor projects are those which cost Rs. 25 lakhs or less each. Ground water is also classified as coming under minor irrigation. Major and medium projects are financed by both Government and private organizations. Thus, the amounts invested since Independence and proposed outlay in the Fourth Plan (1969-74) in the irrigation sectors are shown in Table 2.

The Ministry of Irrigation deals with major and medium irrigation while the Ministry of Agriculture deals with minor irrigation.

In the States, major and medium irrigation is under irrigation department. There are different practices with regard to minor irrigation. These are given in Table 3.

Thus, we see that in most of the States, even minor irrigation is managed by irrigation department.

There has been a considerable debate whether irrigation must go with agriculture or should be under a separate Ministry at the Centre. The Administrative Reforms Commission (1968), appointed by the Government of India to suggest necessary changes in the machinery of the Government of India and its procedures of work, has opined that ground water management must rest with Ministry of Irrigation. Their relevant remarks are given below:

Table 2: Amount Invested (in Rs. Crores) since Independence Including Outlay in Fourth Plan on Irrigating Projects and Achievements Made and Targeted

(in Million Acres)

	Major and Medium Projects	*Minor Projects*		*Total Outlay*
		Government	*Private*	
		(Rupees in Crores)		
1951-69	1.772	851	632	3,255
1969-74	954	511	975	2,440
			Total:	5,695
Achievements in million acres during 1951-69	22	– 15	–	37
During 1969-74	12	– 8	–	20
			Total:	57

"While supporting the existing allocation of major and medium irrigation as a subject to the Ministry of Irrigation and Power and of minor irrigation to the Department of Agriculture, the Study Team has underlined the need for integrated attention being paid to problems like ground water survey, water management and maximum utilisation of irrigation potential. It has, in this connection, suggested the creation of a Water Management Division in the Ministry of Irrigation and Power, to be staffed both by agricultural scientists and irrigation engineers. These proposals merit attention and have our support. The Study Team on Agricultural Administration has also taken up a similar approach. It has recommended that the Ministry of Irrigation and Power (and not the Natural Resources Division of the Planning Commission) should be the coordinating body for all work concerning investigation for underground water resources. The exploratory tubewell organisation may be transferred from the Department of Agriculture to the Ministry of Irrigation and Power."*

In several countries, irrigation is also combined with agriculture, the moot point being that irrigation is not an end in itself but is input for agricultural production and, therefore, it should be managed by the Agriculture Ministry. There is considerable force in this point of view but it is to be noted that achievement of irrigation is essentially an engineering problem and it is, therefore, desirable to have a separate Ministry. This is not necessary where irrigation is not required or where irrigated areas are small. But in India, irrigation is the prime need and makes all the makes all the difference in the prosperity of the people. Scientific analysis has indicated that the most backward areas in India are those where *rice is grown without irrigation*. This

* Administrative Reforms Commission, *Report of the Machinery of the Government of India and its Procedures of Work,* Delhi, Manager of Publications, Government of India, 1968, p. 90.

Table 3: Administrative Arrangements at State Level Pertaining to Minor Irrigation Works

State	*Departments dealing with Minor Irrigation*			
	Irrigation or Public Works Department	*Revenue Department*	*Agriculture Department*	*Others*
Andhra Pradesh	All works irrigating more than 200 acres each in Andhra area and 100 acres each in Telengana area	Works irrigating less than 200 acres each in Andhra area and 100 acres each in Telengana areas	–	–
Assam	All Minor irrigation except tubewells	–	Tubewells	–
Bihar	Some of the works	–	Some of the works.	Directorate of Minor Irrigation also deals with some works
Gujarat	All works irrigating more than 250 acres each	Works irrigating less than 250 acres each	–	–
Himachal Pradesh	All works	–	–	–
Haryana	Tubewells and other minor irrigation works	–	Loans for well sinking and pumping sets	–
Jammu & Kashmir	–	–	–	Panchayats
Kerala	All works dealing with 5 acres and above in old Travancore area and 200 acres in old Madras area	–	–	Panchayats and beneficiaries
Maharashtra	All works irrigating more than 250 acres each	–	–	Zila Parishads for works irrigating less than 250 acres each
Mysore	–	All minor irrgation works	–	–
Orissa	–	Other minor irrigation works	Lift irrigation and tubewells	–
Rajasthan	All works irrigating more than 200 acres each	All works irrigating less than 200 acres each	–	Panchayat Samittees for part of works irrigating less than 250 acres each
Tamil Nadu	All works irrigating more than 200 acres each	All works irrigating less than 200 acres each	–	–
Uttar Pradesh	Tubewells	–	–	Other minor irrigation works under Agricultural Production Commission
West Bengal	All works costing more than Rs. 1 lakh each	–	All works costing less than Rs. 1 lakh each	–

is an important and interesting observation. Rice is grown where there is a possibility of good rainfall and, therefore, the density of population is great in these areas. But when irrigation is not provided, agriculture becomes gamble and in many years the yield is either nil or entirely poor. Therefore, poverty reigns. This is the reason why eastern U.P., northern Bihar and portions of coastal Orissa and Kerala are considered in India as the most backward areas. In India, as stated already, irrigation is provided only for 25 per cent of the cultivated land we have to bring it up to 50 per cent at least, that is, the irrigated area to be further developed is 100 million acres. This is a tremendous task. It will require all the ingenuity of engineers to achieve this, specially as the diversion schemes and easy storage sites are all already exploited.

There should be integrated planning between surface waters and ground waters. Maybe these have to be developed together or sometimes separately. Also, tubewell sinking requires machinery and electrification, which have predominantly engineering content. Again the problems of recharging the ground to replenish ground water supplies and extending the life of tubewells, which, at present, is only 15 years, requires extensive probing and field research in well established hydraulic laboratories. Irrigation in its entirety has to work closely with Agriculture and for this, a close coordinating link will be beneficial.

WATER RESOURCES ADMINISTRATION: OTHER USES

The total utilization of water for irrigation is estimated at 25 million acre ft. There are no accurate figures for other uses of water, but estimates are:

	Million Acre ft.
Drinking water	10
Industries	2
Power stations	6
Total:	18 or say 20

Thus, the total water used at present is 270 million acre ft. By far, the largest use is in irrigation and the industries involve the lows use. The exact quantity of usable water has not yet been assessed. This is assumed as between 800 and 900 million acre ft. Thus, the water utilized in India at present is a third of the available water.

Administrative arrangements for utilizing irrigation waters have been dealt with earlier in the article. The arrangement in regard to other uses are as discussed in following paragraphs.

Drinking Water Supply

The problem of supply of drinking water is important in all parts of the world but in India it assumes special significance because of its vast rural population flung apart in isolated villages numbering more than 5,60,000. Of these, nearly 38 per cent are villages with less than 500 people. Most of the villages depend on wells. In nearly two-thirds of the villages, wells are either inadequate, or they fail just at the time of the greatest need, *i.e.* in summer. Also, some times wells do not yield potable water. Sanitary arrangements are very unsatisfactory in many urban areas. In the field of supply of potable water and arrangements for sewerage disposal, India has to go a long way. Water supply is dealt with by most of the States in their Departments of Public Health Engineering or Local Self Government. In the Centre, the subject is dealt with by the Ministry of Health.

Water Supply for Industries

There is nor systematic channelling of water supplies for industrial uses. The requirements are arranged from time of time in the Departments of Irrigation or in the Departments of Public Health Engineering at the State level. At the Centre, the problems are dealt with in the Ministry of Industrial Development who, however, invariably consult the Ministry of Irrigation for supplies. Research on reuse of industrial waters must be encouraged in the interest of economy of water.

The pollution of rivers in India is due to two reasons. The first reason is the letting down of untreated sewage from towns and cities. The second and more serious is the pollution created by industries. The disposal of effluents from the industries are at present controlled by the respective Ministries. The effluents are either not treated at all or are not treated properly. These require urgent attention. The Ministry of Health is bringing up a bill to regulate pollution.

In order to provide for the prevention, abatement and control pollution of rivers and streams, for maintaining or restoring wholesomeness of such water courses and for controlling the existing and new discharges of domestic and industrial waters, the Bill seeks to: (*i*) establish at the Centre as well as in the States water pollution prevention boards with the necessary complement of technical and administrative staff and to confer on them such powers as are necessary to deal effectively with the problem of water pollution in the country; (*ii*) provide penalties for contravention of the provisions of the Act; and (*iii*) establish Central and State Water testing laboratories to enable the boards to assess the extent of pollution, lay down standards and establish guilt or default. On the whole, it should be accepted that industrial waters have not yet received an integrated consideration either for initial supply or later disposal.

Water Use in Thermal Stations

For cooling purposes, large quantities of water are required in thermal stations. In coal or oil fired type of generation, the requirements of water are about 125 cusecs for 100 Mw. If cooling towers or mechanical cooling is provided, the requirements will be reduced to 12.5 cusecs for 100 Mw. In the atomic power plants, the consumption is about 50 per cent more. We have in India, at present, a total of 10 million Kw of thermal plant and the total requirement of water is about 9 million acre feet assuming straight cooling. Actually a number of stations use cooling towers and the actual use may be about 6 million acre feet. Water requirements for thermal stations are arranged by the Ministry of Irrigation & Power.

NEW PROBLEMS IN WATER ADMINISTRATION

Conflicts between Uses, States and Countries

As water uses are getting diversified and with the growing realization that water is a valuable and scarce commodity, new problems are arising in management.

In some cases, water is required to be released from storages purely in the interests of power that is being generated under a dam. Sometimes, irrigation demands require release of water in excess of requirements of power. Thus, at the Bhakra reservoir, there is often a conflict between water requirements for irrigation and power, specially in years of scarcity of inflow into the reservoir. This conflicts is at present settled on an *ad hoc* basis and keeping in view the relative benefits between the different sectors.

Similarly, conflicts arise in the sharing of water between different States. In India, most of the rivers are inter-State, flowing through more than one State. The existing law provides that the conflicts may be resolved by negotiations and only in cases where the Central Government feels that the dispute cannot be settled by negotiations, Tribunals consisting of three Judges may be appointed. It is generally accepted that settlement by negotiations is the best way of resolving a water dispute as these disputes give rise to emotional approach and the best way of effacing the emotions is by agreement on vital issues. No other method will remove the ill-feelings. In India, most of the differences with regard to use of water of different States are settled through discussions and negotiations.

In recent years, some water disputes have been referred for adjudications. There are at present three Tribunals before which the sharing of waters of inter-State rivers is being argued. These Tribunals were set up more than two years back and are likely to take considerable time before making their judicial pronouncements.

River Damodar was creating a large amount of damage in its valley, which is very rich in minerals, like coal and iron ore. Also, its waters were required for use for irrigating lands. The river passes through two States, Bihar and West Bengal. To achieve the maximum benefits, the management of the Damodar water was entrusted to a specially created statutory body called, the "Damodar Valley Corporation". This Corporation is similar to the Tennessee Valley Authority of U.S.A. The DVC has been responsible for construction of four dams, canal system for irrigating a million acres and development of power, both hydro and thermal, with an installed capacity of a million Kw. Yet another device which proved successful in the implementation of very large projects benefiting more than one State is management by a Control Board. Thus, in Chambal development, which consists of 3 dams, a canal system irrigating 1.5 million acres and a power system of 386 Mw is under the Chambal Control Board. The Board consists of Ministers of Madhya Pradesh and Rajasthan with Central Minister as Chairman. This kind of management is largely used for big irrigation projects.

India is also involved in settling the water disputes of rivers which flow through India and Pakistan. Both these countries were one till 1947 and, therefore, the river systems, Indus and Ganga, were being developed as a single unit. After the partition of the country, disputes arose and a settlement with regard to the Western rivers, *i.e.* the Indus and its tributaries, was achieved through negotiations with the assistance of the World Bank. Attempts have been made to settle the dispute relating to Ganga also by holding discussions between engineers of both the countries. There are a large number of tributaries of the Ganga which flow through Nepal and India and matters that arise are settled amicably between both countries through mutual discussions from time to time.

Management for Flood Control

Due to the large number of the rivers flowing in the country and the highly variable rainfall, which intensifies in different parts of the country at different times, floods occur almost every year in some part of India or the other. Added to this, the east coast of India is subject to cyclones, every year and at times, these become violent and cause immense damages to crops and houses, besides loss of cattle and human lives. The damages are tending to act more and more as a drag on the economic progress of the country. Floods occur in June to September and cyclones either in April and May or in October and November. This year, for example, the damages due to floods which occurred between June and September, and amounted to 6,000 million rupees and the losses due to cyclone which occurred in October was 2,000 million rupees. Floods are dealt with by the Ministry of Irrigation and Power both at the Centre and State level. In case of emergencies, such as closing breaches or attending to relief works in remote areas, the help of the army is sought. The functions of prediction and keeping observations of rainfall are in the Department of Meteorology under the Ministry of Civil Aviation, but relief and rehabilitation is done at the State level by departments of Irrigation and Revenue and at the Centre by the Ministry of Home Affairs.

It appears that systematic administrative arrangements both to fight the floods, such as defence against breaching and breach closing, and to render immediate relief should be in the hands of a coordinating body. This may be called the "Distress Mitigation Committee" or by any other suitable name. It is increasingly felt that for planning and implementing flood control works, specially for big river systems, separate commissions should be set up. Accordingly, for Brahmaputra, a Brahmaputra Flood Control Commission has been set up. The Commission consists of three Members with supporting investigation, design and construction staff. It is advised by a technical advisory committee. Sanction of estimates and policy decisions are made by the Brahmaputra Flood control Board, which has, among its Members, Ministers of the States and Central Governments. A similar organization is being considered for flood control in the Ganga River system.

Transfers of Water and Its Management

There are always areas of scarcity and areas of surplus waters. Transfer of water from one to the other is receiving great attention of the present times. There are good examples in India where for irrigation, waters was diverted from one basin to another. Thus, towards the end of the last century, waters from west-flowing Periyar river were diverted to the east, to feed the parched lands of Madurai District in Tamil Nadu. This has transformed the scarcity areas into flourishing and prosperous areas. Similarly, there are quite a number of other examples where water is conveyed to scarcity areas to relieve the inadequacy of water. A more comprehensive and much bolder scheme is now under contemplation. A portion of the surplus monsoon waters of the Ganga, which flows wastefully into the sea, are proposed to be lifted up and diverted for use in western and peninsular India, where waters in the rivers are inadequated to deal with the extensive areas under crops. When this scheme comes up for detailed investigation, planning and implementation, it will require a new administrative set-up.

Financial and Target Coordination

In India, the planning process is vested in the Planning Commission of which Prime Minister is the Chairman and the Finance Minister a Member. The goals of economic development and national budgeting are thus coordinated. The allotment of funds required for implementing the projects for different uses of water are all done by the Planning Commission. There is a separate Minister for Planning who is able to devote his entire time to periodical review of the implementation of the projects to ensure achievement of targets.

Water Resources Administration in Future

The present water resources administration has been dealt with in the preceding three sections. The problems met with and the need for changes have also been given briefly. The most difficult future problem for the human race is going to be that of supply of quantum of water needed by the population. At the rate of 500 tons per person, the quantity of water that will be needed by the additional people will appear on the earth in the next ten years will be of the order of 45 million acre ft. or approximately the entire water of a river like Krishna. Water is a fixed quantity of earth. It is, therefore, of the greatest importance that water resource management must be most efficiently organized.

As stated earlier, most of water uses, that is more than 90 per cent, are in respect of irrigation. Also in India, drinking water and water required for industries have to be arranged from rivers, canals or wells, all of which are dealt with by Irrigation Departments of the States. It is, therefore, considered desirable to entrust the Ministry of Irrigation and Power at the Centre with arrangement of supplies of water for different uses and rename it as "Ministry of Water Resources" or simply of "Ministry of Water". In view of adequate availability of water in India, there should be no extensive conflict between the different uses except in a few isolated areas. The more difficult is the settlement of water disputes between the States. The control of inter-State rivers may need to be taken over to a large degree by the Central Government.

A national water policy must be set out to ensure the use of water efficiently and with equity. The national water policy must also be flexible as priorities may have to be altered at intervals of time. A national water grid may also be built up if the Government at the Centre is invested with proper authority. National Water Grids are most essential for achieving the best uses of available waters. Like Electrical Grids, water may be sent to any part of the country to overcome the shortages due to seasonal variations. The Grids can equalise the water costs and thus it will help in the country's wide economic development. The national policy must, therefore, enunciate the development of water grids. Thus, the national water policy must lay down guidelines, organizational principles and fundamental procedures for management and utilization of waters. To formulate the national policy and watch its implementation, a high level National Water Resources Council will be necessary.

To implement the water projects, a Ministry of Water will be necessary. The function of the Ministry of Water will be to plan and ensure implementation of water supply projects. The actual use and manner of use will be left to the respective Ministries and Departments. Thus, utilization of irrigation waters would be with the Department of Agriculture; Municipal and Rural Water Supply use would be with the Department of Local Administration or Public Health; and industrial waters with the Department of Industry.

For the present, the "Ministry of Water" can look after power also. Power is expected to grow rapidly in the next ten years (*i.e.* to rise from 17 million kW to 51 million kW). At such a stage, the management of electric supply will require a separate Ministry for Power and the present Ministry of Irrigation and Power can then beome "Ministry of Water." It is very important that the personnel, both technical and administrative, of water management organizations should be up to date with latest knowledge on the subject. This is the only way to ensure economic development. In India, there is one unique organization called Central Board of Irrigation and Power. Members of this Board are all Chief Engineers engaged in the irrigation and power development and Professors. The Board, formed 44 years ago, has been rendering valuable service. Besides this, refresher courses must be organized at all levels to improve efficiency and administrative drive.

Irrigation development in India in the past and in the last two decades has been most imposing and is the largest in the world. The management which has made this possible, can be expected to tackle the tasks in future as well with the modifications suggested. The management of industrial and domestic water supply will need more attention in future as increased industrial activity is necessary to eliminate poverty and unemployment in the country.

14

Inter-State Rivers: Cooperative Approach Essential for Optimum Development

N.D. Gulhati

That our rivers are important to our well-being and economy is only stating the obvious. What is perhaps not adequately appreciated is that this importance has been steadily increasing with increasing population and with the development of the country's economy and must continue to do so for a long time to come. Intensive development of river waters, as of water resources in general, is vital to our growth in agriculture and industry and otherwise influences our lives in many ways. At the same time, this development is itself dependent on our economic resources. It is both the cause and effect of the prosperity of any State, of any region or of the country as a whole.

The British Indian Government, which laid the foundation of modern irrigation in India, spent on this development*, mainly from surface waters, a total of Rs.156 crores. Against this, the expenditure on irrigation, from surface and sub-surface waters, during the five years of the First Plan was Rs. 385 crores, about two and a half times as much as in the preceding hundred years and more[1]. In the Second Plan, the amount spent on irrigation development was Rs. 475 crores and in the Third Plan Rs. 845 crores. Apart from the development of water resources for agriculture, a sum of Rs. 600 crores was spent during the three Plans on new hydro-electric projects on different rivers of the country. The tempo of such developments, both for agriculture and power, since the end of the Third Plan, is even more than in that Plan period and will continue to increase for many years to come. Other demands on river waters are for domestic water supply and for industries. Schemes of flood control and soil conservation represent another phase of water resource development and one must not forget the importance of fresh waters for fisheries, landscaping, scenic beauty and recreation.

---

* In all the provinces of pre-partition India, until 1947.

As in all other developmental activity, the development of water resources raises numerous technical, economic, financial and administrative problems. There are some problems, however, which are peculiar to this development; these arise from the very nature of the natural resource and have facets which attract several disciplines. It is the purpose of this article to deal with these latter problems, describe the difficulties that present themselves in their solution and indicate how they should be resolved.

Nature of water resources

For an appreciation of the problems peculiar to the development of water resources, it is necessary, first of all, to examine briefly some aspects of water as a natural resource, its distribution in time and space and, broadly, the manner in which it serves mankind.

Unlike other natural resources, river waters are not stationary but mobile, yet inexhaustible. River flow cannot be held except by special engineering works and then only to a limited extent, and for a limited time. Unless held or used, river waters flow away. But, in accordance with Nature's hydrologic cycle, river waters keep on reappearing, year after year, in the same place and in more or less the same manner and quantity. While the quantum of flow varies from day to day, seasonal changes, even though regular, are indeed large*. It takes considerable human effort and ingenuity to regulate natural flow to conform to the requirements of use; the proportion that can be so regulated, at any time, is a function largely of the stage of development of related engineering techniques.

The contribution to flow from different parts of the catchment of a river varies widely. In some cases, e.g. the Krishna, the contribution from its catchment in the Western Ghats is very much more than that from the Deccan plateux; however, under virgin conditions, the volume of flow increases as one proceeds from the source of the river to the sea. On the other hand, on the Indus system, the flow is maximum as the rivers emerge from the foot-hills, the large catchment in the plains yields but little additional supply. On account of losses enroute, the volume of flow decreases as one proceeds downstream from the foot-hills.

As indicated above, river waters are used for various purposes: for domestic water supply, for stock breeding, for irrigation, for navigation, for generation of hydro-electric power and for a variety of industrial uses.**

Rivers are also important for drainage and sanitation, for disposal of sewage and industrial waste, for conservancy of ports, harbours and estuaries, for fisheries, for recreation and for landscaping.

---

* Some idea of the magnitude of seasonal variations in Indian rivers would be given by the fact that the four monsoon months, from July to October, account for 75 per cent of the annual flow on the Ganga and as much as 93 per cent on the Mahanadi. On the latter river, most of the tributaries are dry from December to May.

** Ground waters can also be used for all these purposes except, of course, navigation and generation of hydro-electric power.

On the other hand, high floods in river occasionally cause extensive damage to life and property—agricultural, urban and industrial.

Some of the uses mentioned above, like navigation, generation of hydro-electric power and recreation are non-consumptive uses which do not involve any reduction in the volume of water flowing in a river. On the other hand, domestic water supply schemes and irrigation projects may abstract large quantities of water from river flow—in some cases the entire river flow may be so diverted for the greater part of the year. There are developments, like generation of hydro-electric power and some industrial processes, in which river waters can be used again and again; even when these are diverted for consumptive uses like irrigation or domestic water supply, a part of the waters so used must find its way back into the river lower down and may be put to further use.*

Most Indian rivers inter-State

Rivers do not respect political boundaries between States; in India, ever since Independence, the latter have been changing much too fast. As of now,

> the Indus basin lies in Tibet, Afghanistan, India and Pakistan—about 13 per cent in the first two countries and the rest in India and West Pakistan; within India, the Indus basin includes the whole of Kashmir and Punjab and parts of Himachal Pradesh, Haryana and Rajasthan;
> the Yamuna, the largest tributary of the Ganga, runs through Himachal Pradesh, Haryana, Delhi, Uttar Pradesh, Rajasthan and Madhya Pradesh; the rest of the Ganga system in India lies in Uttar Pradesh, Madhya Pradesh, Bihar and West Bengal;
> three of the Himalayan tributaries of the Ganga, the Gogra, the Gandak and the Kosi river in Nepal; the delta of the Ganga includes parts of West Bengal and East Pakistan;
> the Brahmaputra rises in Tibet and runs through Assam, West Bengal and East Pakistan;
> the Narmada and the Tapti both flow through Madhya Pradesh, Maharashtra and Gujarat;
> the Mahanadi drains Madhya Pradesh and Orissa also, small parts of Bihar and Maharashtra;
> the Godavari lies in Maharashtra, Madhya Pradesh, Orissa, Mysore and Andhra Pradesh;
> the Krishna system passes through Maharashtra, Mysore and Andhra Pradesh; and
> the drainage basin of the Cauveri lies in Mysore, Kerala and Tamil Nadu.

---

* According to a U.S. estimate, of the water withdrawn for industrial and municipal use, only about 2 per cent and 10 per cent respectively is used consumptively and of that diverted for irrigation 40-60 per cent is so used.

Some of the smaller rivers like the Damodar, the Mahi and the Pennar also pass through more than one State. In fact, most of India is served by inter-State rivers; some of these are also international.

Accordingly, river waters which are today in the territory of one State, and therefore, under its jurisdiction, will, except to the extent they are used up or held temporarily, flow away into the sea or into the territory of another State and, in the latter case, fall under the control or jurisdiction of the other State. To the extent the upper Slate has made consumptive use of the waters of a river, to a corresponding extent the lower State will have less supply available for use. Similarly, to the extent the lower State has developed a use, the upper State will have less water available for use except at the cost of the developments already carried out in the lower State. Thus, while each State has authority over these waters before they enter its territory or after they have left it, except as may be permitted by the adjoining State.

Modern trends in water resources development

Since the end of the nineteenth century, there has been a large increase in the consumptive use of river waters for domestic water supply, for irrigation and other uses – thus creating competition between different uses of water and between users. For many centuries past, the economic development of river waters progressed comparatively slowly and most exploitation were self-contained isolated units. This is not so any more. During the last few decades, there has been a growing realisation in all progressive countries that, for optimum development, water resources need to be treated on the basis of a whole drainage basin or an entire river system and that surface waters and ground waters must be considered together, in an integrated manner.*

At the same time, there has been an increasing tendency towards multipurpose development of river waters, for maximum overall benefit to the community – the various uses of water together with the requirements of flood control finding their proper position in the scheme of development in accordance with local or regional social and economic needs.

To maximise the use of limited** water resources and in the interest of public hygiene, it is being increasingly realised that sewage and industrial waste, before being let into a river, must be treated and rendered safe for the uses from and of the river below.

Over the last 30 years or so, emphasis is being laid, increasingly, on the inter-connection between water resources and related land resources and the consequent requirement that planning and development of the former should go hand in hand

* It has to be recognised that, since rainfall is the common source of all fresh waters, there is hydrologic unity in all natural water resources, whether surface or sub-surface.

** In most parts of India, total available water supply is much less than ultimate requirements of agriculture, industry, etc.

with that of the latter. It is urged that soil conservation and watershed management is of interest not only locally but for the entire river basin downstream; soil erosion in any part of the catchment increases sediment load in the river below, reducing the useful life of storage reservoirs and increasing flood hazards. Soil conservation and good watershed management also help in conserving water supplies; similarly, keeping the banks and sides of rivers and natural streams clear of aquatic growth and bush help in reducing losses by transpiration and improving on the quantum of utilizable waters.

With the ever-increasing demand for fresh water supplies and the increasing costs of conservation of natural waters, it has become important on the one hand to ensure that the supplies already developed are being put to maximum beneficial use and on the other to look out for new sources of water such as conversion of sea water to fresh water and rendering brackish ground waters fit for agricultural, domestic or industrial use.

ADMINISTRATION OF WATER RESOURCES

Historical

From ancient times, whereas construction and upkeep of wells for irrigation has always been by private endeavour, the development of surface waters for irrigation has been largely a State enterprise, Hindu kings and rulers in ancient India undertook construction of tanks and canals as benevolent works for the benefit of their people. Muslim rulers continued the humanitarian task. The British Government followed suit and undertook, in a big way, construction of irrigation canals, tanks and reservoirs, as state-financed and state-managed public works. From about 1930 onwards, tube-wells also came to be installed by Government, first in western Uttar Pradesh and later in Punjab, Bihar and other parts of the country.

Under British rule, the execution and management of irrigation works was a responsibility of provincial governments; but until 1921, the Government of India and the Secretary of State in London exercised powers of superintendence, direction and control on all activities relating to irrigation through an Inspector General of Irrigation and a Public Works Secretariat at the Centre. The Government of India "always possessed what may be called a common law right to use and control in the public interest the water supplies of the country...."[2]

In 1921, irrigation became a provincial subject but expenditure on it was not subject to the vote of the provincial legislature. Its administration was reserved to the Governor-General in Council and was, therefore, still under the ultimate control of the Secretary of State. All irrigation projects which affected more than one province or the cost of which exceeded Rs. 50 lakhs had to be submitted through the Government of India for the sanction of the Secretary of State. Whatever disputes arose between contending units for the utilisation of water supplies were referred to the Government of India and decisions were given in an executive capacity; in many cases, however, an attempt was first made to secure an agreement between the parties.

From April 1937, with the introduction of provincial autonomy, provincial governments got full powers over irrigation works and development. Only in case there was a dispute between two or more provinces, which could not be resolved by mutual agreement, the matter was required to be referred to the Governor-General who was empowered to appoint a Commission* to investigate all aspects of the dispute. The Governor-General was then to give a decision in the matter of the dispute, not necessarily in accordance with the report of the Commission, but as he deemed fit. If one of the contending parties so desired, the dispute had to be referred to His Majesty's Government.**

All electrical development in the provinces of British India, until 1932, as mainly in the private sector† and was regulated by licenses granted by the provincial governments under the Indian Electricity Act, passed by the Government of India in 1910.[3] In 1921 when, irrigation became a provincial but reserved subject, electricity (and hydro-electric development) became a provincial but transferred subject. However, in the Government of India Act, 1935, while water power was in the provincial list, electricity was placed on the Concurrent List, i.e. it became subject to the legislative powers of both the Central and Provincial Legislatures. Hydro-electric development in India was thus, from the beginning, under the control of management of the Provincial Governments.

As regards navigation, under the Government of India Act, 1935, 'shipping and navigation on tidal waters' was under Central control, but 'shipping and navigation on inland waterways as regards mechanically propelled vessels, and the rule of the road etc.' was subject to concurrent legislation of Central and provincial governments.

---

* "Consisting of such persons having special knowledge and experience in irrigation, engineering, administration, finance or law, as he (*i.e.* the Governor-General) thinks fit..." Only one such Commission was appointed under the 1935 Government of India Act, in September 1941, "to investigate the complaint of the Government of Sind about their interests in the water from the river Indus". The Commission comprised the Honourable Mr. Justice B.N. Rau, a judge of the Calcutta High Court, as Chairman, and Mr. P.F.B. Hickey, retired Chief Engineer, Irrigation Branch, United Provinces and Mr. E.H. Chave, Chief Engineer, Madras, as members.

** The Indus Commission submitted in report in July 1942. It made a number of recommendations. Neither the Government of Punjab nor that of Sind accepted these recommendations and both submitted representations to the Government of India against the finding and recommendations of the Commission. Ultimately, it was decided to refer the whole matter to His Majesty's Government for a final decision. A Number of informal meetings between the Chief Engineers of the two Provinces were also held with a view to finding a solution by agreement. One such draft agreement was prepared in September 1945. No decision was, however, reached either by agreement, or otherwise, up to 15th August, 1947, the date on which the Indus basin was split between two independent countries, India and Pakistan.

† The State of Mysore started to develop electric power as a State enterprise in 1902.

Constitutional position

Under the Constitution of Independent India, adopted in 1949,

> "Water, that is to say, water supplies, irrigation and canals drainage and embankments, water storage and water power...."
> and
> "Land, that is to say, rights in or over land...."

are in the State List (items 17 and 18 of List II of the Seventh Schedule). In other words, the State Legislature has exclusive powers to make laws and the State Government has exclusive powers to administer both the surface and the ground water resources and to generate hydro-electric power. These powers in respect of inter-State rivers are, however, subject to the control of the Union to the extent regulation and development of inter-State rivers and river valleys is declared by Parliament, bylaw, to be expedient in the public interest (item 56 of List I of the Seventh Schedule). The Constitution makers did not engage themselves in laying down any policy or directive principles to guide the Union in respect of the control that may be exercised by it in respect of inter-State rivers but left everything to the discretion of Parliament.

As regards navigation, the Union List includes "... shipping and navigation on tidal waters", "shipping and navigation on inland waterways, declared by Parliament by law to be national waterways, as regards mechanically propelled vessels; the rule of the road on such waterways"; and "carriage of passengers and goods... by national waterways in mechanically propelled vessels" (items 25, 24 and 30 of List I). These activities on other inland waterways are provided for in the Concurrent List (item 32 of List III). The State List includes "inland waterways" other than national waterways "and traffic thereon", by means other than mechanically propelled vessels, fisheries, and "taxes on goods and passengers carried... on inland waterways" (items 13, 21 and 56 of List II).

Apart from the functions allotted to the Union and the States in respect of the use of natural waters, their regulation and control etc. as described above, the Constitution also makes provision for adjudication of disputes relating to water of inter-State rivers or river valleys. Article 262 of the Constitution reads:

(1) Parliament may by law provide for the adjudication of any dispute or complaint with respect to the use, distribution or control of the waters of, or in, any inter-State river or river valley.

(2) Notwithstanding anything in this Constitution, Parliament may by law provide that neither the Supreme Court nor any other court shall exercise jurisdiction in respect of any such dispute or complaint as is referred to in clause (1).

Legislation

It was only in 1956 that, under the provision of Item 56 of List I of the Seventh Schedule, referred to above, Parliament passed the River Boards Act.[4] Section 2 of the Act states: "It is hereby declared that it is expedient in the public interest that the Central Government should take under its control the regulation and development of inter-State rivers and river valleys to the extent hereinafter provided". However, the Act does not give any authority to the Centre to develop or regulate the waters of inter-State rivers nor to control, in any way, the activities of State Governments in respect of these waters nor does it lay down any policy or directive principles relating to the use of these waters. All that the River Boards Act does is to give authority to the Government of India to set up, for any inter-State river, a River Board

> to advise* the States on any matter relating to the regulation and development of the waters of the river, in particular on questions relating to the coordination of their activities in relation to these waters with a view to the resolution of inter-State conflicts; and
>
> to make technical studies, prepare schemes of development and advise* the States regarding their execution including questions relating to allocation of their costs, etc.

The River Boards Act, as passed in 1956, emerged after detailed examination of the technical requirements of developments on inter-State rivers, of constitutional provisions, of the pre-1937 administrative procedures which had led to developments of no mean order, of the relevant provisions of the 1935 Government of India Act and, to a limited extent, of the experience of other countries. Starting in 1949 with proposals which aimed at giving to the Central Government executive powers of direction and control in respect of these developments, after discussion with the States, and between the concerned ministries of the Government of India and the Planning Commission, the conclusion was ultimately reached that River Boards, as described above, should provide an efficient machinery for securing optimum regional development as well as fostering a cooperative approach. It was the intention (as Sir V.T. Krishnamachari started more than once) that River Boards would be set up within a few years for all inter-State rivers. The Planning Commission was all the time keen** on them and so was, for sometime at least, the Ministry of Irrigation and Power. However, the Act was not mandatory in its application; for several years

---

* This advice is not binding but should any dispute arise between two or more States in regard to such advice, any of the States concerned can seek arbitration, under the Act, and the award of the arbitrator shall be binding on the concerned States.

** The Third Five-Year Plan sets out the necessity of inter-State cooperation in the following terms: "River basins, especially those of the larger rivers, naturally extend beyond the boundaries of individual States. In some cases, the most suitable site for harnessing the water resources of a river involving, for instance, less submergence of land or smaller cost of construction, may lie in one State, while the area receiving irrigation or power benefits may lie in another State. *For integrated and economic development of water resources, arrangements for inter-State cooperation are therefore, essential... The setting up of River Boards* for important river basin, as envisaged in the River Boards Act, 1956, *would enable a coordinated view to be taken of the need of a river basin as a whole, including soil conservation in the catchment area.* Steps to establish River Boards for the more important rivers are being taken in consultation with the States". (emphasis supplied)

after it was passed, nothing was done to set up any Board under the Act. In 1961, however, steps were taken to set up River Boards on several rivers, the Mahanadi, the Krishna, the Godavari, the Narmada, the Tapti, the Mahi, the Yamuna, the Sutlej, Beas and Ravi, and the Chenab. After some of the concerned States had indicated their willingness to cooperate, necessary procedural and financial details were worked out in 1963 and, in due course, a supplementary grant was approved by Parliament to meet the expenditure on these Boards during 1963-64. It seems, there was a sudden change of policy thereafter and the idea of setting up the Boards was abandoned.

Along with the River Boards Act, Parliament also enacted the Inter-State Water Disputes Act, 1956 under Article 262 of the Constitution. But provision was made that "no reference shall be made to a tribunal", under the latter Act, "of any dispute that may arise regarding any matter which may be referred to arbitration under the River Boards Act, 1956". It was hoped that, with River Boards established on most inter-State rivers, the provisions of the Inter-State Water Disputes Act would seldom have to be invoked.

The Inter-State Water Disputes Act provides that "neither the Supreme Court nor any other Court shall have or exercise jurisdiction in respect of any water dispute which may be referred to a tribunal under this Act". It authorises the Central Government, on the request of a State Government, to constitute an ad-hoc Water Disputes Tribunal for any dispute between two or more States with respect to an inter-State river; but strange as it may seem, the tribunal under the Act was to consist of one judge of the Supreme Court or a High Court. Recently, the Act has been amended to provide for three judges to constitute the tribunal instead of one as in the original Act. The Act does not lay down any principles or guidelines to be followed by the tribunal. It is difficult to understand the logic of adopting, on the one hand, the permissive clause of the Constitution to debar the Supreme Court from exercising jurisdiction over such disputes and, on the other, to constitute for the purpose ad-hoc tribunals of three judges of the same court or a High Court. The Act is thus contradictory in concept and the recent amendment does not much improve the position. Section 3 below deals further with the employment of the judicial process in resolving inter-State controversies about the use of river waters.

The Electricity (Supply) Act was passed by the Constituent Assembly (Legislative) in 1948, as a Central Act, "to provide for the rationalisation of the production and supply of electricity and generally for taking measures conducive to electrical development."[5] It provides for the formation of semi-autonomous State Electricity Boards "charged with the general duty of promoting the coordinated development of the generation, supply and distribution of electricity within the State in the most efficient and economical manner, with particular reference to such development in areas not for the time being served by any licensee". The Act defines the relations between these Boards and the licensees. The Act also provides for the constitution of the Central Electricity Authority, inter alia, to "develop a sound, adequate and uniform national power policy, and particularly to coordinate the activities of the planning agencies in relation to the control and utilisation of national power resources".

A Board is required under the Act to consult the Authority in respect of every new schemes likely to cost more than 50 lakhs* of rupees and the Authority, before making any recommendation in respect of the scheme, shall "have particular regard to whether or not in its opinion", among other things,

> "any river works proposed by the Board will prejudice the prospects for the best ultimate development of the river or its tributaries for power-generation, consistent with the requirements of irrigation, navigation and flood control, and for this purpose the Authority shall satisfy itself that an adequate study has been made of the optimum location of dams and other river works".

The Authority is required to forward a copy of its recommendation to the State Government.

On the setting up, a few years later, of the Central Water and Power Commission, under the Ministry of Irrigation and Power, many of the functions of the Central Electricity Authority came to be performed by the Commission. As of now, while the constitutional entity of the Central Electricity Authority is being maintained, the Power Wing of the Commission virtually functions as the Authority.

With regard to ground water, even though there has recently been a considerable increase in the effort towards their development, there has so far been no legislation in this connection; no legal or constitutional problems have yet emerged.

There has been little change since Independence about inland navigation. Developments, if any, have been of little consequence. No waterway has yet been declared by Parliament as a national waterway.

Present status not satisfactory

It would appear from the above that, in respect of the development of our river basins, most of which extend beyond the limits of a single State, our Constitution is only permissive and does not, by itself, foster any regional approach. Such water law as operates in the country and the administrative institutions concerned are related to the geographical limits of the States which implement the law or control the institutions. The legislation enacted by Parliament in 1956 to foster a regional approach, the River Boards Act, has not been implemented, and there does not appear to be any intention on the part of the present Government of India to do so. The legal and administrative situation, thus, is not in pace with the modern trends towards water resources development, as described in Section 1 above.

The non-existence of any institution to coordinate developments on inter-State rivers is the prime reason for the large number of current disputes on these rivers which, by their very nature, generate strong emotions**, from time to time, in one

* Since increased to Rs. one crore.

** Referring to inter-State disputes, the Indus Commission (1942) recorded[1]: "cases of this nature, involving, as they do, questions of vital importance to the future development of an entire State or Province, are necessarily fought with great tenacity on each side and often occupy several years in the ordinary courts of law...."

part of the country or another. As already stated, the organisation intended by Parliament to bring about a basin-wise approach for optimum development has not been established on any inter-State river. Instead, the Government of India continues to rely on administrative procedures under which, as part of the planning process, there is an agreement between the Centre and the States to the effect that no large project would be undertaken by a State unless cleared by the Planning Commission and the Government of India. The power so enjoyed by the Central Government has been used, in some cases effectively, to foster cooperation in the development of inter-State rivers. On the other hand, this procedure tends also to complicate the issues if clearance is given to a project on an inter-State river without securing agreement of other States on that river. Such clearance, it may be noted, has no constitutional validity in respect of water rights of any State but, nevertheless, authorities expenditure of large sums of public money.

With no River Board having been set up, no adjudication could be sought under the provisions of the River Boards Act. Some yeas ago, Maharashtra and Mysore requested the Government of India to set up a tribunal under the Inter-State Water Disputes Act in connection with their rights on the Krishna and the Godavari; presumably, the request was not vigorously pursued and the Government of India was reluctant to set up the tribunal. Recently, Andhra Pradesh has, it is understood, also requested for a tribunal and one may be set up soon for the two rivers. There seems to be no move yet for setting up a tribunal for any other river.

Meanwhile, as recorded by the Krishna-Godavari Commission in 1962, State Governments continue to put forward projects assuming for each the highest priority on the available flow without consideration of the requirements of other projects on the same river in adjoining States, or schemes which would submerge large areas in the territory of another State or even adversely affect developments in that State. The result is the ever-increasing number of disputes on inter-State rivers. On some inter-State rivers, while broad agreement have been reached between the concerned States on sharing of waters or other benefits, there is inadequate coordination in the day to day operation, leading to occasional complaints by one State or the other. Under present conditions, these disputes and complaints will increase considerably with increasing use of water by projects now under construction or by new projects which must be taken up. The position is thus far from satisfactory; but the worst part is that, so far as known, nothing is proposed to be done about it except for the Union Ministry of Irrigation and Power to continue with its not very effective mediatory efforts and reference of individual disputes to arbitral tribunals in accordance with the provisions of the recently amended Inter-State Water Disputes Act.

No machinery exists at present for the prevention of pollution of the waters of inter-State rivers or for the coordination of activities of the concerned States in respect of afforestation and control of soil erosion; Parliament had provided in the Rive Boards Act, 1956 for these functions to be performed by River Boards to be set up under the Act. Promotion of inland navigation is likewise receiving scant attention.

JUDICIAL DECISIONS ON INTER-STATE WATER DISPUTES—AN UNHAPPY CHOICE

Constitutional reluctance

That disputes between States with regard to inter-State rivers should not fall within the jurisdiction of the Supreme Court is in accordance with the provision of Article 262(2) of the Constitution; the latter is in turn based on Section 133 of the Government of India Act, 1935 which excluded all matters in respect of water rights from the jurisdiction of the Federal Court. That provision was made after an examination in considerable detail of all aspects of the problem. A Joint Committee of the British Parliament observed:

> "The Federal Court would indeed have jurisdiction to decide any dispute between two Provinces in connection with water supplies, if legal rights or interests were concerned; but the experience of most countries has shown that rules of law based upon the analogy of private proprietary interests in water do not afford a satisfactory basis for settling disputes between Provinces or States where the interests of the public at large in the proper use of water supplies are involved. It is unnecessary to emphasise the importance from the public point of view of the distribution of water in India, upon which not only the prosperity, but the economic existence, of large tracts depends".

Having excluded, for good reasons, the jurisdiction of the Supreme Court over a water dispute between States, to constitute, for its adjudication, a tribunal consisting of three judges of the Supreme Court or a High Court is but a poor substitute. The ultimate settlement of a water dispute seldom lies merely in the determination of legal rights, assuming, which is not true, that a set of inelastic legal principles did exist as a basis of that determination. More often than not, engineering technique, mutual accommodation, quid pro quo or outside financial assistance have provided a basis of settlement with large overall benefits not otherwise possible.

There can be no better way to examine the problem further than to study the developments on some rivers in India and abroad and see if those developments could have been brought about by recourse to the judicial process.

Examples from Indian rivers

Among the earlier developments in India may be noticed the Gang Canal in Rajasthan (erstwhile Bikaner State) which was constructed in 1920-28 to supply water from the Sutlej to Bikaner—a non-riparian State; the canal runs for about one hundred miles through the territory of Punjab. Could this development have been brought about by the decision of a court or through any judicial adjudication? Similarly, could Madras acquire the right, through any judicial process, to divert eastward, across the watershed, for irrigation of a most precarious tract in Madras, the waters of the

Pariyar, a river rising in Travancore and flowing, in its natural state, westward into the Arabian Sea. The answer is obviously no.

Coming to more recent times, could any tribunal direct Bihar to submerge its lands for the development of irrigation and for flood control in West Bengal. This is exactly what the Damodar Valley development has done under Central legislation. The Damodar Valley Corporation Act was passed in 1948 by the Constituent Assembly (legislative); but it could not have been enacted unless the Legislative Assemblies of Bihar and West Bengal had first agreed that the Centre might do so. On the Chambal, the States of Madhya Pradesh and Rajasthan are sharing equally the costs and benefits of

> the Gandhisagar project, situated almost wholly in Madhya Pradesh;*
> the hydro-electric development at Rana Pratap Sagar and Jawahar Sagar, dependent mainly on the storage at Gandhisagar but situated wholly in Rajasthan;
> the Kota barrage in Rajasthan; and
> the canals taking off at Kota one of which runs for 81 miles in Rajasthan territory before entering Madhya Pradesh to irrigate 7 lakh acres of land in the latter State.

It should be obvious that such a development could not result through recourse to the judicial process and, but for the mutual cooperation between the two States, the development described above would not have been possible and the people concerned would have been deprived of the potential benefits from the river resources. Similarly, but for the accommodation shown by Punjab (including the present Haryana) and the persuasion of the Central Government, Rajasthan could hardly have acquired a share in irrigation and power generation from the Bhakra-Beas complex and made possible the vast irrigation development from the Rajasthan Canal; the judicial process could not have led to the happy result.

Practice in the United States

The United States, like India, is a federation of States with many inter-State rivers. The U.S. Supreme Court has jurisdiction over disputes between States relating to the use of waters of inter-State rivers but, in practice, the Court has generally restricted itself to determining whether or not the action taken or proposed to be taken by one State would cause injury to another. According to a study of the decisions of the Court[6];

> "... in the only three instances in which the Supreme Court came to a decision on the merits of the case, this took the form of an interim, rather than a final, decree. In no case has the court laid down a specific formula for the apportionment of the water of an inter-State river. Every case was decided in

---

* To facilitate the construction by Madhya Pradesh of the Gandhisagar dam, Rajasthan transferred a few square miles of its territory permanently to Madhya Pradesh.

the light of its particular circumstances. The reluctance of the court to exercise supervisory control of inter-State rivers is quite apparent. The court has quite consciously left the details of the necessary regulation to the disputing states as this involves an executive and legislative rather than a judicial function, and has restricted itself to stating whether present injuries or injuries to be expected in the future which were clearly defined and whose effects were unambiguous were sufficiently established".

The U.S. Supreme Court has itself stated[7]:

> "The reason for judicial caution in adjudicating the relative rights of States in such cases is that, while we have jurisdiction of such disputes, they involve the interests of quasi-sovereigns, present complicated and delicate questions, and, due to the possibility of future change of conditions, necessitate expert administration rather than judicial imposition of a hard and fast rule. Such controversies may appropriately be composed by negotiation and agreement pursuant to the compact clause of the Federal Constitution. We say of this case, as the court has laid of inter-State differences of like nature, that such mutual accommodation and agreement should, if possible, be the medium of settlement, instead of invocation of our adjudicatory power".

Thus, for adjustment of inter-State issues relating to regional water resource development, there are two channels in the United States: negotiations leading to inter-State compacts and litigation among the States within the original jurisdiction of the Supreme Court. The first represents the 'cooperative' approach; the second the 'contentious'.[8] But, as shown above, in most cases, the apportionment of waters and the details of regulation, etc. are determined by negotiation between the States concerned and embodied in inter-State compacts. These compacts generally make provision for a joint permanent commission or agency.

Examples from international rivers

Before India and Pakistan agreed in 1952 to accept the good offices of the World Bank, and during stalemates in the negotiations that followed, Pakistan had repeatedly urged that the dispute relating to the use of the waters of the Indus be referred for adjudication to the International Court of Justice. But India could not entrust[9] to any outside body the well-being of a large section of her people dependent for their livelihood on the waters of this river. The practical solution to the dispute, which emerged in 1960, after discussions over a period of 8 years, could by no stretch of imagination have been obtained through any judicial process. Had India agreed to Pakistan's request, either the people of India or those of Pakistan or both would have been the sufferers; for the engineering solution, which provides for maximum development in both countries and in the basin as a whole, could have been brought about only by negotiations conducted by a group of persons (engineers and administrators) whose thinking was not restricted by any existing or assumed legal principles. In fact, the Indus Waters Treaty set up new precedents in international relations in respect of the use of river waters of common concern. It is noteworthy that even when the World Bank, acting as a mediator, had on some occasions urged, as a short-cut to the negotiations, that India and Pakistan should agree to accept third party decisions on relatively minor issues, India consistently refused to do so.

On the Nile, the agreement[10] between Sudan and the United Arab Republic (November 1959), which enabled developments to proceed at the High Dam at Aswan, is another outstanding example of mutually agreed basis of development. Apart from arrangements relating to the flooding of Sudanese territory by the High Dam at Aswan in the U.A.R., this agreement gives Sudan the use of 14.5 billion cubic metres out of a net benefit from the dam of 22 billion cubic metres*; the U.A.R. will get the rest of the water and a huge amount of electric power.** Such arrangements between different countries can only be negotiated; these cannot be secured through a judicial process even assuming that there was a court with the jurisdiction to adjudicate and it was possible to enforce its decision.

The negotiations leading to the recent Columbia River Basin Treaty, between Canada and the United States of America, presents some important features which must be noted here.[11] The Columbia river is shared by two highly developed countries, with a long tradition of friendship and trust between them. Also, the developments on the Columbia are relatively free from the difficult problems that arise when relatively large quantities of water have to be diverted for agricultural use. Yet the negotiations leading to the treaty took almost 20 years; it is important to note the procedure adopted.

As early as 1909, Canada and the U.S.A. entered into a treaty laying down principles and procedure for resolving the then existing (and future) disputes between them relating to boundary waters etc. A continuing organisation—the International Joint Commission—was set up under this Treaty to assist the two Governments. In 1944, under the provisions of the 1909 Treaty, the Commission as entrusted with the task of working out the possibilities for cooperative development on the Columbia. Thereupon, a joint Engineering Board was set up by the International Joint Commission. This Board, after extensive field surveys and technical studies, submitted its report in 1959. This report indicated a number of sites in Canada suitable for large storage reservoirs which could be used for regulation of river supplies to the benefit of both countries. It presented three alternative plans of development. The International Joint Commission was then asked to formulate its recommendations concerning the principles by which the benefits to be realised could be assessed and apportioned between the two countries. Its report was submitted in December 1959

---

* The average annual yield of the river at Aswan taken as 84 billion cubic metres, less the "acquired rights" on the Nile at Aswan of 48 billion cubic metres for U.A.R. and 4 billion cubic metres for Sudan, less the estimated annual evaporation loss from the reservoir of 10 billion cubic-metres.

** Installed capacity of 12 units of 175,000 kW each, at the designed head.

whereupon the two Governments appointed delegations to negotiate the terms of a Treaty which was signed in January, 1961. The United States ratified the Treaty soon thereafter but in Canada a number of problems had still to be resolved between the Federal Government and the province of British Columbia. These related to Centre-State relations—the degree of control the federal government was to exercise over the development of power in British Columbia. Two years elapsed before agreement could be reached between the province and the federal government. It was only in September, 1964 that the ratifications were exchanged together with a Protocol Note embodying agreed changes in the Treaty provisions and supplementary provisions to accommodate the point of view of British Columbia. This treaty represents an important step toward achieving optimum development of the river from which either country will receive benefits materially larger than it could obtain independently. From the point of view of Canada[12], the Treaty commits Canada to manage the river in its territory "within general guidelines designed to protect the objectives of the cooperative undertaking, and yet leaves that country with sufficient flexibility to proceed with the optimum power development in its own part of the basin and, even more essential, to use the waters of the Columbia system to meet the consumptive needs of that nation". On the other side, "the United States will secure a large block of power at low cost, substantial flood control benefits, ... at a much earlier date and at a cost materially less than would be the case were they to be a provided exclusively through projects in the United States".[13] Such a result could not be achieved by any judicial process nor could the latter be used to obtain acceptance of the principle adopted in the treaty to the effect that the upstream riparian should receive a share of the benefit which the downstream riparian can get from the activities of the upstream riparian on its reach of the river.

Inherent difficulties

The three international treaties mentioned above created new rules of law between the signatories in relation to the specific rivers. This legislative work cannot be left to any outside agency but has to be evolved by the parties themselves, in the light of the conditions and requirements of each river. While few will contest that negotiation can be the only practical method for resolving conflicts regarding the use of river waters as between independent countries, the position is or should be different, it is often urged, when the contending parties are States within a federation, within the same political and economic unit. Contrary to the position in the international field, it is within the competence of the national legislature to give jurisdiction over such matters to its Supreme Court or any ad-hoc body to be established by law. There is danger, however, as shown above, that recourse to the judicial process might not lead to optimum development of the natural resource with consequent and permanent loss to the well-being and future prosperity of the people concerned. And this danger is particularly significant at the present stage of our development, with inadequate basic data of river flow on most rivers, with no plans or inadequately worked out plans of development, in the absence of any principles laid down either in the Constitution, or by legislation, to guide adjudication, and in face of the serious difficulty of interpreting such principles, even if they did exist.

It has been stated above that, prior to 1937, the Government of India had to be consulted with regard to every major irrigation project. Whenever questions arose of water rights between provinces and states, that Government was guided by two considerations[14]:

> that the waters of a river should be utilised to the best possible advantage (for the maximum good of the maximum number) in the tracts commanded, irrespective of territorial boundaries;*
>
> that it is both just and expedient that each case of dispute between provinces or between a province and a state should be dealt with on the merits of the individual case; the principles on which a decision was based in one case are not necessarily applicable to another.

No general principles could emerge under such conditions as guides for judicial adjudication of inter-State disputes relating to the use of river waters.

The Indus Commission (1942) found that the following general principles for distribution of the water of inter-State rivers seemed to emerge from a study of the practice in other countries[15]:

> "The most satisfactory settlement of disputes of this kind is by agreement, the parties adopting the same technical solution of each problem, as if they were a single community undivided by political or administrative frontiers,
>
> "If once there is such an agreement, that in itself furnishes the 'law' governing the rights of the several parties until a new agreement is concluded.
>
> "If there is no such agreement, the rights of the several Provinces and States must be determined by applying the rules of 'equitable apportionment', each unit getting a fair share of the water of the common river.

---

* An appropriate example is the allotment of the waters of the Sutlej to Bikaner, a non-riparian state. Prior to the preparation of the Sutlej Valley Project (1920), there was a lengthy dispute with the Bahawalpur Durbar in regard to the utilisation of the waters of the Sutlej; the main bone of contention was the inclusion in the project of some areas in Bikaner, a non-riparian state. The dispute was eventually settled at a conference of representatives of the Government of India, the Government of Punjab, and the Bahawalpur and Bikaner Durbars, at which it was emphasised that the paramount power was the sole judge. This decision was eventually accepted by Bahawalpur, and the following formula was agreed to:

"That in considering the method of disposing of the waters made available for irrigation by the Sutlej Valley Project, the general principle is recognised that those waters should be distributed in the best interests of the public at large, irrespective of provincial or state boundaries, subject always to the proviso that established rights are fully safeguarded or compensated for and that full and prior recognition is given to the claim of riparian owners, and that their rights in existing supplies or in any supplies which may hereafter be made available in the Sutlej River below the junction of the Beas and Upper Sutlej are fully investigated and are limited only by the economic factor".

"For purposes of priority, the date of a project is not the date when survey is first commenced, but the date when the project reaches finality and there is 'a fixed and definite purpose to take it up and carry it through'.

"In the general interests of the entire community inhabiting dry, arid territories, priority may usually have to be given to an earlier irrigation project over a later one: 'priority of appropriation gives superiority of right'.*

"As between projects of different kinds for the use of water, a suitable order of precedence might be (*i*) use for domestic and sanitary purposes, (*ii*) use for navigation, and (*iii*) use for power and irrigation".**

The Commission propounded these principles in September 1941, on the first day of its open session, and after hearing all the interested units, expressed its views in the following terms:

> "All parties have accepted the general principles which we tentatively formulated on the first day after examining the practice in other parts of the world. It follows from them that the rights of the several units concerned in this dispute must be determined by applying neither the doctrine of sovereignty, nor the doctrine of riparian rights, but the rule of 'equitable apportionment', each unit being entitled to a fair share of the waters of the Indus and its tributaries".

Referring to the earlier decisions of 1937 regarding the use of the Indus waters, the Commission stated:

> "The orders of the Government of India, March 30, 1937, proceeding, as they did for the most part, on the consent of the unit concerned, must be regarded as having secured the mot equitable apportionment then possible. If owing to material errors in the original data, or a material change in river conditions, or other sufficient cause, those orders are now found to be inequitable, and if a more equitable arrangement can be discovered in present circumstances, with due regard to the interests of all the units concerned, the original orders may properly be modified. This implies, of course, that a modification of the orders in one particular may necessitate consequential modifications in other particulars by way of redressing the balance between the several units".

---

* It may be noted that the Indus Waters Treaty (1960) modified this principle as follows: "Historic withdrawals of water must be continued, but not necessarily from existing sources". No fair and adequate plan could, it was stated, be devised if existing uses must be supplied from existing sources.

** The Commission observed "that the ranking of different uses in a particular order of precedence depends on the circumstances of the river concerned. And even as regards the same river, different authorities may take different views".

Now let us turn to this rule of 'equitable apportionment' which seems to command general acceptance. After several years of debate, in August 1966, the International Law Association defined[16] this rule,* for application to international rivers, in the following terms and this comprehensive definition may, with advantage, be used for inter-State rivers:

> "Each basin State is entitled, within its territory, to a reasonable and equitable share in the beneficial uses of the waters of an international drainage basin".
> "What is a reasonable and equitable share... is to be determined in the light of all the relevant factors in each particular case".
> "Relevant factors which are to be considered include, but are not limited to:
> the geography of the basin, including in particular the extent of the drainage area in the territory of each basin State;
> the hydrology of the basin, including in particular the contribution of water by each basin State;
> the climate affecting the basin;
> the past utilisation of the waters of the basin, including in particular existing utilisation;
> the economic and social needs of each basin State;
> the population dependent on the waters of the basin in each basin State;
> the comparative costs of alternative means of satisfying the economic and social needs of each basin State;
> the availability of other resources;
> the avoidance of unnecessary waste in the utilisation of waters of the basin;
> the practicability of compensation to one or more of the co-basin States as a means of adjusting conflicts among uses; and
> "the degree to which the needs of a basin State may be satisfied, without causing substantial injury to a co-basin State."
> "The weight to be given to each factor is to be determined by its importance in comparison with that of other relevant factor. In determining what is a reasonable and equitable share, all relevant factors are to be considered together and a conclusion reached on the basis of the whole".

It would be obvious that the conclusion, referred to above, cannot be reached nor 'a reasonable and equitable share' determined by any judicial process. Such determination can properly be made only by persons who have special knowledge and understanding of water resources development and must not be made unless and until detailed engineering studies of different possible plans of development have been prepared on a comparable basis and evaluated. It is important to note in

---

* The International Law Association being a non-Governmental organisation, the question does not arise of the rule having been accepted by, or the rule being binding on, the Government of any country or State.

this connection that before one can proceed to determine shares of different States, one must first know the total available or utilisable flow to be shared. This itself is more often than not in dispute and its determination is not a matter of law but of engineering judgment to be based on an analytical study of river flow data and the seasonal variations in flow, on an expert examination of the physical features of the rive and on the ever-developing technique of dam construction.

A plea that is frequently put forward in India is that water resources are national assets; these should be developed in the best interest of the nation. But those who advocate this rely on their own subjective understanding of national interest. It is generally noticed that people of each State, of each district and even a part of a district regard, not without some justification, the particular project of interest to them as one in the best national interest and they would not recognise that any one else has a right to express a contrary view. They would not stop to consider that any project for water resource development, if economically justified, no matter in which Sate it lies, must benefit the country as a whole. It is possible, however, that some plans of development may be more beneficial than others. While few people will not concede that, in such cases, overall national interest should prevail, there must be some objective test for determining which particular plan would be more in the national interest than another.

It would appear from the above that such general principles as one can bring to bear are not, by themselves, of much help in adjudicating on the respective rights of different States in respect of the economic use of waters of inter-State rivers. Under these conditions, the award of a tribunal, even of three judges,* is hardly likely to satisfy all parties, it may not satisfy anyone. On the other hand, it may stand in the way of maximising developments from a river, if for no other reason, by freezing a situation otherwise capable of being improved upon by further study or by development of engineering technique. On matters closely related to the permanent well-being or otherwise of large sections of the population, it is extremely difficult to control emotions and passions that may thus be generated and one cannot hold, with confidence, that the award of the tribunal, the limitations imposed, would be faithfully administered by the concerned State or States on which rest the ultimate responsibility and the authority to control the waters.

A NEGOTIATED SETTLEMENT IS THE BEST SETTLEMENT

As has been illustrated by the examples given above of developments on some inter-State and international rivers, a proper assessment of resources, employment of the best engineering technique to maximise benefits and detailed analyses of alternative plans of development must play an important role in working out a settlement which

* As per recent amendment of the Inter-State Water Disputes Act, 1956. The fact that the Tribunal may have "two or more persons as assessors to advise it" would not materially alter the situation.

would commend itself to the parties and be in the best national interest. Apart from this, conditions vary widely and each river is a law unto itself. It is for these reasons that a negotiated settlement is the best possible solution of a water dispute between States—it leaves no bitterness behind and, having been voluntarily agreed to, carries with it the best prospect of being implemented faithfully; the latter aspect may, in some cases and in course of time, become even more important than the immediate resolution of a dispute. In the ultimate analysis, equity lies in what the parties agree upon as equitable. Accordingly, all the time, energy and thought that may have to be spent to secure a mutually acceptable settlement of a water dispute is worthwhile.

The principal reasons why it has not been possible so far to resolve, by negotiation, the inter-State disputes on the Krishna, the Godavari, the Narmada and several other rivers in India are:

> There do not exist, as basis of negotiation, basin-wise plans of development, or alternate plans, prepared with the participation of the concerned States. Such spasmodic negotiations as have been conducted were apparently not meaningful, were not conducted systematically nor in the proper atmosphere. For example, for the Union Ministry, acting as a mediator, to make a public statement of its proposals to resolve the controversy, as it did in the case of the Krishna and the Godavari, was bad tactics; no wonder, the proposals were rejected by all the parties.
> On these rivers, as well as on the Narmada, some of the principal items in dispute relate to projects which had been framed, sponsored or cleared by the Union Ministry of Irrigation and Power, ignoring in a few instances, the objections raised by some States. For the same Ministry to assume the role of a good officer or mediator can hardly inspire the confidence which the parties must have in a mediator.

Whether the Central Government is a party to a dispute or not may be contended, the fact remains that this Government is, directly or indirectly, so deeply involved in some of the matters under dispute that it would be well advised to stay out of the picture and should urge the States concerned to settle the matter between themselves, directly or with the help of one or more mediators of their own choice. Only if such mediation, given a fair trial fails, should the parties consider recourse to some form of arbitration. It may sometimes happen, when a dispute has been allowed to linger on for long, that a State Government or the party in power, finding it embarrassing to take on itself the onus of agreeing to a solution of the dispute different from its earlier declarations, may want to seek arbitration on the dispute, as a measure of political expediency. This would be nothing short of abrogating the Government's responsibility to the people of the State and the Government may land itself; or its successor, into situations even more embarrassing than that it tries to escape from. In case of an adverse decision by the tribunal, the people affected would, for ever, decry the Government's decision to seek arbitration.

COOPERATIVE APPROACH LIKELY TO PROVIDE THE BEST SOLUTION

Reference has been made in Section 1 above to the growing realisation in most countries that, for optimum development, water resources should be considered on the basis of a whole drainage basin. With all major rivers of the country flowing through more than one State and with States constitutionally semi-sovereign in respect of land and water development, the only practical way to secure basin-wise development of river resources, in the light of the special problems inherent in such development, as briefly described above, lies through a cooperative approach, based on due recognition of the constitutional rights of the concerned States and the reasonable requirements of the people of those States. In this connection, it would be pertinent to refer here to a recent U.S. Act, passed by Congress in 1965, for the establishment of river basin commissions.

River basin Commissions in U.S.A.

The Water Resources Planning Act, 1965, provides, inter alia, for the establishment of Federal State river basin planning commissions for any river basin or group of river basins upon a request, made to the President, by the Water Resources Council* or the Governors of at least half of the concerned States. "With water and related land functions carried out at all governmental levels and by private enterprise, it is important that what is done within the same region in the utilisation of water and related land resources make sense. Conflicts need to be ironed out and opportunities for complementary action fully utilised....

"The functions of a Commission are:

> "To serve as the principal agency for the coordination of Federal, State, inter-state, local and non-governmental plans for the development of water and related land resources";
> "To prepare and keep up to date a comprehensive, coordinated joint plan for Federal, State, inter-state, local and non-governmental development".

"Members of Commissions are one from each State; one from each Federal department or independent agency determined by the President to have a substantial interest; one member appointed by any relevant inter-State agency created by compact to which the consent of Congress has been given; and one member, when appropriate, from the United States Section of a related international commission".

"The chairman is appointed by the President. He is also the coordinating officer of the Federal members.... He represents the Federal Government in Federal-State relations on the commission. State members are to elect one of their number as vice-chairman, and he is to coordinate the State members and represent the States in Federal-State relations on the commission.

---

* Consisting of the Secretaries of Agriculture, the Army, the Interior, and Health, Education, and Welfare and of the Chairman, Federal Power Commission.

"The Act recognises that meaningful collaborative planning requires consensus .... In view of that fact, the Water Resources Planning Act contains no provision for voting within the commission; and indeed, the legislative history makes it clear that it was the intention of the framers that commission decisions would not be determined by voting".

"The requirement of ultimate consensus does not mean, however, that the river basin commissions will face a choice only between unanimity and deadlock. The Act provides that, in the case of failure to reach consensus, full opportunity is to be afforded each member to present his views and have them reported; and, in another provision, the commission is directed to include in its comprehensive plans an evaluation of all reasonable alternatives".

"These provisions mean that a commission, failing to agree, has not reached a dead-end, but has the means for agreeing to disagree, for continuing its activities in the hope of reaching consensus, and for referral of alternatives for legislative decisions at the appropriate level of government".

River Boards

The Rive Boards Act, 1956, as indicated earlier in Section 2, aimed at securing optimum regional development and had in it the potential for fostering a cooperative approach. It was, however, unfortunately worded: ".... expedient ... that the Central Government should take under its control..."; but the Act gave little authority to the Centre. The Act emphasised, and rightly so, the importance of basin-wise development and provided machinery for tendering advice on the subject to the concerned States. However, it did not contain any specific provision for engendering cooperation between these States. On the other hand, Section 22, which enabled any State to seek arbitration on disputes or differences arising out of any advice tendered by a Board, stood in the way of such cooperation. It was because of this shortcoming in the Act that the Krishna-Godavari Commission, while recognising the need for inter-State cooperation, did not show any enthusiasm for creating a River Board under the Act but stated[17]:

> "The Commission recommends that an inter-State body, a River Board or by whatever name called, should be established without any delay, for bringing about a cooperative approach and establishing the necessary coordination in the planning and operation of various developments in the two river basins. The integrated operation of all projects, which is indispensable, would not be possible without such a coordinating body".

Some of the shortcomings of the River Boards Act were, however, made good in 1963, when it was decided to appoint a Chief Engineer to be nominated by each of the concerned States as an ex-officio member of a River Board and provision was made in the revised draft of the Rules, under the Act requiring the Central Government, before appointing an Arbitrator under Section 22, to "take such steps as it may deem fit to settle the matter in dispute by negotiations" and to proceed to appoint an arbitrator only if, in its opinion, the matter in dispute could not be settled by negotiation.

It was the intention in 1963 that after some River Boards had been set up and had begun to function, the Act would be amended in the light of the experience to be gained. With regard to settlement of controversies between States, Sir V.T. Krishnamachari expressed the view that even if the Boards were unable, by themselves, to secure agreement between the States, their objective reports, prepared after a detailed examination, cooperatively made, of the technical issues involved, would help in building up public opinion necessary for reaching political settlements.

An inter-State body like a River Board is likely to provide the best practical approach towards prevention of pollution of river waters, control of soil erosion, optimum development of ground waters and promotion of inland navigation. Some legislation concerning these activities will no doubt be necessary but there would be no better way of drawing up the requisite legislative measures and of implementing them than through regional cooperative institutions which would treat a whole river basin as a single unit. Such institutions would also play an important role in building up public opinion towards making the most economical use of a scarce natural resource, developed at considerable public expense.

Essential elements

To foster a cooperative approach, it is necessary not only to create regional institutions like River Boards but also to adopt procedures likely to engender confidence between different States on a river basin. All relevant facts must be made freely available to all concerned and no attempt should be made, as is sometimes evident, to present a fait accompli.

Based on the discussion in the preceding paragraphs and in the light of the experience and practices on several inter-State and international rivers, the following would appear to be the principal elements essential for promoting a cooperative approach towards optimum and orderly development of our inter-State rivers:

(1) The general approach to the problem should be functional and should, within the framework of the Constitution, aim at accommodating to the maximum extent possible the aspirations of all the concerned states.

(2) As full assessment of a resource is sine qua non of its development, a central independent agency should, on a permanent basis, make periodical observations of river discharges at all key stations on each inter-State river.* Complete statistics of river flow and use must be published; the data cannot be treated as privileged.

(3) For optimum development, to accommodate all existing and proposed schemes, and to guard against potential conflicts, water resources need to

* The Central Government has already taken on itself the task of river gauging at key points on the Ganga, the Krishna, the Godavari and the Chenab.

be treated on the basis of a whole drainage basin or an entire river system. To the extent possible, surface waters and ground waters must be considered together, in an integrated manner. The benefits to be derived may not, however, necessarily be confined to the basin.

(4) For each inter-State river, there must be a permanent body, consisting essentially of engineers of the concerned States, to make a continuous study of all matters relating to, or arising out of, the conservation, development, use, regulation and control of the waters of the basin, for maximum permanent benefit to the community. Such a body may include one or more independent experts.*

(5) Before undertaking any project on an inter-State river, unless the project is part of a master plan of development of the river (see 6 below), a detailed examination must be made:
of the availability of waters required for the project after allowing for all existing and future uses, upstream; and
of the hydrological consequences of the operation of the project on existing or future works, downstream on the river,
and the consent of the concerned States secured.

(6) For each inter-State river a master plan of development of the whole river system, or alternative master plans, should be prepared, cooperatively, by the States concerned with the assistance, if needed of independent experts. In making such plan or plans, the following guidelines are important:
 (*a*) Each State in the river basin is entitled to all the non-consumptive uses it can enjoy in its territory without affecting adversely other States through which the river flow.
 (*b*) Each State in the river basin is entitled to an equitable share of the river flow for consumptive use (under special conditions, areas outside the basin may also be given a share of the waters).
 (*c*) To ensure orderly development and smooth operation, allocation of supplies to each State should be such as will afford to it the greatest possible freedom of action in the construction, operation and management of its projects, subject only to the requirements of coordination of related activities of different States.
 (*d*) The plan should aim at multipurpose development, irrigation, power, domestic and industrial uses, navigation, fisheries and recreation, and should include measures for flood control to the extent possible and necessary. Surface waters, return flow, and underground waters must be considered in an integrated manner.

---

* Such bodies may be formed by agreement between the States concerned or under the River Boards Act (1956). The Act needs to be amended to provide for the establishment of River Boards on a compulsory (not optional as at present) and permanent basis. Section 22 relating to arbitration should be deleted from the River Boards Act and, as a consequence, Section 8 of the Inter-State Water Dispute Act should also be deleted. In other words, the Board should be purely advisory and its advice is not to be treated as a handle for starting arbitration proceedings.

(*e*) Cooperative action, under terms to be agreed upon, must be encouraged when:
   (*i*) conservation storage in one State is needed for the benefit, wholly or partly, of one or more downstream States;
   (*ii*) a storage dam in one State would submerge some territory of one or more upstream States;
   (*iii*) benefits to each participating State from a cooperative undertaking would exceed those available to it from projects within its own territory.*

(*f*) The plan, as a whole and each component of the plan should be technically sound and economically justified. In view of changing economic values and improvements in engineering technique, it will generally be possible to improve upon any plan in course of time. To the extent possible, therefore, some flexibility must be built into the plan.

(*g*) The plan, as a whole, should be politically acceptable to the parties.

(7) A negotiated agreement is the best possible settlement of conflicting claims on, or disputes relating to the use of, the waters of an inter-State river and carries with it the best prospects of being implemented faithfully. This should be accomplished by direct negotiations between the States concerned assisted, when necessary, by one or more mediators acceptable to the parties. Only in extreme cases, when all efforts at settlement by negotiation have failed, should arbitration be resorted to.** Since independence, the Government of India has consistently held the view that water-disputes between independent countries must be resolved only by negotiation. The same position should, ordinarily, apply between States of the Union, quasi-sovereign in respect of land and water resources. In recent times, some of the most complicated water disputes have been resolved, by negotiation, in different parts of the world. There is no reason why it should not be possible for the State Governments in India to find satisfactory solutions for their problems on inter-State rivers provided appropriate conditions are created, as set out above.

(8) Along with the master plan of development, as set out in (6) above, a study should be made of the existing activities in the basin in respect of soil and

---

* This represents an objective test for overall national interest.

** The parties may enter into a special agreement (compromise) specifying the issues in dispute, the composition of the arbitral tribunal and such other matters as may be agreed upon between the parties. Alternatively, the tribunal may be appointed under the Inter-State Water Disputes Act which needs to be amended:
   (*i*) to provide that the tribunal should consist of not less than three persons including a majority of those who have special knowledge of water resources development, and
   (*ii*) to ensure that, to the extent indicated by the nature of the dispute, the problem is first dealt with cooperatively, following generally the procedure indicated in this Section.

water conservation with a view to coordinate and supplement these activities as part of a long-term inter-State plan of land management in the best interests of the basin as a whole.

(9) In view of the fact that water is a scarce raw material in large parts of the country and an expensive commodity, and will be increasingly so in the years to come, as a long-term measure, a plan of cooperative action should be prepared for each river basin:

to make the most economical and beneficial use of the waters already harnessed; and

to create new sources of water to the extent possible.

Practical measures towards these would include:

reduction of seepage losses from canals, distributaries water courses, field channels and from the beds and sides of reservoirs and tanks; removal of weeds and jungle from the sides of canals, reservoirs and tanks to save transpiration losses—at present, more than half of the waters obtained from rivers are being thus lost;

reduction of evaporation losses from reservoirs and tanks;

closed circuit use of water for thermal power plants and in industries;

introduction of good water-management practices in irrigated agriculture;

prevention of pollution of river water, not to permit any sewage or industrial waste to flow into a river, *nalla* or drain without proper treatment;

reduction in transpiration losses from aquatic growth and bush along rivers, natural streams and other natural collections of water;

use of waters of natural and artificial drains for irrigation;

re-use of municipal waste for irrigation;

rendering brackish ground waters fit for irrigation;

conversion of sea water to fresh water, to begin with, for industrial use and domestic water supply.

REFERENCES

1. *Water Resources of India – Their Assessment and National Policy for Their Development*; N.D. Gulhati; Lala Karam Chand Thapar Memorial Lecture, October 1967.
2. International problems relating to the economic use of river waters—A Note by the President, August 1961; International Commission on Irrigation and Drainage.
3. *Waterways of India, Their Problems and the Administrative Machinery Required for Obtaining Maximum Benefits*: Central Board of Irrigation Leaflet No. 4, New Delhi, 1947.
4. Government of India Act, 1935; The Constitution of India (as modified up to 1st November, 1956); the Electricity (Supply) Act, 1948; The River Boards Act (1956); The Inter-State Water Dispute Act (1956) and its amendment (1968).
5. N.D. Gulhati, "Inter-State Water Disputes – I. Three Judges better than one? II. Importance of engineering judgement, and III. Need for integrated approach", *The Hindustan Times*, New Delhi, October 10, 11 and 14, 1968.

6. F.J. Barber, *Rivers in International Law*, The London Institute of World Affairs, 1959.
7. Documents on the Use and Control of the Waters of Inter-State and International Streams—Compacts, Treaties and Adiudications; U.S. Department of the Interior, 1956.
8. Walter Kiechal, Jr. *Regional Water Resource Development in the Federal System*, International Conference on Water for Peace, 1967.
9. Several unpublished notes.
10. The Water Resources Planning Act of 1965; Henry P. Gaulfield; *Water and America's Future*; Proceedings of the 21st Annual Meeting of the Soil Conservation Society of America, August 14-17, 1966.
11. John, V. Krutilla, *The Columbia River Treaty*, Resources for the Future Inc., 1967.
12. Gordon M. Macnabb, *The Columbia River Treaty*, International Conference on Water for Peace, 1967.
13. Treaty relating to international cooperation in water resource development of the Columbia river basin; Memorandum dated January 17, 1961 from the President to the Senate of the United States.
14. N.D. Gulhati, "Irrigation and Power Projects—Their Finance, Administration and Policy—A Historical Review up to 1950-51". *Journal of the Central Board of Irrigation & Power*, New Delhi.
15. Report of the Indus Commission (Volume I), 1942.
16. Helsinki Rules on the uses of the waters of international rivers, as adopted on 20th August 1966; The International Law Association.
17. *Report of the Krishna Godavari Commission*, July 1962.

15

Problems of Water Management – Need for an Integrated Approach

B.B. Vohra

It would be convenient to consider the problems of water management under two broad heads-those which can and should be tackled by existing State irrigation and ground water organisations, with such revamping and re-orientation as may be found necessary, and those which by their very nature are beyond their capacity to handle. Such a review will yield the startling revelation that the most pressing problems of water management, namely, the abatement of droughts and floods, the saving of reservoirs from premature siltation and the replenishment of ground water resources, belong to the second category and can be tackled only by carrying out far-reaching reforms in the entire field of land management, afforestation and rural development.

IMPORTANCE OF GROUND WATER

The problems which it is possible and necessary for existing irrigation organisations to handle are fairly well-known even though for various historical reasons, there is a great reluctance to face them squarely. The storage and distribution of surface water through the construction of big dams and canal networks are our biggest achievement in the field of water management so far. We have spent something like Rs. 25,000 crore between 1951 and 1989 to actually irrigate a net area of something like 16 million hectare through big projects. The sorry state in which this sector finds itself today is, however, best described in the words used by the Prime Minister while addressing the State Irrigation Ministers' Conference in July 1986:

> The situation today is that since 1951, 246 big surface irrigation projects have been initiated. Only 65 out of these have been completed. One hundred eightyone are still under construction. This is not a happy state of affairs. We need some definite thrusts from the projects that we started after 1970. Perhaps we can safely say that almost no benefit has come to the people from these projects. For 16 years, we have poured money out. The people have got nothing

> back, no irrigation, no water, no increase in production, no help in their daily life. By pouring money out to a few contractors or a few thekedars and labourers to build canals and maybe Public Works Departments to construct the dam, we are not really doing our people a favour. The favour comes when the benefits of the project start flowing.

This is a very serious indictment indeed and needs to be taken to heart by all those interested in better water management. The following concrete issues require to be tackled with the utmost expedition in order to improve the working of this sector:

1. The most urgent action must be taken to close the large gap between the gross irrigation potential of around 23 m ha which has been created since 1951 and the potential of around 17 m ha which has been actually 'utilised'. The creation of an additional capacity of six m ha—which represents the size of the gap and is equivalent to around 25 per cent of the total potential created during the 38 years in question—and would require an investment of over Rs. 24,000 crore. It would obviously make better economic sense to make use of available idle capacity than to create additional capacity at a time when we are desperately short of resources.
2. High priority must also be given to the task of making fuller use of the post 1951 potential of around 17 m ha which, although it has been 'utilised' in the parlance of irrigation departments, is in fact grossly under-utilised as is evident from the fact that the productivity of these lands is no more than around one-third of what can be achieved through improved arrangements for distribution and application of water. This means that Command Area Development Programmes must receive much higher priority than is being accorded. However, in the Seventh Plan, out of a total provision of Rs. 13,227 crore for big irrigation projects, as much as Rs. 11,556 crore or over 87 per cent stand earmarked for creation of additional potential and only Rs. 1,671 crore for Command Area Development Programmes. Irrigation departments must overcome their fatal fascination for new projects till such time as existing installed capacity has been put to proper use.
3. The menace of waterlogging (and consequent salinisation of the soil) which has already affected at least seven m ha of good agricultural lands, and threatens many more, must no longer be ignored but tackled in right earnest. It must be clearly understood that we cannot, under any circumstances, permit the blessings of canal irrigation to be turned into a curse and allow our renewable resources of water to damage our non-renewable resources of land. It is, however, surprising that no separate provision has been made in the Seventh Plan for drainage and anti-waterlogging activities—apparently these are meant to be financed, if at all, as part of Command Area Development Programmes.
4. Ways and means must be found to put an early end to the very serious financial losses which are being incurred by irrigation projects. These losses

are already of the order of Rs. 1,000 crore per annum and are steadily mounting.

5. Our costly and irreplaceable reservoirs, which represent not only valuable irrigation potential but very often hydel and flood control potential also, must be saved from the threat of premature siltation. This, however, is a task which demands effective afforestation and soil conservation measures in the catchment areas of reservoirs and is, therefore, beyond the capacity of irrigation departments to handle.

However, the biggest single reform that is required in our irrigation departments is their re-orientation with regard to ground water which is still looked upon as a source of 'minor irrigation' and not considered to be anywhere nearly as important as what is called 'major and medium irrigation'. The fact must be faced that, thanks to the natural advantages it enjoys, ground water has developed extremely rapidly as a source of irrigation in the private sector in recent years. Unlike surface water, which lies at the mercy of Irrigation Departments for its development and is even then available only to areas lucky enough to be situated in the command areas of projects, ground water is available, to a greater or lesser extent, in most parts of the country at fairly accessible depths and can be easily tapped by the farmer with the assistance, where necessary, of nothing more than a short-term loan. The installation of a tubewell can be completed within weeks, if not actually days, and since it begins to yield returns within a single season, it represents a most attractive investment. Above all, ground water represents a source of irrigation which is completely under the farmer's own control and permits him to apply water to the land exactly when and to the extent it is required by the crop. It is this last circumstance, which explains why ground water irrigation has been found to be twice as productive as canal irrigation.

There are today well over 10 million electric or diesel-driven pumpsets in the country. At the end of the Sixth Plan, ground water already served a gross area of 26.1 m ha as against 25.3 m ha irrigated by 'major and medium' projects. However, if the higher productivity of ground water is taken into account, the area served by it in 1985 was equivalent to around 52 m ha of canal irrigated lands. There is, thus, no room for doubt that ground water is no longer a 'minor' but a major and the most productive source of irrigation in the country. It may be mentioned in this connection that while the total storage created by big projects up to the end of the Sixth Plan was around 17 million hectare metres(mhm), the country's ground water resources have an annual utilisable potential of nearly 42 mhm, of which only around 10 mhm have been presently utilised. In the world as a whole, fully 98.4 per cent of all liquid fresh water resources are represented by soil moisture and ground water and only 1.6 per cent by water in streams, lakes and swamps.

Advantages

It is time for irrigation establishments to appreciate the reasons why irrigation from big surface projects has to necessarily yield pride of place to ground water. Big projects require huge public investments, take years and often decades to complete, and demand large areas of valuable land for submergence as well as for distribution systems. Big projects also suffer from serious losses of water by evaporation and seepage during storage and transport on an average less than 50 per cent of the impounded waters reach farmers' fields. Such projects also create grave problems of waterlogging in areas which are not naturally well-drained. Further, they are not easy to operate efficiently and require large additional investments by way of Command Area Development Programmes in order to ensure that water is put to good use. Big projects also pose the most difficult problems of rehabilitation of communities displaced from lands which get submerged by reservoirs. Finally, they are weighed down by large bureaucracies which have become notorious for their corruption and inefficiency.

Thanks to these inherent disadvantages, plus the haphazard manner in which many big surface irrigation projects have been taken up in recent years—without full investigations and surveys and without making adequate provision for the funds required to complete them in reasonable time—the cost of creating irrigation potential per gross hectare of land through the "major and medium" route has shot up from about Rs. 1,200 crore in the First Plan period to around Rs. 40,000 crore in the current Plan. However, if the costs of command are a development and drainage are also taken into account, the cost of creating 'utilisable' irrigation potential in one gross hectare of land will, on an average, be found to be well above Rs. 50,000 per hectare. This is an exorbitantly high figure by any standards and indicates why the future of irrigation in this country will belong increasingly to ground water.

It is, however, necessary to note that—for reasons which are too obvious to mention—the 'big dam' lobby is still extremely powerful and welt-entrenched. This is apparent from the manner in which it has been able to obtain clearance for the Narmada Project in the teeth of opposition by environmentalists throughout the country.

Be that as it may, it is clear that the country's ground water resources should not be taken for granted just because they represent a gift of nature and should be given much greater attention than they have received so far. The neglect which ground water has suffered is apparent from the fact that the Seventh Plan document contains no separate section on this subject, nor any discussion of the problems it faces. It is time that the most serious notice is taken of the steep falls in water-tables which have occurred in many parts of the country as a result of overpumping on the one hand, and on the other, decreasing rates of replenishment caused by increasing deforestation and denudation in our watersheds. In certain areas, such as the coast of Saurashtra, excessive pumping has led to the intrusion of sea water into sweet water acquifers and has turned once blooming agricultural and fruit-growing areas into wastelands.

Some Precautions

It is necessary that such developments should be anticipated and avoided in all sensitive areas so that ground water development does not become its own worst enemy. The following concrete suggestions need to be considered:

1. State ground water organisations should be suitably strengthened and

equipped and made capable of carrying out scientific investigations into the extent and nature of acquifers and their recharge characteristics so that they may be able to monitor their behaviour and sound warning bells in time;

2. State ground water organisations should also be equipped to give competent technical advice to farmers regarding the kind of tubewells and pumpsets they should install in their holdings so that there is no wastage of either scarce materials or even scarcer energy resources;
3. State Governments must empower themselves to impose, wherever necessary, restrictions on pumping by individual farmers in the larger interests of agricultural production, and the farming community as a whole as well as of the health of the resource on which so much depends;
4. State Governments should ensure that installed pumping capacities are not under-utilised for lack of either electricity or diesel; and
5. State Governments should take up time-bound programmes for the consolidation of holdings because this is one of the surest ways of encouraging ground water development on sound lines.

The most important task in the field of ground water management, however, is to ensure that the replenishment of this invaluable resource is increased to the maximum possible extent. However, this is a task which, like the prevention of floods and droughts and the premature siltation of reservoirs, lies beyond the purview of irrigation organisations and belongs to the field of watershed management and soil and water conservation.

PROBLEM OF RUN-OFF AND SOIL LOSSES

The reduction of run-off and soil losses through a greater emphasis on afforestation and better land management must be given pride of place in any overall strategy for water management. They constitute our best insurance against both droughts and floods, the premature siltation of reservoirs and the over-exploitation of ground water resources. Such an approach will not only result in the revival of natural springs in the hills which have dried up as a result of excessive run-off-even in such rain-rich areas as the North Eastern states—but also in the raising of ground water-tables in the plains. What is equally important is that seepage from such acquifers into river channels will increase river flows in the dry season. The reduction of run-off losses is particularly necessary in arid areas where heavy rains may occur only once in three or four years, but are largely wasted on account of denudation and the absence of adequate soil and water conservation works. If every drop of the precipitation, which occurs in such areas, could be conserved locally-preferably as soil moisture and ground water, to avoid heavy evaporation losses—the failure of rains during some years would lose much of its sting.

Need for Control

The control of run-off and soil losses has a very significant moderating effect on floods also, because there is not only a reduction in the amount of water which reaches the river but also in the amount of silt it contains. It is the excessive silt load in waters from denuded watersheds that results in the sedimentation of river beds and reduces their capacity to carry water, particularly during times of heavy precipitation.

The control of run-off and soil losses is also necessary in the interests of preserving the productivity of rain-fed agricultural lands. Not only is top soil the most fertile part of the soil and represents a virtually non-renewable resource—it takes nature hundreds of years to build an inch of it—but the retention of water as soil moisture is also a matter of vital importance to such lands.

It is pertinent to note in this connection that the prevention of neither droughts nor floods figures in the charter of responsibilities of the Ministry of Water Resources. This is the most surprising circumstance indeed because droughts and floods are, without doubt, the most pressing problems in the field of water management today. "Flood control" does feature among the responsibilities of the Ministry, but this only involves protection of certain specified and limited urban areas against floods, through construction of engineering works, such as bunds and dykes. Such measures naturally have no effect on either the incidence or the severity of floods and it is highly misleading to describe them as 'flood control' measures. 'Flood protection' would be a better description for these activities.

Be that as it may, the centre has hardly any choice but to tackle the problems of droughts and floods in right earnest, if the country is to be prevented from continuing to bled white. The extreme seriousness of the situation is reflected by the scale of the demands which the states are making for financial assistance for drought and flood relief—these demands added up to around Rs. 8,000 crore in 1985-86. The annual losses to the economy as a result of excessive run-off and soil losses have never been properly computed but must certainly be of the order oftens of thousands of crore, if account is taken not only of the direct distress caused by droughts and floods but also of the growing losses in production which are being suffered by the 85 odd m ha of agricultural lands which are known to suffer from soil erosion, of the unutilised potential for production represented by the 65 odd m ha of non-agricultural lands which lie almost completely denuded, and if an estimate is also made of the damage suffered by our irrigation projects through premature siltation. It needs to be realised that it is these invisible losses which explain the seemingly intractable poverty of our people and the fact that in terms of per capita GNP India stands 11th from the bottom in a list of 126 nations.

It is most curious indeed—to put it mildly-that while the Centre accepts responsibility for reimbursing the states for a part of the mounting expenditure they incur on drought and flood relief (and is also responsible for maintaining the health of the national economy as a whole), it has yet to evolve an effective strategy for dealing with these most dangerous threats to the country's well-being and indeed its very survival. As of today, there is no national programme for controlling run-off and soil losses and naturally, also, no organisations entrusted with such a responsibility.

Need for Control Mechanism

If we are really serious about tackling these tasks, there is no alternative except to set up, as early as possible, a suitable mechanism which would place under one administrative umbrella, so to say, all the various disciplines, agencies, and programmes relating to management of our inextricably interlinked resources of land, water and forests. It is necessary to stress that the first task of the proposed organisation would be to consider how the total financial resources which are placed at its disposal should be redeployed to serve new priorities and to redress the glaring imbalances which exist in this field of water—and therefore also land-management today. These financial resources, it is needless to say, would include the sums which are allocated to the Ministry of Water Resources and the Department of Forests, as well as for the numerous schemes of the Departments of Agriculture and Rural Development which cover subjects like watershed management, soil and water conservation, soil surveys, special area development programmes and improvement of local natural resources through poverty alleviation and employment generation programmes. Nothing can illustrate the lopsidedness of our existing policies better than the fact that while a total investment of Rs. 2,723 crore was made up to the end of the Sixth Plan in forestry and soil and water conservation programmes to serve the interests of some 150 m ha of denuded and erosion-prone lands, large irrigation projects claimed an investment of Rs. 15,206 crore to serve a net area of only around 13 m ha during the same period. It is this kind of bias which must be immediately corrected if we are to save ourselves from certain ecological disaster.

But all said and done, better management of our water, soil and forest resources is too serious a matter to be left to the tender mercies of government organisations alone. The public, in general, and in particular local communities must take a much greater interest in a matter which concerns their future—and the future of their children and their children's children — than they have done in the past. Voluntary organisations and political parties have a great role to play in educating the people — and for that matter even the government — in managing these basic resources to the best possible advantage. Hope lies in the expectation that they will play this role energetically and fearlessly and help to dispel the 'resource illiteracy' which, to a large extent, has been responsible for creating the tragic situation in which we find ourselves today.

CONCLUSION

To conclude, the major tasks in the field of water — and therefore also land-management may be summarised as follows:

1. State Governments must ensure that their irrigation establishments get over their near-obsession with the creation of additional irrigation capacity through big projects as these have been found to be economically unviable, environmentally hazardous, difficult to manage and very slow to complete

and yield results. They must instead pay greater attention to the early utilisation of existing capacities, to Command Area Development, and to the requirements of drainage in lands affected or threatened by waterlogging.

2. State Governments must appreciate the natural advantages enjoyed by ground water and pay more attention to the scientific management and development of this wonderful resource.
3. By far the most important but also the most neglected task in the entire field of natural resources management is the reduction of run-off and soil loses so that droughts and floods may be contained, ground water recharge may be maximised, the premature sedimentation of reservoirs prevented, rain-fed agriculture made more productive, so that wastelands may be reclaimed quickly through the forces of natural regeneration. There is no alternative for the Centre but to accept responsibility for initiating appropriate action in this critical field.
4. In order to effectively implement such a strategy, it will be unavoidably necessary to create an organisation which can take a synoptic and integrated view of all related matters and deploy-resources to the best advantage.
5. Voluntary organisations and political parties must take greater interest in problems of resource management as this is a matter vital to the country's survival.

16

Governance and Institutional Mechanism for Integrated Water Resources Management

R.S. Goel and V.B. Patel

INTRODUCTION

The distribution and management of available water is highly crucial in a vast country like India, with diverse topography, climate, geology and consequently hydrology; not only for meeting the ever bulging competing demands but also for socio-economic development as well as sustenance of built environment. In the early stages of development, it was generally taken for granted that our large water resources were almost inexhaustible. Consequently excepting in some basins like Damodar, no plans were formulated for long range water resources development. Planning was mostly project specific and often for specific purposes. With the mani-fold increase in population, rapid urbanisation and socio-economic development, the requirement of water has tremendously grown for various uses like drinking and municipal water supply, irrigation, hydropower generation, cooling needs of thermal and industrial plants, navigation, pisciculture, and maintenance of water quality etc. The dominant multi-departmental structure, time consuming consultations, constant inter-departmental references, weak coordination and lack of holistic approach are the main handicaps in fulfilling the needs of water in adequate quantity and of proper quality for conflicting demands of bulging population in India, even after 50 years of Indian Independence. A comprehensive strategic planning for integrated use of water resources has, therefore, now become an urgent necessity. Such need has also been highlighted by the Irrigation Commission, Irrigation Ministers' Conference, National Commission for Integrated Water Resources Development Plan (NCIWRDP) and also in the National Water Policy (NWP). Integrated water resources development and management requires urgent holistic changes in governance and institutional mechanism for water sector.

NATIONAL COMMISSION FOR INTEGRATED WATER RESOURCES DEVELOPMENT PLAN

Government of India had constituted a highpowered NCIWRDP with top multi-disciplinary experts as its members. Union Secretary, MoWR also participated in the meetings as a permanent invitee; while Chairman, CWC and Additional Secretary, MoWR were amongst the members. The Commission in its Report of November 1999 also discussed the subject matter of Legal and Institutional Framework. NCIWRDP has very strongly recommended, "The CWC should be restructured into a statutory high powered inter-disciplinary commission, with maximum autonomy, in order to deal with policy and reforms, Centre-State and Inter-State issues, planning and project finalisation, international aspects, legal, economic and financial issues, water productivity, conservation and management, environmental aspects and rehabilitation, people's participation and communication, coordination and facilitation of inter-disciplinary research, HRD and Training and a National Information/Data System". It is also relevant to note that the Central Water and Power Engineering Services (CWPES) Association, during its Silver Jubilee Celebrations, had organised a National Seminar on `Strength and Weakness of CWC and CEA' (NSSWCWCCEA), on February 7, 1987, which was participated by over 500 delegates, including the then Secretary (Water Resources) and over 25 past Chairmen and Members of CWC and CEA. This Seminar had strongly recommended that CWC should be reorganised as High Powered Autonomous Commission with status of Secretary to Government to its Chairman; to avoid the duplication of efforts and wastage of resources in the present set-up, wherein the cases and matters decided by CWC are processed again through a multi-hierarchical set up in MoWR. The Recommendations of the NCIWRD, 1999 and above Seminar, in 1987 are identical, aimed at granting to CWC, the status of a statutory highpowered inter-disciplinary Commission with maximum autonomy.

STUDY ON RESTRUCTURING OF CWC BY ADMINISTRATIVE STAFF COLLEGE OF INDIA

MoWR has commissioned the Administrative Staff College of India (ASCI) Hyderabad for study on restructuring of CWC in the light of NCIWRDP recommendations. ASCI has submitted First Draft Report in September 2002 wherein it has strongly recommended creation of a corporation.

ASCI's proposal of converting CWC into a Corporation and to work on cost recovery basis has perhaps emanated without appreciating the obligatory and national leadership role of CWC wherein hundreds of crore of rupees have been saved by CWC through timely appropriate techno-economic appraisal, planning, investigations and designs of irrigation, flood control, hydro-power and multi-purpose river valley projects. But for its role tremendous infructuous expenditure might have been incurred through unnecessary components and over designed spillways, gates, power houses and canals. The role of CWC in ensuring hydraulic, hydrologic and seismic safety of various components of river valley projects, publishing state of art design manuals, developing BIS codes and guidelines on various intricate aspects of designs, planning, investigations, appraisal and preparation of project reports, construction equipments, flood forecasting and flood management, etc., has to be properly appreciated for its strengthening. CWC should remain the apex technical supreme organisation at the union level to spearhead all activities under the sphere of water resources development and management.

If, the principles of integrating responsibilities, status and accountability are upheld in water resources sector; CWC needs to be recognised with the status of a full-fledged department of Government of India headed by Secretary to Government of India to deliver the targeted results, since the professionalism has already proved fruitful and highly satisfactory in the sectors of railways, atomic energy, space research, telecom and postal services. The Chairmen of these organisations enjoy a status equivalent to Secretary to Government of India and render the professional competent advice to the respective minister and the Union Cabinet. Similar arrangement is absolutely necessary in water resources sector; keeping in view the deep concern even of Hon'ble President and the Supreme Court for inter-linking of rivers and action plan to implement the National Water Policy.

Since this study on CWC by ASCI, Hyderabad, has its origins in the above NCIWRD recommendations; it is quite necessary and unavoidable that the study should also include the distribution of work amongst various organisations under the MoWR; redefine the domain for CWC; redefine the relationship between CWC and MoWR and find the ways and means to synergise the functioning of CWC and MoWR. The Planning Commission and the Parliamentary Consultative Committee of MoWR and the Vision for Integrated Water Resources Development and Management have underlined that all water related subjects, presently scattered over several union ministries, must be brought under the umbrella of MoWR. The ongoing ASCI Study on Restructuring of CWC should focus on the following thrust areas seriously:

1. To examine the role of CWC in development and management of the water resources of the nation, in three different scenarios:

    (*a*) Enlargement of CWC's responsibilities if the MoWR succeeds in enlarging the role of Central government in water resources management through various legislative and constitutional changes.
    (*b*) Increase in CWC's responsibilities without the legislative changes but within the scope of administrative changes such as bringing all water related issues, presently scattered over several union ministries, under MoWR.
    (*c*) Increase in CWC's responsibilities within the present allocation of business amongst Central ministries.

2. To suggest necessary steps to prepare CWC and Central Water Engineering Service (CWES) to accept the additional responsibilities for the above mentioned scenarios.

3. To advise on the organisational structure required to discharge these functions.
4. To examine the impediments that prevent CWC and CWES from effectively discharging the role assigned to them, at present as well as in future. In doing so *inter-alia* examine:

   - Synergy between functioning of CWC and MoWR.
   - Operational freedom available to CWC officers.
   - Morale of Central Water Engineering Service (CWES) cadre officers.
   - Performance of supporting services.

5. Effective management of CWES cadre w.r.t transfer, promotion, continuing education and opportunities for enriching specialisation.
6. Making use of CWES expertise in:

   - Planning Commission, Ministries and Central government departments and CPSUs dealing with any facet of water resources.
   - To other developing countries, through WAPCOS and CPSUs.
   - State Water Resources Departments.
   - Under Central Staffing Scheme.

7. Providing opportunities to CWES officers for a wider range of experience in fields such as construction; consultancy; ground water; hydraulics; R&D; irrigation and CAD; O&M of projects, watershed development, drinking water, relief and rehabilitation, catchment area treatment, etc.

Vision for Integrated Water Resources Development and Management

While inaugurating the Fresh Water Year the Prime Minister released the MoWR's 'Vision for Integrated Water Resources Development and Management', which emphasises as under, with regard to the institutional mechanism for water sector.

It is desirable that all schemes related to development, management, conservation and protection of water resources and designed to encourage state governments in this direction are handled under one umbrella. All the subject matters related to water resources be brought under one umbrella, both at the centre and the states. The need for RBOs for inter-state rivers has been extensively discussed at Government, non-government and political level in the country. There is broad agreement on the need for RBOs and on their powers and functions. MoWR would help to establish one river basin organisation in each major state for a basin falling within the state, to begin with and create atmosphere of trust among the states so that they donot see establishment of RBOs in interstate rivers as an infringement on their rights and establish RBOs with the consent of state governments".

Accordingly, it is high time that all water related issues are dealt by the Ministry of Water Resources rather than the present fragmented manner wherein the Union ministries of Urban Development, Rural Development, Drinking Water Supply, Transport and Navigation, Agriculture and Cooperation and Environment and Forests deal water related issues in different context without proper coordinating mechanism. NCIWRDP, Planning Commission and the Parliamentary Consultative Committee of MoWR and the Vision for Integrated Water Resources Development and Management released by the Prime Minister have already underlined that all water related subjects, presently scattered over several union ministries, must be brought under the umbrella of MoWR

INTER-STATE WATER DEVELOPMENT

Inter-state Disputes

Water resources of India mainly comprise of 20 such major inter-state river basins, which account for 82 per cent of the country's geographical area. All the issues connected with the development, regulation and management of water resources of the inter-state basins could be broadly termed as inter-state issues. As most of the major rivers in India are inter-state, sharing of water between the upper and lower riparian states has always been a bone of contention. With the riparian states of almost all the inter-state river basins clamouring with their claims for more/additional quantum of water as their share and related apprehensions by other co-basin states inter-state disputes are cropping up every now and then. The projects on inter-state rivers are being formulated by the concerned states as per their needs and inter-se-priority with in their share of water for utilisation for irrigation and other purposes in their respective territories.

As the development of these projects by one state on such inter-state rivers may affect the interests of the other basin states, inter-state differences arise amongst the concerned basin states with regard to its use and distribution. Disputes also arise in connection with the control, operation and regulation of releases for various uses of the co-basin states under the same inter-state project. The aggrieved state/states seek the Center's intervention or approach courts for mitigation of their grievance. All these inter-state differences or disputes are delaying the implementation of the water resource projects thus causing immense harm to the overall development of water resources in the country as a whole. Though a number of inter-state disputes regarding sharing of waters and project related matters have been resolved by reaching agreements mutually between the states with or without the Central Government's intervention, some of them remained unresolved. Five of the inter-state disputes concerning the Krishna, Godavari, Narmada, Cauvery and Ravi-Beas basins have been referred to the tribunals for adjudication. Out of the above five, tribunals for the Krishna, Godavari and Narmada have given their final awards and the final awards in respect of the remaining two are awaited. Concerted efforts are being made by the Central government to resolve the outstanding differences to the use and development of inter-state as well as international waters through negotiations. By the end of 1998, a total of 125 international and inter-state agreements were cumulatively reached and 102 of them were in the Post-Independence era.

River Boards Act 1956

The River Boards Act (RBA) 1956 is an Act to provide for the establishment of River Boards for the regulation and development of inter-state rivers and river valleys. The Central government may, on a request received in this behalf from a state government or otherwise establish a River Board when it is declared that it is expedient in the public interest that the Central government should take under its control the regulation and development of the inter-state rivers and river valleys to the extent provided in the Act. However, no River Boards have been established under this Act so far mainly on account of unwillingness on the part of the states concerned. Some boards/committees have been established (either to deal with specific projects on inter-state rivers or for the preparation of master plans for a basin and its sub-basins) through Government Resolution (*e.g.*, Bansagar Control Board, the Sardar Sarovar Construction Advisory Committee, and the Ganga Flood Control Commission) or through specific legislation by Parliament independent of the River Boards Act (*e.g*,. the Brahmaputra Board, the Betwa Board).

RIVER BASIN ORGANISATIONS (RBOS)

Realising the need for a strong implementing and decision making mechanism for river basin development, the NWP recommended setting up of suitable basin level organisations for the planning and management of water resources of various river basins. NCIWRDP 1999 also strongly recommended that RBOs for each river basin are an essential institutional mechanism for integrated development of water resources and that such RBO should be set up as a body in which the concerned state governments, local governments and water users would have representation and which would provide a forum for mutual discussions and agreement.

NCIWRDP has suggested that RBOs may consist of a "general council" and a "standing committee" with a "permanent secretariat". The "general council" is to consist of two minister representating the state government, leader of the opposition and three representatives of panchayats from each of the districts in the basin, one representative of urban local bodies from each district of the basin and two representatives of water districts from each of the riparian states. In addition, five well-known experts in environment, water laws, health, economics and sociology and another five representatives from other interest groups like NGOs and activists shall be co-opted by each RBO for its general council. For some of the large river basins like the Ganga, it will be necessary to form the general council at the major sub-basin level, with a small coordinating body for the basin as a whole.

The standing committee of each RBO is to consist of one state minister, leader of opposition, three representatives of panchayats, three representatives of urban local bodies and three representatives of water districts for each of the riparian states. All the members of the standing committee will be elected from among the council members. The general council and the standing committee shall have representation for women and SC/ST communities. The secretariat of the RBOs is to be formed by restructuring the field offices of CWC. MoWR and CWC are organizing a National Seminar on River Basin Organisations to take state authorities and various stakeholders into confidence so that much needed RBOs are immediately set up in different river basins. Initially, the regional offices of CWC may facilitate such RBOs as their secretariat, who are also involved in collection, analysis, revalidation, storage, retrieval and documentation of the water related statistics.

INTERLINKING OF RIVERS

NWP has underlined the need for making water available to water scarce areas by transfer from other areas including transfer from one river basin to another, based on a national perspective. Keeping in view the long-term strategy for optimum development and efficient utilisation of country's water resources, MoWR and CWC had prepared in 1980 a National Perspective Plan for Water Resources Development (NPPWRD) disregarding political boundaries of the states. The proposal envisages construction of storages and interlinking of rivers. NPPWRD is in two parts namely, (i) Peninsular Rivers development which is entirely within the control of the central and state governments and (ii) Himalayan Rivers development which calls for co-operation of India, Nepal, Bangladesh and Bhutan. The Himalayan and Peninsular River Plan would add about 35 million hectare (mha) (25 mha by surface water and 10 mha by additional use of groundwater) to the presently estimated ultimate irrigation potential besides providing large quantum of hydropower, flood control and in some reaches, navigation. The National Water Development Agency (NWDA) was set up in 1982 by the Government of India. This Agency is charged with the detailed planning of the link proposals and preparing the feasibility reports of the various components. By now, the NWDA has completed all water balance studies and pre-feasibility studies. It has completed six feasibility level studies and is engaged in 18 other feasibility studies.

Objectives of Inter-Linking of Rivers

Although India receives some waters from the upstream countries, the precipitation is the main source of water availability. This precipitation, as is well known, has a very uneven distribution, with an annual rainfall of more than 10m in parts of Meghalaya to less than half-a—metre in semi-arid parts of Rajasthan and Gujarat. In arid regions it could be less than 10 cm. Much of the water is received in a few months of the monsoon, and that too within around 100 hours of the rainy days. Also, there are very large inter-annual variabilities. The basin is a natural hydrological unit. It is possible to plan an integrated development and management of a basin in such a way as to meet the demands of the various parts of the basin in an equitable way to the extent possible, thus overcoming to some extent the natural inequities in water resources within a basin.These basin plans would have to consider various aspects like the availability of water in different sub-basins, the demands of water in different sub-basins as also within the different political units of the basin and the need for catering to such developments without causing significant harm to others.

There are large inequities in the availability and demand scenario amongst the various basins. Broad objectives of the inter-basin transfers are equitable distribution of available water resources within a region or the nation, increased economic efficiency, self-sufficiency in basic water related outputs such as food and hydro-energy and providing livelihood and employment opportunities *in situ*; so that large scale migration of population (seasonal or permanent, short distance or long distance, in water distress situations) is checked. The world trade in foodgrains is not large enough to meet the needs of a large country like India. World trade in rice for example is only 18 million tonnes at present. Large imports by India would affect the price stability. Infrastructural bottlenecks like port facility, shipping, roads, railways etc. are other constraints on increasing the trade in foodgrains. Next 50 years in India would witness further accelerated urbanisation. Most of the urbanised areas would have to depend on surface water from distant reservoirs. Long distance inter-basin transfers of waters is already common in existing metro cities. Delhi gets substantial part of water from Bhakra reservoir on Sutlej River and Kalagarh Reservoir on River Ramganga; Kolkata from Farakka Barrage on river Ganges, Mumbai from distant reservoirs like Bhatsa and Vaikarna and Chennai from Srisailam reservoir.

Challenges in Inter-linking of Rivers

Proposed water transfers by their nature are inter-basin and may violate the basic premise of 'basin' as a hydrologic unit for water management. These transfers allow the diversion of waters to the 'non co-basin' states or provinces of India. Conformity of these proposals may need review of existing legal system (the International Law, Constitution of India and other relevant laws and policies within India). Methodologies and practices for economic analysis of the conventional in-basin water developments have already been evolved. The applicability of these methods and practice in the inter-basin transfer proposals need to be modified, if required. These transfers being rather large would require technical, social and ecological studies. Water development projects are normally undertaken by a state besides a few inter-state projects by inter-state agencies. If in a state a particular basin is rich in water resources while an adjoining basin is poor, the state may like to transfer the water of the rich basin in its own basin which is not so rich. There is perhaps no case where within the same state, the citizens within the basin can claim the right to the full use of the basin waters by not transferring it to their co-citizens outside the basin. The implementation of these proposals would require great understanding and co-operation among different states. MoWR in its Vision for Integrated Water Resources Development and Management, Feb, 2003, has decided to implement a few important river link-canal schemes under the National Perspective Plan, in a phased manner. Meanwhile, the concept of inter-basin water transfers again came to the limelight and the Government of India, has set up a task force. The task force has to prepare action plans outlining the time schedules and options for funding and execution so as to facilitate implementation of the project by end of 2016. It is heartening that the Supreme Court and all main political parties and Hon'ble President are unanimous for expeditious implementation of national mission on inter-linking of rivers on a war footing through cooperation and consensus of various agencies to avert the fast developing water crisis in many deficit river basins while other rivers are in spate of high floods.

Water Rights and Ownership of Water

Many inter-state issues including the in-basin apportionment and inter-basin transfers of waters arise from different interpretations of the ownership rights in regard to water. Traditionally, the basic elements: space, air, water and energy have been perceived as non-legal objects and as such incapable of becoming property. The Roman Law did not ever classify running water as capable of becoming someone's property. No ancient Indian text mentions property rights to anyone, including the King, in rivers. Though there is in general no international law in regard to water, there seems to be a consensus on treating water as a 'negative community' which indicates that it is meant for all but owned by none. In such a negative community only unfructuous rights can exist; i.e., the right would be linked to a use and right would exist only when the water is in possession of the rightful owner. Krishna water Dispute Tribunal gave a detailed discussions in this regard. The international conventions allow equitable use of water by the basin states, provided such use does not cause any significant harm to others. Thus, absolute ownership of water is repugnant to the principle of negative community.

Socio-ecological Impacts of Inter-basin Transfers

Some people feel that inter-basin transfers may cause socio-economic and environmental impacts much different from those caused by in-basin developments. These differences could be both due to the large size of the project and due to the different nature of the project which involves long distance water transfers through large and long canals. India is familiar with the social and environmental concerns caused by inter-basin projects like BSL, IGNP, Parmbikular Alyar projects as well as small, medium and large in-basin projects. Over the years, the awareness about such concerns and the methods for minimizing the adverse impacts have changed considerably. Acceptable methodology of evaluating and meeting such concerns through legal policy, related guidelines and management measures has already been evolved. Each individual storage dam such as the Ichampally, Polavaram, Manibhadra/Tikarpara etc. in the peninsular links would not be much different from the large reservoirs like Bhakra, Gandhisagar, Sardar Sarovar, Srisailam, Nagarjunasagar etc. Similarly, we have substantial experience about large canals exceeding discharge capacities of 1000 cumecs and the proposed link canals would be not of much larger magnitude. The issue of introduction of alien flora and fauna may need a study. Existing inter-basin transfers in India have not experienced any such problem.

INDIAN CAPABILITIES IN INTER-LINKING OF RIVERS

It is commendable that Indian technocrats, are the first to conceive the Inter-linking of Rivers (ILR), as a solution to meet the impending water crisis. Various proposals in this regard have come up for consideration in last 25 years. NWDA which was set up to study the possibilities and prepare feasibility studies have been working on the various possible links for last 20 years. These studies are now to be firmed up on priority. The international community has now awakened and is becoming active to grab the opportunity of securing consultancy assignments and also construction contracts for these works. Some of the Indians have also been thinking on this line. Attempt has been made in this note to focus the issues which need to be kept in mind while taking policy decisions in this regard.

Indian Experience in Construction

It is known that major constructions like Sardar Sarovar, Tehri, Ranjitsagar, Koyna, Nagarjunsagar have been done by Indian contractors. Given an opportunity they have capacity to match the challenges involved in ILR proposals. They are second to none in the field of construction of dams, power plants and major canals. Infact projects of such huge magnitude in terms of quantities involved are not implemented elsewhere, by the countries likely to advise/claim that India needs to utilise outside contractors. It is known that in other sectors, like roads, most of the work grabbed by international contractors is done by Indian contractors. Our country only ends up in paying higher margins when outsiders are involved.

Indian Experience in Plants and Equipments

The construction equipment and heavy plants are also being manufactured in India. Given prior intimation these companies have capabilities to expand the capacity to meet the demands. Import therefore needs to be restricted to only components and plants not under manufacture in India. Heavy turbines/generators, not presently under manufacture in India could be considered for import. But with India in a very sound position of foreign exchange reserves, one need not think of using foreign funding for plants and equipments otherwise available in India.

Indian Experience in Consultancy Assignments

It is commendable that much of the basic work of conceptualisation of the various links and the preliminary studies have been done over last 20 years by NWDA. Indian consultancy companies have capacity to handle the work of preparing feasibility studies and also preparing the D.P.Rs. In fact, detailed engineering for major dams and powerhouses built in India is done by Indian engineers. In a few cases where foreign consulting firms are tied up with externally funded projects again, most of the work is done by Indian engineers and less than one percent of manpower comes through expatriates, who take away major share of the fees realised. It is thus more a mechanism of siphoning funds in name of International Consultancy. Such tendency needs to be curbed.

Indian Experience in River Basin System Studies

With the definition of objectives, evaluation criteria, supply and demand estimates, system studies need to be conducted for each river basin to determine the sustainable development policy. In basin studies covering a large area over a long time period, infinite variety and variations are possible in development and management strategies. Further, growing complexities of water management, seek various methods for helping water resources engineers in their task. This requires the use of strong technical tools to handle and analyse large amount of river basin data/simulate the whole basin under various hydrologic conditions, make sensible comparison among possible development/management options and evolve information in a presentable manner for supporting decision-making process. For this purpose a number of system studies have been carried out in CWC with available data. UNDP assisted Systems Engineering Project, has also carried out comprehensive studies for the development of Mahanadi basin using system engineering technique during 1982-87.

Recently with availability of more data, a demonstration study namely 'Integrated River Basin Planning and Management of Sabarmati basin' was taken up in April, 2000 under the World Bank aided Hydrology Project. The study is being carried out jointly by CWC and Narmada Water Resources and Water Supply Department, Gujarat. Irrigated agriculture is the main water user of the Sabarmati basin and surface as well as ground water is fully exploited. Besides agriculture, the basin area has been showing a rapid growth in all sectors of economy, particularly in the industrial sector. Since the area experiences a semi—arid climate, limited water resources are now posing conflicting problems among the various users. The basin is considered complex from a water management point of view. The development and sustainable use of water and land resources in the area require appropriate allocation of these scarce resources among competing human activities. This implies decision making in complex situations, often with conflicting interests. Careful planning and analysis are required to support such decisions, taking into account technical, economical and environmental aspects in a specific social-cultural and institutional context.

Thus, there is no need to bank upon the foreign consultancy for planning, investigation, engineering and construction of different links under the interlinking of rivers programme of India. The Central and state agencies have adequate expertise and background in handling such projects during the last 50 years when giant multi-purpose river valley projects like Bhakra, BSL, Tehri, INGP, DVC, Sardar Sarovar etc. have been successfully completed through indigenous expertise. On one side, the foreign consultancy either for planning/designing or construction/supervision adds to the project costs exorbitantly, on the other hand most of the foreign agencies are not experienced with the typical geological, hydrological, seismological, topographical and construction methods relevant to Indian conditions.

CONCLUSION

India is supporting one-sixth of the world's population on 1/50th of world's land with meager one-twentyfifth of the world's water resources. Further, 80 per cent of all diseases and over one-third of deaths are caused by consumption of contaminated water and on an average as much as one-tenth of each person's productive time is sacrificed to water related diseases. Deteriorating water quality has become a serious problem. In such peculiar conditions, the initiative for inter-linking of rivers in India so as to meet the bulging demands of water for various uses even for water starved states is highly commendable and timely. This article has reviewed the vital need of urgent changes in governance and institutional mechanism for ensuring integrated water resources development and management of water for various demands, keeping in view the peculiar socio-political and diverse hydro-meteorological features. It is utmost essential that appropriate RBOs are urgently set up, all water-related subjects are brought under the umbrella of MoWR and CWC is urgently restructured into a high powered commission headed by a Chairman with full status of a Secretary to Government of India and maximum autonomy to carry out all additional functions as recommended by NCIWRDP.

A SELECT READING

1. Administrative Staff College of India, *First Draft Report on Restructuring,* The Central Water Commission, Hyderabad, 2002.
2. Central Water Commission, *Annual Report,* New Delhi, 2002.
3. Central Water Commission, *Water Related Statistics,* New Delhi, 2003.
4. Goel R.S. (Ed.), *Environment Impacts Assessment of Water Resources Projects – Concerns, Policy Issues, Perceptions and Scientific Analysis,* New Delhi, Oxford and IBH Publishing Co. Pvt. Ltd., 2000.
5. Goel R.S. and Srivastava R.N (Ed.), *Hydropower and River Valley Development – Environment Management, Case Studies and Policy Issues,* New Delhi, Oxford and IBH Publishing Co. Ltd., 2000.
6. Goel R.S., "Water Resources Development and National Water Policy", Special Number *Indian Journal of Public Administration* on "Water Resoruces Management: Issues and Strategies", Vol. XLIX, No.3, July-September, 2003.
7. Goel R.S. and Patel V.B., *Ecological Concerns and Challenges in Integrated Water Management in India,* National Workshop on Mountain Environment and Development: Potentials and Prospects, G.B. Pant Institute of Himalayan Environment and Development, Almora, Uttaranchal, December 9-10, 2002.
8. Goel R.S and Patel V.B, "Water Resources Development and Interlinking of Rivers – Challenges And Prospects", *Eighteenth Indian Engineering Congress,* Institution of Engineers (India), December, 18-21, 2003, Lucknow.
9. Goel R.S and Patel V.B, 'Integrated Management For Water Security In India – An

Overview' *36th Annual Convention of Indian Water Works Association*, 10-11th January, 2004, Ahmedabad.

10. Indian Water Resources Society, 1997, *Theme Paper on River Basin Management – Issues and Options*, New Delhi.
11. Indian Water Resources Society, 1998, *Theme Paper on Five Decades of Water Resources Development in India*, New Delhi.
12. Indian Water Resources Society, *Theme Paper on Integrated Water Resources Development and Management*, New Delhi, 2002.
13. Ministry of Water Resources, *Report of the Working Group on Legal, Institutional and Financing Aspects for National Commission for Integrated Water Resources Development Plan*, New Delhi, 1999.
14. Ministry of Water Resources, *Report of the National Commission for Integrated Water Resources Development Plan*, New Delhi, 1999.
15. Ministry of Water Resources, *National Water Policy*, New Delhi, 1987.
16. Ministry of Water Resources, *National Water Policy*, New Delhi, 2002.
17. Ministry of Water Resources, *Vision for Integrated Water Resources Development and Management*, New Delhi, 2003.
18. Ministry of Water Resources, *Agenda Notes for Meeting of Parliamentary Consultative Committee*, New Delhi, 2003.
19. National Water Academy, CWC and Indian Water Resources Society, Pune Centre, 2003, Proceedings of National Seminar on River Basin Organisations, July 10-11, 2003, Pune.
20. Patel V.B and Karajagi B.B., *Water Resources Administration in India*, Proceedings of Seminar on Irrigation Water Management, Vol-I, Water Management Forum, New Delhi, 1992.
21. Planning Commission, *Approach Paper for X Five Year Plan*, New Delhi, 2003.
22. Prasad K. and Goel R.S. (Ed.), 'Environmental Management in Hydro Electric Projects', New Delhi. Concept Publishing Company, 2000.
23. Tungabhadra Board, *Proceedings of Regional Seminar on Management of Inter-state River Valley Projects*, 6-7, November, 2003, Tungabhadra Dam, Karnataka
24. Water Management Forum, *Theme Paper on Inter-Basin Transfers of Water – Challenges and Opportunities*, New Delhi, 2002.

17

Water Resources Management in India: An Introspection

A. Sekhar

GLOBAL WATER SCENARIO

Water, alongwith air, is a basic requirement for sustenance of life on earth. When astronomers search for existence of life on other celestial bodies, they first look for tell-tale signs of the presence of water. The earth has a huge water-resource of 1.39 billion cubic kilometres (bckm). This is not surprising considering the fact that three-fourths of the earth surface is covered with water. Unfortunately, only 2.5 per cent of this is fresh water. Seventy per cent of the available fresh water is locked up in glaciers and as permanent snow cover. It is estimated that all the world's drinkable water can fit inside a cube shaped tank with 150 km side. There is no more fresh water on the earth today than what was available 2000 years ago when the human population was only three per cent of the current population level. The dwindling per capita availability of fresh water has therefore become the most serious crisis the human race is facing today. A per capita annual availability of 1000 cum is considered as the threshold value to avoid a water stress situation. As we enter the new millennium, 26 countries with a population of 300 million already suffer from water scarcity. Projections for the year 2050 show that 66 countries comprising two-thirds of the world population will face moderate to severe water scarcity. About 1.1 billion people have no access to safe and affordable drinking water and nearly twice that number have no proper sanitation. Lack of clean drinking water brings in its wake health problems. Diseases like typhoid, cholera, diarrhoea, jaundice spread mainly due to contaminated water. Eleven million children under the age of five die each year of easily preventable diseases like diarrhoea. The water scenario in India is therefore to be viewed in this backdrop of the global picture.

THE INDIAN SCENARIO

With 2.4 per cent of world's land area and four per cent of its fresh water, India has to support 17 per cent of the world's human population and 18 per cent of its cattle population. India being situated in the monsoon region has to face a paradoxical situation of scarcity amidst plenty. The per capita annual availability of water is 1869 cu m considering all the river systems. However, as bulk of the flows are contributed by thinly populated basins like Brahmaputra and Barak, many basins like Pennar and Sabarmathi are, in fact, severely water stressed already. The spatial and temporal variability in annual rainfall is a well-known fact (11000 mm in Cherrapunji in the north-east to about 100 mm in desert of Rajasthan). The monsoon is confined to four months—: June to September. There are only 75 to 90 days of rain every year. Actual precipitation of significance is only for about 35 days and merely 100 hrs. Although the country receives 4000 bcm as rainfall and snowfall, the actual run off is only 1869 bcm. Only 1122 bcm of this runoff is utilisable (690 bcm from surface and 432 bcm from groundwater sources). The water use in 1997-98 was estimated as 629 bcm of which 524 bcm was for irrigation alone. By 2050, the demand for water has been projected as 1180 bcm. In other words, all the utilisable water resources will have to be put to use by 2050 to meet the demand. This calls for exploitation of all potential storage sites and replenishable ground water resources, which is indeed a tall order. Although about 173 bcm of storage has been constructed, the per capita storage in India is very low compared to many other countries like USA and China.

Development of Irrigation

The irrigation development in our country since Independence has occurred in leaps and bounds. The irrigation potential created was only 21 mha in 1950 but had increased to about 94 mha by the end of the Ninth Five Year Plan in 2002. The ultimate potential from major, medium and minor irrigation schemes has been assessed as 139.88 mha. Minor irrigation (81.42 mha) is the main contributor while the major and medium irrigation sector is expected to account for 58.46 mha. Currently the annual production of foodgrains has touched the 210 mt mark mainly due to irrigation (The foodgrain production was only 51 mt in 1951). Despite these impressive gains, there are many areas of concern in so far as the irrigation sector is concerned. Only 40 per cent of our agriculture has assured irrigation whereas 60 per cent continues to depend on the erratic monsoon. The productivity of both rainfed and irrigated areas continues to be low. This is attributable to poor water management and dilapidated irrigation systems due to lack of maintenance. The gap between the potential created and potential utilised is still uncomfortably large—about 14 mha. Lack of field channels, poor condition of canals, silting of reservoirs, changes in cropping pattern from that envisaged at the time of project formulation are cited as some of the main reasons. A large number of irrigation projects (now assessed as about 390) continue to remain incomplete. Many of them were started as early as in the pre-Fifth and Fifth Plan periods. Their spillover cost is now estimated as around Rs. 95,000 crore. The irrigation water use efficiency in most systems is less than 40 per cent. Low water charges in most states do not convey the scarcity value of water and on the contrary encourage overuse and misuse. The collection of water charges as a percentage of demand is also very low in most states. The establishment component in O&M is very high leaving very little funds for maintenance works.

The Tenth Plan strategy is aimed to link reforms in water sector to Central funding. The accelerated irrigation benefits programme has relaxed lending norms for states agreeing for reforms (4:1 Centre: State lending ratio against 2:1 for non reforming states). Some states have already agreed to carryout required reforms. Participatory Irrigation Management (PIM) is being further promoted through the Command Area Development Programme. It is proposed to set up an Expert Committee to look into the whole gamut of issue related to water charges, O&M and PIM. The lending rate for AIBP has been reduced from 11.5 per cent to 10.5 per cent. Under Rural Infrastructure Development Fund IX, a provision of Rs. 5,500 crore has been made for 2003-04. It has been decided that 60 per cent of this will be allocated to the irrigation sector. Rehabilitation of old tanks is being now included under CAD programme as also under NABARD. All these measures will, it is hoped, help in completion of on-going projects, improve water use efficiency and accelerate pace of irrigation development.

Ground Water

Although the total replenishable ground water resource is about 432 bcm, the present level of ground water development is only 37 per cent. Notwithstanding this fact, the level of development in some states is very high leading to a situation of over-exploitation in certain pockets of the country. Out of 5,711 number of blocks/mandals/taluks/watersheds in the country, 310 are over exploited and 160 are dark where the level of exploitation is 85 per cent-100 per cent of the replenishable quantum. In 19 states, the fall in ground water level in some districts has been more than four meter during the period 1982 to 2001. The unbridled growth of the ground water sector has been mainly due to lack of legislation on control of ground water extraction and provision of free or subsidised power for agriculture sector. The Central government has been urging the states to enact legislation on groundwater. A few states have responded positively while the response from many states has been lukewarm. The Central Government is even contemplating a Central legislation on this subject. A Central Ground Water Authority has been constituted under the Environmental Protection Act to serve as a watch-dog body. The authority does not have policing powers and is dependent on the state governments for implementing its decisions. Under the World Bank assisted Hydrology Project, a National Data Bank on groundwater data is being set up.

One of the steps taken to improve the ground water situation is promotion of watershed programmes and artificial recharge through rain water harvesting. Commendable work on watershed programmes has been done in a few states. Roof top rain water harvesting has been a big success in Mizoram and more recently in Kuttanad area of Kerala. Revival of traditional drinking water sources like tanks, bawlis, khadins is also receiving attention now through a new scheme to revive one lakh traditional sources. Rain water harvesting in urban areas has been made compulsory in many states. However, recharge alone without attendant steps to check over exploitation may not yield the desired results.

Water Supply and Sanitation

In the rural water supply sector, habitations are classified as Not Covered (NC), Partially Covered (PC) and Fully Covered (FC). A NC habitation is one which has no public or private drinking water source point within 1.6 km of the habitation in plain area or 100 m elevation in hilly area. A norm of 40 litre per capita per day (lpcd) has been fixed for a FC habitation while a NC habitation has availability in the range of 10 to 40 lpcd. The Rajiv Gandhi Drinking Water Mission, which operates the Centrally Sponsored Scheme (ARWSP) has done a commendable job in covering fully about 90 per cent of the 14.23 lakh habitations in the country and another nine per cent have been partially covered. The National Agenda for Governance aims at full coverage by 2004. The Tenth Plan strategy is to provide potable drinking water to all villages. It is planned to utilise the period 2004-07 for consolidation and the period upto 2015 for augmentation of per capita availability (to 55 lpcd or more).

One of the problems being faced in the rural drinking water sector is slippage of habitations from fully covered to partially covered and partially covered to not covered habitations due to increase in population, fall in ground water, water quality problems, etc. Water quality is a serious problem with 17 states reporting fluoride and 75 blocks in West Bengal reporting arsenic in ground water. Other water quality problems include iron, nitrates and bacteriological contamination. The recent controversy over presence of pesticides in bottled soft drinks has raised fears that the source is contaminated ground water used for manufacture of soft drinks. Sustainability of assets created is also another issue. The recently launched *Swajaldhara* scheme involving community participation in development and maintenance of rural water supply schemes is a step in the right direction. Sustainability issues are being addressed through focus on revival of traditional rain water harvesting techniques.

On the rural sanitation front, the coverage has been only 18 to 19 per cent. The Millennium Declaration of the United Nations has stressed the global goal of halving by 2015 AD the population without access to water supply and sanitation. The recent launch of the demand driven Total Sanitation Campaign will, it is hoped, help in achieving the Millennium Declaration goal.

The urban water supply sector has done better with 91 to 93 per cent of India's urban population taking their drinking water from protected sources. However, this sector has also been beset with several problems. The low water tariffs have left finances of most the local bodies in a very bad shape leaving no funds for maintenance and new developments. Due to rapid urbanisation and unbridled growth of new localities/colonies, the percentage of 'unaccounted for water' in most cities/towns has been increasing. Delhi can be quoted as an example in this context where revenue expenditure is Rs. 480 crore, earning Rs. 225 crore and 30 to 40 per cent leakage is reported in distribution. The need of the hour is to raise water charges to cover at least the O&M costs and improve distribution efficiency.

While 75 to 81 per cent of urban households have toilets, urban sewerage disposal and solid waste management have assumed alarming problems. The coverage in terms of organised sewerage systems ranges from 35 per cent in Class IV cities to 75 per cent in Class I cities. Studies conducted by the Central Pollution Control Board showed that the total wastewater generated in 300 Class I cities is around 15,800 mld while the treatment capacity is hardly 3,750 mld. A lot of water is wasted due to large-sized flushing cisterns in many houses. There is need to standardise the cistern size to economise the water use.

Municipal Solid Waste (MSW) Management is also becoming a burgeoning problem. The *per capita* generation of MSW ranges from 100 gm in small towns to 500 gms in large towns. Delhi and Mumbai generate about 5,500-6,000 t of MSW each daily. The conventional disposal method of landfill is becoming difficult to sustain due to non-availability of land for new landfills. Composting and generation of power have been tried in a limited scale. Cities/towns are facing health hazards due to uncontrolled dumping of garbage and indiscriminate use of plastic bags which are clogging natural drains. Scientific Solid Waste Management is called for involving segregation of biodegradable waste at source, setting up of sanitary landfills, generation of energy and use of compost as fertiliser.

Even after 50 years of Independence, the obnoxious practice of manual scavenging has not been eradicated, mainly prevailing in the urban areas. Although an Act was enacted in 1993 on this issue, its adoption and implementation by states has been tardy. The Planning Commission has prepared a National Action Plan for eradication of manual scavenging by 2007.

Rehabilitation of Project Affected Families

Most states have now drawn up a reasonably fair rehabilitation policy with the objective of making the displaced person economically better off. The judicial intervention in the Sardar Sarovar case has accentuated the need for rehabilitation before displacement. Resettlement of project affected persons through allotment of land and house plots as due should be done well before actual submergence. Their subsequent rehabilitation though training schemes is equally important to ensure their gainful employment. Only then can the trauma of displacement be minimised.

WATER CODE

Watershed programmes have been launched in many states. While in good rainfall year, watershed structures will minimise wasteful runoff into the sea. The impact of watershed development in upper reaches on water availability in lower reaches, especially in a series of drought years, has not yet been fully studied. A National Water Code will clearly define the parameters within which watershed development should take place. This is also issue of sustainability of an assets created which merit attention before embarking on a massive programme to conserve water.

PRIVATE SECTOR PARTICIPATION

While the private sector has shown some interest in drinking water supply, the irrigation sector has so far failed to enthuse it. It is not difficult to pin-point the reason for this. While the water charges for drinking are a few rupees per kilolitre, for irrigation it is only a few paise which is unremunerative for a private investor to make investments. Even in the drinking water sector, municipalities have been wary of handing over O&M of water supply systems to the private sector for fear of a large hike in water charges. The Cochabamba experiment in Bolivia where a multinational reportedly hiked water charges from 30 per cent to 300 per cent should serve as an eye-opener for all those who advocate such commercialisation of water. Public opinion of water as a practically free commodity is still to change. A person is ready to pay Rs.10 for a litre of bottled water but is reluctant to pay even a rupee for a kilolitre of municipal treated water supply. As in the case of irrigation charges, drinking water charges have remained stagnant in most cities/towns for decades and thus there is stiff opposition to a change. Most urban local bodies do not have funds to improve or expand the water supply infrastructure and it is only a question of time before the private sector will have to step in. In irrigation, while private sector may not immediately enter areas like building of dam or distribution of water, some of the components like tourism can be commercialised. In reservoirs, boating and recreation gardens can be entrusted to private operators who levy an entrance fee. Use of canal banks for billboards, pisciculture in reservoir and canal power house are other areas where private sector can invest.

CONCLUSION

From the forgoing discussions, it is apparent that we have to grapple with a plethora of issues in the water sector in this country. The times ahead are indeed going to be difficult on the water-front. Only with sustainable development objectives and an integrated management approach can the issues be effectively addressed. The Revised National Water Policy lays down the road map for such an approach. It needs to be operationalised quickly with an Action Plan and state level water policies. The subject of water is being dealt at the Centre in too many ministries. It needs to be brought under one umbrella so that a holistic view can be taken of this precious resource. The Prime Minister has recently given a call to make water conservation a national mission. Year 2003 is being observed as the Fresh Water Year. The successive droughts in the past few years have given us the 'wake up' call. This year's good monsoon should not make us complacent. Water is no more a fresh, abundant and bountiful resource to be squandered away. Most of the exhaustible resources like coal, petroleum, minerals would get consumed in the next 200-300 years and posterity would have to plan for using alternate sources of energy like hydrogen and solar energy. Let us not add water to this list as there is no alternative to water.

18

Water Resources Management: Challenges of the 21st Century

T.N. Dhar

Water is one of the most important priceless gifts of nature and an essential need for sustenance of life and civilizations in the world. Most of the wars in the world have, historically been fought for territory and land. This may change in the present century. It is believed that, perhaps, the wars of the 21st Century will be fought not for land but for water.

In its totality the availability of water globally is practically fixed. The variations are in its dispersal and areal availability. Of the total quantity of water available on the earth, 97.3 per cent is contained in the seas. Of the remaining 2.7 per cent most of it is locked up as ice and snow, in the polar regions and on mountain tops. Only one part of water in 10,000 is available above ground, apart from sea water which is not usable as such. What is available is present in river, streams, lakes, ponds and other water sheets. It is the hydrological cycle, which determines the renewal and repleshishment of water all over the globe.

The world's total water, budget is 14,000 cu km of which only about 3,000 cu km is used. About three-fourths of water is utilized for irrigation and the rest for other uses. In India total annual precipitation is 400 million hectare meters (mhm) but surface water availability is only about 178 mhm. Of this, just about half can be put to beneficial uses because of topographical and other constraints, if surface and ground water is put together the potential of use can be raised to nearly two-third. Water availability in the country is uneven in both space and time. Most of the rainfall is recorded during mansoons (about 80% between June and September) and a substantial part of this water flows to the sea as run off. The annual run-off of the river systems in India is 1645 billion cum, of which, nearly two-thirds is contributed by the Himalayan river systems. We are able to use only a part of the total available water and this is where the situation needs to improve.

India has 16 per cent of the world's population but only 2.45 per cent of land area and four per cent of; water resources. According to the Tata Energy Research Institute, the annual per capita availability of water in India was 6,008 cum when the country achieved Independence in 1947. In 50 years after Independence this availability had fallen by 67 per cent. It was about 2,266 cum in 1977 and is now only around 1,800 cum. It is estimated to fall further to the abysmal level of 750 cum in the next 50 years. Thus, we are already at the stage of water stress, and moving steadily to the likely state of water scarcity.

NATIONAL WATER POLICY

Till recently the country was following the National Water Policy (NWP) of 1987 which among other things emphasized maximization of retention and minimization losses. basin-wise planning, water budgeting, reconciliation of uses and proper pricing. The NWP has since been revised in 2002. It recognizes water as a prime natural resource/ the basic human need and precious national asset. Water is a part of the larger ecological system and getting progressively scarce. The new policy emphasizes the need to develop, utilize and manage this important resource in a sustainable manner and in a national perspective. India's population, which is now nearly 105 crore, is expected to reach a level of around 139 crore in 2025. The food production by then would have to be raised to over 350 million tonne from the present level of 200 million tonne. The drinking water needs of people and livestock as also for domestic/industrial purposes will sharply go up. Similarly, there will be very high demand of water for hydro and thermal power generation. The NWP 2002 stresses the development of comprehensive water data systems, basin/sub-basin-wise water planning watershed management, fixation of water allocation priorities, enhancing, project planning and implementation capabilities, the achieving of sustainability in the uses of ground water in conjunction with surface water ensuring that drinking water needs are met, integration of water and land use policies, adequate financial allocations for water programmes and time bound implementation of such projects. The document specially underlines conservation, integrated use of land and water, participatory management, better flood control and management practices, and appropriate legal framework for water sharing and distribution among states regions and al stakeholders. The use of science and technology inputs has also been given priority along with safety of structures and systems. Training and human resource development, are the other two important components of the policy. The policy document concludes by stating that its success will depend entirely on the evolving and maintaining of national consensus and on parallel formulation of State Water Policies to achieve the national objectives in a coordinated and cooperative manner.

World Water Forum 2002

Recently, in the month of March 2003, the, World Water Forum met at Kyoto, Japan. Among the action points outlined at the Forum, the important ones were: (*a*) Water should be recognized as a human right and enforced in each country accordingly, (*b*) Development of reliable data base for water resources and river flows in time series modes and creation of data banks, (*c*) Set up an International Fund for Water and

Sanitation, (*d*) Enhance and intensify user engagement in the management of water resources at local levels in participatory modes, (*e*) Promote real water saving in agriculture as also in commercial, domestic and industrial uses, (*f*) Intensity environmental education and awareness to ensure water quality, (*g*) Technology exchange and exchange of know-how for capacity building, (*h*) Intensify scientific research and application of most modern technologies, (*i*) Develop countrywise action plants and financial mechanisms and SPVs for funding water projects.

Prospect

In India there are 24 basins in which the total availability of water is estimated at 1,853 cu km. As for groundwater, the estimated available quantity is 432 cu km of which 396 cu km is usable. Nearly half the irrigation in the country is done by using ground water. According to the National Commission for Water Resources Development (NCWRD), keeping in view the past trend and incremental changes in land uses, cropping patterns, etc., the water requirement in 2050 will very between 628 to 807 cu km. For domestic needs this requirement will be between 90 and 111 cu km Irrigation will need about 70 per cent of the water. The NCWRD says "The country's total water requirement in the year 2050 barely matches the estimated utilizable water resources." Therefore, there is great need for conservation, efficiency in water uses, minimization of losses and recycling.

Water and Land Use

India's geographical area is 328.73 million ha (mha) of which the net sown area is 142.60 mha. The cropping intensity is 135, while irrigation intensity is just a little lower at 133. We produce about 200 million tonne of food grains. The existing cropping pattern is such that we have surpluses in cereals while there are shortages in, pulses and oilseeds. Most of the cereals crops, as also sugarcane are highly water intensive. It is evident, therefore, that the cropping patterns have to shift so as to achieve nutritional balance on the one hand and reduction in the use of water on the other. We waste a lot of water or overuse it. For example in Japan and China for a crop like paddy they use only about one-third of water than is used in India. Yet their productivity is more than two-and-a-half times of what we have been able to achieve. There is loss of water in its conveyance and through trans-evaporation. There is also unevenness in distribution with the tail ender farmer-beneficiaries in the distribution systems getting a raw deal. We are overdrawing ground water on the one hand and having waterlogging caused by seepages in canal systems on the other. A clear requirement is to plan conjunctive uses of water. There is need for water harvesting on a large scale and, above all, there is need for community management in the maintenance of water systems and distribution at peripheral levels.

Water Wastage

Most of irrigation water is supplied on a fixed rate basis. Even in urban areas, in most cities and towns, water supply is metered either partially or not at al. This encourages wastage. What is required is a shift to a phased, volumetric supply system and link this with suitable pricing mechanisms so that there is much greater consumer and farmer response and sensitivity for the use and conservation of water.

What are the other measures that can be taken to reduce waste in irrigation? For all this we must re-think water management. We no more live in an era in which rivers can be dammed endlessly, acquifers pumped relentlessly and eco-systems degraded and impoverished in the process. The clear message that we have to focus on is how we use water. Among the measures for achieving water saving in irrigation are the adoption of less water-intensive cropping patterns, increasing *in situ* moisture of land, water harvesting, use of drip and sprinkler system, reducing conveyance losses and using water pricing policies to discourage waste. Also a massive community awareness and extension programme would need to be mounted for this purpose.

FLOOD MANAGEMENT AND DROUGHTS

With irrigation is connected the problem of flood management. In India the flood prone area is about 40 mha of which only one-third is protected at present. On an average 7.5 mha are affected by floods each year. In the worst years the affected area can be as high as 25 mha. Between 1983-2000, on an average about 1,500 human lives and 95,000 cattle were lost each year. Floods cannot be eliminated but can be modified and tempered. The strategy should be to improve management, increase protection as far as possible and go in for disaster preparedness, mitigation and response plans. In flood protection, we have mostly remained dependent upon engineering measures so far. The need is to go for a combination of engineering and biological measures so as to reduce run-off, increase infiltration of water and temper peak flows. To an extent storages and detention reservoirs can help, but this is a limited choice on account of environmental safety and human population dislocation factors.

Contrary to floods we have droughts visiting different states from time-to-time. Droughts are caused by server and long precipitation deficits. These are creeping disasters for which preparations can be mounted in time. During draughts water management offers a big challenges. In such areas water harvesting has to be taken up on a large scale and cropping-patterns have to be changed. Water relief becomes an important necessity including transportation of water, food and fodder.

Ground Water

The management of ground water needs far greater attention. A massive community oriented programme for watershed management, water harvesting and re-charging of acquifers needs to be taken up in the country on a national scale. At present we have a situation where ground water levels are going down fast in many states in India. This has caused great alarm. In urban areas the situation becomes much more different because the going down of ground water level directly affected drinking water supply.

In statistical terms we are at present using only one-third of the ground water in the country but the present methods of drawal and uses have become so inefficient and un-scientific that serious problems have arisen in this context in many cities as well as n rural areas.

Half the agricultural land in the country is irrigated by ground water. In cities and towns it is ground water that meets a very substantial part of drinking water requirements. Unfortunately, serious problems have arisen, because, in areas where intensive agriculture is being practiced, there is overdrawal of ground water. This is a worldwide phenomenon. Over-pumping is widespread in India, China and even in USA. For example, in just one year, 1999, the water table under Beijing fell by 1.5 meter. In fact, since 1965, water table under this city has dropped by more than 60 meter. Nearer home, in Punjab, where the double cropping of high yield winter what and *kharif* rice produce substantial surpluses for shipments to other states in the country, the water table is falling, dropping by 0.6 to one meter per year in different areas. In Uttar Pradesh the situation has become difficult because there is lack of integration between the uses of surface and ground water. On the one hand, in dry and drought prone areas—water scarcity is increasing each year while heavy monsoon river flows go down to the sea. Of 806 development blocks in the state water table is falling in as many as 559 blocks. In some areas salinity of ground water has increased making it unfit for drinking and even for agriculture. In other areas high fluoride content in ground, water is creating health hazards. There are several ways in which the recharge of ground water can be achieved. For example in the rainy season when the canals overflow the surplus water can be led through recharge structures to the acquifers below. Water harvesting in urban areas can improve recharge.

Water Conservation

Conserving water is an area of high priority. It can be done in many ways. For example, roof rain water harvesting is possible in the cities and towns. In rural areas similar results can be achieved by construction of ponds, bandhs, the raising of field mud-boundaries and through shallow wells. Percolation tanks can be built. Tanks and ponds can be deeped to increase storage and greater infiltration. The other important approach is that of conserving ground water which will mean that withdrawal will get reduced and the rate of fall of the water level can be arrested or stopped. Water saving is possible in a number of other ways also. We can use less water in our daily chores, reduce the size of flush tanks and avoid use of precious drinking water for gardening and bathing of animals. The plumbing can be made leak proof to eliminate waste. The other important matter is to ensure that waste water, is not allowed to infiltrate underground to avoid contamination of ground water below. Bathtubs can be replaced by showers. Similarly, in rural areas the use of irrigation water can be economized by better technical knowledge and suitable changes in cropping patterns and agronomic practices, Wherever possible drip and sprinkler systems and hydrams can be used for irrigation. All this will need a major educational and awareness programme to be mounted through different media channels and other means of publicity.

Waterlogging

Waterlogging and salinity are different problems faced in some areas in the country. It can result from both natural and man-made causes. For example, poor natural drainage, monsoon over-flows, storm water heavy floods, etc., can cause waterlogging. There are, then many management activities that cause waterlogging, like seepage from canals and distributaries construction of embankments road, rail-lines and brides, over-irrigation poor on-farm water management and providing inadequate drainage in any civil construction work. About 25 lakh hectares of land were reported to be waterlogged n the country in 1991. The stats most effected were Bihar, Uttar Pradesh, Haryana and Punjab. This problem continues and in some areas has worsened. Both preventive and curative measures are required to tackle it. This is possible by developing drainage plans before construction of any projects, lining of irrigation canals, distributaries and channels constructing control structures/escapes, going in for conjunctive uses of water and regulating irrigation water supply. For those areas which are already underwater the prime need is drainage.

Drainage

An important requirement of good water management is the provision for drainage at the very time when surface water projects are constructed or there is construction of embankments, railway lines, bridges and similar other structures. Different agro-climatic zones will need different appropriate drainage technologies. The measures involved are, for example, changes in cropping patterns, providing horizontal and vertical drainage as the case may be, going in for conjunctive uses of water, adopting bio-drainage, where it is found suitable and improving overall water management.

Water Uses

Water has many competitive uses. It is required for agriculture, forestry, horticulture, energy production, growth of bio-mass, commercial and industrial uses and, above all, for drinking and other domestic purposes. It is therefore, very important to determine alocative priorities and tailor water planning and management to respective demands accordingly. Both protective and regenerative approaches are necessary. Pricing must address accessibility in all its different uses. We have to learn to conserve water and eliminate waste. It has already been stated above that, generally, in agriculture, we use much more water than we should. This is partly because of lack of knowledge and partly because water pricing is not volumetric. Similarly, in the industrial filed, too, there is chronic over-use of water. Industries like paper and chemicals use for more water then they should. Very little recycling is done. In urban areas filtered water is utilized for gardening. In allocative planning, therefore, all these factors have to be taken into account and savings and efficiencies introduced in supply and use systems so that more equitable and sustainable distribution of water for different needs and purposes becomes possible.

WATERSHED MANAGEMENT APPROACH

For ensuring the health of water regimes it is essential to adopt what is called the Integrated Watershed Management Approach. Here the core strategy necessarily has to be a combination of protection, re-generation and production. A watershed is a natural eco-geographical unit in which it is both desirable as well as necessary to undertake integrated land and water planning. Watershed management has been recognized world over as a scientific and sensible system of resource management and use. Many such programmes have been undertaken in the country for years now. Recently the *haryali* programme has been announced by the Prime Minister for the whole country. It is a bold approach at integrated micro-level watershed management programming in the country. Here the crux is to undertake local water and land use planning with the help of village communities who would be provided technical assistance but would be fully involved in preparing and executing local area projects. Most water harvesting projects in rural areas would be necessarily a part of the micro-level watershed management programmes and projects.

People's Participation

If the strategy of integrate watershed management, water harvesting and water conservation is to succeed the question that follows then its, what is the best way to implement it. The answer clearly lies is full community participation and involving local people in planning, constructing, managing and maintaining local water projects. They should be make responsible for equitable distribution of water and been for recovery of water charges. This integrated approach is essential for holistic resource management that would naturally include land, water and all other kinds of bio-mass. In this endeavour Village Panchayats, Water User Groups and similar collectivities have a crucial role to play. NGOs can also very considerably catalyse, guide and support such initiatives.

Water Management in Mountain Areas

Mountains are water towers of the world that nourish land, forests grasslands, cropped areas, trees, etc.,—within and outside their bounds. They feed major river systems and are of great significance to the food security of the country. Mountains have their specificities and their district problems. Here, the slopes are often steep and the water rushes 'down fast'. In mountain areas available cropped land is limited, less than ten per cent. Most other land is either forest, grassland or bare rocks. Massive aforestation and grassland development would help increase infiltration, of water and temper the annual intensity of floods. Storage dams, especially the big ones, are not considered safe. Therefore, detaining very large quantities of water in mountain areas is not a feasible proposition. In the hilly areas the obvious priorities are water conservation, harvesting, user participation and the adoption and use of economic water supply systems such as hydrams, sprinklers, drip irrigation, etc.

Production of Energy

One of the very important uses of water is related to the production of electricity. Water is a source of energy. Where it is allowed to fall to a lower level though turbines it generates energy and the same water can be utilized for other beneficial purposes downstream like irrigation or domestic/commercial/industrial uses. India has vast hydro-electric potential which is estimated at about 84,000 MW at 60 per cent load factor. Till now less than one-fourth of this potential has been taped. Hydropower based on storage is required to meet the peak demand of energy. Experts say that an optimal mix of hydro/thermal power is 40:60. The present ratio in the country is adverse because hydropower contributes only about one-fifth of the total electrical energy produced in the country. The slow development of hydro-power can be traced to several reasons such as inadequate project preparation, massive investment requirements inter-state nature of such projects, serious environmental factors which need to be addressed, problems of the land acquisition and difficulties that arise in respect of the rehabilitation of those people who are displaced. In spite of all that it is vital to step up efforts to increase hydropower production in the country so as to remove the serious imbalance in the power mix as it obtains now is also to reduce shortage between the demand and supply of electrical energy.

Water Resources Planning and Budget Analysis

The various important uses of water are public and domestic, municipal and industrial, animal consumption, irrigation hydropower generation, commercial uses, recreation, inland navigation (in the plains), etc. In addition flood management has necessarily to be included in water resource planning—Planning and management of water resources is at present a compartmentalized activity in governments. In terms of policy and planning, water as a resource needs to be put under a single institutional arrangement. This could be in the form of state and Central Level Empowered Water Boards headed by respective heads of governments. The assessment of water demand projections has necessarily to include the analysis of total water supplies available, withdrawals from surface and ground sources, the aggregate volume of waste and the return of drainage effluents into water bodies. All this needs scientific water budget analysis and this involves the preparation of detailed water budget studies for different regions, which could then be consolidated into the water budget of the country as a whole.

An important aspect of water resource planning is the very ambitious plan of interlinking rivers in India. It is massive project estimated at Rs. 5,60,000 crore—a mind-boggling sum. It is expected to irrigate an additional 1.50 mha, generate 35,000 MW of electricity and double agricultural production. A high level takes force has been appointed by the Central Government and a slew of studies commissioned about the cost-benefit analysis of the project, technical and economic feasibility; environmental impact social, ecological and political issues, water Sharing mechanisms, international implication, etc. Many experts are not convinced about the feasibility, desirability and benefits of a project of such dimensions. There are other political discordant notes to be heard but the mounting national needs of water demand a bold solution. All caution must be exercised but boldness and vision are required to meet the challenge.

Environmental Issues

While planning water development projects it is very important to keep in view the environmental and health requirements and the issues of disaster prevention. Water quality management, environmental issues and health aspects need to be included as an integral part of water resources planning. An important tool that can be used for this purpose is Environmental Impact Assessment (EIA) which needs to be incorporated in all water resource development projects which are likely to create adverse impacts.

Environmental management will also need a careful study of the hydrological regime of a river system before and after a large water project is planned and implemented. Another important need is to check and ensure the surface water quality. It would also be necessary to study the biological parameters as well as applicable pollution parameters like BOD, COD, etc. A study would need to be carried out on the new ecology that would emerge as a result of the construction of a water project. There would also have to be monitoring arrangements in place as in integral component of the project operation programme to enable continuing assessment and corrective measures as may be called for. National standards for quality of drinking water are not available at present. This is an issue that needs to be addressed on priority.

WATER QUALITY MANAGEMENT

Water quality management is an inseperable component for proper use of water resources. Many benefits flow if water quality is assured. *First,* there are health benefits—for the consumers. The cost of treatment of water by sown-stream municipalities is reduced the risk of contamination of ground water is less.

Both surface and ground water has to be regularly monitored for quality. Rivers are at present polluted by all kinds of effluents and water most of the large rivers has become unfit for use. A National River Conservation Programme has been initiated but it is applicable only to a selected number of rivers and lakes. This programme needs to be extended to cover all important rivers and water sheets. It would be also necessary to have stringe at laws as well as enforcement so that pollution of water can be minimized and eliminated. Regular monitoring of water quality is most essential so that no risks are created for people from municipal, rive sheet or well water.

Problems of Large Dams

The question of building large water storages for expanding irrigation facilities and generation of power is one that is full of complexity as well as controversy. There are differing views and differing perceptions. The environmentalists are apprehensive of large dams. They are of the given that large dams cause massive human dislocations, increase the incident of water borne disease, give rise to sedimentation, soil erosion, stratification and proliferation of aquatic-weeds. Many such negativities are identified and emphasized. The other side of the coin is represented by technologists, engineers and development planners. The truth may lie some where in between. The issue cannot be approached integrally either from the exclusive point of view of environmental 'extremism' or from that of the 'hubris, of technology which has a 'fix' available for every problem. A touch-me-not policy would be quite misplaced. The water potential of the country must be harnessed but this must be done in environmental-friendly and people-friendly ways. There is no contradiction between these two objectives if the twin objectives of developmental and environmental security are converged in complementary modes.

Legal Framework and Institution Building

Water, in its natural state, is a unique commodity the characteristics of which seem to defy the usual concepts of ownership. It is now generally agreed that the state, as guardian and promoter of public good, should have a clear responsibility of ensuring efficient and equitable use of this critical resource. Increased competition amongst water users leads to a wide variety of disputes of which there are many examples to be observed in our own country today. The governments, therefore, have to intervene to prevent such conflicts from arising or to settle them in judicious ways.

The legal framework has to be strengthened in terms of laws, institutions, and enforcement machinery so that water, as a priceless resource is used for the good of the people in the most equitable manner and also most efficiently.

For efficient management of water as a crucial resource appropriate river basin organizations are necessary. Similarly, there have to be effective and empowered institutional arrangements for sorting out inter-estate water problems and settling of disputes that often arise as regards sharing of water. At the lower end, water users associations have to be strengthened and empowered so that there is full participation in equitable distribution and use of water for different purpose.

Privatization

The NWP states that private sector participation should be encouraged in planning, development and management of water resources for diverse uses wherever feasible. The private sector participation could be in the form of building, owning operating, leasing and transfer of water resources facilities. The issue of privatization has caused widespread and genuine apprehension in the country. Water is a merit good. Its access has to be ensured for all. As such this resource should be in the public domain. Some specific functions like construction of projects or treatment plants or energy producing units can be entrusted to private entrepreneurs but, as a resource, water in its totality, being a human right, must be fully within the preview of the Central and the state governments. The apprehensions of people in respect of privatization need to be dispelled.

Data and Access to Information

The problems of water availability and flow data as well as ground water estimates are difficult and fraught with complexity. While we have adequate data on rainfall and water flows in major rivers and streams, it is still inadequate. Small rivers, tributaries and streams are not covered. Our information about run-off and infiltration is also said to be lacking accuracy. The need is to put on ground a well-developed water information system at the Central, state and decentralized levels with, facilities for networking of data banks and for exchange of information in one-time as well as series modes. The use of modern information technology as also of Remote Sensing and GIS technique would be necessary for developing a reliable and accessible information base. Such base should include mechanisms for reliable projections for future availability as well as demand of water for different purposes.

Science and Technology Inputs

Frontier scientific knowledge and technologies should be utilized for improving water resources management. These for example, include areas like hydrometeorology, snow and lake hydrology; river morphology; water resources assessment; water quality assurance; water harvesting; ground water recharge; water conservation; reducing conveyance seepage; and evaporation losses; better agronomic uses of water; energy saving, structural design material uses etc. While using science and technology inputs there is need to build on such traditional knowledge, which has been found to be beneficial and economic for centuries.

Water Pricing

It is unfortunate that water is being often treated as a free-riding resource in many ways. In urban areas., in most cities and towns water supply is not fully or adequately metered. Similarly, in rural areas, water for irrigation is supplied in a way where there is no relationship between the price charged and the quantity utilized. Then again, there is hardly any regulation of extracting ground water. Many industrial units are treating ground water as some kind of a free resource. This is a situation that possibly can not submit. Water need to be properly priced so that its consumption is regulated and its waste avoided. If any subsidies have to be provided to specific consumer categories like, for example, the urban poor, slum dwellers and small and marginal farmers, then that should be a charge on government expenditure but should not impact the correct water tariff setting. Time has come when, in all the states of the country, Water Tariff Authorities must be set up for regulating the uses and prices of water.

Human Resource Development

A critical input for economic sustainability and efficient utilization of water resources is trained and motivated manpower. Water resources planning requires high quality knowledge in several areas which can be related to different fields—technical, engineering agriculture environmental, economic, organizational, financial or related to social sciences. The issue of providing the required trained and competent manpower in all these fields and disciplines has not received the attention it deserves. This is an aspect that needs to be addressed for improving the management and planning of water in future.

CONCLUSION

As more than 105 crore people living in India, start their march in the 21st Century of mounting complexities, few issues facing them are as critical and fundamental as water. The situation in this context is difficult globally. More than more billion people do not have access to safe drinking water in the world. About 2.4 billion lack sanitation. And four billion live without sound wastewater arrangement disposal. About 3.5 million-people die each year from water related diseases and 12 million of water scarcity, globally. This is needed a bleak picture. In India we have almost a similar situation with regard to the availability of drinking water, its quality and deficiencies in sanitation and waste disposal. Of 180 countries ranked for water availability by the UN, India's rating is 133. As for water quality the ranking is 120th among 122 countries evaluated. A study has shown that raw sewage in Ganga is 50 times above the level deemed acceptable for human contact. It is starkly clear that we have to give high priority to plans and programmes that will ensure availability of water in adequate quantity and of acceptable quality to every Indian citizen. For this purpose the country has to increase resources, enhance project formulation and implementation competence, limit environmental damage and, above all, enlist peoples', full participation in water management and it prudent uses.

The year 2003 has been appropriately declared by the United Nations as the Year of Fresh Water. The Objectives of the YFW are: (*a*) Increased awareness among stakeholders regarding scarcity value of fresh water, (*b*) Conservation and efficient use of fresh water, (*c*) Preservation of freshwater quality and its eco-system, (*d*) Augmentation of fresh water resources, (*e*) Community partnership for informed decision making. This cannot be the responsibility of the government machinery alone. That mindset has to change. There has to be basic paradigm shift to participative and local management of water resources. Both the Central and the state governments must seek and enlist the involvement of communities at all levels. It is time that we responded to this call of the time and addressed the problem fully and squarely.

As a 21st Century issue fresh water scarcity ranked only second to global warming as a critical environmental problem. The third and fourth ranked problems were desertification and deforestation. The urgency with which it needs to be approached and sorted out is evident from this assessment.

It must be said in conclusion that water has necessarily to be recognized as a social good. Its planning must be put above any political controversy. It should be accessible to all, including specially the poor. The uses of water have to be equitably and sustainably democratized putting people squarely in the circle of its planning and management.

A SELECT READING

Aggarwal, Anil (ed.), *Dying Wisdom: Center for Science and (Water Harvesting) Environment*, New Delhi, 2000.

Aggarwal, Anil (ed.), *Making Water Every-body's Business*, 2000.

Brown, Lester and Brain Halweil, *China's Water Shortage*, World Watch New York July-August 1988.

Brown Lester, R., *Eco-Economy, Orient Longman*, 2001.

Dhar, T.N., *Resource Management and Environment*, IIPA, UP, Region, Lucknow, 2001.

Dhar, T.N. *Sustainable Mountain Development*, Sherpa, Lucknow, 1999.

Gelvick, *Rethink Water*, 2000.

Iyer, R. Radhaswami, Water: *Perspective, Issues Concerns*, 2000.

Mc Cully, P., *Silenced Rivers*, Zed Books, London, 1996.

National Water Policy Document, Government of India, 2002.

Scott. C., A Crisis of Management (Need to Manage Inst. Water Judiciously) *Economics Times*, March 25, 2003.

Report of National Commission on Floods, Government of India, 1980.

Report of National Commission on *India's Water Resource Development*, Planning Commission Government of India, 1999.

Tenth Five Year Plan of India (Document), Planning Commission Government of India, 2003.

Vision-2005 (Irrigation) Document, Government of Uttar Pradesh, 2003.

World Water Forum, Session Records March 2003.

World Development Reports, 2001, 2002, 2003.

19

Water and Poverty Alleviation[1]

Kamta Prasad

INTRODUCTION

Poverty alleviation has started receiving attention from water resource professional bodies. This reflects a significant departure from the earlier approach of treating water resource development as an end in itself or as a means for overall increase in food and agricultural production without adequate concern for equity including poverty alleviation. The earlier technocratic approach, in fact, had favoured concentration of efforts on 'progressive' farmers and regions for getting quick results, thereby bypassing the interest of the poor. Can the emerging focus on poverty in the water sector be regarded as a triumph of Integrated Water Resource Management (IWRM) as conceptualised by Global Water Partnership (GWP) wherein the objective of development and management of water is "to maximise the resulting economic and social welfare in equitable manner?" Or is it an attempt by water developers to project a human face for counteracting the increasingly hostile environment which they are facing due to their alleged careless planning and mismanagement of water resources? Or is it the outcome of donor's increasing attention? Perhaps it could be the result of a combination of all these.

While development of water resources in general and irrigation in particular occupy a pivotal position in the overall development strategy, their role in poverty alleviation has not received much explicit attention apart from some general understanding which has remained vague and elusive. The present article is an attempt to throw light on the mechanisms through which water affects poverty alleviation. It also explains how mismanagement of water, far from alleviating poverty, tends to increase it further. The analysis would be based on secondary information sources available at the macro-level mainly for South Asia where a sizeable proportion of the world's poor reside and whose experience in poverty alleviation is probably the longest in the world.

In the context of this article, the concept of poverty is that of absolute poverty which implies non-fulfilment of the objectively determined minimum standard of physiological needs considered essential for human beings. This is usually expressed in terms of nutritional standards indicated by calorie value of food like an average of 2,400 calories per capita per day in rural areas and 2,100 calories in urban areas of India. Its measurement in monetary terms involves stipulation of a minimum level of per capita consumer expenditure considered adequate for purchasing goods and services needed for the purpose. The monetary equivalents are updated from time-to-time on the basis of changes in the price level.[2]

Water is essential for life, livelihood, as well as for the entire eco-system. But it becomes an issue of critical importance when it starts becoming scarce as is the case now in many countries. Scarcity has an ominous foreboding for the poor since it impacts the poor more than those who are better-off. Increasing water scarcity, therefore, accentuates poverty. The effect is more on women since it is they who have the responsibility of fetching water and it is they who use water for their home-based enterprises in addition to normal domestic uses. A specific focus must, therefore, be placed on water for the poor while implementing any scheme of water security or poverty alleviation.

WATER, HEALTH AND POVERTY

Water is more or less synonymous with life and yet it is an irony that adequate availability of suitable quality of drinking water does not form part of the definition of absolute poverty. This definition is based on calorie value of food, and has been criticised by several experts as too narrow and one—sided as it excludes other elements like clothing, education, health care, shelter, etc. But it is yet another irony that even the critics of the above definition of poverty have ignored the role of potable water. This omission might probably be on the presumption that calorie-based poverty might be correlated to deprivation *vis-a-vis* water both in quantity and quality. Another presumption could be that water is a free and abundant commodity and hence everybody including the poor must be having enough of it.

Dimension of the Problem

Municipal agencies in urban areas of South Asia are not able to provide water and sanitation facilities to cope with increasing urban population. Slums and urban fringes, where a significant proportion of the urban population lives, are generally provided with limited or no piped water supply or sewerage facility. The situation is far worse in rural areas. The number of villages having drinking water problem in India has been increasing rather than decreasing.[3] It has been reported by Self-Employed Women's Association (SEWA), a reputed Indian NGO, that in several drought-prone districts of Gujarat, water is so scarce that midwives have limited access to it even to wash their hands after delivering the child. The water used to clean the new born child is not always clean or safe.[4] Unless appropriate steps are taken, the problem is likely to aggravate on account of rising population, rapid urbanisation and increasing pollution of water.

According to a recent publication of the World Bank, "an estimated three million people in developing countries die every year from water-related diseases.... The majority of fatalities are children under the age of five. Water-related diseases impose an especially large health burden in the Africa, Asia and Pacific regions. In India alone, nearly one million people die annually as a result of water-related diseases".[5] The problem is also serious in countries in East Asia and the Pacific. According to the same source, "More than 500,000 infants die each year as a result of waterborne diseases linked to polluted water. About 60 per cent of these deaths are attributable to deficient rural water supplies, while another 30 per cent are caused by the lack of sanitation in urban area. These impacts are equivalent to shortening the average life expectancy of everyone in the region by nearly two year".[6] According to one estimate, about 30.5 million Disability Adjusted Life Years (DALYs) are lost each year in India due to poor water quality, sanitation and hygiene. This is worth Rs. 366 billion. Women are special casualties.[7]

Vicious Circle of Water and Poverty

Inadequacy of safe drinking water and poverty form a vicious circle. Lack of access to safe drinking water is caused by poverty as well as lack of awareness which goes along with it. Poverty induces compromise on water quality which gets further compounded by the overall unhygienic conditions afflicting the habitat of the poor. At the same time, lack of access to safe drinking water has an accentuating effect on poverty. Contaminated or poor quality water consumed by the weaker sections results in diseases which force them to stay off work and lose their earnings apart from spending a part of their meagre earnings on medical treatment. This often leads to a further drain on their meagre resources resulting in indebteness and perpetuation of poverty. Access to safe drinking water would be a great boon, which will help in breaking the vicious circle of water and poverty, by striking at the root cause of the problem.

Role of Pricing and Institutional Factors

The subsidy burden of the policy of providing free supply of drinking water has not permitted the authorities to fulfil their responsibility of providing access to good quality water to the poor. This policy should continue only if the authorities are prepared to increase the subsidy amount to fill in the gaps in availability of good quality water to the poor. But will this have long-term sustainability? The other option is to put a price tag on supply of water for drinking and domestic use and increase its accessibility to the poor. It may be noted that the poor usually pay a price for water even when water is provided free. This is in terms of opportunity cost of fetching water.

Time spent on fetching water reduces the time available for income generating activities as well as household and child bearing responsibilities. In some places, drudgery apart, it may take several hours to fetch a few pots of water. Viewed in this context, the seemingly free supply of water to the poor is a misnomer for those for whom the opportunity cost of fetching water is quite high. Providing good quality water to the poor and charging for it is better than providing them seemingly free but poor quality water. Wherever administratively feasible, such a price could be a graduated one to induce avoiding wastage of water by the more affluent.

Further improvement can take place through institutional adjustments. Private sector participation in urban areas can be considered if pricing regime is made appropriate. In rural areas, the responsibility for providing water at the household level including maintenance of wells or other decentralised structures could be given to community based organisations. This would take care of the perennial problem of inadequate maintenance resulting in persistence of drinking water problem despite governmental efforts. At the same time, vigorous awareness generation campaigns be launched to educate the poor about the advantages of good quality water specially in terms of enormous saving of expenditure on fighting diseases. Formulation of schemes of improved water management must always ask the question as to how would these benefit the poorer sections of the society.

WATER AND FOOD SECURITY

Food Production

The calorie-based definition of poverty puts a focus on food security which is yet to be achieved in large parts of the developing world. Statistics are well known and easily available in publications of both national and international agencies. The continuing increase in population has the effect of increasing the food requirement still further.

Water is an essential input for crops. Its role in food production in South Asia has increased substantially in recent years after the introduction of the HYV technology since the mid-60s of the last century. Bulk of additional production of foodgrains and specially of marketable surplus in South Asia has come mainly from irrigated areas. There has, however, been some controversy with respect to the extent of increase in agricultural production due to irrigation because of the complementary role of seeds, fertilisers, credit, pricing and other factors. There is no time to go into this controversy. Suffice it to say that a 'with' and 'without' methodology often used for estimating the contribution of irrigation to food production shows that yields per hectare have increased substantially due to irrigation.[8] In addition, there are gains due to increasing area under cultivation, rising cropping intensity and improvements in cropping pattern, which are made possible owing to irrigation. Irrigation is also a catalyst for use of other inputs. Development and better management of water resources are, therefore, needed for attaining the objective of food security.

Distribution, Prices, Income and Access

In the context of food security, the issue is not only of production of foodgrains but also of their availability at the household level. Availability is with respect to prices and therefore to the purchasing power of households. As has been highlighted frequently by Nobel Laureate, Amartya Sen, the infamous 1943 Bengal famine was caused not so much by inadequacy of foodgrains which were available in plenty in traders' godowns, but due to lack of purchasing power of the poor *vis-a-vis* food prices which had shot up largely for speculative reasons.

One key element, therefore, is to ensure availability of foodgrains at lower prices, especially since foodgrains constitute a major portion of budget of the poor and the demand for foodgrains is known to be inelastic. Cost of foodgrains can be kept lower by raising agricultural productivity. Water management plays a critical role in this. The second key element is to raise the income and purchasing power of the poor so that they can afford to purchase the quantity of food considered necessary for them. Water, being a necessary input for agriculture and several other activities which provide livelihood to the poor, has a critical role in this. A third element is to raise the food output of millions of small and marginal farmers as well as tenants and share croppers whose production is mainly for self-consumption.[9] Their food security is linked to their own productivity in which water availability has a critical role to play. The key role of water in food security is thus quite obvious from whichever angle we examine this problem.

Food, Water and Environment

Provision of water for food security has been the dominant concern so far. A greater proportion of water, about 70 per cent is used for irrigation; this goes up to 90 per cent in many developing countries. It is also estimated that need for irrigation would increase further by 15 to 20 per cent in the coming 25 years to meet food demand of a growing population.

On the other hand, a view has been emerging that the share of water going to irrigation should decrease rather than increase because the world's ecological systems are already under pressure on account of increasing water diversion for human activities. Wetlands are being threatened. Some of the world's great rivers, the Nile, Colorado, Indus, Amu Darya and Yellow discharge very little water into their final destinations. Underground water tables are also declining. Fresh water aquatic species are in peril. The picture, of course, varies from country-to-country and from one river basin to another. In Nepal, most water remains in nature. In south India, the picture is completely different. There is, however, a global trend towards increasing diversion and overuse of water. Hence, the need to allow water that nature itself requires to maintain its self-purifying power and protect aquatic eco-systems for future generations to flow through these rivers and groundwater basins.

The conflict between the two objectives was highlighted during the Second World Water Forum, which took place in March, 2000 at the Hague (Netherlands). Resolution of the conflict, however, raises complex issues which are examined below.

Less water for irrigation might undermine the food security unless there are significant improvements in irrigation efficiency as highlighted by Kofi Annan's famous word of "more crops per drop". But as pointed out by International Water

Management Institute (IWMI) in its Podium model, meeting food requirements while decreasing allocations to irrigation by 10 per cent would require and increase in productivity of water by 60 per cent on irrigated lands and by 30 per cent on rainfed lands for the period 2000 to 2025. Several methods and approaches suggested in this respect have been summarised by IWMI and are given in Table 1.[10]

Table 1: Means for Saving Water and Increasing the Productivity of Water

1. Increasing the productivity per unit of water consumed	• Change to crop varieties that provide increased yields for each unit of water consumed, or the same yields with fewer units of water consumed.
	• Switch from high-to less-water-consuming crops, or to crops with higher economic or physical productivity per unit of water consumed. • Use deficit, supplemental, precision irrigation or other irrigation strategies that increase the returns per unit of water consumed. • Improve water management to reduce stress at critical crop-growth stages for increased yields or increase water supply reliability so that farmers invest more in other agricultural inputs leadings to higher output per unit of water. • Optimise non-water inputs such as land preparation and fertilisation to increase the return per unit of water.
2. Reducing non-beneficial depletion	• Reduce evaporation from irrigated fields (drip irrigation, use of mulching, changing planting dates, etc.) surface runoff. • Reduce flows through saline soils or saline groundwater. • Shunt polluted water directly to sinks to avoid the need to dilute with freshwater. • Reuse return flows.
3. Reallocating water among uses	• Reallocate water from lower-to higher-value uses. Can have serious legal, equity and other social considerations that must be addressed.
4. Tapping uncommitted outflows	• Improve management of existing facilities. A number of policy, design, management and institutional interventions like water pricing, improved distribution practices may allow for an expansion of irrigated area, increased cropping intensity or increased yields within the service areas. ▪ Reuse return flows through gravity and pump diversion to increase irrigated area. ▪ Add storage facilities of different forms like reservoirs small tanks, groundwater aquifers, etc., to allow release of more water during drier periods.

Source: IWMI.

The suggestions in Table 1 have remained largely on paper in developing countries. Their effective implementation would require enormous changes in business as usual scenarios with respect to policies, institutions and technologies which, in turn, would require a strong political will of a type not usually found in such countries. It is also doubtful whether the micro-level administrative units would be willing to be deprived of the existing quantities of water since the areas to be benefited would be the downstream river regime in which they have little interest. Economic instruments can be helpful, but these remain neglected in the developing would.

Another option is to rely on food imports from water abundant areas. Such a strategy, however, would induce loss of employment or livelihood opportunities for the rural poor due to reduced scope for irrigated agriculture. Food security and livelihood security are two sides of the same coin for the majority of the farming community in South Asia consisting of small and marginal farmers and landless labourers. This suggestion, therefore, has ominous implications; instead of alleviating poverty it may in fact perpetuate or even accentuate it. Besides, too much dependence on food imports exposes consumers to risks of an embargo on exports due to political considerations.

There are two more options, *first,* is to increase the quantity of recycled water through well-known technologies. These are, however, very costly and often beyond the financial resources as well as viability of poor areas. *Secondly,* a review of the emerging water intensive life-style whose spread is a major factor in increasing the per capita requirement of water for domestic uses. It is always easier to moderate additional increases than to make reduction in existing levels of uses. There could be other options. Human ingenuity in its best form is now needed for this purpose. One can only hope that the coming decades might do so.

Water, Livelihood and Poverty Alleviation

Poverty alleviation would need a multi-pronged approach. The key element is the provision of remunerative employment to the poor. The focus is on employment because most of the poor, having little or no assets, have limited access to sources of income which come from command over productive assets. Even those with some productive assets like small and marginal farmers in South Asia are forced to supplement their farm income by working as labourers on large farms. Employment also includes self-employment of small and marginal farmers working for cultivation of their own land and of tenants and share croppers on leased-in land.

Direct Effects

It is with respect to generation of employment, both wage as well self-employment, that water has a major role to play. Water management is crucial to growth of agriculture which is the main source of livelihood opportunity in rural areas where the bulk of the poor in the developing world reside.[11] Agriculture in poorer areas is also an activity which is highly labour-intensive despite limited mechanisation introduced during the last three decades. What is more, agriculture provides employment to the poorest of the poor. Irrigation leads to the expansion of area under cultivation, rise in cropping intensity and increases in per hectare yield. Each result increase the demand for labour. This leads to an expansion of employment as well as rise in real wage rates, both of which prove beneficial to the poor.

Many of the agricultural operations like sowing, weeding, inter-culturing and harvesting are female intensive activities in India and other developing countries. As a result, the real wage rates for female labour have, in general, been rising relative to male labour in the green revolution belt of Punjab-Haryana as documented in a 1991 World Bank Country Study *Gender and Poverty in India.*[12] As a result, the male-female disparity in wage rate in India has been coming down in the decades of 70s and 80s of the last century (Table 2).

Table 2: Trends in Real Agricultural Wages in India (BASE Year: 1970-71)

State	*Index of Real Wage: Male*			*Index of Real Wage: Female*			*Ratio of Female to Male Increase (Col.(2) to Col. (1)*
	1970-1 1971-2	*1987-8 1998-9**	*Per cent Increase (Col. 1)*	*1970-1 1971-2*	*1987-8 1998-9**	*Per cent Increase (Col. 2)*	
High-Wage Areas							
Punjab	99.2	108.2	9.1	112.7	129.2	14.6	1.6
Haryana	98.7	98.1	0.7	99.8	118.9	19.1	27.2
Himachal Pradesh	105.3	119.8	13.8	98.8	119.7	21.0	1.5
Kerala	105.6	161.7	53.6	113.1	168.9	49.3	0.9
Low-Wage Areas							
Andhra Pradesh	97.6	155.4	59.2	97.1	152.9	57.5	0.9
Bihar	98.5	150.0	55.2	97.7	170.2	74.3	1.3
Orissa	99.8	141.7	42.0	99.4	159.0	60.0	1.4
Madhya Pradesh	99.7	158.4	59.0	98.8	175.6	73.7	1.2

Source: A.V. Jose, "Agricultural Wages in India". Reproduced from Government of India, *Report of the National Commission on Rural Labour,* Vol. 1, 1991, p. 74.

*Two-year average in indices.

Performance of irrigation depends on several factors. Income from agriculture for the poor can be raised by changing the cropping pattern in favour of more renumeratives crops like vegetables and flowers wherever markets are available, by better management, by more efficient post-harvest operations, etc. Provision of irrigation along with other complementary inputs and services, raises productivity and, therefore, has a much greater potential for poverty alleviation.

It may, however, be contended that benefits of irrigation go more to the affluent in rural areas like big farmers and less to the disadvantaged like marginal farmers and landless labourers. Irrigation, therefore, increases rather than decreases the inequality of income in rural societies. Statistics are available to support this contention. But there is no denying—the fact that the lot of rural poor does improve because of increases in both employment opportunities as well as real wage rates. Hence, poverty, defined in the sense of absolute poverty, declines even though relative poverty might increase. Empirical evidence supports this contention. In the case of India, areas having prosperous agriculture, *e.g.*, states of Punjab, Haryana, western Uttar Pradesh irrigated areas of Rajasthan, Andhra Pradesh and Tamil Nadu have a low percentage of the poor while areas having depressed agriculture like states of Bihar and Orissa have a high concentration.

It follows from the above that any emphasis on poverty alleviation as an objective would require that future investment in irrigation as well as other elements of water management like reduction of drainage congestion and moderation of flood be targetted specially at poor areas and poor people. This would imply a departure from the past when most of such investment went to better off areas for reasons stated at the outset in this article.

Migration Effects

The beneficial effect of agricultural development on raising the income of the poor is also felt through inter-regional migration. The expansion of employment and rise in real wages attract labour from distant and poorer areas. In case of India, the proportion of migration-prone labour has been quite high in certain areas, *e.g.*, Bihar, Orissa and Rajasthan. As a result of the rise in staying power and supply price of labour, the real wages started rising at a fast rate in such areas between the early 70s and late 80s of the last century.[13] Consequently, the benefit from agricultural development in green-belt areas was derived by the poor in distant areas as can be seen from data in Table 2. It may, however, be noted that the rise in wage rates would take place only in situations where the rate of agricultural growth is higher than the growth of labour force and mechanisation rates, as has been the case in the green-revolution belt of India.

Small Farmers Development Approach

In addition to the landless labourers who have no productive assets, the poor also comprise those having limited productive assets like small and marginal farmers as well as tenets and share croppers. Access to water would enable these people to raise their agricultural productivity and thereby gain additional income. This access can be facilitated by a mix of appropriate technologies and institutions. Empirical studies have demonstrated the superiority of ground water in targeting the poor through micro-diesel pumps, emergence of markets, formation of small farmers association for tube wells, etc. "In recent years, there has been an upsurge in adoption of technologies such as treadle pumps, low-cost bucket and drop lines, small portable pump sets, supplemental irrigation, sustainable land management practices in rainfed areas, recharge and use of groundwater and water-harvesting systems. This wide range of technologies, collectively referred to as smallholder water and land management systems, enables producers to access hitherto unusable water supplies and to compensate for poor levels of services in large-scale irrigation systems".[14] Hence policies to raise productivity of poor farmers must receive high priority specially as these farmers are vulnerable to adverse impacts of water scarcity.

Many examples can be found of small and marginal farmers gaining access to water and raising their income through forming cooperatives or associations to pool adequate resources for investment in tubewells. Well known example in India include Vaishali Area Small Farmers' Association, Vaishali (Bihar), Indo-Norwegian Development Project, Deoria (UP), Indo-UK Agricultural Development Project, Gorakhpur (UP), Sarvangeen Vikas Yojana, Varanasi (UP) and the Green Farm, Kundrakudi (Tamil Nadu)[15], The Ministry of Agriculture in India also has a programme for providing subsidy-cum-credit to small farmers forming small associations to install and operate tubewells on joint-basis.

Full benefit of irrigation can, however, be derived only if measures for providing other inputs and services like better seeds, fertilisers, credit, extension, etc., are taken at the same time. Income of small and marginal farmers would increase substantially if their cropping pattern changes in favour of high value crops. In other words, there is a need for formulating a poverty–oriented farming strategy with irrigation as a key input.

Participatory Approach

Participatory irrigation management has been another development helping the small and marginal farmers. Apart from enhancing the long-term productivity of water resources, there are examples showing preferential treatment to small and marginal farmers or to the tail-end farmers. According to author's all India study, water scheduling rules framed by water users' association often (though not always) take into account the interests of the hitherto neglected sections. Thus, in Parunde and Palkhed projects in Maharashtra, it has been laid down that water would be provided first to tail–enders, then to farmers in the middle reach and lastly to those in the head reach. Better scheduling of water has led to higher agricultural productivity. At the same time, better financial management of the system has led to better maintenance resulting in a better supply of water for the crops. But the experience has been a mixed one.[16] Hence, the programme of participatory irrigation management requires modification if it is to serve as an instrument of poverty alleviation. Some mechanism of priority and assured allocation of water to the poor would be needed.

These innovations, both technological as well as institutional, deserve to be encouraged. A word of caution, however, is needed. Given the size and diversity of a country like India, it is not safe to prescribe uniform solutions for the whole country. Hence, in the case of water management, a location–specific approach is suggested. What is good for one area may not be good for another. Further, what is good for an area is known best to people of that area. Hence, decentralisation of decision-making in the real sense of the term is an important institutional reform that is needed.

Non-farm Employment

Agricultural growth also affects the poor through secondary effects. Rising incomes in agriculture lead to a rising demand for non-agricultural goods and services which in turn increase the demand for labour engaged in producing them. A similar effect takes place through the requirement for additional supply of inputs like fertiliser and persticides as well as through marketing of increased output and expansion of agro-processing units. The low cost food made possible due to irrigated agriculture has the effect of enhancing urban and industrial livelihood which benefit the poor.

Apart from agriculture, the poor, and specially the women among them in both rural and urban areas are also engaged in a variety of activities in home-based enterprises where it is difficult to distinguish between water for domestic purpose and water for such enterprises. According to one estimate, about 30 per cent of poor women in India are home-based workers.[17] Almost 47,000 of SEWA's 2, 11, 124 members are home-based workers.[18] A large number of home-based enterprises make use of water. These include not only processing and sale of food items and related activities but also for other industries like rearing of cattle and softening the leaves used for rolling hand made India cigarettes known as *bidies*, etc. Easy access to water helps the poor to raise the economic viability of their enterprises. For example, "In the desert areas of Banaskantha in Gujarat, where SEWA works, many milk cooperatives were defunct. With the help of sustained supply of water through the regional water supply scheme, many of these milk cooperatives have been successfully revived".[19]

A poverty alleviation-oriented strategy requires that water needs of labour intensive home-based or tiny enterprises in water scarce rural as well as urban area are met on a priority basis. This is all the more necessary since agriculture alone would not be able to provide livelihood opportunities to all the poor in rural as well as urban areas.

General Effects

Finally, water management has a general effect on livelihood opportunities which goes beyond specific activities like agriculture or industry. Easy access to water saves time involved in fetching it and carrying out other domestic chores. This saving in the time can be used for income earning opportunities thereby assisting alleviation of poverty. "In the savings association of Kheda district, which has 1,000 members, access to water and rising income seems to be related. This pattern is also observed among the 1,000 members of Gandhinagar district savings association promoted by SEWA and supported by SEWA Bank.[20]

Raising productivity in poverty concentration areas requires strengthening of the infrastructural base. Power is one of the most important components of infrastructure. Yet power is grossly inadequate in most of the areas having a concentration of the poor in India like in north Bihar, east Uttar Pradesh, Orissa, Assam, etc. Water resource projects have a potential in this respect since they produce hydro-electric power which is less costly, environmentally more friendly as well as renewable source of power. Construction of irrigation and/or hydro—electricity projects also results in improvements in roads and other infrastructural facilities which benefit the poor in several ways.

ADVERSE EFFECTS

Water resource projects are generally presumed to have a benign effect on the poor.

But sometimes these cause or accentuate poverty if adequate care in not taken as has happened in the past. (1) Excessive exploitation of groundwater by rich farmers or water sellers may result in drying up of dug wells or shallow tubewells of small and marginal farmers, thereby adversely affecting their income and employment. (2) It is a frequent complaint in many mismanaged canal irrigation systems that tail-enders do not get water when they need it and get it when they do not need it. (3) Poor farmers are usually at a disadvantage in getting canal water, since they have neither money nor influence to prevent richer farmers cornering a larger share of water when it becomes scarce. (4) Embankments to control flood on one bank of a river might increase incidence of flooding on the other bank or down stream. (5) Embankments create problems of drainage congestion or the landslide as can be seen in the case of Kosi embankment in Bihar. As a result, cultivable land belonging to farmers becomes useless. (6) The reduction in soil moisture and stoppage of fertilising value of silt due to an embankment has the effect of reducing agricultural productivity whose incidence is specially felt by the poorer farmers since the better ones can afford to invest on irrigation and fertiliser. (7) The worst impact is the displacement of poor farmers and landless labourers due to construction of large dams. Thousands who get uprooted and dispossessed of their habitats and permanent sources of income, become poorer than before. This is an example of development-induced poverty. It is true that compensation is paid, but as is well-known, its amount has been far from adequate. This calls for serious rethinking with respect to the entire methodology and approach of planning and implementing a major water resource project. There is no room for business-as-usual scenario if poverty alleviation is the objective.

Apart from the general scarcity of water, the poor are also adversely affected by society's inability to deal appropriately with water related natural disasters like flood and drought which affect developing countries at frequent intervals. Most of the poverty concentration areas in India are suffering from flood and drought. It may be said that floods are physical phenomena which might not distinguish between the rich and the poor. But the habitat pattern is such that it is the poor who are affected more because it is they who generally inhabit the low lying areas which suffer the most. Moreover, the poor also suffer because their houses are made of mud which tend to collapse when floods hit them whereas the dwelling units of the rich are made of bricks, stone and mortar which have better chances of withstanding the flood fury. As a result of flood, fertilisers get washed away from the agricultural fields. Hence, farmers in flood-prone areas have little incentive to use fertiliser which is an essential input for higher agricultural productivity. Flood-prone areas, therefore, continue to have low agricultural productivity for the crops grown during flood seasons. Floods have an adverse effect on quality of drinking water resulting in frequent outbreak of diseases. Further, frequent occurrence of flood, as in eastern parts of India, leads to damage to roads which become full of potholes and broken patches to such an extent that they hardly fulfil the purpose for which they are constructed. Power lines are similarly affected. Frequent repairs of these roads and power lines result in diversion of resources which could have been spent on poverty alleviation measures.

Floods as well as droughts affect the poor further because they have little stocks of foodgrains and other items to fall back upon. Floods as well as droughts result in loss of daily income of the poor, who are often daily wage earners, for the days for which economic activities remain dormant due to flood or drought. The plight of the poor is further compounded by inadequacy or absence of social safety nets that would protect their income and consumption during water related disasters like flood and drought. There is no flood or drought insurance. And the quantum of flood or drought relief provided by government has been found to be quite meagre.[21] Hence, water management designed to moderate the incidence of both flood and drought would have a favourable effect on the poor.

Sometimes, the quality of water may turn out to be harmful. "In South Asia, there are important regions where ground water cannot be utilised for drinking because of its chemical composition. The most dramatic example is from Bangladesh and West Bengal, India, where thousands of recently constructed drinking water wells are producing water with very high arsenic levels. In other words, fluoride and salt levels of ground water are too high to make it suitable for drinking." [22]

CONCLUSION

While water has an unique role in providing food and water security, it shares this role with several other sectors in providing income and livelihood security. Yet, it is the income generating power of water which is most important for poverty alleviation since it helps in the attainment of both water and food security and enables them to be self-sustaining over a long period without any resort to subsidy.

A breakthrough in productivity and income in poverty concentrated areas can take place by creating water harvesting structures through exploiting both rain water as well as river water. Water reservoirs of all types and sizes, watershed management, recharging underground water storage, etc., should be taken up with renewed vigour but without losing sight of the environmental and human aspects. Technologies and institutions appropriate to small farmers may receive special encouragement. Development of power would be needed for exploiting the groundwater potential and operation of grain storage facilities especially the refrigerated ones. Flood moderation measures specially big dams supplemented by non-structural measures like flood resistant and flood escaping cropping pattern would be needed for boosting agricultural production in areas suffering from flood. Drainage schemes would be needed to take care of low agricultural productivity in areas suffering from drainage congestion. At the same time, output from permanent water bodies like tanks and ponds with respect to fishery and other aqvaculture products like *makhana* and *singhara* in India should be raised by appropriate methods including regular desilting and deepening. These measures taken along with those for strengthening institutions of marketing, credit and grain storage would bolster agricultural production in poorer areas. These measures should be taken in an integrated and holistic rather than piecemeal manner and on a wide scale to produce visible impacts in future. The scale of efforts is as important as the components. At the same time, the known adverse effects of water resource projects may be avoided by appropriate policy measures.

Strengthening the role of water in poverty alleviation would require a sharper focus on water for the poor which would include according priority to water needs of small producers in both rural and urban areas along with other complementary inputs. An appropriate pricing strategy to ensure long—term susceptibility would be an integral part of the strategy. A variable mix of technological and institutional interventions of the type mentioned above should be considered for adoption depending upon location-specific situations.

NOTES

1. Keynote address at the First South Asia Water Forum, organised by Global Water Partnership-South Asia Technical Advisory Committee held at Kathmandu, Nepal, February 26, 2002.
2. Kamta Prasad, *Planning for Poverty Alleviation,* (Chapter 1), New Delhi, Agricole Publishing Academy, 1985.
3. Aasha Kapur Mehta and Nikhila Menon, "Drinking Water", in *Alternative Economic Survey* 2000-01, New Delhi. This article provides latest macro-level data on the subject.
4. Reema Nanavoty, "Women, Water and Work: Sewa's Millennium Campaign", paper presented at *2nd World Water Forum,* March 2000, Ahmedabad, Self Employed Women's Asociation (SEWA), p. 7.
5. The World Bank, *Environment Matters at the World Bank,* Washington, World Bank, 2001, p. 15.
6. *Ibid.,* p. 28.
7. Aasha Kapur Mehta and Nikhila Menon; *op cit.,* p. 9.
8. There are several studies analysing the impact of irrigation on agricultural productivity in India. These show that the impact varies from area-to-area and from crop-to-crop. According to a comprehensive study by B.D. Dhawan, *Irrigation in India's Agricultural Development* New Delhi, Sage, 1988 based on 1983-84 data for 17 states, per hectare agricultural output increase from 8.8 quintals in rainfall areas to 22.1 quintals in irrigated areas which indicated an increase of 152 per cent due to irrigation.
9. Small farmers in the Indian context are those who own one to two hectare (2.5 to 5 acre) of land while marginal farmers are those who own zero to one hectare (0 to 2.5 acre) of land.
10. David Molden, Upali Amarsinghe and Imtizar Hussain, *Water for Rural Development,* Working Paper 32, Colombo, International Water Management Institute, 2001, p. 7.
11. This is because (*i*) majority of the population resides in rural areas, and (*ii*) per capita income levels in rural areas are lower than those in urban areas.
12. C.H.H. Rao, *Agricultural Growth, Rural Poverty and Environmental Degradation in India,* Delhi, Oxford Unversity Press, 1994, p. 60.
13. C.H.H. Rao, *op cit.,* p. 55-56.
14. David Molden, *et al., op cit.,* p. 9.
15. Details of the evaluation of these are available in Kamta Prasad, *Economic Viability and Organisational Requirements of Lift Irrigation Technologies for Small and Marginal Farmers in India,* New Delhi, Indian Institute of Public Administration, 1990.

16. Kamta Prasad, *Farmers Participation in Irrigation Management in India: Status Impact and Determinants,* New Delhi, Uppal, 2001.
17. Government of India, *Report of National Commission on Self Employed Women and Women in the Informal Sector,* Delhi, 1987 as quoted in Reema Nanavoty, *op cit.,* p. 4.
18. Reema Nanavoty, *op cit.,* p. 3.
19. *Ibid.,* p. 5.
20. Reema Nanavoty, *op cit.,* p. 6.
21. Kamta Prasad and B.D. Singh, *Drought Disaster and Development,* New Delhi, Mittal Publication, 1994.
22. David Molden, *et al., op cit.,* p. 13.

20

Administering Water in India in 2050 AD*

Rakesh Hooja

INTRODUCTION

Importance of Water in Future

It is clear that increased populations would lead to increased food and fibre needs as well as increased pressure on, and competition for, water for varying uses and for varying regions. Assessments made in Indian Water Resources Society (IWRS)[1] reports indicate that by 2025 AD total annual fresh water requirement of India would be 1050 billion cu. m. This would be almost at par with our currently estimated exploitable water resources of 1122 billion cu. m. By then the average national per capita water availability would have shrunk from today's 2200 cu. m. to 1500 cu. m. Most of the sources (surface and ground water) of water would already have been developed and issues of inter-basin transfers of water (if at all possible as per the efforts of he National Commission for Integrated Water Resources Development Plan) settled by 2050 AD. However, much of the water-related infrastructure developed during 20th Century would require major renovation and modernisation or significant maintenance and repair. Conservation, recycling and optimal use of water, (as also assuring water quality and checking water-borne diseases and problems of water pollution would be major issues requiring technical, administrative and social solutions. (Thus, for example, 'Command Area Management'—which would encompass a balance between development and management—would have become much more important than today). With increasing competition for water for different needs and different regions and lower per capita availability, the nature of water as public (or social) good would have assumed greater importance than its characteristic as all economic good.

---

* This article has evolved out of inputs that the author in his capacity of Executive Member of Indian Water Resources Society (IWRS) was asked to provide for "The IWRS Theme Paper on Water: Vision 2050" being prepared for Water Resources Day in March 1999. Earlier versions of the article have been circulated to some individuals and institutions.

People's Participation

Hence, community (or participatory) management and public or governmental management would be more relevant rather than leaving things to the market. But individual users of water in the domestic and drinking water, health and sanitation, irrigation and agriculture, industry and commerce, energy, transportation, leisure and recreation etc. sectors would continue to have a major impact on how water resources are utilised, as also the individual scientists working on technologies for water availability to be enhanced or for water to be used more efficiently.

MANAGEMENT OF WATER RESOURCE—FUTURE NEEDS

Water Planning and Coordination Mechanism

The legal, political and institutional arrangements required for managing the water resources would have to reflect the above-mentioned concerns. As disputes and conflicts over water increase—even the Ministries of Home and Defence may have to concern themselves more with water-related issues since water riots or conflicts over water may increase. Perhaps the Inter State Council will have to set up a committee on inter-regional water issues. Alternatively, the National Water Resources Council, which has met thrice between 1983 and 1998, may have to be made more active as would the National Water Board. Region based international forums like say a South Asian Regional Cooperation on Water may also have become very vital to sort out cross-border water issues. Clearly, much greater inter-sectoral coordination then is being achieved at present would be required. On the other hand, since water affects all aspects of human life, it would not be possible to integrate all water use related aspects into a single Ministry, either at the Centre or in the States. The present Standing Committee for Assessment of Water for diverse uses in the country may not be able to meet all the requirements. Hence, a permanent Water Planning and Coordination Mechanism (WPCM) would need to be set up both at the Centre and in the States. This would require: (*a*) an inter-ministerial group, (*b*) an advisory support group or sub-group consisting of experts, (*c*) a small permanent secretariat of interdisciplinary specialists and generalist planners, and (*d*) a standing tribunal also comprising interdisciplinary experts, and generalist planners and administrators to which disputes between various alternative uses of water and between various regions for water use, or regarding issues of environment and soil water quality versus developmental and service provision needs of water could be referred. The WPCM should be a part of the Ministry of Water Resources at the Government of India level, which naturally would continue to be government's nodal point for all issues related to water use. Perhaps the mandate and the name of the National Water Resource Development Agency could be changed and it could also be made a part of the WPCM. At the State Government level, such a mechanism would be attached to the State Irrigation Department with a strong link with the Command Area Development (CAD) and Water Utilisation Department (in those states where the CAD Department is separate from Irrigation Department).

Interaction between Government and Agencies Representing Different Water Sectors and Water Users Associations

River Basin Development Agencies, Command Area Development and Management Agencies for irrigated areas, and Watershed Management Agencies for rainfed areas (with an administrative structure which improves upon the present integrated CAD project organisations in CAD-IGNP and CAD Chambal in Rajasthan) would need to be set up to interact with the Central and State Governments on the one hand and with water-users groups, cutting across all sectors, on the other. Such water-users groups could be area based [canal minor or branch Water Users Association (WUAs), catchment committees, Chak committees, irrigation project level federation of WUA's watershed committees, etc. or function based (industrywise users groups or committees of residents in towns and villages). Some such user groups would have come together into federations working for better resource management, while others would be existing only at the grassroot level.

Comprehensive National Water Data Bank

A national data bank on water having links with Central, state and local level governments as also with river basin, Command Area Development, and watershed agencies and WUA's would need to be fully functional long before 2050 AD.

Transforming Water Management into Joint Endeavour

The State Government Irrigation Departments would need to reorient themselves to meet the changed, and changing needs of water utilisation, and water management would have to be seen as a joint endeavour or joint partnership of the government and the water users. Such joint partnerships would hopefully involve greater user organisation/institution role in terms of representation, operation and management responsibility and ownership of water and water storage, distribution and utilisation structures,[2] while the governmental irrigation agency would be more involved in regulation and shared management providing an enabling environment for the user groups to manage the water themselves. In addition to the interfacing mechanisms necessary for such partnership to be successful, the department would need to set up sector-by-sector coordination committees with various other user departments in government. The major interaction would still perhaps require to be between the States Irrigation, Agriculture and Ground Water Departments as well as the CAD and Water Utilisation Department and the district administration in view of the food and fibre needs which would have to be got met through canal and well irrigated, and rainfed farming, as well as with the Public Health Engineering Department, since drinking water and domestic water needs would have increased drastically as even today many irrigation water sources are being diverted from irrigation to drinking and domestic water use. Inter departmental inter-sectoral disputes and those between user groups and government agencies would need to be settled expeditiously, fairly and transparently and devices to ensure this would have to be evolved over the years making use of available social capital to ensure efficient water management and utilisation. Many traditional, but unrecorded uses of irrigation canal waters by housewives, livestock breeders and the local landless may also have to be considered, when water is diverted for more profitable or vital purposes.

Constitution of Support Groups of Inter-disciplinary Experts in Diverse Fields

The State Irrigation Department would perhaps need to constitute Advisory Support Groups of inter-disciplinary experts and generalist planners in fields like: (*a*) alternative and multiple water uses, including water allocation; (*b*) participatory irrigation management; (*c*) waterlogging, salinity and flood control; and (*d*) Command Area Management and Development (encompassing integrated land-water management, the linking of management of surface and sub-surface water resources, and consideration of both water quality and quantity in planning), (*e*) water conservation and recycling of water, (*f*) water and preservation of social and physical environment, (*g*) extension and technology dissemination regarding water use in irrigation and other sectors (with special reference to improved on-field water application techniques), (*h*) renovation and re-development (including technological upgradation or modernisation) of existing water resource projects, etc. Such Advisory Support Groups would also need to be got created in Ministry of Water Resources, Government of India and in Central Water Commission.

Newer Roles for Irrigation Departments

While the specific form and role that irrigation departments would have to play 50 years hence cannot be predicted since the pace of societal change has become such that it is difficult to predict about specific half-a-century hence—however Svendsen, Trava and Johnsons's views about new roles that irrigation agencies would need to play may prove a useful guide.[3] They emphasise river-basin planning, water resource allocation and monitoring, development of new policies and regulations, environment monitoring and enforcement, ground water monitoring and control, project design and construction technology transfer to user associations, advisory services to user associations, monitoring performance of user associations, and arbitrating disputes. As regards encouraging Participatory Irrigation Management and WUAs in addition to providing advisory services and technology transfer to WUAs, government would have to create the enabling environment through policy resolutions, legal and administrative framework, intellectual, academic and administrative leadership, mass awareness and promotional efforts, financial and technical incentives, training and orientation, etc.[4]

Objectives of CAD

I also suspect that the objectives of CAD agencies as envisioned by me would in some form or the other continue to be valid even in 2050 AD. These objectives (slightly modified from those which I visualised in 1995)[5] are: (*i*) full utilisation of irrigation potential, (*ii*) increased productivity per unit of water and per unit of land, (*iii*) provision of predictable water supply to user, (*iv*) efficient use of water with equitable distribution at minimum administrative cost, (*v*) evolving appropriate cropping patterns to suit agro-economic conditions, available technologies and physical and social infrastructure, (*vi*) conservation of soil and water resources, (*vii*) planned and regulated development of command area and its inhabitants in harmony with land, water and agro-climatic conditions, (*viii*) attainment of cost effectiveness and productive returns on investments for the users, (*ix*) protection of the developed command area to avoid environmental damage and loss of valuable command land due to waterlogging, salinity, erosion, gully formation, pest infestation, canal siltation, etc. and integrating drainage into a multidisciplinary and integrated water management strategy of preventive and curative measures to check waterlogging and salinity, (*x*) providing organisational means and incentives for effective and constructive user participation in management, including operation and maintenance, (*xi*) balancing industrial (including energy generation), domestic, livestock, drinking water and irrigation demands for water, (*xii*) providing basic infrastructure, improved amenities, and services, and increased employment opportunities within the command area, (*xiii*) integrated land and water management and surface and sub-surface water management, through adoption of a holistic project approach for each irrigation and command area project, and (*xiv*) creating a coordinated and well-integrated government delivery system for the command area with appropriate emphasis on both development and management.

While details may change, many of the abovementioned concerns should remain valid even 50 years hence. Some examples of the type of changes may be that just as today water needs to be specially provided for irrigation, with increased pressure on water even the quantities and types (quality based) of water to be made available for silvi-pastoral efforts on marginal lands for livestock husbandry may have become as important a concern of irrigation departments as providing of water for crop husbandry and for drinking purposes to the farmers who live on their fields. In addition to technically ensuring that water can physically become available to all individual user, accessibility of water to individuals in terms of social, economic and legal entitlements would also become much more important as time passes and pressure of water increases. Thus, as Hufschmidt[6] has suggested, the policy overlaps between the water resources domain and those related to agriculture, health, human settlements, forestry, energy, transport and environment would continue to grow within the context of changing land-water eco-system-human activity system interactions.

Required Skills of Professionals

Hence, the water professional or irrigation engineer/officer of 2050 AD would need to possess inter-disciplinary knowledge and skills as follows:

1. Technical Skills in Irrigation Engineering (including Civil Engineering and

Water Resources Engineering) Hydrology, Agronomy, Horticulture, Agriculture Engineering, Hydrogeology and Ground Water Management, On-Farm Water Application Techniques and Integrated Water Management, Drainage, On-Farm Development Environmental Protection, Land Use Geography, Soil Science, Natural Resource Management, Data Management, Action Research in Agriculture, Action Research in Irrigation, Land Water Surveys and GIS based Surveys, and Integrated Land-Water Planning.

2. Social Organisational Skills in Irrigation Sociology, Rural Development, Professional Management, Agricultural Economic, Water Law, Cultural Anthropology, Local Administration and Politics, Human Geography, Social Psychology, Agricultural Extension, Irrigation Extension, Decentralised Planning, Project Planning, Community Organisation and Group Dynamics, Conflict Management, Organisational Capacity Building, Administrative Planning, Interdisciplinary Planning and Coordination, Rapid Rural Appraisal and Participatory Rural Appraisal, Area (or Spatial) Planning and Economic Geography, Public Administration, Development Economics, Development Studies and Agrarian Change, Participatory Management, Multidisciplinary Diagnostic Surveys, Studies and Evaluations. For this, the teaching and research institutes and training bodies like WALMIs and IMTIs would also need to be reoriented.[7]

Integration of Management of Water in its Different Sectors

Just as in last 20-30 years, the need for integrated management of surface and ground water and for multiple water from the same source has assumed importance, similarly the future would necessitate integration of ocean water management with water management on land.

As regards funding, the present schemes like NABARDs Rural Infrastructure Development Fund (RIDF) or the Central Government Accelerated Irrigation Benefit Programme (AIBP) would need to be replaced by private and public arrangements for funding for creation and maintenance of water-related assets. Similarly, funding for research and development would become much more vital as the pressure on water increases. Such R&D would not be restricted only to scientific and technological issues since the success of each water-related project would depend upon the various contexts (agro-ecological, technical and technological, economic, historical, institutional, socio-cultural and politico-legal) within which the project operates and, thus, research and trials (including adoptive research) touching on all these aspects would be necessary to ensure optimum utilisation (including recycling and multiple use) of water in society. Research would need to focus not only upon better water use and management, but also upon non-conventional technologies for water availability expansion.

Variable Water Pricing

Variable pricing of water for variable uses to ensure its efficient use would also have become a crucial (with techno-engineering, politico administrative and socio-economic implications) by 2050 AD, which would necessitate administrative and legal arrangements being worked out to enable the same.

Water laws would have to undergo major changes not only to accommodate increased user participation in management, but also pressures of various alternative uses of water and the overall demand for water as our vision about life and importance of water and related water rights undergo changes over the next 50 years. However, keeping in view the fact that the pace of change has speeded up in all sectors of life, the laws would have to be kept flexible to keep pace with technological changes. Flexible approaches would also be necessary to accommodate physical and socio-cultural differences between regions in each state and between various agro-climate regions in the country.

SUMMING UP

Thus, the administration, funding and laws related to water are likely to see much more changes in the next 50 years than those which have occurred in the last 50 years, as society is forced to respond to newer challenges.

A SELECT READING

Diouf, J., "Sustainability of Irrigated Agriculture", Keynote speech delivered at 16th International Congress on Irrigation and Drainage, Cairo, Egypt, September 1996.

Gulati, Ashok; R. Meinzen-Dick and K.V. Raju, *From Top Down to Bottom Up Institutional Reforms in Indian Canal Irrigation*—Preliminary draft of study report made available at a National Workshop at Institute of Economic Growth, Delhi, January 1999.

Government of India, *National Water Policy*, Ministry of Water Resources, New Delhi, 1987.

Government of India, 1988, *Annual Report 1997-98*, Ministry of Water Resources, New Delhi, 1998.

Hooja, Rakesh, "Speculation on the Agrarian Structure and Government Delivery System in 2000 AD" in Rakesh Hooja, *Administrative Interventions in Rural Development*, Rawat, Jaipur, 1987.

Hooja Rakesh, "Transforming Agriculture Extension and Research to Meet Contemporary Needs" in V.S. Mahajan (ed.), *Political Economy of Reforms and Liberalisation*, Deep and Deep, New Delhi, 1997.

Hooja Rakesh, "Tackling Waterlogging Towards an Integrated Operational Strategy"—Keynote Address at National Seminar on Socio-Economic Aspects of Sub-Surface Drainage and Water Management, Jaipur, May 1, 1998.

Hooja Rakesh, "Command Area Development in India—Water Resources Based Development of Irrigated Areas" in T.N. Chaturvedi (ed.) *Fifty Years of Indian Administration – Retrospect and Prospects*, IIPA, New Delhi, 1998.

Hooja Rakesh, Integrated *Irrigation Management—Need for Multidisciplinary Command Area Approach and Improved Farmers Management Interface*, Arihant, Jaipur (forthcoming).

Joshi L.K. (ed.), *Management of Irrigation: A New Paradigm of Participatory Irrigation Management*, WAPCOs and Ministry of Water Resource, Government of India, New Delhi, 1997.

Joshi L.K. and V.S. Dinkar (eds.), *Waterlogging, Saline and Alkaline Lands—Prevention and*

Reclamation, WAPCOs and Ministry of Water Resources, Government of India, New Delhi, 1998.

Kay Melvyn, T. Franks and L. Smith (eds.), *Water Economics, Management and Demand*, E&FN Spon, London, 1997.

Meinzen-Dick, "Farmer Participation in Irrigation—20 Years of Experience and Lessons for the Future", *Irrigation and Drainage Systems*, Vol. II, 1997.

Meinzen-Dick, Ruth and M. Svendsen, (eds.), *Future Directions for Indian Irrigation – Research and Policy Issues*, IFPRI, Washington DC, 1993.

Ministry of Water Resources, *Report of Working Group on Command Area Development Programme*, New Delhi, 1996.

Nawalawala, B.N., "Water Resources: Development Challenges Ahead" Third H.P. Barua Memorial Lecture at Institution of Engineers (India), Assam State Centre, Guwahati, December 30, 1998.

Ostrom E., "Crafting Institutions for Self-governing Irrigation Systems", ICS Press, San Francisco, 1992.

Smedema L.K. and W.J. Ochs, "Impediments to Improved Drainage in Developing Countries" in *Drainage in the 21st Century: Food Production and the Environment*. Proceedings of the 7th Annual Drainage Symposium, Orlando, Florida, March 1998.

Smedema L.K. and Ochs W.J., "The State of Land Drainage in the World" in Rakesh Hooja, S.N. Mundra and Sewa Ram (ed.) *Irrigation Drainage – International and National Perspective*, Agrotech, Udaipur, 1999.

Sivamohan, M.V.K. and Christopher A. Scott (ed.), *India: Irrigation Management Partnerships*, Booklinks, Hyderabad.

Svendsen, Mark and A. Gulati (ed.) *Strategic Change in Indian Irrigation*, McMillan Publishers, New Delhi, 1995.

Uphoff N., R. Meinzen-Dick and N. St. Julian, *Improving Policies and Programmes for Farmers Organisation and Participation*, Water Management Synthesis Project, Paper I, Cornell University, Cornell, 1985.

Uphoff N., Ramamurthi P. and Steiner R., *Managing Irrigation: Analysing and Improving Performance of Bureaucracies*, Sage, New Delhi, 1991.

END NOTES

1. IWRS, "Theme paper on Five Decades of Water Resources Development in India", Indian Water Resource Society, New Delhi, 1998.
2. Ruth Meinzen-Dick, Meyra S. Mendoza, Loic Saddoulet, Ghada Abiad-Shields and Ashok Subramanian, "Sustainable Water User Associations: Lessons from a Literature Review", in Ashok Subramanian, N. Vijay Jagannathan and Ruth Meinzen-Dick (eds.), *User Organisations for Sustainable Water Services*, World Bank Technical Paper, Washington D.C., 1997
3. M. Svendsen, J, Trava and Sam Johnson III, "Participatory Irrigation Management: Benefits and Second Generation Problems—Lesson From an International Workshop—The conference was held at CIAT Cali, Columbia, February 1997.
4. Rakesh Hooja, "Propagating Participatory Irrigation Management", Prashasnika, Vol. 24, No. 2, 1997; and 'Promoting Water Users Association in Participatory Irrigation Management Scheme: Some Reflections", *Indian Journal of Public Administration*, Vol. 43, No. 4, 1997; and "A Strategy for Propagating Participatory Irrigation Management in India", Paper presented at Fourth National Conference on Participatory Irrigation

Management, Hyderabad, January 1999.

5. Rakesh Hooja, "Multi-disciplinary Management of Irrigation Schemes and the Command Area Approach in India", *Occasional Paper No. 2*, Jaipur, H.C.M. Rajasthan Institute of Public Administration, 1995.
6. "See A.K Biswas, Mohammed Jellah and Glen Stout (eds.), *Water for Sustainable Development in the 21st Century*—especially papers by Mohammed T.El-Ashry and Maynard M. Hufschmidt, New Delhi, Oxford University Press, 1993.
7. Clarence Maloney and K.V. Raju, *Managing Irrigation Together—Practice and Policy in India*. New Delhi, Sage; 1994; also see B.N. Nawalawala, "Water Resources Development and Water Conservation Strategy in India", in Rakesh Hooja, R.C. Bower and S.N. Mundra (eds.), *Irrigation Agriculture and Social Development*, Udaipur, Himanshu, 1997.

21

Managing Rajasthan's Scarce Water Resources: Impact of Government Schemes

Sujata Singh

Spread over an area covering 3,42,239 sq km Rajasthan enjoys the unique distinction of being the largest state in the country. Endowed with abundant mineral deposits Rajasthan at the same time suffers from scarce water resources, with more than half its area covered by desert. The water scarcity is especially precarious in western Rajasthan, which has witnessed severe droughts over the centuries. Droughts are a harsh reality for a large part of the state.

As the Human Development Report points out, Rajasthan continues to be in the lowest quartile in terms of major indicators like literacy, per capita income, etc. A large portion of the population suffers from deprivation in matters of health, water supply and other basic necessities, the report observes. Rajasthan was placed 15th in rank among 17 major states. Whereas the all-India literacy rate stood at 52.21 per cent, Rajasthan was at 38.55 per cent. The all-India literacy rate for males was 63.42 per cent and for females 40.05 per cent. Against these figures, the literacy rate for the male population was 54.99 per cent and female 20.44 per cent in Rajasthan. So far as female literacy rate was concerned, Rajasthan ranked 16th out of 17 states.[1]

A large number of schemes having been launched in rural Rajasthan to harness the scarce water resources of the state. These schemes are designed to serve multipurpose requirements—provide water for drinking purposes as well as for irrigation and livestock. A predominantly rural state where out of a total area of 3,42, 239 sq km rural Rajasthan accounts for 3,37,375 sq km and urban 4,864 sq km. From a total population of 44,005,990, the rural population of Rajasthan stands at 33,938.877 and urban at 10,087.13. Only 22.88 per cent of the state's population live in urban areas.[2] The state of Rajasthan is comprised of 32 districts.

The focus of the article will be on projects taken up under the Million Wells Scheme (MWS) in Rajasthan. The MWS was launched in 1988-89 as a Centrally Sponsored Scheme. It was initially a sub-scheme of the National Rural Employment Programme (NREP) and the Rural Landless Employment Guarantee Programme

(RLEGP). With the merger of these two programmes into one wage employment programme christened Jawahar Rozgar Yojana (JRY) in April, 1989, MWS continued as a sub-scheme of JRY till December, 1995. In January 1996, MWS was made a separate independent scheme and continued as such till April 1, 1999.

The MWS, popularly known as "Jeevan Dhara" in Rajasthan, had been in operation in the state since 1988-89. It was flexible enough to accommodate other schemes of minor irrigation such as irrigation tanks, water-harvesting structures, and water storage tanks (tankas). With the inauguration of Swarnjayanti Gram Swarozgar Yojana (SGSY) in 1999 the MWS, along with other schemes is no longer in operation. However, the construction of water harvesting structures (Anicuts) continue to be taken up under SGSY.[3]

The article examines some of the major findings that emerged from the evaluation of MWS in Rajasthan, in order to highlight the pitfalls that need to be avoided in the planning and implementation of water management schemes in future. This is especially important given the fact that the government continues to sponsor water-harvesting structures (Anicuts) in Rajasthan.

THE UNIQUE TOPOGRAPHY OF RAJASTHAN

The Aravalli Ranges form the main water devide in Rajasthan. The only river west of Aravallies is Luni. The remaining part of Western Rajasthan, which is approximately 60 per cent of the geographical area of the state, the drainage is mainly internal. The streams flow only a short distance from the point of origin before they are lost in the desert sands. The Chambal Catchment occupies 72,032 sq km or 21 per cent of the total geographical area of the state. The Yamuna-Ganga, Mahi and Sabarmati constitute the other important catchments in the state. A few salt lakes and depressions exist in the desert area such as the Didwana Lake, Sambhar Lake, Bap, Pachpadra and Rann of Jaisalmer and Pokhran.[4]

Rainfall Pattern

Rajasthan is mainly dependent on rainfall for groundwater recharge. It receives 90 per cent of its rainfall from South-West monsoon between June to September. Rainfall is meagre during winter season. Data collected by the Central Ground Water Board (CGWB) shows that when compared to the Western Part, east of Aravalli receives much higher rainfall. Again, there is a wide variation between different regions of the state. The fact that rainfall varies from 185 mm in Jaisalmer to 1240 mm in Jhalawar best illustrates this variation. Sounding a note of caution the Central Ground Water Board in its 1998-99 report points out that the recharge to groundwater during 1998-99 has been less when compared to 1997-98 as also 1996-97. Not only has the recharge been reduced on account of erratic and deficit rainfall, 19 per cent of the stations has changed status from permissive to non-permissible limits with regard to content of fluoride. Out of 237 blocks, 59 blocks showed a long-term decline in groundwater levels. Major part of the recharge to groundwater in the entire state is through infiltration from rainfall.[5]

Table 1: Average Annual Rainfall and Departure From Normal Rainfall

Sl. No.	District	*Rainfall in mm*				*Depature from Normal*		
		Normal (1901-70)	*Annual (1998-99)*	*Annual (1999-00)*	*Annual (2000-01)*	*(98-99) %*	*(99-00) %*	*(00-01) %*
1.	AJMER	437.0	478.0	381.1	383.8	9.4	-12.8	-12.2
2.	ALWAR	626.0	709.4	517.7	555.7	13.3	-17.3	-11.2
3.	BANSWARA	870.0	949.4	698.7	452.3	9.1	-19.7	-48.0
4.	BARAN	895.3	800.5	952.6	805.5	-10.6	6.4	-10.0
5.	BARMER	260.0	392.8	152.4	258.5	51.1	-41.4	-0.6
6.	BHARATPUR	675.1	730.3	608.3	455.0	8.2	-9.9	-32.6
7.	BHILWARA	603.3	439.5	530.3	453.8	-27.2	-12.1	-24.8
8.	BIKANER	249.8	377.0	201.1	363.6	50.9	-19.5	45.6
9.	BUNDI	715.8	543.9	692.5	590.7	-24.0	-3.3	-17.5
10.	CHITTORGARH	772.3	599.6	788.4	453.3	-22.4	2.1	-41.3
11.	CHURU	337.9	433.5	204.3	292.3	28.3	-39.5	-13.5
12.	DAUSA	625.5	889.4	538.0	507.1	42.1	-14.0	-19.0
13.	DHOLPUR	717.5	778.9	618.0	538.5	8.6	-13.9	-24.9
14.	DUNGARPUR	610.4	735.3	543.0	381.2	20.5	-11.0	-37.5
15.	GANGANAGAR	171.6	221.7	100.5	203.4	29.2	-41.4	18.5
16.	HANUMANGARH	237.5	413.0	157.0	263.0	73.9	-33.9	10.7
17.	JAIPUR	526.8	619.1	438.2	423.3	17.5	-16.8	-19.6
18.	JAISALMER	158.6	377.0	177.9	199.6	137.7	12.2	25.9
19.	JALORE	400.6	302.5	161.5	311.5	-24.5	-59.7	-22.2
20.	JHALAWAR	884.8	683.2	1140.7	724.5	-22.8	28.9	-18.1
21.	JHUNJHUNU	459.5	508.8	293.4	404.8	10.7	-36.1	-11.9
22.	JODHPUR	296.7	367.2	281.0	267.4	23.8	-5.3	-9.9
23.	KARAULI	616.2	978.6	560.4	526.3	58.8	-9.1	-14.6
24.	KOTA	808.7	581.4	926.9	721.4	-28.1	14.6	-10.8
25.	NAGAUR	363.1	399.6	223.7	398.9	10.1	-38.4	9.9
26.	PALI	484.5	416.8	459.4	347.0	-14.0	-5.2	-28.4
27.	RAJASANAND	556.1	556.3	476.8	304.7	0.0	-14.3	-45.2
28.	S. MADHOPUR	655.8	864.3	655.6	446.2	31.8	0.0	-32.0
29.	SIKAR	459.8	490.7	257.8	406.5	6.7	-43.9	-11.6
30.	SIROHI	606.3	670.3	398.3	512.2	10.6	-34.3	-15.5
31.	TONK	598.2	576.0	690.3	527.3	-3.7	15.4	-11.9
32.	UDAIPUR	632.7	774.1	398.4	385.0	22.3	-37.0	-39.1
1	**RAJASTHAN**	**541.1**	**583.1**	**475.8**	**508.9**	**7.8**	**-12.1**	**-5.9**

Source: *Ground Water Year Book*, Rajasthan, 2000-01, Central Ground Water Board.

The *Ground Water Year Book* on Rajasthan for the period 2000-01 again highlights the progressive decline in water levels and degrading water quality. It points out that key factors such as low rainfall, water salinity, limited ground-water storage availability deep water levels especially in Western Rajasthan together with nearly 50 per cent of the state's area under desertic conditions, need to be addressed in the development and management of groundwater in the state. It warns that a few good monsoons should not lead to complacency regarding the groundwater situation in the state. Insofar as the canal command areas of IGNP. Chambal, Mahi and other surface irrigation systems are concerned, the Report stresses on the increasing menace of waterlogging.[6]

Data on the average annual rainfall pattern shows that less than normal rainfall was received in 27 districts during 2000-01. Banswara, Chittorgarh, Rajsamand and Udaipur districts of Rajasthan appear to be worst hit by drought during this period. The rainfall was also very poor in Bharatpur and Sawai Madhopur.[7]

Table 2: District-wise Number and Category of Potential Zones as on January 1, 1998

District	*Number of POT Zones*	*Category of Ptential Zones*				
		Safe	*S. Critical*	*Critical*	*Over Explo*	*Category*
AJMER	20	5	15	–	–	S. Critical
ALWAR	19	–	–	8	11	O.E.
BARAN	18	7	2	8	1	S. Critical
BARMER	31	14	9	3	5	S. Critical
VABSWARA	18	18	–	–	–	Safe
BHARATPUR	11	6	3	2	–	S. Critical
BHILWARA	34	29	3	2	–	Safe
BIKANER	17	16	–	1	–	Safe
BUNDI	13	9	4	–	–	Safe
CHITTORGARH	48	20	15	11	2	S. Critical
CHURU	19	9	5	3	2	Safe
DAUSA	13	3	1	4	5	S. Critical
DHOLPUR	12	7	3	2	–	S. Critical
DUNGARPUR	11	11	–	–	–	Safe
GANGANAGAR	8	8	–	–	–	Safe
HANUMANGARH	4	4	–	–	–	Safe
JAIPUR	28	4	3	5	16	O.E.
JAISALMER	28	25	3	–	–	Safe
JALORE	30	1	–	6	24	O.E.
JHALAWAR	8	2	5	1	–	S. Critical
JHUNJHUNU	17	2	2	4	9	O.E.
JODHPUR	46	16	3	12	15	Critical
KARAULI	13	9	–	2	2	S. Critical
KOTA	15	11	1	1	2	Safe
NAGAUR	45	14	2	9	20	O.E.
PALI	29	16	6	6	1	S. Critical
RAJSAMAND	18	16	1	1	–	Safe
S. MADHOPUR	19	15	3	1	–	Safe
SIKAR	15	4	2	3	6	O.E
SIROHI	16	7	3	6	–	S. Critical
TONK	19	19	–	–	–	Safe
UDAIPUR	25	21	3	1	–	Safe
TOTAL	**668**	**345**	**97**	**102**	**121**	

Source: Ground Water Resources of Rajasthan, Central Ground Water Board, 1998.

Water Quality

Evaluation of water quality for domestic use by the CGWB found that the percentage of four principal constituents is above permissible limits in good percentage of water samples in 32 districts on account of high values of one or other principal constituents. Out of a total number of 668 potential zones, 348 were declared safe, 97 as semi critical, 102 as critical and 121 were placed in the over exploited category. The districts that have been classified as over exploited are Alwar, Jaipur, Jallore, Jhunjhunu, Nagaur and Sikar. In the critical category is Jodhpur. Among those in the semi critical category are Ajmer, Baran, Barmer, Bharatpur, Chittorgarh, Dausa, Dholpur, Jhalawar, Karauli, Pali and Sirohi. In the safe category are Banswara, Bhilwara, Bikaner, Bundi, Churu, Dungarpur, Sri Ganganagar, Hanumangarh, Jaisalmer, Kota, Rajasmand, S. Madhopur, Tonk and Udaipur.[8]

Based on the norms laid down by the Bureau of Indian Standard the National Hydrograph Stations evaluated the five principal chemical constituents for drinking, domestic and irrigation purposes during May, 2000. It was found that when compared to the previous year's chemical analysis data, there is slight deterioration in chemical quality (0.59 to 2.38%) in all five major constituents. The analysis reveals that Ajmer, Bharatpur, Barmer, Jodhpur, Jaisalmer, Nagaur and Hanumangarh districts have a serious salinity problem where 40-60 per cent wells were found having TDS values which were beyond permissible limits. The groundwater is relatively fresh in Banswara, Jhalawar, Dungarpur, Bundi, Kota, Dholpur and Chittorgarh. So far as chloride content is concerned in Banswara, Udaipur, Dungarpur, Rajasmand, Kota and Jhalawar districts it is found within permissible limits. However, the chloride content is beyond maximum permissible limit in the rest of the state.[9]

Table 3: Percentage of Hydrograph Stations Where the Principal Constitutents are Beyond Permissible Limits for Drinking Water

(Based on analysis of 757 NHS water samples collected during May, 2000)

Sl. No.	*District*	*Samples analysed*	*TDS %*	*SO_4 %*	*Cl %*	*NO_3 %*	*F %*
1.	AJMER	30	46.67	39.99	33.33	9.99	73.32
2.	ALWAR	29	31.03	1034	1034	24.14	37.93
3.	BANSWARA	18	0	0	0	0	16.67
4.	BARAN	14	21.43	21.43	0	14.29	0
5.	BARMER	50	58	46	36	50	66
6.	BHARATPUR	28	50	21.42	32.17	14.29	35.71
7.	BHILWARA	25	16	4	8	20	32
8.	BIKANER	1	–	–	–	–	–
9.	BUNDI	11	18.18	18.18	9.09	9.09	27.27
10.	CHITTORGARH	21	19.04	9.52	0	19.04	52.38
11.	CHURU	25	64	24	32	64	64
12.	DAUSA	8	12.5	12.5	12.5	0	25

(Contd.)

(Contd.)

Sl. No.	*District*	*Samples analysed*	*TDS %*	*SO4 %*	*CI %*	*NO3 %*	*F %*
13.	DHOLPUR	11	9.09	0	0	27.27	18.18
14.	DUNGARPUR	13	0	0	0	0	7.69
15.	GANGANAGAR	29	24.14	27.59	17.24	17.24	62.07
16.	HANUMANGARH	17	41.18	23.53	17.65	35.29	47.05
17.	JAIPUR	24	28.83	12.5	8.33	20.73	70.83
18.	JAISALMER	61	34.43	27.86	16.4	6.55	59.01
19.	JALORE	20	35	15	20	15	70
20.	JHALAWAR	21	9.52	19.05	0	14.29	0
21.	JHUNJHUNU	16	25	31.25	0	37.5	93.75
22.	JODHPUR	55	41.82	14.55	27.27	21.82	47.27
23.	KARAULI	18	27.77	16.66	11.11	44.44	16.67
24.	KOTA	18	11.11	22.22	5.56	16.67	0
25.	NAGAUR	46	43.48	21.74	21.74	54.35	52.17
26.	PALI	28	50	39.28	28.57	17.86	46.43
27.	RAJASANAND	20	15	10	5	35	75
28.	S. MADHOPUR	20	20	20	10	20	30
29.	SIKAR	9	22.22	22.22	11.11	11.11	66.66
30.	SIROHI	16	18.75	0	12.5	12.5	68.75
31.	TONK	21	14.29	0	0	4.76	19.04
32.	UDAIPUR	35	2.86	5.71	0	5.71	11.42
	RAJASTHAN	757	**30.38**	**19.68**	**15.59**	**24.04**	**45.97**

Source: Ground Water Year Book, Rajasthan, 2000-2001, Central Ground Water Board p. 42.

Marwar or 'the Region of Death'

Rajasthan is faced with a multitude of problems especially in its arid Western region. The word Marwar or 'the region of death' is widely used to refer to this arid region of Rajasthan.[10] It continues to suffer serious droughts, year after year. In his classic work *Annals and Antiquities of Rajasthan* published in 1829, Colonel James Tod points out that Marwar is the corrupted version of Marusthali which in Sanskrit means mri, 'to die,' and sthala, 'arid or dry land'.[11] Tod also gives a graphic description of famine which he calls 'the grand natural disease of these regions'. They had a pattern of occurring every third year. He recalls the terrible famines that occurred during 1868-69, 1877-78, 1891-92 and 1899-1900, not to mention the several season of scarcity. Tod appears to hold Hamir Sodha, during whose time the desiccation of the Ghaggar River took place, responsible for it.[12]

As Table 4 indicates Jaisalmer has suffered the maximum number of droughts. Out of 67 droughts, it experienced 42 severe droughts and 25 moderate droughts. Jaisalmer is followed by Barmer with 47 droughts—29 severe and 18 moderate droughts. The number of droughts from 1901-99 stand at 45 for Bikaner. Out of these 45, 23 were of moderate density and 22 severe. There were altogether 42 droughts in Jodhpur—26 moderate and 16 serve droughts.

Table 4: Frequency of agricultural droughts in the Western Rajasthan (1901-99)

District	*Moderate Droughts*	*Severe Droughts*	*Total Number Droughts*
Barmer	18	29	47
Bikaner	23	22	45
Jaisalmer	25	42	67
Jodhpur	26	16	42

Source: Report of Central Arid Zone Research Institute, Jodhpur p.10.

The Indira Gandhi Nahar Project

The Indira Gandhi Nahar Project (IGNP) was one of the major initiatives taken by government to mitigate the hardship faced by people in the Western region of Rajasthan. The Canal water was designed to serve many objectives such as providing water for drinking and industrial use; providing irrigation facilities; to check spread of desert; creation of employment opportunities in rural areas; and to provide drinking water, fodder and forage for the animal in the region. Jodhpur city is being supplied water through IGNP. The execution of the Canal work is spread over the districts of Sri Ganganagar, Hanumangarh, Churu, Bikaner, Jaisalmer, Jodhpur and Barmer.

A word of caution needs to be added here. The CGWB report highlights the declines in groundwater levels in the Canal command areas together with increased water-logging. It warns that unless urgent steps are taken large areas will go out of agriculture.[13]

As can be observed from the Zone-Wise information provided by the government of Rajasthan, all the blocks in Banswara, Dungarpur, Rajasmand, Tonk, Bikaner, Ganganagar, Jaisalmer and Hanumangarh districts fall under the category of White Zone. However, in some districts, an overwhelming number of blocks are under the Dark Zone. Out of the 13 blocks in Jaipur district, 12 fall under the Dark Zone. Similar is the case of Alwar where out of 14 blocks, 12 have been certified as Dark Zone. The picture in Jhunjhunu is not rosy either where out of eight blocks, seven fall under the Dark Zone. Sikar and Dausa districts are at the extreme end with all its eight blocks being declared as 'Dark'.

The different blocks in a district have been certified as Dark, Grey and White based on the availability of water. However, during the course of the field survey it was observed that, areas which are now considered as having high potential for groundwater, were not considered so earlier. For instance all the new wells coming up after January 1, 1996 in Sankara block of Jaisalmer district, have been sanctioned in Olan. This is in sharp contrast to previous years when very few wells were sanctioned here. Discussions with officials of the CGWB revealed that this could be on account of change in the methodology adopted for analyzing the water potential in different areas, from time-to-time. Areas which were earlier certified as Dark Zone, have over a period of time been certified as White Zone and *vice versa*.

Table 5: Zone Wise Information of Rajasthan

Name of the District	*No. of Panchayat Samities*	*Dark Zone*	*Grey Zone*	*White Zone*
AJMER	8	3	2	3
ALWAR	14	12	1	1
BANSWARA	8	–	–	8
BARAN	7	–	–	7
BHARATPUR	9	5	3	1
BHILWARA	11	1	5	5
BUNDI	4	–	1	3
CHITTORGARH	14	2	8	4
DAUSA	5	5	–	–
DHOLPUR	4	–	1	3
DUNGARPUR	5	–	–	5
JAIPUR	13	12	–	1
JHALAWAR	6	1	2	3
KOTA	5	1	–	4
PALI	10	4	2	4
RAJASANAND	7	–	–	7
SIKAR	8	8	–	–
SIROHI	5	–	1	4
S. MADHOPUR	10	3	–	7
TONK	6	–	–	6
UDAIPUR	11	–	2	9
BARMER	8	2	2	4
BIKANER	4	–	–	4
CHURU	7	2	–	5
GANGANAGAR	7	–	–	7
JAISALMER	3	–	–	3
JALORE	7	5	–	2
JHUNJHUNU	8	7	–	1
JODHPUR	9	3	1	5
NAGORE	11	6	3	2
HANUMANGARH	3	–	–	3
Total	**237**	**82**	**34**	**121**

Source: Monitoring Division, Government of Rajasthan, Jaipur.

Evaluation of MWS in Rajasthan

The study covered 31 districts of Rajasthan where MWS or "Jeevan Dhara" as it was popularly known in Rajasthan, was in operation. Dausa district was not covered in the survey since all its blocks had been classified as falling under the "Dark Zone". Two blocks were selected from each district. Five village panchayats were then selected from each block. From each village, ten beneficiaries were selected at randon, making a total of 50 sample beneficiaries per block. Overall, 100 beneficiaries per district were selected. There were altogether 2832 beneficiaries who were interviewed—2630 who had been benefited by open well and 202 by group projects. Survey research techniques were adopted for conducting the study. The survey was conducted during 1999-2000.

The district-wise position of physical target and achievement under the MWS for the period 1988-89 to 1998-99, for the entire state of Rajasthan is given in Table 6. Against the targeted 77,398 wells, 57,539 have been completed. This amounts to a shortfall of 19859 wells. The year-wise breakup presents an interesting picture. Whereas the number targeted was 20,000 during 1988-90, the achievement figures for the same period were as low as 13,480. Again, during 1991-92 only 6,755 wells were constructed against a target of 12,350 and a backlog of 6,520 from the previous years. However, during 1991-92, 1992-93,1993-94 and 1994-95 the achievement rate picked up wherein not only the targeted figures were achieved, the backlog from previous years was also cleared. The period 1996-99 is marked by a steep decline in the target-achievement ratio, leading to an overall short fall of 19,859 wells. The overall trend in Dungarpur appears by and large, satisfactory. Though the lion's share goes to Jaipur district, its performance does not match it.

Objectives of the Programme

The primary objective of the programme was to help create assets for the rural poor, especially the Scheduled Castes and Scheduled Tribes (SCs/STs) by providing them with an open irrigation well/irrigation source free of cost.

The secondary objectives included:

(*a*) Provision of additional gainful employment opportunity for the target group.
(*b*) Overall improvement in the quality of life in rural areas.

Target Group

According to the guidelines of the scheme the target group would comprise of poor, small and marginal farmers below poverty line as listed in the IRDP register of the village. It was further specified that not less than two-thirds of the funds utilised under the scheme in any year should be spent on poor, small and marginal farmers belonging to SCs/STs. Priority was however to be given to freed bonded labourers. The other categories included:

(*i*) Poor SC/ST small and marginal farmers who have been victims of atrocities;
(*ii*) Poor SC/ST small and marginal farmers below poverty line with widows and unmarried women heading the households;
(*iii*) SC/ST poor small and marginal farmers who have been affected by fire, flood, earthquake and other natural disasters;
(*iv*) Other SC/ST poor small and marginal farmers below poverty line; and
(*v*) Poor small and marginal non SC/ST farmers below poverty line.

The evaluation of MWS in Rajasthan threw up some interesting findings.

Data pertaining to the status of execution of works undertaken under the MWS

Table 6: Million Wells Scheme

Physical Target and Achievement

District \ Year	88-90		90-91		91-92		92-93		93-94		94-95		95-96		96-97		97-98		98-99		UPTO 98-99 G. TOTAL	
	T	Achi	T	Achi	T	Achi	T	Achi	T	Achi	T	Achi	T	Achi	T	Achi	T	Achi	T	Achi		
Ajmer	890	429	364	415	385	166	375	228	152	85	64	134	472	147	429	110	260	85	150	251		
Alwar	876	530	526	577	438	570	400	121	155	58	80	42	118	52	110	90	70	91	140	88		
Banswara	1538	632	1692	1645	1419	1742	1370	698	132	452	254	144	–	184	–	91	570	177	140	21		
Baran	–	–	–	–	372	240	44	222	122	101	68	59	–	36	–	68	150	–	150	0		
Barmer	460	398	220	26	183	450	235	229	82	241	35	181	341	59	392	248	110	123	140	161		
Bharatpur	568	386	492	141	305	569	325	402	145	259	74	51	448	26	392	29	500	183	580	234		
Bhiwara	624	649	523	949	532	240	420	136	345	264	89	247	376	230	356	146	450	303	550	265		
Bikaner	110	89	73	8	139	582	100	360	36	86	14	139	1210	170	245	89	250	102	250	34		
Bundi	162	44	205	44	171	232	215	92	76	91	31	37	324	94	276	59	170	63	140	71		
Chittorgarh	964	791	397	137	407	664	440	381	239	295	67	149	366	84	318	145	340	138	390	356		
Churu	248	236	133	133	277	196	290	117	49	232	20	60	–	45	–	33	150	2	140	0		
Dausa	–	–	–	–	169	183	180	59	68	43	23	2	–	71	–	–	60	–	140	0		
Dholpur	250	131	160	–	75	211	130	156	291	52	27	26	155	41	99	9	150	12	250	10		
Dungarpur	1436	1022	1110	534	1195	1022	1000	1832	414	583	176	403	511	148	457	186	230	107	210	74		
Ganganagar	60	30	28	–	24	–	20	17	38	7	5	–	–	–	–	–	–	–	140	0		
Jaipur	2022	1468	360	197	263	479	320	174	81	50	37	27	–	15	–	10	170	6	140	0		
Jaisalmer	120	41	39	65	33	55	80	71	88	5	6	1	–	24	–	–	–	–	140	0		
Jalore	684	421	241	311	48	220	150	167	92	58	41	202	275	221	258	203	280	87	170	128		
Jhalawar	708	616	369	7	308	327	250	355	77	137	61	61	387	55	261	50	100	27	150	27		
Jhunjhunu	252	239	129	160	127	167	160	137	57	52	21	126	284	42	272	56	60	37	140	67		
Jodhpur	608	289	236	80	197	245	50	354	110	38	35	47	–	30	–	3	–	–	170	0		
Kota	700	462	625	66	187	115	100	219	103	62	39	18	265	16	231	64	–	9	150	1		
Nagaur	870	771	318	150	336	465	350	396	132	215	50	93	255	208	294	127	180	148	140	61		
Pali	1536	452	564	310	303	549	395	817	97	511	101	167	343	14	318	74	120	111	140	77		
Rajasmand	–	–	–	–	279	183	570	166	6	160	55	234	356	81	321	34	160	74	230	128		
S. Madhopur	1036	1258	828	4	525	397	480	730	110	139	134	83	–	170	–	79	–	22	140	0		
Sikar	376	362	168	174	160	128	190	173	106	43	30	35	231	21	231	68	140	6	150	0		
Surohi	450	450	278	317	232	192	190	120	155	144	51	48	210	44	187	36	430	22	150	0		
Tonk	612	379	384	166	405	404	160	322	48	113	69	151	393	31	362	28	150	10	150	39		
Udaipur	1840	905	1879	189	586	1160	525	714	214	268	265	104	595	125	541	254	520	463	600	140		
Hanumangarh	–	–	–	–	–	–	–	–	–	–	–	–	172	–	196	–	–	–	140	603		
Karoli	–	–	–	–	–	–	–	–	–	–	–	–	–	–	–	–	–	12	170	0		
Total	20000	13480	12350	6755	10082	12150	9910	9973	3820	4844	2022	3071	6898	2457	6546	2389	5770	2420	6550	2838	77398	57530

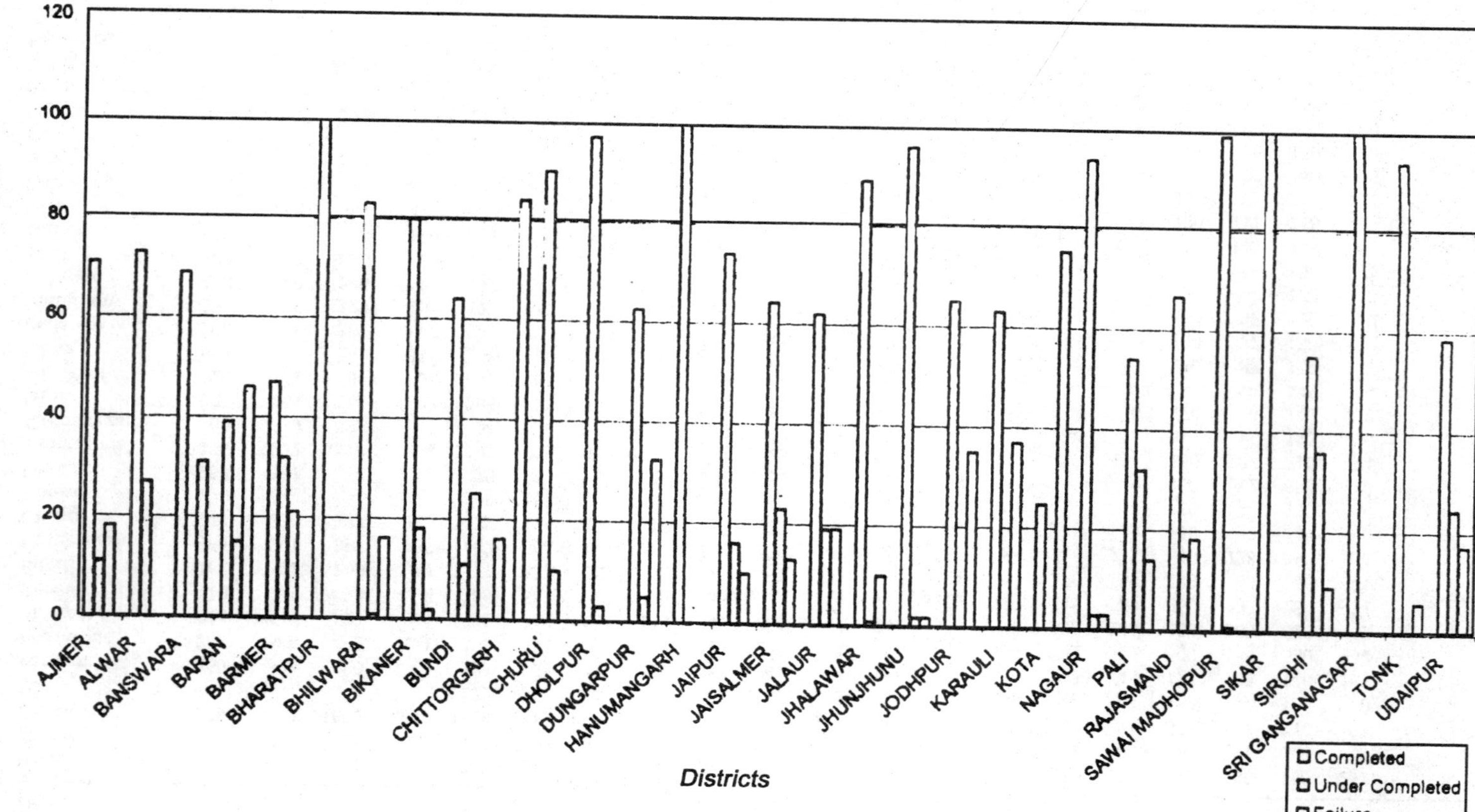

Source: Concurrent Evaluation of Million Wells Scheme in Rajasthan, 2000, pp. 39-40.

Fig. 1: Status of Execution of Wells

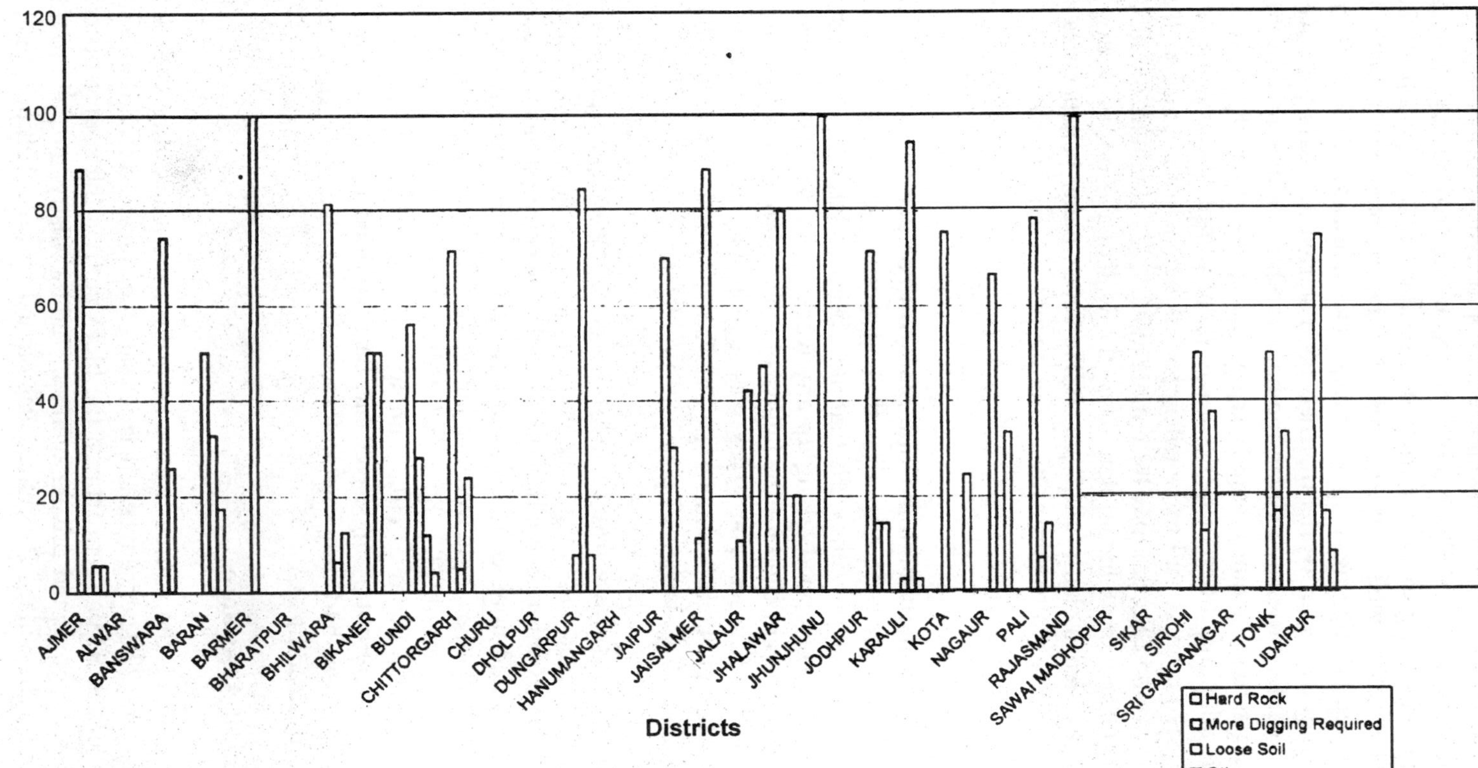

Source: Concurrent Evaluation of Million Wells Scheme in Rajasthan, 2000, pp. 41-42.

Fig. 2: Reasons for Failure

points out that overall 74.07 per cent wells stand completed. Whereas 10.76 per cent wells were under progress, 15.17 per cent have been declared as failure. It may be pointed out that works being shown as completed need not necessarily imply that they are successful. Many of the wells that were considered completed had in fact dried up. They definitely required digging deeper. Another fact that came to light during the course of the survey was that works that had been started 10 years back were still being shown as "Under Progress". Given the hard ground realities relating to water availability in Rajasthan, a many small farmer has given up in frustration. The administration is adopting different tactics to get them complete the work. In many districts notices have been served to beneficiaries asking them to complete the well, failing which they would have to repay the entire amount given to them. In Pali district, old wells are being shown as incomplete since the wells have not been dug to the required depth, in order to claim full payment. However, many beneficiaries are not digging deeper since the water gets salty if dug deeper. Herein lies the dilemma.[14]

Reasons for Failure

The failure rate is particularly high in Chittorgarh with 84 per cent, Kota with 75.38 per cent, Baran with 46 per cent, Karauli with 37 per cent, Jodhpur with 35 per cent and Dungarpur with 32.50 per cent wells that have been declared as unsuccessful. In fact, Jodhpur district has stopped taking up any work under the MWS since 1993.

Two major reasons were cited for the failure of wells. More digging was required felt 43.22 per cent beneficiaries. Hard rock was responsible for the failure of wells, was the view of 40.20 per cent beneficiaries. This is the overall picture for Rajasthan where hard rock as well as loose soil pose real problems.

The position of failed wells gets even more complicated when it comes to certifying by the state agency. Works are being shown as "incomplete" even in cases where they have failed. Whereas 398 wells were considered as "failure", only 25 were so certified. Ajmer with 18 failure cases had not a single one certified as such; Banswara with 31 failure cases had none certified as failure; Baran with as many as 46 failed wells, failed to certify even a single well as a failure case. Similar was the case in Kota with 49 failure cases, Karauli (37), Barmer (21), Chittorgarh (21), Dungarpur (13), Jaipur (10), Jaisalmer (9), Jhalawar (10), Jhunjhunu (2), Jodhpur (14), Rajsmand (12) and Udaipur (12), where not a single well has been certified to be a "failure" case. Pali with 14 failure cases had only one well certified as failed well. Thus, incorrect reporting can be misleading.[15]

Source of Technical Assistance

When asked to indicate the source from where the beneficiary received technical assistance, as many as 42.89 per cent beneficiaries said they received technical assistance from none. Whereas 35.93 per cent named the block staff as the source of technical assistance, 18.25 per cent named private agents including Mistry, etc., as providers of technical assistance. The Village Panchayat was named by only 2.28 per cent sample beneficiaries in the state as a whole. The role of DRDAs/ZPs was even more negligible given the fact that 0.15 per cent mentioned that they have received technical assistance from them. Only 0.49 per cent had taken technical assistance from "others".

Among the large group of beneficiaries (42.89%), who had not received technical assistance from any quarter, were all the beneficiaries from Bharatpur (100%), as also from Bundi (100%), Karauli (100%) and Kota (100%). These high numbers were followed by Banswara where 98 per cent beneficiaries had not received any assistance from any source, as also Jhalawar (97%) and Alwar (83%). Baran and Barmer districts with 79 per cent beneficiaries each, had not provided any technical assistance to the beneficiaries. The position in Sirohi district with 75 per cent, Jodhpur and Sri Ganganagar with 60 per cent each, Rajsmand with 57.58 per cent and Dholpur with 50 per cent was not very different.

In the following districts, the beneficiaries did indicate that the block level staff provided technical assistance, namely, Ajmer (76%), Bhilwara (98%), Dungarpur (97.50%), Jaisalmer (61.43%), Jalaur (87%), Nagaur (96%), Pali (97%), Sawai Madhopur (99%), Tonk (98%) and Udaipur (54.29%). However, the technical assistance provided by the block, the DRDA/ZP and Panchayat put together amounts to less than 40 per cent.[16]

During the course of the survey a common complaint heard was regarding lack of cooperation of technical staff, particularly the Junior Engineer (JE). A large number of beneficiaries complained that they have to spend from their own pockets to get the JE to visit the site. In addition to this, they have to entertain the JE on a lavish scale. Group of beneficiaries pool their resources for this purpose.

In many places JEs are law unto themselves. This is especially the case where the Block Development Officer does not have an engineering background. The JE of Salumber block (Udaipur district) is running a parallel administration. He is proud of the fact that he had been twice suspended from service and claims to have close ties with the local dacoits.[17]

Among the major reasons for the poor performance of MWS in many parts of Rajasthan, is its poor water potential. Second, the amount of digging required can go upto 250 to 300 ft deep. The poor economic condition of BPL families who do not have resources to take care of additional expenses that are involved, is yet another important factor.

The actual cost of the well is much higher than what was assumed. They require blasting, boring and drilling operations as well. It may be noted that though wells required these operations, they could not be undertaken because of lack of finances at the disposal of the beneficiaries.

Technical assistance was not available to the beneficiaries was very obvious to the investigators. A total of 42.89 per cent beneficiaries said they have not received technical assistance from any quarter. They adopt traditional methods for locating water. Only when it comes to denying them the instalments does the technical staff, mainly the JE, step in.

Corruption appears to be widespread through many beneficiaries were not willing to go on record to say so. However, a total of 7.95 per cent beneficiaries, despite the fear of victimisation, let their views be recorded. All of them stated that they had to make a payment in order to get the sanction. Many alleged that they had to give a part of every instalment to either the JE or the Sarpanch. The involvement of Panchayati Raj functionaries in the implementation of rural development programmes appears to have aggravated the problem of corruption. The trickle down in turn is getting thinner with more people demanding a share. It was also observed that women Sarpanch have no direct role in the administration of the programmes as their proxy, the 'Sarpanch Pati' is the one who matters.[18]

The list of beneficiaries provided by DRDAs did not tally with that of the Samiti, in many cases. Given this problem, it was difficult to decide as to which list was authentic. Again, the information provided by the DRDAs and blocks in the respective districts regarding amount sanctioned to beneficiaries, did not match.[19]

MWS Group Projects

Given the mixed results the MWS produced and in keeping with the revised guidelines of the Ministry, which were made more flexible to include other projects under MWS, group projects were taken up in different districts of Rajasthan. These were initially mainly restricted to the mountainous Mewar region comprising Chittorgarh, Dungarpur, Rajasmand and Udaipur. The group projects consists of Water Harvesing Structures or Anicuts wherein a group of beneficiaries are covered under each project. Unlike the open well scheme which caters to individual beneficiary, the group project caters to a group of beneficiaries. The total number of such projects were 19—with five in Chittorgarh, eight in Dungarpur and three each in Rajasmand and Udaipur.

Table 7: Percentage Deistribution of Mws Group Projects By Type

Name of District	*Type of MWS Group Project Works*									*Total No. of Groups Projects*
	Open Well	*Tube Well/ Bore*	*Irrigation Tank*	*Water Harvesting Structure*	*Develop-ment of Land*	*Drainage or consor construction of walls*	*Canals*	*Bandhs*	*Other*	
Chitorgarh	0.00	0.00	0.00	100.00	0.00	0.00	0.00	0.00	0.00	5
Dungarpur	0.00	0.00	0.00	100.00	0.00	0.00	0.00	0.00	0.00	8
Rajasmand	0.00	0.00	0.00	100.00	0.00	0.00	0.00	0.00	0.00	3
Udaipur	0.00	0.00	0.00	100.00	0.00	0.00	0.00	0.00	0.00	5
State Total	**0.00**	**0.00**	**0.00**	**100.00**	**0.00**	**0.00**	**0.00**	**0.00**	**0.00**	**19**

Source: Concurrent Evaluation of Million Wells Scheme in Rajasthan, 2000, p.157.

STATUS OF EXECUTION

In terms of percentage, 60 per cent group projects in Chittorgarh district stand completed whereas 40 per cent are under construction. The figures for Dungarpur are 62.50 per cent completed and 37.50 per cent under progress. In Rajasmand 33.33 per cent have been completed whereas 66.67 per cent are still under progress. The position in Udaipur is exactly the opposite from that obtaining in Rajasamand, in that 66.67 per cent group projects stand completed with 33.33 per cent under progress.

Table 8: Distribution of MWS Group Project Works By Status of Execution

Name of District	*Completed (% age)*	*Under Progress (% age)*	*Failure (% age)*	*Not Yet Started (% age)*	*Total No. of Projects*
Chitorgarh	60.00	40.00	0.00	0.00	5
Dungarpur	62.50	37.50	0.00	0.00	8
Rajasmand	33.33	66.67	0.00	0.00	3
Idaipur	66.67	33.33	0.00	0.00	3
State Total	57.89	42.11	0.00	0.00	19

Source: Concurrenty Evaluation of Million Wells Scheme in Rajasthan, 2000, p.158.

None of the MWS group projects have been declared a failure. At least, this is the perception of the group project administration. But the ground realities present a different picture altogether.

The Village Panchayat, in a majority of cases (52.63%) is the executing agency for MWS group projects. These are being executed under the supervision of the Sarpanch. In the case of Chittorgarh and Rajasmand, all the group projects are being executed by the Village Panchayat. In Udaipur 66.67 per cent are being executed by the Village Panchayat and 33.33 per cent by contractor. In the case of Dungarpur, group projects are either being executed by Line Departments (62.50%), or by Block Staff (37.50%).20

Impact of Group Projects

The benefits flowing from the group projects in terms of availability of water has been far from satisfactory. The combined results from four districts—Chittorgarh, Dungarpur, Rajasmand and Udaipur reveals that the benefit has been either "seasonal" or "not at all". In 52.63 per cent cases the benefit has been seasonal and in the remaining cases no benefit has been recorded so far. These are mainly under different stages of construction. However, in one particular case in Udaipur district (Sulumber Block) the Anicut had already started leaking as a result of poor construction. This, as alleged by the beneficiaries, was built by a contractor, against the guidelines laid down by the Ministry.

An elite group has been involved selectively in the various activities whereas the bulk of the beneficiaries have provided only wage labour. In one particular case in Dungarpur an irrigation department employee drawing Rs.7,500 by his own admission, has been included in the Below Poverty Line (BPL) List. As husband of the Sarpanch (Sarpanch Pati as they are popularly known in Rajasthan) he was the *de facto* Sarpanch and was in charge of constructing the anicut at Outiya, Village Panchayat Gangi. Several of his relatives were beneficiaries of this group project. Many other Sarpanchs and their relatives were beneficiaries of MWS group projects, as was the case with "Open Wells".[21]

As mentioned earlier the MWS group projects in the districts of Chittorgarh, Dungarpur, Rajasmand and Udaipur consists of Water Harvesting Structures. These have been designed on the assumption that they would help store rain water, which in turn will result in water levels rising in individual wells, in the vicinity of the Anicuts.

Water Harvesting Structures have especially found favour in mountainous districts on the assumption that they have a natural advantage in harvesting rain-water.

At the time of the survey, Dungarpur happened to be the only district where 66.67 per cent beneficiaries indicated that the Anicut did promote irrigation in their area. In other districts, Anicuts were either in the process of being constructed or were not producing the desired results on account of Shabby construction and lack of rainfall.

The individual beneficiaries were asked to indicate the extent and nature of benefits they are deriving from the MWS group projects. The combined response from the four districts shows that 69.31 per cent beneficiaries said they have not benefited at all from these projects. However, 75 per cent in Dungarpur and 56.67 per cent in Udaipur did derive benefit from Group Projects which was however seasonal in nature.[22]

Though MWS group projects are to cater to the requirements of BPL families, many families placed above poverty line are deriving benefits from the group projects. The district and block administration point out that it is impossible to exclude them from deriving benefit from the group project given the fact their land holdings fall within the project area. Again, they cannot be forced to contribute towards the construction cost.

The situation regarding MWS group projects is no better. It was found that group projects consisting of Anicuts or water Harvesting Structures are being taken up even in places where it has not rained in years. These appear to have been taken up to utilise MWS funds irrespective of what its benefits were going to be.

The quality of construction is equally questionable. Many beneficiaries complained about the poor quality of construction. DRDA Dungarpur has already entrusted the construction of group projects to the irrigation department. DRDA Udaipur has also initiated steps in this direction. Wherever group projects have been entrusted to the irrigation department, there is a turf war between the elected and government functionaries.

LESSONS TO BE LEARNT

The scope of open wells is rather limited in Rajasthan. First, there is a sharp decline in the groundwater table. Second, the economic condition of the beneficiary does not permit him to bear additional expenses. Extending canal irrigation facilities to larger areas appears to be a viable alternative. Steps may be taken to bring more areas under the Indira Gandhi Canal. At the same time attention should be paid to the warning from the CGWB regarding serious water logging.

Programmes should not be taken up just because there is money that has to be spent. It was found that feasibility and viability were the least important criteria for the selection of site for open wells as well as for Water Harvesting Projects. What mattered most was political connection. In many districts wells had been sanctioned in the name of Sarpanches themselves or their relatives.

During the course of the survey, many cases came to light where despite being on the BPL list and despite getting selected for MWS, many a small/marginal farmer has been excluded. The two reasons generally cited were: they had not backed the candidate who won the Sarpanchship and that the JE for some reason was not giving them the installment money. Many beneficiaries who had borrowed from moneylenders to start the work are now being harassed by them. Some has to sell their land/cattle to repay their loans.

The question of fixing accountability in the case of poor supervision has not been addressed so far. This issue becomes especially crucial in the case of political representatives who unlike government functionaries are not there on a permanent basis. Government functionaries who also have a stake in the successful execution of a programme are in many cases not available because of transfer to another place.

The actual cost of the well is much higher than what was assumed. They require blasting, boring and drilling operations as well. It may be noted that though wells required these operations, they could not be undertaken because of lack of finances at the disposal of the beneficiaries.

A major problem with the implementation process relates to technical assistance. A large group of beneficiaries (42.89%) indicated that they have not received technical assistance from any quarter. In fact, selection of site for digging of wells is not done on the basis of technical advice. Rather it is done on the advice of local 'Popas' who substitute remote sensing devices. To locate water, they use a herb, which is kept behind the ear, and then the person goes around the area. It is believed that the person can thus locate the exact place where water can be found. People appear to have more faith in traditional methods.

Though Jaipur has 12 out of its 13 blocks classified as "Dark Zone", the lion's share of MWS funds have gone to Jaipur district. Again, officials in Pali district admitted that MWS works are sanctioned even in areas declared as Dark Zone because of political pressure. The fact is unless the respective Sarpanch derives the maximum benefit from different schemes for his village; the Sarpanch's image suffers. Hence, irrespective of the viability of a scheme, each nonetheless gets to share the cake.

Reporting failed wells as "wells under construction" provides misleading feedback to the policy makers. In fact, the quality of monitoring by the Ministry of Rural Development is rather poor. Jodhpur district continued to receive funds for MWS projects even though it had stopped implementing MWS projects since 1993. It appears that the district-wise data on the performance of MWS was not reaching the Ministry of Rural Development. Utilisation Certificates for works started ten years ago were still pending.

Some lessons need to be learnt from MWS group projects in Rajasthan, which in many cases are being taken up without any benefit in sight. It was found that MWS group projects are being taken up in regions where it has not rained for years. These group projects need to be entrusted to technical departments like irrigation department. The shabby projects that have come up under the Sarpanch's supervision are not designed tolast. Luckily for the Sarpanch, the shabby work is not getting exposed since it hardly rains in a large part of Rajasthan. Group projects should be taken up only in places they are found viable. The tendency on the part of government is to run the same scheme but under a different name. Unfortunately, the problems fail to disappear with a change in name.

REFERENCES

1. *Human Development Report,* 2000.
2. *Census of India,* 1991.
3. Government of India, *Annual Report 2001-02,* Ministry of Rural Development, p. 41.
4. *Ground Water Year Book,* Rajasthan, 1998-99, Central Ground Water Board, Ministry of Water Resources, 1999, p. 5.
5. *Ground Water Year Book,* Rajasthan, 1998-99, *op cit.*
6. *Ibid.*, p. 7.
7. *Ibid.*, p. 8.
8. *Ibid.*, pp. 29-30.
9. *Ground Water Year Book,* Rajasthan, 1998-99, *op cit.*, p. 42.
10. R.J. Fisher, *If Rain Doesn't Come: An Anthropological Study of Drought and Human Ecology and Human Ecology in Western Rajasthan,* New Delhi, Manohar Publications, 1997, p. 13.
11. James Tod and William Crooke, *Annals and Antiquities of Rajasthan,* Delhi, Low Price Publications, Reprinted 1995, p. 1258.
12. *Ibid.*, pp. 1304-05.
13. *Ground Water Year Book,* Rajasthan, 2000-2001, *op cit.*, p. ix.
14. Sujata Singh, *Concurrent Evaluation of Million Wells Scheme in Rajasthan,* New Delhi, IIPA, 2000, p. 38.
15. Sujata Singh, *op cit.*, pp. 42-43.
16. Sujata Singh, *op cit.*, p. 50-51.
17. Sujata Singh, *op cit.*, p. 5
18. *Ibid.*, p. 60-61.
19. *Ibid.*, p. 86.
20. Sujata Singh, *op cit.*, p. 64.
21. *Ibid.*, p. 73.
22. Sujata Singh, *op cit.*, pp. 73-74.

SECTION VI: IRRIGATION AND PARTICIPATORY IRRIGATION MANAGEMENT

22

Political Economy of Irrigation in India

N.R. Hota

Irrigation is a state subject and except for inter-state utilisation or disputes in regard to river waters, the Centre has practically no control over water-use. Water is also a vital input for agriculture. Thus, the control of water resources and their use gives the State Governments tremendous political power over the economic life of the people in general and the vast majority of the agricultural class in particular.

POLITICAL ECONOMY OF IRRIGATION AGRICULTURE

The utilisation of water has also been conceived in various forms. The ancient and traditional forms of irrigation were through inundation, to which, with improvement in technology, were slowly added tine forms of lift irrigation from wells and streams by means of muscle or animal power with the help of simple gadgets like buckets, baskets, rope, wooden lever (Tenda) and Persian wheel, etc. Further improvements in technology made it possible to have barrages and dams to control the storage, as well as use of mechanical and electrical pumping devices, with the use of diesel or power. The latest in technology are sprinkler irrigation and the seeding of clouds, which simulate natural rainfall to meet the water requirements of crops.

The importance of irrigation in agriculture in Asia can be summed up in the words of Hideo Yamamoto as follows: "Water determines whether there is a harvest or not; fertiliser determines whether the harvest is big or small".[1] This situation applies as effectively to India as perhaps to any other part of Asia. Extremes of dry or high rainfall conditions in India—both make artificial control and use of water essential for agricultural development—much more in fact than fertilisers, improved or hybrid seeds, improved technology or cultural practices. Irrigation can thus be termed as the essential and primary stage of agricultural development, which is to be followed with the intensive stage of new technologies in fertilisation, seeds, weed control, etc.

The very nature of watershed management, involving large-scale construction and management of water-harvesting structures, appears to have made irrigation the sovereign state's prerogative since ancient times, often linked with the despotic rule of monarchs, who used to appropriate the generated surplus. The peasants thus lost initiative in production of surpluses, which they visualised not as fruits of their own labour, but as results of sovereign munificence. Thus, initiative in production was lost, resulting in stagnation in agriculture.[2] The degeneration and fall of despotism left the rural communities helpless. The colonial period-that followed, introduced the concept of private property against community ownership, thus making investments in irrigation by the village community difficult. In any case, high cost river control works required a higher degree of capital formation, which was beyond the farmer or the village community. Even the state was not prepared for such investments in the colony. When Independence came, the need to make public investments in irrigation by the Central and the State Governments became quite apparent. Independence aroused the aspirations of the people for their own sovereign state to take up this function of development again. Besides, in terms of providing work, wages and income in the short-run and increased agricultural production in the long-run, there is no better programme for India's rural community than the development of irrigation. It was, thus, potentially an extremely useful tool in the hands of the political system for winning popularity and franchise and in dispersing a share of the developmental expenditure in the countryside.

Table 1 given below shows the progress made in irrigation, in the country since Independence.

Table 1: Progress in Development of Irrigation in India since Independence

Period	*Outlays/Expenditure (in crore of rupees)*			*Potential Created (million hectares)*		*Cumulative Potential (million hectares)*
	Major and Medium	*Minor*	*Total*	*Major and Medium*	*Minor*	
Pre-plan	–	–		9.7	12.9	22.6
First Plan	380	76	456	12.20	14.06	26.26
Second Plan	380	142	522	14.30	14.79	29.09
Third Plan	581	328	909	16.60	17.01	33.61
Annual Plans (1966-69)	434	326	760	18.10	19.00	37.10
Fourth Plan (1969-74)	1237	513	1750	20.70	23.50	44.20
Fifth Plan (1974-78)	2442	631	3073	24.82	27.30	52.12
Annual Plans (1978-80)	2072	497	2569	26.60	30.00	56.60
Sixth Plan (1980-81)	1225	284	1509	27.55	31.40	58.95

Table 1 shows how during the entire pre-plan period (about 350 years of colonial rule), the irrigation potential created in India was limited to 22.6 million hectares (m.h.), out of the total potential of 107 m.h., constituting thereby a developmental effort of only 21.12 per cent of the available potential. On the other hand, during a period of 30 years of planned development (1950-80), the potential has been raised to 56.60 m.h., *i.e.*, 52.89 per cent of the potential available. The net percentage of increase in 30 years is thus 31.77, which is about 1.5 times more than what had been accomplished during 350 years of colonial rule in India. This clearly shows the influence of political factors in the macro-level development of the irrigation economy in the country. Besides, the race of growth of potential/outlay during the planning era can also be seen in Table 2 from one plan period to another.

Table 2: Growth of Irrigation during Plan Periods in India

(per cent)

Period	*Potential Growth*	*Outlay Growth*
Pre-plan	22.6 m.h.(base)	N A
First Plan	16.19	456 CR (base)
Second Plan	10.77	14.47
Third Plan	15.53	74.13
Annual Plans (1966-69)	10.38	-16.40
Fourth Plan (1969-74)	19.13	130.26
Fifth Plan	17.91	75.60
Annual Plans (1978-80)	8.59	-22.93

Another interesting reason behind such huge state investments is the fact that in every country, including India, the capital cost of irrigation, per hectare of area irrigated, is increasing and thereby bringing such projects more and more within the state's patronage and cutting out possibilities of investments by individual farmers and village communities. Table 3 shows how steep is the rise in per hectare cost of irrigation in different plan-periods in India.

Table 3: Rise in Per Hectare Cost of Irrigation in India during Plan Periods

Period	*Expenditure (in million rupees)*	*Actual Potential Created (in million hectares)*	*Capital Cost p.h. of Potential (in rupees)*
First Plan	3760	3.66	1027.32
Second Plan	5410	2.83	1911.66
Third Plan	10240	4.52	2265.48
Annual Plans (1966-69)	7950	3.49	2277.93
Fourth Plan (1969-74)	24110	7.1	3395.77
Fifth Plan (1974-78)	38530	7.9	4877.21
1978-82	68470	9.47	7230.20

These higher investments require a high level of capital formation and thus give the state greater powers in deciding which projects to select and where to locate them, in keeping with the interests of the political system.

IDENTIFICATION AND SELECTION OF PROJECTS

"Another part of the political economy of irrigation relates to identification and selection of projects. Here, one naturally comes to the streams of costs and benefits or a kind of productivity/financial test. The Royal Commission on Irrigation (1901) was the first body to examine if the financial test was too rigorous and if indirect benefits of irrigation to the Government/people were to be accounted for on the stream of benefits. The Commission finally recommended retention of the financial productivity test. The financial productivity of a project was to be determined as shown below:

(Year X)

Debit	Credit
1. Interest on capital cost as on year of commencement	1. Direct receipts (water rates or charges, rents, fines and Miscellaneous receipts under the Canal Acts).
Plus	Plus
2. Working expenses	2. Indirect receipts (share of enhanced land revenue, interest on sale proceeds of government wasteland, rents from temporary cultivation of Government wasteland, revenue from trees on wasteland, etc.).

Credit minus debit was to show a return on investment of 4 per cent prior to April 1, 1919, 5 per cent up to August 1, 1921 and 6 per cent thereafter. It was refixed after Independence, at 3.75 per cent with effect from April 4, 1949 and at 4.5 per cent after August 1954.

While this financial productivity test remained on the books, in actual practice, to quote K. Puttaswamaiah, "Since 1947, the financial productivity test has not been applied very strictly and projects are generally being sanctioned on the basis of other considerations."[3] He lists out a number of irrigation projects in different states, which were sanctioned by the Planning Commission during the First and Second Five Year-Plans below the productivity test of 4.5 per cent return.[4] It is invariably the 'indirect benefits' or 'multiplier effects' argument (employment, transport, public revenue, etc.) that is thus used in sanctioning projects outside the approved financial criteria or norms, apart from public romanticism and the obvious potential of large irrigation projects for electoral speeches. Colin Clark,' who was Economic Advisor to the Government of Queensland in Australia, Mentions the case of hopelessly uneconomic irrigation project which that government attempted to justify (before he resigned) by setting against its annual cost, "the expected entire gross product of the farms, as if not only labour and enterprise of farmers, but also fertilisers, equipment, transport, etc., were to be had free."[5]

Even now, the Planning Commission in India does not have any strict criterion for sanctioning 'irrigation projects. The projects are examined by the Central Water Commission and the Technical Advisory Committee from broad aspects and a view is taken to recommend them to the Planning Commission.[6] In the final plan discussions between the Deputy Chairman, Planning Commission and the State Chief Ministers, certain adjustments are made and sometimes specific schemes are also mentioned.[7] Since irrigation is a state subject and Central assistance is not tied to any individual project/sector, many State Governments are found to take up execution of certain schemes even prior to their sanction by the Planning Commission, thus pre-empting the latter from sanctioning them sooner or later. "In several cases, the approval of the Planning Commission/Ministry of Irrigation was accorded 3-5 years after commencement of work."[8] The Public Accounts Committee, in its 141st report, however, has recommended that plan projects should be selected in such a manner that "returns, financial, economic and social, on utilisation of our scarce resources, are maximised.[9] See the emphasis on social returns along with financial and economic returns. Obviously, this committee also could not rule out considerations of political economy/ and say that projects should be selected entirely on cost-benefit analysis.

The benefits of irrigation are localised in the farmers' fields in the Ayacut area and, therefore, the smaller a project or the closer it is to the farmers' fields, the greater is its impact on the beneficiaries. It is for this reason that a dugwell, a tubewell or a minor irrigation tank, fire enthusiasm of farmers more than a medium or major irrigation project. Again, due to short gestation period, these modes of irrigation need a low level of capital formation and yield benefits quickly. Puttaswamaiah argues on these considerations that future policy on irrigation "should have an accent on minor irrigation with a modification to the effect that the large and medium projects should also be taken up when the Exchequer is having safe breathing."[10]

While minor irrigation is more populist, major and medium irrigation projects are perhaps hydrologically more stable and less prone to failure in lean years of rainfall. The overall cost-benefit ratio of larger dams is also perhaps more attractive than many of the minor irrigation projects. Carruthers gives the following range of costs for West Pakistan (conversion of one rupee = 25 c)[11]:

	Costs (c/m³)
River Diversion	-0.08–0.20
Canal Remodelling	-0.20–0.32
Surface Storage	-0.32–0.45
Tubewells	-0.45–0.81

In India, cost of irrigation water from large dams and barrages varies from 0.13 to 1.35 (c/m^3) at 10 per cent capital cost.[12] An enquiry in village Danda in Gujarat in 1968 showed cost of water from wells at 1.1 (c/m^3).[13] These show that river diversion and surface storage works are on the whole economically more attractive.

Since it is a question of proper allocation of state resources over competing demands, generally it is better to follow the economic criterion in sanctioning the projects on the basis of their cost-benefit ratio, whether they are major, medium or minor irrigation schemes. This would ensure that the most economically remunerative schemes are taken up for execution and thus the influence of non-economic factors on choice of projects and their location can face substantially reduced. Since dugwells and tubewells require low level of capital, it will also be useful to promote private initiative in their development, and the nationalised banks can play a useful role; in providing credit for such purpose. The state support has, of course, to come by way of groundwater surveys and rural electrification, wherever substantial tubewell development is feasible, and is taken up through emerging private initiative. The working of public sector lift irrigation corporations in many states strengthens such a policy imperative. Such development can also De linked up with a scheme of subsidy for pumpsets, drilling expenses, electricity tariff, etc., for small and marginal farmers or farmers below the poverty line.

The Irrigation Commission (1972) had recommended that the cost-benefit ratio be adopted, in addition to the financial return criterion in sanctioning irrigation projects. They had also suggested that cost of Ayacut development should be included in the cost stream. So far, both these suggestions have not been implemented. The internal rate of return criterion is also not being applied. In fact, to quote the Planning Commission, "There is no regular system of assessing actual economic return of irrigation project."[14] In case of irrigation projects sponsored by international lending institutions, mainly the IDA, the cost-benefit ratio is taken as 1:1.5 and is even relaxed in certain cases.[15]

The Public Accounts Committee has, therefore, recommended in its 141st report that, as in case of public sector industrial projects, suitable investment criterion based on economic return should be adopted for all irrigation projects. The cost stream should take care of all costs, like all inputs for agricultural development and the cost of Ayacut development. There should also be a quinquennial post-facto evaluation of the actual economic returns *vis-à-vis* the estimated one.

This inevitably raises the question of social benefits, which form part of the socio-political ethos. Sometimes, these can be quantified and built into the cost-benefit ratio, and sometimes they can only be appropriately considered. Any practical administrator would easily see that such considerations cannot completely be ignored. Where no other means of irrigation is available, say the Rajasthan Canal Project area, the social value of such an irrigation project is bound to be very high. A classic case in this regard is the Canalisation Project taken up in River Swat in the erstwhile NWFP (now in Pakistan) in 1884 by the British Government. The military authorities felt that the inhabitants of this area were raiding their neighbours and leading generally a turbulent life because they did not have any stable livelihood throughout the year. So the Canal Project was sanctioned at a very high cost of $ 150 per hectare at that time. After the canalisation was completed, Swat became a peaceful agricultural settlement and the people were completely transformed. Such considerations should, therefore, as far as possible, have to be built into the examination of cost-benefit ratios in sanctioning irrigation projects. Economists have been trying to achieve greater sophistication in working out social cost-benefit ratios of projects[16] which no doubt would aid the pragmatic administrators in adoption of workable norms for sanctioning irrigation projects.

UTILISATION OF POTENTIAL

This 'terre-capital-formation' in irrigation in the public sector, as it has been appropriately described by Akira Tamaki, has, however, to be converted into actual 'productive power' by a process of internalisation of investment for operation of individual farms.[17] This raises a number of issues like: (*i*) change in the agricultural environment of individual farms; (*ii*) technical adaptability of producers and motivation for the same; (*iii*) construction of field channels and control of water use; and (*iv*) all these having important bearings on utilisation of potential.

Large irrigation projects invariably have built-in mechanism for flood control and drought prevention through the creation of suitable reservoir capacity, and thus have the effect of changing the agricultural environment of individual farms, which were earlier exposed to the vagaries of nature. Besides, sometimes, the farm environment is completely altered with irrigation water, as it happened, for instance, in the Command Area of the Hirakud Dam Project. The 'banal' and 'berna' lands, which were deep paddy lands, became waterlogged with irrigation and lost productivity while the 'aat' and 'mal' lands, which were highlands, became more productive with irrigation and with better drainage that these lands already had.

Often, there is also a time lag between creation of irrigation potential and its utilisation by the producers in the Ayacut, since the latter need to be adapted to conditions of irrigated agriculture, through education and experience, which take sometime. I had the occasion of working as a DDO in the Ayacut area of the Hirakud Dam Project in the year 1961-62 when the IADP was taken up in that area. In my experience, it was seen that a lot of extension effort was required to educate the farmers in water-use and it practically took a decade to ensure full and proper utilisation of irrigation water in the entire Command Area. One even had to fight a superstitious belief that the water had become all useless for irrigation after generation of electricity. The need for the use of a package of practices, including fertilisers, improved seeds, improved agricultural practices had to be painstakingly sold to individual farmers. The importance of proper water-use and water-control for effective absorption of chemical fertilisers, particularly the need for construction of water-courses rather than using the traditional method of field-to-field inundation, had to be explained.

Motivation also becomes an important factor for technical adaptability of farmers, and is linked with the question of the land-tenure system. Unless the producers own the land and are sure that the fruits of improved production will go to them, they will not have any interest in converting irrigation water to productive power in their individual farms. To quote K.N. Kabra, "In an irrigation project, the additional output is raised by a large number of farmers on farms of varying size, under diverse tenurial conditions. The farmers also display many other socio-economic differences having a bearing on their response to and capacity of using new irrigation facilities. It is on account of such factors that there emerges a timelag between the availability of irrigation facilities and their actual use."[18]

Lag in utilisation results, among others, from:

1. Improper planning and execution of projects, due to which the headworks are completed much ahead of the canal system;
2. Lack of synchronisation of Command Area Development works like land-level ling, drainage, construction of field channels and water courses, etc. with availability of canal water at "the outlet points; and
3. Lack of a proper system of distribution of water or supervision over water-use.

Before the beginning of the planning era, India had a created irrigation potential of 22.67 m.h. (9.7 under major arid medium and 12.9 under minor irrigation) with only two major storage dams at Mettur and Krishnaraj Sagar. During 30 years of planning beginning from 1951-82, a sum of Rs. 16,047 crore has been invested (Rs. 10,090 crore on major and medium and Rs. 5,951 crore on minor irrigation, including institutional outlay of Rs. 2,840 crore). The cumulative target for creation of potential was 59.57 m.h. (29.10 m.h. under major and medium and 30.47 m.h. under minor irrigation). The actual potential created has been only 38.98 m.h. (18.98 m.h. under major and medium and 20 m.h. under minor irrigation). Thus, the total shortfall in creation of potential has been nearly 33 per cent.

The analysis available for major and medium projects reveals that the gap between target and achievement of potential has been considerably narrowed down during the fifth Plan and thereafter, as may be seen from Table 4.[20]

Table 4: Gaps between Targets and Achievements during Plan Periods

	Potential	
	Target	*Achievement (million hectares)*
First Plan	3.4	2.5
Second Plan	4.2	2.1
Third Plan	5.2	2.3
Annual Plans (1966-69)	2.5	1.5
Fourth Plan (1969-74)	2.8	2.5
Fifth Plan (1974-79)	5.8	4.2 (1974-78)
1978-79	-	1.04} 5.16
1979-80	1.13	1.02

As is apparent from the table, the overall position, however, , still remains unsatisfactory.

Stronger political will and administrative support are necessary to improve the economy of irrigation by reducing this lag between potential and utilisation to the unavoidable minimum. The Ministers" Committee set up. in 1973 to study this problem of under-utilisation of created irrigation potential, recommended comprehensive measures, including establishment of Command Area Development Authorities for accelerating utilisation.[21] They also emphasised the need for special legal and financial measures for construction of field channels.[22] Command Area Development Authorities have been created in a number of completed and on-going projects on an experimental basis, with a charter to take up on farm development programmes, including construction of field channels and water courses. In certain states, such on-farm development schemes are being coordinated with consolidation of land holdings (as for example, Hirakud Command Area). Attempts are also being made to introduce warabandi (rotational-system of irrigation) in such Command Areas where it did not exist, with a view to improving utilisation of potential.

The progress achieved, however, is still unsatisfactory and a major thrust towards implementation of these programmes with earnestness is required.

WATER RATE POLICIES

The next important aspect of the political economy of irrigation is the question of water charges as related to the economic returns of the projects and the costs of operation and maintenance.

In India, water charges are fixed based on maintenance costs of the irrigation projects. Very often, these maintenance costs are themselves set quite low and even then are not recovered fully. Therefore, the World Bank has been insisting on revision of such water charges in cases of international funding for irrigation projects in India. But any increase in water charges is a highly politicised decision and is often taken on political rather than economic considerations. Sometimes, even the modest water charges, already in force, are not collected properly and political and administrative will for enforcing such collections is often found wanting.

Though many states have taken recourse to 'betterment levies" in the irrigated areas, in actual practice, it is seen that these laws have hardly been enforced and hence betterment levies have hardly been collected.

As a result, Government irrigation projects are incurring losses in regard to their gross receipts minus total expenditure on maintenance. The actuals of such losses for the year 1980-81 were worked out by the Planning Commission in May 1983 state-wise. There is no state which is not incurring a loss and some of the larger states, like Uttar Pradesh, Maharashtra and Andhra Pradesh are incurring higher losses. States like Orissa, which levy a compulsory basic water race on all ayacutdars in Khariff, show a smaller quantum of loss than other states, which charge for irrigation on the basis of crops or water supplied. In fact, assessments run into difficulties in cases of crop-wise or acre-inchwise charges for irrigation water. Assessments and collections also run into trouble in view of the duality in administration, *i.e.*, water is supplied by the Irrigation/PWD authorities and certification of area irrigated and assessment and collection of water charges is done by the revenue authorities. This duality often suits the beneficiaries and populist Governments and any administration which attempts to raise the water charges or even to collect them effectively, is derided as anti-people. Thus, supply of irrigation water has to reckon with large hidden subsidies by Government to the beneficiaries, at the cost of a large majority of people living outside the irrigated zones (the subsidies are paid out of their tax contributions). The coverage of irrigation on an all-India basis is about 30 per cent of the total cultivable lands and the population benefited may also be around 25-30 per cent.

The range of charges for water according to use, even in USA, shows a hidden subsidy for irrigation (though lesser than power and waste disposal). This is evident from Table 5.[23]

The Planning Commission observed before the 141st PAC that "the main reason for the losses in irrigation projects is that 'water rates are not being revised in keeping with the increasing cost of irrigation."[24] Despite emphasis on this aspect in every Five-Year Plan, every Finance Commission Report, Report of the Irrigation Commission (1972), and the Report of the Raj Committee on Taxation of Agricultural Wealth and

Income, the State Governments have been quite tardy in responding to any upward revision of water rates. Only Orissa and Rajasthan, were able to cover their 'working expenses by the end of 1982-83.[25]

Table 5

Type of Use	*Charges in c/m³*	
	Average	*Maximum*
Domestic	9.0	21.2
Industrial	3.6	14.8
Irrigation	0.15	2.43
Power	0.06	0.53
Waste disposal	0.06	0.23

In 1945-46, *i.e.*, before Independence, the return from irrigation schemes was Rs. 7.93 crore on an investment of Rs. 149 crore, *i.e.*, 5.3 per cent. This came down to Rs. one crore the following year and after Independence, the irrigation and multipurpose projects have been consistently showing losses, as shown in Table 6.[26]

Table 6: Losses in Irrigation and Multi-Purpose Projects

(*in crore Rs.*)

Year	*Losses*
1975-76	154.60
1981-82	424.75
1975-76 to 1981-82 (cumulative)	2053.00

The PAC, in its 141st Report, has, therefore, observed, "this situation cannot and should not be allowed to continue" and has found "no reason why the big landowners who are the principal beneficiaries of the irrigation facilities, should continue to be subsidised any longer, though it may be justified in case of small and marginal farmers and share-croppers."[27]

In the Command Areas of large irrigation projects, there is need to evolve a commercial cropping pattern to consume the large water potential created. In the process, substantial agriculturists, who are often the most adaptable, organised and vocal and have access to centres of political power and patronage, come to control the water and its uses, thereby depriving the bulk of the poorer sections from the benefits of water. These people often join hands with the canal administration in cornering benefits for themselves and also oppose any move to raise the water rates."[28] A progressive administration has to break this vicious nexus of power and bring the economic benefits of irrigation to the common people in the Command Areas.

In India, while major and medium irrigation projects are treated as commercial schemes, minor irrigation projects are not yet treated as such. This is economically not rational since irrigation water is a commercial product and irrespective of the source, the society has a right to get an adequate return from such investment. A rational water-rate policy is, therefore, necessary to ensure an adequate social return on the investment in irrigation. The shadow-pricing of water does not help us in fixing an economic water charge, since the alternative use of such abundant water is often not. available near the points of storage or diversion or lifting. Therefore, a rational water rate policy has at least to ensure that the costs or operation and maintenance are recovered, even if there is no return on the capital invested. Since irrigation projects are basically infrastructure projects, a return on capital can perhaps be sought in the multiplier effects that this investment generates in the economy.

REFERENCES

1. Akira Tamaki, The Development Theory of Irrigation Agriculture, Tokyo, IDE, p. 1.
2. *Ibid*. This concept, extremely well developed by Akira Tamaki, has been adapted from his writing.
3. K. Puttaswamaiah, Irrigation Projects in India—Towards a New Policy, p. 30.
4. *Ibid*., Table 2, p. 78. This list shows that 88 out of 114 projects approved by the Planning Commission were below the productivity criteria.
5. Colin Clark, The Economics of Irrigation, pp. 56-57.
6. The Public Accounts Committee (PAC), (1982-83), One Hundred and Fortyfirst Report on Irrigation Projects, p. 7.
7. *Ibid*., p. 4.
8. *Ibid*., p. 51.
9. *Ibid*., p. 51.
10. K. Puttaswamaiah, *op. cit*., p. 43.
11. Colin Clark, *op. cit*., p. 59.
12. *Ibid*., pp. 130-131.
13. *Ibid*., p. 31.
14. 141st PAC Report, *op. cit*., p. 114.
15. *Ibid*., p. 114.
16. K.N. Kabra, "A Case Study in Social Cost-Benefit Analysis: Kallada Irrigation Project", Paper presented at EDI, Washington.
17. Akira Tamaki, *op. cit.*
18. K.N. Kabra, *op. cit*., p. 24.
19. 141st PAC Report, *op. cit*., p. 46.
20. *Ibid*., p. 23.
21. Report of the Ministers' Committee on Underutilisation of Created Irrigation Potential, June, 1973, Part I, p. 58.
22. *Ibid*., p. 46.
23. Colin Clark, *op. cit*., p. 115.
24. 141st PAC Report, *op. cit*., p. 131.
25. *Ibid*., p. 132.
26. *Ibid*., pp. 135-136.
27. *Ibid*., p. 136.
28. N.S. Joshi and B.R. Dhakney, Irrigation and Agriculture in the First Five Year Plan: An Appraisal, Vol. II, p. 160.

23

Promoting Water-Users Associations for Participatory Irrigation Management—Some Reflections

Rakesh Hooja

INTRODUCTION

Participatory Irrigation Management (PIM) is now being recommended world over as a solution for many problems of designing and operating irrigation systems in a sustainable manner, India's National Water Policy of 1987 had also recommended such efforts based on creation of associations of water-users. However, it is only with the organisation of a National Conference on PIM by the Government of India in June 1995 that a real impetus has been given to this work throughout the country. Before that, we only had some isolated cases of water-users bodies associating with irrigation bureaucracy in the management of irrigation schemes. During 1995-96, 16 regional conferences on PIM were organised throughout the country and a large-scale training programme was also sponsored by the Ministry of Water Resources. Pilot projects have been initiated at many places, including Rajasthan, and much thinking is being generated about legal, technical, organisational and viability related issues which, may influence the success or failure of joint irrigation management efforts whereby water-users bodies and the irrigation (or Command Area Development—CAD) bureaucracy may come together into partnerships of various sorts for managing irrigation schemes.

In the above-said context, this author proposes to set forth his personal views (based on experience of managing CAD schemes, perusal of relevant literature regarding PIM in India and abroad, and attending some workshops, seminars and conferences) on how to propagate Water-User's Associations (WUAs), and makes them successful in the context of one Indian state, *i.e.*, Rajasthan. It is felt that the suggestions being set forth here would be applicable throughout India and may also perhaps have relevance for much of the developing world.

However, as a word of caution, it may be added that while farmers'. participation in irrigation management may help solve many problems, it is not a panacea for *all* the difficulties that may be encountered in managing irrigation schemes. Many issues would have purely technical solutions. Many others would be such as may require governmental action, either directly within the irrigation system management or in the form of influencing the broader environment within which the irrigation system is functioning. However, successful implementation of PIM in India would go a long way towards improved water management and better irrigation system management with all the resultant benefits.

PROMOTING WUAS FOR PIM—AN APPROACH

Functions of WUA

Identification of Functions

There should be no uniform prescription of what tasks a WUA should perform. Each WUA should be free to evolve its own idea of the tasks that it may want to perform through a process of learning from its experience as it experiments with the various responsibilities that it may decide to take upon itself. WUAs or Farmers' Water Management Committees accordingly take up some or all from amongst the following functions:

1. Water distribution, rotational canal running and *Warabandi*—ensuring that water reaches all members as per their due share;
2. Operation and maintenance, and collection (and assessment) of water charges and other special charges that WUAs may levy;
3. Resolution of local disputes amongst members—if necessary setting up of an internal system of penalties and other disincentives or incentives;
4. Agriculture extension and farmers training;
5. Management of inputs and credit supply to members;
6. Irrigation extension and propagation of better on-farm water application and better intra-outlet command water management;
7. Recommending of cropping patterns suitable for WUA farmers;
8. Encouraging and taking up of conjunctive water use, or community lift irrigation, and charging for the same if done on a community basis;
9. Drainage;
10. Provision of drinking water from canals;
11. Soil testing/water quality testing;
12. Post harvest practices (grading, packaging, storage, and marketing);
13. Design and construction of new works (irrigation works, OFD works, drainage works) as well as rehabilitation or deferred maintenance works;
14. Maintenance of commercial, financial and water accounting records; and
15. Any other task as agreed upon by the members.

Flexibility According to the Nature of a WUA

Of course, every WUA would perforce be performing the function of providing an interface between the farmers and the government agencies

In fact, the nature of a particular WUA would depend not only upon the manner in which it gets initiated and the quality of the prime movers behind the formation of the WUA, but also on many other factors.

One such factor could be whether the WUA is being set up in a system which is managed by an integrated, multidisciplinary CAD organisation or whether the WUA would have to separately interact with the irrigation department, the agriculture department, the ground water department, the rural development agency, the land revenue administration and other government departments and agencies working in the command area of the irrigation system.

Another factor could' be whether or not the *Warabandi* system and a *Warabandi* culture already exists in the irrigation project. The example of Chambal-Rajasihan CAD Project informs us that the achievements can be much more dramatic when a WUA comes up in an area lacking in a tradition of *Warabandi* in that in the Arnetha WUA the water saving was substantial (a education of 32 days of watering from 79 days to 47 days) as was the increase in area cultivated (an increase of 145 acre from 660 acre to 805 acre). However, in an area where *Warabandi* already exists, the initial impact may not be so dramatic. However, even in such areas, scope exists for better water management which could lead to more optimal returns for individual members of the WUA as also for the WUA as a whole, based on more equitable and dependable water supplies.

Similarly, a WUA set up before construction starts (the WUA can comment on the need for modification in the designs and oversee the construction and then continue with other tasks), would behave in a very different manner from a WUA set up after construction (which would be more concerned with operation, maintenance and sustainability of the operations).

Of course, a WUA functioning only below the canal outlet level would operate very differently from the one operating above the outlet level, or from the one trying to deal with issues both above and below the outlet through either a system of sub-committees for each WUA created for each outlet command, or a system of a federation of WUAs below the outlet coming together to deal with coming issues relating to a minor or a branch canal.

Flexibility According to the Form of WUA

The flexibility that should be allowed to a WUA to determine its own functions should also be extended to the form of organisation that a WUA wants to create or adopt for itself. There are those who feel that a WUA needs to be a legal entity from is very inception. Hence, one comes across advocates of WUA registering as either a cooperative society, or as a registered society under the Registration of Societies Act or as a company. Others suggest that the CAD Department or the Irrigation Department should formulate its own separate rules for registration of WUAs. On the other hand, many prospective members of WUAs seem to prefer setting up of an informal group, a step also recommended by many irrigation and rural development administrators, experts, and NGOs. The problem of registration as a cooperative, or as a registered society or as a company is that the concerned registering body is not attuned to the problems of irrigation and water management. Hence, the bye-laws for such registration and the system of related inspections may eventually end up hindering the WUA rather than helping it to perform its tasks, Further, by registering a WUA at the onset, the members would restrict or limit the scope of the WUA from evolving, growing, taking up new functions and new organisational structures. It may be appropriate to suggest that prospective members first set up an informal group and later on register it with either Registrar of Cooperatives or Registrar of Societies or Registrar of Companies or with the concerned authority of the Irrigation Department or CAD Department as the case may be. One alternative could also be to permit the cooperative officer in the CAD project or any other designated officer of the CAD or irrigation or Agriculture Department to be authorised to register WUAs as cooperative societies. However (whether an informal group or a body registered somewhere), the WUA should be recognised by the CAD Department or by the Irrigation Department (as the case may be) for purposes of receiving water from the project/department. For this, a Memorandum of Understanding (MOU) (specifically designed for each WUA with ample scope for flexibility and change, based on experience of working the MOU) between the CAD or Irrigation Department and the WUA should form part of the recognition provided to the WUA. If the MOU is not with an integrated CAD Department, then a MOU with the Irrigation Department and Supplementary MOUs with the Agriculture and Ground Water, etc. Department, may also need to be signed.

Since the WUA would need to have some rights to receive a certain supply of water, the WUA should invariably be based on a hydrologically based area unit (outlet command, minor canal command) and should have at least 60 per cent of the area of the command and 60 per cent of the farmers represented on it with the; right of all other farmers in the command to join the WUA remaining inalienable: The WUA could, of course, differentiate between members and non-members as regards charging of fees and provision of services and benefits. However, all members and non-members would have a right to receive their share of the water, with non-members being charged a slightly higher rate since they would not be contributing to the WUAs management.

A mechanism for arbitration of disputes, if any, between the Government department officials and the WUA would also need to be evolved. Here also, if it is an integrated CAD Project, the differences would need resolving between only one Government agency, that is the CAD Project and the WUA. For non-integrated projects, the Government side to the dispute could be the irrigation or agriculture or land revenue, etc. departments, or a combination of some or all of them and the arbitration mechanism would need to be much more complex.

Canal Management and Other Functions

As WUAs take over many functions of management of canals, the Government CAD Department or the Irrigation Department (as the ease may be) would have to gear itself to look more to construction and management of dams and the main canal system (perhaps even to construction of minor canals and to OFD and drainage works), providing technical advice, training, introduction of new technologies, major repairs (if required), creation of an organisation for interfacing between the WUA and the Government and for motivating or catalysing formulation of WUAs. etc. Here, again, while for an integrated CAD Project various functional wings of the CAD organisation could be geared and coordinated for bringing about PIM, for unintegrated projects a number of departments would have to be reoriented to deal with PIM. (It may be added that in Rajasthan. CAD Projects have integrated organisations consisting of Irrigation, Agriculture. Extension. Agriculture Research, On-farm Development. Ground Water. Cooperatives, Drinking Water. Afforestation, Roads, Settlers' Motivation, Drainage. Planning and Monitoring, and related wings, all working under a single project organisation which reports to a separate CAD and Water Utilisation Department at State Government level.)

The WUAs would need to be permitted to fix and levy water charges which are not lower than the Government fixed water rates as also to fix other service and user charges for the WUA to levy.

Based on the performance of WUAs as regards all members (and non-members) receiving their due shares of water even at the tail of the canal, or of canals being maintained up to a particular minimum standard previously agreed upon between WUA and Government or (where the WUA also undertakes recovery of irrigation charges) upon the percentage of recoveries made, some proportion of the receipts to Government of irrigation charges should be returned to the WUA for the tasks to be taken up by it.

Many WUAs would function with the Government continuing to manage, operate and maintain the canals. However, some WUAs would be willing to take over a particular canal(s). In such cases, either the government would have to bring the canal up to a particular standard before it is turned over to the WUA (conducting deferred maintenance and rehabilitation or modernisation of the canal, reduction or removal of oversized and unauthorised outlets, re-determining of canal capacity, fixing of tail guages and measuring devices, as well as proper outlets, *i.e.,* APMs. etc.) or government would have to suggest to the WUA and agree with it as to what sort of improvement would have to be undertaken by the WUA and, *in lieu* of such improvement to be taken up by the WUA, the Government would have to agree to make available to the WUA its share of the irrigation charges for a certain number of years. Government would also have to make available irrigation, agriculture and ground water, etc. related technical advice, and also perhaps some machinery, etc. to the WUAs if the WUA undertakes the canal rehabilitation and modernisation work. Major repairs would still have to continue as a Government responsibility, though minor repairs would be the responsibility of the WUA and if the government undertakes the same, then government should receive payment from the WUA for the work.

As regards deferred maintenance and rehabilitation/modernisation of canals, some pilot projects should be taken up where such rehabilitation precedes formation of the WUA but is taken up where farmers agree to form a WUA upon rehabilitation. Some other pilot projects would be taken up with WUAs being set up first and rehabilitation being subsequently considered, designed and undertaken by WUA and Government jointly. Such pilots would need to be taken up in both integrated CAD projects and in non-integrated projects, as the resultant experiences may differ.

MEETING WUA NEEDS—ROLE OF GOVERNMENT

The post turn-over role of the government *vis-a-vis* the WUA needs to be spelt out in quite some detail.

Role of Local Body

Experience also seems to show that the local (Panchayat) body and the WUA cannot be one and the same. The local body has many other non-irrigation related functions, and its boundaries also are not coterminous with the command areas of either a water course of a canal. Hence, local leaders have concerns and priorities that differ from (or may even come in conflict with) those of the WUA. Also, the interaction between members of WUAs needs to be more frequent and intense than the interaction of the local populace with a local panchayat body.

Hence, a desirable system of WUAs would be as follows:

WUA Below the Outlet

|

WUA Above the Outlet

|

(Possible Association or Federation of WUAs at Minor or Branch Level)

|

Representation of WUAs (as different from representation of local bodies, *Pradhans, Pramukhs* MLAs and MPs) in the Water Distribution or Water Regulation Committees

Role of CADA

For CAD Projects, in the Command Area Development Authority (CADA), in addition to representation of officers representing different secretariat-administrative departments and the executive-field departments and project officers, and Collectors, MPs, MLAs, *Pradhans, Pramukhs,* and nominated farmers, some representatives of the WUAs in the command area should also be made members. However, this would serve the purpose only for integrated CAD projects. For non-integrated irrigation schemes, perhaps a multidepartmental, multidisciplinary coordination committee. would need to be created for each irrigation scheme, or for a group of irrigation schemes in an area, and along with officers and some panchayat non-officials, representation of WUAs would need to be provided for in the multidisciplinary coordination committee.

Coordination of PIM Activities at State Level

At the State Government level, it would be desirable to have a PIM cell created at the Secretariat level in the Command Area and Water Utilisation Department. Two or three multidisciplinary PIM teams should also be created in the CAD and \VU Department which could be sent from project to project to motivate and facilitate the WUAs and to act as catalysts for PIM. These teams could be used to visit and service not only CAD Projects but also non-CAD Projects. For CAD Projects, the PIM cell in the CAD and WU Department would be the coordinating and nodal point for all PIM related activities. However, for the non-CAD Projects, the Irrigation, Agriculture and Ground Water Departments would also need to create an officer-in-charge for PIM in their executive departments to facilitate and propagate PIM. The PIM Cell of CAD Department and the PIM incharges in other departments could also interact with NGOs, experts, and retired officials regarding further steps to be taken to further PIM, The multidisciplinary PIM teams of CAD Department and the officer-in-charge of PIM in each other concerned department would have to work at creating local interface mechanisms between government and the WUA or the farmers in the Command area. NGOs could also prove helpful in this work. The CAD and WU Department should also coordinate PIM related training throughout the State.

A standing high-level Group for PIM has already been set up at the State Government level in many States, including Rajasthan, to ensure interdepartmental coordination.

SUMMING UP

Going by the experience of Chak Committees in CAD, IGNP and Catchment Committees in CAD-Chambal Rajasthan, it is also felt that there should not be any effort to create a large number of WUAs in a short time, nor try to hurriedly cover an entire project by WUAs. Thus, numerical targets for creation of WUAs should not be fixed, This would only lead to creation of associations on paper rather than that of effective WUAs. Instead, the effort should be to propagate PIM and to let effective WUAs emerge at their own speed, in their own style, with their own objectives and tasks as well as their own organisations. The effort should be that initially some pilot WUAs emerge in the integrated CAD Projects and similarly some pilot WUAs come into being in the non-CAD Projects. The experience with them would enable the government to reorient its working in such a manner that genuine irrigation agency-farmer partnerships in irrigation management may emerge.

Similarly, going by past experience, the effort should be to try and discourage formal elections within the WUAs but to try and have consensus based selection of WUA leaders to perform management functions. This may help to control emergence of factionalism amongst the members of the WUA and, thus contribute to greater sustainability.

Similarly, it has to be recognised that financial and infrastructural support may enable WUA to be initially created, but unless major social, institutional and HRD support is made available, sustainability would not be achievable. PIM must not be looked upon as a means to help canal or CAD officers in performing their duties, but as a measure to evolve a sustaining joint management partnership. It should be based not on departmentally or functionally segmented efforts and strategies, but upon a holistic, comprehensive and integrated multidisciplinary approach and strategy aimed at optimal use of precious water resources in the State.

SELECT READINGS

1. CAD and RAJ AD Project, *Workshop on Participatory Irrigation Management,* Kota 5-6 September Workshop Report. Kota, 1995 (mimeo)
2. E.W. Coward Jr. (ed.), *Irrigation and Agriculture Development in Asia.* Ithaca. Cornell University Press, 1980.
3. Government of India, *Proceedings of the National Conference on Participatory Irrigation Management,* New Delhi, June 19-23, 1995 (Ministry of Water Resources).
4. Government of India, *International Seminar on Participatory Irrigation Management, Mexico: Report of Indian Delegation,* New Delhi. Ministry of Water Resources, 1995.
5. R. Hooja, *Administrative Interventions in Rural Development.* Jaipur, Rawat, 1987.
6. R. Hooja, "Command Area Development and Development of Government: Thinking About Its Objectives and Components" in P.C. Mathur and R.K. Gurjar (ed.), *Land and Water Management in Arid Ecology,* Jaipur, Rawat, 1994.
7. R. Hooja, *Multi-disciplinary Management of Irrigation Schemes and the CAD Approach in India,* Jaipur, HCM RIPA, Occasional Paper No. 2, 1995
8. R. Hooja, *Integrated Irrigation Management,* Jaipur, Arihant. (forthcoming).
9. R. Hooja, A- Rai and S.N. Mathur, "Encouraging Farmers Participation in Management of Irrigation Systems in Rajasthan". *The Administrator.* Vol 21. No. 4. October-December, 1995.
10. Irrigation Support Project for Asia and The Near East (ISPAN), *Maharashtra—Policy Options for Participatory Irrigation Management,* 1994.
11. ISPAN, *Participation and Empowerment—An Assessment of Water User Associations in Asia and Egypt,* 1994.
12. C. Maloney and V.K. Raju, *Managing Irrigation Together,* New Delhi, Sage, 1994.
13. R. Meinzen-Dick *et al., Sustainable Water Users Associations – Lesson's from Literature, Review,* presented at World Bank Water Resources Seminar, Virginia (Landsdowne), USA, 1994.
14. R. Meinzen-Dick and M. Svendsen (eds.), *Future Directions for Indian Irrigation,* Washington, IFPRI, 1994.
15. A.D. Mohile and R.S. Pathak, "Theme Paper for National Workshop on Farmers Participation in Irrigation Systems", Roorkee, WRDTC, 1993.
16. N. Pant, "Farmers Organisation in Large Irrigation Projects", *Economic and Political Weekly,* 1986.
17. B.W. Parlin and M. Lusk (eds.). *Farmers Participation and Irrigation Organisation,* Colorado, Westview, 1991.
18. R.S. Pathak, *Farmers Participation on Irrigation Water Management,* New Delhi, Government of India. 1991
19. K.K. Singh (ed.). *Farmers in Management of Irrigation Systems.* Sterling, Delhi. 1991.
20. M.V.K. Sivamohan and C.A. Scott (eds.). *India—Irrigation Management Partnerships,* Hyderabad. Booklinks, 1994.
21. N.R. Uphoff, Mienzen-Dick and N. St. Julien, *Improving Policies and Programmes for Farmers Organisation,* Water Management System's Project. Paper 1, Cornell University, 1995.

24

Revisiting Participatory Irrigation Management in India

Rakesh Hooja

INTRODUCTION

The Middle of 2003 saw an international internet debate conducted through e-mail about the need to 'revisit' Participatory Irrigation Management (PIM) in India and do some soul searching about its status, lessons learnt, prospects, etc. It thus appears to be the appropriate time for one to pen his views on how PIM should be propagated and implemented in India.

Government of India's commitment to PIM and the encouragement of water management being undertaken with the help of Water Users Association (WUAs) is apparent from a perusal of its National Water Policy (2002), the documents related to its celebration of Freshwater Year 2003, the February 2003 booklet of the Ministry of Water Resources (MoWR) on *Vision for Integrated Waters Resources Development and Management*, as well as the agenda notes pertaining to "Command Area Development and PIM" prepared by Ministry of Water Resource Management (MoWR) for the 12th National Conference of Water Resources and Irrigation Ministers held on February 5, 2003.

Similarly many states, (which in the Indian Constitutional set-up have much more influence on whether PIM can be introduced and can work in the water management and irrigation sector) have references to PIM and WUAs in their water policies and irrigation related legislation. Andhra Pradesh (1997), Madhya Pradesh (2002) and Rajasthan (2000) have enacted Farmers Management of Irrigation Systems Acts (the latter two being modeled on APFMIS—The Andhra Pradesh Management of Irrigation Systems Act 1997). Bihar used its experience of the famous Paliganj Distributory WUA to provide for government distributaries, minors canals or water courses to be handed over to WUAs as per the Bihar Irrigation Act, 1997. Gujarat, Maharashtra, Orissa, Uttar Pradesh, Tamil Nadu and Karnataka are amongst the states that have been using the Societies Registration Act or Cooperative Societies Act for the formulation and regulation of WUAs-though now Tamil Nadu Farmers Management of Irrigation Systems Act 2000 has come into force and led to the need to transform the more than 1000 WUAs registered under the Tamilnadu Societies Registration Act 1975 to bring them under the fold of the new TNFMIS Act. Orissa has come up which have many years experience of pilot WUA projects have with the Orissa Pani Panchayat Bill and both Gujarat and Maharashtra have prepared drafts of PIM and WUA related Acts. Karnataka on the other hand brought about amendments through the Karnataka Irrigation and Certain other Laws (Amendment) Act 2000 in the Karnataka Irrigation Act 1965 and the Karnataka (Levy of Betterment Contribution and Water Rate) Act 1957 and have provided for WUAs and federations of WUAs to be registered under the Cooperative Societies Act.

However in actual practice even in the states which have gone in for PIM related legislation, the progress of adoption of PIM and the performance of PIM where adopted, has been uneven in terms of WUAs actually taking over water management functions as also in terms of improved water management.

What Should be Spelt Out in State-level Legislation on PIM in India

The month of November, 2002 saw the organisation of a workshop at WALMI, Aurangabad for discussing the draft Maharashtra Water Policy and two draft Bills including that of a proposed Maharashtra Farmers Management of Irrigation Systems Act, as also the statement of intent at a workshop in Kolkata on the irrigation components of the North Bengal Terai Development Project that the West Bengal Government would constitute a group to draft a Participatory Irrigation Management Act for West Bengal. A couple of months earlier, towards the end of September, the Task Force on Accelerating PIM in the state Through Legislative Approach constituted by Government of Gujarat prepared a final version of a PIM Act as drafted by it for consideration by the state government. Thus more and more states are contemplating the enactment of PIM related legislation.

As already indicated, PIM or Farmers Management of Irrigation Systems (FMIS) or Pani Panchayat Acts or related legislation dealing with transferring of management to WUAs presently stand promulgated in the states of Andhra Pradesh, Madhya Pradesh, Rajasthan, Kartanaka, Orissa, Bihar and Tamil Nadu. Of these, Madhya Pradesh and Rajasthan have modeled their Acts totally on the line of Andhra Pradesh and of the others only Karnataka appears to have followed a totally different approach of permitting flexibility along with legislation rather than going in for a uniform and 'big bang' approach as prescribed by law (for a comparison of these Acts see India NPIM Working Paper 11, 2002). Even Andhra Pradesh (whose PIM efforts are the most talked about in the country) found itself seriously examining the need for substantial amendments of its Acts within five years of its existence and took recourse to an ordinance to carry out amendments as their WUAs moved from first generation problems to second generation problems and it was realised that all the efforts through WUAs had still not resolved the problems of irrigation water supply. Madhya Pradesh has also gone in for amendments recently.

With PIM, or irrigation management transfer, being pushed by donor agencies as part of irrigation sector reform and being part of proclaimed water policies of Government of India and numerous states, it can be expected that more and more states would go in for PIM related legislation, and states already having such laws will consider major amendments as they experience and see the results of field level application of their PIM laws.

Thus many state governments water experts and bureaucrats are grappling at the present with issues about what should form part of PIM related laws. Accordingly it is appropriate to stimulate a debate on the matter by putting down my personal views (based upon many years of experience, study, reflection and writing that the author has done on irrigation systems and PIM) about what should be the components of state level legislations on PIM or Farmers Management of Irrigation Systems.

DEFINITION OF PIM IN INDIAN CONTEXT

A practical definition of PIM in the Indian context is that PIM involves a WUA taking over management (including operation and maintenance) of at least one level of canals above the outlet (*i.e.*, the minor canal) and also being associated with State Irrigation/Command Area Development (CAD)/Agriculture/Water Resources Department in efforts at improved and integrated water and agriculture management. Simultaneously PIM involves a redefinition and refocusing (and not a mere reduction or downsizing) of government's role in irrigation so as to lead to a genuine partnership or joint management between the government and WUAs. Thus PIM involves an approach based upon integrated and joint management of irrigation with the community (in the form of the WUA) and government agencies working together for equitable, rational, timely, and convenient allocation of water and increase in efficiencies both in canal management and on-field water application. The PIM approach allows for flexibility from region to region, irrigation system to irrigation system and even WUA to WUA. It can be applied to major, medium and minor irrigation and even to larger tank or lift irrigation systems.

PIM legislation should specify that regardless of whether the source is lift irrigation (from rivers or from community tubewells), or a tank system or a conventional irrigation system based upon storage and water distribution, wherever water is to be distributed among 30 or more farmers, the PIM and WUA approach should be mandatory.

The organisational structure of WUAs and functions would differ for small river lifts (RLIs) or tubewell lifts, from those for tank systems, or larger irrigation and CAD schemes, for RLIs and community tubewells a number of such contiguous schemes may be grouped into one WUA with each RLI or tubewell having a beneficially group sending one member to the management committee of the WUA. For regular irrigation or command area schemes each canal minor should have a WUA with two members each being provided for in the management committee from head, middle and tail areas respectively of the minor. Each of the head, tail and middle sections could have beneficiary groups covering the outlet (or *chak*) committees in the area. Water distribution below the outlet through water courses is in any case within the purview of the farmers and PIM legislation should instead focus on areas above the outlet from the minor.

In case of very small minors having small commands two minors could be grouped into one WUA. Size of WUAs should be fixed keeping in view future viability and the district collector in consultation with irrigation, CAD and agriculture department staff should determine this.

As long as water rights continue to be linked to land ownership (as is the case in our country), each land holder drawing water from the canal minor (or from the RLIs or community tube wells) would be a member of the WUA. Thus a land owner may be a member of many WUAs but should only be permitted to join the management committee in one WUA. The legislation should specify the rights and duties of both members and non-members in the command area of the canal.

As regards the management committee of the WUA, there could be a provision for half the members to retire every two or three years to be replaced by fresh elected members. The president of the minor level WUA management committee elected from amongst management committee members should automatically be a member of the distributory level users committee, and the president of distributory level users committee should automatically be a member of the project level users committee. The Act should specify that attempts be made to ensure consensus in elections of managing committee members, failing which elections should be held under overall supervision of the district collector.

Functions of WUAs

As regards functions to be performed by WUAs, there are two types of views. Some people feel these should be limited to maintenance of the canal and its structures, distribution of water and resolving disputes related to water distribution and collection of water charges, *i.e.*, only irrigation related functions. However, many experts feel that WUAs can be economically viable and institutionally sustainable only if they also undertake various irrigated agriculture related tasks including input supply and post-harvest activities.

In terms of legislation what it means is that there should be two sets of tasks enumerated: one a core or compulsory group of tasks related to the management and maintenance of the canal (or lift) system which is the bare minimum that a WUA has to take up and the second list of additional agriculture and land-water management related tasks which a WUA could undertake either from its inception, or could gradually add on over the years as it gains in experience and confidence in managing its affairs.

The possible lists of functions that a WUA could perform include the following:[1]

- Acting as an interface between the farmers and the main system management of the irrigation project as well as other concerned government agencies (CAD/Rural Development/Agriculture/Ground Water/Cooperatives Development/(Land) Revenue and Irrigation Departments).
- Water distribution; irrigation scheduling including both rotational running

of canals and warabandi; ensuring that water reaches to all members (as also non-members) as per their due shares.

- Operation and maintenance of the irrigation and drainage system. Collection (and assessment) of water charges and other user charges or special charges that the WUAs may levy.
- Resolution of local disputes amongst members—if necessary setting up of an internal system of penalties and other incentives or disincentives.
- Conflict resolution between members and non-members.
- Agriculture extension and farmers training.
- Recommending of cropping patterns and package of agricultural practices suitable for the WUAs' farmers.
- Management of inputs and credit supply to members.
- Irrigation extension and propagation of better on-farm water application and better intra-outlet command water management.
- Encouraging and taking up of conjunctive water use, or community lift irrigation.
- Drainage.
- Soil testing, water quality testing, water table monitoring, salt-sodic correction (if necessary).
- Provision of drinking water from canal.
- Post harvest practices (grading, packaging, storage and marketing).
- Design and construction of new works (irrigation works, OFD works, drainage works) as well as rehabilitation of canal and structures (deferred maintenance works).
- Maintenance of commercial, financial and water accounting records.
- Cooperating with other WUAs to form federations of WUAs to take over larger canal sub-systems.
- Any other task as mutually agreed upon by the members (*e.g.* canal side plantation, construction/maintenance of farm tracks, providing of matching funds on behalf of the command areas to the district rural development agency, or to Panchayati Raj Institutions as the case may be, for taking up of rural development work).

These broad tasks as suggested above may be divided into core and compulsory or mandatory tasks, and additional optional tasks, while being set forth in legislation. Further refinements in the two sets of tasks could be indicated by having separate lists of tasks for WUAs for RLIs, for community tubewell schemes, for tank schemes and for canal systems. Naturally detailed tasks for distributory users committees or project users committees would differ within the overall framework described above.

There should be provision for each WUA to sign two sets of MoUs—one related to core and compulsory tasks with representative of the Irrigation/CAD/Water Resources/ Ground Water Departments, and the second related to additional optional tasks with the representative of the Agriculture/Rural Development/Panchayats/CAD Department. The legislation should also contain indicative drafts of MoUs delineating the rights and duties of government agencies and of the WUAs and each WUA should have the right to use the indicative draft to evolve actual agreements which they sign with government agencies. This would allow for flexibility to each WUA to evolve as per its own local requirements while adhering to the basic core of PIM.

Functions of Government Agencies

A list of functions that government agencies would need to perform to make PIM effective, as well as an indication of the type of enabling or facilitating role that government should play, and the changes within government agencies required, should form part of PIM legislation. The PIM legislation should specify that it is aimed at participatory, multi-disciplinary and integrated management of irrigated agriculture and of irrigation systems and that accordingly the concerned government agencies need to function in an inter-disciplinary mode.

Experience shows that panchayat bodies cannot perform the functions being expected from WUAs.[2] Accordingly, PIM legislation should specify that WUAs shall work independently from, but in coordination with, the constitutional panchayati raj bodies.

At the state government level each government department having a bearing on PIM should be mandated to designate a nodal PIM officer, with the main department responsible for PIM in each state government constituting a multi-disciplinary PIM cell in the state secretariat. Multi-disciplinary mobile PIM propagation teams should be constituted to move from project to project for creating awareness and orientation about PIM, helping to solve local PIM related problems, communicating government's PIM related policies and supportive measures to farmers and obtaining feedback from the field about policy changes required.

A state level PIM support group consisting of secretaries of concerned government departments, nominated PIM-water management experts, representatives of both state level and national level NGOs directly dealing with PIM, chief engineers of irrigation and CAD, director of rural development, etc., should be constituted to meet periodically to review PIM efforts in the state and suggest measures to make PIM more effective.

Similarly a water users council for coordination of PIM in the state should be set up with minister as chairman, secretaries of concerned administrative deparments, heads of departments of concerned executing departments, a selected number of WUA (as well as distributary and project committee) chairmen, representing RLI, community tubewell, tank and canal irrigation schemes as well as different geographical regions of the state—so as to suggest implementation strategies for PIM and prepare annual action plans for propagating and administering PIM in the state and to review implementation of such annual action plans.

A committee of experts independent of the concerned government departments and agencies should be constituted as per the PIM laws to arbitrate disputes or differences of opinion on specific issues between government agencies and specific individual WUAs, or between two WUAs.

For PIM to be introduced and propagated successfully, awareness generation, capacity building and attitudinal reorientation are extremely important more so than for many other development initiatives. Thus each state needs to provide for a PIM training advisory group and for the preparation of three to five years perspective plans for PIM training and awareness building. This should be in addition to annual PIM action plans.

The PIM Act should take care that WUAs functioning before the enactment of the legislation do not get derailed due to various provisions of the new Act and that there is a transitional period allowed as well as that sufficient flexibility exists to permit the existing WUAs to continue functioning.

We have set forth a brief outline of what could be the contents of an ideal PIM Act for a state in India. The local administrative and irrigation related traditions and agro-climatic conditions would influence what is required for each particular state.

Further Reflections on a Strategy for Propagating PIM

Various state governments in India have gone in either for a 'big bang' approach of uniform and simultaneous introduction of PIM throughout the state based upon and preceded by legislation (the leading example being Andhra Pradesh), or have gone in for some sort of a 'bottom-up' slow and steady approach (starting with pilot projects) of motivating and facilitating the creation of WUAs wherever the farmers agree to voluntarily come together and to form associations so that they gradually takeover some functions on their local irrigation systems. The author refers to the latter as cafeteria approach in that (just like as in a 'cafeteria' or canteen a menu or list of items is displayed for the visitor to choose one or a combination of them) the possibilities of PIM and various functions that WUAs could undertake are made known to farmer water users who can then decide whether or not to form WUAs and what combinations of functions they would like to take up through their WUA and what functions they would like to add-on after a few years of experience of operating WUAs.[3] In the latter approach the WUA would be free to choose its own internal structure and the manner in which it would become a legal entity. Both the above approaches are dependent upon large-scale and repeated training and orientation efforts not only for capacity building but also for spreading the PIM message and thus helping in the propagation of PIM.

It is to be seen to what extent the 'big bang' approach of large-scale creation of WUAs in a uniform manner throughout the state by statutory enactment in Andhra Pradesh shall succeed due to the political will behind it (whereby large-scale training and joint walk through survey-diagnotic analysis of existing irrigation systems are also being carried out on a massive scale).

Atleast Maloney and Raju[4] hold a contrary view and are categorical that each WUA should be spontaneous and not be formed by government orders, should be set up using existing social capital, and should be gradually built up over a period of time and not be based on any single uniform organisational model. As would be obvious, the author does not favour either a uniform, or a big bang approach, and prefers flexibility to choose from a variety of models of WUAs and the gradual adoption of PIM so that it can take strong roots wherever adopted.

The question of which of the two approaches is considered more suitable for each particular state in India, is intertwined with the issue of external donor-driven or government driven-PIM versus internal and spontaneously derived WUAs and PIM-and whether PIM needs to follow the enactment of a special PIM or FMIS Act, or can even take-off without such legislation. A similar question is whether rehabilitation of canals needs to preceed introduction of PIM or not. In both approaches the rights of members and non-members would need to be spelt out in advance and it would also need to be ensured that locally influential people should not be able to capture the WUA, or to grab more than their share of benefits.

Of even more significance is the issue of whether improved water and agriculture management should be the sole objective of PIM, or whether it should be attempted that a host of other societal goals are also simultaneously met through PIM. The author feels that other goals may be left for panchayat bodies and for the government to fulfil. Thus whatever PIM models are propagated should concentrate on the management of water, canals and on irrigated agriculture and related agricultural activities.

No one model of WUA can fit all situations. WUAs need to differ accordingly to whether they are situated on major, medium or minor canal systems, or cover the larger tank or community lift irrigation schemes. A WUA created where a warabandi system and warabandi culture exists would be different from those where other systems of canal irrigation and water distribution have been in force. A WUA set-up before canal construction or rehabilitation and repairs commences would behave differently from one constituted after such works are over. A WUA's nature would also differ based upon the manner in which it gets initiated and the nature of external factors and prime-movers behind the formation of WUAs. Region (and the cultural, socio-economic features of the region) and topography may also influence the nature of a WUA.

However, whatever the type of irrigation systems in existence or model of WUAs being adopted, farmers willingness to undertake PIM and both the initial success and long run sustainability of PIM is dependant upon whether the returns from PIM provide enough incentives[5] to the farmers to offset the substantial costs (monetary and otherwise) of participation and undertaking managerial responsibilities. Physical improvements to the irrigation system in terms of deferred maintenance or rehabilitation works provide only short-term incentives for participation. The farmers need to see possible longer term gains from participation which would depend to a large extent upon the ability of the state to provide a receptive partner bureaucracy and enabling conditions for farmers to take on a greater role in irrigation management which can lead to improvements in water delivery services and system maintenance and the evolution of a feeling amongst the farmers that they can have a genuine voice in water allocation decisions which in turn could lead to increased yields and incomes because of more predictable, reliable and flexible water supplies (including more convenient operation of the irrigation system) and reduction or better resolution of conflicts.

Thus, for the farmers the benefits of physical system improvements, improved water supply, increased farm income, empowerment and conflict resolution obtained through WUAs should offset the substantial time, materials cost and inter-personal transaction costs of being active in local irrigation organisations for them to make the effort of constituting WUAs and of subsequently managing them and the irrigation systems.

An expanded role in main system management through federations of WUAs or through project committees/distributary committees can be a major incentive for farmers to participate on WUAs. As Tang and Ostrom[6] have pointed out, unless the farmers have the freedom to participate in both the governance and management process of their irrigation systems, they will be uncertain about the returns of their efforts and thus have little incentive to participate in collective efforts at operation and maintenance.

The goal of PIM is not the mere transfer or turnover of irrigation systems or sub-systems to WUAs—such transfer is merely a means and not an end. Nor is the goal merely to ensure deferred maintenance or rehabilitation of canal systems. Saving of governmental funds or helping to solve the fiscal problems of state government also is not a basic objective, at least in fact in the transitional phase, when users have to be motivated and trained to set up WUAs which take over systems/sub-systems and when government organisations are being restructured and the staff being retrained or supplemented with personnel having social organisation and other related skills required for PIM, the government expenditure may even go up. Nor should abstract concerns for decentralisation or privatisation be the driving motive for propagating PIM. (Unfortunately many donors like World Bank appear to be more interested today in privatisation oriented goals than in the community and government being used as a means of improved water management.) Nor should PIM be viewed as a mechanism for implementing government schemes or a means for government to pass on its responsibilities to WUAs. The goal instead is improved and integrated management of water and agriculture through a joint partnership of WUAs at various levels and of government agencies—both of whom ultimately represent the community.

Areas where PIM has already been introduced sometime ago face what can be referred to as second generation problems. Svendsen, Trava and Johnson[7] mention insecure water rights, financial shortfalls and lack of financial and administrative experience as amongst the second generation problems of WUAs; need to redefine and to create new roles for itself and for its staff as those of the irrigation department; and the need to increase farm productivity to take advantage of possible improvements in quality of irrigation service and accessing support services (credit extension, newer technologies, markets and market information, access to inputs, post harvest facilities) as that of individual farmers. These issues need to be thought through in advance and planned for before initiating PIM in any area because even one single failed PIM effort at the level of a small WUA can have more of a negative demonstration effect than a hundred successful WUAs. And the impression cannot be permitted to emerge that PIM faces major second generation problems.

It also needs to be emphasised that PIM is not a panacea for all the difficulties being faced in managing irrigation. Many issues have purely technical solutions. Many others would require government action. However, without the userism involved in PIM, technical fixes and governmental actions by themselves may not suffice. Secondly, it needs to be recognised that financial and infrastructural creation/repair support as well as government orders and legislation may enable WUAs to be initially created, but unless major social, institutional and Human Resource Development (HRD) and related support including that of the irrigation and agriculture as well as CAD departments, is made available and farmers are enabled to successfully manage canals on their own, the sustainability of PIM may not be achievable.

Government's Role

It is quite obvious that government and its various agencies and departments have a significant role to play in the initiation, propagation and sustainability of PIM.

The government has to create an enabling environment through: (*a*) policy resolutions, (*b*) specific programmes, projects and activities to be implemented or sponsored by government, (*c*) providing intellectual, administrative and implementional leadership, (*d*) putting into place legal and administrative provisions and procedures including acts, rules, government orders, (*e*) undertaking mass awareness building and promotional efforts, (*f*) providing technical advice and technical back-up as well as funds to WUAs for selective activities while continuing to perform many tasks on its own and initiating newer tasks which were not being undertaken earlier in the pre-PIM era by government agencies, (*g*) ensuring attitudinal and behavioural change amongst employees of all government departments directly or indirectly concerned with canal (and community lift) irrigation, (*h*) creating nodal points of PIM in all concerned government departments both at the Central and state government levels with a multi-disciplinary PIM unit supported by an advisory group of experts being located in the water resources or irrigation/CAD department, (*i*) creating multi-disciplinary mobile PIM propagation teams to move from project to project, motivate as well as orient and train farmers and field/project level government staff, obtain feedback about changes required at the government level, and generally take steps to ensure that PIM takes off and functions properly, (*j*) preparing guidelines and field manuals, (*k*) arranging for various sorts of PIM related training, (*l*) helping WUAs to rehabilitate old irrigation systems to bring them up to at least a minimum operational level, (*m*) involving NGOs and community organisers, and (*n*) providing incentives, monetary, or otherwise for: (*i*) farmers to undertake PIM, and (*ii*) government staff to facilitate it.

As WUAs take over many functions including the management of canals, the government CAD (or irrigation) department would have to gear itself to look more to construction and management of dams and the main canal system or drainage works, providing technical advice, training, introduction of new technologies, major repairs, creation of an organisation for interfacing with WUAs and other government departments and for motivating and catalysing the formation of WUAs, as also undertaking long-term water resource planning.

Statutory and administrative empowerment orders may have to be issued by government to facilitate the adoption of PIM. WUAs should be enabled to charge for services (provided the rates prescribed by them are not less than those of the government), decide about water distribution, impose punishments, and provide rewards and incentives. The duties of government as regards to PIM, and governments responsibilities towards WUAs, would need to be spelt out in Memorandum of Understanding (MoU) between government and each specific WUA so as to act as a supplement to general executive orders and legislation regarding PIM. Such MoUs and orders/enactment would also specify the expectations from the WUAs *vis-à-vis* the government, *vis-à-vis* WUAs members, and *vis-à-vis* society as a whole. If integrated inter-disciplinary and multi-functional CAD agencies exist then one MoU between the agency and WUA would suffice—otherwise a number of supplementary MoUs between the WUA on the one hand and irrigation, agriculture, GWD and CAD Departments (and perhaps even district rural development agency) respectively on the other hand, would be required. The MoU should ensure that no ambiguity remains regarding the rights and duties of the WUA and its members and the rights and duties of those government agencies who are a part of PIM and their employees.

Since the government needs to play the role of the interfacing and catalysing agency, predetermined and transparent provisions and procedures need to be evolved for negotiations/arbitration between WUAs and government whenever required. Provisions would thus have to be put into place for WUAs to, if they so desire, appeal to government agencies in certain situations for help in conflict resolution between the WUA and other agencies/individuals or within WUAs—as also for appeals against government's irrigation, agriculture or CAD department decisions, if required.

A large number of pilot PIM projects, and action research in PIM, as well as PIM orientation, training and implementation review workshops should be supported to provide a positive demonstration affect in favour of PIM, as also to provide experience in the working of PIM which would then be reflected in subsequent legal enactment, and manuals and guidelines on PIM.

As regards technical help to WUAs, government would have to arrange for providing advice; undertaking major repairs and major construction; ensuring the availability of machines on hire basis if required by WUAs; helping the WUAs in the designing of engineering works and in ensuring quality control in works being implemented by WUAs, and help the WUAs and their members in adopting improved on-field water application techniques, and water regulation and distribution techniques as also in other improved agricultural and land-water management practices through irrigation (including drainage) extension and agriculture extension efforts.

A system of payments, incentives, subsidies, grants, etc., would also need to be devised which encourages WUAs to raise their own resources and undertake their own works, yet ensures that WUAs are recompensed for works that should normally be undertaken by government, and also address concerns regarding the viability of WUAs.

One-time functional managerial grants should be made available to WUAs in addition to support for the rehabilitation of the canal and drainage system to bring it up to a minimum functional level. However care should be taken so that the WUA does not get treated like a contractor, but as a user group and stakeholder that is sharing in irrigation management.

Unfortunately, exceptions apart, most states tend to look to Central India or to external funding through aid projects for funds to expend on propagating PIM. Government of India's PIM related assistance is available for a limited number of activities and is channeled through its Centrally-sponsored scheme of CAD and this is restricted to irrigation schemes covered by the CAD scheme and is not available for other irrigation systems. Not all states can obtain external aid for the water sector which includes PIM type components. Hence state governments would need to come forward and commit their own funds for PIM related activities. Government of India should also push through its proposed Centrally-sponsored scheme on PIM which has been on the anvil for the last two-three years.

The government has to agree that part of the water charges recovered shall be the share of the WUA based on the number of activities that it takes over from the government as well as the level of the irrigation system (minor, branch, distributary, main canal, drains, headworks and dam), whose management the WUA takes over. A formula may even need to be worked out for providing O&M grants which could be performance based depending upon ensuring supply of their due share of water to all, the O&M efforts put in, and the recoveries of water charges affected (if the WUA takes upon itself this task) by the WUA. Simple but objectively verifiable criteria for assessing each WUA's performance would need to be established in advance so that both the WUA and the government agency know about these criteria well in advance. It should also be prescribed in advance that if the WUA raises additional resources for certain activities other than the basic O&M of the canal, then the government would make available some matching grants to the WUA.

In the initial stages government would need to finance (and also assist otherwise) forthcoming numerous pilot PIM projects and action research projects. NGOs, research institutes and state government/project agencies could take up such pilot projects jointly with WUAs. For such pilot trials (and demonstration projects) WUAs would need to be given back at least 50 per cent of the water charges (presently being levied at nominal rates) from their areas for managing and carrying out the O&M and other WUA functions.

For areas where WUAs take over the management of canals and other PIM activities, the government could give them a higher priority while sanctioning other development schemes of various government departments. In fact WUAs should be permitted (and perhaps even encouraged) to implement various government schemes not directly related to PIM for which government should make available funds to the WUAs for those activities and their management and supervision.

Government would also need to coordinate so as to facilitate the availability of institutional finance in case WUAs want to take loans for their activities.

Regardless of whether or not PIM is being introduced, government needs to ensure that: (*i*) water charges are raised and a substantial part of the charges recovered are ploughed back into direct action for improved and sustained operation and maintenance of canals, and (*ii*) integrated multi-disciplinary/multi-departmental interaction with farmers and WUAs, and similarly integrated main systems management, is undertaken through integrated project organisations for the larger projects which have strong links with user-farmers and which cut across departmental boundaries. Both these steps would however greatly help in the propagation, acceptance, efficacy, sustainability and success of PIM.

Training for PIM

The success of PIM would also depend upon large-scale training and orientation efforts. The voluntary, bottom up, and flexible cafeteria approach to PIM can only take off through orientation and training efforts. But both the cafeteria approach and the uniform, legislation-driven 'big bang' approach can only work if massive training and capacity building support is provided not only for imparting technical and social organisational and interaction skills but also to bring about attitudinal change amongst all the different categories of actors and stakeholders. Such training would need to be continuous as WUAs move from initial teething problems, to full-fledged operations and then gradually encounter second generation problems. It would also need to cater to new WUA management committee members who get elected in subsequent elections and to the change in government functionaries due to transfers.

While keeping the above in mind, PIM training has to be planned and conceptualised in its broadest sense to include mass awareness-building and attitudinal change in addition to imparting skills and knowledge related to irrigation, participation, group dynamics and conflict resolution, irrigation laws, office procedures, financial accounting, etc. The training has also to be a two-way process serving as an instrument of change in the PIM reform process and making available skills, knowledge and orientation on the one hand, and on the other hand providing a mechanism for feedback from the field whereby policies, procedures, laws, rules, strategies and schemes can be modified and the adoption of PIM facilitated.

The PIM related training would thus need to:

- Create a favourable climate within the country in general for the propagation of PIM.
- Prepare water users to undertake PIM through WUAs
- Enable the government departments and agencies related to water resources and irrigated agriculture to reorient themselves and to adopt new roles, organisational structures, processes and ways of functioning so that they can play a facilitating role for furthering PIM and joint farmer-government agency partnerships.
- Change the orientations and knowledge base of water professionals and policy-makers in the water sector.
- Equip lower level functionaries of government, employees of NGOs and others to be able to effectively facilitate PIM and thus to ensure better water management.

Accordingly, PIM training should include:

- Efforts at general orientation about PIM and attitudinal reorientation about PIM.
- Knowledge and skills in improved water and agriculture management including drainage, *i.e.*, technical matters.
- PIM related procedural, administrative and organisational issues, (including those related to social interactions and group dynamics as well as participation), available incentives, sources of incentives and funding, etc.
- Lessons from a variety of case studies about successes and failures of PIM initiatives and projects in India and abroad.
- Commercial matters and accounting systems (*e.g.*, bahikhata' system) which local farmers may be able to understand more easily.

Training and orientation programmes need to be planned and organised for a variety of categories of people. Such categories of trainees would include: (*i*) politicians (at Central, state and various sub-state—local-self government/panchayati raj institutions/cooperatives, etc., levels), (*ii*) farmers, (*iii*) WUA personnel (elected office bearers as well as WUA employees), (*iv*) NGOs, (*v*) community organisers, (*vi*) senior officers (in Central and state government as well divisional commissioners and district collectors), (*vii*) middle level officers (comprising generalists as well as specialists from agriculture, irrigation, CAD, groundwater, rural development and panchayats, cooperatives, etc., departments and from the district administration), (*viii*) junior level officers (especially those related to irrigation, CAD and agriculture, and such others with whom the WUAs are likely to have regular interaction), (*ix*) officers of registering authorities (since, in may states of India, the WUAs are being registered under either Cooperative Societies Act, or the Registration of Societies Act, or by the CAD authority/irrigation department), (*x*) trainers from WALMIs/IMTIs/WALAMTARIs or other training institutes related to agriculture, irrigation, rural development and panchayats, cooperative, etc., or trainers picked up from amongst government department's implementing PIM, or WUA Chairmen, or NGOs, etc., and (*xi*) mass media professionals and the general public (including students).

At the state level each state should prepare a perspective plan on PIM training orientation and capacity building and ensure that the training becomes a two-way flow of knowledge (technical and policy-oriented) to the field and of feedback to the government and thus can positively influence implementation to PIM. PIM action plans and PIM training advisory groups, as advocated in the earlier section on what should constitute part of a model state level PIM legislation, would also be desirable.

RECENT INTERNET DEBATE ON REVISITING PIM IN INDIA

Now to turn to the informal internet debate on 'revisiting PIM in India' mentioned at the start of this article. This debate had kicked up when the Executive Director of International Network on Participatory Irrigation Management (INPIM) sent an e-mail to the officiating

President of Indian Network on Participatory Irrigation Management (IndiaNPIM) and a few others and lasted over three weeks with most respondents agreeing on the need for a detailed workshop on the subject. The debate, in which this author had also joined and shared many of the thoughts indicated above, dealt in some detail with the participants perceptions of how the Andhra Pradesh 'big bang' effort has been faring (some felt it was a significant success, but others went against it) with brief comments about PIM in some of the other states. Though one of the suggestions was that we need to move beyond the debate on pilot versus 'big bang'.

A view was also expressed that the politics of the reform process in India—which groups or sections of people are pushing for PIM and why, which are resisting and holding it back or are indifferent to it—and their motivations[8] which analyses motivations of different categories of people in propagating or resisting PIM)—needs to be analysed and understood since that would enable us to understand the status of progress in introduction of PIM in various Indian states. Mention was made of the need for a 'political constituency' for PIM reform to evolve.

It was also postulated that PIM should be seen as a part of broader irrigation reform which itself should be situated much more explicitly in the water and natural resource sector and rural development framework.

There was a suggestion that much reliance had been placed on the pilot experiments approach and hoping that governments would help to expand and replicate the same and reflect them in policy. It was also pointed out that the policy advocacy effort has not really questioned expressed policies and that very little experimentation had been undertaken with alternative institutional options other than traditional WUAs. Irrigation departments continue to remain firmly in control and there is little power sharing or the emergence of joint management institutions.

The need for reorientation of irrigation agencies and irrigation administrators was referred to by a number of persons.

A commentator picked on this author's idea expressed during the debate (and also contained in many of his articles including the present one), that PIM is not the panacea for all difficulties of irrigation projects and that many issues have purely technical solutions. The question was raised as to whether PIM would require irrigation systems to be redesigned and rebuilt to enable WUAs to be able to take appropriate decisions related to water distribution. The same commentator went on to state that the manually operated systems found in South Asia/South East Asia are the most difficult to manage. Irrigation agencies have not been able to properly manage these systems. Accordingly, is it fair to transfer management to WUAs and to expect successful water management from them? Most irrigation systems need to be upgraded. Their poor performance is related to faulty designs and unrealistic procedures as well as optimistic assumptions at the planning stage. He further added that physical and organisational improvements are not isolated and separate actions have to be part of a well planned process. The association of technical changes with institutional reforms is required for success. Seeking remedies to poor performance of irrigation systems merely in the institutional sphere will lead to continue lack of attention to operational problems that plague large-scale irrigation systems.

The above observations are interesting since PIM in India is being contemplated either along with some 'deferred maintenance' works on canals or some repairs to restore the canal to a minimum functional level as per existing designs, or even without such works. What the commentator was worried about—institutional PIM reforms being considered and pushed in isolation-appears to a large extent to be true. Water resources or irrigation departments continue to tend to be concerned more with construction and what are referred to as 'technical issues'.

The e-mail debate also saw reference to a view that mere transfer of canal alone (a major component of PIM in India) is just "moving chairs" unless a larger reforms package is undertaken along with the transfer.

There was a view that the fundamental assumption for formation of WUAs—that if all stakeholders come together and negotiate by means of the "rationality of communication" this would potentially resolve various forms of disagreement and enable the WUA to arrive at a mutually accepted notion of 'common good'-requires serious questioning since in reality the formation of WUAs has usually resulted in the elites having captured much of the democratic space. The merits of top town approach and attempt at a uniform model are accordingly questionable.

This was echoed by other participants in the debate who felt the top town 'big bang' approach would have limited impact if it ignores specific and diversified ground realities of social relations, conditions of production, as also sources of resistance to the reform efforts.

It was pointed out that PIM taking place at lower levels (the canal minor) remains a weak, lifeless initiative because higher levels continue to be managed as earlier by the irrigation agency.

On the PIM related Acts one commentator felt that they remain little more than wish lists which spell out governments' keenness for reforms and provide legitimacy to WUAs—they serve as little more than the specifics of irrigation departments commitment to reform so as to please funders and donors and to impress the research and policy community that a lot is happening in PIM. The author felt that the above commentator was being unduly harsh in his views about PIM legislation despite there being a grain of truth in his opinion. After all Andhra Pradesh and Madhya Pradesh have gone through elections as per their Farmers Management of Irrigation Systems Act and a number of other states are working at the operationalisation of their PIM Acts despite resistance from some important quarters in some cases.

A useful contribution on the 'big bang' versus 'slow-learning-by-doing' approaches was that partial coverage under PIM of an irrigation scheme creates disparities in terms of service to users and contributions from the users. Thus creation of WUAs over the entire command area of a particular irrigation scheme should be ensured at the same time. PIM should therefore adopt the concept of full scheme coverage.

The appropriate or optimum size of WUAs and their responsibilities also found reference in the e-mail debate—as did the role of NGOs and of government, and the need for farmers taking greater initiative in the introduction of PIM. The idea of floating and generating farmers networks to lobby for PIM also found mention in the debate.

The need was emphasised for flexible design of reforms using the principle of continuous incorporation of 'learning-by-doing' and that such learnings should not be limited to learnings about administrative measures.

There was widespread agreement that the status of PIM in various parts of the country (most participants were dissatisfied with what has been achieved so far) needs to be understood with strategies for propagating 'revisiting' or re-examining PIM in India.

A SELECT READING

Groenfeldt, D. 1998 (and earlier editions). *Handbook on Participatory Irrigation Management*, The Economic Development Institute of the World Bank, Washington, D.C.

Goldensohu, M. (also ofter referred to as ISPAN, 1994), *Participation and Empowerment: An Assessment of Water Users Associations in Asia and Egypt*. Irrigation Support Project for Asia and the near East (ISPAN) Washington. D.C., 1994.

Gulati, A.R. Meinzen-Dick and K.V. Raju. *From Top Down to Bottom Up: Institutional Reforms in Indian Canal Irrigation*, draft volume circulated for a National Workshop at Institute of Economic Growth, New Delhi, January, 1999. The draft is intended to be got published.

Hooja, R. *Multidisciplinary Management of Irrigation Schemes and the Command Area Development Approach in India*, Occasional Paper No. 2. The HCM Rajasthan State Institute of Public Administration, Jaipur, 1995.

Hooja, R."Objective of PIM" In *INPIM Newsletter*, No. 2 March 1996.

Hooja, R."Promoting Water Users Associations in Participatory Irrigation Management: Some Reflections". *Indian Journal of Public Administration* Vol. 43, No. 4, October.-December, 1997.

Hooja, R. "Participatory Irrigation Management: A Report" *Prashasnika*, Vol. 24, No. 2 July-December, 1997.

Hooja, R. "Command Area Development in India: Water Resources Based Development of Irrigated Area" T.N. Chaturvedi (ed.), *Fifty Years of Indian Administration: Retrospect and Prospect*, Indian Institute of Public Administration, New Delhi, 1998, earlier published in *Indian Journal of Public Administration*, Vol 43, No. 3 July-September 1997.

Hooja, R. "Progogating Participatory Irrigation Management: A Strategy in the Indian Context" *Administative Change*, Vol. 25, No 2, and Vol 26, No. 1, Jan-December 1998.

Hooja R. "Administering Water in India in 2050 AD", *Indian Journal of Public Administration*, Vol. 46, No. 2 April-June 2000.

Hooja R. "Training for PIM in India: A Supplementary Note to IndiaNPIM's Working Paper/ Monograph No. 4", prepared for the workshop on " Capacity Building for Integrated Water Resources Management for Human Development in South Asia", organized by SaciWATERs and Centre for Alternatives at Dhaka, September 22 to 24, 2001.

Hooja, R. *A Strategy for Training of PIM in India – Moving Ahead of Working Paper* 4, IndiaNPIM Working Paper/Minograph No. 7, New Delhi, 2002.

Hooja R. Forthcoming "Two Approaches to Participatory Irrigation Management: Reforming Irrigation in India" S.N.Mishra (ed) *Public Governance and Decentralization*, New Delhi. Mittal Publication, 1993.

Hooja, R., Anjali M. Bhatia and Ganesh Pangare. *Training for Participatory Irrigation Management – Present Status and Needs: A Policy Aid Document*, IndiaNPIM Working Paper/Monograph No. 4, New Delhi, 2001.

Hooja R., R.C. Bower and S.N. Mundhra (ed.). *Irrigation, Agriculture and Social Development,* Himanshu Publication, Udaipur, 1997.

Hooja R., G. Pangare and K.V. Raju (ed.). *Users in Water Management – The Andhra Model and Its Replicability in India,* Rawat Publications, Jaipur, 2002.

Indian Network on Participatory Irrigation Management (IndiaNPIM), *Comparing PIM Legislation in Various States,* IndiaNPIM Working Paper No. 11, November 2002, New Delhi.

IndiaNPIM. *Irrigation Management Transfer: Sharing Lessons from Global Experience* (reprinted from INPIM, FAO International e-Conference on Irrigation Management Transfer) supplement to *India NPIM Newsletter,* Nos 11 and 12, July 2001.

Meinzen-Dick, R., M. Mendoza, C. Sadoulet, G. Abiad Shields and A Subramanian, 1994 *Sustainable Water User Associations: Lessons from a Literature Review* presented at Water Resources Seminar Landsdowne, Virginia USA and reprinted in A. Subramanian, N.V. Jagannathan and R. Meinzen-Dick (ed.) *Users Organisations for Sustainable Water Services,* World Bank Technical Paper No. 354, Washington, D.C.

Meinzen-Dick, R.K.V. Raju and A. Gulati. "What Affects Organizations and Collective Action For Managing Resources? Evidence from Canal Irrigation Systems in India", EPTD Discussion Paper No. 61, IFPRI, Washington 2002.

Meinzen-Dick, R.R. Reidinger and A. Monzardo *Participation in Irrigation,* Environment Department Participation Papers Series, World Bank, Washington, D.C., 1995.

Ministry of Water Resources, India. *Report of the Working Group on Command Area Development Programme,* New Delhi December, 1996. (prepared at behest of Planning Commission)

Ministry of Water Resource, India. *Report of Working Group on Participatory Irrigation Management for Formulation of Plan Proposals for Ninth Five Year Plan,* New Delhi, August, 1996 (prepared at the behest of Planning Commission).

Ministry of Water Resources, India, *Vision for Integrated Water Resources Development and Management,* New Delhi, 2003.

Ostrom, E. *Crafting Institutions for Self-governing Irrigation Systems,* Institute for Contemporary Studies, San Francisco, California, 1992.

Parlin, B.W. and M.W. Lusk (ed.). *Farmers Participation and Irrigation Organisation,* Westview Press, Colorado, 1991.

Planning Commission, India. *Report of the Working Group on Command Area Development Programme (CADP) for 10th Five Year Plan 2002-2007,* New Delhi, September 2001.

Raju, K.V. and J. Brewer. "Types of Irrigation Management Transfer Models in India", paper presented at International Association for the Study of Common Property Resources Meeting, Berkley, California June 1996.

Sampath, R.K. and R.A. Young (ed.). *Social, Economic and Institutional Issues in Third World Irrigation Management,* Westview Press, Boulder, Colorado, 1990.

Sivamohan, M.V.K. and C.A. Scott (ed.). *India: Irrigation Management Partnerships,* Booklinks, Hyderabad, 1994.

Uphoff, N., R. Meinzen-Dick and N. St. Julien. *Improving Policies and Programmes for Farmer Orginatization and Participation in Irrigation Water Management,* Water Management Synthesis Paper 1, Cornell University, 1985.

Uphoff, N.P. Ramamurthi and R. Steiner. *Managing Irrigation: Analyzing and Improving Performance of Bureaucracies,* New Delhi, Sage Publications, 1994.

Note: the views expressed in this article are personal and academic and do not represent those of the organisation where the author presently works.

REFERENCES

1. R. Hooja, *Multidisciplinary and Participatory Water Management for Irrigation Command Areas,* IndiaNPIM Working Paper/Monograph No. 2, New Delhi, 2001.
2. R. Hooja and G. Pangare, "Some Reflections on Software Aspects of Water Policy: CAD, PIM Watershed Development and Management and Water Harvesting", Paper presented at *Round Table on Water Policy* organised by Indian Society of Ecological Economics at India International Centre, New Delhi on May 10, 2002; revised version published as India NPIM Working Paper No. 13, January 2003; and R. Hooja Forthcoming, *Integrated Irrigation Management – Need for Multidisciplinary Command Area Approach and Improved Farmer-Management Interface,* Jaipur, Arihant Publishers.
3. L.K. Joshi and R. Hooja (ed.), *Participatory Irrigation Management: Paradigm for 21st Century,* (2 volumes), Jaipur, Rawat Publishers, 2000.
4. C. Maloney and K.V. Raju, *Managing Irrigation Together: Practice and Policy in India,* New Delhi, Sage Publication, 1994.
5. R.Meinzen-Dick, "Farmer Participation in Irrigation—20 Years of Experience and Lessons for the Future", *Irrigation and Drainage Systems,* Vol. II, 1997.
6. S.Y. Tang and E. Ostron, *The Governance and Management of Irrigation Systems: An Institutional Perspective,* London, ODI Irrigation Management Network (Network Paper 23), 1993.
7. D. Groenfeld and Mark Svendsen (ed.), *Case Studies in Participatory Irrigation Management,* Washington, Economic Development Institute, 2000.
8. R. Hooja and G. Pangare "Participatory Irrigation Management: Issues Related to Policy, Implementation and Research" paper presented at Workshop on *Policy Futures for Water Resource Management in India.* From Prescription and Impact Assessment to Strategic Analysis organised at Hyderabad from October 3-5, 2002 by IWMI India Office, SaciWATER's and Wegeningen University.

SECTION VII: GROUND WATER AND HYDRO-ELECTRICITY MANAGEMENT

25

Creation of Adequate Institutional and Organisational Support for Ground Water Development

B.B. Vohra

The critical importance of ground water to our programmes of intensive agriculture hardly needs to he stressed. The value of ground water as a source of irrigation lies in its availability, in lesser or greater quantities, in practically all parts of the country, the comparative ease and speed with which it can be put to use and the assurance—so vital for the cultivation of the new high-yielding varieties—that it holds of being instantly available whenever it is required to be applied to the soil. It is these reasons, coupled with the extension of electricity to villages during recent years, that explain the rapidly rising demand for ground water development all over the country, not excluding areas long served by flow irrigation systems.

The value of ground water for domestic, industrial and other non-agricultural purposes is, however, of no less importance to the community. In this connection, particular reference needs to be made to the needs of the arid areas where the location and development of ground water can make all the difference in the world in avoiding distress to both human and cattle population, even if the quantities available are neither sufficient nor cheap enough for attempting irrigation on any appreciable scale. There are, thus, strong economic as well as social reasons for ensuring that the fullest possible use is made of the country's ground water resources and that these are managed in a scientific manner so that no over-exploitation takes place.

Very large sums of money will be available for the development of ground water resources during the Fourth Plan. In the Agricultural Sector alone, the amount likely to be invested in ground water development has been estimated to be of the order of Rs.1,400 crores, of which about Rs. 750 crores are expected to come from institutional sources (such as Agricultural Refinance Corporation, commercial banks, land development banks, etc.), about Rs. 300 crores by way of State Plan Outlays and about Rs. 350 crores from the private resources of farmers. However, the World Bank is also showing considerable interest in financing ground water development schemes in various parts of the country and money is, therefore, not likely to be a constraint in this field of activity. In this connection, mention may also be made of the Government's anxiety to come to the help of small farmers and dry areas, both of which interests can be best served if available ground water resources are fully investigated and developed.

In order to review the ground water situation in all parts of the country and to assess the difficulties in the way of development of this resource, a series of regional meetings was held during the second-half of 1969 with representatives of State Governments, the Geological Survey of India, the Agricultural Refinance Corporation and the Exploratory Tubewells Organisation at Hyderabad, Calcutta, Bombay, Jaipur, and Delhi. The overriding impression obtained as a result of these discussions is that the *existing arrangements for the location, development and scientific management of ground water are grossly inadequate and need to be strengthened considerably if our Fourth Plan targets of production are to be achieved.*

The problems of ground water development may be considered under three heads relating to: (a) the discovery and location of ground water, (b) its actual utilisation through construction of wells and tubewells, and (c) its scientific management based on accurate assessments of the capacity and recharge conditions of individual aquifers and the implementation of suitable regulatory measures which would ensure that no indiscriminate pumping takes place. In the paragraphs that follow, an attempt has been made to deal with each of these stages of development and to suggest directions in which improvements in the existing arrangements can be made.

PROSPECTING AND EXPLORATORY DRILLING

At the national level, responsibility for this work is divided between two organisations—the Geological Survey of India (GSI) in the Ministry of Petroleum & Chemicals and Mines & Metals (Department of Mines & Metals), and the Exploratory Tubewells Organisation (ETO) in the Ministry of Food, Agriculture, Community Development & Cooperation (Department of Agriculture). The Geological Survey of India is responsible for prospecting for water by means of geo-physical and other sophisticated methods as well as by reconnaissance surveys on the ground. It also undertakes "systematic surveys" with the object of preparing small scale basic maps which depict geo-hydrological conditions and also contain information with regard to water levels in open wells and the chemical quantity of ground water. At the rate at which "systematic surveys" and hydrological mapping is being done by the Geological Survey of India today, it has been variously estimated that it might take the survey anything between 30 to 50 years to cover the entire country.

The Geological Survey of India has recently drawn up a plan for the expansion of its ground water activities by about 50 percent in the very near future. It has also arranged for part of its staff to specialise in ground water work and has grouped such personnel into 5 Regional Ground Water Directorates located at Calcutta, Lucknow, Jaipur, Nagpur and Hyderabad, However, the number of geologists engaged on ground water work in the GSI is only about 80 out of the survey's total strength of about 1,000 geologists. Groundwater work, therefore, accounts for only a very small portion of the

GSI's total responsibilities as its main pre-occupation is with the discovery of mineral and metal resources.

This matter is of some importance because no exploratory drilling work can be undertaken either by the ETO or any other State ground water organisation unless the area concerned has first been surveyed by the GSI and certified to be likely to contain ground water. (This, of course, is, as it should be, because drilling must follow prospecting and not be carried out in a haphazard way) As far as deep drilling is concerned—up to sometimes as much as 2,000 feet—this is possible (and necessary) only in 30 per cent or so of the country's surface which is classified as non-hard rock area and which comprises mainly of alluvial strata. Such drilling is undertaken mainly by the ETO with the object of looking for water in places where its presence is suspected at great depths. Since the ETO is (for certain reasons which need not be gone into at the moment) capable at present of only a limited programme of drilling, it is not difficult for the GSI to arrange to survey the areas in which it wishes to operate. However, the position would be quite different if the ETO were to increase its efficiency manifold (and there is a scope for such an improvement) and thus needed much larger areas to be prospected by the GSI. In that case, the GSI would have to step up its activities a very great deal indeed in order to keep pace with the ETO's requirements.

Since the ETO, in its 16 or 17 years of existence, has operated only in the non-hard rock areas, it is in these very areas that the bulk of the GSI's ground water work has been done, particularly because the GSI's own ground water specialisation is also of about the same age. In the hard rock areas, water is not to be found beyond the first 250 feet or so and is generally extracted by means of open wells which are being increasingly fitted with pump-sets. Groundwater resources in such areas are naturally limited and the capacity of individual wells depends on such factors as the cracks and fissures which they can tap. Prospecting for water in these areas is in some ways more difficult than in alluvial strata, because hydrological conditions can change within short distances depending upon changes in the formation of rocks and, therefore, require more careful and detailed geo-hydrological surveys than in alluvial areas. The responsibility for exploratory drilling in hard rock areas rests not with the ETO but with State Governments, because drilling up to 250 feet or so does not present any great technical problems and is comparatively easy to organise. The State Governments are also responsible for advising the farmer with regard to the exact location of his well or tubewell in hard rock areas. However, the State Governments would be greatly assisted in their task of carrying out detailed investigations and preparing large-scale maps (8" or 16" to a mile and showing the location of existing wells) if the basic geological maps of at least 1" to a mile could be made available by the GSI. But, as noticed earlier, such maps can be prepared by the GSI for the whole country only in 30 to 50 years at its present pace of work.

The GSI's pace of work in the field of ground water came up for particular discussion in the context of the requirements of the arid areas of the country. These areas are located mainly in Haryana, Rajasthan, Gujarat, Maharashtra, Andhra Pradesh, Mysore, and Tamil Nadu. In accordance with suggestions made by the Ministry of Food & Agriculture, these States have already demarcated their chronically drought-affected areas and have also divided them into 3 categories according to the intensity of the distress suffered by them. The State representatives felt that Category 'A', representing the worst-hit areas, should be completely surveyed by the GSI within two years and the remaining chronically drought-affected areas within five years from now. If these targets are to be met, the Survey will have to undertake a very substantial expansion of its ground water programmes, but this is unlikely to happen so long as its main concern is with minerals and it is part of a Ministry in which ground water figures only as a fringe activity.

On their part, the State Governments need to create efficient ground water organisations which would be capable of preparing large-scale village-wise maps showing local hydrological conditions and of carrying out whatever exploratory drilling is required in hard rock areas. Most of the States have, as of now, made only a beginning towards this goal.

Production and Development

This subject may be considered under two heads, namely, the financing of development works and their actual implementation. While discussing financing arrangements, a distinction may be made between works which are to be executed by State Governments and those which are to be implemented by individual farmers. Provision for State Works exists in their Five Year Plans and is meant primarily for high-capacity tubewells designed to tap deep aquifers and to serve a large number of farmers. Very little investment of this sort is, however, possible in hard rock areas and many States in this region have instead earmarked money for partly compensating private farmers in case of the failure of their wells or tubewells. Provisions in the State Plans are also meant to cover the cost of the building up of adequate ground water organisations.

The bulk of the investment on ground water development during the Fourth Plan will, however be accounted for by private works which will be financed by institutional sources, such as land mortgage banks, cooperative banks, commercial banks and the World Bank. The experience of the last 2 or 3 years, during which these sources have come into existence, shows that while money is available with them in plenty, there are as yet no proper arrangements to make use of it. Thus, the total value of' ground water schemes sanctioned by the Agricultural Refinance Corporation till the beginning of September 1969 was Rs. 132 crores, of which only about 10 per cent had been actually spent. The performance of the States also varied a great deaf and reflected their different degrees of preparedness to take advantage of the opportunities offered. The Punjab stood at the top of the list with sanctioned schemes worth Rs. 24 crores and an actual outlay of Rs. 5.5 crores. At the end of the scale was West Bengal which had sanctioned schemes worth only Rs. 15 lakhs and no actual utilisation. The table given below tells its own story.

In order to take advantage of the unparalleled opportunities which exist today for he financing of ground water development, it is necessary that financing institutions should be presented with viable and adequately documented schemes drawn up on an area basis. The loan proposals should define the extent of the area which is proposed to be developed, it estimated ground water potential (in our present circumstances,

Sl. No.	Name of the State	Schemes Sanctioned as on 5-9-69			Schemes Pending as on 5-9-69	
		No.	Total Financial Outlay (in lakhs)	Outlay incurred (in lakhs)	No.	Total Financial Outlay (in lakhs)
1.	Andhra Pradesh	46	1865.022	27.630	21	1759.07
2.	Assam	–	–	–	–	–
3.	Bihar	4	1013.379	18.000	2	600.52
4.	Delhi	1	8.050	–	–	–
5.	Gujarat	21	1410.200	230.400	24	1365.05
6.	Haryana	5	1103.500	282.897	5	676.00
7.	Jammu & Kashmir	–	–	–	–	–
8.	Kerala	1	87.350	–	–	–
9.	Madhya Pradesh	10	1182.594	31.050	6	666.50
10.	Maharashtra	6	528.970	32.400	35	3302.62
11.	Mysore	4	628.070	–	10	1622.50
12.	Orissa	–	–	–	–	–
13.	Punjab	18	2402.673	549.909	7	2030.00
14.	Rajasthan	4	516.885	5.760	7	396.50
15.	Tamil Nadu	10	1042.000	32.400	10	861.30
16.	Uttar Pradesh	14	1503.236	122.283	15	2365.91
17.	West Bengal	1	15.200	–	–	–
	Total	145	13207.929	1323.729	142	15645.97

this can only be an approximation) the extent to which this has been tapped already and the economies of the suggested investment.

Insistence on an area approach is necessary because compact schemes mean economy in electrification, and resource potentials can be estimated only for areas which are defined. Hardly any State is today fully equipped to prepare area schemes which are backed with adequate hydrological and economic data and can, therefore, be rapidly appraised by financing institutions as being deserving of support. Many States are not even sufficiently aware of the necessity to create organisational structures which will enable them to undertake such work on anything like the scale required. It may be mentioned in this connection that although certain land mortgage banks, cooperative banks and commercial banks do not at present insist on ground water schemes being drawn up on an area basis, as is being done by the Agricultural Refinance Corporation (ARC), they are likely to fall in line with the ARC sooner or later.

During our discussions, delays in the sanctioning of the schemes by the ARC were also gone into. Till very recently, the ARC, which is the principal agency concerned, referred all ground water schemes for technical appraisal to either a panel of private hydrological experts maintained by it or to the ETO. At the instance of the Department of Agriculture, steps have been taken to increase the number of experts on the ARC panel as well as to involve the GSI in the work of technical appraisal along with the ETO. Certain procedures have also been streamlined to ensure that schemes are not delayed by the appraising agencies. However, no real improvement in the rate at which area schemes are sanctioned can be expected till it can be ensured that the States are capable of drawing up and presenting schemes which are complete in all respects and satisfy the requirements of viability. This, in turn, can only be done if adequately staffed and equipped geo-hydrological units are set up in the States to study ground water conditions in detail and to gather the various kinds of data necessary to form even a rough idea of the potential of a given area.

The expeditious implementation of ground water schemes—once they have been sanctioned—requires that Slates should possess adequate drilling (and blasting also, in the ease of open wells in hard rock areas) capacity as well as expertise in the design and construction of tubewells and wells. It is also necessary that there should be close liaison between the State ground water organisations and Electricity Boards, so that the energisation of pump-sets is carried out as soon as possible after they have been installed. Here again, the existing picture is not at all satisfactory. The number of qualified contractors who can carry out a proper job of work is extremely limited with the result that the speed as well as standard of execution is generally poor. Lack of planning and coordination at State Government levels also results in big delays in energisation.

Most of lie States possess some engineering organisations which are equipped to carry out drilling and blasting work, but these are sometimes dispersed over a number of Departments, such as Agriculture, Irrigation, Public Health and Panchayats, and are generally incapable of carrying out a development scheme in an efficient and business-like manner. There is great need to centralise control of all departmental boring and blasting equipment and operations in one place to improve operational efficiency and to develop expertise.

In this context, reference may be made to the present practice in many States for Government organisations to charge subsidised rates for drilling or blasting work. Although this is done with the best of intentions and in order to help the farmer, it has the effect of discouraging private parties from entering this field of activity and thereby depriving the farmer of a useful and competitive service. This matter has been brought to the notice of the State concerned and it is hoped that the rates charged by them will be revised in the ultimate interest of the farmer.

In hard rock areas where open wells fitted with pump-sets are the order of the day, it has been found that the application of improved methods of the 'renovation' of wells results in very great savings. Thus, instead of boring large diameter vertical holes in existing wells whose capacity has decreased on account of the blocking or choking of cracks and fissures, it is much more useful as well as cheaper to carry out slim drillings in various directions at a fraction of the cost of the former. Such techniques need to be propagated widely and backed by adequate organisational arrangements for the execution of work. More research into the ground water problems of hard rock areas also needs to be undertaken—a committee of experts has been recently set up to consider this matter.

In alluvial areas, particularly the Gangetic Valley, fears have been expressed by some experts that the unregulated sinking of a very large number of shallow tubewells might result in lowering of the water table and, therefore, failure of wells and loss of the investment they represent. It has also been pointed out that most of the existing shallow tubewells with a capacity of 0.2 to 0.5 cusecs are under-utilised and that it would be much more economical to the community as a whole to replace them by deeper tubewells of 3 to 4 cusecs each which could be run to full capacity and serve all farmers in their command including small farmers who are today neither in a position to install tubewells of their own nor to get water from their richer neighbours at reasonable rates. These suggestions need to be considered carefully and would be worth adopting if improvements could be carried out in the operation of state tubewells so as to prevent losses in distribution and provide satisfaction to all consumers, and if water rates could be increased to economic levels. Haryana has, in fact, decided to set up a corporation to run its existing tubewells and to construct new ones on strictly commercial lines. Such an arrangement will enable it not only to raise existing water rates but also to find funds for a big tubewell programme from institutional sources, without burdening the Plan.

Visiting experts have also pointed out the need to improve the design of our tubewells and to use new materials like fibre glass in place of steel for pipes as is being done in West Pakistan on a large-scale. The low Level of operational efficiency of rigs operated both by the ETO in the Government of India and by State Governments in another matter which calls for notice. Since Government procedure and regulations are not conducive to efficient commercial operations it may be found that the best way of increasing the efficiency of our rigs might be to make a clear distinction between exploratory drilling and production drilling and to hand over at least the latter type of work to corporations. A step in this direction has already been taken by the Andhra Pradesh Government by making its Agro-Industries Corporation responsible for drilling and blasting work on commercial lines and certain other States are thinking of following this example. The responsibility for giving technical advice and assistance to farmer with regard to the design of their wells and tubewells should, however, remain with the engineering wing of State ground water organisations as this is in the nature of an extensive service.

Whatever the arrangements for execution may be, it is necessary that wells and tubewells should be located at the best possible site from the hydrological point of view. This consideration is not very important in alluvial areas where generally uniform conditions obtain over large distances but has particular relevance to hard rock areas. Such advice can be given only by adequately staffed State ground water organisations which should, thus, have two distinct wings, one to deal with the engineering problems of well designing and construction, and the other with geo-hydrological matters, including the preparation of large-scale maps on the scale of 8" or 16" to a mile showing straight conditions, the location of existing wells, water tables and the chemical quality of water, etc.

The need to ensure the coordination of the financial, hydrological, engineering and energisation aspects of ground schemes pointing to the desirability of creating in each State a ground water organisation which would also include a third wing—responsible for and development. This wing would take the initiative in getting schemes prepared and sanctioned and ensure their timely implementation up to the final stage of energisation.

SCIENTIFIC MANAGEMENT

The scientific management of ground water resources involves two steps, firstly, a quantitative assessment of the capacity and the recharge conditions of aquifers and, secondly, the control and regulation of pumping from them so as to avoid over-exploitation. The quantitative assessment of ground water resources is a rather complex process and has to be based on observations made over a number of years. These observations pertain to the territorial limits and depths of aquifers, the extent to which they are fed by percolation and other sources and the limit to which they can be exploited without causing depletion. Since all ground water was originally surface water, studies have to be made of rainfall, temperature and evaporation conditions as well as of the movement of water in streams, etc. We have so far made only a beginning with quantitative assessment by taking up two projects, one in Rajasthan and the other in Madras, both with assistance of the UNDP. While the final reports of both these projects have yet to come in, interim reports reveal that one of the areas surveyed in Rajasthan is, contrary to popular impression, being already over-exploited and that if the present rate of pumping is continued, stands in danger of not only falling water levels but also of saline infestation. In the meanwhile, reports have also been received from Mehsana in Gujarat and Coimbatore in Tamil Nadu of falling water levels as a result of over-exploitation.

It goes without saying that we must equip ourselves as soon as possible with the expertise necessary to carry out a large number of assessment studies in all parts of the country. This can be done either by sending our own officers abroad for training and/or by giving them on-the-job-training in existing projects as well as in any new projects which may be taken up either with or without foreign assistance. The Department of Agriculture is currently engaged in exploring all such possibilities.

Only after the capacity and recharge conditions of all the aquifers in a given area have been studied, it is possible to plan their optimum development in an integrated manner, and to decide which layers should be tapped and to what extent. Analog models and other scientific aids are of great use in arriving at such management decisions and are, in fact, being already used by the Oil and Natural Gas Commission (ONGC) in the development of oil fields. But management decisions, will require the backing of law before they can be implemented in certain cases, and no such backing is available at present. The whole question of a law to regulate and control the use of ground water in the best interests of the community is, however, being studied by an inter-departmental working group and a model Act is being drafted which is proposed to be circulated to all States for adoption. The implementation of such a law will require an enforcement machinery which again could be most appropriately located in State Ground Water Organisations.

SUGGESTIONS FOR IMPROVING THE SITUATION

(A) At the Government of India Level

It will be seen from the foregoing that not enough attention is being paid to ground water problems either at the Centre or in the States. In the Government of India, problems relating to the development of ground water figure in two Ministries. The Ministry of Petroleum and Chemicals and Mines and Metals (Department of Mines and Metals) comes into the picture as far as prospecting and the preparation of basic maps is concerned. This work, however represents only about 8 percent of the responsibilities of the Geological Survey of India and perhaps 1 percent of the work load of the entire Ministry. The other Ministry concerned is the Ministry or Agriculture, Community Development & Cooperation in which the ETO is located. The ETO, however, claims only about 50 percent of the time of one of the 15 or 16 Joint/Additional Secretaries of the Ministry which works out to about 3 per cent of the attention of the Ministry as a whole.

It is obvious that no great improvement in the existing situation can be expected so long as this state of affairs lasts. The first thing to be done would seem to be to locate all ground water work in one place so far as the Government of India is concerned and to ensure that the new unified organisation has adequate authority and prestige. Such an organisation can very appropriately take the form of a Commission on the analogy of the Oil and Natural Gas Commission and the Central Water and Power Commission (which deals with surface water). Surely, ground water is at least as important as oil and natural gas or surface water for the life and well-being of the community and there is no reason why it should not receive at least as much attention as these resources. The proposed Commission should deal with all matters connected with the search for water, its optimum development and its scientific management which requires attention at the Central level and should take over the duties of the Ground Water Wing of the Geological Survey of India as well as of the ETO. It should be administratively linked to the Ministry of Food and Agriculture (Department of Agriculture) for the simple reason that agriculture is the greatest beneficiary of ground water and therefore, most interested in its development.

With the formation of a National Commission, it would become possible for the first time to obtain an overall view of the country's needs in the field of ground water and to voice the same in an authoritative manner. The latest techniques in prospecting, mapping, resource assessment and management would find it easier to gain acceptance by the Commission than they do with the existing authorities. With a single (and we hope prestigious) body to speak for ground water, it would become possible to draw up policies and plans which are really adequate to meet the challenge of the times and to develop the self-confidence to implement them. Such a body would also provide a convenient point of contact for foreign experts on the subject and make it easier to obtain external assistance in fields of expertise in which we are deficient today. Within the country, the Commission would be a valuable source of advice, information and guidance to various bodies and institutions concerned with the ground water, not excluding State ground water organisations.

Another direction, in which a reform is due, concerns the arrangements in the Department of Agriculture for overseeing the implementation of ground water development programmes in the States. As noticed earlier, the total amount of investment in ground water during the Fourth Plan is expected to be of the order of

Rs.1,400 crores. At present, there are only 2 or 3 officers in the Department of Agriculture charged with the responsibility of ensuring the success of such a huge programme. All of them are headquartered in Delhi and there are no Regional Officers to watch and keep under constant review the progress of each State in the field of ground water development. This kind of supervision—so necessary to ensure the success of the schemes—can be undertaken only if we build up regional organisations and make one senior officer (of the rank of Deputy Commissioner at least) responsible for overseeing not more than 4 or 5 States. A minimum of 5 Regional Officers would thus be required in the Minor Irrigation Division of the Department of Agriculture. The cost of providing this additional support would be negligible when compared to the size of the programme.

(B) At The State Level

The need for State Governments to provide themselves with properly staffed and equipped ground water organisations has already been stressed. The present situation in this regard is quite unsatisfactory and there are only a few States which can claim to have even paid attention to this matter. Rajasthan has the best ground water organisation in the shape of a State Ground Water Board which is equipped for drilling and blasting work as well as for geo-hydrological investigations and works under the administrative control of the Agricultural Production Commissioner. Among the remaining states, only Andhra Pradesh, Haryana, Gujarat, Maharashtra, Mysore, Orissa, Tamil Nadu and Uttar Pradesh have made a beginning with the setting up of ground water organisations, while the rest have yet to make a start. However, conditions vary widely from Stale to State even within those mentioned above and there is no uniformity of organisations. Thus, in Andhra Pradesh, geo-hydrological work has been placed in the Directorate of Agriculture while drilling has been entrusted to the Agro-Industries Corporation although certain departments, like Irrigation, Panchayats and Public Health, also continue to operate their own rigs. In Haryana, a ground water cell has beep created in the Irrigation Department and not in the Agriculture Department. In Mysore, the drilling organisation is in the Department of Agriculture while the geo-hydrological cell is in the Directorate of Mines in the Department of Industries. In Tamil Nadu, the geo-hydrological cell is in the Department of Irrigation.

As a result of our regional discussions, there emerged a consensus of opinion that the State ground water organisations should form part of the agricultural production set up and be directly under the Commissioner for Agricultural Production or where this post does not exist, under the Secretary (Agriculture). The reasons for this recommendation are too obvious to mention.

It is recommended that the State ground water organisation should be headed by a senior officer who may be called Director (Ground Water) and be responsible for all aspects of development. This officer may be assisted by 3 or 4 officers of the rank of Additional, Joint or Deputy Director, depending upon the circumstances of the State. The first of these, who may be called Additional/Joint/Deputy Director (Engineering) should be a senior engineer responsible for all departmental drilling and blasting and for giving technical advice to the farmers on matters relating to the construction and design of wells and tubewells. If the State is situated in the alluvial belt and possesses State tubewells it would be proper to place, the construction and operation of such tubewells under the charge of this Officer unless it is decided to set up a Tubewell Corporation on the lines of the Haryana experiment. The second principal officer, who may be called the Additional/Joint/Deputy Director (Geo-hydrology) should be a senior hydrologist who would be responsible for preparation of large-scale hydrological maps, collection of data pertaining to ground water conditions and for investigations and assessments necessary for the preparation of ARC and other 'area' schemes. In hard rock areas, this officer would also be responsible for advising farmers with regard to the exact location of their wells after examining local geological conditions and the position of existing wells. The third principal officer may be designated Additional/ Joint/Deputy Director (Area Development) and should be responsible for the preparation and processing of area schemes, for watching their implementation and for maintaining liaison with the State Electricity Board for timely energisation. This officer could also appropriately be made responsible for follow-up action, after the scheme has been executed, in such matters as providing enough short-term credit, seed, fertilisers, etc. to farmers. (Since ARC area schemes require the appointment of Project Officers, this State level officer would for all purposes act as their chief.) A fourth officer would become necessary whenever the proposed ground, water legislation comes into force in a State. This officer, who may be designated as Additional/Joint/Deputy Director (Regulation) would be responsible for registering the rights of existing users of ground water, the licensing of new users and the imposition of such restrictions in pumping as may be necessary on technical considerations.

26

Ground Water Development

J.S. Burjia and Saleem Romani

INTRODUCTION

Groundwater development in India is taking place at a very fast pace. The past five decades have witnessed phenomenal increase in growth of ground water abstraction structures due to technically viable schemes backed by liberal funding and availability of power and diesel, good quality seeds, fertilisers, government subsidies, etc. The green revolution in the post-Independence era has also led to excessive development of ground water particularly in northern parts of the country. Groundwater irrigation through dug wells, tubewells and borewells contributes about half of the India's irrigated area. The ground water irrigation received a quantum jump with the advent of high yielding variety crop technology in the second half of 160s. It has been estimated that 70-80 per cent of the value of irrigated production in India comes from ground water irrigation. Around two-fifth of India's agricultural output is contributed from areas irrigated by ground water. The contribution from ground water to India's Gross Domestic Product (GDP) has been estimated as about nine per cent. The tubewell explosion in Punjab, Haryana and Western Uttar Pradesh after 1969 has contributed immensely to food production in India. This effort was facilitated by government efforts through rural electrification and institutional credit support. Even in eastern India, the agricultural strategy launched in mid-1980s mainly based on ground water development has given an unprecedented boost to rice production and the country exported more than five million tonne of rice becoming the second largest exporter of rice in the world.

IMPACT OF DEVELOPMENT ON GROUND WATER RESOURCES

The development activities over the years have adversely affected the ground water regime. Excessive ground water extraction coupled with haphazard disposal of untreated urban and industrial wastes and over application of fertilisers, pesticides/ insecticides in agricultural fields have resulted in ground water depletion and pollution.

With rapid expansion in ground water extraction, development related problems have started emerging. There is continuous growth in dark and over exploited areas in the country. Out of 5,711 Blocks/Mandals/Talukas in the country, 310 are categorised as over-exploited where the stage of ground water development exceeds the annual replenishment. (Table 1). It has been estimated that if the present trend continues, the number of over-exploited and critical blocks would double every 12.5 years. Substantial declines and fluctuations of ground water levels are occurring even in blocks with sufficient ground water resources due to climatic vicissitudes and localised development. Competing users too create problems resulting in social conflicts. Excessive ground water withdrawal for agricultural use can create pumping depression which would adversely affect the drinking water sources in the vicinity. Fluctuations in the water table due to ground water extraction for agriculture reduce reliability of shallow wells as sources of drinking water. Deeper water levels necessitate costly and technologically complex drinking water system due to construction of deep wells and installation of high capacity submersible or turbine pumps. Excessive ground water development has also resulted in ground water quality deterioration especially in coastal areas and those adjacent to areas with saline aquifers. The problem is especially serious in Coastal areas of Gujarat, Tamil Nadu, Orissa and Pondicherry where saline water incursion endangering the fresh ground water has taken place.

GROUND WATER MANAGEMENT STRATEGIES TO MEET THE FUTURE NEEDS

The management of ground water resources is inherently linked with its development. The sustainability of ground water resources is endangered due to haphazard development activities resulting into water scarcity in many areas of the country. The ground water development in a widely varying situation like India needs to be taken up in a regulated and judicious manner. The various issues on ground water management are as follows:

Planned Development of Ground Water Resources

Acceleration of Ground Water Development in Eastern Region

The strong link between ground water and economic growth highlights the development strategy of the country. A special agricultural strategy launched for eastern India comprising eastern Uttar Pradesh, Bihar, West Bengal, Assam, Orissa and eastern Madhya Pradesh in 1980s relied on ground water development. Free boring for shallow tube well and subsidies for pump sets provided in eastern region in 1987 have paid rich dividends and rice production in this region increased rapidly. An accelerating the ground water development through suitably planned strategy cannot only meet the water needs of the eastern region but can add to the total food production of the country.

Exploration of Deeper Aquifers

CGWB has explored the potential aquifers up to the depth of 400 metre in alluvial

Table 1: Categorisation of Blocks/Mandals/Taluks/Watersheds As Over-Exploited and Dark on All India Basis

Sl. No.	States/UTs	No. of Blocks/ Mandal/Taluks/ Watersheds	No. of Block/Taluks/Mandals/Watersheds			
			Over-exploited		Dark	
			No.	%	No.	%
States						
1.	Andhra Pradesh	1104 *	12	1.09	14	1.27
2.	Arunachal Pradesh		0	0.0	0	0.00
3.	Assam	134	0	0.00	0	0.00
4.	Bihar	589	3	0.51	9	1.53
5.	Goa	12	0	0.00	0	0.00
6.	Gujarat	184 **	13	7.07	15	8.15
7.	Haryana	108	33	30.56	8	7.41
8.	Himachal Pradesh	69	0	0.00	0	0.00
9.	Jammu & Kashmir	123	0	0.00	0	0.00
10.	Karnataka	175 **	7	4.00	9	5.14
11.	Kerala	154	0	0.00	0	0.00
12.	Madhya Pradesh	459	2	0.44	1	0.22
13.	Maharashtra	231 **	2	0.87	6	2.60
14.	Manipur	26	0	0.00	0	0.00
15.	Meghalaya	29	0	0.00	0	0.00
16.	Mizoram	20	0	0	0	0
17.	Nagaland	21	0	0.00	0	0.00
18.	Orissa	314	4	1.27	4	1.27
19.	Punjab	138	72	52.17	11	7.97
20.	Rajasthan	236	74	31.36	20	8.47
21.	Sikkim	4	0	0	0	0
22.	Tamil Nadu	384	64	16.67	39	10.16
23.	Tripura	17	0	0.00	0	0.00
24.	Uttar Pradesh	819	19	2.32	21	2.56
25.	West Bengal	341	0	0.00	1	0.29
	Total States	5691	305		158	
Union Territories						
1.	Andaman & Nicobar		0	0	0	0
2.	Chandigarh		0	0	0	0
3.	Dadra & Nagar Haveli		0	0	0	0
4.	Daman & Diu	2	1	50.00	1	50.00
5.	NCT of Delhi	5	3	60.00	1	20.00
6.	Lakshadweep	9	0	0.00	0	0.00
7.	Pondicherry	4	1	25.00		0.00
	Total Uts	20	5		2	
	Grand Total	5711	310		160	

* Andhra Pradesh – Mandal

** Gujarat, Karnataka, Maharashtra – Taluks/Tehsils

areas and 200 metre in hard rocks in the country. However, to increase the availability of water to meet the increasing demands and to retain it for future use, newer potential sources of ground water at greater depth need to he explored. Alluvial basins particularly Ganga basin offer scope for development of deeper ground water aquifers.

Development of Aquifers in Flood Plains

Flood plains in the vicinity of rivers act as repositories for ground water. To meet the additional demands, ground water from the flood plains can be withdrawn during non-monsoon, which gets recharged during the monsoon. Therefore, the flood plains of rivers offer excellent scope for development of ground water to meet the additional demands to some extent.

Development of Ground Water in Water Logged Areas

Large areas particularly in the command areas of major and medium irrigation projects suffer from water logging due to rejected recharge. The water logging conditions have been created due to high intensity of irrigation without adequate drainage, which results in upward movement of water table. As per the assessment made by the Working Group on Problem Identification in Irrigated Area with suggested Remedial Measures (1991), about 2.46 mha of the area under surface water irrigation projects is water logged or threatened by water logging. Such areas offer scope for ground water development by lowering the water table up to six metre or more.

Use of Saline/Brackish Water

It has been estimated that over 1.93 lakh sq km area in parts of Haryana, Punjab, Delhi, Rajasthan, Gujarat, Uttar Pradesh, Karnataka and Tamil Nadu is affected by inland salinity in ground water (EC>4000 micromhos). Saline/brackish ground water resources up to the depth of 450 metre below ground levels in alluvial areas and 100 metre below ground level in hard rock areas have been estimated to be of the order of 1.164 bcm.

Yields of many crops, vegetables and fruit plants, e.g. barley. dates and pomegranate, when irrigated with saline or brackish water are not significantly affected. Saline/brackish water can be successfully used to irrigate such plants and fresh or good quality water can be saved for use by other sensitive crops or for other uses. Brackish water can also be utilised for pisciculture/aquaculture. Therefore, additional resource of 1.164 bcm of saline/brackish ground water resource would be available for use.

Artificial Recharge of Ground Water

Artificial recharge of ground water is one of the most powerful strategy to ensure sustainability of ground water resources. It is, going to be one of the important planning necessities for the country in the times to come. The future food security of teeming millions in the country would depend on the innovative designs and ingenious approach of scientists and engineers to conserve every drop of surplus monsoon runoff flowing into the sea. The ground water reservoir offers technically feasible alternative to store additional quantity of water available in the country during monsoon.

Groundwater augmentation through diversion of rainfall runoff to sub-surface reservoirs by various artificial recharge techniques, has special relevance in India, where due to terrain conditions, most of the rain water is lost as flash floods and local streams remain dry for most part of the year. Central Ground Water Board has identified an area of about 4.5 lakh sq. km. in the country, which shows a declining trend in ground water levels and needs urgent attention to meet the growing needs for irrigation, industry and domestic purpose. It is estimated that in these identified areas of water scarcity, about 361 bcm of surplus monsoon surface runoff is available which can be fruitfully utilised to augment the ground water resources. A twin strategy of adopting simple artificial recharge techniques in rural areas like Percolation Tanks, Check Dams, Recharge Shafts, Dugwell Recharge and Sub-surface dykes and adopting roof top rainwater harvesting in urban areas, can go a long way in redeeming the worsening situation of shortage of ground water. About 2.25 lakh artificial recharge structures in rural areas and about 37 lakh rooftop rainwater harvesting structures in the cities are feasible. The design and viability of various low cost structures have been demonstrated by CGWB by undertaking 174 schemes throughout the country during Ninth Plan under the Central Sector Scheme "Study of Ground Water Recharge". Rainwater harvesting has to be taken up in a big way to solve the crisis of water scarcity.

Regulation of Ground Water Development

The problems caused by unplanned development leading to over exploitation, require specific ground water management options. These are normally: (1) ground water regulation through administrative and legal measures and (2) augmenting ground water availability through artificial recharge. The second option has already been discussed earlier. Administrative measures to regulate ground water development are being taken up mainly through institutional financing for ground water development. The loanees have to observe the technical criteria of 'spacing' between the two ground water structures based on the availability of ground water in the area. However, the private individual investing his own resource is not controlled by these disciplines and can construct wells of any design installing pumps of any capacity. With the advent and proliferation of down the hole drilling technology, construction of borewells in hard rock formation has become an overnight activity. Mushrooming of drilling contractors and farmers affordability to pay for construction of borewells has resulted in over-exploitation of ground water. The withdrawal of ground water has continued unhindered as per the prevailing ground water right, wherein the land owner has an absolute right over the water under his land. These measures can result in distress situation with deleterious effects on ground water regime. Water markets to meet demand of farmers having no irrigation source have developed in many areas like Banaskantha and Mehsana districts of Gujarat. Water lordism has resulted in not only exploitation of needy farmers but also that of the ground water resources.

The Central Ground Water Authority, constituted under Environment (Protection) Act of 1986 is playing a key role in regulating the development for assuring sustainable management of ground water. The Authority is vested with the responsibility of regulation of ground water development and management including conservation, protection and augmentation of ground water through artificial recharge. The approach of the Authority is to place a major thrust on education and bringing in awareness among the people for the need to protect and conserve the resources and their proper utilisation. The Authority is promoting adoption of artificial recharge in water deficit areas.

People's Participation in Ground Water Development and Management

The success of ground water development programme depends on the close and active involvement of beneficiaries. The programme should involve people at different levels with suitable responsibilities at each level. People's participation would be necessary for implementation of schemes related to artificial recharge of ground water, because as discussed earlier, water recharged to the aquifers joins the common pool ground water reservoir and has to be shared by the community. In protection and surveillance of ground water pollution, the local people can play a prominent role. The role of women is crucial in planning and implementing the drinking water schemes. Nobody can better, appreciate the importance and worth of water more than a woman and as such her involvement in planning and management of water resources can provide a workable solution to the satisfaction of the society.

MASS AWARENESS

It is essential to involve the local people/community in water management programme. Central Ground Water Board has taken up 150 mass awareness programmes in rural and urban areas to educate people and seek their active cooperation in ground water management. With availability of experts in different disciplines and experience of working in different parts of the country, the mass awareness programmes of CGWB are widely appreciated. This activity is being expanded by involving electronic media and production of documentary films.

Central Ground Water Board is organising training on rain water harvesting including roof top rain water harvesting in different parts of the country. The objective of these training courses is to educate the masses about the benefits of rain water harvesting in controlling decline of ground water levels and to propagate innovative and economical techniques of rain water harvesting including roof top rain water harvesting in urban environment. Eighty such training courses have been organised throughout the country. Representatives of Central/State Government organisations, institutes, welfare organisations, Group Housing Societies, Panchayats, NGOs, VOs, industries and individuals, etc. have attended these courses.

27

Hydroelectric Power—The Best Use Water can be Put through

Yogendra Prasad

INTRODUCTION

History of mankind shows that all primitive human settlements were based on the criteria of water availability and along the banks of rivers. However, with the progress of humanity and consequent population growth, supplies from local rivers and wells could not satisfy the increasing demand for water. As such the option of water management with available tools and technology were started then. In Middle East, water transfer tunnels were constructed even 3000 years ago. Ancients Romans constructed aqueduct to convey water over long distances.

Indian subcontinent has as many as 12 major rivers, whose total catchment area is 252.8 million hectare (mha). Of the major rivers, the Ganga—Brahmaputra and Meghana have the biggest system with catchment area of about 110 mha. The other major rivers with catchment area of more than 10 mha are Indus (32.1 mha), Godavari (31.3 mha), Krishna, (25.9 mha) and Mahanadi (14.2 mha).

India with a growing population of 1,027 million have to devise her own water management strategy for meeting the water requirement as well as energy requirement. As with other resources, water is not spread uniformly across the country. Both droughts as well as floods have adverse effects ondevelopment of Indian economy. As envisaged by United Nations, water management for development can:

- Improve health through access to safe drinking water and sanitation.
- Enhance food security by providing agriculture with water suitable for irrigation.
- Contribute to diet diversity by preserving fresh water fish habitats.
- Offer employment opportunities if water quality allows fishing stocks to be maintained.

- Protect against damage from floods.
- Safeguard water supplies in time of draught.
- Implement means to adapt water management to the increasing variability of precipitation.

National Water Policy[1] envisaged by Government of India broadly describes the water allocation priority for planning and development as follows:

- Drinking Water.
- Irrigation.
- Hydropower.
- Ecology.
- Agro industries and non-agricultural industries.
- Navigation and other uses.

However, it also says that priorities can be modified or added if warranted by area/region specific conditions. To achieve basic development goals besides meeting the irrigaton and drinking water needs, energy provisions (*i.e.*, through hydro electric power) should also be properly augmented. India being a country of mighty rivers is having immense amount of hydroelectric potential in this direction.

During the recent Third World Water Forum which was held at Kyoto in March 2003 the ministerial declaration indicates the concern of world over the water related issues. Summary of which are given below:

- It recognises the role of hydropower as one of the renewable and clean energy sources and that its potential should be realised in an environmentally sustainable and socially equitable manner.
- Access to clean water is essential for sustainable development and eradication of poverty and hunger.
- The forum notes a report calling for doubling the spending on water infrastructure in developing countries.
- The report calls for private sector participation and public-private partnerships to tackle water issues.
- The report vows to devise integrated water resources management plans by 2005, and to assist developing countries.
- Far more investment in water supply and sanitation is needed to halve the proportion of people without access to safe drinking water and basic sanitation by 2015.
- Collective efforts should be redoubled to mobilise financial and technical resources, both public and private, to achieve the goals.
- Effective and equitable management of water is required to eradicate poverty in rural areas,
- Farm-use water management should be improved *via* innovative investment, research and development, and cooperation.

- Better legislative frameworks are necessary to protect water resources and prevent water pollution.
- Land-use regulation, disaster-warning systems and national risk-management systems are needed to limit the impact of floods and droughts.
- Data and knowledge should be shared between states to minimise disaster damage.

HYDROPOWER—THE BEST USE OF WATER

Hydropower industry is closely linked to both water management and renewable energy production and thus has an important role in sustainable development in a world where billions of people still lack access to safe drinking water and adequate energy supplies. As hydropower doesn't consume the water it uses to generate power it leaves this vital resources available for other uses. Moreover, the revenue generated can fund other infrastructural projects for providing drinking water supply system, irrigation system etc.

During the phases of hydropower development, the option of building dams and reservoirs is often criticised as they profoundly modify the ecosystem where they are created. But this is the option through which unequal distribution of water that occurs in the unmanaged environment can be adjusted. Rejecting the option of a dam is in fact rejecting the opportunity to rectify severe inequalities which are also unsustainable in the long run. Dams thus have an important role to play in integrated approaches, when negative social and environmental impacts can be successfully mitigated or avoided. Dams thus associated with hydropower have an important role in socio-economic and economic development and hence essential to the well being of many millions of people.

The hydropower has several advantages over other forms of commercial power. Besides being inexhaustible, it is pollution free and non-inflationary in character. Moreover, it helps in infrastructural development of the remote and hilly areas. There are several technical merits of hydropower which are required for extending peaking support and for lending reliability and stability to the power system as a whole. And above all, in this age of ozone depletion and global warming, we have to look up to hydropower as the energy source of the future. World over the recent concern has been on the increasing amount of CO_2 in the earth's atmosphere due to excessive burning of fossil fuels and to curb this emission we must switch over from fossil fuel based energy to the clean hydropower.[2]

INDIAN HYDROPOWER SCENARIO

As per assessment made by Central Electrical Authority, India is endowed with economically exploitable hydropower potential to the tune of 84,044 MW at 60 per cent load factor corresponding to 1,48,701 MW of installed capacity. Over and above, 56 number of pumped storage projects have also been identified with installed hydro-potential of 94,000 MW.

Basim/Rivers	*Probable Installed Capacity (MW)*
Indus Basin	33,832
Ganga Basin	20,711
Central Indian River system	4,152
Western Flowing Rivers of Southern India	9,430
Eastern Flowing Rivers of Southern India	14,511
Brahmaputra Basin	66,065

In addition to this hydro-potential from small, mini and micro schemes has been estimated as 6,782 MW. Thus, in totality India is endowed with hydro-potential of about 2,50,000 MW. However, exploitation of hydro-potential has not; been upto mark due to various constraints confronting the sector as well as due to shift in priority for capacity addition in short term, based on exhaustible conventional sources.

Till 2002-03, hydro-potential to the tune of 26,910.23 MW only has been developed which comes to only about 10 per cent of viable potential, leaving gigantic opportunities for developers to exploit. The key issues which led to this low hydro share are time and cost overruns resulting into long gestation periods, financial problems, environmental issues, geological surprises, rehabilitation and resettlement, water sharing disputes among states and detrimental law and order situation in many states. Attributed to some of these issues, hydroelectric power development suffered serious setbacks which resulted in decrease of hydro thermal mix to 26:74 against an optimal mix of 40:60 as on date. Building a good number of hydro projects and pumped storage schemes is a better management of water resource as well as a technical requirement of Indian grid.

RECENT TRENDS IN HYDROELECTRIC SECTOR

Government of India launched "Policy on Hydro Power Development" during 1998 under which impetus is given to development of hydropower in the country. This was a welcome step towards effective utilisation of our water resources in the direction of hydropower development There has been growing concern for meeting out the energy demands of the country and as for now the energy planners have decisively judged development of vast unharnessed hydro potential in the country as national priority. Government has taken strong initiative towards starting new mega hydroelectric projects and completing the ongoing projects well in time. Some of the major hydro projects like Nathpa Jhakri project (1500 MW), Parbati Stage-II (800 MW) and Chamera – II (300 MW) in Himachal Pradesh, Tehri (Stage-l, 1000 MW) project in Uttranchal, Indirasagar project (1000 MW) and Omkareshwar (520 MW) in Madhya Pradesh, Teesta Stage – V (510 MW) in Sikkim, Purulia Pumped Storage (900 MW) in West Bengal and Subansiri Lower (2000 MW) in Arunachal Pradesh are all in different construction stages and will start generation within coming few years.[3]

Special emphasis is laid on development of North Eastern India which is blessed with Bhrahmaputra river system where it has a total drainage area of about 2.65 lakh sq km. It covers the North Eastern states of Arunachal Pradesh, Assam, Meghalaya, Manipur, Tripura, Mizoram, Nagaland, Sikkim and a substantial part of West Bengal. As per the assessment studies, Bhrahmaputra basin is having hydroelectric potential of 66,065 MW of installed capacity. Out of this. NE states along with Sikkim have a potential of 63,257 MW of installed capacity out of which less than two per cent hydro potential has been developed so far. For this underdeveloped part of India, lot of work needs to be done for social and economic development and hydropower could be an excellent option for achieving these objectives as development of hydro projects not only generate clean energy but also provide services such as flood mitigation, water supply, irrigation, improved water quality, navigation and recreation.

Recently the Prime Minister of India during May 2003 launched 50,000 MW Hydroelectric initiative". Under this programme pre-feasibility reports for 162 new hydroelectric projects across 16 states with proposed capacity of over 50,000 MW are to be implemented by the end of 12th Five Year Plan (year 2017). Out of the total 50,000 MW initiative 33,294 MW has been identified in the North Eastern region of the country. Once we achieve this capacity addition programme, the whole outlook of this region will change as more and more economic activity will start in the region and the area will get huge relief from the frequent floods that has been endangering the lives of the people for centuries now.

WHAT NEEDS TO BE DONE FURTHER

Having realised the importance of hydropower development in the country, the present initiatives by the government and other agencies working in this field must be further continued for accelerated hydro-development, some of these initiatives could be:

(*i*) Government in the overall interest of the country must continue support for development of hydro projects.

(*ii*) Basin wise development of hydro projects needs to be implemented for the optimisation of time and resources.

(*iii*) Projects, which are stuck up by inter-state disputes need to be implemented by a neutral agency like NHPC, who have vast experience and capabilities in this field.

(*iv*) Cost overrun and time overrun of project should be eliminated through proactive planning and monitoring use of most modern construction technologies, precise survey and investigation, etc., NHPC has already set such examples through successfully commissioning of projects ahead of schedule some of which are Kurichu HE Project in Bhutan, Kalpong HE Project in Andaman and Nicobar Island, Chamera – II HE Project in Himachal Pradesh.

Awareness needs to be created in the minds of people towards development of hydropower. As issues concerning hydropower development at many times have been totally blown out of portion and only a few pathological cases which are surrounded with controversies are over publicised. People must be made aware of the true benefits of hydroelectric projects through serious campaign.

REFERENCES

1. *National Water Policy* 2002, Ministry of Water resources, Government of India.
2. *The Role of Hydropower in Sustainable Development,* International Hydro Power Association (IHA) White Paper, February 2003.
3. International Hydropower Association (IHA), *Sustainability Guidelines,* 2003.

Section VIII: AGRICULTURAL, FOOD PRODUCTION AND DROUGHT MANAGEMENT

28

Drought Policy Framework – Some Personal Reflections[1]

Rakesh Hooja[2]

INTRODUCTION

Drought is a complex phenomenon.[3] There are agricultural droughts, meteorological droughts, hydrological droughts, etc. (In fact some of the words used in Rajasthan for famines: Ankal great famine, *Jalkal*-scarcity of water, *Tinkal*-scarcity of foder, water and grain, all indicate local perceptions about different kinds of famines.)

A drought affects irrigation and crop production, availability of food, fodder, calorie intake, drinking water, livelihoods, incomes (including incomes in the non-farm sector) in both rural and urban areas since in rural and urban economies are interdependent. Also affected are entitlements, rural indebtedness, health and malnutrition and life expectancies (of both human beings and of animals) , livestock, agro-based activities and allied activities, the State's governmental or administrative machinery (which in periods of server drought turns almost all its attention to and focuses its funding towards providing drought relief in a mission mode, to the detriment of various other regular governmental task), and the overall economy of the region which faces a drought. For anyone living in Rajasthan, the word drought is invariably related to the concept of drought relief. Such, is our present mindset that even the chief government functionary assigned drought related responsibilities is referred to as the Relief Commissioner, and is normally expected to fully activated himself only during periods of server drought.

Three Components of a Drought Policy

Thus we can divide drought policy into three major components: (*a*) drought proofing/ drought prevention whose activities would be chiefly carried out in good years but would also need to be continued in the not so good years, (*b*) mitigation of impact of droughts n years to moderate droughts, (*c*) drought relief operations in years of severe drought. While components (*b*) and (*c*) above can together be viewed as components of Drought Management with difference between the two merely being one of degree, component (*a*) above would involve integrated development and resource management of drought prone areas (which in many ways would encompass much more than the activities that have been part of Government of India's Drought Prone Areas Programme (DPAP) and Desert Development Progamme (DDP) since, as has been emphasised,[4] "life in arid areas is a perpetual struggle where consequences of lack of proper resource management can be very grave". All these components are related to each other and efforts in any one sphere would impact the other two. However the approach to implementing activities as per component (*a*) shall perforce need to be different from that for components (*b*) and (*c*). Activities are per component (*a*) would continue to be carried out concurrently with those under components (*b*) and (*c*). While working out the drought policy framework, one needs to look not only at examples of various government driven interventions across the country, but also at how local populace has been adjusting and adapting to meet drought situations.[5] Such adaptive strategies on the part of local communities can be ecological, economic, social, and the like.

Administrative Arrangements

Before going into details of what the three above mentioned components of a drought policy involve in terms of the activities to be covered, it would be appropriate to briefly look at the implementing and coordinating authorities and structures required for successful implementation (some of this administrative structure already exists albeit in a somewhat different form).

As regards coordination of drought management (including both mitigation and relief), the present Relief Commissioner should be redesignated as the Drought Management Commissioner who would report to the state government's Group of Ministers (GoM) for drought management and to a Committee of Secretaries and Heads of Departments (HoDs) of relevant department (which should be headed by the Chief Secretary, or by the Principle Secretary Disaster Management). The Drought Management Commissioner should operate through the Divisional Commissioners and the District Collectors and activate the concerned HoDs to ensure that the District Level Officers (DLOs) cooperate and accept the supervision and guidance of the District Collector who is the key implementer. The District Collector should also chair a District Drought Management Committee.

The existing system of a very senior state government officer being assigned a district to review and monitor all drought relief activities in severe drought years, and of similarly appointing a Minister in-charge for drought relief work in each district, could also be continued.

As regards the Integrated Development and Resource Management of Drought Prone Areas, the Development Commissioner-cum-Principal Secretary Rural Development should be the key functionary at the State Government level. He should head a Committee of Directions (CoD) for the Integrated Development and Resource Management of Drought Prone Areas comprising selected Secretaries, HoDs, Divisional

Commissioners and experts of Agriculture Universities or regular Universities. The concerned Department through their Dlos and the Panchayati Raj Institutions (PRIs) should implement the various developmental activities with the District Collectors and *Zila Pramukhs* coordinating and supervising/managing them at the district level. There should be Division level and District level Integrated Development and Resource Management Committees in each drought prone district or division with as Divisional/Area Development Commissioner or the District Collector, as the case may be, functioning as its chairman. At the district level an Integrated Development and Resource Management Planning Sub-committee should also be constituted.

In both the above cases, i.e., drought management (including Relief) and Integrated Development and Resources Management of Drought Prone Areas, the roles[6] of community based user groups, panchayat bodies, NGOs, private entities, the institutional credit system (including agriculture and livestock breeders cooperatives), university and research institutions, and various government agencies respectively need to be spelt out as part of the drought policy framework.

In the case of Drought Management (including Relief) the powers and responsibilities of the Drought Management Commissioner and of the District Collector (who could also be designated as ex-officio Deputy Commissioner for Drought Management) may need to be spelt out in a new Drought Management Act which, along with its rules, should replace the Famine Code which is an administrative document having no statutory authority. The District Deputy Commissioner (District Collector) could also, through provisions in the proposed Act, be armed with powers to requisition services of manpower, vehicles and other resources for emergency drought relief operations.

For Integrated Development and Resource Management of Drought Prone Areas, it may not be necessary to go in for a new Act, but government guidelines may suffice.

Now to turn to a consideration of the activities that should be taken up as part of a drought policy.

Activities that form Part of the Various Components of a Drought Policy

Integrated Development and Resource Management of Drought-Prone Areas

The Integrated Development and Resource Management of Drought Prone Areas would need to be taken up on an area basis in a holistic manner. This would involve water harvesting,[7] ground water recharge and efficient use of both surface water and groundwater, diversification of crops and of agriculture, greater agricultural productivity per unit water and per unit land, extension efforts pertaining to agriculture, irrigation and livestock, improved water management,[8] watershed development and management,[9] the spread of irrigation canals into desert and drought prone areas,[10] Participatory Irrigation Management (PIM) canal systems,[11] soil and water conservation in both rain fed and irrigated areas, development of drinking water sources and supply systems, livestock development (cattle, goat, sheep etc.),[12] encouragement of crop-livestock mixed farming, afforestation and pasture development (including sand dune stabilization and fodder development), improved management of common property resources, increasing the efficiency of both human and animal health services, handicrafts and artisan activities, marketing infrastructure for agriculture, livestock, handicrafts etc., rural produce, agro-processing and storage of agricultural produce, non-farm agro based activities like the wool based activities like the wool based activities in the *khadi* sector in Rajasthan non-farm non-agricultural activities (which are less likely to be affected by droughts) like mining, decentralized and alternate energy systems and rural electrification, rural industries, development of the institutional finance network (banks RRBs – regional rural banks–and cooperative institutions) to ensure better supply of credit, and greater people's participation and community management of local land-water assets. Since watershed development forms an important part of both the integrated development and resource management component and the mitigation component, it is proposed at this point to set forth some objectives of watershed development that find common mention in the 2001 and 2003 watershed guidelines of the Ministry of Rural Development. The two guidelines agree on factors like mitigating adverse effects of drought and desertification; need for simple, easy and affordable technological solutions and institutional arrangements; encouraging the village community towards sustained community action for operation and managements of assets and development of natural resource potential in the watershed; promoting overall economic development and improving the socio-economic condition of the resource poor and disadvantaged sections; employment generation; poverty alleviation; community empowerment and development of human and other economic resources in the rural areas; restoring the ecological balance by harnessing, conserving and developing natural resources like land, water, vegetative cover etc. The two guidelines differ somewhat wherein the 2001 guidelines stress developing wasteland/degraded lands, drought prone and desert areas keeping in view the capability of the land and the local needs and conditions, the 2003 guidelines talk of harnessing every drop of rainwater for irrigation, horticulture, floriculture, pasture development/fisheries etc. to create sustainable sources of income for the village community, and provide drinking water supplies.[13]

Planning for Integrated Development and Resource Management

Planning for the integrated development of drought-prone areas would be somewhat similar to district or sub-district planning. It would need to be area specific planning rather than individual beneficiary or beneficiary group planning. It would not be confined to the planning of governmental programmes, but be much broader encompassing the planning for both governmental and private activities at the local or district/regional level and would need to tap into resources available from Central or state government schemes as well as resources available locally. It would need to be guided by advice and guidelines issued at Government of India, or state government ministries and departments and would also be sensitive to local suggestions flowing from the people *via* PRIs or community based organizations and user groups.

The Integrated Development and Resource Management Sub-Committee as suggested above, would need to work in close coordination with the District Planning Committee and District Planning Cell which already exist in each district.

Suggestions[14] of the Economic Area conceipt[15], the Hanumantha Rao Committee which uses the growth center concept,[16] and the 10th Five Year Plan Working Group on decentralized planning and panchayati raj[17] with reference to district planning, can be adapted for use while undertaking planning for integrated development and resource management of drought prone areas.

As the Hanumantha Rao Committee suggests, the plan should not be a mere collection of various departmental or sub-departmental proposal, nor a mere spelling out of targets and financial allocations, but a much more comprehensive document, which, keeping in mind financial constraints, spells out logical relations between sectoral and departmental plans and between various Economic Areas in a district, and which determines the chronological order in which schemes are to be started and implemented. It is to be based on calculations of demand and supply where the need for equipment, trained personnel, buildings raw material, skilled and unskilled labour etc. have been checked against available supply and an attempt made to improve the internal organization of the implementing agencies. The committee goes on to suggest that given the knowledge of Central and state projects n the area and the corresponding inflows of financial outlays, as well as of local natural resources, production, land uses, credit supply, infrastructure and social service facilities, etc., the planner should give priority to the development of socio-economic overheads and to resource development.

Similarly the Hanumantha Rao Committee has set forth the following functions of the planning body; (*i*) crystallization of the local needs and objectives within the broad framework of national and state level objectives, (*ii*) taking stock of the natural and human endowments of the district and regions within the district as well as the level and pattern of development attained so far, (*iii*) listing and mapping of amenities at the village, block and district levels, (*iv*) formulation of plans in their socio-economic, temporal and spatial dimensions along with their linkages with the rest of the economy, (*v*) fromulating of policies, programmes and priorities relevant for the district, (*vi*) coordination and implementation of the plan, (*vii*) monitoring and review of implementation of the plan and programmes with due regard to their linkages and dependencies.

Planning for integrated development and resource management of drought prone areas would adopt the approaches and methodologies being adopted and recommended for district plannnng[18] with the difference that the former concentrates upon drought proofing of the economy and making the area resistant to droughts, while the latter is aimed at the overall development of the district.

DROUGHT MANAGEMENT

Mitigating Impact

Drought Mitigation, or reducing the impact of droughts on an area's economy, involves activities like watershed development, pasture development and afforestation, regulation of use of surface and ground water to ensure water conservation. It may also involve some activities which fall in the nature of relief works. Fodder banks may need to be created. In addition, individual beneficiary schemes of self-employment and poverty reduction based upon credit and subsidies for people below the poverty line to enable them to obtain assets, and employment generation programmes (like the employment guarantee schemes), which are implemented even in good rainfall years, are important for mitigating the impacts of droughts. The employment guarantee schemes find their scope and magnitude extended in times of severe famines when they assume the form of relief works with many of the norms for employment works being relaxed in view of the need for drought relief.

For mitigation of the impacts of droughts which are not too severe but when there is shortage of water and the soils are hard and dry, the scientific establishment should have ready suggestions on practices and cropping patterns (cash crops, food crops, fodder crops) which the farmers could adopt. These would be based upon traditional knowledge as well as modern scientific research. Similarly practices for optimal surface and groundwater management and for modified management and care of the livestock and of common grazing grounds should also be propagated through the agriculture, irrigation and livestock extension networks. In this context initiatives like ITC company's '*e-chaupal*' to provide better information and knowledge to farmers and pastoralists to enable them to take proper decisions as per existing conditions also appear to be worth emulating.

Drought Relief

States having arid or semi-arid ecosystems are prone to droughts which recur with regularly and severity. Thus drills have been worked out whereby the entire district administration gets involved in drought or famine relief as soon as a sever drought becomes imminent. Over the years Famine Codes initially prepared in the directly ruled provinces of British India have been worked upon and rewritten as per experience of famine relief operations. Thus this is a component for which not much new thinking needs to be undertaken, except for trying to increase implementation efficiency and having shelf-of-works (or shelfs-of-projects) kept ready so that relief works leading to construction of productive assets can be undertaken whenever a severe drought occurs.

At times of such famines, when the crops totally fail and fodder ceases to be available, drought relief works are started to provide employment and incomes to the poor. For the infirm, old and the destitute old-age pensions and food doles are distributed. Arrangements for providing drinking water and water for domestic use are made including water tankers by roads or by rail. It is ensured that food stocks are available throughout the state, and that the poor have access to food through the public distribution system. Fodder is imported and fodder depots opened. Land revenue (even though it is now only a nominal amount) collection is suspended, and, if the famine extends over a number of successive years, is even written off Cooperative loans are re-scheduled to ease the problem of rural debt during years of famine. Special medical teams are deputed through out the famine affected areas, as are veterinary teams.

All such steps are undertaken on a war footing with government agencies. Panchayats and NGOs as well as user groups being involved thus GO-NGO-CBO (government organization-non-government organization community based organization) interactions and coordination assumes importance. Action plans for drought relief are prepared and their implementation monitored in physical and financial terms at various levels. In fact in a way the entire state government gets involved in drought relief work.

Monitoring and Evaluation

It will be seen that the drought mitigation component or stage bears a closer relationship to the relief component or stage than to the integrated development and resource management component. Unlike the comprehensive and multi-disciplinary development plans required for integrated development and resource management of drought prone areas, practical action plans are the need for mitigation and relief efforts. The type of monitoring systems required would also differ accordingly particularly since relief (and even, to some extent, mitigation) is taken up as an emergency exercise, while integrated area development and resource management involves regular, on-going and complex efforts.

One activity which has not been receiving sufficient attention is evaluation (both concurrent and post facto) of the impact of the efforts undertaken. This is as important for relief and mitigation activities as for the integrated development and resource management.

There are often charges of corruption in the implementation of drought relief works. Greater transparency in operations and increased peoples' participation should help check possible corruption. However, before concluding, we would like to suggest that a careful listing should be undertaken of all possible leakage points or stages at which leakage can occur in the implementation of the various activities under the three components of the drought policy, so that anticipatory steps to prevent leakage at each such leakage point/stage may be worked out in advance and made an integral part of the policy framework.[19]

REFERENCES

1. A request to prepare a presentation for a National Symposium (since postponed coincided with the return of the author to the Government of Rajasthan after almost seven years in the Government of India where matters like drought did not concern him. It has enabled the author to consider afresh the issue of a drought policy framework based on his earlier 23 years experience in Government of Rajasthan and his reading and writings on issues related to land-water management, rural development and droughts, etc.).
2. The ideas expressed by the author in this note are purely personal and academic and do not represent those of any agency where he has worked. The author has deliberately avoided referring to recent literature regarding drought management in the hope that he would be able to come up with some fresh or new ideas while writing this article.

3. P. Sainath, *Everyone Loves Good Drought: Stories from India's Poorest Districts,* Penguin Book, India, 1996.
4. Rakesh Hooja and Rajendra Joshi (ed.), "*Desert Drought and Development: Studies in Resource Management and Sustainability*", Rawat Publications, 1999.
5. Carol Henderson, "Resource Use, Drought and Desertification: Adaptive Strategies, the Community and Economic Stratification" in Hooja and Joshi, *op.cit.,* No. 4. As Henderson points out, general ecological and economic strategies by which agricultural populations adapt to drought have been documented in Brian Spooner and H.S. Mann "Desertification and its Control: Dry land Ecology in Social Perspective", Academic Press, New York 1982, H.S. Mann (ed.) "The Environmental, Economic and Social Significance of Drought Angus and Robertson Publishers", Sydney, Australia, 1973.
6. In this context, the author's two articles "Administrative Delivery System in Desert Areas (With Special Reference to Western Rajasthan)" and "The development Delivery System in a Desert District" in Horst G. Mensching and RC. Sharma (ed.) Resource Management in Drylands (The Raiasthan Example), Rajesh Publications 1984 may prove interesting. Also see the papers in part II of Rakesh Hooja Administrative Interventions in Rural Development, Rawat Publication, 1987. For the role of panchayat bodies see Meenakshi Hooja and Rakesh Hooja "Institutions of Self-Governance or Agencies of Development: Panchayati Raj in India", in South *Asian Journal of Socio-Political Studies.*
7. Anil Agarwal and Sunita Narain (ed.) "Dying Wisdom: Rise and Fall and Potential of India's Traditional Water Harvesting Systems", Center for Science and Environment, New Delhi, 1997 R.N. Athavale, "Water harvesting and Sustainable Supply in India", Rawat Publications, 2003, and P.M. Natarajan and S. Kallolikar "Rainwater Harvesting: New Approaches for Sustainable Water Resources Development", 2004.
8. "Rakesh Hooja, "The Administration of Water for Agriculture: Essays in Management of Irrigation, "Watersheds and Drainage", Rawat Publications, 2005. Also see Anil Agarwal, Sunita Narain and Indira Khurana (ed.) "Making Water Everybody's Business", *Center for Science and Environment,* New Delhi, 2001.
9. C.H. Hanumantha Rao, "Watershed Development in India-Present Experience and Emerging Issues", Leverage Kumar Memorial lecture, Society for Promotion of Wasteland Development, New Delhi, 2000. (paper based upon the lecture published in Economic and Political Weekly, Vol. 35, No. 35, November 4, 2000.)
10. B.H. Farmer, "Agriculture Colonization in India Since Independence", Oxford University Press, London, 1974 and Rakesh Hooja, "Greening the Desert: Motivating Settlers" in Rawat Publication, 2001.
11. L.K. Joshi and Rakesh Hooja (ed.) "Participatory Irrigation Management: Paradigm for 21st Century (2 volumes) Rawat Publications, 2000, Rakesh Hooja and G. Pangarc," Some Reflections on Software Aspects of Water Policy: CAP, PIM, Watershed Development and Management and Water Harvesting. India NPIM Working Paper/Monograph No. 13, January 2003, Rakesh Hooja, "Revisiting Participatory Irrigation Management in India", *Indian Journal of Public Administration,* Vol. 49, No. 3, July-Sept. 2003, and Rakesh Hooja "Water Users Associations as Part of the Fourth Tier in Indian Federalism", *South Asian Journal of Socio-Political Studies,* Vol. 4, No. 2, June 2004.
12. For integrated development and resource management of drought prone areas it is increased productivity and maximizing of economic returns at the macro level, as well as breed improvement, which would be the goals of livestock activities, while for drought mitigation and relief the focus would need to be on the security and livelihood dependence aspects of livestock as they impact upon rural households. Also see Rakesh Hooja, "Towards a Policy for Livestock in Watershed Development Programme: Livestock-

Environment-Watershed Interactions in India: A Draft Document based on Five State Level Studies", (Draft), unpublished document International Water Management Institute (South Asia Office, Patancheru), 2004. Also see Rakes hat Hooja "The Need for Synergies Between Watershed and Livestock Policies", forthcoming in *Social Change.*

13. It would be interesting to compare the above set of objectives with those worked out by the author in a list of objectives that was initially developed in 1979-80 and published in Rakesh Hooja "Peoples' Participation in Comprehensive Watershed Area Development" in Hoshiar Singh (ed.) "Rural Development in India." Printwell 1985 and the slightly revised for the author's contributions to Social and Institutional Issues in Watershed Management in India OIKOS Delhi and IIRR Philippines, 2000. The list reads as follows: (*i*) conservation of moisture in rainfed areas for optimal production, (*ii*) to check soil erosion, ensure, soil and water conservation, (*iii*) to control problems of drainage, salinity, alkalinity, (*iv*) flood prevention, (*v*) to check siltation in reservoirs, (*vi*) collection of surplus run-off in farm ponds and its recycling for crop use, (*vii*) to recharge groundwater or increase the water-table in wells, (*viii*) collection of surplus run-off for meeting the drinking water requirement of livestock and human population in desert areas, or for partially irrigating a small patch of land, (*ix*) to improve the main and on-farm irrigation systems for increased productivity and increased area under irrigation, (*x*) to achieve optimum productivity per unit land and per unit water, (*xi*) the balancing of non-agricultural (industrial, domestic and human settlement) uses of land and water with agriculture, animal husbandry and allied uses, (*xii*) Generation of income and employment in harmony with land and agro-climatic conditions.
14. D.R. Gadgil "Districts Development Planning", Go hale Institute of Politics and Economics, Pune, 1966.
15. V.K.R.V. Rao "District Planning Concept" in V.L.S. Prakasa Rao *et al*, Working Paper on District Planning Officers Programme, Institute of Social and Economic Change, Bangalore,
16. Report of the Planning Commission's Working Group on District Planning (Chairman C.H. Hanumantha Rao) 1984, Government of India.
17. Report of the Working Group on Decentralized Planning and Panchayati Raj Institutions for Tenth Five Year Plan (2002-07), Planning Commission, Government of India, November 2001.
18. See Rakesh Hooja "Training for and Expectations From District Planner" in Maliipal (ed.) Decentralized Planning and Development in India, Mittal Publications, forthcoming 200C* Rakesh Hooja and B. Yerram Raju (ed.) Decentralized Planning in Multi-Level Framework, Rawat Publications, 1993, and Rakesh Hooja Bibliography on Multi-level and District Planning, Madhya Pradesh Institute of Social Science Research, Ujjain, 1995.
19. This author had, in the early 1980s evolved a similar list of leakage points/stages pertaining to poverty alleviation schemes in the rural delivery system which was originally published in "Machinery for Delivering Benefits to the Rural Poor" *Indian Journal of Public Administration.* Vol. 28, No. 1, Jan-March, 1982, and in "India's Credit Based Anti-Poverty Programme" in The Administrative, Vol. 30, No. 1, Jan-March, 1985.

29

Agriculture, Food Production and Administration

R.N. Chopra

Though science and technology in the sphere of agricultural production are advancing very fast in India—as would be evident from the new hybrid varieties of seeds recently introduced, and what has been prescribed to go with them in the shape of inputs like water, fertilizers and pesticides, etc.—the administrative machinery for agricultural production has not yet been properly geared to the new task, neither at the Government Headquarters' level nor at the District level. This article relates mainly to the District level machine.

NEED FOR A COORDINATED SINGLE-LINE CONTROL

Let it be cleared at the outset that "Agricultural Production" is something much more than mere "agriculture" and what the conventional type of Agriculture Department could perform by itself is not adequate for increasing Agricultural Production by leaps and bounds—an object so desirable and actually possible today. When credit—short, medium or long term—is in the hands of the Cooperative Department and the Governments are withdrawing from taccavi loans for lack of funds; when the extension machinery in the field is controlled by the Development Department and the Panchayati Raj Institutions; when the supply of essential inputs is by and large, arranged by the State Cooperative Supply and Marketing Federations or the State Agro-Industries Corporations, and; lastly, when the agricultural research and education, including extension education, belong to the domain of the autonomous State Agricultural Universities—then what really is left with the Department of Agriculture as such except perhaps the custody of technical "know how", the running of a few seed farms, man-management and self-administration? It is when all these different requirements, viz., factors of agricultural production, are coordinated and controlled by a single Head, both at the political as well as the service level in the Secretariat—that Agricultural Production will get a move on in real terms. Such a Head at the service level may be called the Development Commissioner or the Commissioner of Agricultural Production and Rural Development (C.A.P.D.) according to Ram Subhag Singh Committee of

1963—or it may be a Board of Directors dealing with the operations of the Agriculture, Development Cooperative Departments in the State. Experience has shown that the best arrangement is the C.A.P.D., who apart from being the conventional Development Commissioner, is also Secretary to Government in the Departments of Agriculture, Cooperation and Development—all concerned with Agricultural Production. Such an arrangement exists in many States today.

PANCHAYATI RAJ CANNOT HANDLE AGRICULTURAL PRODUCTION

Experience of the last 5-6 years, since the introduction of Panchayati Raj (P.R.) has shown that agricultural production, as a function, is neither the direct responsibility of the departmental officials, nor have the P.R. institutions, who were given this task by law, been able to perform it in actual fact, for reasons which need not be gone into. The general feeling is that the Raj has failed to make good. Improvements are being suggested now in the shape of the "Maharashtra Pattern" of Panchayati Raj—which reminds one that when the Community Development Programme was gasping for breath in the late fifties, the P.R. idea was trumped with the object of keeping the pot boiling and the hope shimmering on the horizon of our political mass. The fact of the matter is that agricultural production cannot be linked with the slow-moving Panchayati Raj institutions coming to maturity at their own pace. Time has come when we have to choose an agency which would yield results more expeditiously, for the sake of the nation's survival. This work can be handled with success only under a system of single-line control and responsibility. Let us then take away this work from the P.R. elected bodies, who need not meddle in the task of extension, distribution of seed, fertilisers, minor irrigation loans, grants and pesticides, etc.—for reasons of democratic ills still persisting in their functioning. Moreover, in the ultimate analysis, agricultural production in our country will move forward only through the decisions of individual farmers and not by the collective will, wisdom or resolution of the community. Let the P.R. bodies be available for consultation in the planning and programming of agricultural production, their other main activity being to ensure rural municipal welfare and amenities and execute connected scheme requiring collective effort. Let the C.A.P.D. be squarely held responsible for the work of agricultural production and given full authority for the discharge of it. The Department of Agriculture, Cooperation, Minor Irrigation and Extension will have to be put under his control, subject only to the direction of the Minister-in-Charge of Agricultural Production. In short, a single-line administrative framework has to be created, such as is capable of proper definition of functions at all levels and the fixation of responsibility, when necessary.

IMPRACTICABILITY OF "MAHARASHTRA PATTERN"

Before we proceed with the administrative machine at the District level, it is necessary to say a few words regarding the "Maharashtra Pattern" of P.R. which, as indicated already, is supposed to be the greatest panacea for our ills. The Chief Executive Officer (C.E.O.) of the Zila Parishad in that pattern will be the executor of all developmental schemes, coordinating the work of so many departments, including Agriculture, Animal Husbandry, Forests, Irrigation, Electricity, Cooperation, Extension, and Development. It is difficult to visualise how a single officer will be able to manage all his in practice. Certain arrangements are rather easily visualised, but when we come down to the grass-root realities of life, a contrary picture emerges. What, for example, will be the link between the district departmental officers (all lumped under the control of C.E.O.) with their Heads of Departments at the Government Headquarters? "Planning from below" is a set phrase but in reality it is a Pandora's Box and for a long time to come schemes under the Five Year Plans will continue to be formulated at the Headquarters, and supplied down to the districts. The whole administrative machine has yet to travel a long way, and along with that the individual official and non-official's coefficient of ability, application and purposefulness—before a pattern of democratically decentralised local authority can work successfully. We should not be a party to introducing this "Maharashtra Pattern" on the wave of another sentimental escape from reality, merely because the local politicians vote for it, some in the hope of a fixed monthly salary for the Chairman and Vice-Chairmen.

THE PRESENT DISTRICT SET-UP OF AGRICULTURAL PRODUCTION

Usually, the Agriculture Department is represented in the District by a District Agriculture Officer (D.A.O.) who belongs to Class II of State Agricultural Service and has a contingent of Inspectors and Sub-Inspectors under him including the Extension Officers (Agri.) at the Block level—the latter being under the administrative control of the B.D.P.Os./Block Samiti Chairman and the technical control of the D.A.Os. The D.A.O., in addition, may be assisted by 3 or 4 Subject Matter Specialists, appointed by the State Agriculture University for Extension Education and effecting coordination between the Research Organisation of the University and the farmer's problems in the field. He may also have Inspectors in-charge of the departmental demonstration farms, seed farms and nurseries, etc. which may not have been transferred to the P.R. institutions. The Cooperative Department, similarly is represented in the District by an Assistant Registrar, Cooperative Societies (A.R.C.S.), who has a contingent of Inspectors and Sub-inspectors, at the Block level (though for some reasons the Cooperative inspectors may not have been placed under the administrative control of the P.R. institutions), to ensure control and supervision of the Cooperative institutions in his area. It is to be noted that the supply line of inputs—including the most important component of rural credit in all shapes—has come to be controlled directly by these institutions. The State Cooperative Marketing and Supply Federation may be dealing with the entire fertilizers—their procurement, supply and distribution, and also that of pesticides, seeds and pumping sets, etc. The State Cooperative Banks/Central Banks may be distributing a major portion of the rural credit; similarly the State Land Mortgage Banks may, directly through its Primary Banks, be dealing with the medium and long-term credit for the purchase of tractors, sinking of tube wells and land reclamation, etc. Even the Agricultural Refinance Corporation would enter this field only through the Land Mortgage Banks.

Lastly, the head of the field extension agency in the Block, viz., the Block Development Officer (B.D.O.), is to look after many more tasks today than mere agricultural production, and has to please many more masters than the D.A.O. or the Chairman of the Block Samiti. Torn between many equally "pressing" loyalties, he is the most harassed official, who in his efforts to please all, has perhaps succeeded in pleasing none and achieved only a little of the task. The D.C. and the S.D.Os. (Civil) remain responsible on paper for the task of agricultural production in their jurisdiction, with the remote hope, and some possibility, of their "marginal" control, interference and direction, bearing fruit in the desired direction. By definition, the D.C. may have the authority to write the annual confidential reports of the district officials, only insofar as their reputation for honesty and relations with the public are concerned. The S.D.O. (C) may not have even that much given to him and yet he may be meddling in the coordinational aspect of agricultural production in his Sub-Division.

A DEPUTY DIRECTOR, AGRICULTURE SHOULD BE IN-CHARGE OF THIS WORK IN THE DISTRICT

It is not intended that the D.C. may be made directly and wholly responsible for the work of agricultural production in his District and that all the authority may emanate from him, whether administrative, technical or financial. This functionary has to perform other hundred and one jobs and in multifarious spheres, on behalf of Government. The economic development generally, and agricultural production in his district particularly, may be entitled to receive only some of his attention but not entire or main. All the same, his interest in the task of agricultural production must be retained, however, marginal and on the fringes it may be, and his local prestige as well as his link with the officers at the Government Headquarters must be utilised to the maximum. To him would soon be available—if not already be the case because of either I.A.D.P., or H.V.P. and similar other programmes—an officer of the rank of a Deputy Director, Agriculture (D.D.A.) to be entrusted squarely with the task of agricultural production at the District level. It is now seriously suggested that the work of agricultural production be taken away from P.R. institutions and the entire agricultural extension agency, including the B.D.O., Agricultural Inspectorate and the Village Level Workers as well as the Cooperative Department officials in the District must be placed under the control of the D.D.A. (assisted by a D.A.O.), who will be responsible to get work from all the three agencies—agriculture, development, extension and cooperation—coordinate their respective functions in the field, subject to the overall control, direction and guidance of the Deputy Commissioner. A broad-based District Agricultural Production Committee (A.P. Committee), presided over by the D.C., and consisting of 20 or 30 non-officials of the District, including the Chairmen of Zila Parishad and Block Samitis, should assist in the programming and planning of agricultural production for the District, and later in evaluating the actual work. This Committee will have nothing to do with the actual implementation of the programme. That will rest squarely with the D.D.A./D.C., with the respective roles of their subordinates properly defined.

THE PROPOSED ORGANISATION

The organisational picture, at the District level, briefly will emerge as shown on next page.

Of course, through the Agricultural Production Committee mentioned in the preceding para, the D.C. will ensure proper coordination with the other allied Departments, like Irrigation and Electricity. The problems needing such coordination will be thrown up by the D.D.A., who will not only plan the overall agricultural programme for his District in consultation with the Agricultural Production Committee, but also pick up the problems from the field by intensive touring with a view to getting them sorted out and the bottlenecks removed.

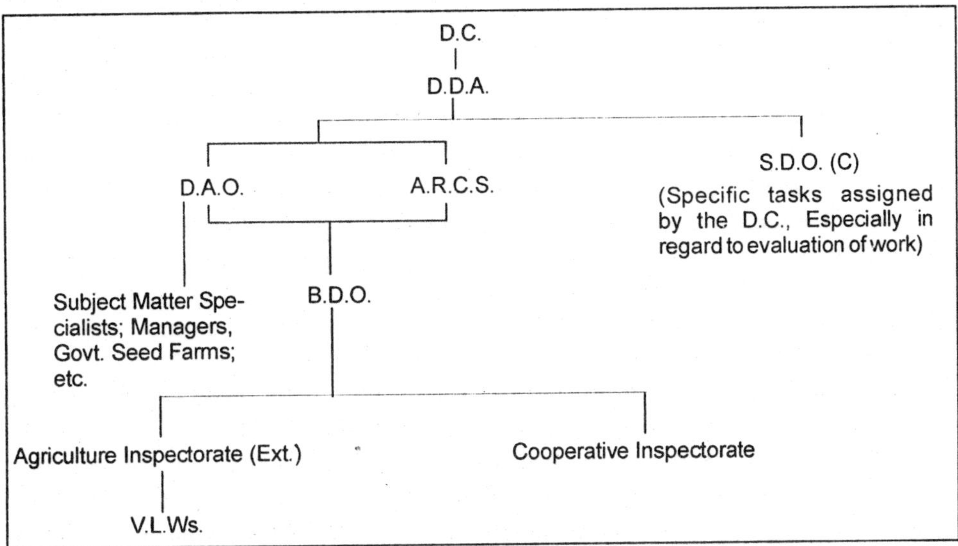

It hardly needs to be mentioned that the District programme, in its broad outlines, will be derived from the overall State Plan of Agricultural Production, chalked out by the Director of Agriculture (D.A.)/Commissioner, Agricultural Production and Rural Development, in consultation with the State Planning Department and the Government of India—the initial formulation of it having been after discussion with the Deputy Directors, Agriculture in the Districts.

LINE OF COMMAND

The channel of writing the annual confidential reports of the officials concerned with Agricultural Production in the District, will be as indicated below. It is important to mention this, so that it becomes clear as to who works under whom and the line of command becomes clear:

(*i*) V.L.Ws. Agri. Inspectors/B.D.O./A.D.O.

(*ii*)	Agri. Inspectors	B.D.O./D.A.O./D.D.A./D.A.
(*iii*)	Coop. Inspectors	B.D.O./A.R.C.S./D.R.C.S./R.C.S.
(*iv*)	B.D.Os.	D.A.O. (jointly with A.R.C.S.)/D.D.A./D.C./C.A.P.D.
(*v*)	A.R.C.S.	D.D.A. (in consultation with D.R.C.S.)/D.C./R.C.S.
(*vi*)	D.A.O.	D.D.A./D.C./D.A.C.A.P.D.
(*vii*)	D.D.A.	D.C./D.A./C.A.P.D.

This set-up need not be spelt out further nor an effort need be made here to define precisely the tasks of each functionary in the proposed chain. All this can be the subject of another article. Suffice it to say that the main object of the above proposals is to ensure a single line of command. The officials of the Cooperative Department may not relish this, but there is no alternative. Moreover, they represent a service agency mainly.

SOME SUGGESTIONS

Summing up, the suggestions are:

(*i*) That a Class I officer of the Agriculture Department (D.D.A.) assisted by a D.A.O. should be made in-charge of the Agricultural Production work in the District, under the direction, guidance and control of the Deputy Commissioner. The latter advised by an Agricultural Production Committee and assisted by S.D.Os. (Civil) in the evaluation and execution of specified tasks only.

(*ii*) The staff of the Cooperative Department and the Extension Agency of the District must be placed squarely under the D.D.A.

(*iii*) The task and responsibility of Agricultural Production in the District should be taken away from the Panchayati Raj Institutions.
It will be a mistake to introduce a new "carrot" under the name of Maharashtra Pattern of Panchayati Raj. The work of Agricultural Production cannot afford the luxury of a slow-moving and cumbersome machinery.

(*iv*) All the same, it will be necessary to consult the grassroot leadership in planning and programming of agricultural production. (Bodies like the Agricultural Production Committee at the District level may be appointed at the Block level also.)

(*v*) The Block as a unit of administration for agricultural production must be retained and not replaced by a Tehsil or a Sub-Division level.

30

Human Environment in India: Some Suggestions for Agriculture Action Programme*

B.B. Vohra

It is curious that the growing pre-occupation of the West with environmental and ecological matters is as yet unmatched by a similar interest in our own country. It is not as if we have no such problems to worry about. It is simply that we, as a people, are neither adequately aware of these nor sufficiently bothered about these. It is perhaps easy to understand why this is so. We have a long tradition of keeping our gaze turned inwards and of pre-occupation with personal rather than social problems. We have also inherited a tendency to accept the things around us as if they were preordained. How else can one explain our quiescent acceptance of the indescribably squalid living conditions that characterise large parts of all our cities and villages and our apathetic tolerance of the filth which litters the banks of even the holiest of our rivers? And, if this is the situation with regard to a simple matter like sanitation, what hope is there that we can take a sustained interest in our less immediate ecological environment which raises no immediate stink but will nevertheless determine the future of our children and of our children's children?

All the more reason that the spotlight should be turned on these subjects and every effort made to educate and interest the public in a matter which concerns them deeply. For one must live in the hope that one of these days we shall outgrow our chronic indifference to our surroundings and make this country fit to be lived in—by Indians at least, if not by heroes.

CIVIC ENVIRONMENT

Let us first consider our immediate physical environment—the state of our cities, towns and villages. An awesome amount of work awaits doing before even the minimum standards of hygiene and housing can be achieved. Yet, even the primary responsibility

* It was presented as a paper at the first meeting of the Indian Committee on Human Environment held in January 1971.

of keeping our streets open spaces and gutters clean is not being carried out properly, not to speak of attention being paid to more sophisticated civic needs, like water supply and drainage, slum clearance, vertical instead of horizontal growth in cities so as to save further encroachment on precious agricultural lands, the segregation of industrial and commercial areas from residential areas and the elimination of speculation in urban and sub-urban lands through well-considered programmes of legal and positive controls. The pollution of air by smoke and exhaust fumes and of rivers by industrial effluents and sewage are other matters which continue to be neglected, as also the unregulated "ribbon development" which not only disfigures our highways by also makes these unfit for fast moving traffic.

What prospects are there that all these jobs will be tackled quickly and efficiently so that we may live with dignity and self-respect if not today, then at least at some foreseeable date and not remain condemned for ever to sub-human conditions of existence? Hardly any, if things are allowed to continue to drift as at present. The only hope lies in an enlightened Government assuming responsibility for a bold programme of civic improvement not only in a few urban centres but throughout the country so that the people are shaken out of their present lethargy and have something to look forward to. Assuming that such a situation will come about sooner or later, let us consider what administrative and organisational problems will have to be faced to achieve concrete results. For it is one thing to talk airily on objectives and quite another to achieve these.

The fact must be faced that the basic cause of the unsatisfactory state of our towns and villages is the poor quality of our local governments. Elected by people who have never known anything better than the dirt and filth they are surrounded with and are, therefore, undemanding in their attitudes, the local bosses who run our civic bodies are under no sort of pressure to perform well. It is no wonder that these elected but honorary posts have come to be looked upon as offices of profit in the literal sense of the word and as a means to political advancement rather than as an opportunity to serve fellow citizens. The result is there for all to see. There is mismanagement of precious financial resources, inefficiency, corruption, petty politics and intrigues instead of purposeful activity and dedicated work. It is, therefore, not surprising that under the care of such men gutters should remain choked and streets unswept. It is also not surprising that there should be a dramatic change for the better whenever a municipality is superseded and its work entrusted to a trained officer.

Although a machinery exists for the constant scrutiny of the performance of municipal bodies and for the enforcement on these of certain minimal standards of honesty and efficiency, recourse is had to it only as a last resort. This is so, partly because of the lack of an effective public opinion on such matters, and partly because even when examples of misdemeanours and mismanagement are brought to light, State Governments are generally reluctant to step in because this might damage their own local bases of power and influence. All this has created such an atmosphere of hopelessness and cynicism that people have begun to look upon inefficiency and corruption in municipal bodies almost as a part of the natural order of things.

Yet it is not difficult to put an end to this state of affairs, provided it is appreciated that local self-government is not an end in itself but only a means to the improvement of the civic environment. In this view of the matter, there should be absolutely no hesitation on the part of the State Governments to impose suitable curbs on the licence which local bodies today enjoy to mismanage the charges entrusted to them. One of the first things that needs to be done in this connection is to take away from local bodies their powers of control over their employees. This has been done in several States already with the provincialisation of municipal cadres and it is time that other States also followed suit. A great deal of improvement will automatically result if municipal employees are not left to the mercy of local bosses and are enabled to work efficiently and honestly in the knowledge that their performance will be judged on merits by people competent to do so. Such a reform will no doubt reduce the status of municipal bodies from full-blooded executive authorities to anaemic advisory bodies. This will, however, be all to the good if the good we have at heart is the good of the man in the street and not of the ambitious politician.

The State Governments must, however, simultaneously take steps to strengthen their machinery for supervising the working of local bodies, including Panchayats (in their role as civic bodies). Adequately staffed Departments of Civic Affairs should be created and encouraged to adopt a positive approach towards their work. Thus, the emphasis should not be on locating where transgression of rules and regulations have taken place but on how local bodies can be assisted to render improved service to their citizens. Needless to say that such departments should be staffed by men who are experienced in municipal government and possess an intimate knowledge of its problems. However, such a department will be only as effective and useful as the technical advice and services which can be made available to support it. Specialised services in the field of roads, construction, and water supply and drainage are already available in the States in the form of Public Works Departments (PWD) which are in-charge of buildings and roads and public health engineering, etc. Advice on medical and educational subjects is also available from the corresponding departments of Government. However, many States do not still possess adequate architectural organisations for the designing of Government buildings, not to speak of dealing with municipal problems. This is a gap which needs to be filled urgently by the creation of an adequately staffed department of architecture in each State. In places, where this discipline exists as part of the PWD, there is an obvious need to ensure that the Chief Architect is in a position to advise freely with regard to the design of buildings and their aesthetics.

Another specialisation which needs to be provided for on an adequate scale, is town and country planning. The designing of town layouts, and the planning of urban reconstruction are matters which require the greatest care from many points of view and can be properly handled only by trained specialists. A great deal of infructuous expenditure on unplanned growth, which it is difficult to rectify at a later stage, can be avoided if new growth centres in the country – side are taken in hand at an early enough stage. Regional studies are required to be undertaken to determine the extent to which the size of existing towns should be restricted and what new urban centres should be developed in the interior. In a situation where agriculture and industry are beginning to develop with some speed, it would be wise as well as economical to take up these activities in right earnest. One has only to look at the numberless new mandi towns, which are springing up all over the country in a haphazard and unplanned way, and the factories, which line our highways, to realise that a little prevention will be better than a great deal of cure later on. An adequate town and country planning organisation should, therefore, be set up in each State.

Town planning by regulation is, however, a difficult matter. Experience in our country shows that town planning succeeds best where it adopts a positive approach. Instead of laying down a large number of restrictions as to what should or should not be done, it is far better from every point of view for the authorities to step in and take positive (as distinguished from legal) steps to ensure that urban growth takes place along the right lines. This can be done quite easily by acquiring and developing suitable areas of land for various needs and selling sites to prospective builders at reasonable rates. If undertaken on an adequate scale, this is also the best way of keeping speculators under control and reserving for the community appreciations inland values. Even better results can be achieved if large scale construction is also undertaken and buildings, complete in all respects, are sold to the public at attractive prices. This is so because economies of scale as well as good architectural designs will both contribute to reduce costs and finished buildings will save the buyer the bother associated with individual construction. However, a separate organisation is needed to undertake such jobs and to ensure that these are carried out honestly and efficiently. Such a department can appropriately be called the Department of Urban Estates.

It is worth mentioning that full-fledged Departments of Architecture, Town and Country Planning, and Urban Estates were set up in the Punjab about ten years ago. All the three organisations have already proved their utility in full measure.

This brings us to the question at finances. Is the lack of finances such a hurdle to effective civic improvement as is sometimes believed. The answer is both yes and no. Yes, if things are allowed to drift as at present, if leakages are allowed to occur both in the collection of revenues and in expenditure, if city wastes are not properly treated and sold and, above all, if the appreciation in land values which continues to take place continuously is allowed to be appropriated by speculators instead of being reserved for the community. No, if none of these things is allowed to happen, if efficient and honest working is insisted upon and full use is made of organisations for developing and selling urban properties. In fact, a State-wide Department of Urban Estates, if properly run, cannot only repay the initial loan which would have to be given to it by way of a revolving fund, but also produce profits which can be used for subsidising slum-clearance schemes.

Imaginative housing schemes aimed at bringing a house of one's own within the reach of all, but the poorest, are also to be welcomed on social considerations. A property-owning middle class, howsoever small the property may be, is the backbone of any nation and a powerful factor for stability and progress. The feeling of security which comes from the ownership of one's home (even if it is a small apartment in a multi-storeyed building) would also help our women to get over their attraction for gold and silver and thus mobilise some of the very considerable savings which are laying unused today in safes and lockers. Finally, the millions of jobs which would be created by a massive housing programme and by the town planning, architectural, road-making and other activities that would go along with it, are something which the country badly needs today.

While the bulk of the responsibility for improving the civic environment must, as has been shown above, rests with the State Governments, it will be necessary for the Central Government to provide the necessary leadership, coordination and guidance. This can best be done through a Central Department of Civic Affairs which can be easily created by separating the portfolio of public works from the existing Department of Works, Housing and Urban Development.

A bold programme for improvement of our civic environment would, thus appear to be within the bounds of possibility. All that is required is the will to improve matters and the organisation to carry out this will. The challenge is worth taking up if for no other reason than that success in this venture will restore dignity and self-confidence to our people and bring about a basic change in their present apathetic and irresponsible attitudes. We have in fact no choice in the matter. For to let matters drift any more would be to invite disaster—the example of Calcutta shows that when physical surroundings deteriorate beyond a certain point, they result in the breakdown of the social order.

ECOLOGICAL ENVIRONMENT

Let us now turn to the much more complicated subject of our ecological environment which is a function not only of our natural resources of land and water but also the manner in which we use or misuse these. Since, in the ultimate analysis, it is these resources which constitute the real wealth of our country, it is easy to see why their proper management should be a matter of the utmost concern to all of us.

It would be useful to illustrate this point by considering situations of both good and bad soil and water management. Good management situations exist in some of our most productive agricultural areas which have been cultivated for centuries and have still not lost their fertility. Here, the lands are invariably level and, therefore, in no danger of losing their fertile top soil, an inch of which it takes nature anything from 500 to 1,000 years to build, by the erosive action of rain-winter. If such lands are irrigated, it will be found that these are either provided with drainage or are naturally well drained on account of the lightness of the soil and, therefore, do not suffer from water-logging or salinity. The fertility of such lands is maintained either by cropping practices which do not exhaust the soil unduly or by the regular addition of manures and fertilisers. Such lands are also so situated that these do not suffer from the effects of wind erosion in hot dry months. All of which adds up to saying that the top soil of such lands is neither allowed to be displaced by erosion nor to lose its fertility by improvident practices.

Bad soil and water management situations may, on the other hand be best observed in marginal or waste lands with little or no productivity. In the hilly areas, the genesis of the trouble usually lies in either the indiscriminate felling of trees or in the overgrazing of pasture lands. The resulting loss of vegetative cover exposes the top soil to the erosive action of rain drops and facilitates its being carried away by fast flowing water into the valleys below. Since there is nothing to impede the flow of rain water along the already denuded slopes, it has little time to percolate into the soil and recharge the ground water aquifers. This, in turn, causes the drying up of natural springs and the lowering of water levels in wells in the plains below. At the same time, the high run-off causes flash floods during times of heavy rainfall. Again, since eroded soils contribute to excessive sediment loads in streams and rivers, tanks and reservoirs get silted up prematurely. Thus, in those parts of the country which have traditionally depended upon tanks for the supply of irrigation water, the degradation of catchment areas has caused tremendous damage to agriculture. However, since such degradation has taken place over a period of decades and not suddenly, it has passed more or less unnoticed. Not only has the command areas of tanks shrunk as a result of the loss of their storage capacity but with the diminution of the recharge of ground water aquifiers, there has also been a failing of the wells below these tanks. The Rajasthan desert offers some of the most striking examples of the aridity which follows denudation.

The damage, which soil erosion has caused and continues to cause to our expensive multi-purpose river valley projects, is equally serious. The rate of siltation of our dams is many times higher than was expected at the time these were designed. If this process is not checked in time, the nation will not obtain the returns expected from these prestigious projects. However, what is perhaps an even more serious matter is the fact that in many cases there are no alternative sites for dams, which means that once the present reservoirs go out of use, the possibility of harnessing these rivers would have been lost for ever. The loss of hydro-electric potential which occurs as a result of the loss of storage potential is an equally serious matter. Apart from the effect that this will have on industrial and other uses of electricity, the loss to agriculture will be particularly serious because we depend to a large extent on hydro-electric power to run the pump-sets in our tubewells.

Soil erosion in the catchment areas of rivers also contributes significantly to a rise in their bed levels in the plain. This, in turn, results in the over-flowing of rivers during periods of heavy rain. The damage which is caused to our economy by floods year after year runs into hundreds of crores, not to speak of the human misery that they leave in their wake. This is, however, not the end of story. The continuous degradation of eroded areas results in the impoverishment of the local people. They have necessarily to look farther a field for their sustenance. Thus, more forests get cut down, more pasture lands get invaded by grazing animals and more marginal lands are brought under improvident cultivation. A vicious circle is set up which can be broken only by the most determined of efforts.

Desert and semi-desert areas in the plains have a similar story to tell. The loss of vegetative cover in such areas as a result of indiscriminate over-grazing by migratory herds of camels, cattle, sheep and goats has exposed the top soil to erosion by strong winds which, due to the bleakness of the landscape, find no impediment in their path.

It has also been found that most of such areas can be easily converted into fairly productive pasture lands if only they are completely closed to grazing for a season or two and thereafter are opened to controlled grazing. The ravines which lie along the banks of many of our rivers are also caused by the erosion of soil as a result of the felling of forests and over-grazing. Waterlogging and salinity are other examples of bad soil and water management and are due, in most of the cases, to lack of proper drainage in heavy irrigated soils.

It needs no special insight to appreciate the fact that we just cannot afford to neglect the loss of our soil and water resources which is taking place in the manner described above. While on the one hand, our total productive capacity is going down as a result of this loss, on the other hand our population continues to increase, thus placing even greater burdens on an already impoverished soil. At the same time, increasingly large sums of money have to be spent on the relief on sufferers from so-called natural calamities, like droughts and floods, although these calamities are very much man-made. The great emphasis which is being placed on the national family planning programme is certainly called for but it must be realised that even if we attain a zero growth rate, our troubles will not be over until and unless we succeed in conserving and building up our natural soil and water resources. Yet, this vitally important matter is still far from the consciousness of even the leaders of public opinion, let alone the general public, and finds almost no mention in an atmosphere dominated by sterile political controversies and day-to-day problems.

A massive programme of soil and water conservation must nevertheless be taken up immediately if we are to face the challenge of growing unemployment and poverty. Such a programme may run into hundreds of crores a year and people who are blissfully unaware of our ecological situation, might well ask whether the country can afford such a heavy outlay. The answer to this lies in the counter question as to whether we can afford not to maintain the productivity of our soil, whatever the immediate cost may be. Can we, in our already impoverished state, really afford to lose the vast quantities of top soil and water which are today flowing into the Bay of Bengal and the Arabian Sea day and night on account of our failure to manage our watersheds properly? Can we afford to continue to shorten the life of our river valley projects into which so much precious money and effort has been sunk? Again, can we afford to pay vast sums of money as relief grants to victims of floods and famines year after year? The truth is that expenditure on a bold programme of the conservation of our soil and water resources can be justified even on strictly financial grounds—it is a different matter that due to a general lack of attention to this subject no such attempt has been made so far. That the issue is not in doubt is, however, shown by the fact that individual farmers find it profitable to get their lands treated for soil conservation through loans which carry normal rates of interest.

Assuming that the will is there—and this is not a. mall assumption in India today—it should not be difficult to find the necessary finances for an imaginative programme either from our own resources or through a loan from an international agency, like the World Bank. The difficulty, which will, however, still remain, is our own unpreparedness to undertake a programme of adequate size. In the paragraphs which follow, an attempt has been made to assess what kind of administrative and organisational arrangements will need to be made before we would be in a position to meet the challenge of our ecological environment.

ADMINISTRATIVE AND ORGANISATIONAL ARRANGEMENTS

The problem is really one of using the land to the limit of its capacity in any given situation but neither below nor beyond this limit. Placed as we are, we cannot afford to let any portion of our resources lie unutilised. At the same time, we must be careful not to resort to short-sighted methods which will permanently deplete the very resources on which we depend for our sustenance. However, it is easier to enunciate such an obvious principle than to implement it. This is particularly so because before we can even begin to talk of resource management at optimum levels, we must know exactly what these resources are. In other words, resource assessment must precede resource management. We must, therefore, ask the question as to whether we possess enough knowledge of our soil and water resources to enable us to use these to the best possible advantage.

Here, it may be mentioned that the only possible strategy in a programme of proper resource management in our situation today will be to aim at the intensification of agriculture and animal husbandry in areas which have a high potential for production so that we may be able to relieve the intolerable pressure which our marginal areas are bearing. By getting more out of the land which is in a position to yield more (if properly handled), we will be able to give our exhausted marginal lands a long-needed respite and enable these to be restored to fertility. To illustrate, if cereals grown in irrigated areas in the plains are abundant enough, people in the hills will be tempted to switch over from agriculture to horticulture, which is much less damaging from the point of view of soil erosion. Similarly, if high protein foods, such as eggs, poultry, piggery products, fish and milk, can be produced in larger quantities in areas of intensive agriculture, there will be an automatic fall in the demand for mutton grown by grazing sheep and goats in the hills. With such a view, we shall have to give equal importance to the assessment of our resources in our good as well as in our marginal lands. However, if a choice has to be made between the two categories, priority shall have to be given to the more fertile areas in order to meet the needs of production in the short run. This point is of some importance because there is a general tendency even among conservationists to assume that our more productive areas are doing fairly well and, therefore, do not need any special attention. It is forgotten that if we are to improve our standard of living to any extent, it will be necessary to increase the productivity of even our good lands many times over, and that in order to do this, we shall have to pay special attention to the management of their soil and water resources.

For obvious reasons, the management of productive areas present much greater difficulties than the management of marginal areas. While all that is necessary in most of our marginal lands is to protect these from indiscriminate felling and grazing and to carry out fairly simple engineering works, like gully plugging, terracing and bunding, to heal scars and open wounds, our productive agricultural lands in the plains need far more sophisticated treatment. Attention shall have to be paid to measures, such as the lining of canals and distributaries to prevent seepage losses and waterlogging, control over the application of irrigation water to ensure that no more water is applied to the land than is required by the crop, the proper levelling of fields and the provision of drainage wherever soils are heavy. At the same time, the soil has to be carefully analysed to find out what additional nutrients (including micro-nutrients) should be supplied to it, and in what exact manner, in order to enable it to yield the maximum of which it is capable in the given conditions of climate, water availability and optimum cropping patterns. Are we today in a position to assist in such a programme? Again, wherever ground water is available, the extent to which it can be safely exploited has to be assessed and its development regulated accordingly through an appropriate legal machinery. Many other supporting measures have to be taken but enough has been said to illustrate that good soil and water management constitute the core of any programme of intensification of agriculture, and that without such management all talk of multiple cropping on a large scale is a little hollow.

Reverting to the question of resource assessment, we may consider it under two separate heads of soil and water. As far as water is concerned, data regarding precipitation is available in a fairly satisfactory degree with the Indian Meteorological Department. Whatever gaps in knowledge exist can be easily filled up by this organisation through a closer network of observatories as well as snow-gauging stations. Data regarding ground water resources is the responsibility of the newly created Central Water & Power Commission (CWPC) and State Irrigation Departments; gaps of knowledge in this field can also be fairly easily filled up by an increase in the number of stream and sediment gauging stations. Data regarding ground water resources is the responsibility of the newly created Central Ground Water Board and State Ground Water Organisations wherever these exist, but it must be stated that it is still largely lacking and will need sustained efforts during the next few years to collect. (How relevant such data can be is illustrated by the discovery of unexpectedly copious supplies of ground water near Jaisalmer in the Rajasthan desert. When developed, this resource will convert this area from an arid desert into a granary).

It is, however, in the field of soils that our organisational arrangements need to be strengthened most. Soil and land capability surveys are a must before programmes of soil and water management can be considered either for productive or denuded lands. In productive areas, such surveys are necessary to determine irrigation practices and fertilisation levels while in marginal areas, these are needed to indicate how the land should be treated for control of soil erosion. However, this subject has somehow not received adequate attention so far. The primary responsibility for coordinating and guiding soil survey work must rest with a Central Soil Survey Organisation. Such an organisation was set up in 1955 but never gathered much momentum. While most of the States do possess soil survey organisations of their own, these are engaged largely in carrying out detailed surveys in connection with irrigation projects, and little effort is being put in on carrying out a reconnaissance sol survey of the country as a whole. At the rate at which work is going on at present, it is estimated that it will take 90 years to prepare a basic soil map of the country. Soil testing facilities, which are so vital to intensive agriculture, are also seriously deficient, and need to be greatly improved.

Let us now turn from resource assessment to resource management. The proper management of soil and water resources—and these must always be considered together—in a given area is, by the very nature of things, possible only after various alternative cropping patterns, agricultural practices, and land treatment measures, etc. have been tried out in actual field conditions. This requires the setting up of research-cum-demonstration centres which could usefully also serve as training centres for extension workers and farmers. Such an approach was, in fact, adopted by the Department of Agriculture some years ago and a beginning was made with the setting up of 8 such centres to investigate and deal with problems of soil erosion in different situations, including those faced in the management of watersheds in our River Valley Projects Recently, ten pilot project have been put on the ground by the Department of Agriculture to deal with problems of soil and water management in irrigated areas—it is proposed to take up additional dozen or so such projects so that there is at least one in each State. How much strengthening these activities will need would be apparent when we consider that the total number of technicians working in such projects and the Soil Survey Organisation under the Centre today is only around 500, about half of whom are engaged in soil survey work and half in soil and water management projects. A comparison with conditions in U.S.A. will show how pitiably small these numbers are. Although that country has land and water resources which are much larger than ours and a population which is barely half of ours, it possesses, as part of the U.S. Department of Agriculture, a unified Soil Conservation Service (responsible for soil surveys as well as soil and water management matters on a countrywide basis), which has a permanent strength of 15,000 men and a temporary strength of about 5,000 men. And this is in spite of the fact that the federating States of the U.S.A. possess far larger organisations of their own in these fields than our States do.

It seems that the time has come when we should take a leaf out of the American book and create something similar to the federal Soil Conservation Service (SCS) which has reached out almost to the last village, as it were, in an effort to save the country's soil and water resources. The SCS has an office not only in each State of the federation but in each of the 3,000 odd countries of the country, so thorough is its coverage. The service is manned by technicians drawn from all the disciplines which are required for the job—soil sciences, engineering, agronomy, hydrology, etc.—and studies (in collaboration with State and University agencies where feasible) soil and water problems in every possible situation in order to find the right answers.

The obvious solution to many of our problems would seem to lie in the setting up of a permanent and prestigious organisation which may appropriately be called the Central Soil and Water Conservation Commission and entrusting to it the same sort of responsibility which the SCS is discharging to successfully in the U.S.A. Such a Commission should naturally be located in the Department of Agriculture and should assume responsibility, at the Centre, for work connected with soil surveys, as well as for all aspects of soil and water management. With the setting up of such an organisation, it would become possible, for the first time, to take up integrated view of the country's need in these related fields and to formulate policies and plans calculated to face boldly and imaginatively the perilous situation in which we are placed today. The creation of strong soil and water management organisations in the States and the allocation of suitable resources to them for the execution of specific schemes would be among the most important functions of the Commission.

The Commission would inherit about 20 regional Soil and Water Management Centres to begin with. This could be quickly increased in number so as to give adequate attention to each type of local situation and to provide a good research and demonstration base for effective extension work. A vastly expanded and time-bound soil survey programme could also be launched so as to provide the necessary basis for area planning in a short time as possible. A massive watershed management programme could also be taken up in a bid to save our reservoirs from extinction before it is too late. Special programmes for the reclamation and amelioration of degraded lands and deserts could also be given adequate attention. Such an approach would not only help to save our soil and water resources from further damage and safeguard the interests of generations as yet unborn but would also create vast and unending employment opportunities for technical and unskilled workers alike. For there is no limit to the loving care we can lavish on the Good Earth—and therefore, on ourselves.

CONCLUSION

Problems, such as the gradual disappearance of forests and wildlife, have not been mentioned separately in this article because these are merely the symptoms of the disease we have to fight, not the disease itself (as they are sometimes made out to be). Problems of the pollution of the atmosphere and of the oceans also do not find any mention here—this is so because a lot of work is being done on these by Western countries and we can make use of their findings without difficulty, provided the desire to do so is there. However, it may be desirable to create a small Bureau of ecological Affairs in the Cabinet Secretariat to keep the Prime Minister and her colleagues informed of the latest developments in these fields and also to ensure that the proposed Department of Civic Affairs and the Soil and Water Conservation Commission at the Centre are not starved of funds and personnel. Another suggestion which may be considered is the formation of a nationwide society, somewhat on the lines of the Red Cross Society, under Government patronage to draw the people's attention to the need of improving their immediate surroundings and conserving the nation's resources in soil and water. Such a society could perhaps appropriately be called the Green Cross Society of India to signify the greenery which we want to see in parks and open places in our cities as well as in the country-side.

31

Food Production Policies and Programmes After Independence: A Historical Review

Ram Saran and H.L. Chawla

Food production is a function of physical factors like soil, topography, rainfall, temperature, humidity and other climatic conditions on the one hand and of technology, organization, Motivations of people working on land, institutions, planning and administration on the other. The term technology in this context covers a wide field of application of past knowledge and experience as also the results of modern scientific research and experimentation. It encompasses a large number of factors, such as irrigation, soil conservation, use of fertilizers, and compost, improved seeds, agricultural machinery and improved implements, use of electricity or other mechanical power for various agricultural operations. The role of administration, organization, institutions and motivational factors is in the final analysis to be reflected in the progress of technology. The purpose of planning and programming is to achieve greater efficiency through coordination based on an overall view of the development process. As such, when we talk of foodgrains production programmes we have to see the broad approach as well as the policy formulation and implementation process that have been followed for influencing the production. We propose to review this process principally for the period since Independence with a brief background in which these efforts have been made.

PRE-INDEPENDENCE BACKGROUND OF FOOD PROBLEM

Food shortages have been endemic in India. The available records for the last one and a quarter century indicate the occurrence of droughts and famines of varying severity in several parts of India. More particularly, between 1860 and 1870 and again between 1890 and 1900 such occurrences were found to be quite severe and frequent. In the present century a number of areas suffered from drought and famine conditions in the first quarter. Again, in 1943 there was a severe famine in Bengal consequent on the cessation of supplies from Burma.

The Government of India started giving attention to agriculture for about 1870. Major efforts bearing on agricultural production included development of canal irrigation systems, undertaking of agricultural research on selected commodities at central research institutes and in the States and attempts to develop cooperative organization to promote self-help and mutual help among cultivators in the supply of credit and marketing of produce. The reports of Famine Enquiry Commissions set up from time to time and the monumental report of the Royal Commission on Agriculture in 1928 contained valuable guidelines for agricultural development in this country. The programmes actually taken up and implemented, however, were not large enough to make a significant mark on the traditional subsistence agricultural economy of India. The net area irrigated by major and medium irrigation works in the Indian Union (Present India) in 1947 was about 20 million acres. Agricultural development was the responsibility of the State Governments, and the Central Government had little direct interest in it. It may be added here that prior to World War II in a normal year, India was marginally surplus after taking into account the availability of surplus rice from Burma (Which was separated from India in early 1937), and pressing need for increased food production was felt only at the occurrence of famines or food scarcity conditions.

During the Second World War, Government of India undertook a Grow More Food (GMF) Campaign which provided for (*a*) Switch-over from cash crops, mainly from short staple cotton to food crops, (*b*) intensive cultivation of cultivated lands through irrigation, better seeds and manures and better farming practices, and (*c*) extensive cultivation by bringing under plough current fallows, culturable waste lands, etc. Loans and subsidies were given by Government of India to the State Governments for implementing these programmes.

In 1946, it was decided to continue GMF Campaign for another five years and a target of additional production was fixed at about 4 million tonnes and contributions of programmes of minor irrigation, land development, distribution of fertilizers, manures, seeds, were fixed.

SITUATION AT THE TIME OF INDEPENDENCE

As the country achieved Independence which synchronized with Partition, the food supplies for Indian Union (present India) were adversely affected to the tune of about 8 lakh tonnes. "While the Indian Union received 82 per cent of the total population of undivided India, it got 75 per cent of the total cereal production, 65 per cent of the total wheat production and 68 per cent of the total rice production." About 31 per cent of the total irrigated area in undivided India went to the share of Pakistan; and as a result while 44 per cent of total agricultural lands in Pakistan were irrigated, in India the percentages was 19.

---

* Page 5, Grow More Food Enquiry Committee Report, 1952.

POLICY, EFFORTS AND ACHIEVEMENTS FROM 1947 TO 1950

The Foodgrains Policy committee appointed by the Government of India in September, 1947, was required, *inter alia,* to suggest measures for increasing domestic production. The important recommendations made by the committee may be broadly grouped as under:

(*i*) greater attention to minor irrigation works, development of local manurial resources and distribution of improved seeds;
(*ii*) plans for production of fertilizers;
(*iii*) survey of ground water resources with a view to undertaking tubewell construction; and
(*iv*) setting up of a Central organization for undertaking reclamation and development of large blocks of culturable waste land.

The committee suggested a target of about 10 million tonnes of increased production of foodgrains, out of which about 3 million tonnes were to be achieved by the reclamation of nearly 10 million acres of land. In 1948, on the advice of Lord Boyd Orr who was invited by the Government of India to review the working of GMF Campaign and to make suggestions, the Government of India appointed a Commissioner of Food Production at the Centre and the States also appointed corresponding officers. It was decided to achieve the objective of self-sufficiency in foodgrains.

In 1949, the rupee was devalued and soon after difficulties developed in getting cotton and jute from Pakistan for the textile mills in India. The programmes for food production had to be reviewed and an integrated production programme was devised. It was envisaged to divert areas from foodgrains to cotton and jute to the extent of about 15 lakh acres during 1950-51 and another 22 lakh acres in 1951-52 Schemes for fisheries, subsidiary food and crop competitions were also added to foodgrains production programme. In the Central Ministry of Agriculture, an administrative apparatus was created for facilitating supplies essential for food production. Financial help was also given to States so as to enable them to meet the cost of additional staff employed and other measures for food production schemes.

According to the Review by the GMF Enquiry Committee, the targets for additional foodgrains production through the GMF schemes were achieved to the extent of about 80 to 90 per cent during 1947-48 to 1949-50 and to the extent of about 65 per cent in 1950-51. According to the same source more than 50 per cent of the achievement in 1949-50 and nearly 65 per cent of that in 1950-51 in terms of estimated additional foodgrains production under the GMF campaign was due to irrigation works. The second important programme related to land improvement which included reclamation of waste lands to the extent of about half a million acres by the Central Tractor Organization and about half a million acres through the State Tractor Organization and certain lands reclaimed by private individuals. The schemes for supplies of manures, seeds and fertilizers were of small magnitudes. In 1950-51 *for example,* the quantity of ammonium sulphate distributed was 99,000 tonnes (*i.e.,* about

20,000 tonnes of nitrogen), of super phosphate less than 1,000 tonnes and other chemical fertilizers 17,500 tonnes. The total quantity of seeds distributed was 59,000 tonnes, of oilcakes 1.1 lakh tonnes and of town compost about I million tonnes.

BEGINNING OF THE PLAN ERA

The general economic setting of the country in 1947 was that the extent of development of basic industries was almost negligible, the transport system was inadequate and over-strained, the levels of general education were very low, the technical (including engineering, agricultural and vaterinary) education facilities were extremely limited, and level of investment, savings and productivity, more particularly in agriculture, were very low. Broadly speaking, the overall picture was one of economic stagnation, inadequacy of economic and social over-heads and prevalence of controls, restrictions and shortages. The economic situation called for a massive attack on the problem of India's poverty.

The Government of India had been giving thought to the problems of reconstruction of the economy in the post-war period and certain development programmes had been worked out. The experience of the Soviet Union in economic development through planning and the desire of the country, after achievement of Independence, to work for economic and social progress led to the constitution of Planning Commission by a Resolution of the Government in April, 1950. The Commission drew up by July 1951 the draft of the First Five Year Plan for the period 1951-52 to 1955-56, which after modifications was finalized by December 1952. The First Plan was "concerned more with effecting the post-war and post-partition re-adjustments required by the economy rather than dealing with the entirety of the country's long-term economic problem".[1] It indicated a broad perspective in respect of levels of income, investment and output for the next twenty years or so and in relation to that objective, laid down programmes for various sectors. The outlays proposed in the First Plan for the Agricultural and other sectors are given in Annexure I (p. 480). While speaking about priorities in the First Plan, the Planning Commission stated "for the immediate five-year period, agriculture, including irrigation and power, must in our view have a top-most priority...we are convinced that without a substantial increase in the production of food and of raw materials needed for industry, it would be impossible to sustain a higher tempo of industrial development".[2]

Out of the total public sector outlay envisaged under the First Plan, 31 per cent was for agriculture, community development and irrigation.

As for the programmes for foodgrains production under the First Plan, on the physical side, the basic approach of the GMF Campaign was followed but the scale of efforts envisaged was greatly stepped up. From 1947-48 to 1950-51 the Government had incurred an expenditure of about Rs. 40 crores on GMF schemes. As against this, the outlay proposed for schemes relating to minor irrigation, supplies of inputs to the farmers, land reclamation and development, agricultural research and education, etc. which came under the head "Agricultural Production" in the First Plan was Rs. 197 crores for the period 1951-52 to 1955-56. The pattern of Central help to States was modified. Under the GMF Campaign, the Central Government used to give subsidy to the States to the extent of 50 per cent of the total expenditure ($66\frac{2}{3}$ per cent in case of Assam and Orissa) in respect of private minor irrigation schemes and non-remunerative expenditure on public minor irrigation and land improvement schemes and for seeds, manures and staff. Under the First Plan, in case of public minor irrigation schemes, 50 per cent Central subsidy was to be given on remunerative* schemes while no subsidy but 100 per cent loan was to be given for remunerative schemes. For private wells, Central subsidy was admissible to the extent of 25 per cent of the cost (up to 50 per cent for backward areas). Fifty per cent Central subsidy was also admissible on the net loss incurred by States on land development schemes and 50 per cent for plant protection schemes. No subsidy was to be given for staff, nitrogenous fertilizers, private tubewells, rural compost and green manuring schemes.

A remarkable new feature of food production programmes in the First Plan was the importance attached to organization, institutions and motivations bearing on agricultural (including foodgrains) production. The Plan stressed the need for "a comprehensive and many sided effort to transform the peasants' outlook and environments".[3] "The development of human and material resources of the rural community"[4] was stated to be an important objective. It was laid down that "community development is the method and rural extension the agency through which the Five Year Plan seeks to initiate a process of transformation of the social and economic life of the villages"[5] The Plan provision for community development and rural extension was Rs. 90 crores, *i.e.*, about half the amount earmarked for various programmes including minor irrigation supply schemes, agricultural research, education marketing etc. The main lines of activity to be undertaken in a community project included agriculture and related matters, irrigation, communications, education, health, supplementary employment, housing, training and social welfare. In relation to agriculture sector, the programmes envisaged were "reclamation of available virgin and waste land; provision of commercial fertilizers and improved seeds; the promotion of fruit and vegetable cultivation, of improved agricultural techniques and land utilization; supply of technical information, improved agricultural implements, improved marketing and credit facilities; provision of soil surveys and prevention of soil erosion, encouragement of the use of natural and compost manures and improvement of livestock..." It was also laid down that "one of the important functions of the agricultural extension worker will be to encourage the growth of a healthy cooperative movement".[6] Land policy was elaborated in the First Plan in great detail. "The future of land ownership and cultivation", mentioned the First Plan, "constitute perhaps the most fundamental issue in national development". The adequacy of land policy was to be judged in the measure in which "it reduced disparity in wealth and income, eliminates exploitation, provides security for tenant and worker and finally promises equality of status and opportunity to different sections of the rural population".[7] The principal programmes included: abolition of intermediaries'

---

* Those schemes which were capable of yielding return of 4 per cent on capital or twenty years were considered remunerative schemes.

rights, limitations on future acquisition of land and on resumption for personal cultivation, providing security of tenure for tenant cultivators and fixation of reasonable rents. Distribution of available lands among landless workers and encouragement to cooperative farming societies were also envisaged. The need for strengthening the cooperative credit, marketing and other societies and regulation of markets was also emphasized.

For foodgrains production, the target fixed in the First Plan was an increase of 7.7 million tonnes including about 4.1 million tonnes of rice, 2 million tonnes of wheat, I million tonnes of gram and pulses and the balance in terms of other cereals. This involved an increase of 14 per cent over the base level production for 1949-50. An increase of 42 per cent in cotton production and 63 per cent in jute production was also envisaged. The major irrigation works were expected to benefit an area of 8.5 million acres, minor irrigation programmes 11.2 million acres and land reclamation programmes 3.7 million acres. For nitrogenous fertilizers the target fixed for 1955-56 was about 1.25 lakh tonnes of nitrogen.

From 1949-50 to 1955-56 a great deal of legislation was enacted by States bearing on abolition of intermediaries, tenancy reforms and relief of agricultural indebtedness. A process of break-up of the past rural structure characterized by landlord-money lender-trader nexus was initiated. As for the operational structure in agriculture, in spite of the use of bulldozers and tractors for land reclamation, undertaking of major irrigation and power development projects and development of tubewells in selected areas, it cannot be stated that there was much change in the agricultural technology. By and large, at the operational level, additional production was being achieved through traditional methods including the cultivation of larger area, expansion of major and minor irrigation facilities, larger use of manures, improved seeds, etc.

SECOND PLAN

After about one decade of strain, India experienced easy supply situation for agricultural commodities in the second half of the First Plan. With a rise of 20 per cent over the base level, the First Plan target of foodgrains production was exceeded. On the eve of the Second Plan the economic situation was considered to be "distinctly better than it was on the eve of the First Plan"; and there was "more confidence and greater readiness all round for a larger effort".[8] Therefore, compared to the First Plan, relatively greater emphasis was placed on development of industries and mining, social services than agriculture, but the outlay for agricultural sector was also stepped up from Rs. 357 crores to Rs. 568 crores. Within this sector, relative emphasis on Community Development and Cooperation, development of animal husbandry and dairying and fisheries was increased. This is evident from the distribution of outlays given in Annexure I.

In respect of agriculture, the Second Plan recorded that the First Plan had "already initiated the process of increasing productivity in agriculture".[9] It also mentioned that "the lines on which efforts have been made for increasing the productivity of land are already familiar. The provision of irrigation facilities, better seeds, fertilizers and the spread of improved techniques of cultivation will offer scope for expansion for many years to come."[10] In this way, on the physical plane, GMF Programme approach got a further lease of life.

The level of additional annual foodgrains production to be achieved by 1960-61 was targeted at 10.2 million tonnes of which about 4.3 million tonnes was expected to be achieved through major and minor irrigation programmes, about 2.6 million tonnes through expanded use of fertilizers and manures, 1.0 million tonnes through land reclamation, land improvement and general improvements in agricultural practices. The overall target of additional foodgrains production was subsequently revised upward to 15.75 million tonnes.

Among the programmes bearing on technology of foodgrains production, improved seeds programme deserves special mention. It was decided to set-up Government Seed Multiplication Farms at the rate of one seed farm of the size of about 25 acres per C.D. Block. The expected advantage was that in each Block, improved foundation seed would be raised on Government farms and it would be multiplied by registered growers after which it could be distributed for sowing in the surrounding areas. During the First Plan also some farms had already been set up but the number was proposed to be raised to about 4,000 during the Second Plan. Need for a much wider use of improved implements and attention to their manufacture and repairs was also stressed in the Second Plan. The use of nitrogenous fertilizers was decided to be stepped up to the level of 5.1 lakh tonnes (actual achievement was, however, 2.1 lakh tonnes only).

The Second Plan placed greater stress than the First Plan on organizational, institutional and motivational factors. It proposed that the Community Development and National Extension Programme which covered nearly one-fourth of the country by 1955-56 should be extended to cover the entire country by 1960-61. The supply of credit through cooperatives was proposed to be greatly enlarged, and for this purpose various measures like Government participation in the share capital of cooperative societies, implementation of integrated scheme of credit, marketing, processing storage, etc., recommended by the All India Rural Credit Survey Committee in 1955 were incorporated in the cooperative development programme. At the Centre, a new Ministry of Community Development and Cooperation was established and most of the States also set up corresponding Departments. To provide the producer with fuller incentives for increasing production, the Second Plan reiterated the stress on abolition of intermediaries and tenancy reforms and also suggested fixation of ceilings on agricultural holdings. In addition, it suggested that agrarian cooperative should be developed in such a way that "within a period of 10 years or so a substantial proportion of agricultural lands are cultivated on cooperative lines".[12] The encouragement to cooperative farming societies through preference in the supply of improved seeds, fertilizers, materials for local constructions, credit from cooperative agencies and special attention in the community development and national extension areas were suggested. Enactment of land management legislation to provide for standards of efficient cultivation and management and fixation of cultivators' obligations for measures like levelling, bunding, fencing, maintenance of irrigation channels, use of improved seeds, etc. was also suggested.

Comming to the achievement, the community development programme was extended and covered 60 per cent villages by 1960-61. (Later, by early 1966 cent per cent villages in the country were covered by the programme.) In the sphere of land reforms, the programme of abolition of intermediaries made a good progress and there was also advance in regard to tenancy reforms. A number of States enacted legislation fixing ceilings on agricultural holdings though little progress was made in its implementation. There was very little of progress with regard to enactment of land management legislation.

Soon after the start of the Second Plan the atmosphere of confidence about steady progress of foodgrains production and steady prices started changing. In 1956, foodgrains prices started rising and the trend was accentuated by a poor crop in 1957. The crop in 1958-59 was quite good and there was again a record crop in 1960-61, the last year of the Second Plan. As shown in Annexure II the target of foodgrains producing was practically achieved. On the whole, the period 1956-57 to 1960-61 broadly marked a period of steady upward trend in agricultural production. However, due to the mounting pressure of demand, prices were rising and the situation called for a review of food production programmes and policies.

As such, various aspects of agricultural production came in for detailed studies. In June 1957, a Foodgrains Enquiry Committee was appointed to assess the food situation and make recommendations, *inter alia*, on prices which provide incentive to producers with due regard to the interest of the consumers. On the production side this Committee noted the delays in the progress of major irrigation projects and the utilization of irrigation potential; delays and inadequacies in the seed production and distribution programme; the difficulties created by indiscriminate import of tractors of unknown makes for land reclamation and development; problems of obtaining spare parts, lack of facilities for training servicing, etc. and lack of follow-up cultivation of reclaimed lands. It also made some suggestions for bringing about improvements.

In 1958, the Government appointed an Agricultural Administration Committee *inter alia,* to suggest a model agricultural organization in the States so that agricultural schemes may be carried out speedily. This committee made a large number of recommendations for strengthening of agricultural departments, better coordination, programme planning, improvements in budgeting, sanctions, procedures and delegation of powers and arrangements for training of staff, etc.

Early in 1959, on the invitation of the Ministry of Food & Agriculture, a Team of Agricultural Experts sponsored by the Ford Foundation studied India's food production problems and targets. The Team reached the conclusion that "an immediate and drastic increase in food production is India's primary problem of the next seven year".[13] An important recommendation of the team was that those selected crops and those selected areas in each State should be chosen (for intensive cultivation) which had the greatest increase potentialities. The Team considered that such areas could "increase India's food production more rapidly than others, if given allocation of fertilizers in combination with other improved practices, such as plant protection measures, improved seeds and water for irrigation."[14] Other important recommendations of the team included fixation of guaranteed minimum prices, improvement in storage and marketing facilities, enlarged supplies of high analysis fertilizers, close attention to water management and drainage facilities, provision of security of tenure to tenant cultivators and substantial increase in the supply of credit.

In 1960-61 the Programme Evaluation Organization in the Planning Commission undertook evaluation studies on the programme for the multiplication and distribution of improved seeds and on the problems of minor irrigation. The study on improved seeds comprehensively dealt with the policies and programmes for setting up of State Seed Farms, production of foundation seed, seed multiplication by registered growers, distribution arrangements at the block and village levels and use of improved seeds by cultivators. It revealed a large number of deficiencies and made various recommendations. For example, with regard to Government Seed Multiplication Farms the study indicated that there was "considerable scope for improvement in economic organization, managerial efficiency, technical supervision and enforcement of recommended measures for ensuring purity in the foundation seed produced."[15] A number of improvements with regard to seed multiplication and distribution arrangements were also made. The study on minor irrigation tried to analyse the impact of minor irrigation programmes on total irrigated acreage and on irrigated area under various crops. This study revealed that in many of the States 3 to 5 different authorities were entrusted with the minor irrigation schemes. In some States, coordination machinery existed at the State or District level but there was no single authority responsible for assessment of the entire irrigation potential in various areas. In the Panchayat legislation of most of the States, responsibility for maintenance and repair etc. of irrigation works was entrusted to Panchayats, Panchayat Samitis or Gaon Sabhas but the actual performance was not considered encouraging.

AGRICULTURAL PROGRAMMES UNDER THE THIRD PLAN

Since the progress in agricultural production achieved during the Second Plan was on the whole satisfactory, the Third Five Year Plan did not recommend any significant fundamental changes in the matter of technology. It laid down that the "crop yields are at present so low that given adequate irrigation, supplies of fertilizers, improved seeds and implements, education of the farmers in using better methods and reforms of land tenures and development of the agricultural economy along cooperative lines, large increases in levels of production can be achieved over relatively short periods".[16] In regard to price policy which has a strong influence on motivations of farmers, the Third Plan recognized the need for providing incentive to farmers for extended use of fertilizers and adoption of improved practices. It also mentioned that "a policy designed to prevent sharp fluctuation in prices and to guarantee of certain minimum level is essential in the interest of increased production. Another objective, on less essential, is to safeguard the interest of the consumer...."[17]

The principal technical programmes for increasing agricultural production were similar to these in the Second Plan. The targets for these programmes are given in

Annexure II. Since a considerable part of the country is likely to be dependent on rainfall for the moisture requirements of crops, the programmes of soil conservation were given comparatively much greater emphasis than in the previous two Plans. On irrigation, the emphasis was continued to be high while for fertilizers, manures and improved seeds further set up over the previous levels were envisaged.

In order to provide incentive to agriculturists to undertake various development and input programmes, the Third Plan enlarged the scope for subsidies which were allowed from the beginning of the First Plan generally up to the end of the Second Plan. It provided for subsidy at the rate of 25 per cent for surface wells, kuhuls, renovation of irrigation tanks (50 per cent for kuhuls in hilly areas), and 2 per cent on phosphatic fertilizers, the expenditure being shared equally between the Central and State Governments. A premium of Rs. 2 per mound for improved seeds of foodgrains (other than hybrid maize for which the States could fix their own rates) was also allowed on the basis of 50:50 sharing between the Central and State Governments. In the matter of plant protection, a Central subsidy of 25 per cent of cost on the supply of pesticides, dusters and sprayers was allowed. Additional subsidy could be provided by the State Governments. A similar assistance was applicable to supply of improved implements to cultivators. Twenty-five per cent Central subsidy on soil conservation and consolidation of holdings was also allowed. The rates of subsidies were more liberal for agricultural research, surveys and statistics (50 per cent) and agricultural education and training (75 per cent on non-recurring cost and 25 per cent on recurring cost). Seventy-five per cent subsidy was allowed for cost of land and seed stores for Government Seed Farms envisaged under Second Plan but still to be completed.

In regard to land reforms, the Third Plan reiterated the need to remove "impediment to increase the agricultural production" arising from agrarian structure and "to eliminate all elements of exploitation and social injustice withing the agrarian system".[18] The Plan suggested the need for "ensuring speedy and effective implementation"[19] of legislation regarding ceilings on agricultural holdings.

The Third Plan period has been characterized by a virtual stagnation in food production except in 1964-65 when it touched a new record of 89 million tonnes, as compared to the previous highest level of 83 million tonnes in 1961-62. In 1965-66 the country witnessed the worst drought of the century leading to a sharp decline in production to the level of 72 million tonnes. Even beyond the Third Plan period the year 1966-67 was the second successive year of drought over large parts of the country and led to even greater consumer hardship than experienced in the previous year. Under these circumstances food production programmes have become a focus of Government and public attention.

In 1963-64 the need for close coordination between various departments whose activities impinge upon agricultural production, such as agriculture, irrigation, community development, cooperation, revenue, panchayats, etc. came up for close consideration. Proposals for administrative coordination were formulated and have been largely implemented. Inter-departmental Coordination Committees have been set up in the States and Agricultural Production Commissioners or Senior Secretaries have been made responsible by State Governments for coordination of various programmes of development, supplies of inputs and credit, etc. Close liaison among the Departments of Agriculture, Community Development and cooperation began at the Central level also and more recently these Departments have been placed under the charge of one Cabinet Minister since 1967 and their activities are being closely linked together. From 1963-64, the need for utilization of large irrigation potential created under the major irrigation projects has come in for increasing attention. The problems of land levelling and shaping, research on cropping patterns suitable for newly irrigated areas, popularization of wet cultivation, training of farmers and provision of facilities for credit and supply of inputs have been all considered important for these areas. Since the closing part of the Third Plan, ayacut development programmes involving the about measures are gaining importance.

The impementation of agricultural (including foodgrains) production programmes has come in for increasing scrutiny by the Central Government since about the third year of the Third Five Year Plan. A number of deficiencies were mentioned in the Mid-Plan Appraisal published by the Planning Commission. The Central Teams of the Ministry of Food and Agriculture visited various States to see the implementation of agricultural programmes at the field level and to take note of problems of agricultural development faced at the village, block, district and State levels. These Teams made a number of recommendations for larger allocations for minor irrigation works, linking up of the programmes of credit and requisites for minor irrigation development as also establishment of irrigation pumping sets or tubewells and the programmes of rural electrification, etc.

One new development in relation to food production programmes was that the Ford Foundation sponsored an Intensive Agricultural District Programme in 7 selected districts in the country. In these districts "Package Programme" approach involving simultaneous use of improved seeds, fertilizers, pesticides, water and other inputs was to be adopted for introducing intensive and more productive agriculture. Gradually, the number of districts under this programme during the Third Plan period was raised to 16. In Mandi district of Himachal Pradesh, intensive programme was taken up under an Indo-West German Agreement.

One development which was quietly taking place during this period was the effort of the Indian agricultural scientists, in collaboration with the scientists of the Rockefeller Foundation and Ford Foundation, to try hybrid varieties of maize and other foodgrains under Indian conditions. The research indicated very promising result and provided a clue to the ushering in an era of biological revolution in foodgrains production.

FOURTH PLAN—ERA OF NEW STRATEGY

Major changes in approach to agricultural development and programmes, therefore, have taken place in the past 2 or 3 years. A new strategy for agricultural development has been formulated so as to bring about massive technological improvements in India's agriculture and to create a dynamic process of change with implications extending considerably into the future. It brings in agriculture the biological, chemical, economic and mechanical innovations which have already revolutionized foodgrains production in Japan, Taiwan, Mexico, U.S.A. and West European countries.

The two principal foodgrains production programmes under this New Strategy are:

(1) Applying a Package of Practices comprising water management, high-yielding varieties of seeds, pest control and a sufficiency of fertilizer application along with good cultural practices reaching an area of 32.5 million acres in 1970-71.

(2) Introducing short-term varieties in the major cereals of the country which are as good yielders as the long-term varieties under a suitable package of practices thereby allowing for the growing of major second crop in the irrigated areas of the country where previously only one crop was being grown under irrigated condition. This programme is expected to reach 30 million acres in 1970-71.

The various important aspects of the Strategy relate to arrangements for the production of nucleus and foundation seeds of high yielding varieties on scientific basis; its multiplication and distribution, use of large doses of fertilizers and close attention to plant protection measures; development of irrigation principally for intensive cultivation close attention to water use and management; adequate arrangement for the production and import of inputs and organization of their timely distribution right up to the village level, provision of adequate credit for supporting investment in intensive cultivations continued stress on agricultural research so as to break new ground as also to solve various problems faced by cultivators in the adoption of new high yielding varieties; close liaison between research and extension efforts and stress on farmers' training for the dissemination of the knowledge of new techniques and new inputs.

The great biological break-through has been achieved due to agricultural research, experimentation and adaptations of high yielding varieties capable of absorbing high doses of fertilizers and giving 100 to 200 per cent higher yields than traditional varieties. The high yielding varieties like the Taichung Native I, Taichung 65, Tainan 3, ADT-27 and IR-8 of paddy, Lerma Rojo and Sonora 64 of wheat and several hybrid varieties of jowar, bajra, and maize are being cultivated over millions of acres. For producing the nucleus and foundation seed of high yielding varieties on scientific lines, large sized forms of 500 to 2000 acres or more, are being set up and the multiplication of foundation seed is being promoted under expert technical supervision in compact areas called "seed villages". The coverage in 1966-67 was about 4.4 million acres and the target for 1967-68 is 15 million acres. The achievements of the past few years have encouraged our agricultural scientists towards opening up further new horizons. While commenting on the future potentialities of rice, Dr. Pal, Director-General of the Indian Council of Agricultural Research, has observed that "floor for rice yields of the future should be what the ceiling is today under general farm conditions." A recent meeting of the research scientists working on wheat has recommended a number of new wheat varieties which give considerably higher yield as compared to the high-yielding Mexican varieties presently giving yield levels of 50 to 80 maunds per acre.

The emergence and spread of high yielding varieties is being accompanied by a fast rising demand for fertilizers. While the consumption of Nitrogen (N) in Indian agriculture increased from 50,000 tonnes of N in 1951-52 to about 6 lakh tonnes of N in 1965-66, the target for 1970-71 is 24 lakh tonnes of N and the tentative target for 1975-76 is 40 lakh tonnes of N. The consumption and demand for phosphatic and potassic fertilizers are also rising fast. Since the rich luxuriant crops of high yielding varieties are more susceptible to damage by crop pests and insects, close attention through plant protection is called for and, therefore, pesticides will also have to be used in large quantities.

The new technology is also of tremendous economic significance in the context of food production programmes. Their cultivation calls for investment in quality seeds, fertilizers, irrigation, pesticides and larger production and marketable surplus the cultivators are expected to be increasingly brought into the vortex of market economy. Naturally this implies a major change from the past subsistence agriculture.

In terms of extension efforts also a new era is getting ushered in. Since 1966-67, Government has taken steps to organize, on a larger scale, the training of farmers in short, medium and long duration courses. Peripatetic teams of experts are also being sent to villages for 2 to 3 days training in the techniques of cultivation and care of high yielding varieties. The atmosphere for the spread of new ideas is thus greatly changed.

In terms of institutional measures for increased food production a number of new ideas and new developments are coming up. Investment being a key factor in intensive cultivation, provision of credit has assumed a great importance. The supply of short and medium term cooperative credit is being stepped up from the level of about Rs. 400 crores in 1965-66 to about Rs. 700 crores in 1970-71. The supply of long-term credit will similarly be raised from Rs. 56 crores to Rs. 350 crores over the same period. Crop loan scheme has been undertaken since 1966-67 under which credit will be advanced by the cooperatives not primarily on the security of assets available with the intending borrower but in relation to production needs of a cultivator. To begin with, this scheme has been undertaken in areas covered by high yielding varieties programme. The Reserve Bank has started assuming a much larger role in providing support to supply of institutional credit. In 1967-68, *for example,* it has allowed higher credit limits to cooperative institutions to support the crop loan scheme. Further, it has allowed a credit limit of Rs. 50 crores for the year for financing, distribution of fertilizers by cooperatives. The State Bank of India, which in the past, along with Life Insurance Corporation, was supporting purchases of debentures of Cooperative Land Development/Mortgage Banks, has now decided to provide a large support to cooperative marketing societies. The commercial banks are also coming forward to finance agricultural production programmes.

Price incentives are known to have a profound influence in motivating cultivators towards increased effort and increased investment for agricultural production. In Western countries this incentive has accounted for large increases in foodgrains production. Uptill the middle of the Third Plan this factor did not play an important role in relation to foodgrains production. Some peripheral action was taken in the second half of the Third Plan. Since the establishment of the Agricultural Prices Commission in January, 1965 and more particularly in the context of new technology adopted from 1966-67, price policy has started assuming its rightful place. Through its effect on motivations of cultivators an appropriate price policy should prove to be an important factor in the achievement of targeted rapid increase in food production.

For the success of the new technology a number of new institutions are necessary. Already, Agro-Industires Corporations are being set up in the States to link up the supply and demand for bullozers, tractors, pump-sets for irrigation, power sprayers and various other types of agricultural machinery and equipment. These Corporations would undertake even the financing and hire purchase of agricultural machinery. For the benefit of small farmers proposals for introducing service stations for providing tractor cultivation, crop spraying, etc. on prescribed rates or provision of such facilities departmentally or through large cultivators on customs basis, are also being considered. Seed Corporations are being set up in States to coordinate arrangements for the production, multiplication and distribution of seeds of high yielding varieties. Cooperative societies are being supported and strengthened so as to undertake the distribution of fertilizers, pesticides and various other agricultural requisites needed by farmers. Development of storage godowns, could storages and marketing arrangements for agricultural commodities is also being given close attention.

* * *

During twenty years since Independence and more particularly since 1951-52, Government efforts to raise food production in the country have been progressively intensified. Development of irrigation has consistently received a high priority. Irrigation potential for 14 million acres has been created through major irrigation works. The benefit of irrigation through minor irrigation works has been extended to 31 million acres. Additional area benefited by land reclamation and development totals nearly 8.5 million acres while soil conservation has benefited 12.5 million acre of agricultural lands. Systematic efforts for the propagation of improved seeds of foodgrains resulted in the extension of their cultivation over about 112 million acres by 1965-66. The use of nitrogenous and other chemical fertilizers which was formerly confined to plantation crops and to a very limited degree to certain commercial crops has gradually been adopted for foodgrain crops also. In terms of nitrogen the consumption of nitrogenous fertilizers has risen from 50 thousand tonnes in 1950-51 to the level of 960 thousand tonnes in 1966-67. Plant protection measures through the use of pesticides and insecticides etc. which were almost unknown before the First Plan, have been gradually catching up and in 1966-67 covered about 63 million acres of area. Through various schemes, green manuring has also been extended and it covered about 20 million acres in 1965-66. As a result of such programmes considerable increases in foodgrains production have been achieved. Taking the average production for three years 1949-50 to 1951-52, as base, the annual linear rate of growth in foodgrains production during 15 years up to 1964-65 was 3.66 per cent.

In the past three or four years, trends towards increasing use of fertilizers, diesel and electric pump-sets for irrigation, construction of private tubewells, increased use of tractors and taking up of plant protection with power sprayers, specially by progressive cultivators, have developed. A New Strategy for Agricultural Development is being implemented since 1966-67. Increasing stress on scientific agriculture and intensive use of land, water and other resources in combination with industrial inputs, is the key note of this Strategy. In five years time, up to 1970-71, the consumption of nitrogen will be raised four times and of phosphatic and potassic fertilizers six to seven times. In the sphere of minor irrigation the use of diesel and electric power will increase rapidly.

For increasing food and agricultural production, a number of supplementary measures, particularly, institutional improvements, have also been introduced. A framework of contact between Government and the cultivators has been created through the organization of community development and national extension service which presently covers the entire country. The technical competence of extension personnel has to be and is being improved. The progress made by credit cooperatives and in some States by cooperative processing and marketing societies has been considerable though much more still needs to be done. On the land reforms side, a great deal of success has been achieved in the abolition of intermediary tenures; some progress in tenancy reforms and consolidation of holdings has also been made. In the sphere of administrative coordination, a great deal of progress has been achieved though further efforts need to be continued. Price policy is playing an increasingly important role in supporting food production programmes.

In brief, India has been making a valiant struggle to raise foodgrains production commensurate with the rising demand resulting from large increase in population and purchasing power. Considerable success has been achieved though it has not proved enough. The programmes of food production have been successively enlarged. New inputs from the industrial, chemical and power sectors and supply of credit to support investment on a large scale are being undertaken. It is hoped that the new intensive approach will help the country soon to turn the corner in the matter of food production. Through progressive application of scientific knowledge to agriculture we are sure to achieve rapid growth in food production which is essential for India's progress and prosperity.

Annexure I(a)
Distribution of Plan Outlay by Major Heads of Development

(Rs. in Crores)

Head of Development	*First Five Year Plan*			*Second Five Year Plan*			*Third Five Year Plan*		
	Plan Outlay	*Per cent*	*Expenditure*	*Plan Outlay*	*Per cent*	*Expenditure*	*Plan Outlay*	*Per cent*	*Expenditure*
(1)	(2)	(3)	(4)	(5)	(6)	(7)	(8)	(9)	(10)
1. Agricultural Programmes	233	10	206	305	6	276	668	9	735
2. Cooperation	7	Neg.	5	47	1	34	80	1	76
3. Community Development & Panchayats	117	5	79	216	4	219	320	4	292
4. Major Irrigation	384	16	434	381	8	272	659	9	{572
5. Flood Control	17	Neg.	*	105	2	48			85
6. Power	260	11	149	427	9	446†	1,012	13	1,262‡
7. Industry & Minerals	179	8	97	890	19	1,075	1,784	24	1,955
8. Transport & Communications	557	24	518	1,385	29	1,300	1,486	20	2,116
9. Social Services & Miscls.	602	26	472	1,044	22	830	1,300	17	1,422
10. Inventories	–	–	–	–	–	–	200	3	116
Total	2,356	100	1,960	4,800	100	4,600	7,500	100	8631

* Included under the head Major Irrigation.
† Including Rs. 75 crores for Rural Electrification.
‡ Including Rs. 125 Crores for Rural Electrification.

Annexure I(b)
Plan Outlay on Major Heads under the Agriculture Sector

(Rs. in Crores)

Head of Development	*First Five Year Plan*			*Second Five Year Plan*			*Third Five Year Plan*		
	Plan Outlay	*Per cent*	*Expenditure*	*Plan Outlay*	*Per cent*	*Expenditure*	*Plan Outlay*	*Per cent*	*Expenditure*
(1)	(2)	(3)	(4)	(5)	(6)	(7)	(8)	(9)	(10)
1. Agricultural Production }	197	85	176	104	34	97	226	33	203
2. Minor Irrigation }				66	21	95	177	26	269
3. Soil Conservation }	10	4	11	20	7	18	73	11	78
4. Forests }				27	9	19	51	7	47
5. Animal Husbandry }	22	9	16	38	12	21	54	8	44
6. Dairying & Milk Supply }				18	6	12	36	5	36
7. Fisheries	4	2	3	12	4	9	29	4	24
8. Warehousing & Marketing	*	*	*	20	7	5	42	6	34
Total	233	100	206	305	100	276	688	100	735

* Not separately reported as this was included under the head Cooperation.

Annexure II

(a) Targets and achievements for production of Foodgrains in the First, Second and Third Five Year Plans

(Million tonnes)

	Assumed base level production	*Target*	*Percentage Increase over base level*	*Achievement*	*Percentage Increase over base level*
(1)	(2)	(3)	(4)	(5)	(6)
First Plan	54.87	62.59	14.07	65.85	20.01
Second Plan	66.04	81.79	23.84	80.75	22.33
Third Plan	77.22	101.6	31.57	72.03*	(-) 6.72

* Partially revised estimates.

Note: Figures of food grains production for different Plan periods are not strictly comparable due to changes in coverage and methods of estimation.

(b) Growth Rates in Foodgrains Production (1949-50 to 1964-65)

(i) Linear Growth Rate:
(1949-50 & 1951-52 = 100) 3.66 per cent per annum.

(ii) Compound Growth Rate: 2.98 per cent per annum.

Source: Growth Rates in Indian Agriculture, Dte. of Economics & Statistics Publication.

Annexure II

(c) Targets and achievements principal Agricultural Development Programmes during First, Second, Third and Fourth Plans Periods

S. No.	Programme	Unit	First Plan		Second Plan		Third Plan		Fourth Plan Tentative Target
			Target	Achievement	Target	Achievement	Target	Achievement	
(1)	(2)	(3)	(4)	(5)	(6)	(7)	(8)	(9)	(10)
1.	Major and Medium Irrigation (gross addl. area benefited)	Million acres	8.4	3.2(a)	10.4(b)	5.4(b)	12.8(c)	(A)5.5(c)	8.9(d)
2.	Minor Irrigation – (gross addl. area benefited)	-do-	11.1(a)	9.4(a)	8.9(b)	8.9(b)	12.8(c)	12.9(c)	17.1(d)
3.	Soil conservation on Agricultural lands (addl. area benefited)	-do-	N.S.	0.7(a)	2.5(b)	2.5(b)	11.0(c)	9.4(c)	20.0(d)
4.	Land Reclamation and Development (addl. area benefited)	-do-	3.7(a)	2.7(a)	1.5(b)	1.2(b)	3.6(c)	4.7(c)	2.5(d)
5.	Improved Seeds of Foodgrains*	-do-	N.S.	4.7	N.S.	48.9	302.0	112.0	N.S.
6.	Consumption of Chemical Fertilizers*								
	(a) Nitrogenous – in terms of N	Lakh tones	1.22	1.07	5.1	2.1	10.2	6.0	24.0
	(b) Phosphatic – in terms of P_2O_6	Thousand tones	N.S.	19	150	70	406	150	1,000
	(c) Potassic – in terms of K_2O	-do-	N.S.	11	N.S.	28	203	78	700
7.	Urban compost*	M. Tonnes	N.S.	2.2	3.0	2.4	5.1	3.0	6.0
8.	Rural compost*	-do-	–	–	N.S.	67	152	117	N.S.
9.	Green Manuring*	M. acres	–	–	N.S.	11.1	41.0	19.7	67.0
10.	Plant Protection*	-do-	–	–	N.S.	16.5	50.0	50.3	136.9

† As in Third Plan Report of the Planning Commission.
‡ Compiled from Draft Fourth Plan/check list of various State Governments/Union Territories.
(A) Anticipated achievement.
* Level reached/to be reached.
(a) Over 1950-51, (b) Over 1955-56, (c) Over 1960-61, (d) Over 1965-66.
N.S. – Not specified.
Source: Indian Agriculture in Brief – Eighth Edition, March, 1967.

REFERENCES

1. Chapter on India by Dr. V.K.R.V. Rao in *Asian Economic Development* edited by Carnley Onslow.
2. First Five Year Plan Report, Para 46, page 44.
3. First Five Year Plan, p. 161.
4. *Ibid.*
5. *Ibid.*, p. 223.
6. *Ibid.*, p. 226.
7. First Five Year Plan, p. 184.
8. Second Five Year Plan, p. 5.
9. *Ibid.*, p. 51.
10. *Ibid.*, p.61.
12. Second Five Year Plan, p. 228.
13. Report on India's Food Crisis and Steps to Meet it, 1959, p. 3.
14. Report on India's Food Crisis and Steps to Meet it, p. 5.
15. Study of the Multiplication & Distribution Programmes for Improved Seeds, Programme Evaluation Organization, Planning Commission, New Delhi, 1961, p. 88.
16. Third Five Year Plan, p. 23.
17. *Ibid.*, p. 130.

18. & 19. Third Five Year Plan, pp. 200 and pp. 229.

32

The Strategy of Food Production

B. Sivaraman

THE intellectuals of the world are talking today of the food famine in the early eighties of the century, if the present trend of population growth and the inability of the developing countries to feed themselves continues. The problem has been stated many times over. As a developing country, we are in the list of possible catastrophe in the early eighties. It is against this background that we have to discuss the strategy of food production. This strategy has to be Indian, though it can certainly be based on experience gained in other countries.

Food has many connotations. The intellectual talks of the balanced food requirement for proper growth of a human being. He distinguishes between the manual worker and the brain worker and talks about calorific requirements and the balance carbohydrates, proteins, vitamins, micro-nutrients, etc. To him food is an intellectual exercise. He talks glibly of the protein value of rat's meat and wonders why the poor Indian would rather starve than survive by eating the equally starving bovines which, according to him, are a drag on the economy of the country. Food for the well-to-do is what is *au fait* with the times and what are the right things to eat. These are the innovators who break through tradition. The middle class of a developing country, who can afford variations in the basic diet because of marginal affluence, are generally overwhelmed by conditions of status, and their food reflects the status requirements of the age. Food for the majority, which is underprivileged in a developing country, means what they can afford out of the traditional food. It is worth repeating here what the Advisers of the President of the United States have recently advised the President in their Report on World Food Problem about this:

> "The obstacles by traditional culture, social structure, religious beliefs, and the long established habits and customs of many developing countries are rarely considered in truly realistic terms."

Food in a country in an age is tradition bound and status bound. This is particularly true of India today. The wants in the eighties require that all possible avenues of food in the larger sense are exploited. Unless the consumer is prepared for a change in his diet, it is also obvious that mere production of food without relation to preferences will not solve the problem of food. A change cannot come unless there is a sustained move from the powers that be, in the right direction.

In today' economy, agricultural produce comprises the bulk of food in India—cereals and pulses, vegetables and fruits. The Plan formulators consider that the *per capita* requirement of cereals in 1970-71 should be of the order of 15.2 ozs. per diem and in 1975-76 16 ozs. per diem. The target for pulses is 2.8 ozs. per adult per diem in 1970-71 and 3 ozs. in 1975-76. Vegetables, which include potatoes and fruits, are only of marginal value in the diet, as far forward as 1975-76. These forecasts of requirements are based on the known preferences of the population for certain types of diet and their expected demand, on the basis of income elasticity for this type of food. Food products of animal husbandry like milk, fats and meat will form a minor fraction of the food consumed in 1975-76. The diet will be protein deficient and far from a balanced diet. *Dr. V.K.R.V. Rao,* in his address at Kerala in 1966, has drawn attention to the constituents of the Indian diet *vis-à-vis* the diets of other countries in carbohydrate content and protein content. The table reproduced on the next page from his address is significant.

One significant feature in these statistics is the role tubers play in many foreign countries in making up the carbohydrate content of food. Potatoes form a significant part of the diet in many countries. Our cereal consumption is out of proportion to what developed countries consume. We want to increase it further. There is a vast protein deficiency either in vegetable protein or animal protein in our diet.

The cost of production of various types of food is of great significance in meeting the food hunger of the masses. Food may be available in plenty, but unless the masses have the wherewithal to purchase the food in sufficient quantity, the hunger remains. The Advisers of the President of the United States, in their Report on the World Food Problem, have drawn attention to the linked problems in the following words:

> "It costs money to produce food, however, and someone must pay the bill. Therefore, no matter what the physiological need may be, the production of food is controlled by effective market demand ......aggregate income must grow at a rate which permits consumers to purchase the projected food requirements"

The Indian strategy of food production has to be planned against the background of all these conflicting requirements. Broadly, we may sum up the problem as follows:

(1) Food in an age is tradition bound and status bound.
(2) Food to be available to the masses has to be at the right cost, which the economy of the masses can bear.
(3) The present diet of the Indian is unbalanced and excessive in cereals and very much defficient in proteins, micro-nutrients and vitamins.

The short-term strategy of food production has to take note of the capacity of the country to produce the traditional requirements of food at a fair cost which is acceptable

Per Capita Availability of food in India and Other Countries

*(in gram per person per day at retail level)**

Item	*India*	*Under-developed countries†*	*Developed countries‡*	*World*
(1)	(2)	(3)	(4)	(5)
Cereal	375	393	328	370
Starchy roots	30	229	316	227
Sugar	45	26	88	47
Pulses and nuts	65	50	16	42
Fruits and vegetables	80	191	362	227
Meat	4	37	152	67
Fish	7	28	34	27
Eggs	1	5	33	12
Milk and milk products	140	64	573	228
Fats and oils	11	12	47	22
Calories	1,970	2,190	3,060	2,420
Animal protein	6	10	44	20
Total protein	51	60	90	68
Fats	27	36	106	56
Overall index of animal food	30	47	233	100
Overall index of total food	54	70	179	100

* Retail level means the food grains and other foods available for consumption and excludes that part of production which is not available for consumption due to seed, feed and wastage.
†Includes Far East, Near East, Africa and Latin America excluding River-Plate countries.
‡ Includes Europe, North America, Oceania, and River-Plate countries.

to the consumer. The long-term strategy has to examine the change in the production pattern that is required for a more balanced and economic food packet which can improve the health of the people. The long-term strategy is also to consider how far tradition and status can be overcome towards better economy and better health and what are the forces to be tackled and what are the experiences of ourselves and others in this problem.

PAST EXPERIENCE OF PRODUCTION

Many people have doubted the capacity of India to produce its food requirements. The Third Plan period from 1961-1966 was a sad experience to the protagonists self-sufficiency. From a production of 82 million tonnes in 1960-61, the production of cereals and pulses rose to 89 million tonnes in 1964-65, but fell drastically to 72 million tonnes in 1965-66. Though the actual production of 89 million tones in 1964-65 was close to the targeted production necessary for self-sufficiency in the country that year, strangely in 1965, we had to import 7.5 million tones of food grains from outside. The drought of 1965-66 was a drought of the century. The year 1966-67 though a little better than

1965-66, was again the season of the worst ever drought in Bihar, eastern U.P. and parts of Madhya Pradesh. The winter rains kept off. These raised grave doubts about our capacity to survive. But this experience has also given us an insight into the basic problems of agriculture in the country.

Good agriculture depends on the involvement of a large number of peasants, both proprietors and tenants all over the country, the majority of whom own less than 3 acres of land. In spite of all the propaganda about better cultivation in the Third Plan, the per acre production was at such low levels in many parts of the country that the majority of the small holders were inefficient producers. They lacked the capacity to invest in inputs for better agriculture. Fertilizers, on which a good part of the programme depended, were at such a high price level that till recently, 3.8 kgs of rice were required to buy 1 kg. of nitrogen and the return was 11 kgs of rice per kg of nitrogen. The vagaries of the climate in many parts of the country made it uneconomic and also risky for the small cultivator to improve production by investing in better inputs. The large farmer, who had surplus for better inputs, found labour rates going up whereas his produce fetched only marginally higher prices in the market. The input output ratio was not very favourable for him to take large risks. Thereby though the extension machinery of Government propagated the theory of better inputs, results were not consonant with the efforts made. This brought out forcefully the need for improving the input output ratio to induce the farmer to invest in better agriculture.

The input output ratio can be adjusted either by raising the prices to be paid for the "Food" or by producing more per unit of investment. A high price for food will reduce consumption and lead to a debilitated nation. Prices have to be kept at a level where the general economy enables the weaker sections of the community to get a reasonably nutritive diet. The long-term strategy, therefore, lies in trying for larger production, per acre, per unit of investment. It is also necessary to production. The farmer must get an incentive price. The balance, no doubt, will be the problem.

Meanwhile, the research scientists of the country were getting slowly an amount of experience which had the nucleus for the breakthrough. The first double-cross maize hybrids, like Ganga-1, Ganga-101, Ranjit and Deccan, were released for commercial cultivation in the country as far back as 1961. The National Seeds Corporation, formed in 1963, took up as one of its first duties, the production of sufficient double-cross hybrid seeds of maize. The initial experience in putting through the hybrids was heart breaking. The economics of seed production was not in favour of the farmer and the production had to be on States' farms. The farmer was still not willing to pay a high price for the hybrid seed. There was also consumer resistance to the variety. But it was established that these seeds gave a very favourable input output ratio to the farmer and the per acre yield came to more than double the best experience so far of the farmer in this crop. Similar high-yielding hybrids of *Jowar* (CSH-1) was issued in 1964 and Bajra (HB-1) in 1965. The National Seeds Corporation planned for a modest programme of seed production in 1966-67. In September, 1964, a few kilograms of seed of the paddy variety Taichung Native-I was brought from the Philippines by *Dr. G.V. Chalam*, who accompanied the Minister for Food & Agriculture on his tour to the International Rice Research Institute. The seeds were sown in the summer of 1965 at three different places in the country, and the response appeared to be so significant that a seed programme of 168 acres was organized for the Kharif of 1965 by importing some more seed from the Philippines through the auspices of the Rockefeller Foundation. In Mysore, in the South Kanara region, the exotic variety of paddy Taichung 65, which is a *Japanica* variety, was found to give good yields in the Kharif of 1965. A similar experience with Tainan-3, another *Japonica* strain, was gained in Kerala. *Dr. Borlaug* of the Rockefeller foundation's Wheat Research Programme in Mexico, who was the pioneer in dwarf Mexican wheat production had sent a number of samples of new dwarf varieties in Mexico wheat production had sent a number of samples of new dwarf varieties in Mexico to the I.C.A.R. Early in 1965, it was learnt that in the Indian Agricultural Research Institute and the Punjab Agricultural University, a significant increase in wheat yields at high-fertility levels was achieved through the use of Sonora 64 and Lerma Rojo, two dwarf wheat varieties introduced from Mexico. On the strength of these figures, arrangements were made to import 250 tons of this seed from Mexico for a large-scale production in the Rabi season of 1965. Experiments done on improved strains of *Ragi* in the Coimbatore College of Agriculture indicated that certain varieties of *Ragi,* like Co. 7 showed uniform increase in yield on increased application of nitrogen nutrient even up to 100 1bs. of nitrogen. All this experience gave the first inkling that the problem of input out put ratio was nearing a solution.

The two droughts brought out four facts. The first was that the irrigation sources considered to be safe for agriculture were found to be wanting in times of greatest distress whereas ground-water resources, wherever available in the form of wells, filter points and tubewells, did yeoman's service. Secondly, the per acre output of cereals and pulses from the entire irrigated acreage was not consonant with the potential of good husbandry. In 1964-65, which was a good year for production, the irrigated area of 59 million acres producted only 29 million tonnes of foodgrains and the balance 60 million tonnes of foodgrains that year was from the rain-fed and dry areas of the country. The average production, per acre, from irrigated area was only about 500 kgs. On the other hand, wherever the farmer utilized his water resources carefully and followed good agronomic practices, the yields in the areas covered by ground-water resources were very significant. In fact, in some areas, the output in the irrigated areas, where water was deficient in 1965-66, gave better yields than in a good year of water availability. Control of water was found to be a significant part of good agronomy. Thereby, the potential of private ground-water resources suddenly became significant. The third revelation was the utility of short-term high-yielding paddy strains *vis-à-vis* the normal long-term paddy grown in many parts of the Central and North India under the impression, that the longer the period the greater the yield. For years, the agricultural administrators have been trying to get it across that with a rainfall pattern of 3-4 months only in the year, growing a paddy crop of 180 days duration is a big risk. During the droughts the short-term crops did uniformly well as against the long-term, because the drought was in the latter part of the rainy season. Fourthly, all the high-yielding varieties tried out in the fields in 1965-66 in paddy, jowar, bajra or maize, uniformly showed a capacity to drought resistance that the ordinary varieties did not posses.

All these four factors, along with the high prices for foodgrains that prevailed because of short stocks, brought an immediate response from the farmer. His investment in private ground-water resources has been stepped up by leaps and bounds. His investment in fertilizers rose steeply. He has accepted the advice of the agricultural administrator to go in for a short-term high-yielding paddy for his Kharif crop and raise a good second crop wherever water facilities allow for this. He has realized the value of soil and water management and good agronomy, and last but not the least, he has opted whole-heartedly for the high-yielding varieties programme when many scientists and agricultural economists were still sitting on the fence.

POTENTIAL FOR PRODUCTION

What is the potential for cereal production in this country on the basis of the existing experience? The high-yielding varieties of cereals are able to give an average yield over large acreage of not less than 1.5 tonnes per acre for wheat, 1.25 tonnes per acre for rice and jowar, 1.33 tonnes per acre for hybrid maize and 0.75 tonnes per acre for bajra. Ordinary intensive cultivation at present can give 0.8 tonnes per acre for rice and wheat and 0.6 tonnes per acre for millets. These are very modest figures. An estimate of the production of foodgrains in 1970-71 from irrigated areas is given in a table on the next page.

By 1970-71, it is expected that 100 million acres gross will be under irrigation out of which 80 million acres will grow foodgrains. On a broad assessment, it is estimated that out of the ultimate potential of net sown area of 350 million acres in this country, only 135 million acres net can be provided with irrigation facilities. By utilizing short-term high-yielding varieties and ensuring a proper crop rotation, it should be possible to bring at least 65 million acres out of the irrigated area into a second crop production. Thereby, 200 million acres of irrigated cultivation can be achieved in this country, by systematic improvement of irrigation and adding ground-water exploitation. It is reasonable to expect that at least 150 million acres out of this can be reserved for foodgrains. In 1970-71, the projected figures are 80 million acres net, under irrigation, with 100 million acres gross. The rain-fed and dry areas in 1970-71 would be of the order of 260 million acres (net) whereas the ultimate will be 215 million acres. In 1970-71, because of limitation of fertilizers and the need for time for all farmers to adopt new measures, only 40 per cent will be under high-yielding varieties and about 40 per cent under ordinary intensive cultivation and 20 per cent under present practices. Even then, an average of 0.9 tons of foodgrains per acre can be achieved and for the ultimate potential we should take note of the adoption of high-yielding varieties generally and better agronomic practices under intensive agriculture. An average production of 1.25 tonnes per acre is not an over ambitious expectation with present scientific knowledge. It should, therefore, be possible to produce 187.5 million tonnes of foodgrains from the 150 million acres of irrigated cultivation ultimately foreseen at present.

It is necessary to digress here a little and point out that high-yielding varieties require a chemical fertilizer dosage of as much as 200 1bs. plant nutrient and intensive cultivation as much as 100 lbs. per acre. A 150-million acre programme comprising of

Estimates of Production of Foodgrains in 1970-71 from Irrigated Areas

Foodgrains	*H.V.P.*			*Double Cropping*			*Other Irrigated Area*		
	Acreage (million acres)	*Yield per acre (tonnes)*	*Total Production (million tonnes)*	*Acreage (million acres)*	*Yield per acre (tonnes)*	*Total Production (million tonnes)*	*Acre (million acres)*	*Yield per acre (tonnes)*	*Total Production (million tonnes)*
(1)	(2)	(3)	(4)	(5)	(6)	(7)	(8)	(9)	(10)
Rice	12.5	1.25	15.63	20.0	0.8	16.0	10.0	0.6	6.00
Wheat	8.0	1.50	12.00	2.0	0.8	1.6	2.0	0.5	1.00
Jowar	4.0	1.25	5.00	–	–	–	–	–	–
Bajra	4.0	0.75	3.00	8.0	0.6	4.8	5.5	0.4	2.20
Maize	4.0	1.33	5.32	–	–	–	–	–	–
Others	–	–	–	–	–	–	–	–	–
Total Foodgrains	32.5	–	40.95	30.0	–	22.4	17.5	0.5	9.20

ABSTRACT

H.V.P.	40.95
Multiple cropping	22.40
Other irrigated areas	9.20
Total	72.55

half intensive and half high-yielding varieties programme will require plant nutrients of the order of 10 million tonnes. Our plans provide for an availability of 4.1 million tonnes nutrient in 1970-71, out of which three-fourths will be used for the intensive and high-yielding varieties programme. With an aggressive indigenous production programme for fertilizers, the target in 2000 A.D. is not beyond our capacity.

At present, 220 million acres of unirrigated area on which dry and rain-fed cultivation is done, produces roughly 48 million tonnes of foodgrains. It is a well-known fact that dry and rain-fed cultivation in the country is based on the food preferences of the population rather than on the capacity of the land to produce that crop. *For example,* paddy is grown on such marginal lands that the average production can be between 4 and 6 maunds, per acre on a seed rate of as much as 1½ mounds, per acre. It is also our experience that, if a crop suitable to the land and the climatic conditions is grown, a good yield can be obtained. Bajra grows with 10-15 inches of rainfall. Jowar can survive and do well with 25-30 inches of rainfall. Suitable conservation measures and terracing along with mulching practices can maintain soil moisture as an insurance against drought periods during the rainy reason. Broadly, areas with low rainfall and the hilly areas are more suited for millet production than rice or wheat production. The new hybrid millets, being also drought resistant, have shown excellent performance in these dry and rain-fed areas. A package approach of soil conservation, terracing, moisture maintenance and the right type of millet crop for the area can certainly push up the yields of the dry and rain-fed areas very substantially. When we talk of the ultimate production potential, we can certainly say that the knowledge we have got today can, if properly applied, produce double of 49 million tonnes in the dry and rain-fed areas.

Cereals are consumed mainly for carbohydrate content. In many countries, we notice that potato consumption substantially reduces cereal consumption. Meat, fish, poultry, eggs, milk and milk products go towards a balanced diet and reduces dependence on carbohydrates alone for the calorific value in the food. Experience in the two drought years, *viz.*, 1965-66 and 1966-67 shows that the people will take to larger consumption of potatoes if there is a scarcity of cereals. It is also our experience that once a new item is added to the food even by compulsion, gradually it gets accepted. Our experience of wheat consumption in the southern region of the country will prove this fact. With intensive cultivation on land where irrigation facilities are available, a 10-ton yield of potatoes is an ordinary feature. If we refer to the statistics given at p. 434, by large-scale introduction of potatoes in the diet, we can reduce pressure on cereal consumption. Fewer acres of irrigated land will be necessary to produce the same tonnage of potatoes as cereals. This increases the capacity of the country to supply sufficient carbohydrates to the population.

With the scientific knowledge now available and with the optimum utilization of the water resources and optimum exploitation of the dry and rain-fed areas, we can reach a production of 280 million tonnes of foodgrains, including cereals and pulses. The present estimate of foodgrains requirements according to the present patterns of consumption and income elasticity is 120 million tonnes in 1970-71 and 150 million tonnes in 1975-76. If the consumption pattern achieved in 1975-76 holds good for the long-term perspective and if the population control measures have a reasonable impact, the production of 280 million tonnes can suffice far beyond the year 2000 A.D. But we have also to recognize that the foodgrains packet will have a substantial part of millets and new pulses, the consumption of which will have to be developed in the meantime.

PROTEIN DEFICIENCY

The Indian diet is highly deficient in protein content. Most of the protein that is available today is in the form of vegetable protein, mainly pulses. Animal protein, *viz.*, meat, poultry, eggs, fish, milk and milk products form only a very minor portion of the average diet. If it is possible to increase food production in the protein sector, the diet of Indian will be more balanced and the pressure on cereal production for human food will go down.

The main form of vegetable protein, which is absorbed in the form of pulses, is one of the items of production which has yet to find a break-through. Pulses are mostly grown in the country as a catch crop or a rainy season crop in marginal lands with low rainfall and the average production per acre is very small. With the introduction of the high-yielding cereal varieties and the second crop programme, there is a danger that pulse production may go down. Though there are some signs of high-yielding varieties, it is very doubtful whether pulses can compete with the high-yielding cereals for land allocation. Some of the cereals also contain protein. Bajra is a good example. But, the main problem in vegetable protein from cereals is the lack of particular amino-acids, like lysene, which prevents the human system from absorbing the protein value. Science has recently achieved a break-through in breeding, by which some of the important amino-acids can be bred into maize. Experiments in wheat are proceeding. It is not unlikely that the scientist will find an answer to the problem of absorbable proteins in cereals. At the same time, we cannot minimize the problem of finding vegetable proteins as an alternative to the existing pulses.

The pulses requirement for human consumption in 1970-71 and 1975-76 can be extrapolated as follows:

	Million tonnes
1970-71	16.2
1975-76	20.0

The production of pulses during the last five years are given below showing the fluctuations in production depending on the seasons:

	Million tonnes
1961-62	11.8
1962-63*	11.4
1963-64*	10.1
1964-65*	12.4
1965-66†	10.0

* Partially revised estimates.

† Final estimates.

It is also experience that average per acre yield of pulses, like cow-peas, filed peas and soyabeans can be raised to levels which cannot be achieved by the present pulses in use, like a moong, urd and arhar. If the consumer can be persuaded to change over to pulses which can be grown on a larger per acre scale, a part of the problem can be solved. Recent research has shown that deoiled groundnut powder and deoiled kernel of cotton seed are both highly nutritive sources of protein. Experiments in cooking have shown that groundnut powder can substantially replace gram dal powder in edible preparations. This is a source which can substantially meet the demand for vegetable protein, if the consumer acceptability can be built up.

A change-over to animal protein is inevitable with rising national incomes and *per capita* incomes. This is what the general trend in the world shows. At the same time, one unit of absorbable animal protein requires four times the vegetable protein in the nature of feed. The animal is an inefficient transformer of nutrition into protein. On the other hand, the animal can consume feeds which the human being will not eat and thereby there may not be a substantial conflict; but we have to admit that this fall has not yet been examined in any depth in this country. Poultry, piggery and sheep rearing for mutton, all appear to have good potential in the country. Consumer acceptability for poultry and eggs is developing very rapidly contrary to initial expectation. Strangely, during the last few years, demand for pig meat is also rising. Consumer resistance, owing to social customs, seems to be disappearing fast. In the 1980's we can certainly expect greater utilization of poultry and piggery, subject, may, only to production capacity. Milk and milk products are readily acceptable, but the production, in the present stage of cattle development in the country, is one of the most difficult. Owing to a long period of development of dual purpose cattle, the milk yielder has not found its place in the breeding programme on its own merits. Breeding schemes have just started on scientific basis for selective milk breeding. This is a slow process and we may not expect spectacular results in the next two decades. Sheep breeding for mutton will certainly be popular and the demand is already evident, but the most probable item of animal protein in the next two decades should to be fish.

Though intensive production of fish in the inland waters has been propagated and developed in the last 15 years, the main source of fish, namely, our coastal waters has not been exploited, even marginally. A lot of work has been done to understand the magnitudes of the problem. Harbour facilities and shore facilities are essential. Efficient trawlers should be able to go out into the sea and remain there for a few days and fish continuously. New types of boats and new techniques and new mechanical competencies are necessary. Now that the magnitudes of the problem are understood, it is expected that in the next two decades fishing in the seas around India can add substantially to the protein diet of the people. At the same time we may not minimize the problems of consumer preference. The main fish-eating population of eastern India prefer inland water fish. Sea fish, which have a good price outside the country, are not appreciated by the consumer. At the sametime, in many markets of the South, sea fish and dried sea fish are accepted by the consumer. It is a matter of price. If effort is taken to market sea fish in the interior markets at reasonable prices, it should be possible to build up within the next two decades a demand for this on a large scale.

MICRO-NUTRIENTS AND VITAMINS

Vegetables and fruits are a necessary part of a balanced diet to give the necessary vitamins and micro-nutrients. Thanks to the efforts of the Community Development Organization, vegetable cultivation has spread to the corners of the country. Horticulture has had a boost with a rising demand. The Indian Council of Agricultural Research is organizing coordinated research in horticulture in the most important of our fruits. Much more can be organized and dones if areas suitable for horticulture concentrated in this field. *For example*, the northern hill areas can grow fruits, like apples and pears in plenty. If the country can organize a fair distribution of cereals and pulses to them, so that they need not divert good horticultural land to growing their requirements of cereals and pulses, the spread of horticulture will be rapid. Results will obviously take time.

HIGHLIGHTS OF THE STRATEGY

In the short term, it will not be realistic to expect too much of a change in the diet pattern in the entire country to warrant playing about with crop patterns which are traditional, or laying stress on new foods. In 1970-71, we require 120 million tonnes of food grains, of which 16.2 million tonnes should be in pulses. In 1975-76, we require 150 million tonnes of foodgrains, of which 20 million tonnes should be pulses. The statistics given in previous part of the paper shows that tonne production in 1970-71 is quite possible if we utilize the existing knowledge and keep up the enthusiasm of the farmer. The only uncertain factor will be the pulses production. Unless a break-through in high-yielding varieties of pulses comes up in the near future, it will have to be new varieties of pulses, like cow-peas, field-peas and soya-beans which have to come to the rescue of those depending upon vegetable protein for their protein requirements. Groundnut flour will also have to be exploited sufficiently quickly. If this change in acceptability can be brought about, it will help in the further production of vegetable protein up to 2000 A.D. without any difficulty.

Between 1970-71 and 1975-76 an increase in the gross irrigated acreage of about 25 million acres should look after the increased requirement of 30 million tonnes of food grains. Expectations are that high-yielding varieties will be grown on a much larger percentage of irrigated area than in 1970-71 and the balance area would be used for intensive cultivation and not haphazard cultivation. The short-term strategy should, therefore, concentrate on pushing through the packages of practices for scientific agriculture, based on water use, high-yielding varieties of seeds, fertilizers and pesticides. Some amount of adjustment in the types of pulses consumed will be useful.

Let us have a look at the long-term requirements. We have to add about 75 million acres gross to the irrigated area, between 1975-76 2000 A.D. There are five quinquenniums and an average increase of 15 million acres gross per quinquennium is certainly not beyond the country's capacity. Summing up the various suggestions made in the previous parts of this paper, we have to aim at:

1. increasing millet consumption in the cereal diet of the country;
2. increasing consumption of tubers in the diet so that carbohydrate requirements can be met from less acres of production;
3. getting the population to accept newer varieties of pulses and alternatives, like groundnut powder and cotton seed protein;
4. increasing production of animal protein particularly in poultry and eggs, piggery and sheep; and
5. exploiting the seas resources in fish.

Whenever one talks of change of diet, there is an intellectual resistance on the ground that food habits are sacrosanct. World experience shows that it is not necessarily so. After World War II in Japan consumption of four-footed animals has increased though there was a sentimental and semi-religious objection to eating four-footed animals. The change has been spectacular. In our own country, between 1959 and today, consumption of eggs and poultry has been accepted in many urban and rural areas where there was a social toboo to eating poultry or eggs. West Bengal and the Southern States of this country which are rice-eating area, have absorbed quite an amount of wheat in their diet out of sheer necessity.

Status is the greatest stumbling block to planned diet. Rice and wheat are considered status symbols. Fresh water fish, particularly of the Carp varieties is considered to be the thing in the fish eating States. Sea fish except for some urban areas used to Western habit, is generally treated as the poor man's fish. This is in this filed where a lot of psychological warfare will have to be attempted. We can learn from past experience. In Mysore, even today, *Ragi* is accepted as the richman's food. This was due to the simple fact that Krishnaraj Wadiar, who was for thirty years ruler of Mysore, made it a point to eat *Ragi* at every meal. The leadership has to come from the top. Can we expect this leadership?

The world will not end in 2000 A.D. Nor is science going to be at a standstill. In the next three decades more high-yielding varieties of cereals and pulses may be developed. New proteins may be added to the food packet. Consumer adaptability to new types of food may be brought about. All this will only stretch the point of "no return" to the middle of the twenty-first century. Unless a new generation of supermen develop who can take sustenance out of rocks the strategy of food production will be of no avail without a strong and effective strategy of population control. So, whilst the Agricultural Administrators devise ways and means of augmenting the supplies in the larder, the nations of the world and India, in particular, must find a population balance long before 2000 A.D. If man fails, nature will take over. Nature's solutions may be catastrophic.

Index